D0205940

HISTORICAL DICTIONARY
OF
STUART ENGLAND,
1603–1689

HISTORICAL DICTIONARY
—— OF ——
STUART ENGLAND,
1603–1689

Ronald H. Fritze and William B. Robison,
Editors-in-Chief

Walter Sutton, *Assistant Editor*

GREENWOOD PRESS
Westport, Connecticut • London

Library of Congress Cataloging-in-Publication Data

Historical dictionary of Stuart England, 1603–1689 / Ronald H. Fritze
  and William B. Robison, editors-in-chief ; Walter Sutton, assistant editor.
     p. cm.
   ISBN 0–313–28391–5 (alk. paper)
   1. Great Britain—History—Stuarts, 1603–1714—Dictionaries.
  I. Fritze, Ronald H., 1951– . II. Robison, Wm. B. (William B.)
  DA375.H57 1996
  941.06′03—dc20   94–39244

British Library Cataloguing in Publication Data is available.

Library of Congress Catalog Card Number: 94–39244
ISBN: 0–313–28391–5

First published in 1996

Greenwood Press, 88 Post Road West, Westport, CT 06881
An imprint of Greenwood Publishing Group, Inc.

Printed in the United States of America

The paper used in this book complies with the
Permanent Paper Standard issued by the National
Information Standards Organization (Z39.48–1984).

10 9 8 7 6 5 4 3 2 1

For

Sir Geoffrey Elton
(1921-1994)

Vir Doctissimus, Magister, et Amicus.

Ave atque Vale.

Contents

Contributors

Dr. John Adamson, Peterhouse, Cambridge University, Cambridge, England.

Dr. Christopher Baker, Department of English, Armstrong State University, Savannah, Georgia, U.S.A.

Dr. Sabrina Alcorn Baron, Washington, D.C., U.S.A.

Dr. Stephen Baskerville, Filozofická fakulta Univerzity Palackého, Katedra Humanitních Ved a Evropskych Studií, Olomouc, Czech Republic.

Dr. A. L. Beier, Department of History, Illinois State University, Normal, Illinois, U.S.A.

Dr. Gary M. Bell, Honors Program, Texas Tech University, Lubbock, Texas, U.S.A.

Dr. Dorothy Boyd-Rush, Dean, Graduate School, James Madison University, Harrisonburg, Virginia, U.S.A.

Dr. Glenn Burgess, Department of History, University of Canterbury, Christchurch, New Zealand.

Dr. William E. Burns, Department of History, University of California, Davis, California, U.S.A.

Dr. Bernard S. Capp, Department of History, University of Warwick, Coventry, England.

Dr. Charles Carlton, Department of History, North Carolina State University, Raleigh, North Carolina, U.S.A.

Dr. Jo Eldridge Carney, Department of History, Trenton State College, Pennington, New Jersey, U.S.A.

Dr. Stanley D. M. Carpenter, Department of History, Florida State University, Tallahassee, Florida, U.S.A.

Dr. Esther S. Cope, Department of History, University of Nebraska, Lincoln, Nebraska, U.S.A.

Dr. Lesley Cormack, Department of History, University of Alberta, Edmonton, Alberta, Canada.

Dr. Neil Cuddy, Department of History, University of Toronto, Toronto, Canada.

Dr. Richard Cust, Department of History, University of Birmingham, Birmingham, England.

Dr. David A. Davis, Department of History, Florida State University, Tallahassee, Florida, U.S.A.

Dr. W. Calvin Dickinson, Department of History, Tennessee Tech University, Cookeville, Tennessee, U.S.A.

Dr. John S. Erwin, Division of Social Science, Illinois Valley Community College, Oglesby, Illinois, U.S.A.

Ms. Connie S. Evans, Department of History, Louisiana State University, Baton Rouge, Louisiana, U.S.A.

Dr. Ann E. Faulkner, Graduate School, Loyola University of Chicago, Chicago, Illinois, U.S.A.

Dr. Mark Charles Fissel, Center for Teaching and Learning, Ball State University, Muncie, Indiana, U.S.A.

Dr. Ronald H. Fritze, Department of History, Lamar University, Beaumont, Texas, U.S.A.

Dr. Elizabeth Lane Furdell, Department of History, University of North Florida, Jacksonville, Florida, U.S.A.

Dr. Edward M. Furgol, Department of the Navy, Navy Museum, Washington, D.C., U.S.A.

Dr. Peter Gaunt, Department of History, Chester College, Chester, England.

Dr. Ian Gentles, Department of History, York University, Toronto, Ontario, Canada.

Dr. Richard L. Greaves, Department of History, Florida State University, Tallahassee, Florida, U.S.A.

Dr. Sheldon Hanft, Department of History, Appalachian State University, Boone, North Carolina, U.S.A.

Dr. Rudolph W. Heinze, Oak Hill College, London, England.

Dr. Mark C. Herman, Social Science Division, Edicon Community College, Fort Meyers, Florida, U.S.A.

Dr. Mark Heumann, Independent Scholar, Riyad Bank, Riyadh, Saudi Arabia.

Richard L. Hillard, Department of Social and Behavioral Sciences, University of Arkansas, Pine Bluff, Arkansas, U.S.A.

Dr. Wilson J. Hoffman, Department of History, Hiram College, Hiram, Ohio, U.S.A.

Dr. Daniel W. Hollis III, Department of History, Jacksonville State University, Jacksonville, Alabama, U.S.A.

Dr. John H. F. Hughes, Boston, Massachusetts, U.S.A.

Dr. Maija Jansson, Center for Parliamentary History, Yale University, New Haven, Connecticut, U.S.A.

Dr. John P. Kenyon, Department of History, University of Kansas, Lawrence, Kansas, U.S.A.

Dr. Newton E. Key, Department of History, Eastern Illinois University, Charleston, Illinois, U.S.A.

Dr. Louis A. Knafla, Department of History, University of Calgary, Calgary, Alberta, Canada.

Father René Kollar, St. Vincent Archabbey, Latrobe, Pennsylvania, U.S.A.

Dr. Chris R. Kyle, Department of History, University of Auckland, Auckland, New Zealand.

Dr. Carole Levin, Department of History, State University of New York, New Paltz, New York, U.S.A.

Dr. Eric N. Lindquist, Independent Scholar, Washington, D.C., U.S.A.

Dr. Joseph M. McCarthy, Education and Human Services Department, Suffolk University, Boston, Massachusetts, U.S.A.

Dr. J. Sears McGee, Department of History, University of California, Santa Barbara, California, U.S.A.

Dr. Martin J. Manning, Library, United States Information Agency, Washington, D.C.

Dr. Roger B. Manning, Department of History, Cleveland State University, Cleveland, Ohio, U.S.A.

Dr. James I. Miklovich, Department of History and History Education, University of West Florida, Pensacola, Florida, U.S.A.

Dr. John Miller, Department of History, Queen Mary and Westfield College, University of London, London, England.

Mr. Paul Miller, Department of History, Southeastern Louisiana University, Hammond, Louisiana, U.S.A.

Dr. David B. Mock, Department of History, Tallahassee Community College, Tallahassee, Florida, U.S.A.

Mr. William Nikides, Department of History, Florida State University, Tallahassee, Florida, U.S.A.

Dr. John Nolan, University of Maryland Overseas, Wurzburg, Germany.

Dr. Myron C. Noonkester, Department of History, William Carey College, Hattiesburg, Mississippi, U.S.A.

Mr. Kenneth Postan, Odom Middle School, Beaumont, Texas, U.S.A.

Mr. John Harrison Rains III, Tampa, Florida, U.S.A.

Mr. Thomas R. Reid, Independent Scholar, Serjeant and Facility Management Specialist, United States Army Reserves, Houston, Texas, U.S.A.

Dr. R. C. Richardson, Department of History, King Alfred's College, Winchester, England.

Dr. William B. Robison, Department of History, Southeastern Louisiana University, Hammond, Louisiana, U.S.A.

Dr. James Rosenheim, Department of History, Texas A&M University, College Station, Texas, U.S.A.

Dr. Vivienne C. Sanders, Head of History, Dame Alice Harpur School, Bedford, England.

Dr. Paul Seaward, Clerk, House of Commons, London, England.

Dr. Malcolm Smuts, Department of History, University of Massachusetts, Boston, Massachusetts, U.S.A.

Dr. Johann P. Sommerville, Department of History, University of Wisconsin, Madison, Wisconsin, U.S.A.

Dr. Margaret R. Sommerville, Independent Scholar, Madison, Wisconsin, U.S.A.

Dr. Victor L. Stater, Department of History, Louisiana State University, Baton Rouge, Louisiana, U.S.A.

Dr. S. J. Stearns, St. George Campus, City College of New York, Staten Island, New York, U.S.A.

Mr. Mark Stoyle, Department of History, University of Southampton, Southampton, England.

Dr. Fredrica Harris Thompsett, Episcopal Divinity School, Cambridge, Massachusetts, U.S.A.

Dr. Janet A. Thompson, Department of History, Tallahassee Community College, Tallahassee, Florida, U.S.A.

Dr. Robert Tittler, Department of History, Concordia University, Montreal, Quebec, Canada.

Ms. Nancy Vannett, Groves Middle School, Groves, Beaumont, Texas, U.S.A.

Dr. William T. Walker, Department of Humanities, Philadelphia School of Pharmacy, Philadelphia, Pennsylvania, U.S.A.

Dr. Dewey D. Wallace, Jr., Department of Religion, George Washington University, Washington, D.C., U.S.A.

Dr. Daniel R. Woolf, Department of History, Dalhousie University, Halifax, Nova Scotia, Canada.

Dr. Austin Woolrych, Department of History, Lancaster University, England.

Dr. Jenny Wormald, St. Hilda's College, Oxford University, Oxford, England.

Dr. Robert Zaller, Department of History, Drexel University, Philadelphia, Pennsylvania, U.S.A.

Introduction

Historical scholarship dealing with the British Isles during the years 1603-1689 has been in a state of flux for a number of years. Scholarly debate over the interpretation of the nature and the significance of that era and its various events ranges from polite, to vigorous, to even savage in its tone. Controversy appears at every stage of the study of the events of seventeenth-century British history. Regarding the reign of James VI and I, it used to be thought that when this bumbling Scot arrived in England, he quickly proceeded to weaken the stable regime he inherited from Elizabeth I. In this way England started its slide down the slippery slope leading to the Civil War. This view is now in full retreat. James VI and I is now increasingly seen as a monarch who knew and accepted the limitations of his power and his kingdoms. While he may have had his quirky ways, he bequeathed his heir, Charles I, as strong a government as could be hoped for in the tumultuous 1620s.

Charles I and his reign have always been the subject of controversy and probably will always remain so. The culminating event of his reign was the outbreak of the civil strife that led to his execution by his own subjects. That conflict divided the peoples of the British Isles into royalists or parliamentarians, with many bewildered neutralists watching on the sidelines. The same conflict has also tended to divide historians along similar lines because the temptation to take one side or the other is rather difficult to avoid, no matter how objective the scholar. Hence there is the question of what to call the conflict that intermittently raged over the British Isles with greater or lesser intensity between 1639 and 1660. Was it a civil war or a revolution? Another debate rages over the causes of the Civil War or Revolution. Were there long-term causes (the rise of the middle class or the decline of the aristocracy) or were there short-term causes (the rise of Arminianism), and which were the most important? This type of approach tends to make the conflict appear to have become inevitable at some point. Other historians argue that the violent upheavals of the mid-seventeenth century were not inevitable but an unfortunate accident that could have been avoided. If Charles I had avoided stirring up the problems in Scotland that led to the Bishops' War or if he could have smoothed things over and prevented the Irish Rebellion, then everything would have been all right, or so some historians suggest.

Other historical debates enliven the study of the reign of Charles I. Judgments about the quality of Charles I's kingship have been shifting over the years. Fortunately for his own historical reputation, Charles I made his death the finest moment of his life by his dignified bearing. As a result, a cult of the martyred monarch has tinted the way people have looked at the man Charles Stuart from the day of his death to the present. Recent historians have tended to be less sympathetic, however, and are increasingly seeing him as a rigid and uncompromising ruler who brought many of his troubles down on his own head. Other issues involve evaluating the government of England during the years 1629-1640, the period known as the Eleven Years Personal Rule or the Eleven Years Tyranny. Were the policies of Charles I's ministers effective? Could they have kept the system going if the Scottish crisis of 1639 had not upset the balance? The answers to these questions have not yet been satisfactorily settled.

The religious history of the British Isles is a topic of particularly fierce debate among historians. The classic but outmoded version of seventeenth-century religious history presented a picture of freedom-loving Puritans coming into increasing conflict with tyrannical Anglicans, who were in turn falling under the baleful influence of crypto-papist Arminians. Pushed beyond endurance, the Puritans rose in a rebellion that its historians commonly refer to as the Puritan Revolution rather than the English Civil War. This approach was a way of looking at the English Civil War that made religion a prime cause of the conflict. On the other hand, it has recently been suggested that it was actually the Arminians who were the revolutionary force in these events and that the Puritans and other Calvinists were counterrevolutionaries who opposed the religious innovations of Charles I and William Laud. These Puritans were protecting the status quo of a Calvinist consensus within the Church of England rather than staging a revolution against an entrenched Anglican establishment.

Other debates swirl through the religious history of seventeenth-century Britain. Historians continue to argue about how to define Puritans and Puritanism while going on to new debates over whether there was really a Calvinist consensus, what were the origins of Arminianism, and even whether William Laud was truly an Arminian. Most scholars agree that the term *Anglican* is an anachronistic usage before 1660, and many further insist that it is an anachronistic usage before 1689. The result of this agreement, however, has been to create a terminological void since no satisfactory replacement for *Anglican* has been found to describe those mainstream members of the Church of England who were neither Puritans nor Arminians. Another contentious question is the optical illusion of Puritanism's virtual disappearance after 1660. That date has been a sort of historiographical chasm in the study of British history, particularly religious history. Many scholars would like to see that chasm bridged and so create a better understanding of the significant links between the religious conflicts of the early Stuart and Civil War eras and the religious concerns and conflicts of Restoration Britain.

Meanwhile the people of the British Isles found themselves without the rule of a king from 1649 to 1660. This period, known as the Interregnum, has also been the occasion of much historical debate. How effective were the governments of the English Republic and the lord protector, Oliver Cromwell? Could the Republic have survived and avoided the Restoration? What were the true motives and goals of Oliver Cromwell? These questions and many others remain contentious topics for scholars of that era.

The Restoration and the reigns of Charles II and James II have not attracted nearly the scholarly attention that the early Stuarts and the Civil War and Interregnum have always commanded. That situation, however, has been changing significantly. The anti-popery of the years 1660-1689 has been well studied, but other questions still remain. What did the reforms of the Civil War and Interregnum era actually accomplish in terms of the relations between the monarchy and the political elite? Formerly it was thought that the power of the British monarchy had been irreparably weakened by its defeat at the hands of parliament and that James II's reign was a doomed attempt to revive its fortunes. In contrast, many recent scholars have contended that the restored monarchy was actually quite strong. The parliamentary victory in the Civil War did not settle the issues of royal and parliamentary powers. Some historians have gone so far as to suggest that the British Isles possessed great potential for being converted into an absolutist state along the lines of Bourbon France in the years following 1660. It is even claimed that the Glorious Revolution, long considered a watershed in the growth of parliamentary government, was not actually a decisive defeat for the monarchy.

Other, lesser debates also enliven the study of Restoration Britain. The complex character of Charles II has been well studied by biographers, but he will probably always remain something of a mystery. Other historians have shown an interest in tracing the very real continuity of radical republican and religious sentiments into the Restoration era. The appearance and growth of the political parties of the Whigs and the Tories have been well studied for this era, but much disagreement continues among historians.

This survey has by no means exhausted the richness and the diversity of scholarship on seventeenth-century Britain or the disagreements among its historians. Those interested in learning about the latest trends of research and in studying the historiography of seventeenth century Britain will find these books helpful: R. C. Richardson, *The Debate on the English Revolution Revisited* (1988); Ann Hughes, *The Causes of the English Civil War* (1991); Michael G. Finlayson, *Historians, Puritanism, and the English Revolution* (1983); Ronald Hutton, *The British Republic, 1649-1660* (1990); and Paul Seaward, *The Restoration, 1660-1668* (1991).

Meanwhile, all of this debate makes the need for a comprehensive reference book for Britain between the years 1603 and 1689 all the more imperative. This book makes no claim to be exhaustive. No single-volume reference work consisting of 611 pages on a topic as broad as the British Isles from 1603 to 1689 could hope to be exhaustive in its coverage. Students and the general public are constantly in need of brief introductions to various topics. They are the main audience for this book, although professional historians might also find it useful for checking the occasional fact. Like its predecessor, the *Historical Dictionary of Tudor England* (Westport, CT: Greenwood, 1991), this volume is designed to serve as a handy ready-reference work. It contains 320 entries written by 80 scholars. The primary focus of coverage has been political and religious history, although important cultural, social, economic, and intellectual topics have been included. Individual entries range from 250 to 2,500 words in length and include selected bibliographies for additional reading. Cross-references are indicated by the related term followed by an asterisk (*) when it is mentioned in another entry. The Chronology provides an overview of the important events in the history of seventeenth-century Britain, and a select classified bibliography points out some of the more important books to study that era.

We decided to make 1689 the terminal date for this work. Some people have objected to that choice and suggested (even demanded!) that the terminal date be 1714. In fact, we would have liked to have made the terminal date 1714, but considerations of the size of the volume and the economics of publishing made that choice impractical. At the same time, we do not see 1714 as an intrinsically superior terminal date. Both dates mark significant points in history, and both have been used frequently as the beginning or ending points of books. The great F. W. Maitland long ago warned his fellow historians about rending the seamless fabric of history, but necessity forces practicing historians to do it all the time. We only hope that our break has done as little damage to the web of the past as possible.

Scholars studying British history rank at the top of the academic world in terms of the quality of their scholarship, their conscientiousness, and their collegiality. The quality of the entries we received for the volume has been superb overall. Most people also managed to meet their deadlines, which helped to minimize the delays in publishing this book and kept the wear and tear on our nerves at a manageable level. We thank everyone who so graciously contributed to this volume. Their efforts and scholarship have made this work possible.

During the course of work on this project our home institutions Lamar University and Southeast Louisiana University provided crucial support. The staffs of the respective university libraries have struggled on through years of neglect in terms of crucial funding from the state legislatures. One can only wonder at the great scholarship that might be accomplished if libraries were supported properly. Lamar University has a long and respectable record of supporting scholarship. The College of Graduate Studies and Research provided support through an organized research grant. Its dean, Robert Moulton, has shown consistently good instincts for supporting worthwhile scholarship in diverse disciplines. The History Department, under the former leadership of Adrian Anderson and the present leadership of John Storey, generously provided release time for work on this project, a policy graciously supported by Dean Kendall Blanchard of the College of Arts and Sciences. At Southeastern Louisiana University, the Department of History and Government also provided release time for this project, and Professor Roman Heleniak, the department head, was particularly supportive from its inception. Though he arrived in the latter stages of its production, Dean John Miller of the College of Arts and Sciences was very helpful. All have richly earned the editors' sincere gratitude. We also thank the general editor at Greenwood Press, Cynthia Harris, for her support throughout the completion of this book, as well as the production editor, Dina Rubin, and the copy editor, Beverly Miller, for their assistance in the final stages of preparation. Professor Christine Bridges of Lamar University, Ms. Leslie Lawhon, and Mr. Ted Mead generously proofread portions of the final manuscript. Professor Walter Sutton

proved once again that he is a wizard of the word processor as well as being a most
congenial and conscientious partner in an academic enterprise. Bill Robison also
thanks Bibbet, Matthew, and Zoe for their indulgence while this project was
completed. Flacius, the literary critic cat, continues to supervise Ron Fritze while he
works. Although Sir Geoffrey Elton did not serve as the advisory editor for this
volume, he generously provided advice and suggestions. He will be greatly missed
by his many friends in the historical profession.

Ronald H. Fritze, Lamar University

William B. Robison, Southeastern Louisiana University

A

Abbot, George (1562-1633). Archbishop of Canterbury from 1610 to 1633, Abbot was born in Surrey to a Protestant cloth worker. At sixteen he left Guildford Grammar School for Balliol College, Oxford, where he gained a B.A. (1582), M.A. (1585), B.D. (1593), and D.D. (1597). His lectures and sermons won him a reputation and the patronage of Oxford's chancellor, Thomas Sackville, Lord Buckhurst, subsequently earl of Dorset. Abbot became master of University College (1597-1610), dean of Winchester (1600), and vice-chancellor of Oxford (1600, 1603, and 1605).

After Dorset's death in 1608, Abbot acquired another influential patron, George Hume, earl of Dunbar, a man favored by James I*. Abbot helped Dunbar reestablish episcopal authority in Scotland*. This, along with Archbishop Richard Bancroft's* favor, impeccable anti-Catholic credentials, a pamphlet flattering James, and possibly popularity in parliamentary circles, led Abbot swiftly to the bishoprics of Coventry and Lichfield (1609) and London* (1610) and thence to Canterbury. Contemporaries attributed James's unexpected choice to Dunbar's influence. By 1611 Abbot was a privy councilor.

Abbot favored the theology of Calvinism* and promoted a preaching ministry. He valued seemliness and uniformity, for instance, in 1633 insisting on parishioners in Kent kneeling at the altar. Like James, he often tolerated moderate Puritanism* but had no patience with extremists.

Abbot's relationship with James was amicable despite some disagreements. In 1613 James appointed a commission to judge in favor of a divorce for Lady Frances Howard, who wanted to marry Robert Carr*, the royal favorite. Abbot's opposition irritated James. Abbot's desire for a "Protestant" foreign policy led to antagonism with Carr and Catholic* councilors like the Howards, whom he publicly criticized. He believed England's interests required Carr's fall, which would improve James's relations with parliament*. Therefore, in 1615 Abbot successfully promoted a new favorite, George Villiers*, later 1st duke of Buckingham. Abbot also supported the marriage of the Calvinist Elector Palatine and Princess Elizabeth* (1613) but disagreed with James over assisting Frederick in the Thirty Years War* and over the proposed Spanish match* for Prince Charles* (1617-1623).

Abbot's Protestant foreign policy activism differentiated him from his immediate archiepiscopal predecessors, but his clashes with Sir Edward Coke* and the common lawyers were very much in the Bancroftian tradition. Coke attacked High Commission (see Ecclesiastical Courts*), but James's general impatience with him led to Coke's dismissal in 1616. Controversy over High Commission then decreased, possibly because both sides exercised more caution.

In 1621 Abbot accidentally killed a gamekeeper while hunting. A commission of inquiry debated the canon law precept that homicide merits suspension from exercising ecclesiastical functions, with James casting his vote in Abbot's favor. However, Bishops John Williams and William Laud* refused consecration at Abbot's hand. Abbot's influence at the royal court* never recovered, especially as James's authority slipped into the hands of Charles and Buckingham, by now unsympathetic to the primate. Thus Abbot turned to parliament as his vehicle for political influence. In the parliament of 1624* Abbot supported Buckingham and Charles's anti-Spanish policy and took the official line in the debate on Lionel Cranfield* but was increasingly anxious about Buckingham's power and the rise of Arminianism*. Charles and Buckingham made their Arminian sympathies clear, while the Commons opposed Arminianism and wanted Abbot to silence Richard Montagu, who had written against predestination. Charles's accession ensured Abbot's powerlessness therein.

Abbot blamed Buckingham and Laud when he was sequestered from his ecclesiastical jurisdiction and told to keep away from the privy council* in 1627. Charles, doubtless infuriated by Abbot's refusal to license the publication of Robert Sibthorp's sermon justifying the forced loan*, told Abbot to absent himself from High Commission, convocation, and parliament in 1628, but relented when the Lords requested that Abbot and other excluded Lords be allowed to attend the latter.

In the parliament of 1628*, Abbot supported the Petition of Right*, criticizing imprisonment without trial. However, when John Pym* attacked Roger Manwaring, a clerical supporter of the forced loan, Abbot was critical of Pym *and* Manwaring. Abbot missed most of the 1629 parliament because of increasingly poor health. He had clearly outlived his time. As early as 1626 Charles had promised the primacy to Laud, with whom Abbot had the first of many clashes at Oxford in 1603.

Committed to maintaining an English church in the tradition of Edmund Grindal in particular, but also of John Whitgift and Bancroft, Abbot died knowing his successor would alter its character. Abbot might have been more successful had he not expended so much energy on promoting Protestantism abroad, attempting to use parliament to influence royal policies. Coupled with his uncompromising personality, this embroiled him in court factionalism and seemed to put him on the "wrong" side of a court-versus-country* divide, positions Whitgift and Bancroft had avoided. It seemed the established Church of England (see Anglicanism*) had no choice but to stand (or fall) with the monarch; Abbot's independent stance was unworkable.

Bibliography: Kenneth Fincham, "Prelacy and Politics: Archbishop Abbot's Defence of Protestant Orthodoxy," *Historical Research* 61 (1988): 36-64; Conrad Russell,

Parliament and English Politics, 1621-1629, 1979; P. A. Welsby, *George Abbot: The Unwanted Archbishop*, 1962.

Vivienne C. Sanders

Abhorrers. Name given to those who produced "abhorrences" or "abhorring" petitions during the Exclusion Crisis* (1678-1681) to counter the Whig* petition campaigns. The abhorrers, or Tories* as they came to be known, called for the protection of the Anglican* church and protested the pressure put on Charles II* to agree to the exclusion of his brother, the duke of York (the future James II*) from the succession.

The first of the Tory petitions signed by court supporters, Anglican clergy, justices, and packed grand juries appeared in April 1680. In general these abhorrences were signed by fewer people and attracted less attention than the Whig petitions. The Whigs claimed that these abhorrences interfered with the rights of subjects to petition, and the Whig-dominated second Exclusion Parliament in October 1680 expelled one of the Tory members of parliament* behind the abhorring petitions. After the dissolution of the Oxford Parliament*, the Tories in April 1681 produced a petition, containing 2,000 signatures, that thanked Charles II for dissolving parliament*. Tories claimed that the signatures had been collected within twelve hours. The Whig petitions and the Tory abhorrences continued in 1682 as the Tories planned to produce a petition abhorring a Whig-proposed association to protect Charles II and Protestantism; the Whigs had promoted a petition calling for the meeting of parliament. Tory addresses and counterpetitions were used by Charles II in his campaign in autumn 1682 to secure the selection of two Tories as sheriffs* in London* as part of his effort to break the Whig control of the political machinery there. The Whig petitions and Tory abhorrences brought about a heightened political excitement as both parties sought to demonstrate that their positions had greater support.

Bibliography: Keith Feiling, *A History of the Tory Party, 1640-1714*, 1924; K. H. D. Haley, *The First Earl of Shaftesbury*, 1968.

Mark C. Herman

Absolutism. The word *absolutism* was coined in the nineteenth century as a pejorative label for conservative autocracy and soon passed into historiographical usage to describe a trend toward more powerful kingship in early modern Europe and the system of government this trend created, especially in Habsburg Spain and Bourbon France. Recent scholarship has rendered the concept of absolutism problematical by revealing the enormous variety of governmental practices throughout Europe and the limits that entrenched privilege, geographic obstacles, and bureaucratic inefficiency imposed on the power of even the strongest kings. Most historians, however, continue to use the term to refer to several related developments fostering extensions of royal power: (1) the elaboration of theological, legal, and philosophical arguments elevating royal authority above all political constraints; (2) attempts to curb or eliminate elected assemblies and other institutional limits on monarchy; (3) heavy arbitrary taxation*; and (4) the development of more centralized administrative systems to enforce the royal will.

The most distinguished exponent of absolutist theory in early seventeenth-century Britain was James I*. He argued that monarchs derive their power directly from God and are ultimately accountable to God alone. Rebellion or active resistance to royal authority, even under extreme circumstances, is sacrilege. This doctrine, commonly known as the divine right* of kings, was endorsed by a number of early Stuart clergymen including Roger Manwaring and Robert Sibthorpe in provocative sermons justifying arbitrary taxation during the forced loan* controversy of 1626-1627 and by convocation in 1640. After the Restoration* divine right doctrine received unequivocal support from the Anglican* church and formed the ideological bedrock of Tory* support for the future James II* during the Exclusion Crisis* in 1678-1681. The secular justifications of absolutism advanced by civil lawyers like William Fulbecke and John Cowell, the patriarchalism of Sir Robert Filmer, and the highly controversial arguments of Thomas Hobbes* had less political impact.

Neither James I nor Charles I* began his reign with an absolutist program of eliminating parliament*. Both grew impatient, however, when parliaments criticized their policies and refused them supply, and both ruled for extended periods without calling parliament into session (1614-1621 and 1629-1640). James rather cautiously raised new impositions* (customs duties) without parliament, while Charles substantially increased royal revenues through nonparliamentary taxes, notably knighthood compositions, ship money*, and fines for violating forest laws*. Doubts about parliament's survival developed under James and increased in the 1630s. During the Tory reaction of the 1680s, the Crown sought to control parliamentary elections by remodeling borough charters, and in 1686 James II launched a campaign to pack the Commons through systematic electoral interference.

England's unique administrative system, with its reliance on unpaid local magistrates rather than professional officeholders, precluded the sort of bureaucratic centralization that characterized French and Spanish absolutism. England's gentry magistrates, however, implemented the Personal Rule* of the 1630s and the Tory reaction. The Crown's administrative dependence on local elites placed some practical limits on its actions but did not necessarily rule out nonparliamentary government.

Used incautiously, the term *absolutism* can disguise assumptions and beg questions about the intentions and character of Stuart rule. Nevertheless, in a number of theoretical and practical features, Stuart kingship did resemble continental absolutist states. It is a legitimate question how far these similarities justify speaking of British absolutism.

Bibliography: Nicholas Henshall, "The Myth of Absolutism," *History Today* 42 (1992): 42-47; John Miller, ed., *Absolutism in Seventeenth Century Europe*, 1990; J. P. Sommerville, *Politics and Ideology in England 1603-1640*, 1986.

Malcolm Smuts

Addled Parliament. The parliament of 1614—the second of James I* —was short-lived and produced no legislation or other result. It was first called "addled" (meaning empty or fruitless) by contemporaries.

The king, deeply in debt, summoned the parliament in the hope that it would grant him a large supply, of which he was greatly in need. At least one privy councilor, the earl of Northampton, was doubtful of success, although there is no evidence that he schemed to sabotage the meeting, as was once widely supposed.

The parliament assembled on 5 April, when the king addressed both houses and appealed for supply. The House of Commons debated his request on 12 April, but the general feeling was that supply should be postponed. The house turned its attention to other matters, including reports of various improper attempts to influence its composition and proceedings. After an investigation, it expelled Sir Thomas Parry, chancellor of the duchy of Lancaster and a privy councilor, for having applied undue pressure in the election in Stockbridge. However, it found no evidence of widespread or concerted efforts to pack the house and concluded that there was no substance to the rumors that certain men called "undertakers" had arranged to manage the parliament for the king.

These matters did not disturb the parliament unduly, and for a time the session went on peacefully enough, though there was no haste in the Commons to give the king his subsidies. Both the Commons and the House of Lords paid a good deal of attention to ordinary legislative business. Some 109 bills, most of them relatively uncontroversial, received at least one reading in the Commons and some eighteen in the Lords (there was some overlap as each house sent bills it had passed to the other).

This peace was precarious, dependent upon the Commons's (temporary) forbearance in bringing up the dangerous matter of impositions*. These unparliamentary customs duties, introduced by Robert Cecil*, the earl of Salisbury, in 1608, had already helped wreck the previous parliament (of 1604-1610*), and some observers had predicted that the present parliament would also eventually come to grief over them. While the Commons regarded the impositions as a grave threat to property rights and parliamentary control of taxation*, the king could not afford to surrender them. The Commons were slow to make an issue of impositions in 1614; once they did, disaster followed quickly. Having resolved to petition the king, on 21 May they asked the upper house to confer, hoping to persuade the Lords to join them. However, the Lords declined even to confer, and the two houses then became embroiled over speeches critical of the lower house made by the bishop of Lincoln. This dispute brought all other proceedings to a halt. On 3 June, the king informed the Commons that if they did not turn to the consideration of his supply, he would dissolve the parliament. When the house insisted on first receiving some satisfaction in the matter of impositions, the king carried out his threat on 7 June.

Following so closely upon the debacle of 1610, the events of 1614 seem to have soured James on parliaments*, and he did not call another until a foreign crisis forced him to summon the parliament of 1621*.

Bibliography: Maija Jansson, ed., *Proceedings in Parliament 1614 (House of Commons)*, 1988; Thomas L. Moir, *The Addled Parliament of 1614*, 1958; Linda Levy Peck, "The Earl of Northampton, Merchant Grievances and the Addled Parliament of 1614," *Historical Journal* 24 (1981): 533-552.

Eric N. Lindquist

Adventurers (Ireland). A term applied to English investors of the 1640s and 1650s who provided funds for the suppression of the Irish Rebellion* (1641-1653) in exchange for a share in Irish lands confiscated in its aftermath. Usually taking the form of cash payments, occasionally the shares were issued in compensation for expenses in active service against the rebels. The sale of shares continued throughout the English Civil War* and eventually raised £306,718, making it the second largest joint stock enterprise of the seventeenth century, after the East India Company*. Approximately 1,530 individual adventurers can be identified. The vast majority were parliamentary supporters, especially Puritans*, and there were several Dutch investors. Prices were not especially favorable compared to other colonial projects, and the investors tended to be speculators who planned to serve as absentee landlords or pass Irish estates on to their offspring.

First proposed to parliament* by the City of London* in December 1641, speculation was probably encouraged by the Old English Lords' joining the rebellion early the same month, for only their estates in the Pale were prosperous enough to attract investors. By the time "An Act for the Speedy Supply and Effectual Reduction of the Rebels in his Majesty's Kingdom" (known as the Act for Adventurers) was passed on 19 March 1642, it was viewed as a thinly veiled means for parliament to raise funds for the coming struggle with Charles I*. It allotted 2.5 million acres (18 percent of all profitable land in Ireland) for speculative investment and valued the shares to raise a total of £1 million. In actuality the size of the eventual confiscation was ultimately determined by the financial needs of parliament. This can be seen in an act of 1643 that doubled the shares received in exchange for investment. The Act of Adventurers assumed that the rebels would be totally dispossessed. This made a negotiated settlement of the rebellion unlikely, for parliament and the investors had a tremendous financial stake in such a confiscation, while the rebels would certainly never agree to it.

The land designated available for adventure was divided equally among the four provinces. The values were rated according to which province the land was located in, with Leinster acres (the highest, at 12 shillings) being worth three times Ulster acres (the lowest, at 4 shillings). Although there were some extremely large investments, the average holding was about 700 acres at the time of distribution. The land was distributed among the adventurers in several lotteries, which began in 1653, despite the lack of an accurate land survey. The adventurers pressed for this quick settlement, in fear that the claims of Oliver Cromwell's* soldiers, who were also being paid off in Irish land, would supersede their own. As a result, many holdings were poorly defined and the subject of resurvey and litigation for many years. At the Restoration*, Charles II* recognized the holdings of approximately half the adventurers who received land in 1653, the remainder somehow having lost or given up tenure during the previous seven years.

Bibliography: Karl S. Bottigheimer, *English Money and Irish Land: The "Adventurers" in the Cromwellian Settlement of Ireland*, 1971.

John Nolan

Agitators. Not long after the New Model Army* began to resist the Long Parliament's* attempt to disband it in the spring of 1647, the soldiery of the cavalry regiments elected "agitators" as spokesmen for their interests, and the foot regiments soon followed suit. The word *agitator* carried no subversive overtones and was interchangeable with *agent*. The original agitators had a close rapport with many sympathetic officers and were wholly loyal to the army's* commanders. Hostile observers attributed their emergence to the Levellers*, but it was spontaneous. A few agitators, notably Edward Sexby, showed Leveller leanings from the start, and the Levellers subsequently attempted to indoctrinate the rest, but they had only partial success. By May the agitators had a closely knit organization; when the regiments were asked to draw up statements of their soldiers' grievances, agitators played a major part in preparing them and were admitted to the subsequent meetings between officers and parliamentary commissioners at Saffron Walden. Only three of the statements that survive (from thirteen regiments and the life guard) show specifically Leveller influences.

The agitators' organization was chiefly responsible for the abduction of Charles I* from Holdenby House on 2-3 June. This may have induced Lord Thomas Fairfax* to give it formal recognition and bring it under control, for the *Solemn Engagement of the Army*, which was approved by the assembled regiments at the general rendezvous on 5 June, announced that the satisfaction of their grievances must be ratified by a new general council of the army, including two officers and two soldiers elected by each regiment. The general council's first debates at Reading in July, in which the Heads of the Proposals* were considered, and the even more fascinating Putney Debates* of late October and early November, were recorded in a primitive shorthand by its secretary William Clarke; the published *Clarke Papers* transmit the authentic voices of a number of agitators, as well as many officers. By September, however, John Lilburne* and other civilian Levellers had become disappointed with most of the agitators, finding them too submissive to Oliver Cromwell* and Henry Ireton*, so they organized the emergence of new agitators in five cavalry regiments. These "agents of the five regiments" were almost certainly never formally elected by their units, which continued to be represented by their authentic agitators in the general council. But they put their names to the Levellers' Agreement of the People*, and their spokesmen were admitted to defend it at Putney. Even while the debates were in progress, however, they were stirring up serious unrest among the soldiery, and on 8 November the general council agreed to send the representative officers and soldiers back to their regiments. A week later Fairfax and Cromwell nipped an incipient Leveller mutiny in the bud, and the unity and discipline of the army were rapidly restored. It was high time, for Charles I had just escaped from the army's custody, and the Second Civil War* was soon to follow. The agitators never returned to the general council, which became an assembly of officers. The Levellers made some attempt to revive them in the early months of 1649, but where they appeared they were plainly identified with subversion and had no officer support. After the repression of the Leveller mutiny in May, their memory was occasionally invoked but never to much effect. Several ex-agitators, however, made interesting careers as officers.

The historiography of the agitators belongs almost entirely to the last hundred years, for until Sir Charles Firth published the first volume of *The Clarke Papers* in 1891, they were little known.

Bibliography: C. H. Firth, ed., *The Clarke Papers*, vols. 1 and 2, 1891-1894, rprt. 1992; Austin Woolrych, *Soldiers and Statesmen: The General Council of the Army and its Debates, 1647-1648*, 1987.

Austin Woolrych

Agreement of the People. A Leveller* constitution written in late October 1647, published by early November, and modified in December 1648 and May 1649. Attributed to agitators* from five New Model Army* cavalry regiments, the first agreement's actual authors are unknown, though John Lilburne* and John Wildman may have written it, perhaps aided by Richard Overton and William Walwyn. Assuming the old state to be dead, the Levellers offered the agreement as a social contract for a new society and the common soldiers' alternative to the officers' Heads of the Proposals*, which would have created a constitutional monarchy. The agreement distilled arguments in *The Case of the Army Truly Stated* (15 October), which argued for the existence of a "law paramount" based on reason, superior to parliamentary law, and guaranteeing popular sovereignty.

Clause I called for proportional representation in parliament*, clause II for the dissolution of the Long Parliament* on 30 September 1648, and clause III for biennial parliaments. Clause IV stated that parliament's powers, inferior only to the electorate's, should entail both legislative functions and executive, the latter including creation of offices and courts, appointment of officials, making of war and peace, and diplomacy. It also reserved to those represented certain essentially inalienable rights: religious toleration, freedom from impressment, equality before the law, and indemnity for acts committed during the war. Clearly there was to be no king or House of Lords.

Clause I became the focal point of the Putney Debates* held in the general council of the army from 28 October until early in November. Henry Ireton*, speaking for the officers, took it to imply universal manhood suffrage; *The Case of the Army Truly Stated* had called for enfranchising all free-born men twenty-one or over save for "delinquents" (royalists*). It emerged in debate that the Levellers meant to exclude servants and recipients of alms (see Poor Laws and Poverty*), who would be too dependent on their masters to vote freely (though there is some question whether "servants" included all wage earners or only those living in their masters' homes). The Levellers would have given the franchise to craftsmen, shopkeepers, copyholders, and leaseholders, whereas the officers or Grandees wished to restrict it to freeholders, as well as preserving monarchy and the Lords. Attempts at compromise bore little fruit, and Oliver Cromwell* ultimately ordered the soldiers at Putney back to their regiments. Colonel Thomas Rainsborough attempted to present a copy of the agreement to General Thomas Fairfax* at Ware on 15 November, but to no avail.

The Levellers' fortunes fluctuated over the next year, but by December 1648 they appeared to be in a strong position. The army* seized the king, Fairfax took London*, and Pride's Purge* left the Rump Parliament* dominated by Independents*. The need for concessions to the Independents led Lilburne, Walwyn, Wildman, and Maximilian Petty to draft a second agreement, which explicitly denied the vote to wage earners, accepted a council of state* to govern between parliamentary sessions, provided for the reserved powers to include strict separation of executive, legislative, and judicial branches, prohibited "leveling" of wealth (thus deflecting the inaccurate charge that they were communists), and listed various grievances, while retaining the original guarantees of individual rights. But in the council of officers, the Independents rejected the complete religious toleration insisted on by the Levellers, wishing to exclude Catholics* and atheists. On 15 December the Levellers withdrew from the meeting and published the second agreement, a week later Lieutenant-Colonel John Jubbes produced his own agreement in a failed attempt at compromise, and on 20 January 1649 the officers presented their heavily amended version to parliament, where it was ignored amid the furor surrounding Charles I's trial and execution*. The Levellers had lost again.

On 1 May, seeking to exploit mutinous sentiment among soldiers ordered to Ireland*, Lilburne, Overton, Walwyn, and Thomas Prince—all imprisoned in the Tower—published the third agreement. It called for dissolving the Rump in August; annual parliaments; enfranchising all men twenty-one and older who were not servants, recipients of alms, or royalists; strict separation of powers; rotation in office; prohibition of membership in consecutive parliaments; and an increased number of reserved powers (or fundamentals), which were to be beyond the scope of legislation. These included the ban on excise taxes (see Taxation and Revenue*), monopolies*, and tithes; such legal reforms as exempting defendants from self-incrimination, requiring legal proceedings to be conducted in English, abolishing imprisonment for debt, and limiting capital punishment to murder and other "heinous offenses"; and various others. Religious toleration remained, but Catholics, though to be free to worship, were banned from holding public office. However, the Grandees more tightly restricted the Leveller leaders in the Tower, easily crushed the mutiny at Burford on 15 May, and charged Lilburne with high treason on 24 October. Though he was acquitted two days later amid popular rejoicing, the Levellers were never a power in English politics after 1649, and the third agreement went the way of its predecessors.

Bibliography: G. E. Aylmer, ed., *The Levellers in the English Revolution*, 1975; H. N. Brailsford, *The Levellers and the English Revolution*, 1961; Howard Shaw, *The Levellers*, 1968.

William B. Robison

Agriculture. Agriculture remained the most important sector of the Stuart economy, producing almost all of the raw materials for industry and overseas commerce as well as the food supply. England was more self-sufficient than any other country of Europe in food production, but rapid demographic expansion stimulated a 600 percent increase in food prices between 1520 and 1640, and this expanding market provided the incentives for the agricultural revolution.

The main features of agricultural innovation were discernible by 1600 and made rapid progress after the middle of the seventeenth century. Generally the yields of grain and animal fodder per unit of land at least doubled, and as a consequence the crises of subsistence and the accompanying mortality crises, which still characterized comparable continental European countries in the seventeenth century, totally disappeared from England after the crises of 1629-30. The agricultural revolution was based on the practice of convertible husbandry, which banished the wasteful medieval practice of leaving arable fields fallow every third year, and substituted a system of continuous cultivation, alternating the growing of grain with the sowing of nitrogen-fixing grasses and legumes such as clover, lucerne, and sainfoin and tubers such as Swedish turnips. The increase in production of these fodder plants allowed farm animals to be fattened at all seasons of the year, resulting in increased production not only of meat but also of greater quantities of tallow for soap and candles and manure for fertilizer. The application of fertilizers, together with the practice of marling and the increasing cultivation of artificially planted nitrogen-fixing grasses, increased the fertility of arable fields and made fallowing unnecessary.

England had been a net exporter of grain up to the crises of the 1590s, when it began to import cereals despite the onset of a period of demographic stagnation. The disappearance of measurable famine from England in the first half of the seventeenth century suggests that a more highly developed marketing system allowed remote parts of the highland zone to absorb the surpluses that had formerly been exported. The export of grain resumed at midcentury when a population* decline caused domestic grain prices to subside. England became self-sufficient in all agricultural commodities except naval stores (which included hemp and flax as well as timber), wool, and the exotic commodities, such as tea, coffee, cocoa and sugar, that could be produced only in tropical climates. Tobacco was grown in the American colonies as a matter of mercantile policy (see Mercantilism*) rather than of necessity, and domestic cultivation was discouraged.

The increase in agricultural productivity also resulted from an expansion of the land under cultivation. The significant features of this movement include the draining of fens and marshlands (see Fen Drainage*), especially prominent in East Anglia and Lincolnshire; the disafforestation of royal forests, notably in the Midlands and the west of England, where the Tudor and Stuart monarchs had ceased to hunt; the disparking of private game reserves (i.e., ending their status as parks); and encroachment upon and enclosure of common wastes. Enclosure was promoted by manorial lords who wished to change to convertible husbandry, which required substantial investment of capital, or who saw the opportunity to make large profits by subdividing commons and erecting large numbers of cottages. The latter course, which did not require large capital outlay, was associated with the phenomenon of impopulation, or the rapid and uncontrolled influx of population into a particular community, and the growth of rural industries. Disafforestation often caused environmental degradation, and the land reclaimed for cultivation could be made fertile only by heavy applications of marl and manure. The draining of the fens was undertaken by Dutch hydraulic engineers such as Cornelius Vermuyden. The fens proved more fertile but were enormously expensive to drain and keep dry and have never been totally free from flooding. Drainage also provoked violent protest from the fenlanders, as did most projects that radically altered land use. Altogether land reclamation increased the area under cultivation by 25 percent between 1500 and 1700, with most of the increase occurring in the seventeenth century. The increase in productivity from this source, however, barely kept pace with demographic expansion.

There is also an important social dimension to the increase in agricultural productivity. The transition from a peasant economy based on subsistence farming to commercial agriculture, resting on capitalist principles and ownership of the land by large proprietors, degraded the status of peasants to that of agricultural laborers or cottagers. Family-sized holdings of 15 to 50 acres, which had been bequeathed from one generation to another, were sold off, thus reducing the standard of living and food consumption of smallholders. It is generally agreed that as less food went into the bellies of peasants, more food was freed up for the market economy. These smallholders were especially vulnerable to repeated harvest failures, such as occurred during the crises of the 1590s, and they often sank under the burden of indebtedness. Although enforced only sporadically, the tillage statutes of the sixteenth century had protected peasant holdings against depopulating enclosures and consolidation into larger farms. With the collapse of the prerogative courts*, especially the court of Star Chamber, which had enforced these laws, another obstacle to thorough agrarian change was removed. Thus, peasant proprietors steadily lost ground to large farmers, who were more oriented to commercial production and invested their profits in more land. During the economic stagnation that prevailed from the war years of the 1640s to the end of the century, the larger farmers found it more difficult to purchase additional land, and available land was usually snatched up by the great landed families, a trend that continued into the eighteenth century. Thus, agricultural land and wealth became increasingly concentrated in fewer and fewer hands, and the social gulf in rural society between the owners of the great estates and the agricultural laborers who cultivated those lands continued to widen. The English peasantry disappeared in the process. With the progress of the agricultural revolution, food production became more capital intensive but required less labor. Especially hard hit were laborers in closed villages, where seigneurial control was strong, enclosure ate away at common wastes, and few alternatives to agricultural employment existed. The surplus population was compelled to emigrate to areas of woodland pasture, to squat on common wastes or rent cottages, seek employment in rural industries such as textiles and the secondary metal trades, migrate to towns, or make their way overseas.

By contrast to the regions of mixed farming where peasant proprietors had largely disappeared, in pastoral regions such as the East Anglian and Lincolnshire fens and the northern highland zone, the small family farm remained strong through the end of the seventeenth century. An increase in population in these areas stimulated production by small farmers, and common wastes were more accessible for cottagers to graze their animals upon. In these areas manorial lords were less able to control population growth and the erection of cottages on the commons. Many of the small farmers and cottagers furnished the labor for the expansion of rural industries and created a distinct proto-industrial society. It was in the woodland and pastoral societies of the West Midlands, in counties such as Shropshire and Staffordshire, that the Industrial Revolution began.

Bibliography: Joan Thirsk, ed., *The Agrarian History of England and Wales,* Vol. 4: *1500-1640,* 1967, Vol. 5: *1640-1750,* pts. 1 & 2, 1984-1985; C. G. A. Clay, *Economic Expansion and Social Change, 1500-1700,* Vol. 1: *People, Land and Towns,* 1984; R. B. Manning, *Village Revolts: Social Protest and Popular Disturbances in England, 1500-1640,* 1988.

Roger B. Manning

Allegiance, Oath of. The oath of allegiance originated in "An Act for the Better Discovering and Repressing of Popish Recusants" (3 Jac. 1, c. 4) passed by the parliament (of 1604-1610*) in 1606, after the Gunpowder Plot*. It could be extended to all recusants* except peers and included clauses repudiating the pope's power to depose kings and stating that the recipient did "abhor, detest, and abjure, as impious and heretical, this damnable doctrine and position, that princes which be excommunicated or deprived by the Pope may be deposed or murdered by their subjects." Its emphasis on the political doctrines of Catholicism*—especially the medieval claim that the pope might depose rulers and sanction rebellion, which Jesuit theologians had recently reasserted—was designed to exploit divisions within the recusant community between laymen and secular clergy eager to prove their loyalty and more intransigent Jesuit missionaries. The oath also lent color to James I's* assertion that his policies toward Catholics sought only to defend against potential traitors, not to infringe in matters of conscience.

Pope Paul V quickly issued a breve condemning the oath and forbidding Catholics to take it. Many nevertheless did so, including the nominal head of the English Catholic community, the Archpriest George Blackwell, who wrote an open letter justifying his submission. This elicited a second papal breve and a reply from the great Jesuit theologian Cardinal Bellarmine. In 1607 James himself responded to the pope and Bellarmine in *Triplici Nodor triplex cuneus or An Apology for the Oath of Allegiance,* which he published anonymously in English, Latin, and French. Besides defending the oath, he asserted his own orthodoxy and argued that the pope was the Antichrist. Bellarmine replied under the name Matteo Torti, whereupon James reissued his treatise, acknowledging his authorship and adding a prefatory "Premonition" to the rulers of Europe.

This exchange began an international controversy that continued for over a decade, resulting in the publication of more than 150 books and pamphlets in English, Latin, French, and other languages. Apart from Bellarmine the most important Catholic participants were Martin van der Beek or Becanus, Jean l'Heureux or Eudaemon-Joannes, and Francis Suarez. The English Jesuit Robert Parsons also entered the controversy. The most substantial defense of the oath was Lancelot Andrewes's* *Tortura Torti Sive ad Matthaei Torti Librum Responsio*, composed at James's command and published in 1609. Several other English bishops and clergymen also defended the king's position, as did the French Protestant theologian Pierre du Moulin and the great Huguenot scholar Isaac Casaubon, who became absorbed in the controversy after immigrating to London* in 1611. John Donne* supported the cause with *Pseudo-Martyr* (1610) and *Ignatius His Conclave* (1610 or 1611).

The oath of allegiance controversy became intertwined with a related debate stemming from a posthumous book of the Scottish Catholic William Barclay, *De Potestate Papae* (1609), which denied that the pope had any power in temporal affairs. Bellarmine replied to Barclay and elicited a number of responses in turn.

In France the English position met with sympathy from Gallican Catholics anxious to uphold the liberties of the French Crown against ultramontane pretensions, especially after Henry IV's assassination in 1610, which many Frenchmen blamed on Jesuit influence. In the Estates General of 1614, the Third Estate proposed an oath for French officeholders similar to the oath of allegiance. In the ensuing debate, the spokesman for the clerical First Estate, Cardinal du Perron, charged that this proposal had originated in England as a plot to destroy the unity of French Catholics and reignite the wars of religion. After the measure was defeated and du Perron's oration appeared in print, James responded with *A Remonstrance for the Right of Kings* (1615), his longest political treatise.

Bibliography: Charles McIlwain, *The Political Works of James I*, 1918; Peter Milward, *Religious Controversies of the Jacobean Age: A Survey of Printed Sources*, 1978.

Malcolm Smuts

Amboina Massacre (1623). Incident in which officials of the Dutch East India Company executed ten English employed by the English East India Company* along with ten Japanese mercenaries and a Portuguese for allegedly conspiring to seize the Dutch fortress of Fort Victoria on Amboina in the Moluccas.

The growing rivalry between the English and the Dutch East India Companies for control of the Indonesian spice trade broke out into open hostility during 1618 and 1619 (see Trade, Foreign*). Both sides agreed to peace in the accord of 1619, which conceded a third of the spice trade to England. The Dutch, however, continued to harass English traders, and English imports of pepper showed a severe decline between 1619 and 1623. Bad feelings and suspicion grew between the two sides, and by early 1623 the outnumbered English decided to abandon some of their more vulnerable trading posts. Before that withdrawal could be accomplished, a tragic incident occurred at the important spice island of Amboina in the Moluccas.

The European trading factory at Amboina contained eighteen Englishmen at the beginning of 1623. English sources put the strength of Dutch forces at 200 Europeans and 300 native troops along with some Japanese mercenaries. Dutch sources number their own forces at 150 Europeans and 50 native troops. There were also eight Dutch ships in the harbor. But in spite of their overwhelming numerical superiority, Dutch officials remained nervous. On 23 February 1623, a Japanese mercenary in English service was caught scouting the Dutch fortifications and asking suspicious questions. Taken into custody by Dutch officials, he revealed under torture an English plot to seize the Dutch Fort Victoria upon the arrival of a single English ship. The Dutch governor, Herman Van Speult, had other Japanese soldiers questioned under torture, and they too confessed to the English plot. Finally the Dutch interrogated the chief English factor, Gabriel Towerson, and the other English traders. Some admitted to the plot only under torture, although a few acknowledged it of their own free will. Those who confessed to the conspiracy on their own were spared and allowed to leave Amboina. As for the rest, Van Speult decided to execute ten English, ten Japanese, and a Portuguese by beheading on 9 March.

In England, outrage greeted the news of the executions on Amboina. The Dutch claims about the existence of an English conspiracy seemed preposterous given the situation. Certainly the public in England thought so, although the Dutch did not. The Dutch government supported its representatives in Amboina, and some modern historians supporting the Dutch position argue that an actual conspiracy existed. Van Speult, the man most responsible for the tragedy, died in 1626 on the way home to answer English charges of a massacre. Otherwise Dutch investigators acquitted the remaining officials at Amboina of any crime.

The Amboina massacre had no effect on the English decision to close their trading posts in the Moluccas. It did, however, contribute to the growth of anti-Dutch feelings in England for many years. It was not until thirty years later, in 1654, that a clause in the Treaty of Westminster ending the First Dutch War* required that the Dutch pay £3,615 in compensation to the families of the victims. Charles II* in 1665 still claimed the Amboina massacre as one of the causes of the Second Dutch War*.

Bibliography: D. K. Bassett, "The 'Amboina Massacre' of 1623," *Journal of Southeast Asian History* 1, no. 2, 1960: 1-19; Holden Furber, *Rival Empires of Trade in the Orient, 1600-1800*, 1976.

Ronald H. Fritze

Andrewes, Lancelot (1555-1626). Scholar, court preacher, and bishop, Andrewes played a key role in the transmission and development of a distinctively Anglican* piety from the Elizabethan to the Caroline era. Andrewes was born in London in 1555 and educated at Merchant Taylors' School and Pembroke Hall, Cambridge. Elected a fellow of Pembroke Hall in 1576, he was offered two bishoprics by

Elizabeth I, which he refused because he objected to her insistence that he yield episcopal revenues in return for the positions. In 1601, however, he accepted appointment as the dean of Westminster and ascended steadily after James I's* arrival in England, becoming bishop of Chichester in 1605, bishop of Ely and member of the privy council* in 1609, and dean of the Chapel Royal and bishop of Winchester in 1619. Having mastered fifteen languages, his linguistic skill made him an obvious choice to help translate the authorized version of the Bible*. When the Jesuit controversialist Robert Bellarmine attacked the oath of allegiance* that James I required in the aftermath of the Gunpowder Plot*, Andrewes wrote two powerful treatises in its defense.

James loved Andrewes's preaching so much that he said that no one had spoken as well "since the days of the Apostles," and the king kept a copy of one of the sermons under his pillow. But James did not approve of Andrewes's inclinations toward an Arminian* position on predestination and enjoined him to silence on the subject. Andrewes obeyed but nevertheless inserted numerous barbs against Calvinists* and Puritans* into his sermons, and, unlike his royal master, he never distinguished between moderate and radical Puritans. Andrewes denounced a piety that emphasized the hearing of sermons (especially those containing speculation about absolute predestination) and altered the liturgy contained in the Book of Common Prayer. For him attendance at a sermon was not to worship God but to prepare to do so in the Church of England's prescribed prayers, ceremonies (including bowing at the name of Jesus), and sacraments, especially the Eucharist (which should be received kneeling). According to Andrewes, liturgical prayer and the Eucharist were sources of divine grace, not preaching. For him the Puritans had taken the Protestant Reformation too far and become a threat to order in the church and royal power in both church and state. James's policy of balancing Calvinists and anti-Calvinists against each other and the bishop's own dislike of controversy acted as a brake on the desire of Andrewes and his friends to harry both Calvinists and Puritans. But their efforts put them in position for rapid advance after James's death in 1625. Andrewes died on 26 September 1626, but his ideas powerfully influenced the work of two of his most fervent admirers, Charles I* and William Laud*.

Bibliography: Kenneth Fincham, *Prelate as Pastor,* 1990; Peter Lake, "Lancelot Andrewes, John Buckeridge, and Avant-Garde Conformity at the Court of James I," in Linda Levy Peck, *The Mental World of the Jacobean Court,* 1991, pp. 113-133; Paul A. Welsby, *Lancelot Andrewes, 1555-1626,* 1958.

                                                                    J. Sears McGee

Anglicanism. A term used to represent an understanding of Christian faith and practice that evolved in England particularly during the Reformation. Today Anglicanism claims to represent a body of Christendom distinct from Orthodox, Roman Catholic*, and Protestant traditions. It refers to the practice of Christianity in Churches of the Anglican Communion, which at the end of the twentieth century is a worldwide affiliation of 70 million members in over 160 countries.

The word *Anglicanism* appeared only in the nineteenth century. The *Oxford English Dictionary* records an earliest written use by John Henry Newman in 1838. Uses of the adjective *Anglican* date from 1635 onward. Both words derive from the Latin word for the English, *anglicanus*. The phrase *ecclesia Anglicana* was used to refer to the medieval English church, and during the Reformation, Henry VIII was legislatively acknowledged supreme head of the Church of England, *Anglicana ecclesia*.

Although there was no common usage of the term *Anglicanism* before the nineteenth century, historians and theologians continue to address past roots of this concept. Debate continues today about how early to begin the study of Anglicanism, with some saying as early as Roman Britain. Most historians, however, concur that the sixteenth and seventeenth centuries were foundational for the historical development of classical Anglicanism. Certainly the Reformation period was formative. It is clear, retrospectively, that leading statesmen, ecclesiastics, reformers, and theologians of the sixteenth century established the vision, structures, and basic principles for worship and teaching in the reformed English church.

The process of religious reform in England did not begin exclusively at home, though the Lollard tradition of dissent and late medieval anticlericalism provided indigenous evidence of dissatisfaction with religious life on the Reformation's eve. Tudor scholars and reformers were well informed by and contributed to Renaissance humanism. Early English reformers also incorporated fundamental insights from continental reformers (e.g., Martin Luther, Martin Bucer, and Huldreich Zwingli), particularly the central place they gave to the authority of Scripture and their affirmation of justification by faith from which works would freely flow. As on the Continent, accessibility to vernacular Bibles* in England was central for new religious understanding. Key to the eventual provision of printed English Bibles were biblical translations by the reformer William Tyndale (c.1494-1536). Authorized use of the Bible in English was permitted in parishes from 1538.

In the sixteenth century, three English leaders had the most influence on the eventual character of Anglicanism. Chief among these primary early architects of Anglicanism was Thomas Cranmer (1489-1556), skilled liturgical scholar and archbishop of Canterbury (1533-1555). Late in the reign of Henry VIII, Cranmer worked on drafting vernacular liturgies. He was able to present a more coherent program of reform during the reign of the child king, Edward VI (1547-1553). In 1549 a new vernacular liturgy, the Book of Common Prayer, replaced its Latin predecessors. Three years later Cranmer and his associates, working in response to English and continental reformers, enhanced the Protestant character of English liturgy with authorized use of the new 1552 prayer book. The doctrinal framework of this new-reformed church was also influenced by Cranmer in the Forty-two Articles of 1553 (the basis of the Thirty-nine Articles in 1571). Collectively, these articles came to represent not precise confessionalism; instead they provided broad assertions of belief and practice. By the end of Edward VI's reign nascent Anglicanism rested on its great books: the English Bible and the common worship in accord with the Book of Common Prayer. The experience of those Edwardian laity and clergy persecuted in the reign of Edward's successor, Mary Tudor (1533-1559), was narrated and amplified in another of the English Reformation's "great books," John Foxe's *Acts and Monuments*, popularly named *Book of Martyrs* (first printed in English in 1563).

Elizabeth Tudor (1533-1603) was the second primary architect of early Anglicanism. Adroitly this monarch, who did not seek "windows" into her subjects' souls, worked to establish an ideal of comprehensiveness designed to encompass England's Catholics and Protestants. The Elizabethan Settlement of 1559 rested, as her father's had, on a reassertion of royal supremacy and, as her brother's had, on promulgation of the new Book of Common Prayer publicly enforced by an Act of Uniformity. The 1559 prayer book, a conservatively revised version of the 1552 text, established norms of worship that were more traditional than those desired by returning reformers who had been persecuted or exiled during Mary Tudor's reign. The polity of the Elizabethan church was maintained through episcopal church governance and enforced by Elizabeth's unyielding assertion of royal supremacy.

In practice, however, these tenets and other hallmarks of early Anglicanism were far from amicably settled. At least since 1572, an organized body of lay persons and clerics, who came to be known as Puritans*, energetically sought to purify further—with scriptural and Calvinistic* perspectives similar to those used in reformed churches of the continent—what they viewed in England as a "halfly-reformed" church. Meanwhile many English Catholics, called recusants* for their refusal to attend services of the established church, were tenacious in practicing the old faith, despite penal laws increasingly enforced against them in the latter half of Elizabeth's reign. For recusants the English reformation was a disaster; for Puritans it was unfinished.

The central advocate and apologist for Elizabethan Anglicanism was scholar, theologian, and preacher Richard Hooker (c.1554-1600). This third architect of classical Anglicanism in his central work, *Laws of Ecclesiastical Polity* (1593 and 1597), defended the reason and order of England's ecclesiastical practice. Like the apologist John Jewel (1522-1571) before him, Hooker called on scriptural and patristic sources to illustrate and defend the church's authority. He argued that the church in England had departed from the errors of Rome and the extremes of continental reformers and Puritan reformers alike, but not from essential Catholic faith. Hooker, the most widely read Anglican theologian in succeeding centuries, provided a theological framework that grounded the church's judgment in the authority of Scripture, reason, and tradition. While not disputing the supremacy of Scripture, his method gave room for various interpretations and applications in church life and teaching.

At the century's end, the ideal hallmarks of early Anglicanism were a faith conveyed in Scripture and creeds and embodied in the Book of Common Prayer, prescribed liturgical practice of word and sacrament governed through episcopal oversight and defended by royal supremacy, nonconfessional teaching officially open to wider understandings, and the assumption of a nationally ordered society where loyal citizenship and church membership cohered.

In seventeenth-century England, each of these assumptions proved troublesome, underscoring the increasingly fractious nature of religious life in England and throughout early modern Europe. Indeed, in Anglicanism's second formative century, the stage was set for continuation of the struggle between supporters of the establishment and more militant reformers, including those who effectively encouraged concessions to Puritan consciences, those with Presbyterian* leanings, as well as those who labored for more toleration for English Catholics.

Religion continued to be one focus for the long-apparent constitutional battles between king and parliament*. During the later years of James I* and under Charles I*, the alliance of crown and miter was increasingly tested. Charles I's appointment of William Laud* as archbishop of Canterbury in 1633 and the promotion of other clerics who in Puritan eyes favored "popish" doctrines and ceremonies continued, amid other tensions, to fuel suspicion and resentment. Eventually with the execution of Laud in 1645 and Charles I in 1649, Anglicanism was disestablished: episcopacy, the Book of Common Prayer, and the Articles of Religion were replaced at first by a Presbyterian ministry and later in Oliver Cromwell's* Commonwealth* by liberty for congregations as long as they were neither Roman Catholic nor Anglican. With the Restoration* in 1660, episcopal polity was rapidly reasserted and Laudian influences generally triumphed. Although Charles II* in the Declaration of Breda* attempted to extend broad toleration for those who were not Anglicans, the Act of Uniformity of 1662 (14 Car. II, c. 4) and restrictive statutes known as the Clarendon Code* emphasized adherence to church structures (episcopal leadership and prayer book liturgies) and disadvantaged non-Anglicans. Later under William III* religious freedom was granted to all trinitarians (those who accepted the doctrine of the Holy Trinity) except Roman Catholics. By the end of the seventeenth century Anglicanism and the Church of England remained established but within the context of a religiously pluralistic society.

The history and further evolution of Anglicanism under the Stuarts are especially noted for literary and theological contributions. Chief among the classics of seventeenth-century Anglicanism was a new biblical translation, which won James I's early support. This project, entrusted to scholars organized by Bishop Richard Bancroft, resulted in 1611 in the Authorized, or "King James," Bible*. This literary masterpiece of early Anglicanism became the Bible of English-speaking Protestants for centuries. Like Foxe's *Book of Martyrs,* it was frequently carried by religious refugees and colonial adventurers to the New World.

The seventeenth century was also a golden age of classical Anglicanism in the lives and writings of its major divines. Collectively known as the "Caroline Divines," several church leaders and theologians (many of them bishops) stood firm in refuting the errors of Roman Catholics and Puritans alike. They turned to the testimony of Scripture and the traditions of the first four centuries to explicate the Catholic context of the English church. Chief among them was Lancelot Andrewes* (1555-1626), a scholar, outstanding preacher, and apologist for Anglicanism. Andrewes was best known for his *Ninety-Six Sermons* and *Preces Privatae* (posthumously published in 1628 and 1648). His profound piety, like Hooker's, emphasized reason as part of the created order and focused on the essential character of grace, which perfects creation. His works evidence an essential appeal to learning as a profound basis for private prayer.

Likewise, Jeremy Taylor's (1613-1667) prolific works (sermons, manuals for prayer, and other books for daily devotion) emphasized concern for "Holy Living" and "Holy Dying." His popular works, many still read as classics of Anglican spirituality, underscore the practical and moral thrust of Anglicanism. Unlike Puritan contemporaries, in practicing the faith Taylor saw little division between religious and secular life; humanity was called every minute to do the work of God when serving others and even ourselves. The essential optimism about lived faith in this world, evidenced in Taylor and other early Anglican theologians, is far from the pessimism of Puritans and those sectarians inclined to see the world and worldly affairs as a swamp of evil.

Delight in the divine generosity of creation was also underscored by Thomas Traherne (c.1637-1674). Although Traherne was known and admired by contemporaries, appreciation for his devotional and inviting mystical reflections on creation awaited publication early in the twentieth century of his greatest work, *Centuries of Meditation.* During his lifetime he worked similarly to recall the ideal of felicity, elevating happiness to a theological principle. To the names of Traherne, Taylor, and Andrewes should be added those of Anthony Sparrow and Thomas Ken, among others, for their contributions to Anglican devotional life. The metaphysical poets, especially George Herbert, Henry Vaughan, and John Donne* (in prose as well as verse), were also among the foremost interpreters of Anglican spirituality (see Literature*).

In the Restoration church, impressive intellectual vitality was represented in the Latitudinarians* led by Edward Stillingfleet and John Tillotson, themselves influenced by the Cambridge Platonists' call for rationalism and an open spirit of inquiry. These churchmen favored moderation and latitude of opinion in religious life; they affirmed diversity so long as public order prevailed. Gilbert Burnet*, an author and bishop appointed by William III*, defended Latitudinarianism against the rigid divisions in church parties. In 1701 Burnet coined the terms *High* and *Low* used in successive centuries to describe variable affiliations within Anglicanism (see High Church*). These Latitudinarian bishops, characterized as "Broad" churchmen, were largely sympathetic to the intellectual climate of the ensuing Age of Reason.

Zeal for constructive education in the Anglican faith was represented at the end of the century by the 1698 establishment of the Society for the Promotion of Christian Knowledge, which published popular Christian literature, and the Society for the Propagation of the Gospel, which from 1702 on promoted colonial chaplaincies in the Americas, India, Asia, and Africa. For some scholars the resulting expansion of Anglicanism and the development of its evangelical character in the eighteenth century have come to represent the basis of modern Anglicanism as it developed into a worldwide communion of churches. Still other scholars point to nineteenth-century developments as formative for modern Anglicanism.

Yet for some contemporary authors, the seventeenth-century legacy of Anglicanism remains most important for its demarcation of Anglican theological method. This expression is apparent in its wide breadth of theological voices and perspectives, its appeal to sound learning, as well as to reasoned moderation, pragmatism, and the ability to reflect openly amid the competing tensions of a catholic and reformed thought. Today Anglicanism as a concept generally refers to these components of its method and ethos rather than to specific historical ingredients from its classical sixteenth- and seventeenth-century legacies.

Bibliography: H. R. McAdoo, *The Spirit of Anglicanism: A Survey of Anglican Theological Method in the Seventeenth Century*, 1965; S. Sykes and J. Booty, eds., *The Study of Anglicanism*, 1988; W. L. Sachs, *The Transformation of Anglicanism: From State Church to Global Communion*, 1993.

Fredrica Harris Thompsett

Anne (1665-1714). Anne's reign from 1702 to 1714 marked the end of the Stuart dynasty. It was characterized by the War of the Spanish Succession (1702-1713), battles between Whigs* and Tories*, and the union of England and Scotland* in 1707. Anne's role prior to the Glorious Revolution* is less well known. She was born in 1665, the third child of the duke of York (see James II*) and Anne Hyde*, daughter of Edward Hyde*, earl of Clarendon. Of their children only Mary* and Anne survived to maturity. Anne grew up in relative obscurity in the royal nursery at Richmond and did not develop a close relationship with her parents. The deaths of her grandmother (Henrietta Maria*), aunt (Henrietta Ann), and mother during an eighteen-month period in 1669-1671 and her own poor health gave Anne a feeling of insecurity and possibly caused her antisocial behavior.

York secretly converted to Catholicism* in 1669 and married the Catholic Mary of Modena* in 1673. But anti-Catholic sentiment in England convinced Charles II* to have Mary and Anne brought up as Anglicans*. Henry Compton, bishop of London, was the primary figure who influenced Anne to be faithful to the Church of England, teaching her that the papacy was evil and Dissenters* a threat to the Crown. Anne was confirmed in 1676, an insult to her father, who stopped attending Anglican services the same year.

Religion aside, Anne developed distaste for the Whigs because of their opposition to her father. Charles sent James to the Netherlands in 1679 after the Popish Plot* and the passage of the second Test Act* (30 Car. II, st. 2, c. 1) the previous year. The Exclusion Crisis* (1678-1681) kept James from returning home permanently until 1682 and prevented Anne from marrying. However, her marriage was increasingly important politically, and Charles searched cautiously for a suitable husband. This became more urgent in 1682, when it was rumored that Anne and John Sheffield, Lord Mulgrave, had become very friendly. In July 1683 she wed the Protestant Prince George of Denmark. Among their close friends in the "Cockpit Circle," foremost were John Churchill (later duke of Marlborough) and his wife, Sarah, who greatly influenced Anne. Others were the Berkeleys, the Bathursts, and the dukes of Grafton, Ormonde (James Butler*), and Queensbury.

When James came to the throne in 1685, Anne became the leading Protestant in England, as Mary had married William of Orange* in 1677. The Protestant majority looked to Anne to produce an heir, but despite her numerous pregnancies, none of her children reached adulthood. James's pro-Catholic policies alienated his people, and

Anne—no exception—moved closer to the Protestant camp. After a series of personal tragedies in 1687, she and George moved to Richmond, to recover and to be away from James. Many believed the Churchills were behind this move.

James's second Declaration of Indulgence*, the trial of the Seven Bishops*, and the birth of his son in 1688 caused leading Whigs and Tories to appeal to William of Orange for help. Anne and the Cockpit Circle were not directly involved, but it was widely known that they would support any move to prevent the reintroduction of Catholicism in England. Shortly after William's landing in November, the prince of Denmark, Churchill, Berkeley, and the dukes of Grafton and Ormonde defected to his side. James was extremely hurt by Anne's desertion.

William was given civilian and military control immediately after James's flight to France, but the Convention Parliament* waited to decide upon the constitutional situation until 1689. After a weak push to have parliament* provide for her succession upon Mary's death, Anne gave in to the Whig plan that William and Mary rule jointly, with William and their heirs (if any) succeeding Mary, and Anne and her heirs to follow William (see Bill of Rights*). For their role in the Glorious Revolution, she and George were given apartments in Whitehall, George was made duke of Cumberland, and Churchill became a member of the privy council*.

Bibliography: Edward Gregg, *Queen Anne*, 1980.

Paul Miller

Anne of Denmark (1574-1619). Queen consort of James VI and I*. Born on 12 December 1574, she was the daughter of the Lutheran King Frederick II of Denmark and Norway and Queen Sophia, whose father was Ulric III, duke of Mecklenberg. A popular tale claimed that until she was nine, attendants carried her about, refusing to let her walk. Sporadic negotiations for the marriage began in 1585—against the will of Elizabeth I of England—and James and Anne were married by proxy on 20 August 1589. After the ship carrying her to Scotland* disappeared in a storm, James sailed to the coast of Norway, where he found her and married her in person on 23 November. They spent the winter at the Danish court, where there was apparently a third ceremony. In May 1590 they were back in Scotland, where in 1591 the earl of Bothwell was charged with using witchcraft* against James during his journey to Denmark.

James and Anne's children included Henry, Prince of Wales*, in 1594, whose death in 1612 she mourned deeply; Elizabeth* in 1596, who married Frederick, the elector of the Palatinate in 1613; Margaret (died in infancy) in 1598; the future Charles I* in 1600; Robert (died in infancy) in 1601; and Mary in 1605 (died in 1607). Against Anne's wishes, James gave custody of Henry to the earl of Mar in 1595; she finally secured his return in 1603. Elizabeth was placed in the care of Lord Livingstone, whose wife was Catholic*, causing great uproar among the ministers in the Kirk*, who also complained of Anne's vanity and immorality (both exaggerated). Though she was later accused of popery, being Lutheran among Scottish Calvinists* was bad enough.

James became king of England in March 1603; Anne followed him there in June with Henry. Her lavish expenditures, constant indebtedness, and receipt of monopolies* were unpopular in England. So was her flirtation with Rome, though she apparently died a Protestant. Anne's influence over James should not be overemphasized, but neither was it negligible, though his affection for her perhaps declined with the rise of his favorites, the duke of Somerset (Robert Carr*) from 1607 to 1614 and the 1st duke of Buckingham (George Villiers*) from 1615. She intrigued against the earl of Salisbury (Robert Cecil*), detested Somerset, and worked to advance Buckingham. On good terms with Sir Edward Coke*, she also befriended Sir Walter Raleigh*. Though early on she favored Spain and supported a Spanish match* for Charles, late in life she became more sympathetic to France. She died of dropsy on 2 March 1619.

Bibliography: Gordon Donaldson, *Scotland, James V to James VII*, 1965; Leslie Stephen and Sidney Lee, eds., *Dictionary of National Biography*, 32 vols., 1908-1909.

William B. Robison

Argyll, 8th Earl of. See Campbell, Archibald, 8th Earl of Argyll.

Argyll, 9th Earl of. See Campbell, Archibald, 9th Earl of Argyll.

Arlington, Earl of. See Bennet, Henry.

Arminianism. This doctrine took its name from the Dutch theologian Jacobus Arminius, whose rejection of the high Calvinist* doctrine of absolute or double predestination in favor of human free will and the universality of Christ's atonement for human sin led to the calling of the Synod of Dort* in 1618. Although Arminian doctrine was condemned by that assembly, the reaction against Calvinist soteriology (which had begun before Arminius himself in any case) did not end.

The difficulty with *Arminian* as a term is that both contemporaries and modern historians use it to mean several different things. In the narrowest and most precise sense, it refers to those theologians who read the books written by Arminius and his Dutch colleagues and were directly influenced by them to reject double predestination and the doctrinal positions associated with it in favor of Arminian free will, universal grace, and the possibility that individuals might reject divine grace or have it but later fall away from it. In this restricted sense the number of Arminians in early Stuart England was small. More broadly it includes those who held to such doctrines whether they had read Arminius or not. Certainly some did so in England as early as the 1590s. There was a small but growing number of anti-Calvinists, especially in the universities*, by the turn of the century. James I* admired and advanced some of them (e.g., Lancelot Andrewes*) and even advanced some he did not particularly admire (e.g., William Laud*), but he prevented them from addressing the debate on predestination publicly. He also gave ecclesiastical preferment to Calvinists, such as his archbishop of Canterbury, George Abbot*, so long as they conformed to the ceremonies of the Church of England (see Anglicanism*).

Theological Arminianism first became a public issue, disputed in print and parliament*, as a response to the books of an anti-Calvinist cleric, Richard Montagu, beginning in 1624. John Pym* sounded the alarm in parliament*, and from 1624 through 1629 its importance as a grievance gained strength. At the tumultuous close of the parliament of 1629*, a Commons protestation called for the execution of anyone who sought to "extend or introduce Popery or Arminianism" because both departed from the doctrine of "the true and orthodox Church."

The main reason that the fears of Pym and his friends mounted during Charles I's* reign was that it seemed to them that the new king listened not to Calvinists like Archbishop Abbot, but to Laud and other anti-Calvinists. Some modern historians (among them Peter Lake, Conrad Russell, and Nicholas Tyacke) see Laud and Charles as initiating a major religious shift. They rejected the Calvinist theological inclination and relative liturgical simplicity of the late Elizabethan and Jacobean church. From this perspective, James's careful balancing of Calvinist and anti-Calvinist factions yoked both in the service of his purposes and kept their differences of opinion on the back burner and out of the public eye. But Charles abandoned his father's policy and handed the reins of the church to the anti-Calvinists. He encouraged Laud's campaign for the "beauty of holiness," meaning liturgical reforms emphasizing elaborate and uniform ceremonies in richly refurbished churches and envisioning the sacraments as sources of saving grace. As Laud himself put it, the "altar is . . . greater than the pulpit" and "the holy table is the greatest place of God's residence on earth."

Moderate Calvinists who had conformed to the earlier and less ambitious ceremonial requirements but disliked the new ones suddenly found themselves denounced as "Puritans"*, and they responded by counterattacking with the charge that the "Laudians" or "Arminians" were highjacking the church and taking it back toward Rome. Although Laud was not in fact a covert Catholic*, underpinning his liturgical program was a theology of free will that Calvinists correctly saw as more consonant with Rome than Geneva. In other words, theological Arminianism lay behind and informed Laudian ritualism. In this formulation, Arminianism in England came to have a liturgical as well as a theological character. The result is a much broader and more politicized conception of the meaning of Arminianism in early Stuart England.

Other historians (such as George Bernard, Kevin Sharpe, and Peter White) reject the notion of an "Arminian" takeover of the English church after 1625. They argue that the extent of Calvinist influence on the Elizabethan and Jacobean churches has been greatly exaggerated. There were Calvinist and anti-Calvinist factions, but Elizabeth, James, and Charles all followed a similar middle-of-the-road policy on the controversial theological issues and avoided commitment to either side. The Caroline liturgical reforms were not novel in their substance; they were for the most part merely canons* and rubrics or logical extensions of them that nonconformists had gotten away with ignoring in the past. Neither Charles I nor Laud was a theological Arminian, and behind their program lay not a theology of free will but a set of aesthetic preferences and a thirst for order and uniformity in worship. What was innovative was not, for example, the policy that communion tables be placed altarwise rather than tablewise, but the energy and thoroughness of the king and the archbishop in their enforcement of this and related requirements. On this account Arminianism was a purely theological issue, unrelated to liturgical matters, and it was not an important bone of contention in 1640-1642.

Choosing between the broad (theological/liturgical) and narrow (theological only) definitions of Arminianism presents considerable difficulties. How many contemporaries perceived a connection between free will theology and Laudian liturgy? Was the connection real or illusory? One thing is clear: fair or unfair, the belief in "Arminian innovation," broadly defined, was present in the Long Parliament*. For men like William Prynne*, John Pym, Sir William Brereton, and other parliamentarian* activists, the connection among theology, liturgy, Laudian episcopacy, and "popery" was not in doubt.

Bibliography: Kenneth Fincham, ed., *The Early Stuart Church, 1603-1642*, 1993; Nicholas Tyacke, *Anti-Calvinists: The Rise of English Arminianism, c.1590-1640*, 1987; Peter White, *Predestination, Policy and Polemic*, 1992.

                                                                                    J. Sears McGee

Army. Between 1600 and 1700 the English armed forces degenerated into perhaps the most dismal condition since before the time of Alfred. But after learning the "modern" art of war by fighting the Civil Wars*, the English army emerged at century's end in a form recognizable as that which would conquer the largest empire in the history of civilization. The overall trend of the Stuart period was toward centralization and nationalization of armed force, based after 1640 on parliamentary statute and designed to safeguard parliamentary sovereignty. These developments were neither smooth nor inevitable.

James I* inherited a military system designed for defense. Elizabethan practice had dictated that the trained bands, whose drilling and arming received close government scrutiny after 1573, were to protect their respective shires. Overseas expeditions could press men of marginal value to the local community. Only in rare instances had the queen allowed militiamen to be sent abroad to fight. Defense took precedence over foreign military expeditions. English offensive capabilities had been questionable since the Treaty of Troyes (1420), and it is significant that most, if not all, Tudor battlefield successes were in defense of the kingdom: the repulse of the Scots at Flodden in 1513, the expulsion of French interlopers in Scotland* in 1560, the scattering of the Armada in 1588, and the counterinsurgency against Catholic* threats in Ireland* at the end of the dynasty. Since James I expected to have no enemies, for he had no intention giving offense, he had no need of a formidable military force. It was still thought that the navy* and the English Channel provided sufficient defense. The first Stuart reduced the English military presence in Ireland and allowed militia preparedness to slacken. The nadir was reached in 1606-1608, with corrective measures to stiffen the militia implemented first in June 1608 and then with more stringency from 1612 to 1623.

It was the accession of Charles I* that rekindled the beacons and saw the revitalization of the trained bands into a "perfect militia." The husbandmen and skilled artisans of the militia experienced greater rigor in their drilling and the upkeep of their weapons, but Caroline expeditionary forces, like their predecessors, were regarded as expendable, and soldiers sent overseas in 1624, 1625, and 1627 suffered because of royal recklessness and a foolish foreign policy compounded by the obstinacy and callousness of parliament*. The failures of the 1620s were the legacy of Jacobean sloth and Caroline bellicosity. With the confrontation between Charles I and his Scottish subjects in 1638, a test of the efficacy of the English militia seemed likely. The religious and political uncertainties that had festered during the Personal Rule* (1629-1640), however, made the assemblage of an army to fight an English-speaking Protestant neighbor a matter of concern to those who would do the fighting. Not surprisingly, the definition of the military obligation became a pronounced political issue in the parliaments of 1640 and after, as had happened in the Middle Ages and to an extent in the 1620s. As it worked out, the English army of 1639 was an amalgam of coerced nobles, reluctant militiamen, and forcibly conscripted unfortunates. Whether this army would have prevailed against the Scots is unknown, for a peace was signed after no more than an impromptu skirmish. Less than a year later the Short Parliament* would wrestle with the legality of the military obligation. The earlier Stuarts, in fact, conducted their military activities without benefit of statutory legislation. The militia statute of Philip and Mary had not been reaffirmed by the first Jacobean parliament (of 1604-1610*), which meant that there existed no current legal basis for military service, be it for militia service or impressment. When the cooperative business of government broke down in 1642, it is not at all surprising that the crisis grew out of the struggle for control of the English armed forces.

Serious doubt about the Crown's intentions in the use of the armed forces had arisen in 1640, during the Second Bishops' War*, largely in a religious context. Was it right to wage a war against good Christians (i.e., Protestants) who professed their loyalty to the state? Suspicion grew even greater during the Long Parliament*, the episode of the army plots*, and then ultimately in the strategy for extirpating the Irish Rebellion* of 1641. By this time some members of parliament dreaded the Crown's unrestricted use of armed forces even in a campaign against Catholic Ireland. The debate over the militia ordinance brought these controversies into sharp focus. As a number of contemporaries acknowledged, the key issue was the control of armed forces (in the guise of the militia), for until the Roundheads* and Cavaliers* had the opportunity to forge their own military instruments, it was the militia that comprised the most formidable armed might of the realm. Yet the militia was an amateur force, its command shared by the governed, if shaped by the government. In that sense the modern English army finds its origins in the Civil Wars of 1642-1648, for more Englishmen gained military experience in that span than at any time previous. The Civil Wars made soldiers out of civilians who in normal times would have eschewed the military. This generation then spawned a Britain that prized military excellence, as had been the case in the Middle Ages.

The mobilization of English armies at the outset of the Civil Wars followed predictable patterns. Charles I issued commissions of array and looked to his nobles and gentry on an individual basis to cooperate in the creation of royal regiments. Parliament, "possessing" London*, recruited a force of over 10,000 from the vast human resources of the metropolis commanded by Robert Devereux*, the 3d earl of Essex. But other parliamentary armies contended with localism by reliance on county associations*, creating armies amalgamated from the militia and volunteers from regional areas who were in effect protecting their corner of the realm as much as supporting parliament. Early reverses and the incompatibility of local and national strategies ultimately provoked the establishment of the New Model Army*, which in composition was traditional but in command unusual, for its parliamentary commanders (especially those of noble birth) were put aside in the interests of safeguarding command from political bickering. Ultimately the New Model triumphed on the battlefield, supported administratively and financially from Westminster. But the apparent depoliticization of command led to the creation of a new political constituency, the army itself, which engaged in lobbying and threatening parliament once the war was won in 1645, with the years 1647-1648 being the most disruptive.

The Cavalier army, on the other hand, never perfected a bureaucratic apparatus to rival that of the Roundheads. Although the royalists* too created associations to raise and support troops, they did so in a more gradual way, without imposing their will as systematically on the county communities. Given their territorial position, they could not afford to act as arbitrarily as could a government seated at London. The tenuousness of royalist authority in the countryside in fact hampered the efforts of the Cavaliers. In contrast the parliamentarian* army ultimately turned on its creator and became a major political force in the settlement of the kingdom. From 1646 onward, England discovered what happened when an army was an active participant in domestic politics; thus, the rule of the major generals* and the accompanying ubiquitous soldier convinced Englishmen that the army should be divorced from politics.

The Restoration* achieved that. In 1661 England had its first peacetime standing army. Although anti-army sentiment persisted, Charles II's* army was clearly subordinate to the royal will, thanks to his choice of officers. It thus quite easily became an instrument of royal foreign policy in quarters throughout the globe. It was expensive, if relatively small, costing no less than £140,000 per annum. As the troops escorted bullion, broke up illegal assemblies, and personified royal authority, the existence of the army sat uncomfortably with many members of parliament. This, along with Charles II's apparently hereditary predisposition to rule without parliament, made his six standing regiments symptomatic of another potential constitutional breakdown within the ruling elite. That fear did not become a reality until the accession of James II*. Although the armed forces in early 1685 amounted to fewer than 9,000 men, Monmouth's Rebellion* precipitated an increase to nearly 20,000 by year's end. By the time William of Orange* set foot in England in November 1688, James II had massed 30,000 men, with another 10,000 in garrison or training. These were not trained band soldiers, for the militia had virtually disappeared in most parts of England by 1688. Although most army officers were Protestant, there were enough

Catholic officers, some newly commissioned, to give the impression that a Romanist army was coalescing.

On the other side of the Channel, the Anglo-Dutch brigade, its exploits in the name of Protestantism recognized, provided a nucleus for William's invasion. This brigade, and a conspiracy among the officer corps of James II's army, made possible the bloodless coup of 1688 (see Glorious Revolution*). Although increasingly professional, the army still was not immune to the powers of politics and religious sentiment. The crisis of 1688 in effect disintegrated the national army wrought by James II, and the accession of William and Mary* brought a new army into being. The new monarchs inherited the throne along with the political nation's mistrust of any government in possession of a standing army. William III saw the English army as a tool of his foreign policy, and when it was not needed, he allowed partial disbandment. At century's end, the regular army had dwindled to its smallest size in at least thirty years. Then events outside England led to the army's resurgence. Fear of French aggression overruled suspicion of military force. The ensuing victories overseas won for the army a respect it could never have earned in peace.

During the reign of Anne* the partnership of the duke of Marlborough and the earl of Godolphin* hastened the development of a regular army whose exploits equaled those of their forbears in the Hundred Years' War. In 1702 roughly 30,000 British subjects served in the regular army; four years later the number of troops approached 50,000 and grew ultimately to just under 75,000 by 1711. Significantly the nation, especially the Whigs*, now asserted the indispensable need for the army and was prepared to provide money and arms. As has always been the case, successful armies needed a substantial commitment from the resources of the realm. By the later years of Anne's reign, British arms had distinguished themselves, the size of armies reached new heights (though there was significant disbandment in the year before the queen's death), and a national English army, essentially British in composition, was a foretaste of what would be achieved in politics in 1707. One might argue the commonplace that military developments reflected changes in the whole of the polity. A professional army in the service of what would become an imperial state had evolved from amateur and local origins, not wholly unlike Rome. By the end of the reign of the Stuarts, the army was national, and the future lay in empire.

Bibliography: John Childs, *The Army of Charles II*, 1976; *idem*, *The British Army of William III* ,1987; Sir Charles Firth, *Cromwell's Army*, 4th ed., 1962; Ronald Hutton, *The Royalist War Effort, 1642-1646*, 1982; R. E. Scouller, *The Armies of Queen Anne*, 1966.

Mark Charles Fissel

Army Plots. The two failed army plots of 1641 helped convince parliament* that military force would be used irresponsibly if left in the hands of Charles I*. They also illustrated how the controversy between king and parliament, which at first had been largely religious (i.e., anti-Catholic* and anti-Arminian*), had become overwhelmingly a political and ultimately military confrontation. In the long term, the plots were symptomatic of the lack of trust, disintegrating since Charles's accession, between the king and a significant stratum of the traditional ruling elite. On the other hand, they were peculiar to the months prior to the outbreak of the Civil War* in that the king had so frightened his natural supporters that men who under normal circumstances never would have considered taking up arms against the government now believed that Charles had to be saved from himself, for the Crown's actions threatened religion, law, order, and property.

The first plot ran from about 21 March to 4 May 1641. Initially the plotters were involved in several conspiracies, which then coalesced into a single plot. The English and Scottish armies, lacking pay and losing patience with parliament, were ripe for intrigue. A few English officers, some of whom sat in parliament, got the idea that by bringing the English army* up to London*, they might, through threat of force, make the assembly more pliable to their demands and perhaps accommodate the king. Others contemplated occupying the Tower of London. A strong case has been made for Charles's orchestration of these activities. As events turned out, the Tower was secured by the installation of the earl of Newport there, which not only denied the plotters a London stronghold but also prevented the escape of Thomas Wentworth*, the earl of Strafford, destined to die on the block.

The second army plot came about in July 1641. Its significance is inextricably woven into the debate over the Ten Propositions. The king had employed one Daniel O'Neill to present proposals to the English army, suggesting among other things that the army might intervene in the political struggle by providing security for king and parliament in London. It was alleged that subversive elements threatened the state and that the army might safeguard against anarchy. O'Neill hoped to ensure that the Scots would not interfere further in English domestic politics and thus allow the English army to intimidate parliament to the benefit of the king. John Pym* and his allies saw through this and proposed that the counties of England and Wales* be put on alert, in effect readying the militia for the repulse of any royal coup d'état against parliament and its constituencies. In that sense, the army plots prefigured the debate over deployment of forces against Ireland* later that year and the struggles over recruitment and supply depots in 1642. Lofty political concepts and ideology had given way to concern for survival, and control of the armed forces was the critical issue. It would not be resolved until the end of the century.

Bibliography: Conrad Russell, *The Fall of the British Monarchies, 1637-1642*, 1992; *idem*, "The First Army Plot of 1641," in *Unrevolutionary England, 1603-1642*, 1990, 281-302.

Mark Charles Fissel

Art. With few exceptions the Stuart monarchs of England, like the Tudors before them, looked to the Continent for the artists deemed to be talented enough to preserve their royal images, enhance their private collections, and design their palaces. Those close to the throne were similarly inclined. Where the royal court* led, the country followed. It has been rightly stated that the Elizabethan genius was more literary and musical than visual. Not until the later Stuarts, William* and Mary* and Anne*, did English names begin to occupy a prominent place among those who constituted the elite of the visual arts in England, and even then competition from abroad remained significant.

The first of the Stuart line to rule in England was James I* (1603-1625). As king, first in Scotland* and later in England, he and his court patronized various continental artists, many of whom are little known today (e.g., Jan de Critz and Paul van Somer). Only in the realm of portrait miniatures did James—like his predecessor, Elizabeth I (1558-1603)—occasionally recognize English talent. For example, many superb portrait miniatures of James, his wife, Anne of Denmark*, and children were commissioned from Nicholas Hilliard (1547-1619), the son of an Exeter goldsmith who fashioned such superbly crafted miniature portraits that they adorned the most important individuals then as splendidly as they do the premiere galleries today. James's successor similarly patronized the London* workshop of John Hoskins (?1590-1664/5), an Englishman born and bred.

Since the days of Henry VIII (1509-1547), portrait miniatures have been uniquely popular in England. Building on foundations laid by Hans Holbein (?1497-1543), portrait miniatures quickly captured the imagination of those who led the kingdom, both at court and in the cities and counties. Meticulously painted on ivory or parchment, often with a brush made from a single hair, most miniatures of the seventeenth century were intended to be worn as jewelry or carefully displayed in appropriately crafted frames, many being little more than two inches in diameter and three in height.

James's son and heir, Charles I* (1625-1649), undoubtedly selected his painters and architects with far greater skill than he did his friends and ministers. The London-born Inigo Jones's (1573-1652) architecural talents, which had been carefully honed in the warmth of Italy, were put to work by Charles almost as soon as he came to the throne. Inspired by the work of Andrea di Pietro Palladio (1508-1580), Jones used the so-called Palladian style in constructing his great Banqueting House at Whitehall in London during the early 1620s, thus bringing the influence of the Italian Renaissance directly to bear on British architecture. The Italian influence that Jones introduced would be perpetuated by his immediate successors and culminate still later in the work of Sir Christopher Wren (1632-1723). Ironically Charles I would be executed (1649) at the Banqueting House he so much admired.

While Charles I is recognized along with George IV (1820-1830) as one of the true founders of the royal art collection and his name is therefore associated with many artists, his association with the painter Sir Anthony van Dyck (1599-1641) overshadows all the rest. Originally from the Netherlands, Van Dyck's meteoric career took him to the Antwerp workshop of Peter Paul Rubens (1577-1640), the Venetian palace of the Doge, the papal curia, and eventually the courts of James and Charles. It was Charles who succeeded in keeping Van Dyck in England for almost nine years (1632-1641). Charles designated Van Dyck "principalle Paynter in ordinary to their Majesties," a position he occupied until his unexpected death in 1641. Van Dyck's carefully posed, clothed, and idealized figure of the king depicted in *Charles I Hunting* has overshadowed all other visual representations of the man who became "Charles Stuart, late king of England." It has been suggested by many that Van Dyck tended to depict his subjects as they ought to have been rather than as they were.

While Charles I's execution* in 1649 ushered in an era when religion, war, and politics rather than the arts dominated, even the lord protector, as Oliver Cromwell* (1599-1658) came to be called, appreciated the talents of the miniaturist Samuel Cooper (1609-1672). Cooper's portrait of Cromwell in the National Portrait Gallery is well known. Cromwell's fondness for the work of Cooper was one of the very few traits that he shared with the future Charles II* (1660-1685). Cooper painted both men and captured the essence of each. Effectively utilizing the rich colors of Van Dyck and his own mastery of effective lighting, Cooper was appointed to be "His Majesty's Lymner" in 1663.

The nation's appreciation for miniaturists had obviously survived the Civil Wars*. Their patronage of and preference for English miniaturists had similarly emerged intact. Interestingly, the influence of the Continent on large-scale painting in England also remained strong throughout the rest of the seventeenth century. Sir Peter Lely (1618-1680) and Sir Godfrey Kneller (1646-1723) are merely the most obvious examples of continental artists who were in demand at court after the Restoration*. Both were born in Germany and had studied in the Netherlands and elsewhere on the Continent. After the long years of Puritan* domination, many undoubtedly wanted to see themselves writ large. It was certainly true of the new king. The lavishly framed portrait of Charles II by Lely in the National Portrait Gallery in its size, color, pose, and boldness proclaims the very spirit of the Restoration.

From the beginning of the Stuart period until the Glorious Revolution* in 1688, the artists who enjoyed royal patronage and hence popularity tended to be from the Continent and trained there. Only in the areas of miniature portrait painting and architecture were Englishmen able to come to the fore, generally after study abroad. The Renaissance came to England relatively late, and perhaps as a consequence Englishmen tended to look to the Continent for mature talent longer than might have been reasonably expected. Accordingly, England's artistic indebtedness to the Continent remained largely intact throughout the seventeenth century.

Bibliography: John Murdoch, Jim Murrell, Patrick J. Noon, and Roy Strong, *The English Miniature*, 1981; John N. Summerson, *Architecture in Britain: 1530-1830*, 8th ed., 1971; Ellis Waterhouse, *Painting in Britain: 1530-1790*, 4th ed., 1978.

Dorothy Boyd-Rush

Aubrey, John (1626-1697). Antiquarian, biographer, and bon vivant, John Aubrey was born in Wiltshire in 1626. After attending Blandford Grammar School, he entered Trinity College, Oxford at the age of sixteen.

A "modest, kindly, and generous" man, Aubrey had many friends and patrons, including a lifelong close friendship with Thomas Hobbes*, of whom he wrote a biography. His wide and powerful circle, combined with his skillful pen, enabled him to write vivid portraits of his contemporaries. Aubrey's portrayals contain a degree of verisimilitude that courted scandal, a fact he recognized when he asked that his notes be kept hidden as they "are not fit to let fly abroad, till about thirty years hence, for the Author and the Persons ought to be rotten first." From among the materials he did choose to print came *Brief Lives*, upon which Antony à Wood drew for *Athenae Oxonienses* in 1691-1692. The friendship and collaboration with Wood had begun in 1667 and continued for over twenty-five years until, in a fit of anger, Wood ravaged Aubrey's manuscripts.

In 1663 Aubrey found honor as an original fellow of the Royal Society*. This brought him into contact with several potential patrons, including Charles II*, who often attended meetings. In 1673, the king commanded Aubrey to write "a discourse on Stonehenge," a project he was particularly qualified to undertake having just completed topographical surveys of north Wiltshire and Surrey.

As the heir of his family's estates, he was less successful; his financial mismanagement led to their ruin and eventual sale. Even his love affairs failed, one ending only after three years' litigation. By 1677 all was gone, even his books, and he spent the rest of his life dependent on writing commissions and the generosity of friends. Aubrey died in 1697 at Oxford and was buried in the Church of St. Mary Magdalene. There is no good biography of Aubrey; the reader is directed to the standard reference works and Britton's *Memoir*.

Bibliography: John Britton, *Memoir of John Aubrey, FRS*, 1845.

Ann E. Faulkner

B

Bacon, Sir Francis (1561-1626). Bacon was born on 22 January 1561 at York House in London*, the second son of Lord Keeper Sir Nicholas Bacon and his second wife, Ann Coke, sister-in-law to Sir William Cecil, later Lord Burghley. He went up to Cambridge with his elder brother, Anthony, in 1573, and in 1576 he accompanied Sir Amias Paulet on an embassy to France. His father's death in 1579 left him in straitened circumstances, and he enrolled that year in Gray's Inn, becoming a barrister in 1582. By that time he had already sat in his first parliament*, representing the Cornish borough of Bossiney in 1581; he served in every one thereafter until 1621.

Bacon's quest for preferment bore little fruit under Elizabeth, although he gained a reversion to the lucrative clerkship of the Star Chamber (see Prerogative Courts*) in 1589. Burghley regarded his precocious nephew as a threat to his own son, Robert Cecil*, and Bacon attached himself to the earl of Essex in 1591. He was passed over for attorney general in favor of Sir Edward Coke* after unadvisedly questioning a subsidy bill in parliament, and he failed to obtain even the lesser post of solicitor. Bacon's unconcealed view of his own desserts continued to irk many, but after these reversals he was far more politic, lobbying for Crown bills in the parliament of 1597 and against a monopoly statute in 1601. In the latter year he joined Coke in prosecuting Essex for treason. Coke allowed his junior colleague to take center stage in this unpopular proceeding, and Essex taxed him famously for ingratitude: "I call forth Mr. Bacon against Mr. Bacon." The case haunted Bacon, though he stoutly defended his role in it in an *Apology* (1604).

Bacon was knighted at James I's* coronation in 1603, no great distinction, as he observed, among some 300 others. Past forty and deeply in debt, he hoped to impress the new monarch by serving as point man for the Scottish union* in parliament and by dedicating to him *The Advancement of Learning* (1605). He was finally rewarded with the solicitorship in 1607 and in 1608 became treasurer of Gray's Inn, but further advancement was blocked until the death in 1612 of his cousin Robert, latterly earl of Salisbury, an event he celebrated with a spiteful essay, "Of Deformity." Thereafter his rise was rapid. Elbowing Coke upstairs to the King's Bench (see Common Law and Courts*), he was appointed successively attorney in 1613, lord keeper in 1617, and lord chancellor in 1618. Honors accrued correspondingly; he became Lord Verulam in 1618 and Viscount St. Albans in 1621. Coke's dismissal from the bench in 1616, in which Bacon was a principal, removed his perennial rival, seemingly forever.

Bacon's fall was sudden. The unexpectedly severe attack on monopolies* in the parliament of 1621*, engineered by Coke, left Bacon exposed politically. When accusations of bribery surfaced, he was impeached (see Impeachment*), forced to resign the great seal, sentenced to imprisonment and a fine of 40,000 marks, forbidden access to the royal court*, and disabled from sitting in parliament. All but the last of these penalties was remitted, but Bacon never again served the state. His last years were devoted to a multifarious intellectual agenda, and he died, still in debt, on 9 April 1626. In 1606 he married Alice Barnham, the fourteen-year-old heiress of a London alderman; there was no issue.

"I have taken all knowledge for my province," Bacon wrote in 1592, and he made good his boast. The first ten of his celebrated *Essays*, brilliant literary performances in the manner of Montaigne, appeared in 1597; their number had grown to fifty-eight by the edition of 1625. His other major works, besides *The Advancement of Learning* (expanded as *De Augmentis Scientiarum*, 1623), were the *Novum Organum* (1620), his chief treatise on method; the *History of the Reign of Henry VII* (1622), written in a final bid for favor; and the *New Atlantis* (1627), a utopian fable whose proposal for an intellectual division of labor in the sciences echoed the classificatory system of knowledge laid out in the *De Augmentis* and found acknowledgment in the creation of the Royal Society*. In addition there were important legal treatises and miscellaneous literary, ecclesiological, and scientific works. Overarching all was Bacon's grand project for a redefined natural philosophy based on the empirical method, *The Great Instauration* or *Instauratio Magna*. Only a twenty-page epitome appeared under that title, published in 1620 as a pendant to the *Novum Organum*, but in a sense it lies scattered through most of his other writings.

Bacon's influence on later thought was vast. Immanuel Kant dedicated the *Critique of Pure Reason* to him, and David Hume, John Stuart Mill, and Karl Popper all acknowledged him as the founding figure of modern British philosophy. The criticism of Bacon's method is now familiar: that it neglected the role of hypothesis in knowledge formation and mathematics as a descriptive tool and, more broadly, that it promoted an imperial approach to the natural world. Nonetheless, his emphasis on experiment and induction and his trenchant critique of received thought was a critical move in the Western tradition and a necessary if not sufficient condition for the development of modern science*.

Since Alexander Pope described him as the "wisest, brightest, meanest of mankind," Bacon has attracted passionate admirers and detractors. Perhaps the greatest compliment is paid him by those who regard him as the author of William Shakespeare's* works; two great minds were never more unalike. There is no fully adequate modern biography.

Bibliography: Lisa Jardine, *Francis Bacon: Discovery and the Art of Discourse*, 1974;
J. Martin, *Francis Bacon, the State, and the Reform of Natural Philosophy*, 1992;
Paolo Rossi, *Francis Bacon: From Magic to Science*, 1968.

Robert Zaller

Bancroft, Richard (1544-1610). James I's* archbishop of Canterbury, whose
reputation as the hammer of the Puritans* obscures some notable work for a well-
educated and diligent clergy within a relatively comprehensive Church of England (see
Anglicanism*).

Bancroft was born in Lancashire, probably into a lesser gentry family. Educated
at Christ's College, Cambridge, he obtained his M.A. in 1572 and was ordained in
1574. A pluralist, he became chaplain to Bishop Richard Cox of Ely and then to
Elizabeth's favorite, Christopher Hatton. He co-wrote Hatton's effective
parliamentary speech against Presbyterianism* (1587) and assisted John Whitgift,
archbishop of Canterbury, in answering "Martin Marprelate," finding the press and
prosecuting the suspects. Bancroft's anti-Presbyterian tracts, *Dangerous Positions* and
A Survey of the Pretended Holy Discipline (both 1593), effectively exploited lay fears
of clericalism and anarchy. Whitgift rewarded Bancroft with the bishopric of
London* (1597). Bancroft's 1589 sermon at Paul's Cross had revealed his unusually
elevated view of episcopacy.

Bancroft and Whitgift were nervous at the accession of James I, particularly when
the king agreed to hear the Puritan case at the Hampton Court Conference* (1604).
Bancroft denounced Puritan views on predestination and their elevation of preaching
above the Book of Common Prayer, trying unsuccessfully to halt the conference with
claims that Puritans were schismatics whose attacks on bishops should be ignored.
James's chief minister, Robert Cecil*, felt that Bancroft was diligent and successful
at the conference.

Whitgift died in March 1604, and James chose the equally authoritarian Bancroft
to succeed him. This appointment suggested James's determination to follow
Elizabeth's religious policies and possibly his own fear of Puritans. Significantly,
James's subsequent episcopal appointments were in the earlier Elizabethan
latitudinarian* tradition.

Bancroft formulated England's first Protestant canons* in 1604. They signaled his
desire for clerical conformity. Canon xxxvi required subscription to the assertion that
there was nothing contrary to God's word in the prayer book and the Thirty-nine
Articles.

Puritanism had been relatively quiescent since the 1590s, but disappointment with
the Hampton Court Conference, coupled with Bancroft's new conformity campaign,
led to a resurgence. In Lincoln diocese alone, 746 ministers petitioned against
Bancroft's proceedings, although ultimately the number of beneficed clergy preferring
deprivation to subscription was probably under 100. The success of this conformity
drive probably varied according to the sympathies of individual bishops and lay
patrons toward these "good" Protestants. James, like Elizabeth, supported the
primate.

Parliamentary bills in 1604 and 1610 against Bancroft's canons revealed tension between primate and gentry over this conformity issue (see Parliament of 1604-1610*). Bancroft, always quick to consult with the king's judges, rejected members of parliament's (MPs) claims that only parliament* could give canons force of law. They also clashed over other issues. In 1603-1604 Bancroft accused MPs of encroaching on church liberties when they discussed reform; royal support ensured no act impinging on those liberties was passed during Bancroft's archiepiscopate. When MPs attacked pluralism and nonresidence (1610), Bancroft criticized lay "pluralists" who received impropriated tithes from several benefices. He correctly diagnosed that lay economic interests were a major problem for the church, but his attempts to remedy this were unpopular with the property-owning classes who dominated parliament.

Bancroft's resentment of writs of prohibition, which called cases out of ecclesiastical courts* to common law courts*, resulted in clashes with the common lawyers championed by Sir Edward Coke*. Bancroft complained to the privy council* (1605 and 1607), insisting on the separate and independent nature of ecclesiastical and common law jurisdictions, while recognizing that both were subject to the Crown. He defended the unpopular views of the civil lawyer John Cowell in the Commons (1610), although James's proclamation against Cowell's writings suggests that James felt it impolitic to emphasize clerical independence under the protection of enhanced royal authority.

Bancroft's clashes with the Commons and common lawyers might appear to reflect some of the divisions that led to the Civil War*. However, Bancroft's chosen successor, George Abbot*, was in the mold of the Puritan Edmund Grindal rather than the authoritarian Whitgift. It is noteworthy that the relatively comprehensive Jacobean church could accommodate both Bancroft and Abbot, and even William Laud*. When Bancroft died in 1610, the English church was not irrevocably set along any road to civil war.

Bibliography: S. B. Babbage, *Puritanism and Richard Bancroft*, 1962; Patrick Collinson, *The Elizabethan Puritan Movement*, 1967; K. C. Fincham, *Prelate as Pastor: The Episcopate of James I*, 1990; J. P. Sommerville, *Politics and Ideology in England, 1603-1640*, 1986.

Vivienne C. Sanders

Baptists. The name for several similar religious groups that broke away from the English Separatists* during the early seventeenth century to found churches practicing adult or believer's baptism. They rose to prominence during the Civil War* and Interregnum* along with the other radical religious sects and were supporters of the English Republic. After the Restoration* they suffered periodic persecution along with the other Protestant Dissenters* until the Glorious Revolution* established limited toleration for them.

All Baptist groups practiced adult baptism as opposed to the infant baptism common in most other Christian churches. Baptism is the sacrament that admits a person to membership in the Christian church; the first Baptists contended that only those people willing and able to make a conscious commitment to Christianity should be baptized, and they rejected infant baptism as invalid. True churches were voluntary associations (referred to at that time as gathered churches). To emphasize their separation from the Church of England (see Anglicanism*), many early Baptists underwent rebaptism, which had the unfortunate effect of associating them with the despised and feared Anabaptists of the sixteenth century in the minds of many authorities. Baptists also placed a great emphasis on the study of the Bible* and on using it as the sole source for recreating the authentic apostolic church.

Two main groups of Baptists arose in early seventeenth-century England. One was known as the General Baptists, a name that derived from their belief in the general redemption of humanity. This belief reflected the influence of the Dutch theologian Jacob Arminius (1560-1609), who taught that Christ had died for all people. As a consequence General Baptists believed that individuals possessed the free will to accept or reject salvation. In contrast, the second group, known as the Particular Baptists, were strict adherents of Calvinism* and its version of predestination, which asserted that Christ had died only for the elect, i.e., those particularly picked out by God for salvation at the beginning of time. There was no room for belief in free will among the Particular Baptists. A third, minor group that appears to have evolved out of the Particular Baptists during the 1650s were known as the Seventh Day Baptists. They insisted on returning to the Jewish practice of celebrating the Sabbath on the seventh day of the week, Saturday, rather than on the first day of the week, Sunday. Apart from those significant but limited differences, the various Baptist groups were quite similar in their beliefs and organization.

The General Baptists were the older of the two main groups founded by English Separatist exiles in Amsterdam in 1609. The group's minister, John Smyth (c.1554-1612), reinstituted adult or believer's baptism as part of an effort to return to the purity of primitive Christianity. It appears that he was encouraged in that belief by the close connections he had developed with neighboring Dutch Mennonites. When Smyth died in 1612, Thomas Helwys (c.1550-c.1616) and other members of the exile community, who found the full range of Mennonite beliefs to be unacceptable, returned to London* and founded the first General Baptist congregation at Pinner's Hall, London. This London congregation maintained a precarious existence during the 1620s and 1630s but managed to found other congregations at Lincoln, Salisbury, Coventry, and Tiverton. The early General Baptists consisted of a minuscule body of about 150 people prior to 1640.

The Particular Baptists first appeared in 1633, when a group calling for the return to believer's baptism broke away from the Separatist church founded in London by Henry Jacob (1563-1624). As more people joined them, the Particular Baptists decided to formulate their own confession or statement of their beliefs in 1644. Although much of the Confession of 1644 was taken directly from the Separatist Confession of 1596, the Particular Baptists did make three significant changes. Their adoption of adult baptism is the most obvious difference, but they also deemphasized both the role of the ministerial office and the secular state's right and duty to protect Christianity from heresy.

As the events of the English Civil Wars and the Interregnum unfolded, conditions became ripe for various religious sects of varying degrees of radicalism to appear and to flourish. The Baptists benefited from these conditions and were at the forefront of the calls for toleration of religious diversity among Protestants. Compared to the other so-called sects, such as the Fifth Monarchy Men* and even the Quakers*, the Baptists were relatively conservative, not differing markedly from their Independent* allies. At the same time individual Particular Baptists flirted with or moved on to uphold revolutionary Fifth Monarchist ideas and so tended to discredit their fellow Baptists, particularly at the time of the Restoration. The regicide Major-General Thomas Harrison (1616-1660) is a good example of a Baptist who rose to prominence in the parliamentary cause but later became a Fifth Monarchy Man.

Charles II's* restoration as king of England in 1660 brought an end to the religious toleration of the Commonwealth* and the Protectorate*. The Baptists, along with other dissenting Protestants, faced persecution because of their supposed associations with the political and religious anarchism of the radical sects and the desire for revenge among the royalists* returning to power after years of political impotence. Because they did not depend on a trained ministry and already rejected association with the hierarchical Church of England, the Baptists were largely unaffected by the great ejections of dissenting ministers. The Act of Uniformity of 1662 (14 Car. II, c. 4) and the Conventicle Act of 1664 (16 Car. II, c. 4) did leave Baptist congregations vulnerable to the suppression of their meetings and the imprisonment of their preachers, with John Bunyan's* tribulations providing the most famous example (see Clarendon Code*). The Particular Baptists appear to have withstood the persecutions better than the General Baptists, a circumstance at least partially attributable to the presence of such outstanding leaders as William Kiffin (1616-1701), Hanserd Knollys (?1599-1691), the redoubtable John Bunyan (1628-1688), and others. Some relief came when Charles II issued the Declaration of Indulgence* in 1672, which suspended the penal laws against Roman Catholics* and Dissenters. Persecution resumed for about a year in early 1675, when a royal proclamation voided the relief provided by the Declaration of Indulgence. After that, persecution did not resume again until the summer of 1680, although it continued until the death of Charles II in 1685. Dissenting Protestants, including the Baptists, were very fearful of a Roman Catholic restoration under the future James II*, Charles's brother and heir. Therefore during the Exclusion Crisis* (1678-1681), they supported the Whig* party's unsuccessful efforts to bar James from the succession. Unfortunately, that action cost them the protection of the normally tolerant Charles II. Still, when James II finally succeeded his brother in 1685, he proceeded to court the dissenting Protestants by policies of religious toleration for them and Roman Catholics. Most Baptists and other Dissenters, however, feared far more the potential persecution that a Roman Catholic restoration might bring than the present persecutions conducted by the Church of England. As resistance to James II mounted, the Baptists supported the Glorious Revolution*, which replaced James II with William of Orange*. They and other Dissenters had been promised formal religious toleration by some Whig leaders, but the resulting Toleration Act of 1689 (1 Gul. III & Mar., c. 18) disappointingly provided only religious toleration, not political equality for Dissenters. Still by 1688-

1689 the Baptists had become firmly rooted in British society and were organized for long-term survival as a denominational church.

Bibliography: J. F. McGregor, "The Baptists: Fount of All Heresy," in McGregor and B. Reay, eds., *Radical Religion in the English Revolution*, 1984; B. R. White, *The English Baptists of the Seventeenth Century*, 1983.

Ronald H. Fritze

Barebone's Parliament (1653). After the closure by the army* of the Rump Parliament*, Lord General Oliver Cromwell* and the council of officers assumed the governorship of the Commonwealth* from April to July 1653. During this period, Cromwell was encouraged by radical sectarians and millenarians*, especially Major-General Thomas Harrison and the so called Fifth Monarchy Men*, to establish a government of saints. Millenarian enthusiasm within the army and among sectarians led to the establishment of Barebone's Parliament in July 1653. Cromwell and the officers evidently saw this as a transitional regime, to sit no longer than through 4 November 1654.

In character, Barebone's Parliament was more moderate than its enemies or historians often have assumed. Its members were chosen by the army council, not, as is often stated, by nominating congregations of sectarian radicals. Congregations were both encouraged to forward nominees' names to the council and may have done so spontaneously in some cases; however, of all the parliament's members, perhaps only Praisegod Barebone, whose name was given to the assembly, came from outside the traditional governing elites. Contrary to royalist* aspersions, Barebone's or the Little Parliament was composed mostly of gentry and urban patricians. Still, there were a significant number of religious radicals, whose policies and proposed reforms antagonized moderate members of parliament.

Instead of seeing themselves as an interim regime, the radicals assumed that they would exercise power permanently, and they favored diplomatic, legal, and religious policies unacceptable to moderates. Believing that Christ's millennial kingdom was at hand, radicals called for a crusade against the Antichrist, starting with the Dutch Republic; however, moderates like Cromwell saw the Dutch as natural allies. The radicals also contemplated reform of the common law*, especially the laws of property, which antagonized the moderate gentry. But it was religious reform that proved the most acrimonious issue: the radicals wanted tithes and government support of the ministry abolished. Divisions in the parliament became bitter and irreconcilable, and on 1 November the moderates elected a new council of state* dominated by their confederates. A shadowy conspiracy to overthrow Barebone's Parliament emerged at the same time. Colonel John Lambert, a confidant of Cromwell, was recalled to London* from retirement in his native Yorkshire and offered command of a punitive expedition into the Scottish Highlands. Lambert refused this commission but proposed a new constitution to the council of state, which allegedly included a provision that would have made Cromwell king. On 10 December moderates in Barebone's Parliament voted to dissolve the assembly, and shortly thereafter the council of state handed power over to Cromwell. The Instrument of Government*, a modified form of Lambert's proposal minus monarchy, was adopted on 16 December 1653, and Cromwell was made lord protector.

Bibliography: B. S. Capp, *The Fifth Monarchy Men: A Study in Seventeenth Century English Millenarianism*, 1972; Conrad Russell, *The Crisis of Parliaments*, 1981; A. H. Woolrych, *Commonwealth to Protectorate*, 1986.

John H. F. Hughes

Bate's Case (1606). In one of the most significant legal decisions of the seventeenth century, the court of the Exchequer* established the Crown's right to levy impositions*, customs duties above and beyond the ordinary customs (the subsidies of tonnage and poundage) authorized by parliament*. This did not go unchallenged.

The imposition on currants, the matter at issue in Bate's case, had a complicated history. It began in Elizabeth's reign as a royalty collected by the Venice Company from nonmembers and aliens importing currants into England; only later, at the start of James I's* reign, did it become a duty collected by the Crown on all currants imported into England. There was much grumbling at the imposition (which at 5s. 6d. per hundredweight was substantially larger than the statutory subsidy of 18d.) since it had not been authorized by parliament, and a prominent London* merchant named John Bate refused to pay. When in April 1606 he resisted the impoundment of a cargo of his currants seized for nonpayment of the imposition he was committed by the privy council*, and the attorney general, Sir Edward Coke*, exhibited an information against him in the Exchequer. His case was heard from 30 June to 7 July 1606, and judgment was delivered in November in the next law term. All four barons of the Exchequer pronounced in favor of the king's right to levy the imposition on currants. One of their chief arguments was that the ports of the kingdom belonged to the king and that he therefore had the power to prohibit (or regulate) the commerce that made use of them. It was also claimed that even the ordinary customs, though now authorized by parliament, had originally been levied by the Crown's authority alone and that the king's predecessors had levied impositions without any protest.

The decision in Bate's Case had far-reaching consequences. Hitherto impositions had been used very sparingly, and they were not a significant source of revenue (the imposition on currants was worth only a few thousand pounds a year to the king). However, with the king's financial situation rapidly deteriorating and his ministers seeking new sources of revenue, the unanimous decision in Bate's Case pointed to an expansion in their use. Whether the king's ministers, anticipating a favorable judgment, had been planning on this all along is unclear, but in any case the earl of Salisbury (Robert Cecil*), the lord treasurer, in June 1608 introduced impositions on almost all commodities subject to tonnage and poundage.

Worth about £70,000 per annum, the new impositions represented a substantial addition to the king's revenues, but he was to pay a significant political price as impositions became one of the most contentious issues in parliament in the period. In 1606 the House of Commons had complained of the imposition on currants but had apparently been satisfied when James invoked the favorable judgment in Bate's Case. However, when the king claimed in 1610 that the decision also justified general impositions, the house was not at all satisfied. The Commons emphatically opposed the impositions, which they regarded as a grave threat to property rights and parliamentary control of taxation*, and the last session of the parliament of 1604-1610* and the Addled Parliament* of 1614 came to grief over the issue.

Bibliography: Pauline Croft, "Fresh Light on Bate's Case," *Historical Journal* 30 (1987): 523-539; G. D. G. Hall, "Impositions and the Courts 1554-1606," *Law Quarterly Review* 69 (1953): 200-218; Linda S. Popofsky, "The Crisis over Tonnage and Poundage in Parliament in 1629," *Past and Present* 126 (February 1990): 44-75.

Eric N. Lindquist

Baxter, Richard (1615-1691). Baxter was a controversial voice for church union throughout the religious turmoil of the Interregnum* and the Restoration*. A non-separating Puritan* who became a reluctant Dissenter*, he once labeled himself an "Episcopal-Presbyterian-Independent." Though he wrote unceasingly, he considered himself primarily a pastor and never accepted a position higher than curate or chaplain.

Baxter was born in a small Shropshire village on 12 November 1615. His father, a freeholder with tenants, was mocked as a Puritan. Largely self-educated, Baxter was ordained in December 1638, taught briefly in Worcestershire, and returned to Shropshire as a curate. In 1641-1642 and 1647-1654 he was lecturer in Kidderminster, Worcestershire, which he considered his greatest achievement; extra galleries were constructed to accommodate listeners. The Civil War* interrupted his tenure; local royalist* hostility drove him to parliamentarian* strongholds. He preached at Coventry through 1645, then served as chaplain in the New Model Army* until his health failed in 1647. Disputes with army* radicals sharpened his casuistry, he became an energetic foe of Separatists*, and he opposed killing Charles I*.

He became famous with his devotional classic, *The Saints Everlasting Rest* (1650). In 1654 he sat on a London committee to determine the fundamentals of religious orthodoxy. He became prominent in national religious affairs, vying for the attention of Oliver Cromwell* with Calvinist Independents* such as John Owen*. In Worcestershire he initiated the first county association, a voluntary union among moderate Presbyterian*, Independent, and Anglican* clergy. Through these "reconcilers," Baxter sought religious unity and (voluntary) parochial discipline and combated godlessness and the onslaught of Quakers* and Ranters* (groups Baxter considered inspired by Catholic* prodding) in the localities.

With the Restoration* Baxter returned to London, preaching to the Convention Parliament* and the lord mayor shortly before Charles II's* return. He was appointed royal chaplain and offered the bishopric of Hereford. Though desire for a more limited episcopalian structure forced him to decline the offer, Baxter continued working for a moderate church settlement. At the Savoy Conference* (1660), Baxter demanded reform of the Book of Common Prayer and penned a substantial "Reformed

Liturgy," but the bishops conceded only slight changes. Baxter preached his farewell sermon in London in May 1662, prior to massive ejections under the Act of Uniformity (14 Car. II, c. 4) (see Clarendon Code*). He married his "meetest Helper," Margaret Charlton from Shropshire, on 10 September.

The Restoration began Baxter's persecutions. When the former vicar of Kidderminster was restored in 1660, he denied Baxter a chance to preach, as did George Morley, bishop of Worcester. Living in or near London until 1669, Baxter preached at home and was imprisoned briefly under the Five Mile Act (17 Car. II, c. 2) in 1669. He distrusted the Declaration of Indulgence* (1672) because it granted freedom to Catholics as well as Nonconformists. He eventually applied for a license to preach without declaring his denomination (otherwise required under the indulgence). He preached briefly to Nonconformists at Pinner's Hall, but strict Calvinists opposed him. In 1675, after the Cavalier Parliament* rejected the declaration, Baxter again faced government persecution, this time under the Conventicle Act of 1670 (22 Car. II, c. 1). He was tried in 1685, before a hectoring Judge George Jeffreys, on the unlikely charge that he "libeled the Church" in *A Paraphrase on the New Testament* (1685). Released from prison in 1686, Baxter briefly assisted Presbyterian Matthew Sylvester in London. He died on 8 December 1691.

Baxter's legacy lies in nearly 140 published works, his voluminous correspondence, and unpublished treatises. His earliest publication, *Aphorismes of Justification* (1649), was a liberal interpretation of Calvinism whose discussion of good works led to charges of Arminianism*. One of his greatest works, *Gildas Salvianus: The Reformed Pastor* (1656), a primer of pastoral care, circulated throughout Europe and New England. He wrote *A Holy Commonwealth* (1659) during Richard Cromwell's* brief protectorate, hoping that peace would return to the English church and a Christian empire would begin. Baxter later renounced this plan for a Christian polity, proscribed by the Tory* *Judgement and Decree of the University of Oxford . . . against Certain Pernicious Books* (1683). After his wife died on 14 June 1681, Baxter preached little but continued to write. *The Certainty of the Worlds of Spirits* (1691) and his unpublished thoughts on the Apocalypse reveal millenarian* interests at odds with his outward rationality. He continued to plead for church unity in *Christian Concord* (1691). His posthumously published autobiography, *Reliquae Baxterianae* (1696), remains a vital narrative of the Interregnum and Charles II's reign and a fine defense of Puritanism.

Bibliography: N. H. Keeble, ed., *The Autobiography of Richard Baxter,* 1974; Geoffrey F. Nuttall, *Richard Baxter,* 1965.

Newton E. Key

Behn, Aphra (c.1640-1689). Spy, political activist, and the first professional woman writer in England.

Accounts of her early life are contradictory. She was possibly the daughter of James Johnson, a Canterbury barber, but other sources suggest she was the daughter of John and Amy Amis. Whatever her background, she seems to have been well educated for a woman of the time, though as an adult she wrote of her distress for the deficiencies in her and other women's* education. As a young woman, Aphra traveled to Surinam, where her (perhaps adoptive) father had been appointed lieutenant-general; he died on the voyage over. Surinam (later Dutch Guiana), a newly established colony on the coast of South America, at that time was British. More than twenty years later Aphra wrote about her experiences in Surinam in the novel *Oroonoko* (1688), the title character of which is a black slave. In 1664 Aphra returned to London*, where she married a Dutch merchant named Behn, who left her widowed a year or two later. Aphra Behn secured entrée to Charles II's* royal court* through Sir Thomas Killigrew, Charles's groom of the bedchamber and a friend of her mother. Killigrew asked Aphra, after her husband's death, to go to Amsterdam as a spy during the Second Dutch War* (1665-1667).

When the war ended she returned to London. Since her husband had left her penniless, Aphra had to earn her living and decided to do so as a writer. A tragicomedy, *The Forc'd Marriage*, about a woman trapped in a loveless marriage, was produced in 1670 and ran six nights. The theme of the need for women's equality in marriage is expressed in a number of Behn's works. Six months later another tragicomedy,*The Amorous Prince*, was staged and soon after a third, *The Dutch Lover*, which had several couples embroiled in intrigue and mistaken identity, but which had problems in its staging. It was clear that Aphra intended to stay in the theater permanently, and she claimed at the time that there was a deliberate attempt to sabotage her work and eliminate her as competition to male playwrights. Aphra, however, was determined to continue. *The Rover* (staged 1677) was even more popular, as was her adaptation of Molière's *Le Malade imaginaire* as *Sir Patient Fancy* (staged 1678). Behn also used her dramatic talents for political caricature. Her comedies *The Roundheads* (staged 1681) (adapted from John Tatham's *The Rump*) and *The City Heiress* (staged 1682) (adapted from Christopher Middleton's *It's A Mad World*) satirized Whig* politicians for the pleasure of Tory* audiences. Altogether Aphra wrote or produced eighteen plays and fourteen prose romances, as well as poetry and translations. She died 16 April 1689. She is noted for her prose romances, especially *Oroonoko*, as well as her plays, and as the first professional woman writer in England (see Literature*).

Bibliography: Angeline Goreau, *Reconstructing Aphra*, 1980; Frederick Link, *Aphra Behn*, 1968; Sara Mendelson, *The Mental World of Three Stuart Women*, 1987.

Carole Levin

Bennet, Sir Henry, Earl of Arlington (1618-1685). A diplomat and minister, Bennet was a natural courtier. From his first employment in 1643 with Charles I's* secretary of state until his last, honorific post as lord chamberlain, Bennet spent his life around central government and the royal court*. Known as an intriguer and one who worked well backstairs, he exhibited political realism, moderation, and flexibility. Able to cooperate with his rivals, he used his friendship with Charles II* to advance during a long career that made him extremely wealthy.

From 1644 until 1661 Bennet served the Stuart monarchy in exile, acting as a reluctant secretary to the duke of York (see James II*) between 1648 and 1657 and then from 1658 to 1661 as envoy in Spain. There he failed to obtain formal recognition for Charles but gained reputation and, inspired by the Spanish example, developed a taste for secrecy, stateliness, magnificence, and Roman Catholicism*.

Bennet returned to England in 1661 and secured a seat in the House of Commons. Aided by Sir Thomas (later Baron) Clifford*, Bennet quickly built an interest in parliament* and became a ministerial spokesman, but he never respected the institution. Appointment as a privy councilor (see Privy Council*) and secretary of state in 1662 (advances on positions as gentleman of the privy chamber and keeper of the privy purse) provoked the jealousy of Edward Hyde, earl of Clarendon*, Charles's leading minister. In office Bennet drafted the first Declaration of Indulgence*, promoted the Second Dutch War* (1665-1667), and worked for Clarendon's removal. Elevated to the peerage in 1665 as Lord Arlington, he replaced Clarendon as the leading voice in foreign affairs when the latter fell in 1667. The Triple Alliance* with the United Provinces and Sweden, which Arlington crafted in 1668, demonstrated this ascendancy.

Arlington's influence with Charles derived from his industry, mastery of inside politics, and willingness to bend to the king's desires. It fluctuated over time but between 1668 and 1672 was unrivaled. Although suspicious of France, Arlington acquiesced when the king's secret conversion to Catholicism forced an accommodation with that country. He felt uneasy about the Treaty of Dover* (1670) and renewed war against the Dutch, but he was too much the politician to obstruct either and helped to draft the Anglo-French pact. As a reward, his only daughter, Isabella, was married to the king's illegitimate son, Henry Fitzroy, yet Arlington's lukewarm support for war weakened his ministerial supremacy.

In 1672 Arlington was elevated to an earldom, but he became the target of parliamentary attacks and had no decisive role in the great decisions of that year: the Stop of the Exchequer*, the Declaration of Indulgence, the declaration of war. Clifford's appointment as lord treasurer (a position Arlington coveted) destroyed a friendship already decayed and presaged Arlington's gradual loss of power. Clifford resigned in June 1673 to conform to the Test Act* (25 Car. II, c. 2), but Charles replaced him with Thomas Osborne*, earl of Danby, not Arlington. While Arlington easily survived attempted impeachment* for his conduct as minister and helped draw the peace treaty at the end of the Third Dutch War* (1672-1674), he had clearly lost his preeminence. In September 1674 he traded his post as secretary of state for that of lord chamberlain, which reduced him to a marginal public figure. Still he continued to advise the king as asked and to snipe at Danby. He voted against excluding York from the throne (see Exclusion Crisis*), gathered further minor positions, and even hoped for a return to power. Confirmed as lord chamberlain at James II's accession, he died in July 1685, formally embracing Roman Catholicism on his deathbed.

Bibliography: Violet Barbour, *Henry Bennet Earl of Arlington*, 1914; Ronald Hutton, *Charles II*, 1989; Maurice Lee, Jr., *The Cabal*, 1965.

James Rosenheim

Bible, Authorized Version (1611). Commonly known as the King James Bible, this has been the most famous and popular version in English for over three centuries.

At the beginning of James I's* reign, the Geneva Bible was the best and most popular translation. It first appeared as the New Testament alone in 1557 and as a complete Bible in 1560. Secular and religious authorities disapproved, however, regarding it as a radical Protestant icon and objecting particularly to its marginal notes, which they considered religiously and politically subversive. To counter its influence, Matthew Parker, archbishop of Canterbury (1559-1575), organized a rival translation known as the Bishops' Bible, which appeared in 1568 but failed to supplant its Puritan* rival. Official discontent continued, and John Whitgift, archbishop of Canterbury (1583-1604), went so far as to formulate a draft act for parliament* authorizing yet another translation, but nothing came of this plan.

One of James's first acts as king of England was to comply with the clergy's call for a conference to settle religious differences between radicals and conservatives. The Hampton Court Conference* took place during January 1604, and among the many proposals discussed, John Rainolds, radical president of Corpus Christi College, Oxford, called for a new English Bible. Rainold wanted to eliminate citations of insufficiently Protestant translations of the Bible used in the Book of Common Prayer. Some conservatives like Richard Bancroft*, soon to obtain the see of Canterbury, were suspicious of the plan, but James I seized on it as an opportunity to displace the Geneva Bible.

By 30 January 1604 James and Bancroft chose teams of translators, and by 22 July the king officially appointed fifty-four men, although only forty-seven actually served. These were among the finest scholars of biblical languages in England and included the entire spectrum of English Protestantism from radical to conservative: Lancelot Andrewes*, John Rainolds, Laurence Chaderton, Sir Henry Savile, and Hadrian Saravia. Not every great scholar participated, however, and the brilliant but cantankerous Hebraist Hugh Broughton was not even invited. The translators were divided into six companies. Two met at Westminster and translated Genesis to II Kings and Romans to Jude, respectively; two at Oxford were responsible for Isaiah to Malachi and the Gospels, Acts, and Revelation; and two at Cambridge handled I Chronicles to Ecclesiastes and the Apocrypha.

Their instructions confirmed the conservative direction of the enterprise. They were to base their translation on the Bishops' Bible rather than the Geneva Bible whenever possible. Traditional English terminology for church matters was to be utilized rather than the innovative vocabulary favored by radical Protestants; for example, *church* was to be used rather than *congregation*. Marginal notes were to be limited to philological explanations and variant readings. In this way the controversial and partisan notes of the Geneva Bible were to be avoided. Each scholar was to translate his company's whole assignment on his own. Then company members were to meet as a group and produce a text commonly agreed upon. Originally the text produced by each company was to be sent to the other five groups for approval, but that plan was abandoned. Instead twelve translators—two from each company—met to revise the whole translation. Individual work on the initial translations took about three years, and the meetings to create the final version took another three. Robert Barker, the king's printer, published the finished product in 1611. It included Miles Smith's lengthy and informative preface, "The Translators to the Reader," which explained their methods.

The scholarship embodied in the Authorized Version was good for its day, linguistic studies having advanced steadily during the sixteenth century. But the translation of 1611 suffered because of the translators' dependence on defective original texts in the biblical languages and their inadequate understanding of some aspects of ancient Hebrew. Although the Bishops' Bible was supposed to serve as the model for the new version, the translators made extensive use of the Geneva Bible and the Rheims New Testament, a translation produced by English Roman Catholic* exiles. The latter was the source for much of the Authorized Version's Latinate English, which, interestingly, was somewhat old-fashioned even in 1611.

The Authorized Version was far more successful than the Bishops' Bible, though it took a generation to supplant the hardy Geneva Bible, whose final (and at least 140th) edition appeared in 1644. Oddly enough, the Authorized Version translator and proto-Arminian* bishop of Winchester, Lancelot Andrewes, continued to use the Geneva Bible in preparing sermons, as did William Laud*, Charles I's* steadfastly Arminian archbishop of Canterbury, during the 1630s. Not surprisingly the irascible Hugh Broughton attacked the Hebrew scholarship of the Authorized Version. None of these things, however, stopped the Authorized Version from becoming the premier English Bible. Its masterful prose, eminent suitability for public reading, and non-partisan Protestantism ensured its unprecedented popularity. It has been challenged but never entirely superseded by the Revised Version (1885), the Revised Standard Version (1952), the New English (1970), and the Revised English (1990) Bibles.

Bibliography: F. F. Bruce, *History of the Bible in English*, 3d ed., 1978; S. L. Greenslade, ed., *The West from the Reformation to the Present Day*, Vol. 3 of *The Cambridge History of the Bible*, 1963; A. W. Pollard, ed., *Records of the English Bible: The Documents Relating to the Translation and Publication of the Bible in English, 1525-1611*, 1911, rprt. 1974.

Ronald H. Fritze

Bill of Rights (1689). A statute based on the Declaration of Rights* promulgated by the Convention Parliament*, the Bill of Rights was formulated to protect England from monarchical and ministerial policies that in the past had jeopardized the Protestant religion and the nation's rights and liberties.

Following the Glorious Revolution* of 1688, a decision had to be reached quickly on the disposition of the Crown, and the grievances that had spawned the revolution had to be redressed. To that end, the Convention was called for 22 January 1689, and its members moved swiftly to fill the vacuum created by James II's* precipitous departure. On 28 January the Commons declared that by his flight James had abdicated the throne, which was therefore vacant. Debate ensued over who was to inherit the throne and under what conditions and limitations. Decisions on these matters formed the core of the Declaration of Rights, which was formally presented on 13 February to William of Orange* and Mary Stuart (Mary II*), the chosen recipients of the throne. The Bill of Rights, the statutory enactment of the declaration, took longer to achieve and was not passed until 16 December. The bill echoed the declaration on many points, but the essential difference was that the bill represented a formal contract between crown and parliament*, whereas the declaration was primarily informational. William and Mary did not agree to abide by the provisions of the declaration but did give formal assent to the Bill of Rights, thereby binding the Crown to the tenets contained therein.

The bill's preamble assigns to James the blame for the governmental problems that led to the revolution. Anticipating John Locke's* contract theory of government, it noted that James had failed to respect the constitution in overriding established laws with absolutist* royal decrees. The bill's thirteen articles dealt with these and other grievances at length and proposed solutions. A protracted discussion on the grant of the Crown to William and Mary and the issue of the succession formed a significant portion of the bill. William and Mary were to rule jointly, and William was to exercise governmental powers. The Crown was to pass to any children born of their marriage, with Mary's sister, Anne*, and her progeny to follow; if Mary predeceased William, any children of a subsequent marriage made by him would follow Anne and her heirs. The bill forbade the throne to pass to a Catholic* or anyone married to a Catholic, thereby effectively barring James and his descendants from the throne.

The bill limited royal authority to dispense with laws (see Dispensing Power*) and prohibited the Crown from suspending laws (see Suspending Power*), levying money, or raising a standing army* in peacetime without parliamentary consent. It called for frequent parliaments, free elections, and freedom of speech in that institution. The bill declared the court of commissioners for ecclesiastical causes and similar courts to be illegal, provided for due impaneling of juries, and forbade excessive bail or fines, cruel and unusual punishments, and fines or forfeiture prior to conviction. It also asserted that Protestant subjects might have arms for defense.

The problem with the bill, as with the declaration, was its vague treatment of some issues. The thirteen articles seemed ambiguous since they dealt only with existing rights and not new ones; based on the hurriedly composed declaration, they were intended as guides for future legislation. References to issues such as free elections and frequent parliaments were not precise, but the convention assumed that these issues would be developed by statute. Only concerns for which there seemed but one solution appear unequivocal, for example, the limitation on standing armies. Subsequent statutes did deal with many of the issues raised by the bill (e.g., elections), but other points were left to stand on their own. Further, the bill contained no means of enforcement.

None of these shortcomings detracted from the bill's constitutional impact at the time of its formulation, nor do they detract from it currently. The bill provided stable government for England during a troubled period, and there is no question but that it influenced the framers of the United States Constitution, particularly in the first ten amendments to that document (another "Bill of Rights"). Taken in context, the bill must be considered a significant contribution to constitutional history.

Bibliography: J. R. Jones, *The Revolution of 1688 in England*, 1972; John Miller, *The Glorious Revolution*, 1983; E. N. Williams, ed., *The Eighteenth Century Constitution: Documents and Commentary*, 1960.

Connie S. Evans

Bishops' Wars (1639-1640). In response to the Scottish Prayer Book Rebellion of 1637, Charles I* mobilized England in 1639 in an effort to overawe Covenanter* resistance. As he would do in 1642, he attempted to rally support for his cause by planting the royal standard. An army of around 20,000 gathered at York and then advanced to the Borders in spring 1639. Aside from an inadvertent skirmish, violence was avoided, and a treaty was signed at Berwick in June 1639. The political settlement foundered, however, largely because the king had no intention of compromising and thus admitting religious heterodoxy within his British kingdoms. Turning to Sir Thomas Wentworth* (now elevated to the earldom of Strafford) and Archbishop Laud*, the king decided to summon parliament*, which had not sat for the eleven years of his Personal Rule*. Charles hoped to solicit sufficient subsidies to fight a major Scottish war in summer 1640, but he dissolved the troublesome assembly known as the Short Parliament* in May without obtaining funds.

The campaign of 1640 was fraught with dissension among soldiers and civilians. Churches were "reformed" by iconoclastic troopers who smashed communion rails, tore up surplices, and committed other violent acts. Mutinies erupted over pay shortages, and two officers were murdered by their own men. The mobilization was delayed primarily due to shortages of weapons and pay. By the time the Scots crossed into Northumberland, determined to make a preemptive strike on English forces, the royal artillery train was for the most part stuck at Hull and the bulk of the regiments held back in Yorkshire staging areas, waiting for more firearms and arrears of pay. A small force met the Scots when they forded the Tyne at Newburn on 28 August 1640. The badly deployed royal infantry, belatedly but valiantly seconded by cavalry, failed to withstand the momentum of the Covenanters' charge across the river. The ensuing retreat compelled the king to sue for peace, and the Treaty of Ripon was signed in October. This obligated Charles to pay the Scots £850 a day until a new parliament met and further negotiations undertaken. That assembly, which convened in November, would become known as the Long Parliament*, and from its conflict with the king came the Civil Wars.*

The Bishops' Wars were neither; they were precipitated by a bellicose prince rather than the episcopate, and they cannot be called wars since only a single battle was fought, a brief affair resulting in several hundred casualties. Their significance lies in how they exposed and aggravated the political and religious divisions within Britain, which for the most part had been camouflaged by the Personal Rule. The

Scots' refusal of the Arminian* prayer book angered Charles I, who responded personally to this affront to his government. Yet the Covenanters cannot be blamed for the recourse to arms. They tried for three years to reach a negotiated settlement that might protect the Kirk*. Ironically, bloodshed was ensured by Charles's actions, which determined that the religious issue (and subsequent political issues) would be settled by the sword. Once the violence began, it would not be stilled until the final act was committed against Charles himself upon the block outside the Banqueting House on 30 January 1649 (see Charles I, Trial, Execution, and Cult of*).

Bibliography: Mark Charles Fissel, *The Bishops' Wars: Charles I's Campaigns Against Scotland, 1638-1640*, 1994; Conrad Russell, *The Fall of the British Monarchies, 1637-1642*, 1992.

Mark Charles Fissel

Bloody Assizes (1685). A notorious series of judicial sittings in southwest England under Chief Justice George Jeffreys, held to try nearly 2,000 prisoners taken in the failed Monmouth Rebellion*.

The complete rout of Monmouth's forces at Sedgemoor on 5-6 July 1685 ensured victory for the Catholic James II*. James, duke of Monmouth, was executed on 15 July. The king was anxious to deal quickly with Monmouth's adherents and strike fear into the hearts of his sympathizers.

Lord Jeffreys opened the first assizes at Winchester on 25 August. It was notable for the trial of the elderly Lady Alice Lisle, whose only crime was unknowingly providing shelter to a rebel fugitive. Convicted chiefly on the testimony of a rebel who turned state's evidence, Lady Lisle was sentenced to be burned alive; a desperate plea to the king resulted in a commutation to beheading. Her execution is symbolic of the ruthlessness of the Bloody Assizes.

With 2,000 persons to try within three to four weeks, Jeffreys devised a plan to speed up the process. Rebels pleading guilty without trial were offered the hope of the king's mercy, while those pleading not guilty were promised summary execution if subsequently found guilty. The first mass convictions and executions began at Dorchester on 5 September, with further sessions at Exeter, Taunton, Bristol, and Wells.

Despite their cooperation with the court, some who pleaded guilty were executed. The great majority of the rebels were whipped or transported, approximately 250 were executed, and a number died due to prison conditions. The gruesome manner of execution—hanging, drawing, and quartering—was compounded by the order to display the mutilated remains in various towns, where they remained until James ordered them removed in 1687. The barbarity and breadth of the punishment gained Jeffreys and ultimately James reputations as cold-blooded murderers.

Bibliography: R. Milne-Tyte, *Bloody Jeffreys, the Hanging Judge,* 1989.

Connie S. Evans

Book of Orders (1630-1631). Charles I's* Books of Orders of 1630-1631 have been interpreted as part of the policy of "thorough"* by which the central government regulated local government*, as an example of efficient local administration of social and economic policy and as a vehicle for securing social stability in times of economic crisis. The minutely detailed books were issued in three installments during 1630 and 1631, although the January 1631 Book of Orders is best known. Each dealt with a specific policy matter: dearth from bad harvests in 1629 and 1630, social unrest relating to the plague (see Epidemics and Plague*) and hunger, and special aspects of the poor laws*. The orders required the justices of the peace to make monthly reports and the sheriffs* to submit quarterly reports to the privy council*.

Dispensing central administration policy to the local community through the justices of the peace began with the Tudors; hence, Charles's orders were traditional, though they lacked a comprehensive framework for planning to meet social and economic emergencies. All matters in the 1630-1631 orders had been addressed by previous administrations in some fashion—for example, during earlier poor harvests, regulations had punished those hoarding or exporting grains. Only the third set of orders—for enforcement of closing of alehouses, suppression of vagrancy, relief of the feeble poor, and work details for the able-bodied poor—could be considered in the least novel. But even though previous central government directives to the JPs had not included these subjects, the justices had been administering the poor laws for decades.

The reasons for issuing the 1630-1631 orders were also comparable to those for previous proclamations, i.e., bad harvests and/or epidemics, which increased the numbers of poor and created conditions of unrest. Such innovations usually originated not with the central government but with the localities or from abroad. With the 1630-1631 orders, the chief influences were not the directors of thorough, Sir Thomas Wentworth* and Archbishop William Laud*, but the king's French physician, Sir Theodore de Mayerne, and the lord privy seal, Henry Montague, earl of Manchester. As a model of how London* and the rest of England should deal with the plague, Mayerne used a French plan developed in 1607. The brother of the earl of Manchester, a Northamptonshire justice of the peace, convinced the earl to advocate new provisions for dearth based on revised methods for distributing grains.

The Books of Orders did not produce major differences on policy between central and local government or between Puritan* and Laudian elements. Except for occasional quibbles, all elements of authority supported the general aims of the Books of Orders. Fear of social unrest by mobs caused even ideological antagonists to agree on most policy strategy. Later the Puritan-controlled Long Parliament* in 1646 issued plague regulations that closely resembled the 1630 Caroline order. Even so, the Books of Orders exemplified a regime that vigorously pursued centralization of government justified by the royal prerogative*. Evidence suggests that they did not improve the Crown's reputation with those who questioned prerogative methods. Thus, while there was common agreement concerning social policy, the Books of Orders exacerbated dissatisfaction with Charles I's often unpopular policy of thorough.

Bibliography: B. W. Quintrell, "The Making of Charles I's Book of Orders," *English Historical Review* 95 (July 1980): 555-572; Paul Slack, "Books of Orders: The Making of English Social Policy, 1577-1631," *Transactions of the Royal Historical Society,* 5th series, 30 (1980): 1-22.

Daniel W. Hollis III

Book of Sports (1617, 1618, 1633). This was at the center of three religious conflicts concerning acceptable Sabbath activities. The issue emerged in 1617 when James I*, returning from Scotland*, quashed an order issued by Lancashire magistrates that prohibited piping, dancing, animal baiting, or any profanation of the Sabbath. James rebuked the magistrates for restricting "our good people for using their lawful recreations and honest exercises on Sundays," and celebrations resumed.

Unfortunately, other abusive Sunday celebrants profaned church services and stirred protests from fearful citizens. James and Bishop Thomas Morton acted quickly to punish abusers. Morton constructed a description of legal recreations and presented it to James, who rewrote and expanded Morton's draft. He barred nonconformers and armed men from participating in these sports, which were permitted only in the participant's home parish.

This Book of Sports was issued in 1617 with a declaration that condemned both Catholics* and Puritans* and threatened both with exile if they violated the church's canons*. James's actions polarized opinion, created local conflicts when abuses occurred, and associated Puritanism with strict Sabbath observance.

It is not known why James's Book of Sports was reissued or promulgated nationally in 1618. The new declaration required its publication in all parish churches and directed all judges and justices of the peace to study it. Whatever James's intent, the proclamation incited disorders, produced many disputes, and reinforced the view that James defended wickedness. The association of Puritans with strict Sabbath observance was strengthened. Despite strong parliamentary support of bills to enact most provisions of the Book of Sports in the parliaments of 1621* and 1624*, James refused his assent.

In 1633 Archbishop Laud*, concerned with ecclesiastical jurisdiction and episcopal authority, convinced Charles I* to reissue the Book of Sports. These concerns were prompted by actions of the lord mayor of London* and Lord Chief Justice Richardson's prohibition against Sabbath wakes in Somerset. After he dealt with the mayor and Richardson, Laud used Richardson's obstructions to convince Charles to reissue the Book of Sports with an amendment protecting wakes. His goal was not to defend wakes but to urge the prosecution of Puritans if they did not conform themselves to the canons of the church. The 1633 Book of Sports included a short preface protecting wakes and urging officials to protect lawful exercises after Sabbath services. Unlike the 1618 declaration, this promulgation more heavily burdened those within the church who were more concerned about protecting Sabbath piety than was Laud.

Reading the Book of Sports in church became a test of conscience that many ministers failed, and those who did were quickly suspended by their bishop. While hundreds remained to face the persecution that was quickly visited on them, many accepted voluntary exile in America. Between 1633 and 1640 a substantial theological controversy ensued in print between Laud's supporters and Nonconformists, which discredited some Laudians.

By 1636 Nonconformists were driven from the church, Sabbatarianism* was firmly associated with Calvinist* Puritans, and the church leadership was mistrusted. Laud tried to make an example of Henry Burton by imposing a £5,000 fine, having him pilloried with his ears cut off, and imprisoning him for life. The sympathetic crowd that accompanied Burton through his ordeal stood in sharp contrast to the abuse and invectives directed against the archbishop. In November 1640 Burton was exonerated and released by parliament*, which ordered all copies of the Book of Sports to be publicly burned in 1644.

The Book of Sports controversies undermined public confidence in the church and government, sharpened the public perceptions of the wickedness of Laud's innovations, and increased the desire for revenge among those in the Long Parliament* who sought his execution and church reform.

Bibliography: Kenneth L. Parker, *The English Sabbath*, 1988.

Sheldon Hanft

Booth's Rising (1659). A royalist* rising in Cheshire in August 1659 for the Restoration* of Charles II*. It was led by Sir George Booth (1622-1684) of the Cheshire gentry, an active royalist named by Charles as commander of the king's forces in Cheshire, Lancashire, and north Wales.

With increased political instability after the death of Oliver Cromwell*, the abdication of Richard Cromwell*, and the reinstatement of the Rump Parliament* in May 1659, it is not surprising that royalists again tried to overthrow the republic. They were divided, however, about what course of action to take. The "Sealed Knot," always cautious, opposed a rising and advised waiting for the government to disintegrate. Members of the "Trust," commissioned by Charles in March 1659 to act in his interests, thought rebellion would hasten his restoration. Booth was closely associated with the Trust, though not a member. The action-oriented Trust, dominated by the impetuous John Mordaunt, ignored warnings from the Sealed Knot and planned simultaneous risings throughout England in coordination with a promised landing by Charles and his forces at a western port. The council of state* knew about their activities by early July and took extensive precautions to thwart them, except in Cheshire, Lancashire, and north Wales due probably to faulty intelligence.

Booth was in charge of the rising in Cheshire, where he was influential. A Presbyterian*, he sought support from members of his sect as well as the discontented in the area. He issued three pamphlets appealing to all classes and malcontents to join him, but his appeals were so broad and disparate that they were suspect and had little impact. He apparently wanted a free parliament*, impartial laws, and freedom of religion. He did not mention the restoration of Charles. Booth, ignorant of the failure of risings elsewhere and assured by Mordaunt of Charles's landing, raised about

4,000 troops. He captured Chester (except the castle) on 2 August, Colonel Ireland secured Liverpool, and Sir Thomas Middleton rashly proclaimed the king at Wrexham. John Lambert, commanding the Rump's forces, met Booth's troops at Winnington Bridge outside Northwich on 20 August and completely routed them. Thirty of Booth's men were killed and 300 captured. Lambert had one soldier killed and three wounded. Booth escaped but was apprehended in female attire at Newport Pagnell when one of his friends asked for an extra razor. He was the butt of many jokes and scurrilous pamphlets. It was perhaps a fitting end to an amateurish and ill-considered endeavor. He was imprisoned in the Tower but survived to win a peerage at Charles's coronation. The dream of the pro-action royalists that Charles could be immediately restored vanished "under a wench's petticoat."

Booth's rising was rash, badly planned, and severely hampered by bad weather. Its fate was sealed by the failure of risings to occur elsewhere, and Booth considered himself "basely deserted." It was the last royalist rising before the Restoration. The Rump treated Booth and his troops leniently; no one was executed, and captured troops were released eventually. The Rump's plans to sequester royalist estates were ended by its expulsion by the army* in October 1659. The rising achieved nothing of consequence.

Bibliography: Godfrey Davies, *The Restoration of Charles II, 1658-1660*, 1955; David Underdown, *Royalist Conspiracy in England, 1649-1660*, 1960.

Wilson J. Hoffman

Breda, Declaration of (1660). Following Oliver Cromwell's* death in September 1658, England experienced a series of short-lived unstable regimes. Nevertheless, as late as February 1660 the prospect of restoring Charles II* appeared as bleak as ever. By then, however, General George Monck*, who had led his army out of Scotland* on 1 January, arriving in London* on 3 February—and whom the Rump Parliament* had tried to use for its own purposes—had reluctantly concluded that only the monarchy could provide the legitimacy the government needed. Yet many, especially in the army*, disagreed, and others favored returning the king only if his authority was severely limited. The soldiers, who had not been paid, and others worried that the king might seek revenge against those who had opposed him or his murdered father, Charles I*. Finally the religious situation in England remained troubled. Therefore Monck wrote urging Charles to quiet the country's fears.

Charles responded with the Declaration of Breda on 4 April 1660, addressing only those immediate problems. He pardoned all of England except those whom parliament* would later except. Second, he promised broad religious toleration, granting liberty to those of "tender consciences." Finally, he accepted existing land titles, but left parliament to resolve any inequities. The declaration was an astute political move, for it allowed Charles to avoid being entangled in messy settlement details that could only cost him popularity. At the same time he involved the Convention Parliament* and committed it to the settlement by leaving to it those details that the declaration suggested needed further resolution.

Charles tried to keep his promises, and the declaration formed the basis for the Restoration* settlement. During spring and summer 1660, he repeatedly urged the Convention to pass the Act of Indemnity and Oblivion* (12 Car. II, c. 11), which would punish only certain regicides*, and in 1662 and 1672 he attempted greater religious toleration, though these efforts were rebuffed by a Cavalier Parliament* bent on squelching religious dissent. Charles returned only the lands of those who had been forced off their property. Where it had been voluntarily sold, even to pay fines imposed upon royalists*, the Crown refused to oust current occupants in favor of loyalists. If Charles failed to deliver all that the declaration promised, it was not entirely his fault.

Bibliography: Godfrey Davies, *The Restoration of Charles II 1658-1660*, 1955; Ronald Hutton, *The Restoration. A Political and Religious History of England and Wales: 1658-1667*, 1985; James J. Jones, *Charles II: Royal Politician*, 1987.

David A. Davis

Buckingham, 1st Duke of. See Villiers, George, 1st Duke of Buckingham.

Buckingham, 2d Duke of. See Villiers, George, 2d Duke of Buckingham.

Bunyan, John (1628-1688). Best known for writing *The Pilgrim's Progress* (1678-1679 and 1684-1685), he also was a member and later served as a minister for the Baptist* congregation of Bedford from the late 1650s until his death.

John Bunyan was born during November 1628 at Elstow, Bedfordshire, to Thomas Bunyan, an itinerant brazier or tinker of yeoman rank. Receiving a modest elementary education from the local school, he apparently became estranged from his father and joined the parliamentarian* forces during the Civil War* and performed garrison duty at Newport Pagnell from 1644 to 1646. After leaving the military he took up the tinker's craft and married in 1649. During these years he also began to experience the psychological crisis over his salvation that eventually led in 1653 to his conversion. He joined the Separatist*/Baptist congregation at Bedford, where he became a deacon and soon started preaching. While fervent in his faith, Bunyan provided a good example of a conservative sectarian by his rejection of the antinomianism and other excesses of the Ranters* and early Quakers*. Although he believed in the impending Second Coming of Christ and the end of the world, he refused to support the efforts of the Fifth Monarchy Men* to hurry the process along or the predictions of other zealous millenarians* who sought to identify exactly the time and the date of the approaching Apocalypse.

His first wife died in 1656, leaving Bunyan with the care of four small children. He married his second wife, Elizabeth, in 1659 just before the Restoration* of Charles II* began a period of persecution for Protestant Dissenters*. The authorities imprisoned Bunyan in 1660 for holding an illegal conventicle and for preaching without a license. He spent most of the years 1660-1672 in the Bedfordshire jail, although there were brief periods of freedom. Apparently his captors were fairly kind and allowed him to make lace to support his family. Bunyan also used his captivity to study closely the Bible* and John Foxe's *Book of Martyrs,* as well as doing quite a bit of writing himself. One product of his enforced leisure was his spiritual autobiography, *Grace Abounding to the Chief of Sinners* (1666). Besides completing a number of other minor works, most scholars believe that Bunyan wrote most of the first part of *The Pilgrim's Progress* during the late 1660s and early 1670s. Thanks to Charles II's Declaration of Indulgence* in 1672, the authorities released Bunyan and he returned to Bedford, where his congregation made him their official preacher. A second brief imprisonment occurred in 1675.

During the last two decades of his life, Bunyan earned a well-deserved reputation as an evangelist and organizer for his church, in both Bedford and the surrounding counties. Admiring contemporaries even nicknamed him "Bishop Bunyan" in recognition of his great efforts as a pastor. It was during a pastoral visit to Reading in 1688 that he was caught in a rainstorm and came down with the fever that killed him.

The Pilgrim's Progress was Bunyan's masterpiece. It is an allegorical novel that tells of the journeys of Christian and his family from the City of Destruction (damnation) to the Celestial City (salvation). Written in powerful but plain prose, it serves as a model for the struggles of all peoples in all ages. Bunyan had a deep sympathy for the poor and powerless of his day, particularly since he was one of them. He did not glorify the rich and powerful; instead, he saw them as sources of evil. Similar themes run through his other writings. These characteristics made *The Pilgrim's Progress* very attractive reading for the middling and poor people of England. The elite culture largely held Bunyan's writings in contempt until critics in the nineteenth century embraced *The Pilgrim's Progress.* It is now a classic of English literature. In 1811 an early settler in Ohio observed about his fellow settlers that if they owned one book, it would always be the Bible, and if they owned a second, it would be *The Pilgrim's Progress.*

Bibliography: John Brown, *John Bunyan (1628-1688): His Life, Times and Work,* 1928; Christopher Hill, *A Turbulent, Seditious and Factious People: John Bunyan and His Church, 1628-1688,* 1988.

Ronald H. Fritze

Burnet, Gilbert (1643-1715). Bishop of Salisbury, clerical politician, and historian, he opposed the re-Catholicizing policies of Charles II* and James II*, and as an adviser to William of Orange*, he helped to bring about the Glorious Revolution*.

Born in Scotland* on 18 September 1643 and educated at Marischal College, Aberdeen, Burnet pursued a career in the Scottish clergy. He gained the friendship of John Maitland*, the duke of Lauderdale and the ruler of Scotland for Charles II, and the two worked together to reconcile Presbyterians* and Episcopalians (see Anglicanism*) during the 1660s. Burnet also managed to develop a friendship with Charles II, and in 1669 he became a professor of divinity at the University of

Glasgow. When his patron Lauderdale began to persecute Scottish Presbyterians in 1672, the two men's friendship ended. Burnet moved to England, where in 1675 he became chaplain of the Rolls Chapel and also soon began work on his *History of the Reformation in England,* with the first volume appearing in 1679. The book supplied a well-reasoned refutation of Roman Catholicism*, which earned the author votes of thanks from parliament*.

Although he was a moderate in religion, Burnet grew increasingly wary of the future James II during the last years of Charles II's reign. His close friendship with William Lord Russell, who in 1683 was executed for treason in connection with the Rye House Plot*, also brought Burnet under suspicion. In 1684 he was deprived of his office of rolls chaplain, and upon the succession of James II, he went into self-imposed exile in Holland. There he became an adviser to the stadholder William of Orange and his wife, Mary*. In that position he helped William to negotiate the agreement that led to his being invited to invade England and depose James II.

After the Glorious Revolution, Burnet possessed great influence with Queen Mary and was quickly appointed bishop of Salisbury. When the queen died in 1694, his influence faded. In 1698 the Latitudinarian* opinions of his *Exposition of the Thirty-Nine Articles of the Church of England* created a controversy between the upper and lower clergy. He was conscientious in his pastoral duties and argued for the augmentation of the stipends for the poorer clergy, which eventually resulted in the establishment of Queen Anne's Bounty in 1704. After his death on 17 March 1715, his *History of My Own Time* was published. It still serves as an important source for the history of the years 1660-1689.

Bibliography: Thomas E. S. Clarke and H. C. Foxcroft, *A Life of Gilbert Burnet,* 1907.

Ronald H. Fritze

Bushell's Case (1670). By the later seventeenth century England had largely abandoned its old form of proof in jury trials (see Common Law and Courts*). Originally juries had been composed of men with knowledge of the particular facts of the case being tried. There thus arose the practice of punishing jurors when they returned a verdict at odds with these facts. The trial judge could jail them for a year, forfeit their property, eject their wives and children, and lay waste to their property if they had agreed to this form of perjury or fraud.

By 1670 jurors were chosen not so much for what they knew but for their ignorance of the details of the case. Their knowledge of the facts came from the evidence presented at trial. This radical shift in what the jury was expected to know concomitantly increased the trial judge's ability to control that body, and during the seventeenth century judges had several techniques to ensure the desired verdict was returned. For example, they often commented on the nature and quality of the evidence presented. They could also instruct the jury on the law and, where the facts were strong in favor of an acquittal, direct them to return a verdict of not guilty.

Finally the court was able to punish a jury for reaching a decision it thought was contrary to the facts.

In 1670 two Quakers*, one of them William Penn, were tried for unlawful assembly and acquitted by a jury in the face of overwhelming evidence of their guilt. The trial court, outraged at this verdict and relying on precedent, jailed the jury. Bushell, one of its members, filed a petition for a writ of *habeas corpus* challenging the continuing validity of that law on which he had been placed in confinement. The court that heard the writ agreed that the trial court had erred and ruled that the jury are judges in matters of fact, and relying on their ancient role, they may have knowledge of the case of which the court is ignorant and therefore cannot be fined or jailed for returning a verdict contrary to the court's instruction.

In time the case came to stand for the jury's unfettered right to decide matters of fact. In the short term—at least one hundred years—the case had little effect on most trials. Courts still had other, more effective ways to control juries, which usually were all too willing to follow the court's suggestions as to the verdict they should return. This made judges unwilling to fight for their previously unchallenged power to punish disobeying juries. Nevertheless, the case has become part of the legacy of criticism of the Stuart judiciary and an important signpost along the road to removing politics from the courtroom.

Bibliography: John H. Langbein, "The Criminal Trial before the Lawyers," *The University of Chicago Law Review* 45 (Winter 1978): 263-316; T. F. T. Plucknett, *A Concise History of the Common Law*, 5th ed., 1956.

David A. Davis

Butler, James, 1st Duke of Ormonde (1610-1688). An influential Anglo-Irish statesman noted for devotion to the Stuarts and the Anglican* church, he was an important figure in Irish history from the 1630s through the 1680s. Born 19 October 1610 as the eldest son of Thomas Butler, viscount Thurles and Elizabeth Poyntz, he became a royal ward after his father's death in 1619 and was raised a Protestant. In 1629 he married his cousin, Elizabeth Preston. Upon the death of his grandfather, Walter Butler, 11th earl of Ormonde, in 1633, he succeeded to the Irish earldom of Ormonde and Ossory and went to Ireland*.

There Ormonde actively supported Lord Deputy Thomas Wentworth*, who appointed him commander of all forces in Ireland when he returned to England in 1640. After the outbreak of the Irish Rebellion* in October 1641, Ormonde was appointed lieutenant-general of the army in Ireland under the lord lieutenant and won several victories over the rebels in 1642. Charles I* rewarded him with elevation to marquis and made him lieutenant-general under direct royal authority. In January 1643 Ormonde forwarded to Charles the grievances of Catholic* nobles and gentry from the general assembly at Kilkenny, initiating a period in which he negotiated with the rebels on the king's behalf. Ormonde acquitted himself well, producing a one-year cessation of arms signed on 15 September 1643, which enabled 5,000 Irish troops to be sent to aid the royalist* cause in England. However, he was unable to end the hostilities permanently because of the presence of parliamentary forces in Ulster and a papal nuncio who urged Irish Catholics to reject Ormonde's proposals. In July 1647 Ormonde arranged with parliamentary commissioners to give up his offices and return to England. After an interview with Charles, who approved his conduct, Ormonde escaped to France, having been warned that parliament* would seize him. In France he met with Charles's wife, Henrietta Maria*, who authorized him to return to Ireland to negotiate with representatives of the general assembly at Kilkenny. Ormonde also negotiated with other Irish leaders and brought about a general peace between the Irish rebels and the royalists. After Charles's execution*, Ormonde proclaimed the prince of Wales as Charles II* and attempted to conquer Ireland in his name. Defeated by parliamentary forces, Ormonde left Ireland in 1650 to attend the prince in his continental exile. He was involved in correspondence with General George Monck* and negotiations that led to the Restoration*.

Charles II rewarded him with many honors, including elevation to the dukedom of Ormonde in the Irish peerage and the lord lieutenantcy of Ireland. Ormonde governed Ireland justly and promoted Irish interests and the economy as far as possible under restrictive English policy. A staunch Anglican, he worked to restore the Irish episcopacy and implement the Restoration land settlement. Sir Henry Bennet* and the earl of Shaftesbury (Anthony Ashley Cooper*) intrigued against Ormonde, and in 1669 Charles dismissed him. In 1670 he survived an attempt on his life by the notorious adventurer Thomas Blood. He was reappointed lord lieutenant in 1677 and kept Ireland at peace during the Popish Plot* and the Exclusion Crisis* (1678-1681) by expelling clergy whose authority derived from Rome, dissolving Catholic societies, convents, and schools, and disarming Catholics. However, Shaftesbury and the Whigs* criticized him for not enacting more stringent measures. In 1682 he went to England, helped secure election of Tory* sheriffs* in London*, and assisted in the prosecution of Shaftesbury. That year Charles elevated him to an English dukedom. In 1684 he was recalled as lord lieutenant, but before he could turn over control to his successor, Charles died in February 1685. Ormonde's last official act was to proclaim James II* in Dublin. In 1687 he opposed James's attempt to assume dispensing power* in the Charterhouse case. Ormonde died on 21 July 1688 and was buried in Westminster Abbey.

Bibliography: Thomas Carte, *The Life of James Duke of Ormonde*, 2d ed., 6 vols., 1851.

Mark C. Herman

Bye Plot. See Main and Bye Plots.

C

Cabal (1667-1673). Edward Hyde, earl of Clarendon's* dismissal in 1667 for mismanaging naval affairs in the Second Dutch War* (1665-1667) cleared the way to prominence for a clutch of ambitious courtiers. Henry Bennet*, Lord Arlington, a member of Clarendon's informal parliamentary committee and already the king's principal adviser on foreign affairs, took direction of foreign policy, assisted by George Villiers*, 2d duke of Buckingham. Sir Thomas Clifford*, another of Clarendon's parliamentary managers, assumed control of the treasury along with Anthony Ashley Cooper*, Lord Ashley. Together they increased the yield from customs and excise taxes and adopted new methods of scheduling payments to improve the government's credit (see Taxation and Revenue*). John Maitland*, earl of Lauderdale, became high commissioner for Scotland*. Arlington and Clifford were particularly effective in creating a court party* to manage Charles II's* business in parliament* (see Cavalier Parliament*). The only common focus the five had was serving on a standing committee of the privy council* known as the "committee for foreign affairs."

Anxious for the security abroad that a close political alliance with France would bring, Charles pursued secret negotiations in 1669. Outmaneuvered by the French, he brought Arlington and Clifford into the scheme, and in May 1670 they—with others, all Catholic or with strong Catholic sympathies—signed the treaty of Dover* (1670) with France, in which both powers pledged to join in a war against the Dutch, the French undertook not to rupture the peace with Spain, and Charles promised to declare his adherence to Roman Catholicism* in return for £140,000 and 6,000 French soldiers to protect him from his Protestant subjects. A bogus version of the treaty that omitted the section relating to the king's profession of Catholicism was signed in December by Arlington and Clifford, as well as Buckingham, Ashley, and Clifford, who had been duped into thinking this was the real treaty. Buckingham was a staunch foe of Catholicism, Lauderdale was an ex-Covenanter*, and Ashley was interested in freedom of conscience for Protestants only. Nonetheless, the arrangement of their names Clifford, Arlington, Buckingham, Ashley, Lauderdale to produce the unfortunate acronym "CABAL" made it appear as though they were a ministry united in political agreement, which they were not. The obvious sympathy of Clifford and Arlington for Catholicism, taken together with the signature of the five to the French treaty, led to their being branded as agents of Catholicism. This perception deepened at the beginning of the Third Dutch War* (1672-1674) in March 1672, when a Declaration of Indulgence* suspended the penal laws against Catholics and nonconformists. Soon afterward Clifford was elevated to the peerage and made lord treasurer, Arlington was made an earl and given the garter, Ashley was made earl of Shaftesbury and given the lord chancellorship, and Lauderdale was made a duke and given the garter.

In February 1673 parliament met and Commons refused supply for the war, forcing Charles in March to cancel the Declaration of Indulgence and accept a Test Act* excluding Roman Catholics from office. Clifford resigned in June rather than receive communion according to the ritual of the Anglican* church. The session of parliament that met in October was even more antipapist and anti-French. To conciliate parliament, Shaftesbury suggested that Charles back out of his marriage to the Catholic Mary Beatrice of Modena*, and he established back-channel contacts with the Dutch. He was dismissed and became one of Charles's most dedicated opponents. In January 1674 parliament met again and Commons threatened the impeachment* of Buckingham, Lauderdale, and Arlington. The Cabal collapsed, one of the last casualties of the war from which England withdrew via the Treaty of Westminster on 9 February. Buckingham was removed from all offices and dismissed from the privy council soon afterward. Arlington resigned his last government position in September.

Bibliography: Ronald Hutton, *Charles the Second, King of England, Scotland, and Ireland*, 1989; Maurice Lee, *The Cabal*, 1965.

Joseph M. McCarthy

Cabinet Government. In its modern sense there was no cabinet government or ministerial responsibility in Stuart England. There are many problems, particularly for the seventeenth century, concerning use of the word cabinet and the appearance of a cabinet that regularly formulated policy. Even after the Glorious Revolution*, William III* regularly acted without taking the advice of his ministers and very often against their counsel. It is clear, however, that the growing complexity and size of the government made the privy council* increasingly ineffective. As a result, temporary and permanent committees within the privy council were established. The more significant ministers served on the most important committees. The term cabinet council was used initially to describe the king's secret advisers and later those who sat on many of the important privy council committees.

There was continuing tension because of the king's reliance on secret "cabinet councils" instead of the "public" advice of the privy council or parliament*. In 1642 the Long Parliament* presented the Nineteen Propositions*, seeking to require that the king consult parliament in the choice of his ministers; Charles I refused to accept them. But not until after Charles's execution* and the fall of the Commonwealth* did any real movement begin toward making the king's ministers responsible to parliament.

By the Restoration* the size of the privy council had increased further, and it was less workable. Charles II* worked instead through privy council committees or "cabinet councils." He also revealed secret plans, such as the Treaty of Dover* (1670), to an even smaller group of advisers. The House of Commons became increasingly suspicious of these "secret" councils and sought to discover who had advised the king concerning such matters as the Declaration of Indulgence* in 1672 and the dissolution of the Triple Alliance*.

In response to this lack of direct accountability, parliament used the power of impeachment* as a weapon, with two attempts to impeach the earl of Clarendon (Edward Hyde*), three against the earl of Danby (Thomas Osborne*), and numerous others. Charles II sought to protect his current and former ministers through pardons on eight different occasions. The most noteworthy and contested was the pardon of Danby in 1679. The House of Commons stood its ground, declaring the pardon illegal. Ultimately the House of Lords sent Danby to the Tower, where he was to stay for five years. Eventually the Act of Settlement of 1701 (12 and 13 Gul. III & Mar. II, c. 2) established that the king's pardon was not a defense to impeachment by the House of Commons.

During the Exclusion Crisis* (1678-1681), in an attempt to placate his opponents, Charles II remodeled the privy council to conduct "all business both domestic and foreign." The king named the Whig* exclusionist earl of Shaftesbury (Anthony Ashley Cooper*) as its lord president but dismissed him within six months. It was soon apparent that Charles continued to rely on his "cabinet council." The privy council was not even consulted when he prorogued and later dissolved parliament.

The House of Commons also sought to control royal ministers through addresses to the king. For example, in 1680 the Commons questioned the "pernicious counsels" of the earl of Halifax (*Commons Journal* XI, 630). In addition Commons attempted to exercise control through its authority to raise taxes, designating the proceeds of particular taxes for special purposes, and began to take regular accounts of the king's finances though the use of an audit commission.

James II* increased the privy council's size from thirty-five to forty-nine; however, he continued Charles's practice of having its actual work performed by temporary and permanent committees. Contemporaries continued to note the functioning of the king's "cabinet" as being distinct from the privy council as a whole.

After the revolution, William allowed the privy council, which grew to over sixty members, and its committees to deal with some matters, but he also continued to maintain a sort of cabinet council of his most important ministers, and his ministers still viewed themselves as responsible not to parliament, but to the king. As a result parliament's challenges to the king's ministers continued, and the issue was not resolved until well into the eighteenth century.

Bibliography: Clayton Roberts, "The Growth of Ministerial Responsibility to Parliament in Later Stuart England," *Journal of Modern History* 28 (1956): 215-233;

Clayton Roberts, *The Growth of Responsible Government in Stuart England*, 1966; E. R. Turner, *The Cabinet Council of England in the Seventeenth and Eighteenth Centuries 1622-1784*, 2 vols., 1930-1932.

John Harrison Rains III

Cadiz Expedition (1625). A miserably failed attempt to recapture the glories of the Elizabethan era. In contrast to Sir Francis Drake's raids, it was remembered by the English people ignobly for decades.

The expedition grew out of renewed conflict with the Spanish, with whom the English had been at peace since 1604. Then James I* had styled himself a peacemaker, but peace with Spain was never popular with the English people or parliament*, and James changed his diplomatic stance after the rude treatment Prince Charles and the duke of Buckingham (George Villiers*) received in Spain in 1623 while negotiating unsuccessfully for a Spanish match* between Charles and the Infanta. When James died in March 1625, conduct of a Spanish War* was left to Charles I* and to Buckingham, friend and principal adviser to the new king as he had been to his father.

After attempts to damage Spain indirectly by attacking its European domains failed, Charles and Buckingham conceived the Cadiz expedition to satisfy parliamentary demands for direct action. Cadiz was the most desirable target since it was the port through which naval traffic proceeded to and from the New World. Attacks on Cadiz became legendary after 1587, when Drake boldly "singed the king's [Philip II's] beard," sailing into the harbor to burn ships and provisions for the Spanish Armada. Historians have credited the resulting delay and disruption with aiding the defeat of the armada the next year.

Charles and Buckingham appointed Sir Edward Cecil, a relative of Elizabeth's Lord Burghley, to command the 1625 attack. Although he had earned a credible military record in the Low Countries, he was totally inexperienced in naval operations. The bulk of the fleet consisted of conscripted merchantmen's ships, filled with troops raised mainly from the gaols and streets. Its meager resources resulted from parliament's refusal to grant further subsidies after Count Mansfeld's expedition into Germany, which Buckingham had organized, failed early in 1625.

The Cadiz expedition set sail in October with about 10,000 men. The English landed in the vicinity of Cadiz, and after capturing Fort Puntales, a small outpost at the harbor mouth, the troops marched south and west around the bay to San Fernando. There they encountered vast stores of wine intended for Spain's New World fleets. Becoming drunk and unruly, the soldiers had to be put back aboard the ships. On the return trip to England, shortages of food and water and poor sanitary conditions reduced the army to shocking conditions of illness and want.

When the fleet reached Plymouth, Sir John Eliot*, vice-admiral for Devon and a former client of Buckingham, observed the evidence of failure and mismanagement. What Eliot saw turned him against his former patron and the government; in subsequent parliaments in the 1620s, Eliot was a ringleader against Charles.

The expedition increased Buckingham's unpopularity. Because it foundered under Cecil (who was nonetheless rewarded with a viscountcy), Buckingham led the next expedition, to the Isle of Rhe, himself. When it fared no better, John Felton, an unpaid, disgruntled officer, assassinated him in 1628. Felton instantly became a national hero.

Although Eliot died in 1632, imprisoned for opposing Charles, the ignominious character of the expedition was not forgotten during the Personal Rule*. When the Long Parliament* drafted the Grand Remonstrance* in 1641, it was third on a list of 204 grievances. Sixteen years after the event, parliament remembered that the expedition "was so ordered as if it had rather been intended to make us weary of war than to prosper in it."

Bibliography: John Bowle, *Charles I*, 1975; P. Gibbs, *The Romance of George Villiers*, 1930; John Glanville, *The Voyage to Cadiz in 1625*, Camden Society, 1883; Roger Lockyer, *The Early Stuarts: A Political History of England, 1603-1642*, 1989.

Janet A. Thompson

Calvin's Case (1608). Determined by the common law* and equity judges in Exchequer* chamber, this was the second controversial judicial ruling of James I's* reign concerning the extent of the royal prerogative* (the first was Bate's Case* in 1606) and caused lasting distrust of the king's attitude to the common law. It ruled that Scots born since 24 March 1603, the "post-nati," were automatically naturalized subjects in England by virtue of the Scottish James VI's accession to the English throne as James I.

The issue had a controversial prehistory. James's 1604 scheme for the union* of England and Scotland* had depended on recognition of an existing "union and incorporation" established by his accession. The Commons mauled it by distinguishing between the "king's two bodies," private and public—the accession of a private man who was also king of Scotland had no automatic effect on the public kingdom of England (effectively "king-in-parliament"). The keystone of the 1604 commission's proposed legislation was a naturalization bill, based on a judicial opinion (announced by proclamation in 1604) that the post-nati were already naturalized by the accession. In 1607 its program asked parliament* merely to confirm this by statute. The Commons appealed to the judges: allegiance was due not to the king's "private" body but to his "public" body; thus, Scots, whenever born, needed a statute to be naturalized, and that would stop any Scot from receiving English land or office. They also argued that if the royal prerogative* was "British" in scope, above English and Scottish laws and parliaments, then the impositions* recently set in England should also apply to Scotland (as they did not). The judges found for James: allegiance depended on the body natural and the prerogative. But the Commons rejected this and refused further discussion, much less legislation, unless the legal principle was surrendered. At this impasse James dropped naturalization in parliament.

Calvin's Case was the result, a collusive action to set a legal precedent, where an English land grant to a three-year-old Scot (Robert Colville, or Calvin) was challenged on the grounds that he was an alien. Counsel against Calvin had spoken against naturalization in the Commons in 1607 and used the same arguments; with the majority judgment (twelve to two), James triumphed over both. This was made explicit in the judgment of Lord Chancellor Ellesmere, published by royal authority in 1609, which also denounced the "two bodies" distinction as potentially treasonable.

The reversal in law of a clear Commons stance and the assertion that James's highest prerogatives did have concrete consequences brought distrust of the prerogative to new heights, which despite the efforts of James and the earl of Salisbury (Robert Cecil*) at reassurance helped cause breakdowns in the parliaments of 1610* and 1614* and which (in principled resistance to impositions) persisted into Charles I's* reign. In retrospect Ellesmere saw Calvin's Case as the beginning of his parting of the ways with Sir Edward Coke*, the champion of the common law. Conrad Russell observes that "a very large proportion of the parliamentary arguments in 1642 seem to have been drawn from the losing side in Calvin's case."

Bibliography: Bruce Galloway, *The Union of England and Scotland, 1603-1608*, 1986; Louis Knafla, *Law and Politics in Jacobean England: The Tracts of Lord Chancellor Ellesmere*, 1977; Conrad Russell, *The Causes of the English Civil War*, 1991.

Neil Cuddy

Calvinism. *Calvinism* is a conventional and convenient name for Reformed theology, the position originally of the Swiss and Rhineland Reformers, as distinct from the Lutherans. Reformed theology began with Ulrich Zwingli, Heinrich Bullinger, and Martin Bucer, the last of whom especially influenced John Calvin. However, Calvin was its principal formulator, though others made significant contributions, such as the exiled Italian theologians Peter Martyr Vermigli and Jerome Zanchi and Calvin's Genevan successor, Theodore Beza. In the seventeenth century many theologians, both continental and British, developed Calvinism beyond Calvin. But Calvinism, through all its development, although recognizing an inchoate natural knowledge of God, centered on a piety and theology of divine grace nourished by the Pauline Epistles and St. Augustine, which it expressed through an order of salvation that proceeded from election to effectual calling, justification, sanctification, and glorification.

Calvinists agreed with the Lutherans in affirming justification by faith and the primacy of Scripture but differed in rejecting the Lutheran Eucharistic doctrines of consubstantiation and the ubiquity of Christ's body (instead teaching receptionism, the view that by the power of the Holy Spirit the saving benefits of Christ are conveyed to those receiving the bread and wine in faith), in denying that Christ's descent into hell pertained to his exaltation rather than his humiliation, in emphasizing predestination, and in teaching the indefectibility of the elect. Also in distinction from Lutheran theology, the Reformed affirmed a "third use" of the law (the necessity of the law as a guide for believers), a point related to their emphasis on personal sanctification and the construction of a Christian social order.

Swiss theology (to call it Calvinism at the beginning is anachronistic) emerged as an important theological current early in the English Reformation (as with William Tyndale), was promoted during the reign of Edward VI (bishops such as Thomas Cranmer and Nicholas Ridley were by then adherents of receptionism), and became the regnant theological school in the Elizabethan age with both conformists and nonconformists (though nonconformists tended to be more ardent in their espousal of Calvinism and more active in amplifying it as a piety and ecclesiology). William Whitaker and William Perkins were leading expositors of Elizabethan Calvinism.

In the seventeenth century English Calvinism developed in ways stimulated by both continental Reformed currents and the English religious experience. Among the continental currents was the emergence of Reformed scholasticism, as theologians, under the pressure of controversy, sought to present more tightly knit systems than those produced early in the Reformation. The first Protestants had deplored medieval scholasticism as barren, but later Protestant theologians returned to Aristotelian scholasticism, or else like William Ames developed a scholastic theology on the basis of the new more rhetorical logic of the Huguenot martyr Peter Ramus.

Scholastic Calvinism emphasized predestination, sometimes in its supralapsarian form (God's decrees of election and reprobation preceded the Fall) and placed it in the context of a whole pattern of divine decrees concerning creation, providence, and redemption. But English Calvinists continued to relate predestination to piety as a guarantee of the gratuitousness of salvation.

Another continental influence on English Calvinists was Federal Theology, a development of the covenantal emphasis of such early Reformed theologians as Bullinger. Federal Theology taught two covenants, those of works and grace, of which Adam and Christ were, respectively, the "Federal" heads, rather than one covenant of grace differently administered, as taught by Bullinger and Calvin. The double covenant, derived from Zacharias Ursinus at Heidelberg, was first taught in England by Dudley Fenner and Thomas Cartwright and appeared in many Puritan* writings as well as in the Westminster Confession of 1646 (see Westminster Assembly of Divines*). In an influential view, Perry Miller interpreted covenant theology as modifying strict predestinarianism, but Michael McGiffert has shown that the doubling of the covenant paralleled the doubling of the divine decrees and intensified the theme of unmerited grace.

Arminianism* was the main challenge stimulating Calvinist response and development in England in the first half of the seventeenth century. Though arising on the Continent, it developed in distinct ways in England, being connected there both with Laudian sacramentalism and ecclesiasticism (salvation through a sacramental system fit uneasily with predestination) and with sectarians resistant to the hegemony of Calvinist theologians.

During the reign of James I*, Calvinism continued as the prevailing outlook of the Church of England (see Anglicanism*), as shown by the Irish Articles (1615), English participation in the Synod of Dort's* condemnation of Arminianism (1619), and the archiepiscopate of the staunchly Calvinist George Abbot*. But opposition was growing, as some conformists sought an outlook more compatible with their appreciation of traditional elements retained by the English church of the sort to which Puritans objected. Hence Bishop Thomas Bilson, in publications of 1599 and 1604, adopted the Lutheran rather than the Calvinist interpretation of the descent of Christ into hell, while others questioned limited atonement and the indefectibility of the elect.

With the ascendancy of Charles I* and William Laud*, the opponents of Calvinism came into favor, driving a theological wedge between conformists and nonconformists who previously had differed mainly over ceremonial and discipline, disrupting the relative ecclesiastical stability of the Jacobean years, and giving rise to fears of "popery." The divisiveness created by such widespread alienation from the ascendant party in the established church contributed to the coming of the Civil War*, as Nicholas Tyacke and Conrad Russell have argued. Anti-Calvinism of a different sort from that of the Laudians appeared in the ferment of sectarian ideas and groups during the 1640s, exemplified by the Independent* John Goodwin and the General Baptists*.

In response to Arminianism, Calvinists defended their theology at the challenged points, such as unconditional predestination and limited atonement. This defense, along with scholastic method and the doubling of the covenant, characterized the High Calvinism of midcentury, of which John Owen* and Thomas Goodwin were leading exponents.

Antinomianism, which caused alarm in both the 1640s and the 1690s, was another stimulus to the development of English Calvinism. Though sometimes mistakenly regarded as a libertarian protest, it was actually an extreme version of High Calvinism, its central insistence being that the redeemed were justified as well as elected from eternity, prior to their effectual calling. By the end of the seventeenth century, Hyper-Calvinism, which discouraged general offers of salvation, represented a further development of High Calvinist and Antinomian tendencies, but it was restricted to some Particular Baptists who maintained it through the next century, while it was deplored by all other Calvinists.

Calvinist theology was eclipsed at the Restoration*, discredited by association with rebellion, the Cromwellian church, and sectarian excess. It seemed out of tune with the new spirit of reasonableness. A dwindling force within the church, it was opposed by High Churchmen* and Latitudinarians* alike, though still represented by some bishops, such as Edward Reynolds and Thomas Barlow. Thus after 1660 it was mainly identified with dissent. The Congregationalists*, led by John Owen, were firmly committed, especially after their Savoy Conference* of 1658, to High Calvinism, as were the Particular Baptists, including John Bunyan*.

However, a moderate and Latitudinarian Calvinism, fearful of Antinomianism and resistant to High Calvinism, emerged with the Presbyterian* group centered around Richard Baxter*, John Howe, and Daniel Williams. They minimized predestination and, at least in Baxter's case, followed the French Calvinist Moses Amyraut in teaching a hypothetical universalism of grace with respect to the atonement. Baxter and his circle also wrote on natural theology, echoing some of the earlier themes of Calvin and paralleling the interests of the Anglican Latitudinarians.

In their homiletic and devotional writings, however, Baxter and the other moderate Calvinist Dissenters* remained faithful to the Reformed insistence that the holy life resulted from a conversion and renovation through supernatural grace effected by the Holy Spirit. Indeed throughout the century English Calvinists of all sorts were industrious in the production of an extensive literature of practical "affectionate divinity" focused on providing comfort and assurance to believers, as well as exhorting unbelievers to conversion. The development of a rich piety centered on divine grace was a principal achievement of English Calvinism.

Bibliography: R. T. Kendall, *Calvin and English Calvinism to 1649*, 1979; Nicholas Tyacke, *Anti-Calvinists: The Rise of English Arminianism c. 1590-1640*, 1987; Dewey D. Wallace, Jr., *Puritans and Predestination: Grace in English Protestant Thought from 1525-1695*, 1982.

Dewey D. Wallace, Jr.

Campbell, Archibald, 8th Earl and 1st Marquis of Argyll (1598-1661). Scion of the Highlands' most powerful clan, Argyll played a major role in the upheavals of the 1640s throughout the British Isles. The Roman Catholicism* of his father, the 7th earl, propelled Lord Lorne (honorific title of the heir) into the position of clan leader as early as the 1620s. The death of the 7th earl legalized his position as Campbell overlord and opened the path for his extensive role in Scottish, English, and Irish affairs.

The Campbells were neither a simple Highland clan nor a geographically consolidated kin group. Their lengthy conflict against the MacDonalds had enlarged clan territories and developed an extensive alliance system with middle-sized clans such as the Lamonts and MacDougalls. Unlike other clan chieftains, the earls had maintained tight control over their junior branches (principally in the shires of Perth and Nairn). In 1638 this formidable clan was estimated to possess 5,000 well-trained fighting men, making the loyalties of its leader of vital importance to Charles I* and the Covenanters*. The ancient feud with the MacDonalds and the earl's strong Protestant predilections meant that County Antrim, Ulster, with its royalist Roman Catholic MacDonnell (MacDonald) earl, was a threat to the security of the Campbell heartland of Argyll. In addition to Highland concerns, the 8th earl inherited a landed estate (Castle Campbell) and a legacy of involvement in national politics (embodied by the hereditary title of lord justiciar of Scotland*).

The 8th earl's education directly reflected a duality of outlook. Educated to speak Scots, Gaelic, and Latin, Lord Lorne studied at the University of St. Andrews. He became imbued with Protestant piety, commencing each day of his adult life with two hours of private prayer. With experience as a military leader in carrying out royal commissions of fire and sword, as well as membership on the Scottish privy council, Lorne had a thorough preparation for the tempest of the 1640s.

After succeeding his father in 1638, the new earl lingered with the royalist* cause by attending council meetings. When the Covenanters* defied the royal commissioner's order to dissolve the Glasgow general assembly of the Church of Scotland (see Kirk*) in December 1638, Argyll immediately voiced his support for the opposition. His status propelled him to the front rank of the Covenanting movement. Between 1638 and 1641 Argyll was instrumental in establishing Presbyterian* church government, creating a noble-dominated parliamentary civil government, and securing Scottish assistance to crush the Ulster rising. Argyll's prominence led to allegations that he intended to usurp the king. This is unlikely, although charges that he aimed to share ruling Scotland with Hamilton are more plausible. Throughout the period Argyll ensured that his loyalty to the Covenanters benefited the Campbells.

Assessing Argyll's role in the 1638-1660 period is complex. Despite numerous military and honorific commands, his martial abilities were limited. In the two Bishops' Wars* Argyll secured the southwest and central Highlands, even capturing Dumbarton Castle (1640) by a policy of alliances and destruction. His regiment of clansmen secured the Antrim lands in 1642. Two years later the marquis (promoted 1641) defeated the marquis of Huntly's rising. Campaigns in summer and autumn 1644 failed to defeat James Graham, marquis of Montrose, and Alasdair MacColla MacDonald's forces. With their ravaging of Argyll in December 1644 and a disastrous defeat of the Campbells at Inverlochy on 2 February 1645, Argyll's military power disintegrated. The clan lands were devastated in 1644-1647. Argyll's attempt to join the Kirk party's* Whiggamore raid in September 1647 fell to pieces when Engager troops (see Engagement and Engagers*) surprised his men at Stirling.

Although pushed into political leadership due to his military power, the marquis's skill as a politician preserved his leading role in civil affairs. In 1642-1643 he successfully battled Hamilton's attempts to neutralize Scotland and threw his weight behind the Solemn League and Covenant*. From summer 1643 until the Engager coup in spring 1648, Argyll led the Covenanter government. That provided him with a voice in English affairs, where he urged the adoption of Presbyterianism. His return to power after the fall of the Engagers was not absolute due to the hostility of the Kirk party to nobles and to any accommodation with Engagers. The defeat at Dunbar in September 1650 and the Public Resolutions of December 1650 ended Argyll's dominance of civil affairs. The 1652 campaign by the New Model Army* in the Highlands led to his capitulation to General George Monck* in October. Subsequently the marquis assisted the English regime, even opposing his heir's attempts to raise the Campbells for the royalists* during Glencairn's Rising. Argyll's efforts to make peace with the Restoration* regime failed, because the royalists sought his death and Charles II* hated him for his Kirk party loyalties. Argyll was tried for treason and executed in 1661. Thus ended the career that prefigured that of his eighteenth-century successors, the great political dukes of Argyll.

Bibliography: Ian Cowan, *Montrose for Covenant and King*, 1977; David Stevenson, *Revolution and Counter-Revolution in Scotland 1644-1651*, 1977.

Edward M. Furgol

Campbell, Archibald, 9th Earl of Argyll (1629-1685). While the 8th earl had effortlessly entered into his inheritance, his son had an unconventional path to power. Enjoying the favored upbringing of a major Scottish noble family, the 9th earl also had been schooled in the traditional ways of a Gaelic Highlander. To preserve his heir from the upheavals of the mid-seventeenth century, Argyll sent him to Italy and France from 1647 to 1649. Returning to Scotland*, Lord Lorne (courtesy title of Argyll's heir) received command of His Majesty's Life Guard of Foot in July 1650 from Charles II*. Lorne survived its engagement at Dunbar and escaped from the regiment's destruction at Worcester. Abandoning his father's policy of accommodation with the English regime, Lorne joined Glencairn's Rising in 1653. Although the 8th earl actively disapproved, Lorne tried to recruit Campbells for the royalists*. When his allies sought to attack clansmen and Lowland settlers loyal to Argyll, Lorne intervened on their behalf, preventing the revival of the successful anti-Campbell coalition of the 1640s. The failure of the rising led to Lorne's submission in 1655. Throughout the Interregnum* he remained loyal to Charles II, enduring constant surveillance, as well as occasional fines and imprisonment by the English.

The Restoration brought a sharp decline in Campbell fortunes. The royalist regime of the earl of Middleton carried out the execution and forfeiture of the 8th earl in 1661, secured the death sentence for Lorne in 1662, and levied crippling fines on numerous Campbell lairds. A combination of the clan's traditional role in securing peace in the Highlands and the lobbying of the king's favorite and secretary, the earl of Lauderdale (John Maitland*), caused the revival of Lorne's fortunes. In 1663, with his death penalty removed, Lorne became the 9th earl and regained the earldom's lands. However, the marquis of Huntly's lands, granted to the 8th earl, were not restored, though the debts pertaining to them were assigned to the new earl. Serving the government by pacifying the western Highlands and Isles helped maintain Lauderdale's regime but brought complaints from royalists (especially the MacDonalds) that Argyll was serving clan interests. Faced with massive debts, Argyll harshly tried to collect them. Attempts to gain repayment from the Macleans caused open warfare over their lands, which secured the loans in 1674 and 1679. The downfall of Lauderdale in 1679 provided the anti-Campbell clans with a chance to paint the earl as an oppressor of royalist clans. Argyll's road to Whig* martyrdom was built on the Highland policies of the duke of York, vice-regent in Scotland and the future James II*. Although the duke had no personal animosity against the earl, he wanted to settle the Highlands by curbing Argyll's authority. York's plans became entwined with the passing of the Scottish Test Act, whose oath Argyll would take only "as far as it was consistent with itself." In 1681 he was imprisoned in Edinburgh, tried, and condemned for treason, yet the earl's life and estates were spared. He escaped to the Netherlands, where British exiles hostile to Stuart policies were gathering. As a result the king forfeited Argyll's title and lands but partially restored his heir. The succession of York as James II and VII led to an ill-fated attempt by Argyll to raise his clan for Charles's bastard, the duke of Monmouth. Good planning and a massive turnout of anti-Campbell clans led to a rapid collapse of Argyll's rising (Monmouth's Rebellion* failed also). Argyll was executed, and his clansmen were pillaged ruthlessly, ensuring undying loyalty of his heirs and the Campbells to the Whig cause.

Bibliography: David Stevenson, *Alasdair MacColla and the Highland Problem in the 17th Century*, 1980; J. Wilcock, *A Scots Earl in Covenanting Times,* 1903.

Edward M. Furgol

Canons of 1604, 1606, and 1640. Medieval England recognized the laws, or canons, of the Catholic* church in religious and moral matters. Henry VIII accepted canons that were not "contrary or repugnant to the laws, statutes and customs of this realm" or against "the King's Prerogative Royal*," but there was considerable confusion as to which canons came into those categories. The Act for the Submission of the Clergy (25 Hen. VIII, c. 19, 1534) said future canons should be enacted by convocation with royal assent and that existing canons be revised by a royal commission containing lords, members of parliament*, and clerics. Despite much discussion, however, there was no official new codification of canon law under the Tudors, so the ecclesiastical courts* eclectically combined canons and statutes in occasionally confused fashion.

Protestant England's first official and systematic modification of canon law occurred after the Hampton Court Conference* (1604) confirmed the desire for clarification. In April 1604 James I* authorized convocation to prepare canons under the presidency of Richard Bancroft*, about to become archbishop of Canterbury. Most of the 141 canons are still technically in force, but appeal is rarely made to them in the present day Anglican* church. Issued on the authority of Crown and convocation, they constituted a rather sketchy codification of existing ecclesiastical law. They defined the characteristics of England's church, reaffirming the rectitude of its practices in general (III) and the royal supremacy in particular (I and II). Attacks were punishable by excommunication (V-VIII). Matters about which "hotter" Protestants had reservations, such as the Book of Common Prayer (IV), episcopacy (VII), the cross in baptism (XXX), and the surplice (LVIII), were set out as correct and essential, although significantly even some of the episcopate in convocation had been divided over some of these issues. Abuses relating to church courts, pluralism, and nonresidence (XLI) and to inadequate ministers (XXXIV, XLV, XLVI) were attacked. Some canons dealt with comparatively trivial matters such as the provision of "good wholesome" communion wine in a "clean" pot of pewter or some "purer metal." Canon XXXVI was particularly controversial. It required clerical subscription to the royal supremacy, the Thirty-nine Articles, and the prayer book. Aspects of the latter offended some clerics; roughly 100 clergy refused to subscribe and consequently lost their livelihoods. Loopholes enabling malcontents to infiltrate the church were closed; for example, strangers could not preach without displaying licenses (L, LVI). Such canons probably precipitated Separatism*, as with the many parishioners of Sandwich who sailed on the *Mayflower* in 1620. Much depended on local circumstances; sympathetic bishops and lay patrons could and did protect nonconforming clerics.

Lay hostility erupted in parliament in 1604, 1607, and 1610 (see Parliament of 1604-10*). MPs resented canons issued on the authority of Crown and convocation without parliamentary approbation. The common lawyers among them declared clerical deprivations under the canons were against fundamental rights, for bishops were taking property (benefices). Similarly, laymen should not be punished by laws drawn up by the clergy.

In 1606 convocation had drafted more canons, which James rejected. Perhaps he considered references to *jure divino* ministry unnecessarily provocative to the Commons. Canon XXVIII contended that "new forms of government" arising after a rebellion were legitimate once "thoroughly settled," which no doubt unnerved James. The Commons reacted with a bill against "substantial changes" in religion unless effected "by parliament* with the advice and consent of the clergy in convocation." The checkered history of Bancroft's canons thus reflects constitutional tension between MPs and common lawyers on the one side and church on the other. It also suggests the greater wisdom of the first Stuart, who in rejecting the 1606 canons blurred possible demarcatory battle lines. Under James, church and Crown constituted a more flexible partnership than under the second Stuart. James, for example, soothed MPs' religious sensibilities by appointing Archbishop George Abbot* in 1610. Robert Cecil* rightly diagnosed that controversy over the ecclesiastical authority exercised in the issuing of canons touched too closely upon the royal prerogative*. Wisely, Abbot let sleeping canons lie. Significantly, the controversy revived under his more provocative successor, William Laud*.

In April 1640 Laud and Charles I* took the unprecedented step of keeping convocation in session after the dissolution of the Short Parliament*. Despite vociferous minority opposition, convocation passed a series of canons advertising Laud's religious ideas. Canon VI aroused special unease because its oath bound clerics to support episcopal government "etcetera." The vagueness of that "etcetera" suggested tyrannical plans to suspicious minds in the heated atmosphere of 1640. The requirement that clerics read and preach in favor of the divine right* of kings (I) completed the identification of an increasingly unpopular Laudian church with an increasingly unpopular Stuart monarchy. When the Long Parliament* met in November 1640, the Commons condemned these Arminian* canons (15-16 December) and declared that convocation lacked the power to bind clergy or laity without parliamentary consent. The Lords echoed this. About 15,000 Londoners meanwhile called for the extirpation of episcopacy "root and branch"* (11 December). Once again the passage of canons reflected and exacerbated the tensions that brought England to the Civil War*.

Bibliography: J. P. Kenyon, *The Stuart Constitution*, 1986; J. R. Tanner, *Constitutional Conflicts of the Reign of James I*, 1930.

Vivienne C. Sanders

Carleton, Dudley, Viscount Dorchester (1573-1632). One of the second tier of Stuart officialdom, whose exchange of letters with John Chamberlain and his official diplomatic dispatches provide a rare and consistent view both of the Stuart royal court* and of the European context in which it existed. He represents, although not by his own choice, one of the earliest British examples of a professional diplomat. He yearned instead to be the provost of Eton, a vice chamberlain, or at the pinnacle of his aspirations one of the secretaries of state. He succeeded to most of these positions but only by doggedly pursuing a diplomatic career as the means to his more cherished ends. His career bears witness to the value that diplomatic assignments had for ultimate career enhancement. It also demonstrates that there was a cadre of men on whom the Crown relied consistently and repeatedly for its international contacts.

After the prerequisite foreign tour to acquire languages and experience, Carleton early on begged assignment to some overseas post. Success there provided him with first a secretaryship to the English resident at Paris, Sir Thomas Parry, and then the assumption of a residency in his own right at Venice. To be sure, there had been seven years between his service in Paris and his appointment to the Venetian Doge and Senate, but an apparently innocent association with the Gunpowder Plot* goes far to explain the hiatus. He passed the time in the employ of Henry Percy, 9th earl of Northumberland, and as an aide in scholarly pursuits to his father-in-law, Sir Henry Savile, provost at Eton.

From there it was a steady, albeit frustratingly slow, rise in the estimation of both James I* and the 1st duke of Buckingham (George Villiers*). After five tedious years in Venice, he was advanced to the key diplomatic residency at the Hague. There his negotiating skills, which developed notably in work at Savoy while assigned to Venice, earned approbation and advancement. After ten years in the post (1615-1625), he undertook several significant missions to France in 1625-1626 and served another longish stint in the Low Countries from late 1626 through 1628. He became vice chamberlain, was appointed to the privy council*, and became secretary of state to Charles I* in December 1628. He served as the principal among the two secretaries and was a key advisor and policy maker for foreign affairs.

Along his career path he earned a knighthood (to accompany the Venetian responsibilities), and the distinction of Baron Carleton of Imbercourt (to carry with him in his various missions to France). Just prior to the secretaryship, he became Viscount Dorchester. Both he and his wife found their final resting spots in Westminister Abbey. Although he did not die a rich man, he did die honored.

Insofar as anything has been made of Carleton, it is because of his correspondence. However, his career can be seen as a microcosm of patronage and job seeking in the era. He was an effective, albeit not flamboyant, diplomat, and it is one-sided to attribute his rise merely to a well-placed gift of marbles here, a key friendship there, or a timely death overall. Ability counted, experience earned credit and preferment, and he is much more accurately seen as an exemplar of diplomatic professionalism than as simply the long-importuning placeman.

Bibliography: *Dictionary of National Biography*; John H. Barcroft, "Carleton and Buckingham: The Quest for Office," in Howard S. Reinmuth, ed., *Early Stuart Studies*, 1970; Maurice Lee, ed., *Dudley Carleton to John Chamberlain, 1603-1624: Jacobean Letters*, 1972; Wallace Notestein, *Four Worthies*, 1957.

Gary M. Bell

Carr, Robert, Earl of Somerset (1586-1645). The favorite of James I* from 1607 to 1614. James became infatuated with Carr when he saw the handsome young Scotsman thrown from his horse in the tiltyard. The royal physician was ordered to care for Carr, and James himself remained in attendance while he recovered from a broken leg. For the next seven years, Carr became the center of James's personal life. Although Carr did not possess the intelligence and competence necessary to influence important government policy, he received numerous lucrative positions and honors and was embroiled in court politics.

In 1609 James took the imprisoned Sir Walter Raleigh's* country estate, Sherbourne, and gave it to Carr; this gift was followed by the title Viscount Rochester in 1611. During this time Carr fell in love with the scandalous Frances Howard, who was then married to the 3d earl of Essex (Robert Devereux*). The countess of Essex decided to file for divorce so she could marry Carr, claiming that Essex was impotent and that the marriage had never been consummated.

Carr's confidant and ally, Sir Thomas Overbury*, opposed the marriage because he did not want to lose his control over Carr to the powerful Howard family. James was persuaded to put Overbury in the Tower, where Frances Howard had him poisoned. Various rumors surrounded his death, but the controversy eventually died away. James, who supported Carr's proposed marriage, oversaw the divorce proceedings of 1613; due to royal pressure, the commission returned a verdict favorable to the countess. In November James awarded Carr the title earl of Somerset. In December Somerset and Frances Howard had a lavish wedding, paid for from the royal coffers and attended by the king and queen (Anne of Denmark*).

Somerset's rise in fortune reached its zenith in 1614, when he was appointed lord chamberlain, but his downfall quickly followed. His arrogance began to frustrate the king and opened the way for another court faction to advance George Villiers* as the new favorite. Moreover, gossip about Overbury's murder resurfaced, with enough evidence for James to order an investigation.

In 1616 Somerset and his wife were both found guilty; she admitted her crime, but Somerset steadfastly maintained his innocence. They were condemned to death, but James commuted their sentences to imprisonment. Their love did not survive the scandal; their greatest punishment was said to be each other's company. In 1622 they were allowed to retire to the country, where Somerset lived in obscurity until 1645.

Bibliography: M. A. Deford, *The Overbury Affair*, 1960; P. R. Seddon, "Robert Carr, Earl of Somerset," *Renaissance and Modern Studies* 14 (1970): 48-68.

Jo Eldridge Carney

Catherine of Braganza (1638-1705). Catholic* queen consort of Charles II*, Catherine was the daughter of John, duke of Braganza, who became king of Portugal in 1640. Five years later he suggested Catherine as a bride for the prince of Wales. The Civil War* and Interregnum* put the plan on hold, but when plans for the Restoration* were in the air, the Portuguese ambassador raised the issue of the marriage with General George Monck*, and the English were willing. Catherine and Charles were married in 1662; part of her dowry was Tangier and Bombay.

Despite her father's long-term plans to have Catherine become queen of England, she was not properly educated for the role. She knew nothing about affairs of state and spoke neither English nor French. Charles enjoyed Catherine's company and taught her English soon after the marriage, but his affection for Catherine did not keep him from having mistresses or parading them at the royal court*. Catherine fainted dead away when Charles presented Lady Castlemain to the court but eventually came to realize that tears and anger did not move Charles; she showed an outward calm and treated his bastard children with kindness. This may have been particularly difficult for Catherine, as she had no children of her own, suffering from three miscarriages. Despite his rampant infidelity, Charles remained fond of Catherine and refused to consider divorce despite her childlessness, saying he would not be another Henry VIII. Charles also defended Catherine during the Popish Plot* of 1678, when she was accused of plotting to have him murdered. Charles stated he would never see an innocent woman wronged. When that November the earl of Shaftesbury (Anthony Ashley Cooper*) proposed a bill in the House of Lords to grant Charles a divorce so he could marry a Protestant, Charles actively opposed the bill, and the matter was dropped. With the strong anti-Catholic feeling in the country, Catherine was suspected of trying to influence Charles in Catholic interests, but in fact Catherine was not politically powerful. Her interests were centered on dancing, masquerades, and games of chance. Those who wanted political influence ignored Catherine in favor of Charles's various mistresses.

Catherine was greatly pleased when Charles accepted Catholicism on his deathbed in 1685 but went into deep mourning after his death and lived in seclusion, distressed by the Glorious Revolution* of 1688 and the subsequent harsh measures against Catholics. In 1692 William III* gave Catherine permission to return to Portugal, where she lived quietly, encouraging Anglo-Portuguese friendship. In 1704 Catherine became regent for her brother Pedro during his illness, but her regency was short lived. She died on 31 December 1705.

Bibliography: L. C. Davidson, *Catherine of Braganza*, 1908; Hebe Elsna, *Catherine of Braganza*, 1967; Janet Mackay, *Catherine of Braganza*, 1937.

Carole Levin

Catholicism. Whatever illusions some English Catholics may have entertained about the status of their religion after Elizabeth I's death, they were shattered during the early years of the reign of James I*. During the first thirteen years of his reign, the government added three new anti-recusant statutes. The most significant enactment was an Act for the Better Discovery and Repressing of Popish Recusants (3 Jac. I, c. 4), which was passed in 1606 and required an oath of allegiance*. Another law of the same year levied restrictions on Protestant husbands of Catholic wives. The third, enacted in 1616, called for stricter enforcement of the oath of allegiance by specifying that anyone over the age of eighteen might be required to take it.

From the national perspective, the most significant development within the context of the Catholic question during the reign of James I was the Gunpowder Plot* of 1605. Initiated by Robert Catesby (1573-1605), it was designed to eliminate the king and parliament* and, in the subsequent turmoil, to allow the Catholics to seize control of the government. The conspiracy was foiled by information provided to the government by a relative of a conspirator; most of those involved were executed in 1606. This plot heightened anti-Catholic fervor among the public and caused Catholics to examine their own movement; this resulted in a polemical campaign that was characterized by denunciations of anti-Catholic leaders and by internal factionalism. The controversy over the oath of allegiance, the continuation of the publication of recusant* works, and the debate that focused on the episcopate of Richard Smith were the dominant issues associated with English Catholicism during the early decades of the seventeenth century.

In response to the Gunpowder Plot, parliament in February 1606 began the debate on articles designed to identify Catholics through the enforcement of oaths. In May 1606 the legislation embodying the oath of allegiance was passed. The most significant clauses of the oath specified that James I was king and could not be deposed by the pope. Pope Paul V condemned the oath in two separate declarations in 1606 and 1607. The most intriguing development related to the oath crisis occurred when the Catholic archpriest George Blackwell was captured, took the oath, and invited the English Catholic clergy to do the same. The reaction to these developments extended over several years. Within the Catholic camp, confusion reigned; some people supported Blackwell and the oath, others were in clear opposition to it, and still others were not sure which position was correct.

The crisis over the oath was significant primarily because it demonstrated the growing strength of the Catholic laity and the decline of Catholic clerical influence. The oath caused the Catholic polemicists considerable concern, and several significant works resulted. In 1606 Robert Parsons's *An Answere to the Fifth Part of Reportes* was published; it included a general discussion of the jurisdiction of a monarch over religion and specifically addressed the continuing difficulties the Jesuits were having with the English Catholic secular clergy and the general Catholic response to the oath. Other works condemned Blackwell and the oath, including *A Directorie Teaching the Way to the Truth in a Briefe and Plaine Discourse Against the Heresies of this Time* by John Radford (1561-1630) and *A Briefe and Cleare Declaration of Sundry Pointes* by Anthony Hoskins (1568-1615). Other English recusant writers and polemicists of the era were Edward A. Maihew, John Percy, Thomas Fitzherbert, Richard Broughton, Laurence Anderton, Anthony Champney, and John Heigham. During the early seventeenth century, the Jesuits expanded their "mission" in England; in 1600 there were about a dozen Jesuits operating in England, by 1620 there were more than 100, and by the 1640s their number reached 150 to 200, where it leveled off for the remainder of the century.

During the early seventeenth century, the secular clergy advanced the implementation of the decrees of the Council of Trent more than any other element within the English Catholic community. The most significant attempt to conform with Tridentine degrees was the temporary restoration of "ordinary" episcopal government to the church in England. This effort, referred to as the Chalcedon controversy, was based as much on the need to provide adequate pastoral care for English Catholics as on the jurisdictional and historical claims that had been the basis of the earlier Appellant claims. The plan to reestablish an "ordinary" episcopate was not welcomed by all English Catholics. Catholic aristocrats and gentry enjoyed the flexibility of the selection of their priests and were quite unwilling to surrender the control over their religion that they had acquired as a result of the absence of a strong, centralized episcopal establishment.

Nonetheless, with the death of Pope Paul V in January 1621 and the succession of Pope Gregory XV, archpriest William Harrison (1553-1621) sent John Bennett, one of his assistants, to Rome to request that the system of archpriests be replaced by an "ordinary" episcopal structure. Bennett succeeded in persuading Gregory XV to reverse the existing policy; in 1622 the pope announced that a bishop would be appointed to replace Harrison, who had died in May 1621. In March 1623 Gregory XV appointed William Bishop to lead the English Catholic church; he was given the titular see of Chalcedon. During his brief tenure (he died in April 1624), Bishop was able to achieve several objectives. He established a chapter (ordinarily referred to as the Old Chapter) for the purpose of advising and assisting him and for providing continuity in the event of his death. The chapter consisted of twenty canons. Bishop requested that Rome formally approve the chapter; while official approval was never granted, Propaganda—the Sacred Congregation for the Propagation of the Faith— permitted it to continue operating.

Bishop's successor, Richard Smith, enhanced the power and responsibility of the chapter when he allowed it to elect its own canons and dean and directed that it should exercise jurisdiction over the English Catholic church in the event that a successor was not appointed. Since there would be a prolonged vacancy between 1631 and 1685, the chapter provided continuity of leadership during that period. Bishop also succeeded in reaching agreements that reduced the difficulties between the secular clergy and the religious orders. Smith's tenure (1625-1631) as bishop of Chalcedon was characterized by turmoil and a general deterioration of the unity of English Catholicism. Smith's autocratic style resulted in troubles with the Jesuits and Benedictines; they resented his involvement with their finances. Smith alienated the laity by planning to establish church courts to handle matters relating to tithing, matrimony, and defamation. The result of the disenchantment with Smith was a Catholic coup directed against him. Catholic aristocrats arranged for Smith to be charged with treason; a warrant was issued for his arrest. Smith found sanctuary in the French embassy in 1629 and remained there for two years; in 1631 he fled to France.

During the period from Smith's flight to the Restoration* in 1660, English Catholics were focused on their own internal problems. The chapter survived and provided the continuity that Bishop had planned. From 1636 to 1642 foreign agents attempted to gain power at the royal court* by exploiting the Catholicism of Henrietta Maria*. This so-called Popish Plot (of 1636-1642*) collapsed with the queen's departure from England in 1642. During the Civil War* and Protectorate* English recusants* were persecuted but survived. After the Restoration Catholics anticipated a more tolerant era under Charles II*. In the secret Treaty of Dover* (1670), Charles agreed to attempt the restoration of Catholicism in England. But while he did indicate his intent to eliminate penal laws against the Catholics in the Declaration of Indulgence* of 1672, he was forced to abandon that policy because of virulent anti-Catholicism. This public hysteria manifested itself clearly with the circumstances surrounding the Popish Plot of 1678*. This was fabricated by Titus Oates and Israel Tonge, who stated that Jesuits planned to murder Charles II, burn the city, and place the Catholic duke of York (the future James II*) on the throne. The so-called plot resulted in more than two dozen executions and a new series of anti-Catholic measures. Test Acts* passed in 1673 and 1678 excluded Catholics from serving in the government (25 Car. II, c. 2; 30 Car. II, st. 2, c. 1).

Upon the death of Charles II, his brother, James II, became king of a Protestant nation. During his brief reign (1685-1688) James removed the penal laws and restrictions against Catholics and supported the establishment of a vicar apostolic for England and Wales; Bishop John Leyburn held this position from 1685 to 1688. In 1688 the ecclesiastical administration was reorganized; Leyburn was assigned to the London District, Bishop Buonaventura Gifford was consecrated as vicar apostolic of the Midland District, Bishop James Smith led the Northern District, and Bishop Michael Ellis was installed as the vicar apostolic of the Western District. It was the birth of a Catholic male heir that led to the ouster of James II and the invitation to William* and Mary* to take the throne jointly. The exile of James and other events associated with the Glorious Revolution* eliminated the "favorable" treatment Catholics had enjoyed during this brief reign, but the structure of the vicars apostolic and the elimination of many of the anti-recusant laws were sustained. As the Stuart era closed, English Catholics were less visible and vocal than they had been at the beginning of this period, yet they continued to be penalized for their religious affiliation.

Bibliography: John Bossy, *The English Catholic Community, 1570-1850,* 1976.

William T. Walker

Cavalier Parliament (1661-1679). The Cavalier House of Commons was elected early in 1661. Unlike its predecessor, the Convention*, it was summoned in the traditional way, by the monarch, and there was no attempt to exclude particular groups from voting. Its composition reflected the public mood: former parliamentarians* sought to forget their past and keep a low profile, while the royalists*, especially after Thomas Venner's abortive rising, demanded firm action against "disaffection." Unlike the Convention, therefore, the new House of Commons had a strong royalist majority.

From the start its attitude was partisan. Doubts about the legal status of the Convention offered a pretext to overturn or drastically amend its legislation, including the Act of Indemnity and Oblivion* (12 Car. II, c. 11). At Charles's insistence the indemnity was confirmed, but it became clear that although the Commons were strongly royalist, they had definite ideas of their own about the form of the new regime.

The Commons were eager to rebuild the power of the Crown in order to guard against the threat of revolution from below. To this end they denied that parliament* could legislate without the king; reaffirmed that the king had sole right to direct the armed forces; tacitly abandoned any claim to influence the king's choice of ministers or to exercise executive authority (whereas the Convention had taken charge of paying off the New Model Army*); and gave the king power to censor the press (see Printing*) and to appoint commissioners to purge borough corporations of "disaffected" persons. They also revived the principle that the king should have revenue for life sufficient to support the costs of government (see Taxation and Revenue*).

Yet at the same time the Commons were careful not to enlarge the king's power too far. The power to purge corporations and to censor the press was only temporary. The Commons did not accept that the king needed a standing army*. Above all they were careful not to give him such a large revenue that he would have no need of parliaments. While they wanted a king capable of maintaining order and undertaking the burdens of government, they did not want him strong enough to threaten the liberty and property of the landed classes.

The divergence of attitude over the indemnity became more marked on the issue of the Church of England. Many members of parliament (MPs) were firm Anglicans*; many others saw the church as an essential instrument of social and political control. In addition, while the Act of Indemnity made it impossible to prosecute former parliamentarians for their past activities, it was still possible to proceed against many of them for their present religious nonconformity. MPs were therefore determined to reestablish the church in its traditional form and to suppress all religious gatherings outside the church in groups larger than a single family.

Charles shared the Commons belief that Dissenters* were subversive, but his response was one of conciliation rather than repression. He wished to make the church's liturgy and government more flexible, in order to accommodate Presbyterians*, but was defeated by the Commons's insistence in the 1662 Act of Uniformity (14 Car. II, c. 4) that the church should remain essentially unchanged (see Clarendon Code*). He also at times granted toleration to all Nonconformists, notably in the Declaration of Indulgence* of 1672; again, faced with the Commons's resistance, he backed down.

The struggle over the Act of Uniformity showed that from the outset the Cavalier House of Commons was capable of standing firm against the king. Although it could still show itself effusively loyal, it became disillusioned with Charles's rule. The mismanagement of the Second Dutch War* (1665-1667) deeply angered MPs, and they became still more suspicious of the king and his government after the Declaration of Indulgence, the French alliance (see Treaty of Dover*), and the conversion to Catholicism* of the duke of York (the future James II*) revived fears of "popery and arbitrary government." The earl of Danby (Thomas Osborne*) tried to overcome these suspicions by an apparent switch to anti-French and pro-Anglican policies and to maximize support for the government through careful parliamentary management, but the suspicions remained and burst into the open with the Popish Plot* in 1678. When Danby fell from power after revelations of his secret dealings with France, Charles finally dissolved this, the most long-lasting of English parliaments.

The history of the Cavalier Parliament shows that an effective monarchy was restored because MPs felt that it was in their interests to do so and that the effectiveness of that monarchy depended on the king's being able to work with parliament.

Bibliography: Paul Seaward, *The Cavalier Parliament and the Reconstruction of the Old Regime 1661-7*, 1989; D. T. Witcombe, *Charles II and the Cavalier House of Commons, 1663-74*, 1966.

John Miller

Cavaliers. During the English Civil Wars* the supporters of Charles I* quickly came to be called Cavaliers by their opponents, much as they had, perhaps slightly earlier, begun referring to the supporters of parliament* as Roundheads*. As with the later terms for parties after the Restoration* (Whig* and Tory*) the intention was to deride those so described, but the usage became so widespread in all these cases that over time the names lost their sting and simply became the generally applied label.

The use of *cavalier* as a synonym for royalist* goes back to the beginning of the Civil Wars in 1642. The word *cavalier* earlier had passed into English from French as a corruption of *chevalier*, but was generally understood to be an unflattering label for the swaggering militarized gentry of the Continent, like the Spanish *caballero*. In its Romance language forms, the term originally referring to a horseman or mounted warrior came to be the equivalent of the English "knight" and was not necessarily unflattering. Its negative connotation in English usage was due to its foreign reference, particularly as Catholic foreigners were regarded with the greatest possible suspicion and hostility at the time. While the earliest application of the term specifically to the royalist party is uncertain, it seems likely to have been applied first to unemployed military officers discharged from Ireland*, who were loitering about London* in the winter of 1641-1642, loudly proclaiming their fidelity to the king and looking for employment, possibly hoping that a royal suppression of parliament would require their services. Their swagger earned them the name, and it was not long before all the members of their party were so labeled.

Bibliography: *Oxford English Dictionary*.

S. J. Stearns

Cecil, Robert, Earl of Salisbury (1563-1612). The dominant political figure in the first decade of James I's* reign (after the king himself), Cecil was the second son (by a second wife) of the famous Lord Burghley, longtime minister to Queen Elizabeth. He served his political apprenticeship by helping his father execute the office of secretary of state, becoming secretary in name as well as fact in 1596. Following

Burghley's death two years later, Cecil succeeded to much of his influence with the queen. He also succeeded his father as master of the Court of Wards, a powerful and lucrative office. His position was strengthened further in 1601 when his chief rival, the 2d earl of Essex, was executed following his disastrous rebellion. At the same time that position was somewhat precarious since the queen was aging and her likely successor, James VI of Scotland*, was thought to be prejudiced against him. However, the king came to see that Cecil was well placed to help him secure his claim to the English throne, and the two men reached an understanding before the queen's death.

Meanwhile Cecil had married Elizabeth Brooke, daughter of Lord Cobham, in 1589. She bore him a son and a daughter before she died in 1597. He never remarried.

James's accession was untroubled, and Cecil was well rewarded for the helpful part he had played, being confirmed in his offices and promoted to the peerage as Baron Cecil of Essendon in May 1603. He became earl of Salisbury in May 1605. He retained the position of trust he had established under Elizabeth and soon emerged as the king's chief English adviser. He was the obvious choice to succeed the earl of Dorset as lord treasurer when Dorset died in April 1608. He now held three great offices of state (in addition to a host of minor offices and titles), a perhaps unprecedented concentration of authority.

As lord treasurer, Salisbury found himself responsible for the king's mounting financial problems. In contrast to James's later lord treasurer, Lionel Cranfield*, whose preferred remedy was a program of reform and retrenchment, Salisbury's main efforts were directed toward increasing the king's revenues (see Taxation and Revenue*). Among other things, he attempted to improve the yield from the Crown lands*, although he also resorted to land sales, which meant a reduction in land revenues in the long run. His most profitable improvement was the impositions*, customs duties on top of the subsidies of tonnage and poundage granted by parliament*, which were worth about £70,000 per annum to the king. However, these were to prove highly controversial.

Despite all of Salisbury's efforts, the king's troubles persisted, and in 1610 an appeal was made to the parliament (of 1604-1610*). Instead of a traditional grant of one or more subsidies, however, Salisbury proposed that (in addition to subsidies) parliament give the king an annual revenue, something that was entirely unprecedented. The House of Commons insisted on obtaining something in return, notably the abolition of wardship, the king's right to control the estates and marriages of his tenants in chief when they were minors, which Salisbury administered (to his great personal benefit) as master of the Court of Wards. An agreement, known as the Great Contract*, was slowly negotiated in the first session of 1610. However, when parliament met again in October 1610, the Great Contract collapsed, and shortly afterward the parliament itself was dissolved, in large part because of continuing disputes over impositions, which the Commons emphatically protested.

The failure of the Great Contract was a terrible disappointment to Salisbury, who had striven mightily to manage the scheme through parliament from his seat in the House of Lords, although it does not seem to have led to his political downfall, as was once widely supposed. He kept his vast accumulation of offices and, by most accounts, the confidence of the king. Nonetheless, not long afterward his health, which had never been very good, became even worse. He sought a cure in Bath but died on 24 May 1612.

Although he seems to have retained the king's confidence until the end, Salisbury died a very unpopular figure, blamed for monopolizing power and oppressing the people with impositions and other exactions, among other things. He has also long been a controversial figure among historians. While some have argued that he profited excessively and in dubious ways from his position, helping to bring public ethical standards to new lows, others have seen him as more statesmanlike, citing in particular his willingness to surrender the mastership of the Court of Wards to promote the Great Contract.

Whether they were ill or fairly gotten, his gains from office were substantial. He used them to acquire a large landed estate centered in Hertfordshire, Dorset, and London*. He was also a great builder, erecting a palatial town house and the New Exchange (dubbed "Britain's Burse" by James) in London, Cranborne House in Dorset, and, the greatest of all his buildings, Hatfield House in Hertfordshire.

Bibliography: Eric N. Lindquist, "The Last Years of the First Earl of Salisbury, 1610-1612," *Albion* 18 (1986): 23-41; Menna Prestwich, *Cranfield: Politics and Profits under the Early Stuarts*, 1966; Lawrence Stone, *Family and Fortune: Studies in Aristocratic Finance in the Sixteenth and Seventeenth Centuries*, 1973.

Eric N. Lindquist

Charles I (1600-1649). Born in Dumfirmline on 19 November 1600, Charles was the second son of James VI, king of Scotland*, who became king of England as James I* in 1603. A sickly child, he was brought up by Sir Robert and Lady Elizabeth Carey. His early years were far from happy. His father disliked him, and his elder brother, Prince Henry*, teased him mercilessly. The claim of his mother, Princess Anne of Denmark*, that Charles was her favorite is credible only because her relations with her other children were particularly venomous.

Between the ages of ten and eleven Charles suffered three major losses: Prince Henry died suddenly in 1611, Charles left the security of the Carey household, and his sister Elizabeth married and departed England. As an adolescent he initially quarreled with his father's possibly homosexual favorite, George Villiers*, the 1st duke of Buckingham, but at the age of eighteen they formed a friendship that dominated his life for the next decade.

In 1623 the two went to Madrid to court the king of Spain's daughter. Their attempt to obtain a Spanish match* was a humiliating failure, forcing them to scuttle back to England, where to their surprise they were welcomed home as heroes. Following James I's death in March 1625, Charles let Buckingham rule England (as he would have permitted his elder brother had he lived to become Henry IX). The duke pursued an aggressive and expensive foreign policy. It failed disastrously, causing a constitutional crisis that climaxed with the Petition of Right* on 7 June

1628, in which the king reluctantly agreed not to tax without parliamentary approval (see Taxation and Revenue*).

But Charles neither kept his word nor bowed to parliamentary demands to dismiss Buckingham. The latter's assassination on 23 August 1628 and the consequent public jubilation were a turning point in Charles's life. After the Commons rioted on 2 March 1628, rather than obey his order to adjourn, he tried to rule without parliament* for the next eleven years, a period known as the Personal Rule*. The king retreated to the world of the royal court*, where he fell in love with his wife Henrietta Maria*, patronized poets and dramatists, and collected paintings.

Although Charles dabbled in affairs of state, he was not the architect of consistent, comprehensive policies. His inclinations ran toward absolutism*, but he was too lazy to become an effective autocrat. The most important case wherein he initiated policy ended in disaster. In 1637, erroneously interpreting the Presbyterian* Scots' refusal to accept an Anglican* (even papist) form of church worship as an excuse to establish a republic, Charles refused to concede, no matter the cost.

The cost eventually became a Civil War* that engulfed the whole of the British Isles. After his defeat in the two Bishops' Wars* and his failure to obtain revenue from the Short Parliament* in 1640, Charles had to call the Long Parliament*, which met on 3 November 1640. For the next two years king and parliament tried to work out a compromise, but the king negotiated in bad faith, convinced that any concessions extracted under duress from a divine right* monarch were invalid. The outbreak of the Irish Rebellion* in October 1641, with much exaggerated stories of atrocities against Protestant settlers, severely worsened relations with parliament. The king's botched attempt of 4 January 1642 to arrest the "five members"* leading the opposition in the House of Commons by marching into their chamber with a company of musketeers made war inevitable.

For seven months the two sides shadow-boxed, issuing pamphlets to explain their stances. For the king his cause was simple, even simplistic: by defying their divine right ruler and by misleading naive subjects into rebellion, the opposition were evil men who richly deserved punishment. In declaring war against the rebels on 22 August 1642, Charles found a simple solution to a complicated problem. As one of the flags his soldiers carried into the Battle of Edgehill* on 23 October proclaimed, the king was cutting the Gordian knot of treason.

But as Charles was to learn, civil war was far more complicated and bloodier. Lacking the ruthlessness to follow up Edgehill with the immediate capture of London*, he lost his only real chance of victory, and the First Civil War* dragged on for four more years. As a military leader the king lacked an overall strategy, being unable to coordinate the efforts of his forces within England, let alone Scotland and Ireland*. He failed to adopt a unified command and allowed his generals to squabble among themselves. While personally brave, he was a poor leader of men. His battlefield performances were mixed: brilliant at Lostwithiel, he was ineffective at the first Battle of Newbury, incisive at the second, mediocre at Cropredy, and faltering at Naseby*.

Naseby (14 June 1645) signaled the beginning of the end. Eleven months later Charles surrendered to the Scots Covenanters*, who tried to force him to become a

Presbyterian. "I never knew what it was to be so barbarously baited before," Charles wrote to his wife. In January 1647, the Scots handed him over to parliament, from whose safekeeping he was seized by Cornet George Joyce on June 3. In November Charles escaped from army* custody, fleeing to Carisbrook Castle in the Isle of Wight.

There he remained for two years, as the conditions of his confinement became stricter. He tried half-heartedly to escape a couple of times but failed. After secret negotiations with the king, the Scots invaded England in July 1648, but were routed by Oliver Cromwell* at Preston. The army put down royalist* risings in south Wales*, Kent, and Essex with equal brutality, now convinced that Charles Stuart was "a man of blood" who deserved to die for again taking up arms after he had surrendered. The Treaty of Newport*, which the king signed in November with the Rump Parliament*, confirmed their convictions. The army arrested Charles and brought him to be tried in London.

At his trial* in late January, Charles defended himself ably, without the stutter that had bedeviled him for his whole life and with an unwonted dignity. Although in court he made a legal argument, in private Charles believed he was a martyr for the Church of England (see Anglicanism*) and divine right monarchy. "A king and subject are clear different things," he declared from the scaffold in Whitehall moments before his head was chopped off on 30 January 1649.

The most important thing about Charles's life was the manner of his death. He died bravely, and yet more than anything else, it was character flaws that went back to his earliest years—stubbornness, aloofness, an inability to make friends or chose good advisers, inflexibility, and untrustworthiness—that brought him to the scaffold and set off a series of Civil Wars, of which he was both the best-known victim and the most significant cause.

Bibliography: Charles Carlton, *Charles I: The Personal Monarch*, 1983; John Reeve, *Charles I and the Road to Personal Rule*, 1989; Kevin Sharpe, *Charles I and the Personal Rule*, 1992.

Charles Carlton

Charles I, Trial, Execution, and Cult of. The first public trial and execution of a reigning monarch by his own subjects. Both proponents and opponents of the act acknowledged it to be unprecedented. That it was "not a thing done in a corner" was what most ennobled it in the eyes of supporters and most shocked those who opposed the proceedings. With the defeat of the royalist* forces, the parliamentary army* seized the king and purged the House of Commons of all members still willing to support a treaty with him (see Pride's Purge*). Petitions to the House from the army and from several counties urged that "justice" be done on the king and his adherents. Various compromises were mooted, such as a purely ceremonial monarchy or deposition of Charles I* in favor of his youngest son, Henry, duke of Gloucester, but none of these came to anything.

When the House of Lords refused to concur in the trial, the Commons proceeded on their own to erect a High Court of Justice, presided over by John Bradshaw after the lord chief justice and other legal luminaries refused. The prosecutor was John Cook, and the charge against the king was high treason, defined as "to levy war against the parliament* and the kingdom of England." In more religious terms Charles was also designated a "man of blood" and held to be guilty of all the blood shed in the Civil Wars*. The trial was held in Westminster Hall, the venue used for trying traitors and for the trials of the earl of Strafford (Thomas Wentworth*) and Archbishop Laud*.

Charles refused to recognize the jurisdiction of the court and to plead to the charge. He was therefore denied permission to speak at the trial, and the court proceeded to sentencing. On 27 January he was convicted, and on 30 January, in the presence of a large crowd, he was beheaded on the scaffold at Whitehall.

The public reaction was profound though muted. There were no public demonstrations either way, though people on both sides expressed enormous shock. Probably no other event in English history was more disturbing politically and emotionally. Charles had been both tried and executed as "king of England," and the Commons had proclaimed the sovereignty of the English people and ordered the making of a new great seal. They had already prohibited the proclamation of the king's successor. Shortly afterward the House of Lords and monarchy were abolished, and the Commons declared itself the supreme power in England. A public funeral according to the Book of Common Prayer was prohibited.

From the time of his death, royalist propagandists began to create the cult of the "royal martyr," as a result of which Charles achieved more popularity in his death than he ever commanded in life. Most notable was the *Eikon Basilike* (1649), ostensibly a collection of royal devotions but in fact probably written by John Gauden. The book proved enormously popular and rapidly went through numerous editions. Other royalist literature depicted Charles as a Christ-like figure and likewise held England collectively guilty of his blood. The notion of blood guilt thus played a conspicuous role on both sides, and the entire ordeal might be seen as the quasi-sacramental climax of a revolution in which questions of ritual and ceremony, both sacred and secular, were central throughout. In 1661 a parliamentary statute proclaimed January 30 a fast day, and sermons on this occasion were popular, though also often controversial, through the time of the French Revolution. The practice was discontinued in 1858.

At the Restoration* several of the fifty-nine regicides* who signed the death warrant, along with some others, were themselves tried and executed as traitors, though others received pardons.

Bibliography: C. V. Wedgwood, *The Trial of Charles I*, 1964.

Stephen Baskerville

Charles II (1630-1685). Charles was born on 29 May 1630, the eldest son of Charles I* and Henrietta Maria*. In royalist* eyes he became king of England on 30 January

1649, following parliament's* execution of his father in the aftermath of the Civil Wars*, but his actual reign began only after the Restoration* in 1660.

While his early childhood was relatively uneventful, the events of the 1640s shattered his family and put young Charles's life in jeopardy on more than one occasion. He assumed an early role in his father's military campaign to retain the throne and in 1645 took command of the West Country operations. By 1646 he was on his way to exile in France. In 1648 Charles began a series of attempts aimed first at returning his father to complete royal authority and later at placing himself on the throne abolished during the Interregnum*. Charles I's execution* was a great blow. In the 1650s it proved difficult to obtain foreign aid sufficient to recover the Crown, and royalist efforts therein came to nothing. Though he was recognized as king in Scotland*, that kingdom's resources were inadequate to allow Charles to penetrate the English Republic's defenses. In the end it was Oliver Cromwell's* death in 1658 and the factionalism which subsequently developed in the army* that made the Restoration possible.

Returning to England in triumph on 26 May 1660, Charles, who was naturally indolent and devoted to pleasure, wanted to revel in his new position. Nevertheless, he moved energetically to form an administration, rewarded those who had supported him in exile with political appointments, and pursued a moderate policy in dealing with the republican remnants of the Interregnum. The Cavalier Parliament* repealed most of the constitutional changes made since the early 1640s; however, while securing the new king's position, parliament was careful not to relinquish all the progress made during the Interregnum. Inevitably there were clashes over the issues that had provoked the Civil War. For example, Charles, who personally leaned towards Catholicism* without actually converting, was inclined to broad toleration, but the Anglican* majority favored prosecution of Dissenters*, and Charles was constrained to follow this policy. Nevertheless by the mid-1660s a relative stability had been achieved, allowing foreign affairs to take precedence.

Disputes over trade led to the Second Dutch War* (1665-1667), which ended in a humiliating defeat and led to the fall of the king's chief minister, the earl of Clarendon (Edward Hyde*). The vacuum was filled chiefly by the earl of Arlington (Henry Bennet*), who pursued a policy of pragmatic caution into the early 1670s. Legacies of this period include the secret Treaty of Dover* (1670), which bound Charles to convert to Catholicism in exchange for French aid. The Declaration of Indulgence*, issued in 1672, suspended penal laws against Protestant dissenters and Catholics* and showed that Charles was determined to follow his own course in religious matters.

Shortly afterward the Third Dutch War* (1672-1674) broke out, and Charles was short of money to prosecute it. However, Charles's marriage to Catherine of Braganza* had proved childless (despite his string of bastards), and by 1673 his brother and heir apparent, the duke of York (see James II*), was known publicly to be a Catholic. Parliament was not inclined to support the war policies of a king with a Catholic heir. Further, the widowed James had recently married the young Catholic princess Mary of Modena*, and parliament feared that a Catholic Stuart dynasty would be created. Thus in 1673 it passed the Test Act*, which made Anglican communion a requirement of all officeholders and forced James to resign from the navy*. In fury Charles sacked his minister, the earl of Shaftesbury (Anthony Ashley Cooper*), who opposed James's succession. But to placate parliament, Charles was advised to end the war and disavow James and his marriage. Though he found both suggestions repugnant, it became expedient to conclude peace with the Dutch after parliament reconvened early in 1674.

The years between 1674 and 1678 saw a return to relative stability under the auspices of the earl of Danby (Thomas Osborne*), but English policy remained bound up with the fortunes of France and its continuing war with the Dutch and their allies. Charles tried to mediate between Louis XIV of France and William of Orange*, but the latter would not abandon his allies in order to make a separate peace with France. Charles held out to William the hope of a marital alliance with the Stuarts in the person of Mary*, James's Protestant elder daughter, who was next after her father in the order of succession. William still refused to make peace with the French but did conclude an alliance with Charles, resulting in his marriage to Mary in late 1677.

The concentration on foreign affairs up to 1678 had overshadowed the domestic issues that had caused such problems in 1673-1674, the chief of which was a strident anti-Catholicism. The discovery of the Popish Plot of 1678*, a largely unsubstantiated intrigue supposedly aimed at murdering the king and replacing him with the Catholic James, fueled anti-Catholic feeling in parliament; the outcome was a more restrictive Test Act. In the aftermath of the plot, Charles decided to exile James from England for his own safety; he did likewise with his illegitimate son, the duke of Monmouth, whom some saw as the Protestant alternative to James.

During the years between 1679 and 1681, parliament made three attempts to exclude James from the succession on account of his religion, the so-called Exclusion Crisis.* Party alliances began to develop during this period, when the country party or Whigs* became known as supporters of exclusion, and the court party or Tories* as supporters of the monarchy, including the Catholic heir to the throne (see Court versus Country*). Charles allowed James to return home sporadically during this period, but parliamentary pressure precluded his permanent repatriation until May 1682. Charles had previously prorogued the Oxford Parliament* of 1681 after one week and vowed not to call another one. Upon James's return, the Tories moved into political ascendancy; their vigorous pursuit of the Whigs culminated in the Rye House Plot* of 1683, when the Whig leadership was effectively decimated.

After 1683 James assumed a much stronger role in governmental affairs, with Charles relying on him as one of his chief advisers in the administration of the kingdom; indeed, Charles came to depend more and more on James's circle for posts in his administration and ideas about policy. It was this reliance that smoothed James's accession to the throne at Charles's death on 6 February 1685. Charles converted to Catholicism on his deathbed, publicly revealing at last his own personal preference.

Historical assessments of Charles have varied, but most agree that as king he pursued no grand design. His political shortcomings and his great need to be liked made him appear indecisive at times and precluded the development of a coherent approach to disparate situations. Some historians see him as weak at the beginning of his reign and strong at the end; others reverse that assessment. It is indicative of the man himself that he remains the subject of such debate.

Bibliography: Ronald Hutton, *Charles II, King of England, Scotland, and Ireland,* 1989; John Miller, *Charles II,* 1991.

                                                                                    Connie S. Evans

Church of England. See Anglicanism.

Church of Scotland. See Kirk.

Civil War, Causes and Historiography. Widely divergent interpretations of the English Civil War have been struggling for supremacy ever since the 1640s, when royalists* and parliamentarians* began to seek for ways of blaming each other for what had happened. The process continued in the decades after the Restoration* and into the eighteenth century, with the publication of a series of accounts and memoirs of the Civil Wars. By the early decades of the eighteenth century, a relatively stable pattern of interpretation had evolved. The Tory* view, fueled by the publication in 1702-1704 of Edward Hyde*, earl of Clarendon's *History of the Rebellion,* argued that the Civil War was primarily the product of the actions, mistakes, and wickedness of a few key people. It was an avoidable conflict, though what prevented its actual avoidance was the deliberate refusal of Charles I's* enemies to accept their duty of allegiance to the Crown. The Civil War was an act of illegal rebellion, motivated by greed and ambition. For many Tories, it was also a divine punishment of human sin. There were variations on this royalist-Tory version of events—Thomas Hobbes* in *Behemoth* (1679) stressing, for example, the role of mistaken beliefs about religion and politics in shaking men's proper allegiance to their sovereign—but the general features were common to such writers as Clarendon, Hobbes, and Sir William Dugdale.

The eighteenth-century Whig* interpretation was very different. Much of it was similar to the views of the parliamentarians themselves, and there is much truth in the remark that the Whig interpretation was invented by the Grand Remonstrance* of November 1641. It tended to stress the legitimacy of the Long Parliament's* actions in the 1640s, often arguing that Charles I had contravened the fundamental principles of the English constitution or the terms of some original contract. He thus became a tyrant, and this justified resistance to him. Unlike the Tory account, this one tended to portray the king rather than his opponents as an innovator. It also tended to be more favorable to the idea of long-term causation. The Civil War became the culmination of a process of constitutional struggle and conflict that went back perhaps to the beginning of the reign of James I*. In this struggle parliament*, especially the House of Commons, was attempting to resist the Stuart drive toward arbitrary and absolute monarchy.

The Whig interpretation of the Civil War became the dominant one, but in 1754 the historian and philosopher David Hume attempted to bring together the chief elements of both the Tory and the Whig accounts. He argued that there was no straightforward constitutional precedent that could be appealed to for a solution of the problems faced in the mid-seventeenth century, and this made it difficult to say that Charles's actions were clearly wrong. If this might be thought to ally him with the Tories, Hume was Whiggish in his belief that the Civil War was progressive and brought improvement in its wake.

Hume's effort at balance failed. Early nineteenth-century Whigs such as Henry Hallam and Thomas Babington Macaulay (wrongly) saw Hume as a simple Tory and themselves accepted a simple Whig account of the English Civil War. The French Revolution also helped to stimulate accounts of the Civil War that began to uncover some of its more radical dimensions, and this increased hostility to the "Tory" Hume. William Godwin's *History of the Commonwealth of England* (1824-1828) directed attention to England's only experience of republican government. Godwin, along with Catherine Macauley and Thomas Carlyle in his edition of the speeches and letters of Oliver Cromwell*, were among early users of the Thomason Tracts, a collection of materials acquired by the British Museum in 1762 which revealed the radical ideas that had flourished in Civil War England and contributed to increased awareness of the depth of the challenge to established institutions found there.

The development of academic historiography on the German model had an immediate impact on interpretations of the Civil War. Leopold von Ranke himself produced a history of seventeenth-century England that placed it against a European background, breaking down some of the Whig insistence on the uniqueness of English history. More important, Samuel Rawson Gardiner set out in the 1860s to write a scholarly account of the Civil War and its background that would free the subject from Whig myth making. Not unlike many later historians who have seen themselves as reacting against the Whig interpretation, it has been Gardiner's fate to become known as the archetypal Whig historian himself. His view of the Civil War, or the "Puritan Revolution" in his own phrase, was strongly political and constitutional in character, but he recaptured some of the subtlety of Hume. Gardiner believed with the Whigs that the Civil War was instrumental in the achievement of parliamentary government in England, but he hesitated to say that justice was entirely on parliament's side and attempted to portray fairly the noble intentions of men on both sides of the seventeenth-century conflicts. Like Hume, he was aware that legal precedent did not favor just one side, though he was inclined at moments of rhetorical excess to forget some of his own scholarly insights. Gardiner also boosted the habit of seeing Puritans as leaders of the fight against the Stuart monarchy, while doing scant justice to their religious beliefs and motivations. This way of viewing Puritanism*, in terms other than religious ones, began to be challenged in the twentieth century, particularly by American historians (Perry Miller, William Haller), but only very recently has genuine religious motivation been seen to play a large role in causing the Civil War. In the end, Gardiner's work possesses a hybrid character: it maintains the older Whig obsession with determining where moral blame for the outbreak of Civil War should be laid, but grafts onto it some of the features of twentieth-century academic historiography (rigorous and extensive employment of primary sources, especially unpublished ones; attention to factual accuracy and detail).

The twentieth-century historiography of the Civil War has been characterized by continuous reaction against the "Whiggism" of Gardiner, though many of his critics have themselves ended up bearing the Whig label. One of the most important criticisms of the Gardiner approach has come from Marxist historians like Christopher Hill. Gardiner, it has been argued, took too much at face value the idea that the Civil War was in the interest of the whole nation and ignored the social conflict that underlay it. In his early work (*The English Revolution*, 1940) Hill advanced the view that the English Civil War was a classic bourgeois revolution in which a rising middle class overthrew the hegemony of a reactionary feudal class. In subsequent work Hill has revised this view but still maintains that the Civil War was a bourgeois revolution in that it fostered the long-term development of capitalism in Britain. He has also stressed (especially in *The World Turned Upside Down*, 1972) the ferment of radical aspirations in the 1640s and their defeat by more conservative forces. This latter work completes the rediscovery of the radical dimension of the Civil War that began in the late eighteenth century and accelerated in the early twentieth century under the impact of Marxist and socialist thinking. It has done much to convince many that the Civil War was a genuine revolution.

Hill's work has owed much to the work of R. H. Tawney, who in 1941 identified sections of the gentry as part of the rising middle class and thus initiated a lengthy and inconclusive debate on the relationship between the Civil War and preceding changes in social structure*. The attempt to link the political history of the Civil War to trends in social and economic history has been one of the chief themes in twentieth-century discussion of the subject. In 1972 Lawrence Stone, one of the participants in the debate on the gentry sparked off by Tawney (see Gentry Controversy*), published a synthesis of work done on the social history of the period before the 1640s in which he portrayed the Civil War (drawing on sociological models of revolution) as the result of "multiple dysfunction," which produced a deep crisis in early Stuart society. Existing institutions— Crown, the aristocracy, church—lost their legitimacy and were challenged by newer social groups. Stone and others have been important in viewing the Civil War against the background of a non-Marxist social history, but like Hill and others they see the events of the 1640s as having a social and not just a political character.

Although Stone's work, like that of Tawney and the Marxists, was an attempt to break down the Whig concentration on political-constitutional history, the "revisionist" historians of the 1970s and 1980s have taken his work as the apotheosis of the Whig interpretation. Revisionists, a rather loose collection of historians that includes John Morrill, Conrad Russell, Kevin Sharpe, and Nicholas Tyacke, have in common mainly a rejection of previous perspectives, especially of the view that the Civil War was the product of long-term social change or of long-term constitutional conflict. They have not agreed, however, about what the Civil War was and have seen it variously as "the revolt of the provinces"; a localist reaction against the centralizing tendencies of early Stuart government; "the war of three kingdoms," a crisis in the government of a mosaic state in which the difficulties of simultaneously governing England, Scotland*, and Ireland* would have defeated a better king than Charles I; a "baronial revolt" of the medieval sort, in which the king's leading noblemen banded together to save the realm from misgovernment; and, like Gardiner, a "Puritan revolution" or war of religion, though with the proviso that Puritanism is now to be seen as a motivating force in its own right and not as a cloak for political, economic, or social interests. In particular, stress has come to be laid, following the lead of Tyacke, on the religious outrage that followed the rise of Arminianism* under Charles I and Archbishop Laud*. But more than anything else, historians have become aware of the immense complexity of the Civil War: it had a different character for different participants.

Arguably, revisionism marks one of the sharpest breaks in the historiography of the Civil War. Whereas Whig, Marxist, and sociological accounts tended to stress the progressive and subversive character of the Civil War, making it a genuine revolution, the various revisionist accounts take as their themes popular conservatism rather than radicalism, consensus rather than conflict, the search for godly and just authority rather than anti-authoritarianism, the desire to avoid innovation and change rather than to bring it about. The result is the portrayal of a series of events far from revolutionary: hesitant, muted in ideological justification, the work of men reluctant to challenge authority but forced into it by the pressure of events. Revisionist views come closer to Tory views of the Civil War than to Whig ones, though this similarity should not be exaggerated. They lack, of course, the strong moralizing streak of Tory history.

These revisionist interpretations have not gone unchallenged. J. H. Hexter has resolutely defended some aspects of the Whig account, while a younger generation of historians, including Ann Hughes, Richard Cust, and Johann Sommerville, have in various ways attempted to move beyond revisionism. In particular they have attempted something close to a synthesis of revisionist political history with the social-conflict perspectives of Hill, Stone, and others. It is impossible to say where this conflict of interpretation will lead, but it remains undeniable that, for better or worse, the 1980s and 1990s have seen greater diversity in the interpretation of the Civil War than any other time since the mid-eighteenth century.

Bibliography: J. C. D. Clark, *Revolution and Rebellion: State and Society in England in the Seventeenth and Eighteenth Centuries,* 1986; R. C. Richardson, *The Debate on the English Revolution Revisited,* 1988; Roland G. Usher, *A Critical Study of the Historical Method of Samuel Rawson Gardiner, with an Excursus on the Historical Conception of the Puritan Revolution from Clarendon to Gardiner,* 1915.

Glenn Burgess

Civil War, First (1642-1646). Neither royalists* nor parliamentarians* wanted civil war, and both hoped to get it over quickly, so their initial strategy was simple and direct. In July and August 1642 the Long Parliament* raised 20,000 men from London* and the Home Counties, ostensibly for defense. Robert Devereux*, 3d earl of Essex, was appointed commanding general. Charles I* raised his standard at

Nottingham on 22 August, declaring parliament* in rebellion, then struck west to Shrewsbury, where he could draw on ample supplies of money and men from Wales*, Lancashire, and Cheshire, as well as Shropshire and Worcestershire. On 9 September Essex marched out of London to confront him but got no farther than Worcester; Charles left Shrewsbury on 12 October with an army* roughly equal to Essex's, heading for London. The two armies clashed at Edgehill* in Warwickshire on 23 October. After a scrappy but ferocious battle, both sides retained their ground, but next morning Essex decamped north, sacrificing most of his artillery and supplies and leaving the road to London wide open. Charles missed this golden chance, which never recurred; he went first to Oxford to establish his headquarters, and by the time he reached Turnham Green on the western outskirts of London on 13 December, the city militia was mobilized against him and Essex had returned with parliament's main army. Charles withdrew to Oxford, only about sixty miles from London, and never made another attempt on the capital.

The next year, 1643, both sides were intent on conquering territory, though this was never openly stated, and both began to raise regional armies. For the royalists Sir Ralph Hopton recruited an Army of the West from Devon and Cornwall; William Cavendish, earl of Newcastle (soon promoted to marquess), raised another in the border counties of the far north; and later in the year Sir John Byron began to pull together another from Cheshire and Lancashire. Parliament began to group counties into regional associations, each with its own army, though the only one of any lasting importance was the Eastern Association—Norfolk, Suffolk, Essex, Cambridgeshire, Hertfordshire, and later Lincolnshire—which by the fall began to raise a crack army of 20,000 men under the earl of Manchester, with Oliver Cromwell* as his lieutenant-general of horse.

The royalists were quick to seize the advantage. After a dogged campaign up and down Somerset, Hopton conclusively destroyed parliament's Western Association army under Sir William Waller at Roundway Down on 13 July, while Newcastle marched south to defeat the Yorkshire rebels under Lord Fairfax and his son, Sir Thomas Fairfax*, at Adwalton Moor near Bradford on 30 June. Hopton's army, reinforced by contingents from Oxford under the king's German nephew, Prince Rupert, went on to storm Bristol on 26 July, giving the king possession of a major port and the second city in England. Meanwhile, the earl of Essex's advance down the Thames valley toward Oxford got bogged down halfway at Reading, and Charles decided to launch another attack, this time on Gloucester, which would give him control of the west Midlands. Essex was forced to go in pursuit. He raised the siege of Gloucester on 6 September but then became the pursued as he strove to regain his base at Reading; Charles brought him to bay on 20 September at Newbury in Berkshire. No clear victor emerged from a hard-fought, destructive battle, but the next day the king retired to Oxford, leaving Essex free to make for home.

Already both sides were finding it difficult to replace battle casualties and deserters; the enthusiastic volunteers of 1642 were no longer to be found, especially for the infantry, and both introduced conscription almost simultaneously in the fall of 1643, although to little avail. But since the spring they had also been seeking outside help, parliament from Scotland* and the king from Ireland*. On 1 September parliament signed the Solemn League and Covenant* with the Scots, and on 19 January the veteran Alexander Leslie, earl of Leven, invaded northern England with nearly 20,000 men. Meanwhile, on 15 September 1643 Charles had signed a "cessation" (or armistice) with the Irish rebels and had begun to withdraw 17,000 troops from the Army of Ireland, sent over the previous year to suppress the Irish Rebellion*. However, though the unified Scots army played a significant role in the campaign of 1644 (at least initially), the Irish army had to be brought over piecemeal and merged with existing royalist forces, and the main contingent attached to Sir John Byron's army in Cheshire was destroyed or dispersed at Nantwich on 29 January 1644 by parliament's Yorkshire army under Sir Thomas Fairfax. Another scratch army assembled for Hopton with an Irish component (his Western army had returned to Devon) was routed by Waller at Cheriton near Winchester on 29 March.

Cheriton lost the king the whole area south of the Thames valley, Nantwich lost him Cheshire and Lancashire, and he now stood to lose Yorkshire and the northeast. Newcastle's army was squeezed between the Scots advancing south, the new Eastern Association army coming up through Lincolnshire, and Fairfax's army in south Yorkshire; June found him penned up in York. Rupert, sent from Oxford to relieve him, recruited fresh troops in the west Midlands, rallied the remains of Byron's army, and took over Newcastle's cavalry, but he was handsomely defeated at Marston Moor* on 2 July, and York surrendered. This was the first encounter in which Cromwell distinguished himself at the national level. His army virtually destroyed, Newcastle went into exile, and Rupert returned south.

At this stage, parliament's strategy began to unravel. The Scots retired north to besiege Newcastle, and thereafter they were to be distracted by a long-running royalist revolt in Scotland under James Graham, marquess of Montrose. Manchester led his Eastern Association army south slowly and reluctantly. In May the king emerged from Oxford with his main army, and Essex and Waller dogged his tracks through the Midlands, but on 6 June Essex turned southwest on a wild goose chase into Devon and Cornwall, leaving Waller to contain the king. In fact Waller was thrashed at Cropredy Bridge north of Oxford on 29 June, and his army fell apart. Parliament tried to recall Essex, but he refused, and the king set out after him, picking up the remnants of the old Western army as he went. At the end of August, bereft of local support, Essex found himself penned up at Lostwithiel, on the Fowey peninsula in Cornwall. His cavalry broke out of the ring, and the general himself escaped in a fishing boat, but he left his infantry to surrender on 1 September.

Worse was to come. The news of Lostwithiel brought Manchester hurrying south to cover London, and the king, returning victorious from the west, decided to challenge him at Donnington Castle just outside Newbury. After a confused struggle against superior numbers (the second Battle of Newbury) on 27 October, he withdrew to Oxford in good order and unpursued. But on 9 November he brazenly returned to retrieve his guns from Donnington Castle under the eyes of the parliamentarians and retired without a shot fired.

This fiasco led to a violent clash between Manchester and Cromwell in the council of war, continued at Westminster over the winter. Not only were the strategy and tactics of the noble generals in question but also their commitment to outright victory.

In the end the Self-Denying Ordinance* of 3 April 1645 obliged members of both houses of parliament to resign their commissions, sweeping away Essex, Manchester, Waller, and (for the time being) Cromwell. Meanwhile on 15 February parliament had already decided to incorporate the remains of Manchester's and Essex's armies in a new strike force of 22,000 men, the New Model Army*, under the command of Sir Thomas Fairfax, who had an almost unblemished war record and was not a member of parliament. After some fumbling, parliament also decided in the spring that this army's function was to seek out and destroy the king's forces, irrespective of territory gained or lost. After further hesitation it also reinstated Cromwell as lieutenant-general of horse and second-in-command.

Fairfax duly finished the task, though he was helped by Charles's folly in dividing his field army and sending nearly half of it into the west under George, Lord Goring. Charles sustained an irrecoverable defeat at Naseby* in Northamptonshire on 14 June 1645 and Goring at Lamport in Somerset on 12 July. Fairfax doubled back to retake Bristol on 10 September and then proceeded methodically to reduce Devon and Cornwall over the winter. In August Charles scraped together a few thousand men in south Wales and made for Yorkshire; repelled there, he swung over to Cheshire, only to be defeated by local rebel units at Rowton Heath outside Chester on 24 September, the last pitched battle of the war. He took refuge in Oxford for the winter unmolested, but in the spring the very last royalist army, a mere 3,000 men under Sir Jacob Astley, was forced to surrender at Stow-in-the-Wold in Gloucestershire on 21 March 1646. On 27 April, with the New Model Army marching relentlessly back from the west, the king slipped out of Oxford incognito with a couple of servants and, striking north, gave himself up to the Scots, who had now returned to besiege Newark, Nottinghamshire. Oxford opened its gates to Fairfax on 24 June. A few scattered royalist garrisons still held out (the last, at Harlech Castle in north Wales, did not surrender until 16 March 1647), but the war was effectively over.

Bibliography: Ian Gentles, *The New Model Army*, 1992; J. P. Kenyon, *The Civil Wars of England*, 1988; Peter Young and Richard Holmes, *The English Civil War 1642-51*, 1974.

John P. Kenyon

Civil War, Second (1647-1648). In 1646 royalist* forces had been defeated in every part of England, and Charles I* had surrendered himself into the hands of the Scots. Yet less than two years later, armed conflict broke out again. How can the renewal of the Civil War in 1648 be explained? One reason was economic hardship. The harvest of 1647 had been bad, but there was no letup in the financial burdens parliament* placed on the population*. The maintenance of a standing army* and the persistence of the practice of free quarter by parliamentary soldiers, as well as the tyranny of county committees (see County Associations*) over their local communities caused many to yearn for monarchical rule. The Second Civil War was more than a localist revolt against authoritarian centralism, however. It also possessed an ideological dimension, since the king's restoration to his former power and dignity and the reestablishment of the Church of England (see Anglicanism*) were seen as prerequisites if the imagined harmony and stability of the past were ever to be recovered. Charles's stubbornness in negotiation, moreover, produced increasing exasperation on the parliamentary side, not least among the officers of the New Model Army*.

The Second Civil War may be said to have begun on 11 November 1647, the day that Charles fled from his parliamentary captors at Hampton Court. The king had ample reason for thinking that a second appeal to the sword might have a different outcome. Not only had many grown weary of parliamentary dictatorship, the Thirty Years War* was almost at an end in Europe, and soon there would be plenty of soldiers looking for work. Maybe those who had promised to send aid would at last make good on their word. More important was the change in attitude of the Scots. Active combatants on the parliamentary side in the First Civil War*, many Scots were profoundly disenchanted by parliament's failure to institute a true Presbyterian* church, the de facto tolerance toward radical religious sects, and the increasingly revolutionary character of parliament's military leadership.

After his flight from Hampton Court, Charles blundered in allowing himself to be taken to the Isle of Wight and the custody of Colonel Robert Hammond. He would have been much safer on the Continent. But this did not prevent him from signing a secret Engagement* with the Scots commissioners at the end of December 1647. By its terms the Scots were to supply military aid in return for Charles's confirming Presbyterianism in both countries for three years. The Scots commissioners quit England at the end of January 1648, having completed, they thought, arrangements for a coordinated rising in Kent and the Eastern Association when their army should cross the border.

Knowledge of Charles's conspiracy, however, had hardened Oliver Cromwell*, Henry Ireton*, and other parliamentarians* against him. In December the Four Bills were passed, the most important of which called for parliamentary control of the militia for twenty years. Charles's refusal to countenance this demand led to the severance of talks by the Vote of No Addresses*. This breakdown of negotiations had the unexpected effect of restoring unity in the New Model Army.

Portents of the coming conflagration were the Canterbury riot against the Long Parliament's* attempt to enforce the abolition of Christmas, the celebrations in London* of Charles's coronation in March, and the Easter riot by apprentices against the suppression of their traditional Sunday recreations on 2 April. The ideological content of resurgent royalism was frequently expressed in cultural terms.

Alarmed at the signs of violent hostility on every side, the officers of the New Model Army met at Windsor for an intensely emotional three-day prayer meeting at the end of April. Amid the shedding of copious tears, they once again steeled themselves to risk their lives in the godly cause, resolving to bring "Charles Stuart, that man of blood" to account for his crimes.

That the royalists were crushed was due in part to the implacable resolution of these officers and the men they commanded and in part to the disarray of their adversaries. The royalist rebels were geographically divided, politically incoherent, and strategically uncoordinated. English royalists feared their Irish Catholic* allies and were cool toward their newfound Scottish Presbyterian friends. The Scots themselves were also divided. The new alliance forged by the commissioners in London fractured the Covenanter* leadership. While the duke of Hamilton strove to mobilize an army for the invasion of England, the Kirk* denounced the alliance as a mockery of the Solemn League and Covenant* and did everything in their power to block recruitment. The consequence was that Hamilton's army was ill organized and late in taking the field.

Poor timing was one of the fatal flaws in the royalist war effort. Impatient for action, the Welsh royalists rose in April, but were soon trounced by Thomas Horton and Cromwell. In the north, royalist insurgents appearing from nowhere seized Carlisle, Pontefract, and Berwick with what seemed like laughable ease. Yet the royalist risings in Norfolk and Suffolk around the same time were too early to help the serious insurrection being concerted by the men of Kent. Unable to wait for the Scottish invasion, the royalist rebels rallied at Rochester at the end of May and profited from the revolt in the navy* by seizing county magazines and coastal castles. But then they dispersed their 11,000-strong army among several towns. Sir Thomas Fairfax*, with only 4,000 seasoned troops, was able to overpower them in a critical engagement at Maidstone at the beginning of June. Most of the Kentish royalists then went home, but 3,000 of them trudged north with the earl of Norwich hoping to use Essex as a springboard for an attack on London. Fairfax was able to bottle up most of the rebels in Colchester in a bitter siege that lasted until the end of the summer. Meanwhile, Major-General Philip Skippon kept a firm grip on the capital, also strangling the flow of royalist recruits and supplies to Colchester. Nonetheless, the royalists in Essex could boast the negative achievement of pinning down nearly half of parliament's mobile forces for three months. Thanks to their perseverance the northern royalists and Scots invaders were handed a matchless opportunity.

That they made so little of it is attributable to their divided counsel and military incompetence. Hamilton's ramshackle army, fewer than 10,000 strong, had crossed the border on 8 July. Cromwell, having smashed the revolt in Wales*, moved north to meet the invader and the northern English royalists under Sir Marmaduke Langdale. The decisive battle of the Second Civil War took place near Preston on 17 August. There Cromwell and his troops, almost 14,000 strong, pounced on Langdale's compact force of 3,600, wiping it out after a strenuous battle that lasted six hours. Hamilton's army, stationed nearby, played no part in this engagement. His cavalry were strung out in a twenty-mile line stretching north toward Lancaster, while his infantry were trudging across the bridge over the River Ribble at the very moment that Langdale's forces were undergoing their agony a scant three miles away.

Having brilliantly divided his enemy, Cromwell had no trouble mopping up the larger but profoundly demoralized Scottish force as it fled southward during the following seven days. Charles I, who during all the fighting had been kept a close prisoner on the Isle of Wight, would soon be brought to trial by the now twice-victorious army for the blood that had been shed on his behalf (see Charles I, Trial, Execution, and Cult of*).

Bibliography: Ian Gentles, *The New Model Army in England, Ireland and Scotland, 1645-1653*, 1992; Brian Lyndon, "Essex and the King's Cause in 1648," *Historical Journal* 29 (1986): 17-39.

Ian Gentles

Civil War, Third (1649-1651). The execution of Charles I* on 30 January 1649 precipitated renewed hostilities known as the Third Civil War of 1649-1651. The prince of Wales, proclaimed as Charles II* on 5 February 1650 by the Scottish Covenanters*, appointed James Graham, marquis of Montrose, as lieutenant-governor and captain-general of all royal forces in Scotland*. Montrose immediately set about reconstructing a royalist* force in Scotland, built upon a nucleus of Danish and German mercenaries, native Scots from the Orkney Islands, and royalist refugees. Landing first at Kirkwell to rally the Orcadians, Montrose crossed Pentland Firth and landed his vagabond force near John o' Groats on 12 April 1650.

David Leslie (Baron Newark in 1661), the parliamentarian* commander, ordered a concentration of forces to oppose Montrose. No Highland clan troops joined the royalists as Montrose expected; nonetheless, he resolved to confront the enemy at Corbisdale. Montrose expected that a victory would attract desperately needed Highland support. Lulled into attacking a superior force on open ground without effective cavalry support, Montrose was beaten, captured, and executed in May at Edinburgh.

With the defeat of Montrose, Charles resolved to regain Scotland by accepting the Covenant*. He landed at Spey Mouth in Moray on 23 June 1650, immediately drawing support from both royalists and recent Covenanter foes. Fearing the actions of the newly formed Scottish force supporting Charles, parliament* resolved to destroy the royalist uprising.

The New Model Army*, reduced through disbandment of units and the detachment of troops to Ireland*, could muster only twelve regiments of horse (cavalry), half a regiment of dragoons (mounted infantry), and eleven regiments of foot (infantry). New regiments were raised, and on 12 June 1650, Lord Thomas Fairfax* assumed command as general of the field, with Oliver Cromwell* as lieutenant-general. Parliament resolved on a thrust into Scotland, a policy to which Fairfax objected, arguing instead for awaiting a probable Scottish royalist/Covenanter invasion. Parliament overruled Fairfax, who resigned his command. Cromwell took charge of the expedition, with John Lambert as second in command and major-general of the horse, Charles Fleetwood as lieutenant-general, and George Monck* (later duke of Albemarle) as major-general of foot.

On 22 July the army*, consisting of 5,000 horse and 10,000 foot, crossed the Scottish border, opposed by a Scottish force nominally under the earl of Leven but effectively commanded by Leslie, now in the king's service. After several sharp engagements around Edinburgh, Cromwell, unable to reduce Leslie, retired to Dunbar for reinforcement and resupply by sea. Goaded by overconfident ministers of the Kirk*, who accompanied the Scottish force and urged an abandonment of the strong defensive position in the hills south of Dunbar, Leslie deployed his army into the open country, an area ideal for cavalry action. Observing this mistake, Lambert proposed a cavalry assault on the exposed Scottish right wing, which occurred on 3 September. Lambert's assault required only an hour to rout the surprised Scots. The Battle of Dunbar devastated the Scottish royalist/Covenanter army, the remnants of which—perhaps 4,000 troops—retreated west to Stirling. Cromwell occupied Edinburgh on 4 September, and in his dispatch to parliament called Dunbar "one of the most signal mercies God hath done for England and this people."

On 1 January 1651 Charles was crowned king of Scotland at Scone, the traditional coronation site. He appointed the duke of Hamilton as lieutenant-general of the newly raised royal army with Leslie as major-general. Scant action other than raids and harassment operations occurred throughout the autumn of 1650 and into the late spring of 1651.

On 28 June 1651 Leslie deployed out of Stirling Castle into the hills south of the city, hoping to lure Cromwell into battle. Cromwell reacted by sending Lambert into Fife to disrupt Leslie's food supplies, an action that resulted in Lambert's victory at Inverkeithing over Sir John Brown. Stung by Brown's defeat, Leslie withdrew and marched south to invade England, an action that set in motion the Worcester campaign.

Charles II counted on significant royalist support in the northern English counties and marched into Lancashire. To raise troops, particularly among English Presbyterian* supporters, he sent Major General Edward Massey ahead of the army with instructions to announce the arrival of the king. The committee of ministers accompanying the army supplied Massey with a "declaration" (of unrestrained zeal for the Covenant and the king's acceptance of it) and with orders not to enlist any man who would not swear the Covenant. Charles, on hearing of the declaration, ordered Massey to desist, but it was too late. The declaration had been published and few volunteers appeared.

Cromwell detached Lambert with five regiments of horse to pursue the royalist force. On 13 August Major General Thomas Harrison joined Lambert with four regiments of horse near Preston. Fleetwood remained in the northern counties to muster loyal militia and to suppress royalist recruiting. Cromwell followed Lambert with seven regiments of slower-moving foot, while other forces departed to deal with royalists mustering under the earl of Derby. These Lancashire royalists were beaten and dispersed at Wigan on 24 August. This dispersion of parliamentary forces might have been critical had not the invading Scottish army been depleted by desertion and demoralization before reaching Worcester on 23 August.

On 28 August Lambert secured a bridgehead over the Severn River, which allowed Cromwell to attack in three bodies on 3 September. The Scots formed up north of Worcester, but disintegrated under the three-pronged assault. Charles, viewing the debacle from the tower of Worcester cathedral, mustered his reserve horse and attacked the parliamentarian troops gathering outside the city. After some initial success, the weight of the opposing numbers told, and Charles had to flee. The action at Worcester on 3 September 1651 ended the Third Civil War.

Bibliography: Peter Young and Richard Holmes, *The English Civil War: A Military History of the Three Civil Wars*, 1974.

Stanley D. M. Carpenter

Claim of Right (Scotland, 1689). After William of Orange's* invasion and James VII and II's* flight to France in late 1688, the English Convention Parliament* met on 22 January and by 13 February had declared the English throne vacant, offered the crown to William and Mary*, and settled other constitutional questions in the Declaration of Rights*, later enacted as the Bill of Rights* (1 Gul. III & Mar., sess. 2, c. 2) on 16 December.

Scotland's* response to the Glorious Revolution* was somewhat slower. There a convention of estates met on 14 March, in which neither James's supporters nor William's initially held a clear advantage. The marquis of Hamilton, chosen by William to represent him in the convention, won the presidency of the convention by a narrow margin over the marquis of Atholl, who had associated himself with James. The real victory for William, though, came on 16 March, when the body read letters from both claimants to the throne. Whereas William's was conciliatory, confined itself to general statements, and promised to protect Protestantism, James's epistle was threatening in tone and was interpreted by some as requiring "natural allegiance" not only to the king but also to the pope. Thereafter most of James's supporters defected, except for a small group headed by Viscount Dundee, who quickly withdrew and by 30 March was declared to be in rebellion. On 27 March the convention appointed a committee of the estates, composed of supporters of William, to serve as a temporary executive and direct the convention's business.

The committee was unable to heed William's suggestion that it simply follow the English precedent, for the Scots objected not only to James but also to the form of the monarchy. Though some Scots were receptive to William's proposal for union* of the two kingdoms, the English were not. Therefore the convention was left to its own devices. On 4 April it passed a resolution (with only five nay votes) stating that James had forfeited the crown, and on 11 April it approved the Claim of Right. This document listed James's faults, among them his Catholicism*, his failure to take a coronation oath, and his attempt to overthrow Scottish Protestantism and convert a limited, contractual monarchy into despotism. It also enunciated the principles that a Catholic could not occupy the throne or any other public office, that royal prerogative* was not superior to the law, that parliamentary authorization was necessary for taxation, that there should be frequent parliaments, that members of parliament should have freedom of speech, and that torture should not be used as it had been. It also condemned prelacy.

On the same day the convention proclaimed William and Mary to be king and queen, on 13 April, it passed the Articles of Grievances, which dealt with relations between crown and parliament, and on 11 May William and Mary accepted the crown from a Scottish delegation in London*. As in England, the Scottish convention was converted into a regular parliament. Unfortunately, the Claim of Right and the Articles of Grievances did not solve all of Scotland's problems. Many in the convention expected William to treat the two documents as a contract between Crown and parliament, but the king did not entirely share that view, and he and his Scottish kingdom were plagued by a variety of constitutional and political disputes, many of which persisted into Anne's* reign.

Bibliography: William Ferguson, *Scotland 1689 to the Present*, 1968.

William B. Robison

Clarendon Code. In preparation for the Restoration*, Charles II* issued the Declaration of Breda*, in which he promised "a liberty to tender consciences" and an indulgence for differing opinions in religion, subject to passage of such an act in parliament*. But the Convention* of 1660 had no success in passing measures for toleration or for comprehension providing for more flexibility on doctrinal and liturgical points so as to widen the Church of England (see Anglicanism*) nor did the Savoy Conference* (1660) achieve compromise between leaders of Laudian (see William Laud*) and Puritan* positions. And in 1661 many members of the Cavalier Parliament* did not share Charles's enthusiasm for a tolerant religious settlement. They ignored the Declaration of Breda and focused directly on the issue of conformity. The five repressive acts regarding religion passed between 1661 and 1665 have become known collectively as the Clarendon Code. Though the legislation was named for the earl of Clarendon (Edward Hyde*) and supported by many of his strongly Anglican backers in the House of Commons, Lord Chancellor Clarendon repeatedly criticized and attempted to moderate the "sharp laws."

The Corporation Act (13 Car. II, st. 2, c. 1) of 1661 required town officers to renounce the Presbyterian Solemn League and Covenant* and to receive the sacrament according to Anglican rites. Local gentry served as commissioners to vet and, in some cases, thoroughly purge the corporations. Though some historians have not included it as part of the code, the Quaker Act of 1662 (13-14 Car. II, c. 1) was certainly part of the religious repression. It deemed guilty any persons who met together for worship outside the parish church in groups of five or more and who refused to plead in court (Quakers* refused to swear oaths). Thus, when the Uniformity Act received royal assent on 19 May 1662, the metes and bounds of the Restoration religious settlement were already in place.

The Uniformity Act (13-14 Car. II, c. 4), the central plank of the code, defined the ordination and activities of all future Church of England ministers. All ministers, professors, and schoolmasters had to swear oaths repudiating the Solemn League and the taking of arms against the king. Most important, it required the use of the restored Book of Common Prayer for all church services, and each minister had to swear consent to "all things" in the prayer book by 24 August 1662 ("black Bartholomew") or be deprived of his living. Local magistrates could commit to prison any deprived ministers who continued to preach. In effect the act created nonconformity by testing for outward conformity of practice. Nearly 1,000 clergymen, about one-tenth of the total in England and Wales*, were removed by the act. Altogether about 1,760 clergy were forced out of their livings between 1660 and 1663. In some dioceses, London* especially, the bishop and local magistrates oversaw a severe purge; in others they allowed a degree of latitude in the wearing of the surplice, bowing at the name of Jesus, and other matters prescribed by the prayer book.

Though Charles II and Clarendon still hoped for tolerant religious legislation (partially for theological reasons, partially to defuse Civil War* factionalism), a short-lived rising against the government, the Yorkshire Plot of October 1663, encouraged parliament to pass the Conventicle Act in 1664 (16 Car. II, c. 4). This act ordered huge fines (and transportation for the third offense) for those attending Nonconformist meetings where five or more persons not of the same household met. The act permitted justices to break into houses upon information of a conventicle there. Finally, in 1665, when even Clarendon denounced Nonconformist "scorpions," parliament passed the so-called Five Mile Act (17 Car. II, c. 2). It prohibited Nonconformist preachers from coming within five miles of their former parishes or of an incorporated town unless they took an oath stating that it was unlawful to take arms against the king. Enforcement of the Clarendon Code depended largely on local gentry serving as justices of the peace. Prosecution under the Conventicle Act was intensely localized and sporadic; under the Five Mile Act virtually no record of prosecution survives for the first year. In any case the initial repressive mood of the Episcopalian gentry in the House of Commons and the bishops in the House of Lords had run its course.

The Conventicle Act lapsed in 1667 but was replaced by the more finely tuned Conventicle Act of 1670 (22 Car. II, c. 1). Nonconformist ministers found restrictions eased, temporarily by the Declarations of Indulgence* in 1672 and 1687, more lastingly by the Toleration Act (1 Gul. III & Mar. II, c. 18) of 1689. But the Clarendon Code or what one historian has labeled the "Cavalier Commons Code" and another has called the creation of Gilbert Sheldon*, bishop of London* and his supporters was not fully repealed until the nineteenth century.

Bibliography: Ronald Hutton, *The Restoration: A Political and Religious History of England and Wales, 1658-1667*, 1985; John Spurr, *The Restoration Church of England, 1646-1689*, 1991.

Newton E. Key

Clarendon, Earl of. See Hyde, Edward.

Clifford, Thomas, Baron Clifford of Chudleigh (1630-73). Clifford emerged from an obscure background into political life in 1660. In the Convention* he obtained a reputation for hard work and financial knowledge and was made a gentleman of the privy chamber in December. Returned for the Cavalier Parliament*, he was an extremely active member, named to over 300 committees before entering the House of Lords. His remarkable energy, his dislike for the earl of Clarendon (Edward Hyde*), and a measure of self-promotion brought him the attention of Sir Henry Bennet*, future earl of Arlington, who secured a small royal grant for Clifford and engaged him as a parliamentary manager. By 1664 Clifford, now knighted, was an acknowledged court dependent, a designation earned by his support for government measures in parliament*. Hostile to the Dutch, he directed parliament's drive for war and then in 1665 served in the naval campaign in the Second Dutch War* (1665-1667) and as an envoy to Sweden and Denmark. His reputation thus enhanced, he resumed parliamentary work in 1666, when he also became comptroller of the household and a member of the privy council*.

Although Clifford played no major role in Clarendon's fall in 1667, Arlington's consequent advancement helped make Clifford a lord of the treasury that year and a commissioner for trade in 1668, when he also advanced from comptroller to treasurer of the household. Despite this close identification with Arlington, Clifford's final rise came at the former's expense. The two were the only ministers to whom Charles II* originally revealed his conversion to Catholicism*, and they reacted differently, although each was at least a crypto-Catholic. Unlike Arlington, Clifford sought closer ties with France to secure Charles's independence from parliament, and he enthusiastically endorsed alliance with France by the Treaty of Dover* (1670).

Where Arlington hesitated, Clifford rushed ahead, urging renewed war against the Dutch and searching for ways to finance the conflict. His nonparliamentary expedient, the Stop of the Exchequer*, declared a moratorium on payment of Crown debts in January 1672. Although unpopular with bankers and disowned by others on the treasury board, the Stop helped to finance the navy* for the Third Dutch War* (1672-1674). This work and Clifford's instrumental part in issuing the second Declaration of Indulgence* brought ennoblement as Baron Clifford in April 1672. Appointment as lord treasurer followed in November, finally wrecking Clifford's friendship with Arlington, who had coveted the office. The appointment also marked the apex of Clifford's career. When parliament reconvened in 1673, hostility to indulgence and suspicions of France led to passage of the Test Act*, which Clifford vehemently but futilely opposed in the Lords. The act provided a sacramental test for officials, thus barring Catholics from office and forcing his resignation that June. Within four months of his career's demise, Clifford himself was dead. When he had formally converted to Roman Catholicism is unknown, as in the 1660s he had practiced a High Church* Anglicanism*, although advocating toleration. Nonetheless, by 1671 his Catholicism was widely assumed.

In parliament Clifford was active in debate and generous with secret service payments to members, and was therefore powerful. His influence with the king, however, was never unalloyed, and the two were not close. Clifford was in ways a mediocrity who lacked vision, and his knowledge of financial affairs was shallower than appeared. Yet he was loyal, honest, committed to the royal prerogative*, and extremely industrious. These characteristics, perhaps along with his Catholicism, recommended him to the king and account for his impressive, if brief, success.

Bibliography: C. H. Hartmann, *Clifford of the Cabal*, 1937; B. D. Henning, ed., *The House of Commons 1660-1690*, 1983; Ronald Hutton, *Charles II*, 1989.

James Rosenheim

Cloth Trade. At the beginning of the seventeenth century, the cloth trade was the biggest employer in England after agriculture*. In foreign trade* England was dangerously dependent upon wool cloth, which constituted about three-quarters of all English exports. This was predominantly in the form of the "Old Draperies," fine, heavy cloths made from carded short staple wool and often expensive. A monopoly*, the Merchant Adventurers (see Trading Companies) controlled all trade from London* to northern Europe, which amounted to about half. Most of the cloth shipped was unfinished, and much went to Holland, where it was dressed and dyed, with the Dutch reaping much of the profit. This system was sharply criticized in the 1620s and after by Thomas Mun and others, who insisted on the importance of a favorable balance of trade (see Mercantilism*). At home wool was still spun all over England, by now with a spinning wheel rather than a distaff, but the industry was concentrating in three areas: Norfolk and Essex in the east, the West Riding of Yorkshire in the north, and an area stretching from Gloucestershire to Devon in the west.

After a boom in the first decade of the century, the industry crashed in 1614, beginning over half a century of difficult times. One of the most immediate results was James I's* withdrawal of the Merchant Adventurers' monopoly and the launching of the Cockayne project*, which purportedly was intended to add the finishing of cloth to the English industry but actually was an attempt by rivals of the Merchant Adventurers to usurp their trade in unfinished cloths. However, the Dutch retaliated by prohibiting the import of finished cloths, the trade dropped by a third, and the new King's Merchant Adventurers failed so miserably that by 1617 the project was discontinued and the old Merchant Adventurers restored. There was no real increase in the export of finished cloths to Europe until late in the century, at least partly because England lagged in technology.

The industry continued to suffer from tough Dutch competition, as well as the perils of the Thirty Years War* and currency fluctuation on the Continent. There was also a shift in the wool supply and in fashion that favored the "New Draperies," cloths of the worsted type that were made from coarser, longer-staple wool and were lighter, more brightly colored, and usually cheaper. A new wave of depression in the early 1620s led to a decline in the trade and threats of disorder from unemployed workers. One result was that the government ended monopolies on all but the export of undyed cloth. Another was the emergence of Mun and other like-minded thinkers, often referred to as "mercantilists." After a brief recovery in 1624, there was renewed depression, accompanied by plague (see Epidemics and Plague*) in 1625, and another dip in 1629 probably due to the Spanish War of 1625-1630* and the French War of 1627-1629* which affected even the New Draperies.

During the 1630s the industry remained stagnant at home and faced tough competition abroad. The Old Draperies were particularly hard hit, while the New gradually gained ground. These included such cloths as the bays and says made in East Anglia by the descendants of sixteenth-century Dutch immigrants and the mixed serges and "Spanish" cloths made in the west. Adversity persisted as the result of the continuing war on the Continent and the Civil War* in England in the 1640s, as well as increasing competition for shrinking markets. But the English inflicted real harm on the Dutch by forbidding the export of wool from England, and by the 1650s the

English were gaining in the market for inexpensive wool thanks to lower wages and taxes and abundant raw wool, and there was even some progress with finer cloths.

After the Restoration* the proportion of cloth to total exports dropped from about three-quarters to less than half, but the cloth industry remained the largest in England. East Anglia and Devon gained in terms of the concentration of the industry, with increased demand for worsteds and mixed cloths. Devonshire serges acquired a bigger share of the market at home and abroad and by 1700 boosted Exeter to the third largest exporter after London and Bristol. Norwich also gained, specializing in light worsteds, which were often made from wool mixed with cotton or silk; the West Riding profited from shifting to the New Draperies; Lancashire employed the Dutch loom in the production of linen (especially in Manchester), fustian, and woolens; and the stocking frame was adopted in the Midlands, especially Nottingham and Leicester. Technologically the English remained behind the Dutch, though they learned a great deal from them. Also important in the late seventeenth century was the influence of Huguenots, who contributed to the development of the silk industry in and around London and linen manufacturing in Scotland* (Edinburgh) and Ireland* (near Belfast).

Bibliography: Peter J. Bowden, *The Wool Trade in Tudor and Stuart England*, 1971; Charles Wilson, *England's Apprenticeship, 1603-1763*, 2d ed., 1984.

William B. Robison

Clubmen. Rural insurrectionaries determined to protect their homes, goods, and families from the depredations of plundering soldiers, the Clubmen were chiefly a phenomenon of the chaotic final year of the First Civil War*, first appearing on the scene in large numbers at a time when law and order had all but broken down across large areas of western England. Unable to gain redress through the normal channels, the Clubmen resorted to physical force instead, banding themselves together in large groups or associations (usually based on distinct rural territories) and bidding defiance to the soldiers of either side. The insurgents derived their name from the wooden clubs seven feet long and liberally studded with glass and iron spikes that many of them used as weapons. Their philosophy was well summed up by the rhyming couplet allegedly inscribed on one of their makeshift banners: "If you offer to plunder or steal our cattle / Be assured we will bid you battle."

During 1645-1646 Club risings occurred in at least sixteen counties throughout the south and west of England. Many thousands of countrymen took part in these disturbances. In June 1645, the Clubmen of Somerset alone were estimated to be around 5,000 strong. Yet despite their impressive numbers, the Clubmen were poorly armed and almost wholly untrained. As a result, they were seldom able to defeat large bodies of regular soldiers in battle. When they did try to engage their enemies on equal terms, as at North Molton in August 1645 or at Hambledon Hill during the same month, the results were usually disastrous for the countrymen. Nevertheless, it would be a mistake to dismiss the Club risings as ineffectual or unimportant. By tying down large numbers of troops and disrupting the collection of men, money, and supplies, the Clubmen did a great deal to dislocate the already faltering war effort of

Charles I*, in whose territories most of the risings occurred. The Club risings undoubtedly hastened the war's end then, and in this sense at least the disturbances helped to secure a return to the peaceful and settled conditions for which the countrymen so desperately longed.

The political attitudes of the Clubmen have been the topic of a good deal of debate among historians. On one point there is general agreement: the Clubmen's program was essentially a conservative one; they acted in defense of the accustomed ways and the status quo. That this was so can be seen from their frequent appeals for a return to prewar conditions, their nostalgia for the days of "Good Queen Bess," and their concern that the established laws should be upheld. About the Clubmen's attitude toward the issues that lay at the heart of the Civil War itself, however, there is rather more disagreement. One school of thought holds that the Clubmen were genuine neutrals, equally hostile to both the warring sides. But other historians regard this view as too simplistic and point to the fact that different Club groups acted in very different ways, some entering into temporary alliances with the royalists*, others with the parliamentarians*.

It is possible, of course, that these alliances were purely tactical, yet an increasing body of evidence suggests that they were not. Instead, the differing behavior of the various Club groups would appear to reflect long-standing political divisions at the popular level. In areas of the country that had consistently supported the parliament* during 1642-1644—north Devon and north Somerset, for example—it is notable that the Club groups of 1645-1646 were overwhelmingly anti-royalist. In areas that had previously favored the king, however—like the Dorset downlands—local Clubmen were often prepared to cooperate with the royalists. It is tempting to conclude that while Clubmen everywhere were desperate for peace, different groups had very different ideas as to how that peace should be brought about, some favoring a more broadly "royalist," some a more broadly "parliamentarian" solution to the conflict.

Bibliography: Ronald Hutton, *The Royalist War Effort, 1642-46*, 1982; J. S. Morrill, *The Revolt of the Provinces*, 1976; David Underdown, "The Chalk and the Cheese: Contrasts Among the English Clubmen," *Past and Present* 85 (1979): 25-48.

Mark Stoyle

Cockayne Project (1613-1617). The decade preceding the Cockayne project was one of continued prosperity for the English textile industry and the Merchant Adventurers, sustained by a boom in drapery exports that peaked in 1614 (see Cloth Trade*; Trade, Foreign*; Trading Companies*). As most fabric exported to Germany and the Low Countries prior to 1614 was unprocessed ("white") cloth, many schemes to increase English wealth and employment by marketing manufactured goods were proposed. Alderman Cockayne's project for the dyeing and tailoring of cloth exports to Germany and the Low Countries was one of the most significant.

By 1613 Alderman Cockayne gained the support of James I* for his scheme. Cockayne's "projectors" convinced James that England possessed adequate men, materials, and technology to restructure the trade without damaging England's monopoly of wool manufacturing. Their project entailed great risk by requiring the replacement of the Merchant Adventurers, which had record-setting sales in 1614, with a new company capable of purchasing most of the available white cloth and coordinating its manufacturing and marketing abroad. Claiming a subscription of £1 million, they predicted that they would market 50,000 finished cloths. James, hoping to raise an additional £40,000 of revenue, prodded a hesitant privy council* to approve the scheme.

In July 1614 the Merchant Adventurers were prohibited from exporting white cloth after 2 November, and licensed merchants were given until 20 September to underwrite specific quantities of fully processed cloth for export over the next three years. In December the Merchant Adventurers' charter was suspended.

Once empowered the new King's Merchant Adventurers expended little effort to produce or market finished goods in German-speaking Europe. Government pressure forced the Adventurers to manufacture cloth, but they marketed only 6,000 pieces by autumn 1616. The project produced a greater change in the personnel of the trade than in the products exported.

A chief goal of Cockayne and the major projectors, many of whom were involved in the Baltic and Levant trade, was to secure control of the profitable white goods trade with Germany and the Low Countries. They also gained the privilege to market finished goods in eastern Europe and Turkey in 1616.

Crucial to the success of Cockayne's project was the involvement of a substantial number of the old Adventurers. While a variety of inducements attracted some old investors, most of the wealthier merchants declined. Their failure to cooperate left the project inadequately funded and vulnerable when subscribers failed to meet their promises.

From the outset the company was unable to purchase all available cloth at the 1615 spring and summer markets, causing a decline in exports and a drop in cloth prices. While they struggled to get the needed cash and credit to make the white goods trade profitable, the government demanded an increase in the export of manufactured cloth, which resulted in a promise to increase exports by 6,000 units in each of the next three years. In return the Adventurers received extended powers and promises of government aid in fighting Dutch restrictions. With James's support the project survived mounting criticism as most exports continued to decline.

Throughout 1616 the Adventurers' inability to profit from white cloth sales or expand the markets for manufactured cloth deepened, and complaints increased. By the fall the decline affected most aspects of the cloth trade and the stock of unsold textiles further strained resources.

By early 1617 the project failed, and the old Merchant Adventurers were restored. The project demonstrated that the old international division of labor in the cloth trade was a valid reflection of economic realities, while the English belief in their monopoly of wool manufacturing was misplaced. The western counties suffered severe depression and extensive unemployment that was part of a decline in traditional drapery manufacture, from which the textile trade never recovered.

Bibliography: Astrid Friis, *Alderman Cockayne's Project and the Cloth Trade*, 1927; B. E. Supple, *Commercial Crisis and Change in England, 1600-1642*, 1959.

Sheldon Hanft

Coffee Houses. An innovation in seventeenth-century England. Coffee had been unknown in the sixteenth century, and only scattered instances of its consumption are recorded for the first few decades of the Stuart era, the great anatomist William Harvey being one early coffee drinker. The first English coffee house, the Angel, was founded in Oxford in 1650. Two years later it was followed by the first London* coffee house, the Greek's Head. These early establishments were managed by people from the Near and Middle East, the area with the longest coffee drinking tradition—the Angel by a Lebanese Jew and the Greek's Head by the Greek servant of an English Turkey merchant. Over the following decades English people entered into the coffee house trade, and hundreds of coffee houses spread over urban England. Some became centers of political discussion—James Harrington's* famous political club, the Rota, met at the Turk's Head coffee house. Others catered to business; bankers and goldsmiths sometimes carried on business at coffee houses; and the insurance underwriting syndicate Lloyd's of London began as a coffee house. For literature* Will's was the gathering place of the poet John Dryden* and his coterie, and for science* the Grecian was frequented by the Fellows of the Royal Society*.

Coffee houses, often converted taverns, were relatively egalitarian in regard to class. Patronage extended from nobility and gentry down to urban artisans, and persons of lower rank were not expected to give up their seats to those of higher. This egalitarianism did not extend to gender, however; patronage was entirely male. Coffee houses usually charged a penny for admission—hence the term "penny university"—and served tea and chocolate and sometimes ale and wine, as well as coffee. A great deal of tobacco was also smoked at coffee houses, and observers sometimes describe the walls as being black with smoke.

The egalitarianism of coffee houses and the ease with which news and gossip was circulated in them made them suspicious to the Restoration* government. Their novelty and the stimulating properties of coffee made coffee houses much more threatening to public order in the eyes of the government than taverns. Coffee houses were identified as places where seditionaries gathered, particularly during times of political tension, such as the Popish Plot* (1678) and the Exclusion Crisis* (1678-1681). In 1666, during the Second Dutch War* (1665-1667), the government considered suppressing coffee houses, and in 1675 Charles II, after legal consultation, went so far as to issue a Proclamation for the Suppression of Coffee Houses. Coffee houses were so deeply entrenched in English urban society by that time, though, that the proclamation was wholly ineffective and was withdrawn eleven days after it was issued. Coffee houses were permitted to stay open provided their proprietors took the oaths of allegiance* and supremacy (see Clarendon Code*) and posted a £500 bond. This last clause was never enforced.

Besides the government the other great enemies of coffee houses were the tavern keepers, who saw coffee as an economic threat. In pamphlets, coffee was accused of being a foreign, Eastern, and Moslem usurper of the place rightly belonging to English ale and even of causing male impotence. Coffee's defenders fought back by praising its alleged healthful and invigorating qualities and the sociable atmosphere of the coffee house.

In a period with few sanctioned outlets for public opinion, the relatively free circulation of pamphlets, newspapers, and conversation in coffee houses made them important spaces for the creation of an informed, and sometimes misinformed, public.

Bibliography: A. Ellis, *The Penny Universities*, 1956; U. Heise, *Coffee and Coffee Houses*, 1987.

William E. Burns

Coinage and Monetary Policy. At the outset of James I's* reign, the 22-carat gold coins of the realm included the 30 shilling rose royal, 20s. unite (which replaced the gold sovereign), 10s. angel, 10s. double-crown, 5s. Britain crown, 4s. thistle crown, and 2s.6d. half-crown. The silver coins were minted in denominations of 60s., 30s., 12s., 6s., 2s., 1s., and 1/2s. Copper coins included the twopence and penny. English coins of the same denomination were worth twelve times the Scottish coins. James I authorized the minting of gold coins in 1603, 1604, 1605, and 1619 (a total of £3.5 million worth); silver coinage occurred in 1603 and 1604; and copper coinage was limited to 1613. Because the coins were hammered instead of being milled at the edges, the illegal practice of clipping coins caused the issues to lose value over time.

The traditional ratio of silver to gold at twelve ounces to one ounce was undermined in the early seventeenth century by the influx of precious metals from other countries, as well as by the drain of English coins to the Continent. At the beginning of James I's reign, silver comprised more than half of the total coinage of the mint, but silver coinage declined considerably in later years (1611-1630). Although part of the reason was a decline in the mint ratio, another factor was the change in the balance of payments. The end of the Spanish War in 1604 (see London, Treaty of*) helped to achieve a favorable balance of payments for the next few years, but economic and trade problems later eroded English exports, especially cloths (see Cloth Trade*; Trade, Foreign*), which had a negative impact on the balance of payments. Circumstances changed again by the 1630s, when there was a decline in the issue of gold coins and a corresponding increase in the amount of silver coins issued. Much of the reason was an improving trade balance.

The English ambassador to Spain in 1630, Sir Francis Cottington, negotiated a lucrative arrangement for English monetary interests. The Spanish had been financing a lengthy military operation against the Dutch, which previously transferred the money, mostly silver, through Genoa, Italy. Cottington persuaded Spain to divert those shipments to the English mint in English ships, which provided England with a handsome profit while guaranteeing greater security for the Spanish shipments. Perhaps £10 million worth of Spanish silver was minted in England between 1630 and 1643. Yet knowledgeable English goldsmiths sifted out the new silver coins and sold them abroad for profit. The Crown prosecuted and imprisoned several goldsmiths in the 1630s for illegal exports of coin. When Charles I* temporarily stopped the coinage of the Tower mint in 1640, he startled the London* merchants, who feared that the king's desperate gambit for revenues might jeopardize the security of their accounts at the mint. During the Civil Wars* of the 1640s, the Crown was forced to use alternative mints since parliament* controlled London. At varying times during the war, coins were issued from provincial mints at Aberystwyth, Bristol, Chester, Colchester, Combe Martin, Coventry, Exeter, Lundy Island, Newark, Oxford, Pontefract, Scarborough, Shrewsbury, Truro, Weymouth, Worcester, and York.

Although a machine to produce coins with milled edges was demonstrated in the Tower as early as the 1550s, the traditional coinage interests blocked the replacement of the hammered method of coinage. By the 1640s the French government had adopted the new coinage machine and even banned hammered coins. After a suspension of coinage from 1646 to 1649, a committee of parliament gave a favorable review to the new technology in 1649. However, it was not until 1656 that the first official English coins were minted with the machine. Finally, in 1663 Charles II* authorized the machine-stamped, milled-edged coins to replace the hammered coins. Although clipping of the new coins was eliminated, the practice continued for the hammered coins that remained in circulation.

By the Restoration* many merchants and goldsmiths urged that the mint charges, typically 45s. per pound of coin, be reduced or eliminated. An act of 1666 allowed individuals to bring bullion to the mint for coinage without charge. The measure also prevented cessation of the minting of coins for any reason. The price of gold appreciated during the 1650s so that in 1661 the value of gold coins was raised an average of 1s.6d.

The development of credit in England was dramatic in the second half of the seventeenth century. Although bills of exchange had been used for several hundred years to accommodate private debts, promissory notes did not have the protection of common law until 1710. Prior to the Civil War era, public debts were issued in the form of wooden tallies (notched wooden sticks split into two parts, half held by the Exchequer* and half by the creditor), which could be redeemed only at times designated by the Crown. In 1667, at the instigation of Sir George Downing, parliament authorized the issue of paper "Exchequer Orders" to creditors, but after the Third Dutch War* (1672-1674) broke out, they were terminated by the Stop of the Exchequer* in 1672, which damaged the government's credit rating. The tallies reappeared as credit instruments after 1672. The improvement of trade and reduction of debt in the late 1670s and 1680s allowed the government to recoup its credit rating. Although tallies and Exchequer orders carried interest, they were not payable on demand and were limited to very large amounts.

Concurrent with the expansion of credit was the emergence of banking. Initially controlled by scriveners, brokers, and goldsmiths, private banking provided opportunities for the government as well as creditors. The notes issued by these agencies were soon exchanged in the financial markets. Goldsmiths utilized checks, defined legally as bills of exchange, for the first time during the Civil War.

The years 1694-1696 were crucial for coinage, credit, and banking in England. The silver coinage was in considerable disarray since Charles II's milled coins mingled with the older hammered coins, which remained subject to clipping. Further, the fact that the value of silver was greater than the silver coins in circulation led to the disappearance of milled coins, which were melted down and sold. The government ordered all silver coins demonetized in 1696 and gold coins revalued so that all hammered coins were removed permanently from circulation. Five new mints were established in addition to the Tower mint in order to speed the recoinage process.

The fundamental reason for creating the Bank of England was the debt issuing from the Nine Years War (1689-1698) against France. The cost of the war, including foreign subsidies, was over £49 million, whereas revenues in the period, including major tax increases, totaled only £32.7 million. The recoinage of 1696 significantly reduced the amount of coinage in circulation, exacerbating the financial situation. Innovative financial measures such as the "Million loan" of 1693 and the "Million lottery" of 1694 were operated by the Million Bank until 1696. Yet these measures were only temporary solutions.

In 1692 parliament interviewed banking authority William Paterson regarding the establishment of a permanent national debt. The parliamentary committee and Paterson could not agree on the question of bank notes becoming legal tender, so the matter was delayed. When the Bank of England was chartered by parliament in 1694 and authorized to lend the government £1.2 million at eight percent interest, the legislation was intentionally vague about the bank's privileges to issue notes as legal tender as advocated by Paterson. As a joint stock company and a monopoly (see Monopolies*), the bank bought up approximately £5 million of outstanding tallies (i.e., debts), some at seven and others at eight percent. The bank was not very successful in underwriting long-term loans, but short-term loans flourished. The inflation of credit caused by the Bank of England was the most notable in the history of the nation. Responding to the continuing funding crisis caused by the war, the bank agreed to issue interest-bearing, transferable £5 and £10 Exchequer notes in 1696, which were eagerly accepted by the financial markets.

An act in 1697 reinforced the bank's monopoly by preventing parliament from creating any other national bank. The act resulted from several challenges to establish other banks, including the idea of provincial banks with a central headquarters in London. The specialized Orphans' Bank, established in 1694 by Paterson, began to issue notes in 1695, but opposition by the Bank of England caused its banking functions to cease by 1697. The Bank of Scotland was chartered by the Scottish Parliament in 1695 to aid business rather than finance government debt. The Scottish Bank remained conservative and lacked influence upon the currency during its history. The Bank of England's charter was renewed in 1710 until 1732. By the end of the Stuart era, it was clear that the bank would be a permanent English institution.

Bibliography: Albert Feavearyear and E. Victor Morgan, *The Pound Sterling: A History of English Money*, 2d ed., 1963; John Keith Horsefield, *British Monetary Experiments, 1650-1710*, 1960.

Daniel W. Hollis III

Coke, Sir Edward (1552-1634). Born on 1 February 1552, Coke rose to prominence under Elizabeth and became the preeminent lawyer of the early Stuart period. To parliament* men he was an oracle of the law whose wisdom inspired confidence amid the changing personnel and uncertain tenure of the House of Commons. To succeeding generations accustomed to reliance on his writings and judicial decisions, he was a reliable authority. To litigants he was an attorney capable of turning a doubtful case into a dramatic triumph. To the Crown, however, he was a troublemaker whose cooperation as a client of the royal court* was preferable to the threat afforded by his precarious application of ancient legal precedents to contemporary policy.

Coke sat in six parliaments between 1589 and 1628 and also served as attorney general from 1594 to 1606, as chief justice of the Common Pleas from 1606 to 1613 and of the King's Bench from 1613 to 1616. Coke's rise to prominence suffered a setback in 1616 when James I* removed him from the bench, banishing him to his county house to rid his legal writings of "errors" prejudicial to the royal prerogative*. Upon returning to make amends, however, Coke found his ambition unequal to his vanity, insisting that he could discover only five errors, a conclusion that did not improve his reputation with the king. Consequently, except for service on the privy council until 1622 and as a parliamentary client of the 1st duke of Buckingham (George Villiers*) and Prince Charles in the parliament of 1624*, Coke never regained sufficient credit at court to realize the high political attainments that his early career seemed to presage.

In the parliament of 1592-1593 Coke had served as Speaker of the Commons, but after the parliament of 1621* he was imprisoned for misconduct. Always Hispanophobic, Coke noted in 1624 that the prospect of war with Spain made him feel seven years younger. By 1625, however, he had begun to entertain doubts about the new king's military policy. After the parliament of 1625* ended, Charles I*, probably in a deliberate allusion to Coke's desertion of his former patron, pricked (i.e., appointed) him sheriff* of Buckinghamshire for 1626. Not only did the office of sheriff relegate its holder to his county during his year of office, it was also illegal for a sheriff to return himself to the Commons as a knight of the shire for his county. When Coke was selected knight of the shire for Norfolk, however, he returned to the Commons, insisting that sheriffs had served as members of parliament in the past and could still do so legally. In 1628 Coke was one of the MPs who drew up the Petition of Right*, which apparently confirmed his belief that law, as embodied in an ancient constitution, was the source of all authority. The acceptance of the petition mitigated Coke's anxieties for the fate of the common law*, but subsequent years were to show that many at the court of Charles I did not share his attitudes.

Coke's reports and commentaries, particularly his *Institutes*, inspired a reverential attitude toward the common law. But perhaps it was as a practitioner and the embodiment of that law that Coke scored his greatest triumph with posterity. In his wake, a profession whose membership was once reviled as "pettifoggers" and "vipers of the commonwealth" at last acquired an invincible respectability. Coke died on 3 September 1634.

Bibliography: C. Gray, "Reason, Authority and Imagination: The Jurisprudence of Sir Edward Coke," in Perez Zagorin, ed., *Culture and Politics from Puritanism to the Enlightenment*, 1980; Stephen D. White, *Sir Edward Coke and the Grievances of the Commonwealth*, 1979.

Myron C. Noonkester

Colonization. In the practice of seventeenth-century England, this process meant establishing a colony for purposes of trade* or for the settlement of a specific population*, often incorporating agricultural plantation* or exploitation of other natural resources. Colonies had strategic political as well as economic importance and were usually equipped to perform limited military operations.

In spite of the Tudors' interest in and patronage of discovery and exploration, James I* (1603-1625) was heir to only embryonic colonial holdings. Contact had been lost with the first English settlement in Virginia. The East India Company* was having some successes but was threatened by the Portuguese in India and confronted by the Dutch in the Spice Islands. While interest in colonial expansion was clearly evident, the Crown's limited financial means made individual investment the primary source of capital. James's first colonial interest lay in the orderly plantation of Ireland*. Virginia remained neglected until 1606, and even then pressure from the Spanish to withdraw was given serious consideration. By 1609, however, Robert Cecil*, earl of Salisbury, convinced James that national interests and prestige outweighed foreign policy objections. The Virginia Company was then given greater royal support (see Trade, Foreign*; Trading Companies*).

Charters granted to investors gave them considerable sovereignty in the internal affairs of their colonies. For this reason control exercised by the government was concerned primarily with economic considerations. Both during this period and for some time after, distance and travel time made centralized control difficult or nearly impossible.

By 1621 the productive output of colonies in the Far East, the Indies, and North America had become sufficiently significant that the privy council* ordered that all goods would be landed in England first. Despite the king's objections to its use, tobacco rapidly became the prime cash crop of the Americas, but even this success could not save the financially troubled Virginia Company. Its bankruptcy in 1623 made that territory a Crown colony. In the Far East Thomas Best's naval victory over the Portuguese near Surat at Swally Roads allowed the expansion of British interests in the region and enabled Thomas Aldworth to establish the trading center at Surat. A second battle at Swally Roads in 1615 by a fleet commanded by Nicholas Downton again resulted in victory and granted a measure of security to Surat. Despite the Amboina Massacre* of English traders by the Dutch off the New Guinea coast in 1623, trade in the Far East continued to grow.

By the time of James's death in 1625, the successes of expansion were mixed. Attempts to penetrate South America by Sir Walter Raleigh* and Captain Roger North of the Amazon Company failed. The North West Passage Company sent William Hawkridge on a last fruitless voyage of discovery in 1619. The plans for the plantation of Ireland, constructive and reform-oriented upon their introduction in 1609, were made a failure as the Crown allowed expedient private interests to triumph over public ones. Also, exploration and expansion caused constant friction with Spain, Portugal, France, and the Dutch. On the positive side, new colonies were planted in the Indies, and the value of North American fisheries off Newfoundland and agriculture to the south were constantly increasing. Virginia contributed 60,000 pounds of tobacco to the London* markets in 1625. The East India Company was expanding its sphere of influence, but at great risk.

The administration of the colonial empire inherited by Charles I* in 1625 was seriously flawed. Although a success by mercantilist* economic standards, power was so decentralized as to grant virtual independence to many colonies. During the decade preceding the Civil War*, Charles pursued the goal of a self-sufficient empire and attempted to increase his control as earlier, overly generous charters expired. As in other areas of attempted expansion of royal power, the Crown's efforts were hampered by the lack of any constitutional basis for colonial administration. In 1634 Archbishop William Laud* headed a committee to regulate overseas interests. The committee was given broad powers to govern and to legislate for the colonies, but since Charles did not have the resources to enforce its enactments, its power was largely illusory.

With the Convention of Goa in 1635, the Portuguese formally granted the English trade rights in West Indian ports. These concessions made the position of the East India Company more secure. In 1639, following the acquisition of Madras, construction began on the first fortified factory, Fort St. George. This development marks a point at which English interests began to turn from seeking open trading markets to overt colonial actions.

The emigration of religious dissenters increased during Charles's reign. Charters were granted for Catholic* colonists in Maryland, dissenters in Rhode Island, and Puritans* emigrating to the Indies. Of these all were successful except the colonization of the islands of Tortuga and Santa Catalina by the Providence Island Company. A successful agricultural endeavor at first, these settlements degenerated into little more than pirate camps raiding on unprotected Spanish shipping. This led to their loss to Spanish reoccupation between 1635 and 1640. Also in 1640 the introduction of sugar planting in Barbados gave birth to an export crop whose importance rivaled tobacco and briefly made that small island Britain's most valuable single colony. The development of intensive single-crop agriculture put an end to the transplanted small-scale peasant farmer in favor of large plantations using slave labor.

During the years of the Civil War, royal influence in the colonial arena ceased. The Irish Rebellion* broke out in 1641, and in the Caribbean colonists ceased payments to the proprietorship the Crown had granted Carlisle. Charles's execution* in 1649 caused further rebellion in Maryland, Barbados, Antigua, Bermuda, and Virginia, which openly broke with the Commonwealth* and supported Charles II*.

The centralized power and regulation of colonial holdings that had eluded James I and Charles I were forged during the Interregnum*. Enactment of the Navigation Acts* of 1650-1651 forbade colonial trade with foreign ships or shipment of goods in ships whose crews were not predominantly English, Irish, or colonists. These acts, enforced with greater effectiveness as British naval power increased, provided the basis for imperial control for over a century. The establishment of the commission for plantations in 1649 provided the constitutional framework for colonial administration that had been lacking. The Commonwealth mounted successful military actions against rebellious colonies with Oliver Cromwell's* campaigns in Ireland in 1649-1650 and Sir George Ayscue's expedition to the Caribbean in 1651-1652.

Although it failed its stated purpose, the conquest of Spanish Hispaniola, Cromwell's "Western Design" task force did seize Jamaica, later an important sugar and tobacco producer. In addition, increases in the power of the navy*, demanded by the First Dutch War* (1652-1654), ensured that British colonies in the Caribbean would be less threatened by foreign interests. This period witnessed the initial colonization of Surinam and North Carolina. Cromwell's reorganization of the East India Company in 1657 strengthened it and ensured its monopoly in Far East trade. During both the Commonwealth and Protectorate*, the importance and desirability of the overseas empire was appreciated, and appropriate policies were enacted to protect it.

The Restoration* of Charles II* brought about few changes in colonial administration. Colonial holdings continued to grow, initially as the result of the dowry of Catherine of Braganza*, with the addition of Tangier and Bombay in 1660. Recognizing the East India Company's financial success, Charles confirmed privileges granted to it by Cromwell. Although administration changed little, major changes were seen in the pattern of emigration from Britain. Earlier perceptions of overpopulation were replaced by feelings that colonization was depleting a valuable resource. Later colonies drew their settlers in large measure from existing colonies. In 1662 the notorious slave trade with the colonies of the West Indies and North America from Gambia and other West African ports was granted a charter and monopoly* as the Royal Adventurers to Africa. Renewed hostilities of the Second Dutch War* (1665-1667) allowed an English military force commanded by Colonel Richard Nicholls to take New York, but this gain was offset by the loss of Surinam as a result of the Treaty of Breda in 1667.

The granting or annulment of charters to the North American colonies allowed Charles II further accumulation of power. The constant assault on the traditional rights of colonists was not always made without resistance. In the Crown colony of Virginia, attempts to limit the representative assembly by the royal governor, Sir William Berkeley, led to open rebellion in 1676. This consolidation of power was expanded in the latter years of Charles's reign with the withdrawal of the charters of the Somers Islands Company of Bermuda and of the Massachusetts colony in 1684. The death of Charles II and accession of James II* in 1685 witnessed no change in policy. Consolidation of royal power was promoted by annulment of the charters of Rhode Island in 1686 and that of Connecticut in 1687. James took the process one step further in that year with the establishment of the Dominion of New England, a brief and unsuccessful attempt to unite those colonies with a single government under Governor Sir Edmund Andros.

The brief reign of James II witnessed important events in the colonial arena, including the occupation of Calcutta and the return by the French of the seized forts of the Hudson Bay Company in Canada. As the Glorious Revolution* drew near, the East India Company began its military struggle with the Moguls. Colonial expansion under the Stuarts transformed England from a secondary player in European politics to the world's greatest imperial power.

Bibliography: R. S. Dunn, *Sugar and Slaves: The West Indies, 1624-1713*, 1972; Ephraim Lipson, *The Economic History of England*, vol. 2: *The Age of Mercantilism*, 1961; David Quinn and A. N. Ryan, *England's Sea Empire*, 1983.

Thomas R. Reid

Committee of Both Kingdoms (1643-1648). One of the few federal institutions ever created in Great Britain, the committee arose as a direct result of the Scottish Covenanter*-English parliamentarian* alliance of 1643. The impetus for the organization came chiefly from the Scots, who saw federal bodies composed of Calvinist* landowners and burgesses as the best means of preserving their national interests within the setting of the triple monarchy. The Covenanters initially attempted to form international councils during the Treaty of London negotiations (1640-1641), when they advanced and had recognized claims for representation at court and for the formation of a new body styled the conservators of the peace. The conservators never met. The formal alliance between the Covenanters and parliamentarians, signified by the Solemn League and Covenant* of 1643, raised the possibility of reviving the concept of a federal body for Britain. The necessities of coordinating the war effort against the royalists* and possible negotiations with the king provided further stimulus for founding a committee composed of leading delegates from both countries.

The English parliament* formally established the committee in February 1644. Its sessions, held in secret, commenced in London* at Derby House, hence the nickname Derby House Committee*. The Scots commissioners sought English acceptance of the Covenant*, the establishment of Presbyterianism*, security for the liberties of both kingdoms, and the restoration of peace. English commissioners were more concerned with military operations and coordinating negotiations with the king.

Commissioners from the two countries included some of the leading figures of the period. The Scots, three to four commissioners at a given time, included the marquis of Argyll (Archibald Campbell*); the earls of Loudoun, Lauderdale (John Maitland*), and Lanark; Lord Balmerino; and Sir Archibald Johnston of Wariston. Their English counterparts, mustering seven from the Lords and fourteen from the Commons, included the earls of Essex (Robert Devereux*), Manchester, Northumberland, Pembroke, and Warwick*; Lord Say and Sele (William Fiennes*); Sir William Armine; Sir John Clotworthy; Sir Arthur Haselrig; Sir William Waller; Oliver Cromwell*; Denzil Holles; Oliver St. John; and Henry Vane the younger.

Initially, the committee primarily sought to coordinate military operations against the English royalists. Given the slow communication between London and the field armies, the effort was fraught with hazard at best, and more than likely to prove absolutely futile since the military situation changed even as the committee discussed options. Circumstances were complicated in 1645 when the Scots commander, Alexander, 1st earl of Leven, retained his army in northern England as a precaution against a union of Charles I's* and Montrose's armies, despite orders from the committee to assist with elimination of the royalist bastions in the south. With the arrival of Charles in the Scots camp outside Newark in May 1646 suggesting a secret deal, English distrust of their allies accelerated.

The committee transformed into an English national executive committee, which accomplished little for the Scots save the settlement of their military pay claims. The allies' negotiations with the king deepened divisions and weakened the committee as the English strove for parliamentary control of the militia, while the Scots fastened onto a religious settlement as the best means of restraining the king. The Scots' secret negotiations with Charles—leading to the furtive signing of the Engagement* in December 1647 and the departure of the commissioners home in January 1648, followed by the treaty's public acceptance—led to the dissolution of the committee and the practical end of federal government in Britain.

Bibliography: Lawrence Kaplan, *Politics and Revolution during the English Revolution: The Scots and the Long Parliament 1643-1645*, 1976; David Stevenson, *Revolution and Counter-revolution in Scotland, 1644-51*, 1977.

Edward M. Furgol

Common Law and Courts. The old forms of action lay at the heart of civil suits at common law, and the court of Common Pleas was its primary repository (for criminal prosecutions at common law, see Law Enforcement*). Suits before Common Pleas grew significantly from the mid-sixteenth to the mid-seventeenth century with the rise of commercial society in the provincial towns, a fleet of attorneys to service its actions in the countryside, and a shift in lodging writs of debt from local courts to Westminster. While its business did not grow as much as that of Chancery or King's Bench, it still had twice the litigation of King's Bench in 1650. Falling upon lean years in the third quarter of the century, its revival by 1700 was aided by a change of proof in debt from wagermen to jurors, by legislation that caused more land transactions and oral contracts to be made in writing, and by the use of legal fictions as a gateway for actions to be sued by bill.

The court of King's Bench was the fastest growing court in England in the early seventeenth century. Possessed of the procedure of the bill of Middlesex, once a person arrested for a fictitious trespass was gaoled in the court's prison (the Marshalsea), he could then be sued by bill for any common plea. The court, by lowering its costs and adopting the advantages of Chancery procedure, cut dramatically into the original writ business of the Common Pleas. The court's calendar increased tenfold from the mid-sixteenth to the mid-seventeenth century, when it heard over 20,000 bills a year, and its clerks made fortunes from their fees. The court was also aided by Slade's Case (1602), whereby it won the right to allow plaintiffs to try cases of assumpsit (trespass on the case) to recover debts. The century also witnessed the full development of ejectment, which allowed freeholders to recover possession in Common Pleas as well as King's Bench by an action of trespass instead of under the old forms of action. This spawned the fictitious lease for a trial of title using the famous pseudonyms of John Doe versus Richard Roe.

The Exchequer of Pleas was a small common law court that had expanded business in the sixteenth century with the writ of quominus, which allowed plaintiffs to sue in debt on the fiction that they were unable to pay their own debts or taxes to the king. The real, solid growth of the court came in the seventeenth century, when the barons of the Exchequer* refused to allow defendants to challenge the fiction. And by the later years of that century, plaintiffs were using the court's subpoena with the same allegation. Therefore, by 1700 all three common law courts were hearing common pleas with common procedures. Each court, however, remained with a central core of business: Common Pleas for real actions, King's Bench for personal actions and jurisdiction in review, and Exchequer for revenue cases. All three courts also began to experience contraction. Socioeconomic changes, together with an as yet unexplained change in litigation mentality, led to a long-term secular decline in litigation that began in the 1680s and continued well into the eighteenth century.

The critical piece in the puzzle of common law litigation was the court of Chancery. Arising out of the royal secretariat through the king's residual personal power to give justice when it could not be obtained in his other common law courts, its procedure was by bill instead of by writ. Not restricted to the law terms and always open for business, it could hear cases in either Westminster or the countryside by a commission of dedimus potestatem. The chancellor or his master in the sixteenth century, playing judge and jury, was more concerned with the circumstances of individual cases than with general legal rules and precedents. Between the late sixteenth and the late seventeenth centuries (from the time of Lord Ellesmere as chancellor to that of the earl of Nottingham), the court developed common remedies for commonly recurring cases to meet the demands of the litigants who flocked to its doors. The regular reporting of Chancery cases from 1660, and the development of a scientific jurisprudence by the 1700s, brought the evolution of equity into a set of legal principles in a legal development parallel to that of the earlier common law courts. Thus throughout the seventeenth century Chancery expanded its handling of complaints concerning property and commercial matters: bonds, conveyances, trusts, and mortgages. By 1700 there were over 10,000 cases pending in any given year.

One of the great episodes in English legal history was the clash between the Chancery and the King's Bench in the early seventeenth century. The clash involved personalities as much as legal principles and the competition between two of the most successful courts in the era. Since most decisions of fact at common law were made by wagermen and jurors, such courts could not handle questions concerning the conscience or good faith of the parties. The powerful injunction of the Chancery allowed the court to intervene in any cause on the basis of "conscience." This did not suit the combative Chief Justice Edward Coke* or the financial interests of the King's Bench and its clerks and practitioners. The conflict arose in the years 1612-1616, when the chief justice used the writ of habeas corpus to release persons committed by the chancellor for winning cases by fraud or deceit. The matter was resolved by the privy council* in 1616. The chief justice, having alienated many of his own supporters by the authoritarian control he exercised over his court and by threatening jurors to secure "correct" verdicts, was dismissed. As a result, the Chancery injunction became supreme in matters of equity, and within two centuries Chancery procedure became part of the common law.

The common law was as dependent on its practitioners as it was on its doctrines and procedures. In the seventeenth century, the law profession entered the modern age of specialization. Serjeants at law declined as early Stuart kings sold their offices for money and bribes, discrediting them with the inflation of honors* that soiled the aristocracy. In their place rose the barrister at law to appear in practice at the central courts, with solicitors to instruct them on behalf of clients and attorneys to appear for them. The title of the modern king's counsel also originated in the early 1600s. It enabled successful barristers to gain the "silk" (gowns) with precedence in the common law courts by 1670. The century was also an age of great judges, lions on the throne. Lord Ellesmere and Sir Edward Coke in the early years, Sir Matthew Hale in the middle ones, and Sir Francis North and Lord Nottingham afterward represented a great age of jurisprudence. Apart from Coke's monumental four-part *Institutes of the Laws of England* (1628-1644), the really bold and imaginative jurisprudence came from the pens of renaissance jurists such as Sir Francis Bacon*, Sir Henry Finch, John Selden*, and Hale. Bacon perhaps represented the most forward looking of this work: reflective, analytical, comparative, and elegantly written.

The growth of litigation, coupled with the development of increasing complexities in both procedural and substantive areas of the law, enabled the political revolution of the 1640s to be extended into an attack on and reform of the law and the courts. Dissatisfaction with the role of the king in the conciliar courts and with increasing costs and delays in the common law courts led to a virtual legal revolution, which included the abolition of the Star Chamber, High Commission, councils of the north and the marches of Wales in 1641, and the House of Lords, ecclesiastical courts, court of Wards, feudal tenures, Latin, and Law French by 1650 (see Ecclesiastical Courts*; Prerogative Courts*). Only the Lords, a modified ecclesiastical jurisdiction, and the old languages were restored in the 1660s. Meanwhile, hundreds of revolutionary pamphlets called for the abolition of the common law, and major law reform programs were written by Sir Matthew Hale and William Sheppard. Few were enacted, and none survived the Restoration*. They did, however, find warm currency in the law reform movement of the late eighteenth and nineteenth centuries, which brought the common law into the modern world.

Bibliography: J. H. Baker, *Introduction to English Legal History*, 3d ed., 1990; J. G. A. Pocock, *The Ancient Constitution and the Feudal Law*, 2d ed., 1991; Wilfrid R. Prest, *The Rise of the Barristers: A Social History of the English Bar, 1590-1640*, 1986.

Louis A. Knafla

Commons Protestation of 1621. This occurred in the parliament of 1621*, during the second session in November, for which the privy council* had prepared poorly, while James I* resided at New Market.

Earlier James had appealed for supplies to aid the Protestant cause in the Thirty Years War*, and the Commons responded with a grant of two subsidies (£140,000) in economically troubled times. During the debate over grievances, monopolies* and impositions* were attacked, and events were manipulated to cause the impeachment* of Lord Chancellor Francis Bacon* with the connivance of privy councilors and the king's tacit acknowledgment. It recently has been argued that the government used initiative and principles of harmony, in contrast to traditional interpretations stressing the Commons's innovation and assertion of its powers to press a national grievance, with Bacon sacrificed in the process.

The main reason for calling parliament* was to pressure Spain and the Holy Roman Emperor, while helping the Protestant cause by appearing to prepare for war. At the suggestion of the duke of Buckingham's (George Villiers*) spokesman and despite the deepening depression troubling the nation, the Commons approved one subsidy (see Taxation and Revenue*) to use to pressure Spain to restore James's son-in-law Frederick in the Palatinate of the Rhine, with Catholic* recusants* paying double. Tied to the grant was a petition attacking the proposed marriage of Prince Charles (see Charles I*) to the Spanish Infanta (see Spanish Match*). James harshly rebuked parliament and rejected their right to consider the marriage. He asserted his generosity in not imprisoning transgressors of his royal prerogative* after the first session.

After a lull, former speaker Sir Robert Phelps reminded the Commons that in the parliament of 1604* the king's threats and assertion that their privilege derived from his sufferance were answered with an "Apology and Satisfaction," which traced their ancient liberties. He now urged a similar course. Soon business was suspended, and a protestation was drawn with many parallels to the 1604 petition that defended the House's moderate proceedings on monopolies, impositions, and other national grievances and asserted its ancient privileges, especially free speech and its confidentiality. The protestation was hastily constructed and entered into the Commons's *Journal* to avoid adjournment.

James believed that the protestation challenged his authority. Assertions of accepted privilege for unrestricted parliamentary debate and absolute immunity entailed an exercise of power he was unwilling to share or transmit to parliament. After parliament's adjournment and dissolution, James ripped the protestation out of the *Journal* and imprisoned several of its authors.

The events of 1621 have been interpreted in different ways. Traditional historians over the last two centuries perceived the protestation as a milestone in the growth of democracy, with parliament asserting initiative and confronting the king's government in defense of its right to open debate of any subject without fear of reprisal. Since the 1970s revisionist scholars have stressed the Crown's use of initiative and the defensive posture of parliament, noting that consensus rather than confrontation best describes their strategy. Regardless of which side more strenuously exercised initiative and innovation, the protestation resulted in the destruction of the king's foreign policy, and parliament did not meet again for three years.

Bibliography: Conrad Russell, *Parliaments and English Politics, 1621-1629*, 1979.

Sheldon Hanft

Commonwealth. The Rump Parliament*, which was what was left of the House of Commons after Pride's Purge* removed all the members who had pursued the Treaty of Newport* with Charles I*, voted on 4 January 1649 "that the people are, under God, the original of all just power; that the Commons of England, being chosen by and representing the people, have the supreme power in this nation," and that whatever the Commons enacted had the force of law. Upon this claim, made by a fragment of one house of a parliament* first elected over eight years earlier, the Commonwealth was founded. Two days later, the first act to be passed by the Commons alone erected a high court of justice to try the king for waging war against the parliament and kingdom. Oliver Cromwell's* protracted efforts to find some course that would spare his life had run out two weeks earlier in the face of Charles's steadfast refusal to compromise his divinely ordained authority. Charles's trial and execution* inexorably followed. Votes shortly afterward to abolish the monarchy and the House of Lords (despite Cromwell's desire to preserve the latter in some form) were translated into acts of parliament on 17 and 19 March, and a brief act on 19 May, declaring England to be a Commonwealth, completed the formalities.

But the constitutional form of the new republic (a word that the Rump avoided) was still largely undefined and would remain so, for it presented formidable difficulties. The Rump's invocation of the sovereign people was risky rhetoric, seeing that the great majority of both the propertied political nation and the populace at large were outraged by the king's death and did not want a republic at all. Its basis of authority was perilously narrow, for only just over seventy members risked remaining active between the purge and the execution, and some did so more to prevent the army* from assuming any more power than from any commitment to republican principles. The army itself was largely united about abolishing the monarchy, with the significant exception of its general, Lord Fairfax*, but less so about what to put in its place. The Levellers* were renewing their agitation in the ranks, hoping to raise pressure through the soldiers for a far more radical settlement than Cromwell and Henry Ireton*, the army's effective political leaders, cared to contemplate. To hold the army together, Ireton had agreed just before the purge to the drafting of a New Agreement of the People* by a committee of Levellers, officers, members of parliament, and London* Independents*. The draft was debated at length by the general council of officers, modified in particulars, and presented to the Rump on 20 January as the army's agreed proposals for the constitution of the Commonwealth. The Rump, it desired, should dissolve itself by 30 April; thereafter single-chamber parliaments (their constituencies radically reapportioned) should be elected on a broad franchise at two-year intervals, sit for no more than seven months, and appoint a council of state* to govern until the next parliament met. The Leveller leaders, however, were so incensed by the officers' modifications of the agreement that they wrecked any prospects it had of acceptance by publicly repudiating it and reverting to their old tactic of stirring up the soldiery. The resultant mutiny in May 1649 was serious, but

Fairfax and Cromwell easily quelled it, and it proved to be the self-inflicted death blow to the Levellers as a coherent political movement. The suppression of the communistic Diggers* began at about the same time.

Meanwhile the Rump, conscious of its unrepresentative character, was broadening its membership. It was prepared to readmit the many members who had absented during the proceedings against the king, provided that they formally declared their dissent from the vote (accepting Charles's response to the Newport terms as satisfactory) that had triggered Pride's Purge. Within five weeks of Charles's execution, the newly readmitted members outnumbered the Rump's original nucleus, and a further eighty-six resumed their seats at some later date. Many of the latecomers attended only rarely, but inevitably the Commons took on a more conservative complexion, and it cooled toward the army, by whose sufferance it sat. When it set up a council of state in mid-February to exercise a strictly controlled executive authority, only two of its forty-one members besides Fairfax and Cromwell were serving army officers in the field army. Ireton and Major-General Thomas Harrison were nominated but rejected, and the military councilors were outnumbered by five peers. The council was entrusted for one year only, and fresh elections followed at yearly intervals.

Despite its sensational inauguration with the act of regicide, the Commonwealth regime was far from revolutionary. Fine though S. R. Gardiner's account of it remains as a political narrative, our knowledge of it has been transformed by David Underdown's masterly reexamination of its inception in *Pride's Purge* (1971) and by Blair Worden's close investigation of its factions and policies in *The Rump Parliament* (1974).

The army's influence in politics was much reduced while it was engaged in meeting threats of royalist* invasion, first from Ireland* and then from Scotland*. The consequent conquest of both countries extended the Commonwealth's authority to the whole of the British Isles, but it kept Cromwell from Westminster (apart from one short break) from July 1649 until September 1651. Fairfax resigned his command in 1650 and retired from politics. Left to itself, the Rump forgot its promises of early general elections and settled down to the business of survival. Being very aware of its own unpopularity, it risked offending conservative opinion as little as possible. The Rump was so far from sharing the aspirations of sectaries and radical Independents to create a New Jerusalem that it contemplated reestablishing the Presbyterian* national church of the later 1640s; only the speaker's casting a vote quashed the move. Its belated repeal in 1650 of the penal laws that punished nonattendance at parish worship was counterbalanced by a Blasphemy Act aimed against the more extreme sects. Its record in social and legal reform was meager, and its preoccupation with material and mercantile interests produced the Navigation Act* of 1651. This was one of the steps that led to the First Dutch War* (1652-1654), to the dismay of Cromwell and others who sought a united Protestant interest in Europe. The war also worsened its chronic financial problem, which remained unsolved even after vast sales of Crown, church, and royalists' lands (see Crown Lands*).

When Cromwell finally returned to the Rump, he pressed it to name a date for its own dissolution. Powerful though he was, before 1653 he was never the master of the Commonwealth's politics that folk history has supposed. The house voted that it would not sit beyond 3 November 1654, a full three years ahead. Moreover, it was much drawn to a scheme whereby elections would be held only to those seats that stood vacant; the sitting members would go on sitting. This was a crude solution to the problem of preserving a republic that seriously lacked committed republicans, even among its rulers, and it angered the army, whose mounting discontent boiled over in a comprehensive petition from the council of officers in August 1652. This called upon parliament to speed the process of religious, legal, financial, and administrative reform; to restrict public office to "men of truth, fearing God, and hating covetousness" (a thinly veiled reflection on the Rumpers); and to take measures to ensure the election of pious and faithful men to a new parliament. The house was goaded at last into preparing a "bill for a new representative" and under further pressure took it into debate in February 1653. Worden has established that it did provide for a new parliament, not (as used to be thought) merely for the recruitment of the existing one, so it is far from obvious why Cromwell, in a thunderous temper, violently expelled the Rump on 20 April. Worden thinks he was temporarily converted to the belief of the Fifth Monarchy Men* that the prophesied thousand-year kingdom of Christ was imminent and that its people must prepare for it by establishing a "rule of the saints"; elected parliaments belonged to the outworn age of mere "carnal" government. Austin Woolrych has argued in *Commonwealth to Protectorate* (1982) that the evidence is against such a conversion and that Cromwell was probably moved by something objectionable—real or imagined—in the bill itself, which he destroyed.

After much debate as to what to do next, the council of officers proceeded to nominate a new "supreme authority" of 140 men (later raised by co-option to 144), drawn from all the English counties and from Scotland, Ireland, and Wales*. For Harrison and a few fellow Fifth Monarchists, it was the nearest they could get to a rule of the saints, but for Cromwell and most of the officers who chose its members, it was a temporary surrogate for a parliament, entrusted to govern the Commonwealth in a godly manner for a limited period until the people should be settled enough to elect their own representatives again. Gardiner and many subsequent historians were mistaken in supposing that the millenarian* "churches of Christ" had more than a marginal influence on its composition. Barebone's Parliament*, so nicknamed after one of its members, met on 4 July, and set to work with a zeal that the Rump had never known. It was not the conventicle of base-born fanatics of royalist legend, for five-sixths of its members ranked as gentlemen or above, almost as many were justices of the peace (see Local Government*), and over forty had been to university*. It enacted more than thirty statutes. But increasingly it polarized between a moderate majority and a radical minority. The latter, centered on a dozen professed Fifth Monarchists, aimed to abolish any publicly maintained ministry in the church and, instead of reforming the common law*, sought to replace it with a brief written code based on the law of Moses. They also seriously impeded Cromwell's efforts to end the Dutch War.

Cromwell was deeply disillusioned with his pseudo-parliament, but he would not break it by force. The moderate majority solved his problem by staging a well-planned walkout on 12 December and resigning their authority back into his hands. They were almost certainly colluding with Major-General John Lambert and other senior officers, who had recently approached Cromwell with the draft constitution of a limited monarchy, known as the Instrument of Government*. He had then rejected it, but faced with the fait accompli, he at last accepted the headship of state under the terms of Lambert's Instrument, though as lord protector, not as king.

Bibliography: S. R. Gardiner, *History of the Commonwealth and Protectorate*, 4 vols., 1903; David Underdown, *Pride's Purge: Politics in the Puritan Revolution*, 1971; Austin Woolrych, *Commonwealth to Protectorate*, 1982; Blair Worden, *The Rump Parliament*, 1974.

Austin Woolrych

Commonwealthmen. The earliest direct antecedent of the use of the term *Commonwealthmen* during the Interregnum* was among Tudor reformers associated with Thomas Cromwell in the 1530s. After that the term *commonwealth* or *commonweal* was often used in a traditional sense to suggest a common or national interest that superseded narrow interests. Commonwealthmen are identified most closely with a group of republican political writers, members of parliament*, and army* officers who adhered to various notions of the Good Old Cause* during the 1650s. The term is not necessarily interchangeable with *republican* and probably represents only a branch of republican thought expressed by writers such as James Harrington*, Edmund Ludlow, Henry Nevile, and John Streater. Historians have sometimes included Commonwealthmen in a modern category of "classical republicans." This term is misleading, emphasizing a secular classical outlook that contributed to but did not define the actions or writings of this group.

According to the regicide* and republican Ludlow, his political allies in the first Rump Parliament* (1648-1652) were Commonwealthmen. Later Commonwealthmen were defined as opponents to Barebone's Parliament* (1653) and the Protectorate* (1653-1659). Commonwealthmen were associated with calls for the return of the Rump Parliament. They considered it the only assembly that could legitimately design a permanent new constitution. Harrington's *Oceana* (1656) provided much of the historical theory and republican ideals later expressed by Commonwealthmen in 1659-1660 in propositions for a constitutional settlement.

Although Commonwealthmen were active in conspiracies against the Protectorate in England, Ireland*, and Scotland*, particularly in the army, they failed to discredit the regime. Several leading Commonwealthmen were elected to Richard Cromwell's* parliament in late 1658, including Ludlow, Nevile, Sir Arthur Haselrig, Thomas Scot, and Colonel Matthew Alured. Their influence over the majority of conservative MPs was limited. Only in alliance with sectarians and discontented senior officers known as the Wallingford House party were the Commonwealthmen able to overthrow Richard Cromwell and restore the Rump Parliament in April-May 1659.

During debates for a new constitution in the summer of 1659, the Commonwealthmen opposed the adoption of a "select" or nonelected senate. Although not a party or even a constant faction, several key civilian Commonwealthmen were members of Harrington's Rota Club in London*. Harrington's ideas were translated into constitutional proposals, including the establishment of a single elected house, perhaps an elected senate with debating powers, and a system of rotational officeholding. These theories became distilled into popular, simplified versions by pamphleteers known as "Harringtonians." In contrast to the elected model, the MP Sir Henry Vane, a republican sectarian leader, proposed a government of saints with an appointed senate. Vane's ideas were supported by John Lambert and other senior officers, who saw the senate as a means to buttress their influence in government. When the army council overthrew the Rump again in October 1659, Vane was given a constitutional committee to establish a modified version of his constitution. After the return of the Rump in December, the Commonwealthmen were unable to stop General George Monck* from reinstating the purged Long Parliament* MPs, which led to the Restoration* of Charles II*. Throughout the Interregnum*, the Commonwealthmen were a minority in parliament, with uncertain popular support.

Bibliography: J. G. A. Pocock, *The Political Works of James Harrington*, 1977; A. H. Woolrych, "The Good Old Cause and the Fall of the Protectorate," *Cambridge Historical Journal* 13 (1957): 131-161.

John H. F. Hughes

Congregationalism. Congregationalism was a religious expression that placed great importance on the independence and autonomy of individual congregations in matters of governance and doctrine. Some trace Congregationalism to medieval protests against the Roman Catholic* church, while others believe it began with the writings of John Wycliffe (c.1330-1384) and the Lollards. The English Reformation established a state church and began to correct abuses. The Puritans*, however, protested against the Elizabethan church and its emphasis on uniformity. They wanted to institute instead a Presbyterian* system, which would eliminate, among other grievances, the episcopal structure. Some saw no need for a national church. These opponents to Elizabeth's church were driven underground by statute law and persecution, only to surface during the weak reign of the Stuarts.

Robert Browne (c.1550-1633) was the earliest proponent of separation from the Anglican* church (see Separatism*), and his writings became the classical statement of Congregationalism, also called Brownism. At Cambridge University he came under the influence of Puritanism, especially the thought of Thomas Cartwright (1535-1603). He soon began to preach without the permission of the bishop of Ely and attacked the prerogative of bishops to license. In 1580 he joined his friend Robert Harrison (d.1585) at Norwich, where he founded his first church. He came into conflict with the bishop and was imprisoned because of his teaching. Browne argued that the true church was a voluntary association of believers in a congregation who came together in a covenant with one another and with Christ. Each congregation had sovereignty over its life and worship and elected its own leaders. Bishops and ecclesiastical courts* consequently had no authority in the governance of the church, and civil magistrates exercised no role in affairs of religion. As stipulated by the New Testament, leaders within the congregation were the pastor, elder, teacher, deacons, and widows, and they exercised authority only within their congregation. Browne also attacked the idea of a national church and criticized Puritans who wanted reform at the hand of the Elizabethan church.

Because of persecution, Browne, Harrison, and some followers fled in 1581 to Middleburg in Holland, where Browne expressed these religious views in *A Treatise of Reformation without Tarrying for Any* and *A Book Which Sheweth the Life and Manner of all True Christians*. Quarrels broke out which split the group, and Browne and some followers left for Scotland*, where he soon came into conflict with the Kirk* and was imprisoned. In 1585 he returned to England, made his peace with church officials, and was ordained an Anglican priest in 1591. Imprisoned for striking a local constable, he died in jail in 1633.

During the reign of James I* (1603-1625) the Independent* or Congregational movement was still small, but churches were established at Gainsborough by the Rev. John Smyth (c.1554-1612), at Scrooby where one of the most prominent members was the Rev. John Robinson (c.1575-1625), and in Southwark by the Rev. Henry Jacob (1563-1624). Members from the first two churches sought freedom of religion in Holland. The Scrooby exiles moved to Leyden, and from there William Brewster (c.1560-1644) led some of the members across the Atlantic in the *Mayflower* in 1620 to establish their religious principles in New England.

The distrust associated with the reign of Charles I* (1625-1649) and the repressive policies of Archbishop William Laud* (1573-1645) forced more people into opposition against the state episcopal church; some followed the example of the Scrooby congregation and fled to the colonies or to Holland to find a religious refuge. With the advent of the Long Parliament* in 1640 and the beginning of hostilities between the king and parliament*, numerous "congregational men" returned from the Continent and helped their countrymen to form an important part of the opposition to the king. In 1643 the Long Parliament authorized the Westminster Assembly of Divines* to convene and to reform the state church, and the resulting Westminster Confession emphasized the principles of Presbyterianism. Although the majority of the members favored change along Presbyterian lines, a small minority—"The Five Dissenting Brethren"—unsuccessfully argued for church reformation according to Congregational guidelines.

When Oliver Cromwell* (1599-1658) seized power after Charles I's execution*, Congregationalists began to exert influence on the political and religious life of the country. Papists and High Church* Anglicans were excluded from Cromwell's policy of toleration, but Congregationalism experienced the rewards of religious freedom for the first time. Mandatory attendance at Anglican church services, for example, was revoked. Congregationalists also enjoyed the favor of Cromwell, and he appointed them to important posts in government, religion, and at the universities*. Independent congregations grew throughout the country and took part in nominating members to the unsuccessful "Barebone's Parliament"* in 1653.

Influenced by the Congregational traditions in Holland and North America, representatives of approximately 120 congregations met in London* at the old Savoy

Palace in 1658 for a national conference to draw up a statement of policy. The resulting Savoy Declaration consisted of a preface, profession of faith, and principles of discipline. The section dealing with faith drew heavily upon the Westminster Confession, but there was a clear break with regard to church structure and organization. It proclaimed that Christ had given all necessary power and authority to individual local churches. Again departing from the Presbyterianism of the Westminster Confession, the Savoy Declaration believed that church membership should be limited to the elect who could be identified by their loyalty to the word of God and their virtuous life.

With the Restoration* of Charles II* in 1660, Congregationalism suffered as did the other Nonconformist churches. The Clarendon Code* sought to bring uniformity back into English religious life, and the 1662 Act of Uniformity (13 and 14 Car. II, c. 4) in particular was directed against Presbyterians and Congregationalists. As a result over 2,000 clergy were expelled from their livings. In 1689 the Toleration Act (I Gul. III & Mar., c. 18) granted a degree of religious freedom to Nonconformists. Congregationalism consequently became an important part of English religious life.

Bibliography: Daniel Jenkins, *Congregationalism: A Restatement*, 1954; Geoffrey Nuttall, *Visible Saints: The Congregational Way, 1640-1660*, 1956.

René Kollar

Convention Parliament (1660). The Long Parliament* ended on 16 March 1660 with a call for elections, which it was widely expected would lead to Charles II's* recall from continental exile. Although it attempted to exclude royalists* from election, the restriction was ignored, and those chosen for this Convention "Parliament" generally supported the Restoration*, while republicans and supporters of the army* were rejected by the electorate.

The Convention, with a restored House of Lords, first met on 25 April 1660, and immediately the issue of returning the king dominated the debates in the House of Commons. An influential group there known as the Presbyterian* Knot wanted Charles to resume the throne, but only with severe limits on his authority (many of these men had failed to impose similar conditions upon Charles I* twelve years earlier). But the Commons voted that the government was in the parliament* and the king, who should resume his throne without restrictions.

Even before Charles returned, parliament began considering bills to settle English affairs. The most important was the Act for Indemnity and Oblivion* (12 Car. II, c. 11.) Despite the king's repeated calls for swift passage, the Commons and then both Commons and Lords spent the summer wrangling over who should benefit from the king's general pardon in his Declaration of Breda*. When the bill finally passed in August, only a relatively small number of regicides* and a select group of key Interregnum* officials were denied royal mercy. The rest of England was forgiven so the king could get on with governing. The Convention later attainted these same men, providing a vindictive tinge to a generally lenient treatment of the king's opponents.

The land settlement proved more difficult to resolve, and in general individual grievances were sacrificed for the greater good. Although no statute was enacted regarding church and Crown lands* seized during the Interregnum, the principle was established that the king should have all his property returned to him. Proclamations generally sympathetic to the clergy and antithetical to former republicans also passed. Relying on these, the Crown and the church began reclaiming property and leasing it to former owners under favorable terms. Thereafter the issue faded from the Convention's concern.

Similarly the religious issues were beyond this body's abilities. Divisions existing before the Civil Wars* had not been resolved, and the Convention was unable to pass any bill of religious comprehension. Compounding this problem, early signs of intolerance of radical sects, especially Quakers*, emerged among Convention members and the king's closest advisers. The Convention, however, did resolve the festering problem with the army by taxing the country sufficiently to pay what it owed the military and immediately thereafter disbanding its units. This removed a major source of unrest. Finally that body considered but never passed a bill that would have established its rights and the fundamental laws of the land.

Yet the Convention did what it was supposed to do. It returned England to its traditional form of government, pretending, as the Lords blithely assumed, that 1660 was the twelfth year of Charles II's reign. Its accomplishments evidence its desire to erase the memory of the Civil Wars and subsequent governments, but its failures show the difficulty of doing this. It would remain to the Cavalier Parliament* to resolve problems that the Convention could not.

Bibliography: Ronald Hutton, *The Restoration: A Political and Religious History of England and Wales 1658-1667*, 1985.

David A. Davis

Convention Parliament (1689). When James II* fled to France upon William of Orange's* invasion in 1688, England had to reestablish legitimate government (see Glorious Revolution*). On the recommendation of peers in London* and with the concurrence of nearby members of the House of Commons elected prior to James's accession, William issued writs for the election of a special Convention Parliament. Meeting from 22 January to 13 February 1689, this irregular assembly resolved several fundamental issues and dramatically changed England's government. Its modest intent was to create a parliamentary monarchy (the king under the law). It did not foresee the shift in the balance of power from Crown to parliament* that evolved in succeeding decades.

There was broad consensus in both houses that James had threatened English liberties and the Anglican* church. Commons quickly agreed that James had broken the contract between king and people and, having fled the kingdom, had abdicated and left the throne "vacant." The Lords, more concerned about the hereditary principle, debated longer and more heatedly about using such words as *abdicated* and *vacant* but ultimately concurred.

The next problem was filling the throne. The majority in both houses wanted to retain some remnant of hereditary right. To that end the Convention invited Mary*, James's eldest daughter and William's wife, to take the crown. However, she refused to be the sole sovereign, and William refused to be merely her consort or regent. The solution was to offer the crown jointly to William and Mary. While this amounted to a constitutional monstrosity, in practice it worked well. Mary had little interest in government, and it was agreed that William would exercise the powers of sovereign. This suited William, whose primary reason for wanting the throne was to bring England into the League of Augsburg to defend his beloved Netherlands against Louis XIV of France.

The Convention also addressed the problem created when James II attempted to legalize Catholicism*. On 29 January Commons passed a resolution stating that England was a Protestant kingdom and henceforth could have only a Protestant prince. When Lords agreed, any claim to the throne by James or his heirs was set aside. The resolution also solved the problem of establishing the succession, which would run from William and Mary to their heirs, then to Mary's younger sister, Anne*, to Anne's heirs, and to any heirs of William by any wife after Mary. Since all living members of this line were Protestants, the heirs would most likely be Protestant. Some historians think that disinheriting all Catholic princes was the most radical act of the Convention.

It was accepted in the beginning that to redress the grievances against James, the Convention must define the rights, liberties, and privileges of Englishmen and the powers of the Crown. A committee of thirty-nine established for this purpose reported twenty-three "Heads of Grievances" to Commons on 2 February 1689. Many concerned problems recurrent for centuries, including suspension of laws (see Suspending Power*) and judicial decisions, nonparliamentary taxation*, and manipulation of elections, plus various common law provisions for criminal procedures. Others involved fundamental constitutional questions on which there was no consensus and new ideas such as a requirement for frequent elections of parliament, religious toleration, and requiring that judges be appointed on good behavior instead of at the pleasure of the Crown. However, there was considerable pressure from William and various Convention leaders to avoid protracted debate and resolve the crisis of no government as soon as possible. Therefore the Convention reduced the list to those on which there was consensus and left the others for later debate. The resulting Declaration of Rights* was accepted by both houses on 12 February, averting a crisis with William, who perceived the longer version as a list of stipulations that reduced the Crown to a mere contractual kingship. The Convention leadership convinced him that the declaration contained only old laws and was merely a statement of fact, an arguable interpretation.

On 13 February 1689, the Convention Parliament presented a document to William and Mary that contained the Declaration of Rights and other resolutions and offered them the throne, which they accepted. On 22 February the Convention transformed itself into a regular parliament, which lasted until 27 March 1690 and enacted numerous important laws, including the Bill of Rights* (1 Gul. III & Mar. II, Sess.

2, c. 2, the statutory form of the declaration), the first Mutiny Act (1 Gul. III & Mar., c. 5), and the Toleration Act (1 Gul. III & Mar., c. 18).

Bibliography: W. A. Speck, *Reluctant Revolutionaries: Englishmen and the Revolution of 1688*, 1988.

Richard L. Hillard

Cooper, Anthony Ashley, 1st Earl of Shaftesbury (1621-1683). Brilliant politician, courtier, and founder of the Whig* party, he consistently supported moderation and toleration in religion and government by England's traditional landed elite in cooperation with a limited monarchy.

Born on 22 July 1621, the son and heir of the wealthy Sir John Cooper, young Anthony was orphaned at age ten. Later while at Oxford University and Lincoln's Inn, he showed great ability. Although underage, he was elected to both the Short Parliament* and the Long Parliament* but was not allowed to take his seat. During 1643 he fought with the royalist* forces in the Civil War* but switched to the parliamentarian* side in 1644. After the defeat of the king in 1646, Cooper sided with the Political Presbyterians* and upon their defeat in 1648 went into political retirement for several years. During the early part of the Protectorate* he served in Barebone's Parliament* and on the council of state*, where he was an ally of Oliver Cromwell*. Later Cromwell's exercise of the arbitrary powers of the lord protector pushed Cooper into opposition, and by 1660 he was advising General George Monck* on the restoration of first the Rump Parliament* and then of Charles II*.

A grateful Charles II pardoned Cooper for his previous actions against the Crown, appointed him to the privy council*, and promoted him to be Baron Ashley of Wimborne St. Giles. Like his master, Charles II, Cooper supported moderate religious policies, toleration, and reconciliation with other former rebels. In 1663 he helped to found the Carolinas colony in North America (see Colonization*). He also joined the group of young politicians opposed to Lord Chancellor Edward Hyde*, the earl of Clarendon. After Clarendon's fall, he was a member of the group of royal ministers known as the Cabal*. During these years he also began patronizing the young political theorist John Locke*. Cooper supported an anti-Dutch and pro-French foreign policy but was not privy to those clauses of the secret Treaty of Dover* (1670) with Louis XIV of France, which called for the restoration of Catholicism* in England. He supported Charles II's Declaration of Indulgence* in 1672, including the contention that the king possessed the power to dispense and to suspend statutes (see Dispensing Power*; Suspending Power*). That same year he reached his pinnacle of royal favor, when Charles II created him earl of Shaftesbury and made him lord chancellor.

Shaftesbury soon found his political fortunes going into decline as the excesses of Charles II's pro-Catholic and pro-French policies aroused the fears of the Protestant political nation in Britain. The Cabal fell apart, and various royal ministers faced impeachment*. Shaftesbury himself was suspicious of the royal heir, the future James II's* willingness to engage in arbitrary government and the re-Catholicizing of

England. So Shaftesbury's support for royal policies weakened, and a disgruntled king dismissed him as lord chancellor in November 1673. From that point onward Shaftesbury was a leader of the opposition. During 1677 he and several other politicians were imprisoned for agitating for the calling of a new parliament. The next year he exploited the popular anti-Catholic hysteria of the Popish Plot* to bring about the dissolution of the Cavalier Parliament*. During the parliament of 1679 and the Exclusion Crisis*, Shaftesbury led the forces seeking to bar James from the royal succession. This controversy resulted in the formation of the Whig party, which favored limitations on royal power and was fearful of re-Catholicizing by Charles II and James. Unfortunately for Shaftesbury, the wily Charles, with the aid of financial subsidies from France, managed to undermine support for the Whigs. By 1681 the king had Shaftesbury arrested for treason and imprisoned in the Tower of London, but when a pro-Whig grand jury refused to indict him, Shaftesbury went free. Charles II continued to hound his enemies and so goaded Shaftesbury into an unsuccessful conspiracy, which forced him to flee in late 1682 to Holland, where he died on 21 January 1683.

Bibliography: K. H. D. Haley, *The First Earl of Shaftesbury*, 1968.

Ronald H. Fritze

Cotton, Sir Robert (1586-1631). Antiquarian, courtier, and politician, Sir Robert Cotton was born of a Huntingdonshire gentry family, educated at Westminster School under the antiquarian William Camden, attended Jesus College, Cambridge, and read law at the Middle Temple, London*. Together with Camden he founded the Society of Antiquaries. He moved freely between the worlds of politics and scholarship and corresponded with scholars on the Continent. Camden and Cotton helped to break down the insularity that prevailed among English antiquarians by promoting an awareness of trends in historical scholarship in Europe and by using the tools of archaeology, philology, and etymology to illuminate the many continental influences on English language and institutions. Thus they helped to develop among their fellows in the Society of Antiquaries a sense of comparative historical perspective. Following Machiavelli and Guicciardini, Camden and Cotton also secularized and humanized the study of the past by rejecting a providential interpretation of history.

Early Stuart England was still essentially a traditional society, and the weight of the past remained heavy. But since events in that age began to move so rapidly, precedents from the past afforded fixed guideposts to which men could cling in such insecure times. Consequently an antiquarian was a useful person for government officials to consult. Cotton was called upon to render advice concerning the duties and jurisdictions attached to ancient offices and the precedents, ceremonies, and procedures employed in coronations, parliamentary proceedings, chancery practice, and ancient feudal exactions. The latter expertise he also employed in trying to squeeze more rents and seigneurial dues out of the tenants on his Huntingdonshire estates. Cotton also gave useful advice on economic and monetary policies and invented a new honor of baronets which, when suitably clothed in the aura of antiquity, proved a very profitable scheme. From his study of the past, Cotton acquired a knowledge of political behavior, which helped him to be a skillful politician in a society torn by factionalism. He increasingly placed his knowledge of ancient precedents at the disposal of parliament*, not because he identified with the parliamentary opposition but because the privy council*, dominated by George Villiers*, 1st duke of Buckingham's faction, consulted him less. Cotton continued to believe that harmony between king and parliament was essential to good government.

Cotton never held high office and spoke little during the times he sat in the House of Commons, apparently because of a stutter, but he was nonetheless very influential in parliamentary politics. In large part this was because of the many people combining an interest in politics and antiquarianism who gathered in the library at his house in Old Palace Yard, Westminster. This collection, which later became the foundation collection of the British Museum, was different from the libraries of peers and universities* in that it was devoted to manuscript sources of British history rather than to the classics or theology. Historical studies of previous reigns undertaken by Cotton's circle furnished a yardstick with which to measure the performance of James I* and Charles I*. As the achievements of the Stuart monarchs were found wanting in comparison, these writings came to be perceived as seditious and provided the pretext for the Crown to close the Cottonian library in 1629.

Bibliography: Roger B. Manning, "Antiquarianism and the Seigneurial Reaction: Sir Robert and Sir Thomas Cotton and Their Tenants," *Historical Research* 63 (1990): 277-288; Kevin Sharpe, *Sir Robert Cotton, 1586-1631: History and Politics in Early Modern England,* 1979.

Roger B. Manning

Council of State (1649-60). Although many forms of government were tried during the Interregnum*, all incorporated an element known at the time or since as a council of state, that is, a fairly small, select body of politicians exercising a range of executive, administrative, and even quasi-legislative powers. The councils fall into one of two main types.

The first are those that acted in tandem with a parliament* in more or less continuous session. The clearest examples are the five successive councils of state set up by the Rump Parliament* between February 1649 and April 1653. Each was established under an act of parliament, which specified its duration—ten to twelve months' membership, forty-one members chosen by and largely from the Rump—and powers. The councils met almost daily, usually at Whitehall. Each council set out its own business methods and procedures in a series of self-regulations and possessed its own staff, including secretaries and clerks. The impression of an increasingly assured and established body is strengthened by the detailed written records each council maintained, by its use of its own mace and seals, and by the growing power of its chief secretary to handle some business largely on his own initiative.

These councils exercised extensive powers. They were to coordinate opposition to the Stuarts, resist invasion or insurrection, preserve peace, order the militias, encourage trade, maintain foreign relations, and—most wide-ranging of all—advise and consult on any matter concerning the good of the Commonwealth*. The councils could appoint their own committees, send for people and papers, administer oaths, take securities, and imprison any who refused to obey them. In practice, each council handled a broad array of business, important and trivial. The Rump and its councils worked in close and generally trouble-free cooperation, the latter handling a mass of business that would have overwhelmed the slower and more formal mechanisms of parliament, exercising wide administrative and executive powers and often working largely on their own initiative. However, superior and ultimate power always rested with the Rump Parliament, to which difficult or contentious matters were referred for final decision. This sort of relationship, in which a council worked with an ever-present and superior parliament, also occurred during the rule of Barebone's Parliament* (July-December 1653) and of the restored Rump (May-October 1659 and from January 1660).

The second type of council was that which did not have to work with an ever-present parliament. For example, an interim council of state met from late April to early July 1653 to oversee routine governmental and administrative affairs in the aftermath of the Rump's ejection, while the army* officers planned a new government. Chosen largely by the lord general, its thirteen members comprised a mixture of soldiers and civilians, former Rumpers, and other associates of Oliver Cromwell*. Again, in October 1659, after the second ejection of the Rump, a similar body was established, though it was generally known as a committee of safety, and its work and records are shadowy and confused. It collapsed at the end of 1659. But the most powerful and durable of this type of council was that which worked with Protectors Oliver and Richard Cromwell* between December 1653 and April 1659.

The Protectorate council was a small, powerful, permanent body. Membership was stable, and just twenty men served during the Protectorate*. The council met several times a week and was supported by secretaries, clerks, and messengers. It offered counsel and advice to the lord protector, often present in person, in all aspects of government, and it oversaw a mass of routine administration and the formulation and execution of policy. In many ways it was similar to the monarch's privy council* and was often known by that name. But the council's role went much further. Under the written constitutions of 1653 and 1657, the protector alone could exercise only limited powers, and in many vital areas, particularly control over finance and the armed forces and appointment to senior offices of state, he had to obtain the consent of the majority of the council. The council's principal role was as a check on the head of state; its real power lay in its ability to prevent the protector acting in a whole range of fields unless he first obtained its consent. Some conciliar checks acted at all times; others temporarily lapsed when Protectorate parliaments were in session. To bolster conciliar power, the constitutions not only obliged the protector to seek and obtain his council's consent, but also prevented him appointing and dismissing councilors at will. On paper the Protectorate council was a powerful, independent supervisory body.

How these provisions worked in practice is hard to judge. Unlike the public role assigned to the protector, the council worked behind closed doors; its deliberations were secret and largely remained so, and even its official records, from which politically sensitive matters were omitted, give a limited picture. The council certainly spent a lot of time on routine administration and local and private business. But sufficient evidence survives to indicate that it also handled the very highest matters of state, that the protectors usually observed the constitution and sought conciliar consent where required, and that occasionally the council deflected the protector from his preferred path by persuasion or prohibition. The role of the council within the Protectorate regime is often underestimated by historians, and that of Protectors Oliver and Richard Cromwell correspondingly inflated.

Bibliography: G. E. Aylmer, *The State's Servants*, 1973; Peter Gaunt, "'The Single Person's Confidants and Dependents'? Oliver Cromwell and His Protectoral Councillors," *Historical Journal* 32 (1989): 537-560; M. A. E. Green, ed., *Calendar of State Papers Domestic Series 1649-1660*, 12 vols., 1875-1886.

Peter Gaunt

County Associations. On the outbreak of the Civil War* both the parliamentary party and the supporters of the king were obliged to reconstruct a system of local government* for those parts of the country they controlled. The king had been forced to flee from Westminster to Oxford, where he set up as much of the old central administration as had accompanied him and tried to carry on as before. Parliament*, as a representative body and a lawmaking institution, had not been designed to exercise authority and needed to invent its own institutional framework to execute policy. Both sides had to scramble to assert authority over the surviving institutions of local government. The highest priority for both king and parliament was the mobilization of troops for the regions under their control and the collection of taxes to pay for them (see Taxation and Revenue*). When either lost local power struggles to control the machinery of county government, they created parallel institutions from scratch to oppose each other. Where parliament controlled the militia, the king issued commissions of array (see Army*), and where the king controlled the commission of the peace, parliament created the county committee.

The intense localism in each county meant that there was a powerful tendency to insist that men and funds raised in the county be used primarily, if not exclusively, for its own defense and remain under its own control. Given such constraints, when at first it was necessary to build political support and there was no inclination to alienate local supporters, the central authorities on both sides had only modest numbers of men available for field forces under their direct command to move freely in an offensive capacity. It was difficult for either side to develop a coherent nationwide military strategy to win the war with large numbers of troops tied up in purely local defense. By late 1642 it became clear on both sides that for any individual county, security lay in mutually supporting arrangements with neighboring shires, and voluntary county associations linking them in larger units for self defense were the result. The Southeastern Association of Kent, Sussex, and Hampshire was quickly created in 1643 only because of the danger posed by Sir Ralph Hopton's invasion of the region from his base in the royalist* west country.

To the competing central governments, the county associations represented a modest reduction in localism and a limited but welcome gain in flexibility using local resources for national purposes. On the parliamentarian* side the regional forces in East Anglia under the earl of Manchester, with Oliver Cromwell* commanding his cavalry, in Yorkshire under Sir Thomas Fairfax*, and in the southwest under Sir William Waller were as important as parliament's main field force under the earl of Essex (Robert Devereux*) and on balance more successful. As the war dragged on into its second full year in a military stalemate, the pressure grew for a more efficient and centralized authority to overcome the limitations of localism. The loose cooperation among the associated counties was inevitably subjected to considerable strain whenever there were competing dangers to be worried about. Some counties were secure, others buffeted from every direction. Many of the associations simply collapsed as counties failed to respond to their neighbors' emergencies. Some associations were too large to be effective. In others, jealousies between local commanders inhibited cooperation. Overburdened Shropshire was linked to five neighboring associations and so could hardly be counted on for assistance by any of them.

Parliament, impressed with the relative success of the Eastern Association in maintaining an effective force in East Anglia, turned to it as a model for the other associations, but unlike the others, the forces of the Eastern Association were in effect nationalized and became the core of the parliament's newly created New Model Army*. Only the relative security of East Anglia from royalist incursions made it possible to strip that area of its own defensive force to carry on offensive operations directed by the central government. On the parliamentary side the effectiveness of the central administration first in collecting taxes and levying men, then in beginning to win the war, eventually reduced the ability of local authorities to resist direction from Westminster in defense of more local interests.

Bibliography: Clive Holmes, *The Eastern Association and the English Civil War*, 1974; John Morrill, *The Revolt of the Provinces: Conservatives and Radicals in the English Civil War, 1630-1650*, 1976.

S. J. Stearns

Court versus Country. Contrasts between "court" and "country" were drawn by contemporary English poets, commentators, polemicists, and politicians, from the 1540s into the eighteenth century. But the particular currency of this terminology among historians originated in the gentry controversy*, a debate conducted between the 1940s and 1960s about the origins of the "English Revolution" of 1640-1660. It was sparked by R. H. Tawney's seminal article, "The Rise of the Gentry, 1558-1640" (*Economic History Review*, 1941). Tawney did not oppose "court and country" explicitly, but in identifying a horizontal social cleavage leading to "revolution" in the growth of two opposed social and economic entities—a declining feudal Crown and aristocracy and a rising bourgeois gentry—he implied something like a court-country split. The full deployment of the terminology came in H. R. Trevor-Roper's response (1953, 1965), which reversed Tawney's progressive dynamic—the court was capitalist and modern, the country landowning and backward looking—and shifted the axis of social cleavage toward the vertical, opposing a declining "mere" country gentry (often also dissident Puritans* and Catholics*), who revolted in desperation against an Anglican* greater gentry and nobility waxing rich on the patronage and offices offered by a newly centralizing Renaissance court.

In the 1960s and 1970s, while the "storm over the gentry" blew itself out, the trail blazed by Trevor-Roper was pushed onward by others. Alan Everitt's work on county history (which inspired many later local studies) emphasized the isolationism of the "county community" and appeared to strengthen the case for a prewar divergence between a royal court* paying little heed to the concerns of the country and a "country" dissociating itself (notably by parliamentary opposition) from an abhorrent "court." Perez Zagorin's ambitious *The Court and the Country: The Beginning of the English Revolution* (1969) set out to demolish "horizontal" class-conflict explanations of the "revolution" and to characterize the vertical division within the noble-gentry elite, using court-country terminology as an organizing principle (and providing evidence of its contemporary currency). For Zagorin the divide was not economic but ideological, between those "diffuse, yet real...collectivities" that were "recognized partisans in a political struggle" beginning in 1603, accelerating in the 1620s, and ending only in a wholesale regrouping that led to the Civil War* in 1641-1642. The country was a continuous identifiable group in parliament*, in Lords and Commons, composed of substantial men with solid local power bases but national horizons and concerns; the court was broadly (but problematically) defined as all those who held paid offices under the Crown. If the content of ideological division was relatively meager—a dispute over the boundaries between law and the royal prerogative*, with no serious attempt (before 1640) to raise the issue of sovereignty—this was partly because the country was conservative, aiming to restore a traditional balance upset by Stuart innovation. Religion, in the shape of the "Puritan" reaction to Laudianism (see William Laud*), was not fully related to the court-country dichotomy and remained largely subordinated to constitutional struggles in parliament. But Zagorin did posit a wider cultural division, between the foreign art, fawning poetry, and fantastic masques of an isolated and self-obsessed court on one hand and country reality on the other. This last theme was developed by P. Thomas (1973) into a comprehensive clash between "two cultures," literary and visual.

The 1970s saw this picture become textbook orthodoxy. Lawrence Stone, drawing together the results of the gentry controversy (in which he had been a key participant) in an ambitious survey, *The Causes of the English Revolution* (1972), used the court-country division (though with greater caution than Zagorin) to describe a large part of the "multiple dysfunction" in the English polity after the 1580s: "by the reign of Charles I* . . . the two words Court and Country [had] come to mean political, psychological, and moral opposites." Robert Ashton's *The English Civil War* (1979) also used the concepts prominently as part of its explanatory basis.

But in the late 1970s, with the advent of revisionism, came a comprehensive assault on the court-country antithesis, in the form of a critical dissection of the monolithic integrity of the two entities. This exploited the contradictions between the localism of the Everitt school of county studies and the parliament-centered country movement for reform of the court described by Zagorin and Trevor-Roper. John Morrill (1976) distinguished between an "official" country, which approximated to Zagorin's "party" in parliament, and a "pure" localist country, as represented on the backbenches and in the constituencies. The first stood for a change of policies at court (in favor of parliamentary and against prerogative finance) and their own promotion to office, but the second nursed localist suspicion of all central politics and fiscal demands and allied with the "official" country only when the latter were in opposition. Derek Hirst (1978) argued further that, at least during the 1620s, pure country localism and disaffection was largely "earthed" to leadership at court and in the privy council*, which in turn was linked with and in some cases identical to the alleged parliamentary country leadership. In addition "the need to present an effective case by means of addresses to the center undermined the coherence of localism"; an "unmitigated espousal of the 'country' position" was, in terms of local political survival, "non-viable." Despite the storms in parliament, there was thus basic ideological consensus and no breakdown in local government* before 1639-1640.

Conrad Russell (1976, 1979) administered the most wide-ranging attack on the court-country dichotomy as the product of hindsight reading back the deep divisions of 1640-1642 into the preceding period. Russell denied any long-established structural or ideological conflict between either government and opposition or court and country parties, and instead identified the parliamentary cacophony of 1604-1629 (where not itself exaggerated by hindsight) as a product of two phenomena: (1) the ephemeral chatter of the shifting (and non-ideological) factional disputes of a many-faceted court which, even under the 1st duke of Buckingham (George Villiers*), still maintained healthy links with the localities being played out in parliament; and (2) a constant background noise of localist resistance to any fiscal demands, whether imposed by parliament or prerogative. Again Russell's "revision" owed much to the growing body of local studies, highlighting with new precision the complex political interaction between center and locality. To this was added the insights of Sir Geoffrey Elton and David Starkey on the political workings of the Tudor court. The result was a picture of essential continuity with the late-Elizabethan world, of a "permanent" politics of king, court, and council extending into the occasional assemblies of Lords and Commons in parliament, all of which was periodically (but neither consistently nor continuously) divided by essentially unthreatening factional conflict and (more seriously) subject to strain (especially in wartime) due to the burden imposed on the localities by the fiscal and administrative demands of the center. Contemporary references by members of parliament to the need to square themselves with the country—their neighbors, constituents, or both—show their awareness of these competing forces, not the existence of any country party. "Even in 1628, there was not so much an ideological gulf between court and country, as ideological gulfs within the court itself." Overall revisionism, where it admitted court-country conflict, saw it as a center-locality conflict whose competing demands were played out in the minds of individual councilors, peers, and MPs, who were not divided into hard-and-fast political groups but rather united in broad ideological outlook and interests. Kevin Sharpe (1978, 1979) added further arguments against any long-standing court-country division before 1640 by drawing attention to personal factional conflicts in court and council spilling into parliament and to a shared world of political and cultural ideas underpinning the politics of both center and locality. Sharpe (1987) later extended this to a comprehensive denial of any court-country divide in literary culture.

By the late 1980s the revisionists in their turn had drawn criticism, from post-revisionists (a term evidently coined by Christopher Hill). This body of closely related work by Richard Cust, Anne Hughes, Peter Lake, Thomas Cogswell, Johan Sommerville, and others (e.g., Cust and Hughes eds., 1989) accepted and accentuated the revisionist picture of structural unity of the worlds of center and locality. Indeed Hughes decisively rejected the revisionist stress on pure backwoods localism and found national awareness at the lowest levels of local politics. But in place of the ideological unity that revisionism claimed followed from this interpenetration of court and country, post-revisionists have stressed a ubiquitous and developed political vocabulary of division, current over the 1603-1640 period in the politics of the counties, parliament, and privy council alike and applied to both local and national issues. They use the contemporary terms *court* and *country* to describe these complexes of political attitudes. A country stance at the hustings, in the Commons, or on the lips of a "popular" lord or councilor stressed the centrality of parliaments in political life as a forum of wide consultation to check the narrow self-interest of the court; a continuing belief that the rights of the subject were threatened by the prerogative, both fiscal and legal; and, increasingly in the 1620s, a religious perspective opposing "popish" (Arminian*) counsels at court with staunch Protestantism. An opposing view was present in county politics and in parliament but was most closely associated with influential voices at court and on the council (and with the basic beliefs of James I* and Charles I themselves). This distrusted country ideas and agitation as dangerously "popular" and instead stressed order, obedience, hierarchy, and prerogative power; from the early 1620s the group of counselors sponsoring this drew extra theoretical ammunition from Arminian divines.

These opposed positions are seen as based on a fundamental divide in political theory, identified by Sommerville (1986), which Cust and Hughes see hardening by the late 1620s into rival conspiracy theories. Yet rather than rebuild the monolithic "parties" of earlier accounts, post-revisionism has retained a revisionist view of fluidity between them. Country rhetoric in particular was "vague and ambiguous" and its relation to clear constitutional ideas "blurred." In county and parliamentary politics, accusations of excessive "popularity" or of association with the court could be used interchangeably to smear an opponent. Moreover, divisions between these attitudes split the privy council itself, in the struggles over Charles I's "new counsels" of 1625-1626, between "popular" or "authoritarian" sympathizers (Cust, 1987). The revisionists' structural and ideological "one world" is thus replaced in post-revisionism by a similarly unified political structure, extending from privy council to quarter sessions, but split at every level by real ideological division. One aspect of post-revisionism has been to resume the search for social and economic change as an explanation for these political phenomena, particularly in the development of a broad and growing, well-informed political nation below the level of the gentry, committed to Protestantism and parliament, to which a sector of the nobility and gentry formulated in this period a popular appeal. But overall, like the revisionists, post-revisionists have been primarily concerned to characterize and explain the distinctive politics of the 1603-1640 period. Their use of court-country terminology (like Zagorin's indeed), though meant to explain the breakdown of royal government in 1640-1641, does not claim to explain allegiance in the Civil War (Hughes, 1991).

John Morrill's comment on court-country historiography in 1976 remains true: the country has received far more attention and been worked out more convincingly than has the court. Here a fruitful approach may lie in a distinction between the "public" apparatus of privy council and great officers and the monarch's "private" personal agents and agendas, operating through his bedchamber.

Bibliography: Richard Cust, *The Forced Loan and English Politics, 1626-28*, 1987; Richard Cust and Anne Hughes, eds., *Conflict in Early Stuart England*, 1989; Derek Hirst, "Court, Country, and Politics before 1629," in Kevin Sharpe, ed., *Faction and Parliament: Essays on Early Stuart History*, 1978; Anne Hughes, *The Causes of the English Civil War*, 1991; John Morrill, *The Revolt of the Provinces: Conservatives and Radicals in the English Civil War, 1630-50*, 1976; Conrad Russell, "Parliamentary History in Perspective, 1604-1629," *History* 61 (1976); and *Parliaments and English Politics, 1621-29*, 1979; Kevin Sharpe, "Introduction: Parliamentary History 1603-1629: In or Out of Perspective?" and "The Earl of Arundel, His Circle, and the Opposition to the Duke of Buckingham, 1618-28," in *Faction and Parliament: Essays on Early Stuart History*, 1978; Kevin Sharpe, *Criticism and Compliment: The Politics of Literature in the England of Charles I*, 1987; J. P. Sommerville, *Politics and Ideology in England, 1603-40*, 1986; Lawrence Stone, *The Causes of the English Revolution*, 1972; H. R. Trevor-Roper, "The Gentry, 1540-1640," *Economic History Review Supplement* 1 (1953); "The General Crisis of the Seventeenth Century," in T. Aston, ed., *The General Crisis of the Seventeenth Century*, 1965; Perez Zagorin, *The Court and the Country: The Beginning of the English Revolution*, 1969.

Neil Cuddy

Court, Royal. The definition of the Stuart court has been much debated (see Court versus Country*). Contemporaries sometimes used the term court to describe the permanent complex of palaces, government departments, and aristocratic town houses in Westminster and the West End of London* or (especially post-1660) to refer to a political grouping, primarily in parliament*. But there was also a precise contemporary usage: the court was wherever the king was lodged—at an inn, on board a ship, at one of his greater subjects' country seats, or at a royal hunting lodge or palace. This "institutional" court consisted of three divisions: the household, under the board of greencloth; the chamber, under the lord chamberlain; and the bedchamber, under the groom of the stool/first gentleman of the bedchamber. It was the latter two departments, especially the bedchamber, that invariably accompanied the king. The household operated at full strength only when the king was occupying one of his palaces or (pre-1642) when formally "on progress" during the summer months.

Between 1603 and 1642, the household continued, as it had since its last major reorganizations in 1471 and 1526, to express traditional "magnificence" in lavish feasting at about eighty communal "tables" provided to the king's officers at his expense. The board of greencloth—presided over by the lord steward (filled 1615-1625, 1626-1630, 1660-1688), the treasurer and comptroller (the steward's deputies during vacancies), the cofferer, masters of the household, and so on—administered this, overseeing about twenty service departments (kitchen, larder, buttery, pantry, etc.), which provided and prepared the food. It also enforced purveyance, the royal prerogative* to take up supplies at fixed (and, due to inflation, by now beneficially low) prices. This was probably the country's biggest single financial and logistical undertaking and certainly the largest item of royal peacetime expenditure.

But by the 1600s the household was something of a dinosaur. In 1526 it had been identical to the greater nobility's households, but bigger—"the house of houses principal of England." But after 1550 it stood still while noble households shrank to become cheaper and more efficient. England was also out of date compared to the much wealthier monarchy of France, which did not maintain tables, but instead paid courtiers dining expenses or "boardwages." English "magnificence" was thus widely seen as anachronistic. One wit described the household as an agency for putting money down the privy. From 1604 to 1610 attempts were made to replace most tables with boardwages and exchange purveyance for a parliamentary tax. But since they failed, "magnificence" persisted until Charles I* abandoned London in 1642. At the Restoration* purveyance was exchanged for a parliamentary revenue, yet the prewar tables were fully revived. This soon proved insupportable. In 1663 all but a handful of tables for above-stairs attendants on duty were replaced with boardwages. The greencloth now oversaw a mere staff canteen; the household, its cost cut by two-thirds, was no longer the largest item of peacetime expenditure; and the Restoration monarchy had ceased to invest chiefly in magnificent hospitality as a means of confirming its political links with the nation.

The second department was the chamber, under the lord chamberlain, vice-chamberlain, gentlemen ushers (daily and quarter waiters, and of the privy chamber), and the treasurer of the chamber. The lord chamberlain controlled several offshoots: the offices of the revels, tents, ceremonies, and jewels (each under their respective master), and of works (under a surveyor). But the core of the department ran the "public" court of ceremony and display, a sequence of state apartments in each royal residence (and always improvised elsewhere), consisting of the guard chamber, presence chamber, and privy chamber. Here they regulated access. In addition, guard and presence, open to the gentry and above, each had a security force—the yeomen of the guard, under their captain (considerably augmented after 1660), and in the presence, fifty gentlemen pensioners (attending in quarterly shifts), under a captain and a lieutenant.

The chamber under the early Tudors had provided a focus for the royal retinue by attaching substantial gentry to the court as gentlemen pensioners and gentlemen of the privy chamber. The latter had been of particular importance, monopolizing as members of a separate department the king's "private" body service and sharing their close access only with the privy council*. But during 1553-1603, the reigns of two women, the privy chamber and its personnel had joined the "public" outer court under the lord chamberlain. As reinvented in 1603, the privy chamber did retain some of its former distinctly private character, restricted to its own staff of four gentlemen ushers, forty-eight gentlemen (thirty-two between 1610 and 1625), four carvers, cupbearers, and sewers (added about 1610 to serve at privy chamber dinners, when spectators might also be admitted), and eight grooms—a quarter of whom attended at any one time—together with the privy council, some legal and administrative officers, and others named in an entrée list.

By the early 1620s all peers and bishops also had privy chamber access, and Charles I's* ordinances officially sanctioned this. Since the gentlemen of the privy chamber had lost both their fees and their efficient duties—in body-service (effectively in 1553, finally to the bedchamber in 1603) and in serving at dinner (to specialists like the cupbearers)—the importance of the place as a means of retaining the locally important declined. What attraction lingered was negative: immunities from taxation*, arrest for debt, jury service, and local office, which Charles I increasingly defined and enforced. By 1641 the gentlemen proper shared these cheap favors with about 250 extraordinary gentlemen, who did not even have to attend. In 1660-1661 the privy chamber establishment was restored, with its immunities (which remained important into the next century), while any distinction between privy chamber and the other outer chambers was abandoned, since its access was now formally open to "any gentleman of good rank and note."

The bedchamber formed a private inner sanctum at the end of these public chambers. Though closely based on Henry VIII's privy chamber (which had also been independent of the lord chamberlain's control), the bedchamber was effectively a new department, set up by James I's* ordinances (which were confirmed, with minor amendments, by subsequent monarchs up to the Hanoverians). Its territory comprised the withdrawing chamber (next in sequence to the privy chamber), the bedchamber itself, and the privy galleries and lodgings, a complex of private apartments (libraries, closets, bathrooms, and so on). Its personnel consisted of the groom of the stool/first gentleman of the bedchamber (head of department), six (rising to ten) gentlemen, the gentleman of the robes, eight grooms of the bedchamber, and six pages. The first gentleman lodged closest to the king's bedchamber, and the other gentlemen and grooms depending on the palace or lodge also had quarters in the privy lodgings. At night one of the gentlemen slept at the foot of the royal bed; two grooms slept in the withdrawing chamber. By day the bedchamber dressed, fed, and constantly attended the king.

Only the bedchamber's staff enjoyed this close access as of right. All others had to ask for an audience, and the withdrawing chamber was set aside for this. Councilors and some other officers had a right to wait there to be called in; audiences were often conducted there. The bedchamber's constant private access gave its members a large role in patronage, administration, and politics. Before 1615 they were almost all Scottish. Dunbar, James's chief minister in Scotland* in the late 1590s, supplied after 1603-1604 the bedchamber foundation for Robert Cecil*, earl of Salisbury's regime as conciliar chief minister in England. After Salisbury's failure in the parliament of 1610*, the center of gravity swung from the privy council to the successive bedchamber favorites, the earl of Somerset (Robert Carr*, 1611-1615) and the 1st duke of Buckingham (George Villiers*, 1615-1628).

Buckingham's rise brought into the department his kin and dependents, so that by 1622 the bedchamber was split almost equally between English and Scots. Buckingham became still more powerful in Charles I's bedchamber after 1625. He was made first gentleman in a department now composed of domestic retainers and under-age royal kin (like the duke of Lennox and the marquess of Hamilton). Buckingham's monopoly of close access and the great power over counsel and administration that came with it may account for much of his acute unpopularity in 1625-1628. But after his assassination, the bedchamber's active administrative and political role declined, largely because Charles I kept his distance even from his closest attendants. Successive grooms of the stool/first gentlemen—the earls of Carlisle (1631-1636) and Holland (1636-1642)—were important figures but not the great powers James I's favorites had been.

In 1660-1661 the pre-war bedchamber ordinances were reenacted and the bedchamber set up anew. It was larger than before, with twelve (rising by 1682 to seventeen) gentlemen, including supernumeraries, and twelve (rising to eighteen) grooms. Its political role revived, largely due to Charles II's* propensity to pursue a secret policy at variance with that of his formal privy council. The phrase "backstairs intrigue" entered the language. Indeed Charles at once withdrew further into bedchamber privacy and gained greater freedom to act independently of his official ministers. By 1662 he had retreated to a new private withdrawing chamber and bedchamber (where the bedchamber's staff continued to serve him). The old withdrawing chamber enlarged its former function to become the central public audience chamber of the court (the "drawing room," which developed further as an event under Anne* and the Hanoverians), and the old bedchamber effectively became a state bedchamber for formal audiences. All this followed the French model, which Charles had experienced first hand in exile.

The difficulties of Edward Hyde*, earl of Clarendon and his fall in 1867 were partly due to his lack of control of the bedchamber. In the Cabal* ministry two gentlemen of the bedchamber, the 2d duke of Buckingham (George Villiers*) and the earl of Lauderdale (John Maitland*), respectively, represented the Dissenters* and ran Scotland, while the Catholics* were represented by Lord Chamberlain Arlington, who had subordinate bedchamber contacts. (Buckingham and Arlington indeed promoted rival royal mistresses—the former, Nell Gwynne*, the latter, the duchess of Portsmouth.) In 1673 the Cabal's fall and the rise of the Anglican* parliamentary manager, the earl of Danby (Thomas Osborne*), coincided with revised bedchamber ordinances, which took account of the earlier changes in palace geography and buttressed Charles's withdrawal. The Popish Plot of 1678* and Exclusion Crisis* (1678-1681) resulted in both a tightening of bedchamber security and a further disjunction of Charles's backstairs policies from those of his formal showpiece council (revamped in 1679 with the king's chief opponent, the earl of Shaftesbury (Anthony Ashley Cooper*), as president). Charles's retreat culminated in 1682-1685 in another move to new lodgings and further restrictions on access.

James II* confirmed these changes, but made a significant new departure in immediately allowing the privy council foreign affairs committee to attend in the state bedchamber. That eroded the distance between the traditional spheres of public and private, in both access and politics, and gave an ominous sign that under James, Charles II's usually hidden agenda of Catholic and Dissenter toleration would remain hidden no longer.

Bibliography: G. E. Aylmer, *The King's Servants: The Civil Service of Charles I, 1625-42*, 1973; David Starkey, et al., *The English Court from the Wars of the Roses to the English Civil War*, 1987.

                                                                    Neil Cuddy

Courts. See Common Law and Courts; Ecclesiastical Courts; Prerogative Courts.

Covenant (National, 1638). In February 1638, seven months after the first anti-prayer book agitation in Edinburgh, the leadership of the supplicants (opponents of the Anglican prayer book) decided to produce a document that would allow them to face an intransigent Charles I* with the unity of Scotland*. The nobles, lairds, burgesses, and ministers selected the Rev. Alexander Henderson and the lawyer Archibald Johnston of Wariston to draft the National Covenant. Johnston, inspired by a fanatical Presbyterianism* and a masterful legal mind, had the lion's share of drafting the Covenant. Work started on 23 February and was completed two days later, with redrafting on 26 and 27 February by the earl of Rothes and Lords Balmerino and Loudoun.

The National Covenant consisted of two portions. The lengthier, the confession of 1581 and a recitation of the acts of the Scottish estates since 1567 against Roman Catholics*, provided the legal undergirding of what could be considered a treasonous activity. The document contained no promises to uphold a Presbyterian ecclesiastical government but explicitly rejected Catholicism, implicitly denying the king's religious policies: "The same cause of maintaining the true Religion and his Majesty's Authority" provided the basis for future controversy within the movement, with religious interests firing the radicals and some form of royalism* inspiring the moderates and conservatives.

The National Covenant had firm roots in Scottish political and religious culture. From the 1400s to about 1603 nobles and lairds had regularly drawn up bonds (of manrent) to create alliances against rivals. The bonds of the Lords of Congregations in the 1550s and more importantly the Negative Confession of 1581, signed even by James VI (see James I*), formed the basis for the new religious bond. The Reformed concept of federal (contractual) theology, in which the God-man relationship had become envisaged as a two-way street in salvation (as opposed to John Calvin's view of unconditional election by God), had spread among the anti-prayer book clergy before the 1630s. Thus the National Covenant in religious terms asserted Scotland's special relationship with the Divinity and thereby made its adherents a new group of Israelites. Therefore, the Covenant fused a powerful positive current to the negative charge of anti-Catholicism.

When the National Covenant first appeared publicly on 28 February 1638 in Greyfriar's Kirk, Edinburgh, the anti-prayer book petitioners had a document that would be easily recognized within the Scottish politico-religious milieu. Nobles and lairds signed the National Covenant; the following day ministers and burgesses subscribed. Once these groups had signed, the Covenanters* quickly carried copies throughout most lowland shires with success, excepting Aberdeen and Banff, and in the Highlands, save for Argyll. In March 1638 an altered version of the Covenant was circulated in the royalist shires of Aberdeen and Banff. Covenanters solicited signatures or marks of all males of a parish. Their success in this endeavor was singular, which allowed the opponents of Charles I to present evidence of nearly unanimous national backing.

The Crown unsuccessfully attempted to counter the National Covenant by two policies. When asked whether the document was treasonable, the king's advocate, Sir Thomas Hope of Craighall, stunned his royalist colleagues on the Scottish privy council by denying that it constituted an illegal act. In September Charles, spurred by James, 3d marquis of Hamilton, offered the King's Covenant to the nation to mobilize his supporters. The Covenanters sabotaged the royalist maneuver by allowing their supporters to sign it, making it impossible to distinguish the king's adherents from his opponents. Furthermore, the King's Covenant lacked the dedicated support of the ministers in gathering signatures.

Bibliography: J. S. Morrill, ed., *The Scottish National Covenant in its British Context, 1638-51*,1990; David Stevenson, *The Scottish Revolution, 1637-1644*, 1973.

Edward M. Furgol

Covenanter Rebellion (1679). Covenanters* were Presbyterian* adherents of the Covenant* of 1638 opposing Charles I's* attempt to Anglicanize (see Anglicanism*) the Scottish Kirk* and of the Solemn League and Covenant* with the English parliament* in 1643. They opposed Charles II's* restoration of episcopacy in Scotland*, and attempts to suppress nonconformist conventicles led to minor rebellions in 1666. Letters of Indulgence restored some banished ministers in 1669, but conventicles continued. In 1679 violence flared over measures against nonconformists, including the death penalty for preaching at a field conventicle, heavy fines for absence from Sunday church, and free quartering of troops on the Covenanter southwest. To prevent further rebellion, troops were increased by order of the earl of Lauderdale (John Maitland*), a former Covenanter who became commissioner of Scotland in 1669.

Open revolt erupted with the murder on 3 May 1679 of James Sharpe, archbishop of St. Andrews and a former Covenanting minister, hacked to death on Magus Muir by nine Covenanters led by John Balfour of Kinloch, his brother-in-law Hackston of Rathillet, James Russel, and Robert Hamilton. The assassins and their troops were pursued into Hamilton by a small force of dragoons under John Graham of Claverhouse (later Viscount Dundee), who planned to attack the armed conventicle at Loudoun Hill on 1 June 1679. But the Covenanters, warned of his approach, deployed three squadrons of horse and four battalions of infantry at Drumclog, a moorland on the borders of Ayrshire and Lanarkshire. The rebels outnumbered Claverhouse's troops almost ten to one, although the Covenanters were poorly armed and encumbered with several thousand noncombatants. However, they had a strong position, with their front covered by marshy ground impassable to a mounted force. Undismayed, Claverhouse dismounted his dragoons and advanced them within pistol shot of the enemy. Incensed by their accurate fire, the Covenanters charged across the marsh, striking Claverhouse's center and left flank with considerable force. Seeing Claverhouse carried away by his wounded and uncontrollable horse, the government troops fled; over forty fell in the battle or the pursuit. Emboldened, the Covenanters attacked Glasgow the next day, though unsuccessfully.

A thoroughly surprised and alarmed government sent James, duke of Monmouth, to command the royalists. Monmouth fielded about 5,000 militia and regular troops against the unprepared and largely leaderless Covenanters at Bothwell Bridge. The rebels were seriously divided between moderates (including most of the ministers), who were prepared to recognize royal authority and sought only a free parliament and a general assembly, and extremists, who deplored the acceptance of indulgences by some of the clergy and whose loyalty to the Crown was questionable. Monmouth routed the Covenanters on June 22, killing between 600 and 700 and taking 1,200 prisoners to a camp near Greyfriars Kirk in Edinburgh. Toward the remainder, Monmouth adopted a conciliatory policy, which permitted among other things indoor conventicles. The wounded were lodged in George Heriot's Hospital and attended by town physicians. Within two weeks all but 340 signed a bond not to take up arms against the king. In November, 210 who refused were put on a ship bound for West Indies plantations*; all perished in a storm near the Orkneys on December 10.

The defeat and Monmouth's leniency (opposed by Claverhouse) broke the movement; only hard-core irreconcilables continued the struggle during the 1680s (the "Killing Time"). A minor rising led by preacher Richard Cameron in 1680 was easily suppressed, the Test Act* of 1681 which required ministers and officeholders to repudiate covenants heralded further repression, and the support of the 9th earl of Argyll (Archibald Campbell*) for Monmouth's Rebellion* in 1685 led to intensified persecution. Presbyterianism was finally restored in Scotland by William * and Mary* after the Glorious Revolution*.

Bibliography: Ian Cowan, *The Scottish Covenanters*, 1976; J. D. Douglas, *Light in the North*, 1964; J. K. Hewison, *The Covenanters*, 1913.

Martin J. Manning

Covenanters. The Covenanters represent one of many attempts by early modern Europeans to cope with the problem of an unsympathetic absentee monarch. James VI and I*, having established royal control of Scotland*, counseled his heirs to prevent a union of the nobles and Presbyterians* (clergy, burgesses, and minor gentry). His own policies after 1616 and those of Charles I* from 1625 facilitated an alliance of the two groups. The imposition of a prayer book in July 1637 provided the spark that ignited the smoldering discontent into open defiance of the king (see Bishops' Wars*). Charles's opponents (initially called supplicants, from their process of petitioning against the prayer book) were called Covenanters after the promulgation of the National Covenant* in February 1638.

The Covenanters were a nationally oriented party seeking to create the impression that all of Scotland was opposed to royal religious policies. Between 1638 and 1641 the Covenanters sought and gained religious and constitutional reforms that transformed Scotland into a noble-dominated state. The need to establish a Presbyterian system of church government followed from the nobles' desire to eliminate bishops (the monarchy's most loyal ally in national and local politics) and the Presbyterians' wish to create the Melvillian church (one independent of secular control). In step with the religious change was the political alteration of a country utterly dependent on royal prerogative* to one where landholders initiated policy. The Covenanters had commenced the secular revolution in 1638 with the creation of the tables (a committee of nobles, lairds, burgesses, and ministers at the national level) and civil presbyteries in the localities. The royal privy council, while functioning for much of the 1638-1641 period, became a cipher. With the meeting of the Scottish estates in 1638-1641, the Covenanters established the committee system for governing Scotland. Locally, committees of war or the shire carried out instructions from the estates. Charles, desperate for assistance against the English parliament*, assented to the Covenanters' changes in 1641.

To ensure the survival of their revolution, the Covenanters required a British federal system relying on supranational committees. In addition, Ireland* demanded the Covenanters' attention because the king could use troops raised there to invade Scotland. While Scotland was the stage of the Covenanters, they could not ignore the other two kingdoms. Of equal importance was the Covenanters' recognition that they must create a reliable military force (on the model of Sweden's) to count in British affairs. From 1638 they successfully pursued that goal, the aim of any self-respecting early modern state.

The Covenanters' first foray outside Scotland after 1641 was into Ireland. After the Irish Roman Catholic rising in Ulster in October 1641 (see Irish Rebellion*), the Scottish estates speedily accepted the king's request for an army to subdue the rebels. Negotiations with the English followed, and in March 1642 the Covenanters began sending forces into Ulster. For the next six years Ulster and the army there would be an important focus of Covenanter policy.

Initially the Covenanters were neutral when the English Civil War* began. In August 1643, fearing that a royalist* victory in England would lead to royal interference in Scotland, the Covenanters accepted the Long Parliament's* request for alliance in the Solemn League and Covenant*. The Covenanters willingly supported efforts to defeat the king until the animosity of the English Independents* toward a Presbyterian Church of England (see Anglicanism*) became impossible to ignore. For the Covenanters, only a single religious settlement could ensure the stability of the united kingdoms. The king's arrival in the camp of the Scots army at Newark in May 1646 complicated relations with the parliamentarians*. With the Covenanters continuing to demand Presbyterianism as the established religion for the three kingdoms, negotiations with Charles and their allies faltered. Arranging a settlement of back pay owed to the Scots army in England further complicated matters. Eventually, by late December, arrangements for payments to the army had been made; the king was to be handed over to the English when the army departed in January 1647.

Meanwhile in Scotland, the marquis of Argyll (Archibald Campbell*) maintained the control he had been exercising since 1643. However, he faced opposition from more conservative Covenanters, who had opposed the surrender of the king. The division in the movement, enshrined in the National Covenant's dual loyalties to king and religion, as well as discontent with their former allies, created a political crisis. The Covenanters split largely along class lines, with nobles and lairds and Scots supporting accommodation with the king, while lesser lairds, burgesses, and a tiny fraction of nobles led by Argyll argued for a Presbyterian settlement above all else. The former triumphed in 1648 when parliament accepted the Engagement* but fell from power as a result of military defeats.

The opposition Kirk party* ruled Scotland until late 1650, when power sharing became necessary. It followed a policy of severe ecclesiastical discipline combined with total enmity to Engagers (see Engagement and Engagers*), royalists, and English sectaries. Avoidance of conquest by the English became the priority of all save the radical Covenanters (Remonstrants, Protesters). Possibilities for prolonging resistance to the English following the defeats of September 1651 foundered on distrust. The nightmare of direct English rule (albeit by sectarian Protestants, not Laudian* Anglicans*) became reality. By 1660 most surviving Covenanters had shelved dreams of a triune Presbyterian monarchic state (with British committees freely chosen by parliaments checking royal power) for the vain hope of Scotland as a special case receiving Presbyterianism by royal assent.

Bibliography: J. S. Morrill, ed., *The Scottish National Covenant in Its British Context, 1638-51*, 1991; David Stevenson, *The Scottish Revolution, 1637-1644*, 1973.

Edward M. Furgol

Cranfield, Lionel, Earl of Middlesex (1575-1645). Cranfield was apprenticed to Richard Shepard, one of the Merchant Adventurers (see Cloth Trade*; Trading Companies*), whose daughter Elizabeth he married, thereby escaping two years of service. With Shepard's assistance, he traded profitably with the Merchant Adventurers and became a member of the Company of Mercers, whom he later represented at the royal court*. The handsome Cranfield proved an astute merchant and investor. He eclipsed his mentor and acquired a substantial fortune and influence in London's* commercial circles. He gained the earl of Northampton's sponsorship at court and a knighthood in July 1613. He was appointed surveyor-general of the customs and elected to the Addled Parliament* of 1614 for Hythe. After Northampton's death, which was followed by that of Cranfield's wife, he cultivated the 1st duke of Buckingham (George Villiers*), James I's* favorite, who profited from investments Cranfield and Northampton had suggested. James noted that Cranfield "made so many projects for my profit that Buckingham" supported him.

Aided by Buckingham, Cranfield became master of requests in 1616, keeper of the great wardrobe in 1618, master of the court of wards and chief commissioner of the navy* in 1619, and a member of the privy council* in 1620. He worked prodigiously to end corruption, reduce expenses, eliminate waste, duplication, and extravagance, and impose a degree of accountability. In 1621 he married a cousin of Lady Buckingham, Anne Bret.

In the contentious parliament of 1621*, Cranfield's reputation as a reformer and his financial skills enabled him to mediate between the interests of the government and the House of Commons. He was made Baron Cranfield and named lord high treasurer in 1621 and then given the first earldom of Middlesex in 1622.

At the pinnacle of power, Cranfield was often forced to give unwanted advice. He could neither provide adequate rewards for Buckingham's ever-increasing entourage, nor supply the king's extravagant generosity, nor meet the promises of financial assistance both made to participants in the Thirty Years War*. Along with opposing land sales, Cranfield angered both Buckingham and Prince Charles by the slow delivery of funds supplied for their trip to Spain (see Spanish Match*). His consistent opposition to war earned him enemies in parliament* and at court. While his many reforms and innovations failed to satisfy the expanding financial needs of the government during his treasurership, Cranfield increased the value of his own lands from £33,000 to over £100,000.

Amid the clamor for war in 1624, Cranfield's numerous enemies, including Sir Edward Coke* and Sir Edwin Sandys, accused Cranfield of taking bribes and of mismanagement of military ordnance, the wardrobe, and wardship. Buckingham joined the popular cry for war with Spain and the attack against Cranfield, its chief opponent. In May Cranfield was impeached (see Impeachment*), deprived of all his offices, fined £50,000, and imprisoned in the Tower of London. He was soon released and secured a full pardon from Charles I* in 1625, at the cost of some property.

Cranfield spent the next two decades protecting his investments and attending to the problems of his family. He was restored to his seat in the House of Lords in May 1640, and he died on 6 August 1645, survived by his wife and two sons.

Bibliography: Menna Prestwich, *Cranfield, Politics and Profit under the Early Stuarts*, 1966.

Sheldon Hanft

Cromwell, Oliver (1599-1658). Cromwell was born on 25 April 1599 in Huntingdon, the only surviving son of Robert Cromwell, a gentleman of limited means. He was educated at the Huntingdon Free Grammar School and Sidney Sussex College, Cambridge. He married Elizabeth Bouchier, the daughter of a wealthy London* fur dealer, in 1620. Relatively little is known about Cromwell's life, but he was clearly a man of humble circumstances, with an income that fluctuated between £100 and £300 per annum. He seems to have had neither the experience in governing nor the military training to prepare him for the role he would play during the Civil War*. Most of the first forty years of his life were spent in relative obscurity in Huntingdon, where he lived until 1631, and St. Ives, where he lived from 1631 to 1636. Although he was elected to the parliament of 1628-1629* as a member for Huntingdon, he played a very minor role in that parliament, which produced the Petition of Right*. More significant for explaining his actions later in his life was the spiritual crisis that he probably underwent in the 1630s, resulting in a Calvinist* conversion experience that was to dominate the rest of his life by giving the assurance of his personal salvation through God's grace. In response, he sought to serve God and became convinced that he would be guided to carry out God's purposes in his life. In 1640 he was elected to parliament* by the borough of Cambridge.

Although not yet a figure of major importance in the leadership of the Long Parliament*, Cromwell was active in committee, moved the second reading of the Triennial Bill (see Triennial Act*, 16 Car. I, c. 1) and brought forward the petition for release of John Lilburne*. When on 4 January 1642 the king attempted to arrest those he considered the leading members of the opposition to him, Cromwell joined those supporting military measures. In August Cromwell left London for Cambridge, where with a small troop of solders he seized Cambridge castle and prevented plate belonging to the college from being sent to the king. A week after the start of the Civil War, Cromwell raised a cavalry troop at Huntingdon and joined the main parliamentary army* in the Battle of Edgehill* on 22 October 1642. Having become convinced that parliament needed a well-disciplined force of godly men to stand against the royalists*, in 1643 he raised such an army, the Ironsides, who proved themselves in battles in 1643 and 1644.

In 1644 Cromwell was appointed second in command to the earl of Manchester, and in July 1644 he commanded the left wing in the Battle of Marston Moor*. He came into conflict with Manchester over his failure to follow up success at Marston Moor and later at the Battle of Newbury, attacking him in parliament for his ineffectual command. He convinced parliament to establish a professional army, and the enactment of the Self-Denying Ordinance* forbade members of the parliament to hold commission in this New Model Army*. Cromwell, however, was excluded from its provisions and became lieutenant-general to the new commander, Sir Thomas Fairfax*. On 14 June 1645 the New Model Army won the decisive victory over the king at the Battle of Naseby*.

In the years following the end of the First Civil War*, Cromwell worked to achieve a settlement that would provide for religious liberty, parliamentary reform, and the return to power of Charles I*. These principles were embodied in the Heads of the Proposals*, officially published on 2 August 1647. Faced with a parliament whose

Presbyterian* leaders wished to impose a strict Presbyterian settlement and disband most of the army, radicals in the army who presented the Heads of Proposals as an alternative to the Agreement of the People*, and the intransigence and duplicity of the king, Cromwell's efforts failed. The king's alliance with the Scots and his subsequent defeat in the Second Civil War* convinced Cromwell that the king must be brought to justice. This led to Pride's Purge* of parliament in December 1648, followed by Charles's trial and execution* in January 1649.

In the period following the execution of the king, Cromwell sought to win conservative support for the new republic by suppressing the radical elements in the army and using foreign threats as a unifying element. Between August 1649 and May 1650 he suppressed the seven-year-old Irish Rebellion* with terrible brutality, massacring great numbers of defenders and civilians at Drogheda and Wexford. He followed his successes in Ireland* by defeating the Scots, who had recognized Charles II* as king. His victory at the Battle of Worcester in September 1651 was followed by an eighteen-month period in which he sought to work with the Rump Parliament* to bring about reform. When the Rump proved intractable, Cromwell turned again to the army. On 20 April 1653 he used soldiers to expel the Rump. Following the dismissal of the Rump, Cromwell accepted Thomas Harrison's advice to establish a "godly parliament." However, the experiment in godly government failed and the nominated Barebone's Parliament* was dissolved in less than six months.

On 16 December 1653 Cromwell was installed as lord protector under the Instrument of Government*. During the final five years of his life, he sought to erect a constitutional system that would retain the support of the traditional ruling classes of England while simultaneously pursing his commitment to reform. This included a concern for social justice, moral reform, and a limited form of religious liberty. Despite a series of political adjustments, he was unsuccessful in achieving these goals. The first Protectorate* parliament was followed by a short-lived experiment in personal rule in which the country was divided into eleven districts, each ruled by a major-general*. Financial pressures necessitated the calling of the second Protectorate parliament, which sought to restore the monarchy by offering Cromwell the crown, but he refused in May 1657. Cromwell died on 3 September 1658 and was succeeded as lord protector by his son, Richard Cromwell*. After the Restoration* his body was disinterred and hanged.

Bibliography: Barry Coward, *Cromwell*, 1991; C. F. Frith, *Oliver Cromwell and the Rule of the Puritans*, 1900; Christopher Hill, *God's Englishman*, 1970; J. S. Morrill, ed., *Oliver Cromwell and the English Revolution*, 1990.

Rudolph W. Heinze

Cromwell, Richard (1626-1712). Richard was the third son of Oliver Cromwell*, but with the premature death of his older brothers, he became his father's heir. He may have served briefly in the army*, and he studied for a short time at Lincoln's Inn. In 1649 he married into the gentry to Dorothy Major and he spent his time at Hursley Manor hunting and leading the life of a country squire.

Richard was a gentle, meek, pleasant, quiet man who had a mediocre education and little experience or interest in politics. He preferred the life of a country gentleman and was known for his love of hunting, preoccupation with race horses, drinking, gambling, inability to manage his financial affairs, and indiscreet association with royalists*. When in his cups, he was likely to toast King Charles*. His father often chided him about his behavior, but to no avail.

When Oliver died on 3 September 1658, Richard succeeded him as lord protector. The succession, though it went smoothly, was flawed, and the events surrounding it remain unclear. By the Humble Petition and Advice* of 1657, Oliver had the right to choose his successor, but it is uncertain if he actually did so. The letter in which he named his heir was never found, and it was only on John Thurloe's* word that Oliver had named Richard that the latter became lord protector. Rumors immediately circulated that Richard was not his father's choice.

Richard was lord protector between September 1658 and April 1659. He acquitted himself better than was expected but could not reconcile the various political, military, and religious factions. By April 1659 he had lost the support of the army upon which his power depended. He was deserted by all but a handful of troops, and the army officers forced him to dissolve parliament*. By 22 April he was powerless. In May he recognized the Rump Parliament* and was ordered to leave Whitehall.

Richard's tenure as lord protector was brief for a number of reasons. He was in an impossible situation politically; probably no one could have saved the Protectorate*. As a non-military man, he could not command the respect of the army. His flawed succession immediately raised questions about his legitimacy. His background did not prepare him for his unsought position, and because of his indiscretions in the past, his adherence to the "Good Old Cause"* was suspect. Richard himself doubted his abilities to be protector. He was known popularly as "Tumble-down Dick" and in royalist satires as "Queen Dick." In 1660 Richard fled to Paris to escape the Restoration* and his creditors. He lived abroad as John Clarke until 1680, when he returned to England and lived under the same name at Cheshunt until his death.

Bibliography: Earl M. Hause, *Tumble-Down Dick: The Fall of the House of Cromwell*, 1972; Robert Ramsey, *Richard Cromwell, Protector of England*, 1935.

Wilson J. Hoffman

Crown Lands. At various times before the seventeenth century, the Crown lands constituted a central aspect of royal finance. Although the medieval notion that the monarch should "live of his own" landed income reappeared during the first half of the seventeenth century, the Crown actually had not received even half of its income from the royal estate since the early medieval era. While the potential wealth represented by the Crown lands remained significant, the early Stuart monarchs followed the pattern of Elizabeth I by selling the lands for ready cash rather than improving the income from the estates through efficient management. There were two problems with the sales of Crown lands. Because the rents were based on antiquated values, the sales receipts did not produce nearly as much as if the rents had been improved. Moreover, once the lands were sold, it was not possible to recover any future value from rents, either antiquated or improved.

Although James I* continued to sell Crown lands at a brisk pace, in 1619 the Crown's income from its estates was £73,000, which represented about one-fourth of the total royal income. During the early 1630s, Charles I's* income from Crown lands averaged £89,000 per annum, or about twenty-two percent of his total income. In addition to their annual income from rents of Crown lands, the early Stuarts netted large sums from sales. In the first decade of his reign, James I sold Crown lands with a per annum rental of £27,311 for a total of £654,952. In the first decade of Charles I's reign, he sold lands returning about £27,000 per annum for £642,000. Once the lands were sold, they no longer counted as Crown assets.

Even with the deleterious sales of James I and Charles I, at the time of the Civil War* the Crown still owned in England alone almost 400 manors; 200 parcels; 175 urban properties; 60 parks, woods, and chases; 30 honors; and about a dozen courthouses. The Crown also possessed extensive forests and valuable fee-farm rents, a type of permanent lease usually associated with royal boroughs. Most of these properties were leased, often to court favorites, officeholders, and regional elites. Because of the political nature of the leases, they were undervalued and issued for extremely lengthy terms, which allowed the leaseholder rather than the Crown to realize the profits.

The efforts at reform of the management of Crown lands were ill fated. James I's lord treasurer, Robert Cecil*, attempted to revalue the Crown lands in 1609 through extensive surveys, but the king disrupted the plan, preferring to rely on the more expedient method of land sales to gain instant income. A later lord treasurer, Lionel Cranfield*, also designed a reform policy, calling for letting some properties in fee-farm, enclosing some parcels, and improving royal forests. Cranfield's proposals,too, were ignored, and the king continued to sell the properties, on one occasion directing Cranfield to return the sales receipts directly to the royal favorite, George Villiers*, 1st duke of Buckingham.

During the Civil War, parliament* ordered the seizure of Crown, church, and royalist* lands so that their income could help finance the war. Because the collection of rents proved difficult, when the war ended in 1649 parliament ordered the confiscated estates sold in order to pay its debts, especially to the army*. However, realizing that the Crown rents were undervalued, parliament authorized extensive surveys of the lands to revalue them before sale. The parliamentary surveys (1649-1651) were the most thorough and detailed examination of the royal holdings since Domesday Book. Virtually all of the remaining Crown lands were sold between 1650 and 1653 for a total of £1,425,000 from revised rental rates, which would have produced approximately £75,000 per annum. The vast majority of the purchasers were soldiers who cashed in debentures held from their military service. Parliament also surveyed and sold the fee-farm rents and royal forests in the 1650s.

At the Restoration* of Charles II*, parliament ordered the lands returned. While the Crown recovered its estates, many of the Interregnum* purchasers remained as tenants. The Crown utilized the Commonwealth* parliamentary surveys to bring rental rates closer into line with market values and also tended to offer shorter-term leases to tenants. However, it became apparent that Charles II, like his predecessors, did not believe that income from the Crown lands made them worth retaining. Thus in the early 1670s, the king sold most of the remaining lands and fee-farm rents, for a total of £800,000. By the end of Charles II's reign, the Crown lands amounted chiefly to those estates which the royal family used. The alienation of the Crown properties ended permanently the historic revenue production from them.

Bibliography: Gordon Batho, "Landlords in England: The Crown," in Joan Thirsk, ed., *The Agrarian History of England and Wales (1500-1640)*, 1967; Sidney J. Madge, *The Domesday of Crown Lands*, 1938.

Daniel W. Hollis III

D

Danby, Earl of. See Osborne, Thomas.

Declaration of Rights (1689). In 1688 William of Orange* summoned a Convention Parliament* for January 1689 to resolve the crisis of no government created by James II's* flight to France. One of its major achievements and the core of the revolutionary settlement was the Declaration of Rights. It established political safeguards that parliament* had been demanding in its long conflict with the Stuarts over abuses of the royal prerogative*.

Early in the session, the House of Commons created a committee of thirty-nine members chaired by Sir George Treby to draft a list of James II's abuses. The result was twenty-three "Heads of Grievance" reported to the whole Commons on 2 February 1689. After some debate, the grievances were sent back to committee to sort out those based on old law and set aside for later consideration those that required new legislation or involved new interpretations of existing laws. There was considerable pressure from William and some of the Convention's leaders to proceed quickly to a settlement, and this limited debate to issues where broad consensus existed. The result was the Declaration of Rights, which was enacted into law on 16 December 1689 as the Bill of Rights* (1 Gul. III & Mar., Sess. 2, c. 2).

The final version of the declaration approved by Commons and the House of Lords opened with a long section on James's abuses of royal prerogative, followed by a statement that his flight constituted "abdication" and that the throne was therefore "vacant." It then listed the "true, ancient, and indubitable rights of the people of this realm." It was declared illegal for the Crown to enact or suspend a law without parliament's consent (see Suspending Power*); "dispense" (exempt) people from the application of a law (see Dispensing Power*); maintain an ecclesiastical commission or other similar religious courts; set and collect taxes without the consent of parliament (see Taxation and Revenue*); refuse petitions or persecute the petitioners; maintain a standing army* without parliament's consent; and inhibit free debate in parliament in any way. These were not the rights of "the people of this realm" but of parliament. Others concerned individuals directly and included the rights from the common law* to keep arms, to no excessive bail, to trial by jury, and to protection against forfeiture of property prior to conviction. To these rights were added admonitions that parliaments should be freely elected and held frequently. The declaration also included the Convention's resolutions offering the throne jointly to William and Mary*, the line of succession, and the requirement that the sovereign be Protestant and be married to a Protestant.

The declaration was limited in scope and did not settle several important issues. There were no provisions for the frequency of parliamentary meetings and elections or for freedom from royal interference and manipulation. No restrictions were placed on the Crown's power to appoint people to offices in the church, government, or military. The Convention completely ignored the promise of religious freedom for all Protestants made by political leaders in the months just preceding the Glorious Revolution*. When a Toleration Act (1 Gul. III & Mar., c. 18) was passed on 24 May 1689, it offered limited freedom for Nonconformists and left the Test Act* technically in force until 1828. Full civil rights for Catholics* were not granted until 1829. William and Mary accepted the Crown and only then would acknowledge the Declaration of Rights.

Many politicians, lawyers, and scholars have since valued the declaration highly and proclaimed it a major turning point in the evolution of English government, although it contained no new or radical ideas. John Locke's* theories concerning the social contract, inalienable rights, and the right of revolution were not included. The significance of the declaration was that it powered parliament's evolution from a medieval assembly into a full-blown legislature by requiring that no tax be levied without its consent. No English sovereign after 1689 succeeded in contesting that prohibition. While royal prerogative was still formidable, parliament could effectively limit any exercise perceived as an abuse by refusing to grant the Crown money. When parliament did grant monies, it did so only for a limited and specified time. This forced the king to call parliament on a regular basis to keep the government funded. Where parliament had been ephemeral and irregular before 1689, it thereafter became a permanent fixture of English government. The permanence of parliament and its control of the taxing power transformed English politics.

Bibliography: L. G. Schwoerer, *The Declaration of Rights*, 1981; W. A. Speck, *Reluctant Revolutionaries: Englishmen and the Revolution of 1688*, 1988.

Richard L. Hillard

Derby House Committee (1648). The term Derby House Committee is sometimes used to describe the Committee of Both Kingdoms*, which met in Derby House. The Long Parliament* established a different Derby House Committee in January 1648 to act as an executive governing body, replacing the Committee of Both Kingdoms, which had been dissolved after parliament* enacted the Vote of No Addresses*, ending all official negotiations with Charles I*. The Derby House Committee was composed of the English peers and members of parliament who had been acting members of the Committee of Both Kingdoms; the four Scottish commissioners who had sat on the joint committee were excluded. Parliamentary action later added three Independents* to replace three Presbyterian* members who had either become ineligible or who had died. Although the Derby House Committee was to rule in an executive capacity by supervising public matters, it was not designed to control or dictate parliamentary actions. After the renewed outbreak of the Civil War*, the committee served as an official liaison between parliament and the army* commanders, coordinated the military campaigns, helped acquire military supplies, and facilitated cooperation among the army high command. The committee also acted as a storehouse of intelligence information, especially in regard to the covert activities of Charles at Carisbrooke Castle, as well as the actions and movements of the prince of Wales (see Charles II*).

Bibliography: S. R. Gardiner, *History of the Great Civil War 1642-1649*, 1893.

Nancy Vannett

Devereux, Robert, 3d Earl of Essex (1591-1646). Son of the 2d earl, who was executed for treason by Elizabeth I in 1601. The title and estates of which he was deprived at that time were restored by the parliament of 1604*. His 1606 marriage to Frances Howard was humiliatingly annulled in 1613 (see Carr, Robert*; Overbury, Murder of Thomas*); his 1631 marriage to Elizabeth Paulet ended in an unhappy separation after she was charged with adultery. He had one child, a daughter who did not survive infancy. Trained in the military arts, he briefly commanded a company of English volunteers in the Palatinate in 1620, campaigned in 1621 with the prince of Orange, and was a vice-admiral in the 1625 Cadiz expedition*. During the First Bishops' War* in 1639, he was appointed second in command, but there was no fighting.

Essex was active in parliament* from 1614 until his death, and from supporting the power of parliament in general and Lords in particular, he came to oppose Charles I* consistently. In 1640 he voted against Charles's appeal for the backing of Lords against Commons and was one of twelve peers to join John Pym*, Oliver St. John, and John Hampden* in calling on Charles to summon parliament. Named to the privy council* in 1641, he nonetheless favored executing the earl of Strafford (Thomas Wentworth*) in a widely quoted remark that, compared to exile, "stone-dead hath no fellow." With a bloc in Lords to call his own and the backing of Pym's followers in Commons, Essex worked to remove royal councilors, abolish prerogative courts*, and end extraparliamentary taxation*. Because of his retiring disposition, most of this activity was undertaken in committee and by personal meetings with others of like mind rather than by public speeches.

Appointed in July 1642 to raise and command a parliamentary army of 5,000 horse and 25,000 foot, Essex had only half that number when he survived near disaster at Edgehill*, the first battle of the Civil War*. He achieved greater success in 1643 in capturing Reading, relieving Gloucester, and surviving the first Battle of Newbury despite fighting cautiously, defensively, almost lethargically, while continuously bickering with the Long Parliament* about his relationship with other generals. This style accorded both with his personality and with his goal of limiting the royal power while strengthening a parliament in which the aristocracy would occupy a key position mediating between king and Commons. In 1644 he was trapped by the king's army in Lostwithiel after an ill-advised march into Cornwall and had to escape by sea, leaving his cavalry to escape as best they could and his infantry to surrender. Too ill to take the field again, he intrigued against Oliver Cromwell* and opposed the formation of the New Model Army*. He resigned his commission in April 1645, one day before the second Self-Denying Ordinance* prohibited members of parliament from holding public office. He ended his days defending the king and the monarchy against Puritan* political attacks. With his death on 14 September 1646, his title became extinct.

Bibliography: H. C. B. Rogers, *Battles and Leaders of the Civil Wars*, 1968; Vernon F. Snow, *Essex and the Rebel: The Life of Robert Devereux, the Third Earl of Essex*, 1970.

Joseph M. McCarthy

Diggers. The Diggers were an amorphous collection of agrarian communists who appeared in England following the Civil War*. They are difficult to define clearly, for there was considerable overlapping of membership and ideas among radical movements during the English Revolution. The Diggers' goal of abolishing private property went well beyond the political egalitarianism of most Levellers*, but the line between the two groups was sufficiently blurred that the former sometimes called themselves True Levellers.   Where religion was concerned, mysticism, millenarianism*, anticlericalism, opposition to a state church, and belief in spiritual freedom and equality were shared by Quakers*, Ranters*, Seekers*, Fifth Monarchy Men*, some Baptists*, and other Dissenters*. What distinguished the Diggers—or at least Gerrard Winstanley, their most prominent spokesman—was the combination of a rational, secular approach to politics, a highly radical theology, and a commitment to both political and economic equality.

Winstanley was born in Wigan, Lancashire, in 1609. After an unsuccessful career in the London* cloth trade* between 1630 and 1643, he became a cowherd in Walton-on-Thames in Surrey. In 1648 he published several mystical tracts containing a pantheistic notion of God, as well as the idea that God and reason are synonymous. By early 1649 he had embraced communism. This can be seen in a series of Digger manifestos written between then and 1652, in which he maintained that natural law conferred equal economic rights on all men and advanced a new interpretation of the myth of the Norman Yoke that blamed William the Conqueror for importing the concept of private property into England. He called on the poor to seize all common and waste lands, to be followed by common ownership of Crown lands* and ecclesiastical holdings and ultimately abolition of all private property.

On 1 April 1649, Winstanley, William Everard (a radical ejected from the New Model Army*), and about thirty impoverished laborers began an attempt to cultivate the waste (common land) on St. George's Hill at Walton-upon-Thames in Surrey.

Though General Thomas Fairfax* questioned Winstanley, the main opposition to the Diggers came from nearby residents. In August the community moved to Cobham, where it contained at least seventy-three members and enjoyed some support from the local populace. But there it ran afoul of the local gentry and was eventually suppressed in April 1650. At least nine other Digger communities appeared at Barnet in Hertfordshire, Bosworth in Leicestershire, Cox Hall in Kent, Dunstable in Bedfordshire, Enfield in Middlesex, Iver in Buckinghamshire, Wellingborough in Northamptonshire, and unidentified locations in Gloucestershire and Nottinghamshire but these were also unsuccessful.

Later in *The Law of Freedom in a Platform*, written in 1652 and dedicated to Oliver Cromwell*, Winstanley proposed the abolition of money, wages, and commerce; distribution of goods from a common storehouse according to need; an annual parliament* elected by universal manhood suffrage; strong local government*; elimination of the church, clergy, and religious observance of the Sabbath; and free and compulsory education. But he failed to win official support, and the remainder of the 1650s saw political radicalism on the retreat. Winstanley's later life is obscure. It has been suggested that he became a Quaker, but this has never been proved.

Bibliography: F. D. Dow, *Radicalism in the English Revolution, 1640-1660*, 1985; John Gurney, "Gerrard Winstanley and the Digger Movement in Walton and Cobham," *Historical Journal* 37, no. 4 (1994): 775-802; Christopher Hill, *The World Turned Upside Down: Radical Ideas During the English Revolution*, 1972; George H. Sabine, ed., *The Works of Gerrard Winstanley, With an Appendix of Documents Relating to the Digger Movement*, 1941.

William B. Robison

Dispensing Power. A royal prerogative* through which the monarch could excuse or dispense an individual or a group from compliance with a particular statute. Many regarded this as an unconstitutional encroachment on the authority of parliament*. Following the Restoration*, Charles II* and James II* attempted to use the dispensing power to circumvent anti-Catholic legislation.

In March 1662 Charles, who had promised liberty of conscience in his Declaration of Breda*, tried to get the Cavalier Parliament* to include in the Act of Uniformity* (14 Car. II, c. 4) two provisions, allowing him to dispense from the act Catholics* who were not clergymen and to dispense loyal ministers from wearing the surplice or making the sign of the cross during baptism. The House of Lords rejected the first almost immediately, and the Commons the second in April. Charles considered suspending the entire act (see Suspending Power*) but was dissuaded by the judges' doubts about the legality of such action. In December he issued his first Declaration of Indulgence (technically to benefit Dissenters*) and proposed an act broadening the dispensing power; however, Commons rejected it in February 1663. Parliament did not challenge Charles's right to dispense individuals from some statutes occasionally, and he sometimes used the power on behalf of individual Catholics, though this had no effect on ministers deprived under the Act of Uniformity. But when Charles attempted to suspend the entire act in 1672 with his Declaration of Indulgence*, the judges opposed him, and in 1673 Commons forced him to back down, and parliament passed the first Test Act* (25 Car. II, c. 2), which affected both Catholics and Dissenters.

The accession of the Catholic James II brought a new round in the dispute. In subduing Monmouth's Rebellion* and the concomitant rising of the 9th earl of Argyll (Archibald Campbell*) in Scotland in 1685, James tripled the size of the army* and appointed a number of Catholic officers in new regiments, dispensing them from the Test Act (supplemented in 1678 by 30 Car. II, st. 2, c. 1, in response to the Popish Plot*). The parliament of 1685*, however, refused his request to repeal the Test Act, and James prorogued it in November. In 1686 the court of King's Bench (see Common Law and Courts*), which James controlled, ruled in the case of Godden v. Hales that the king could dispense from the Test Act and rejected the popular idea that the dispensing power could not be applied to ecclesiastical matters. In 1686 and 1687 James used the power to dispense Catholic officers from penalties under the Test Act and admit new Catholic officers to the army, which was purged of his opponents; to admit Catholics to the commissions of the peace, which were also purged (see Local Government*); to Catholicize the privy council*; and to allow converts to Catholicism to retain or obtain benefices in the Church of England (see Anglicanism*) and the universities*. In related actions James suspended penal legislation against Catholics and Dissenters in his Declarations of Indulgence* of 1687 and 1688, the latter of which was required to be read in churches, provoking the refusal of the Seven Bishops* and ultimately contributing to the Glorious Revolution*.

As a result, the Convention Parliament of 1689*, in its Declaration of Rights* and subsequently the Bill of Rights* (1 Gul. III & Mar., sess. 2, c. 2), abolished the suspending power and limited the dispensing power.

Bibliography: John Bossy, *The English Catholic Community, 1570-1850,* 1976; J. P. Kenyon, ed.,*The Stuart Constitution: Documents and Commentary,* 1966; J. R. Tanner, *English Constitutional Conflicts of the Seventeenth Century, 1603-1689,* 1928; E. N. Williams, ed., *The Eighteenth Century Constitution: Documents and Commentary,* 1960.

William T. Walker

Dissenters. A broad categorization of British Protestants distinguished by their variance from the Church of England's (see Anglicanism*) leadership following the Restoration* of the monarchy in 1660. The term encompasses a wide spectrum of religious standards of worship established by parliament* in the wake of Charles II's* return to England. It includes formerly conforming Church of England congregations, Presbyterians*, Puritan* nonconformists, Baptists*, Congregationalists*, Quakers*, and other religious or political radicals. Therefore, the term *Dissenter* refers to a multitude of religious sects and political orientations ranging from conservative to radical.

Charles II had hoped to chart a moderate course of modified episcopacy assisted by the existing presbyteries. Preliminary optimism stemming from Presbyterian statements of willingness to conform to the prewar prayer book (with some omissions) evaporated, however, with the failure of Presbyterian leaders to accept episcopal titles.

The failure of this leadership to compromise with moderate Episcopalianism led to the ascendancy of more strident Episcopal spokesmen and demands. A clerical conference distressed Presbyterians with its strident episcopacy. The king responded by sponsoring new discussions that led to the October 1660 Worcester House Declaration, requiring the bishops to cooperate with presbyters in the ordination of clergy and allowing the clergy to use as much of the prayer book as they wished. The initial compromise, however, was overwhelmed by the militancy of the new parliament*, concerned with the fear of religious radicals and determined to exact revenge on nonconformity.

Venner's uprising (January 1661), Presbyterian militancy in the London* elections, and the disbanding of the army* led to an extreme backlash with the election in May 1661 of the Cavalier Parliament*, which was not only overwhelmingly Episcopalian but committed to enforcing a rigid adherence to Episcopal standards. This parliament set out to destroy the king's moderate religious policies and the entire body of the Interregnum's* constitutional reforms.

The Cavalier Parliament set the tone with the public burning of the Solemn League and Covenant* and the repeal of the Bishops Exclusion Act (17 Car. I, c. 27) of 1642, which had excluded bishops from the House of Lords. The passage of the Clarendon Code* introduced the exclusive parliamentary sponsorship of militant Episcopalianism and rigorous repression of opposing views. The Act of Uniformity (14 Car. II, c. 4) demanded allegiance to the entire new Book of Common Prayer, recently revised in convocation, and required a bishop's license for public ministry or teaching. Ministers were deprived of their churches for failing to adhere to the stipulations of the act.

Dissenters were identified by their failure to conform to this body of legislation. Nearly 2,000 clergy were forced from their charges. Parliament drove the wedge between the Dissenters and episcopal hierarchy still deeper with additional legislation. Beginning in 1664 the Conventicles Act (16 Car. II, c. 4, replaced in 1670 by 22 Car. II, c. 1) introduced legal measures to suppress dissenting congregations, such as John Bunyan's*, and in 1665 the Five Mile Act (17 Car. II, c. 2) threw a legal roadblock in the way of dissenting ministers in order to restrict their freedom of movement.

Over time, however, this repressive legislation was neither consistent in its severity nor uniform in its execution. Dissent was kept off balance with a mixture of bloody repression, administrative confusion, and the lack of a consistent governmental response. The result of severe parliamentary legislation, periodically modified and inconsistently applied, was the eventual growth of separate religious denominations and the diffusing of the political threat offered by religious radicals. Such measures as the Declarations of Indulgence* (1672, 1687) and the Toleration Act (1689, 1 Gul. III & Mar., c. 18) also periodically eased the repression of Dissenters without increasing their political franchise.

Most Dissenters, in fact, did not directly threaten the new regime, but the possibility of such a threat remained a paramount concern of government. Religious moderates such as Richard Baxter*, John Howe, and Stephen Charnock were deprived but continued to minister through an impressive body of theological and devotional writing. Others such as John Owen*, Thomas Goodwin, and Thomas Brooks maintained stronger ties with religious radicals, possibly indulging in some seditious behavior but not open rebellion. These typically preferred to undermine legislation by failing to obey it.

Genuine political radicals such as Thomas Venner, Thomas Blood, and George Ayres hatched plots to unseat the government. They not only failed in their attempts but sparked campaigns that repressed both radicalism and more moderate dissent as the government used any excuse to suppress its critics. It is not clear that the government totally fabricated plot rumors in order to suppress dissenting congregations. It is clear, however, that they lent great credence to unsubstantiated rumors, vastly overestimating their threat in order to obtain an excuse for increasing pressure on the Dissenters.

One of the dissenting groups most feared by the Cavalier Parliament and most vulnerable to its repressive tactics was the Quakers. They entered the Restoration period with the most radical spiritual and social ideas. Quakers were implicated in the Northern Rebellion and other violent acts through 1670. Their militancy faded, however, as they fell under the sway of George Fox*, adopting a religious ethic of suffering and forsaking their radical political aims. This gradual lessening of stridency consequently allowed the king to reintroduce a policy of limited toleration.

Restoration government legislation eventually eliminated the universality of the Church of England, introducing what Christopher Hill has termed "the consumer's choice in religion" and perhaps undermining the power of religion in the public forum.

Bibliography: Richard L. Greaves, *Deliver Us From Evil: The Radical Underground in Great Britain, 1660-1663,* 1986; Christopher Hill, *The Century of Revolution, 1603-1714,* 1980; Ronald Hutton, *Charles II: King of England, Scotland and Ireland,* 1989.

William Nikides

Distraint of Knighthood. Henry III began the practice in 1227 of creating knights from among subjects with sufficient income to support the nation's military needs. By the Tudor-Stuart period, the granting of knighthoods was used by the Crown to raise revenue (see Taxation and Revenue*) and by subjects to obtain social status. It was customary for monarchs to grant a certain number of knighthoods at the outset of a reign, usually at the time of coronation, and sometimes when the heir to the throne married.

Although the early Tudor monarchs had continued the practice of creating large numbers of new knights, Elizabeth I parsimoniously created only 878 knights, which did not compensate for losses by death of existing knights. By contrast James I* and Charles I* together created 3,281 knighthoods between 1603 and 1641. At the outset of James's reign in 1603, a call went out to all who owned £40 of real property to be nominated for knighthood. Although James created over 900 knighthoods in the first few months of the reign, no effort was made to enforce the payment of the fines for not appearing at the king's coronation to be knighted.

When Charles I ascended the throne in 1625, there was no immediate attempt to invoke the ancient practice. Finally in 1627 Chancery requested the Exchequer* to take action against those identified by the sheriffs* in 1626 as eligible for knighthood. The decree was not enforced until 1629, after the Crown failed to reach agreement with parliament* regarding national finances.

Because the Crown's primary concern was raising revenues outside parliament, previous collections for distraint of knighthood were insufficient.   An enlarged commission pressed the sheriffs to search more diligently to secure the fines. By mid-1630 the Crown had raised almost £12,000, an amount much greater than any Tudor monarch had acquired. Nevertheless, the Crown remained unsatisfied because many sections of the nation still had not responded.

The privy council* determined that reliance on the sheriffs' collections was inadequate. County commissioners were appointed to draft a list of delinquents and ensure compounding of the fines. The commissioners were given fifteen-part instructions and broad powers to gain the cooperation of local officials in their labors. Continued resistance to payment of the fines caused the commissioners to reduce the numbers of delinquents on their lists in order to avoid the charge of failure. Eventually 9,280 paid the fines by 1640, but they constituted fewer than half of those initially assessed. All but a token amount of the approximately £175,000 raised from distraint of knighthood was paid before 1635.   Knighthood fines were the fourth largest source of extraparliamentary revenue in the 1630s after the sale of Crown lands*, forced loans*, and impositions*.

Yet for all of the money raised, the Crown alienated an important segment of the populace against its use of the royal prerogative*. Distraint of knighthood combined with other unpopular feudal fiscal measures to help create conditions for a national crisis by the 1640s.   Because it was a major grievance of members, the Long Parliament* abolished the ancient feudal privilege in 1641, and an act passed at the Restoration* in 1660 confirmed the termination of all feudal perquisites of the Crown.

Bibliography: H. H. Leonard, "Distraint of Knighthood: The Last Phase, 1625-41," *History* 63 (1978): 23-37.

Daniel W. Hollis III

Divine Right Monarchy. According to the theory of the divine right of kings, God gives sovereigns the right to rule; this power is hereditary and absolute. Although this doctrine did not originate with James I*, he was a principal exponent of the theory, which was advanced by his heir, Charles I*. James described his ideas on divine right in many of his speeches and several works, including *Trew Law of Free Monarchies* (1598), *Basilikon Doron* (1599), and *A Defense of the Right of Kings* (1616).

Soon after his accession, it was apparent to James's new subjects that he saw himself as an unimpeachable ruler, whose power was just but God given and uncompromising. In a famous speech given before the parliament of 1610*, James told the members that kings are God's lieutenants who exercise divine power on earth and that the royal prerogative* is superior to the ordinary law of the land. He added, however, that kings should not rule alone, but with the help of parliament*. He acknowledged that without parliament's aid, he could not make law or collect subsidies.

James had a difficult time working with parliament. His view of the body was based on his experience with the smaller, less complicated Scottish parliament; its larger English counterpart required more adroit handling and compromise than James was willing to give. By the time of his reign, the English parliament had become a powerful representative assembly, expecting to participate fully in government policy. James's adherence to royal prerogatives and the divine right doctrine created many long-term problems during his reign, particularly as it led to conflict with parliament over various religious, financial, and legislative matters.   With the king and parliament disagreeing about their respective powers, it was inevitable that parliament would be forced to formulate theories on the limitations of monarchy; thus the stage was set for the constitutional battles of the next reign.

Charles I, the second Stuart king, emphasized even further the idea of unlimited kingship. From the beginning of Charles's reign, the Crown and parliament came into disagreement over the king's right to pursue his policies in religion and foreign affairs; parliament's response was to withhold taxation*.   After the disastrous parliament of 1629*, Charles dissolved the body and began the eleven-year Personal Rule* without it. When parliament reconvened in 1640, it established a series of regulations to reduce the powers of the monarchy, but this did not resolve the struggle for power, and the conflict led to the Civil War*.

Charles was not as pedantic and philosophical as his father and did not express his views on the divine right doctrine as thoroughly as James did throughout his reign. Nonetheless, he was extremely devoted to the theory. He insisted that his actions were accountable only to God, and he went to the scaffold insisting that the people could not properly claim a voice in government. Although Charles II* personally believed in absolutism*, by the time of the Restoration* in 1660, royal power was considerably restricted.

During the seventeenth century, numerous works were written responding to the frequent constitutional changes and propounding various theories of government (see Political Thought*). Most of these argued for a constitutional system of checks and balances; only a few supported the belief in divine right.   Sir Robert Filmer's *Patriarcha* is usually considered the standard work advocating the theory of divine right monarchy; it was written in 1642 and published posthumously in 1680. Filmer's work was attacked by John Locke's* influential *Two Treatises of Government,* published in 1690, which completely refuted absolutism. In practice divine right was destroyed by the Civil Wars and the Glorious Revolution* of 1688, which overthrew its last English royal exponent, James II*.

Bibliography: G. R. Elton, "The Divine Right of Kings," in *Studies in Tudor and Stuart Politics and Government*, vol. 2, 1974.

Jo Eldridge Carney

Donne, John (1573-1631). The most famous English nondramatic poet of the first quarter of the seventeenth century. To Thomas Carew he ruled the "monarchy of wit"; to Ben Jonson* he was "the first poet in the world in some things." He is remembered as England's foremost metaphysical poet and one of Anglicanism's* outstanding preachers.

Born into a Catholic* family, Donne was the son of a merchant father; his mother was the daughter of playwright John Heywood and granddaughter of Sir Thomas More. After leaving Oxford without a degree (still a Catholic, he was barred from receiving one), he entered Lincoln's Inn in 1592 to study law. Because Donne did not write for publication, the dating of his work, especially the lyric poems, is difficult, but by this time he had begun work on the elegies, satires, and possibly *Paradoxes and Problems*, together with many of the poems later published posthumously in *Songs and Sonnets* (1633). After voyaging with the 2d earl of Essex to Cadiz in 1596 (which resulted in the poems "The Storm" and "The Calm"), he joined the Anglican church and, becoming secretary to Lord Keeper Sir Thomas Egerton, appeared bound for a government career. However, in 1601 he secretly married Ann More, the niece of Egerton's wife. He lost his post, was imprisoned for marrying a minor without permission, and, in a letter to her in 1602, summed up their straitened predicament in the quip "John Donne, Ann Donne, Un-done."

Now with children to support, Donne found employment with Thomas Morton, later bishop of Durham. He also gained the patronage of Lucy, countess of Bedford, and in 1610 that of Sir Robert Drury, with whom he traveled the Continent in 1611-1612. In 1610 his *Pseudo-Martyr* appeared, an argument that Catholics should adhere to the oath of allegiance*. At about this time he also wrote, but did not publish, *Biathanatos*, a prose defense of suicide. His anti-Jesuit essay *Ignatius His Conclave* was published in 1611, as was the poem *The First Anniversary*, written in memory of Robert Drury's daughter Elizabeth, who died at fifteen. Its sequel, *The Second Anniversary*, was published the following year. Sometime during this period Donne also completed the so-called Divine Poems, notably "A Litany" and the sonnet cycles "La Corona" and the "Holy Sonnets." On 23 January 1615, after the urging of Morton as well as James I*, Donne became a priest in the Church of England. Six years later, after holding several minor posts, he became dean of St. Paul's Cathedral. His *Devotions upon Emergent Occasions*, meditations composed during a serious illness, was issued in 1624. Between 1622 and his death, over a dozen sermons were also published; his collected sermons fill ten volumes. He died on 31 March 1631 and is buried in St. Paul's.

The apparent contrast between the pious "Dr. Donne" of St. Paul's and the famed sermons and the carefree, profligate "Jack Donne" of the Inns of Court ("a great visitor of Ladies, a great frequenter of Playes," said a contemporary) suggests a career of two contrasting halves. However, Donne's work retains a continuity beneath the apparent contrast. His early love poems often raise spiritual issues, and his later religious works employ an intense awareness of the physical, so that it is more accurate to speak of a single poetic intensity that gradually focused on a long-standing religious awareness without abandoning his early concern with individual human experience. Donne is an author of emotional and intellectual vigor, whether occasioned by a woman's love or by God's. For example, in "The Canonization," two lovers are consumed by their mutual love: "The Phoenix riddle hath more wit/ By us, we two being one, are it. . . . We die and rise the same, and prove/ Mysterious by this love." In becoming "canonized" as saintly examples of love to others, they achieve a level of religious mystery, having endured a death and rebirth. Conversely, in Holy Sonnet 10, physical violence and passion serve a religious theme. The sinful soul prays to God: "Take me to you, imprison me, for I/ Except you enthral me, never shall be free/ Nor ever chaste except you ravish me."

Donne's metaphysical conceits, ingenious metaphors that find comparisons in unlikely objects, reflect the correspondences that Renaissance thinkers believed inhered in all of creation. This system of relationships, based on a classical heliocentric cosmology, had begun to lose its authority as empirical science in Donne's era made the newer Copernican model of the universe more plausible. To this clash of paradigms, his poetry characteristically records an intensely personal response: "The new philosophy calls all in doubt/[this world is] all in pieces, all coherence gone" (*The First Anniversary*). Donne was able, in F. Scott Fitzgerald's famous phrase, "to hold two opposed ideas in the mind at the same time, and still retain the ability to function." His conceits function as a poetic means of investigating the polysemous nature of the world and experience. Thus a flea containing the blood of two lovers is their "marriage bed and marriage temple" ("The Flea"); the faces of lovers reflected in their eyes are hemispheres of worlds ("The Good Morrow"); the poet's mistress is the center of a universe: "This bed thy center is, these walls they sphere" ("The Sun Rising"). It is this constantly inquisitive, allusive quality, coupled with emotional directness, that helped make Donne, in T. S. Eliot's estimation, "difficult" and thus modern.

Donne's religious prose is a monument of English baroque style. It is self-consciously Latinate and artistic yet conveys a powerful immediacy of feeling. His most famous prose passage, later appropriated by Ernest Hemingway, is from the seventeenth meditation of the *Devotions upon Emergent Occasions*: "No man is an island, entire of itself; every man is a piece of the continent, a part of the main . . . any man's death diminishes me, because I am involved in mankind, and therefore never send to know for whom the bell tolls; it tolls for thee." There is a clearly self-conscious, almost theatrical, quality in Donne's portrayal of the experience of love, death, and sin, yet his work should not be judged insincere. His artistic rendering of the soul's acute awareness of itself is one of Donne's most characteristic and enduring traits. (See Literature*.)

Bibliography: John Carey, *John Donne: Life, Mind and Art*, 1981.

Christopher Baker

Dort, Synod of (1618-19). This synod, which debated aspects of the Calvinist* doctrine of predestination during 154 formal sessions, was an assembly of the Dutch Reformed church that also included English, Swiss, German, and other delegates. It was called by the States-General of the United Provinces to deal with the crisis created by a bitter feud between the followers of Jacobus Arminius (Remonstrants) and Franciscus Gomarus (Contra-Remonstrants), both professors of theology at the University of Leyden early in the seventeenth century. Gomarus led the defense of a rigidly Calvinist soteriology against Arminius, who had begun to doubt Calvinistic predestination some time after 1587. Before his death in 1609, Arminius had gained many adherents, whose views were promulgated in their Remonstrance (1610). The Remonstrants rejected both Calvinistic supralapsarianism (that by divine decree individuals were either elect or non-elect before Adam's sin) and sublapsarianism (that election or non-election came after the Fall). Therefore, human free will is potent and meaningful, and Jesus Christ died for all (and not merely for the elect).

This theological quarrel was inextricably connected with domestic and international politics, since the Contra-Remonstrants were backed by the Dutch military leader, Prince Maurice of Orange, and the Remonstrants by the civilian leader, Johan van Oldenbarnevelt, advocate of Holland. These men were battling over whether to renew the nine-year truce with Spain that had begun in 1609. Both parties sought support in England. James I* favored Maurice and the Contra-Remonstrants, partly for theological reasons and partly because Maurice wanted to maintain the Dutch alliance with England, whereas Oldenbarnevelt leaned toward France. James I sent a delegation of divines (initially four Englishmen, later joined by one Scot) to the synod, which convened in the town of Dort (Dordrecht) on 13 November 1618.

Maurice's overthrow of Oldenbarnevelt in August 1618 guaranteed both resumption of war and Calvinist domination of the synod. By concluding on 23 April 1619 that election is without conditions, that Christ's atonement for human sins is limited to the elect, that humankind is totally depraved, that saving grace cannot be resisted, and that the elect cannot fall away from the state of grace which ensures salvation, the Calvinist majority categorically rejected Arminian* contentions.

Historians disagree over how fully James I himself and the British delegates agreed with the result. For Peter White, the views of James's delegation represent a retreat from an earlier high English Calvinism and a movement toward a middle way between Calvinist and Arminian positions of which the king himself approved. Nicholas Tyacke argues that the delegates were solidly Calvinist despite differences on certain points and that the Synod of Dort actually stimulated the growth of anti-Calvinism in England because of the prominence the debates gave to the issue of predestination.

Bibliography: Nicholas Tyacke, *Anti-Calvinists: The Rise of English Arminianism, c. 1590-1640*, 1987; Peter White, *Predestination, Policy and Polemic*, 1992.

J. Sears McGee

Dover, Secret Treaty of (1670). The secret Treaty of Dover, with interest fueled by a Whig* interpretation that sees Charles II* selling his nation to France and

Catholicism,* has provoked endless speculation about the king's motives. Personally concluded between Charles and Louis XIV, it included items that if known at the time would have generated intense, perhaps fatal, controversy for the restored Charles. That he pledged to convert publicly to Catholicism was the most serious. Though the treaty did not mention converting the realm, this bears little significance for a time when the prince's religion still influenced that of his subjects. Public opinion would have been further inflamed by Louis' pledge of 6,000 French troops to quell any domestic rebellion that this Stuart *volte-face* might incur.

Perhaps more palatable was the clause requiring Charles to dovetail his foreign policy, an area where the monarch was still autonomous, with France, though there were substantial reservations in England about French intentions. That policy's aim, according to the treaty, was a perpetual alliance and an Anglo-French war against the Dutch. This was consistent with the last two decades, wherein hostilities with the Dutch were assumed to be inevitable and even desirable (see First and Second Dutch Wars*).

In truth, the treaty, if known, would have been far more threatening in contemplation than in reality. Charles left himself ample time and room to fulfill his side of the bargain. The clause that committed Charles to embrace Catholicism publicly left the timing entirely to his discretion, and he announced only on his deathbed. War with the Dutch was left to English initiative, and English naval officers would command both French and English fleets.

Charles was willing to pledge a great deal in theory, so long as there were no deadlines and the promised French payments appeared. The cash-starved king became a substantial beneficiary of Louis (2 million *livres* or £140,000) simply by signing the treaty. Moreover, additional subsidies were guaranteed for fighting the Dutch. Louis also pledged to maintain the Treaty of Aix-la-Chapelle, honor the Triple Alliance*, and generally—with clauses on territorial compensation and dynastic integrity—maintain the European balance of power.

For such negotiation, the usual diplomatic channels were not open to the two sovereigns. Charles instead entrusted the initial contact to Henry Jermyn, duke of St. Albans, and then employed his beloved sister, Henrietta Anne (Minette), who was also Louis's sister-in-law, to settle the actual details. He also utilized a Catholic favorite, Sir Richard Bellings, secretary to Queen Catherine (of Braganza*), for carrying messages. Henrietta, the duchess of Orleans, brought the treaty to the port of Dover, where Charles signed it on 22 May 1670.

Given the potential for trouble, Charles deemed it prudent to negotiate a similar treaty for public consumption. The 2d duke of Buckingham (George Villiers*), a Protestant member of the Cabal*, was the vehicle for this. It said nothing about conversions, French troops in England, and perpetual alliances; its focus was anti-Dutch sentiment. The English signed this public treaty on 21 December 1670. When Louis later required Charles to repudiate secretly the "Protestant" version, Charles shrewdly refused. He had advantages playing both against each other: the French payment of money was underscored twice, while the English king's conversion was obfuscated once and had no place in the second treaty at all.

It is curious that Charles, in response to legislative remonstrance, banned all Jesuits and Romish priests from England by 1 May 1671 and asked royal judges to enforce the recusancy* laws. This was necessary to encourage parliament* to grant the necessary taxation* to pay Charles's debts and maintain the navy*, the hammer behind his diplomatic initiatives. But he neatly balanced this act, just before announcing the Third Dutch War* (1672-1674), with the Declaration of Indulgence* (1672), which suspended through royal prerogative* the penal laws against recusants and Nonconformists (see Suspending Power*). We are therefore left to speculate about his true sentiments in pledging to profess Catholicism publicly.

The other major obligation of the Dover treaties evolved less ambiguously. After making much of negligible provocation, England declared war on the Dutch Estates-General on 17 March 1672. Louis XIV thus achieved at least half of his purpose. In the last analysis, both kings got some of what they wanted. Charles may have been more the inspired manipulator of his French cousin than the craven betrayer of his country.

Bibliography: Keith Feiling, "Henrietta Stuart, Duchess of Orleans, and the Origins of the Treaty of Dover," *English Historical Review* 47 (1932): 642-645; Ronald Hutton, "The Making of the Secret Treaty of Dover, 1668-1670," *Historical Journal* 29 (1986): 297-318; Maurice Lee, "The Earl of Arlington and the Treaty of Dover," *Journal of British Studies* 1 (1961): 58-70; A. A. Nitchell, "Charles II and the Treaty of Dover, 1670," *History Today* 17 (1967): 674-682.

Gary M. Bell

Dryden, John (1631-1700). The English foundation upon which Augustan poetry of the eighteenth century is grounded. Alexander Pope acknowledged his debt to Dryden, and Samuel Johnson asserted that before Dryden, English had "no poetical diction."

Dryden was born to Puritan* parents at Aldwinkle in Northamptonshire, attended Westminster School, and later matriculated at Cambridge, receiving a degree in 1654. A small bequest from his father's estate enabled him to live independently for a time after his degree, but around 1657 he settled in London* in the house of his publisher. In 1662 he became a member of the Royal Society* and the next year married Lady Elizabeth Howard. In 1670 he was named poet laureate and historiographer royal, posts he held until 1688. Having converted to Roman Catholicism* in 1685 in the reign of the Catholic James II*, Dryden was thereafter stripped of his posts and spent his remaining days in more modest circumstances; however, he still continued to enjoy the adulation of younger writers in the London coffee houses*. Though accused of being an opportunist in religious and political allegiances (moving from Puritan to Anglican* to Catholic), his changing affiliations were always in a more conservative direction, sparked by his growing philosophical skepticism and conviction of the rightness of established authority. He was buried in Westminster Abbey on 13 May 1700.

After leaving Cambridge, Dryden supported himself by writing plays. From 1666 until 1681 he wrote only dramas, being retained from 1667 to 1678 as author for the king's theater. Of the ten plays produced while on retainer, *Sir Martin Mar-All* (1667) was the most successful; the same year he revised William Shakespeare's* *Tempest* with William Davenant. The spotty success of other comedies (*The Wild Gallant*, 1663; *The Rival Ladies*, 1663; *The Assignation*, 1673; *The Kind Keeper*, 1680) showed that his talent lay with heroic tragedies. His first success in this genre was *The Indian Queen* (1664), noted for its spectacular staging, followed by *The Indian Emperor* (1665). Other notable tragedies were *Tyrannic Love* (1669), *The Conquest of Granada* (1669 and 1670), *Amboyna* (1673), and his last and best tragedy in heroic couplets, *Aurengzebe* (1675). His operatic version of John Milton's* *Paradise Lost* (1677) was never performed. *All for Love* (1678) is an effective retelling of the story of Antony and Cleopatra along neoclassical dramatic principles, an interesting contrast to Shakespeare's play. Nine more dramas followed before his death.

Dryden's poetry is of more lasting value, his satires among the best in English literature*. *MacFlecknoe* (written in 1678, published in 1682) is a mock-heroic attack on the ineptitude of a minor poet, Thomas Shadwell, whom Dryden crowns king of dullness. *Absalom and Achitophel* (1681 and 1682) attacks Edward Hyde*, earl of Shaftesbury's pro-Catholic politics four years before Dryden himself converted. *The Medall* (1682), a satire occasioned by a medal struck in Shaftesbury's honor, denounces democratic factionalism and praises a "rightful monarch." *Religio Laici* (1682) is a defense of Dryden's Anglican latitudinarianism*, a *via media* between Catholic and Puritan extremism. A second religious poem, the beast fable *The Hind and the Panther* (1687), records his shift in belief as the hind (Roman church) defeats the panther (Church of England) in religious debate. Dryden's numerous translations of various classical authors, especially Virgil, are marked by the same carefully phrased and intellectually astute versifying that mark his best poetry.

Dryden's prose, a skillful blend of stylistic grace and Baconian directness (see Francis Bacon*), conveys his critical principles memorably. The *Essay of Dramatic Poesie* (1668) is a dialogue in which four travelers discuss the nature of English drama. Crites (Sir Robert Howard) favors classical theater, Lisideus (Sir Charles Sedley) the French adherence to consistent rules, Eugenius (Lord Buckhurst) the contemporary stage, and Neander (Dryden) the native English drama best exemplified by Jonson, but with due respect for the unique achievements of every age, including Shakespeare's brilliant defiance of classical principles. In various prefaces, Dryden also outlined his theory of translation, his support of tragi-comedy as a form, and his praise of Geoffrey Chaucer. Dryden's best work is controlled, topical, urbane, and neoclassical. He is the supreme literary figure of the later seventeenth century, a writer of intelligent reflection on his contemporary scene.

Bibliography: Philip Harth, *Contexts of Dryden's Thought,* 1968; Earl Miner, *Dryden's Poetry,* 1967.

Christopher Baker

Dutch War, First (1652-1654). A naval war between England and the United Provinces of the Netherlands that resulted in a marginal English victory. It had little impact on the English struggle to surpass the Dutch commercially.

During the Commonwealth* period, the Rump Parliament* sought an alliance with the Netherlands on the basis of their shared Calvinism*. When the Dutch rejected their overtures, the Rump Parliament passed the first Navigation Act* on 9 October 1651, severely curtailing the profitable Dutch carrying trade with England. This action pleased some London* merchants, who were eager to expand their profits at Dutch expense, but it greatly aggravated the Dutch commercial oligarchy, who recognized that international trade* was their country's lifeblood. Other English complaints against the Dutch included their fishing for herring too close to the English coast and their ships' refusal to salute English naval vessels by striking their flags and dipping their topsails as a recognition of English sovereignty over waters around England.

Fighting broke out off Dover on 19 May 1652, when English vessels commanded by Robert Blake attacked a Dutch East Indies convoy and its escorts for refusing an inspection. Both countries declared war during July. The battles of Kentish Knock (28 September) and Dungeness (30 November) were strategically inconclusive, although tactically the superior size and armament of the English warships was already starting to tell. English pressure on Dutch shipping increased in early 1653. Blake with sixty English ships engaged a Dutch convoy of 150 to 200 merchantmen, which was escorted by seventy-five warships under Maarten Tromp in a three-day running battle off Portland during 18-20 February. The English eventually broke through the screen of Dutch warships and sank forty to fifty merchantmen and ten to seventeen warships. In spite of these substantial losses, Tromp still got the bulk of his fleet safely home, while Blake was badly wounded.

The English navy* in March 1653 adopted the new line-ahead formation, which helped to maximize the effect of their cannon. Their admirals Richard Deane and George Monck* employed the new tactic at the Battle of Gabbard Bank against the Dutch under Tromp on 2-3 June. Although Deane was killed, the Dutch withdrew to Holland. Pursuing their advantage, the English fleet commanded by Monck followed and established a blockade of the Dutch coast during June and July. On 25 July Tromp broke out and joined a second Dutch fleet. The combined Dutch fleet attacked on 30 July in an attempt to end the blockade, but the fighting was inconclusive. On the following day the engagement resumed between roughly equal fleets of 100 ships each. After twelve hours of bitter fighting, the English under Monck won the Battle of Scheveningen (or Texel) and drove the Dutch back to their base at Texel Island. Dutch losses were between thirty and forty ships and 1,600 men, including their great admiral Tromp. Although the English lost almost as many ships, they lost only about 400 sailors. After Scheveningen there were no more significant battles.

English blockades and attacks on Dutch commerce were having an adverse effect on the Dutch economy. At the same time the naval war was an unneeded expense for Oliver Cromwell's* government. Both sides were anxious for peace, which was signed at the Treaty of Westminster on 5 April 1654. The Dutch agreed to pay an annual fee to fish in English waters, to adhere to the first Navigation Act, and to salute English naval vessels, along with other minor concessions. Militarily the war was a draw or at best a marginal English victory that had little immediate impact of the growth of English commerce.

Bibliography: G. E. Aylmer, *Rebellion or Revolution? England from Civil War to Restoration,* 1986; J. R. Jones, *Britain and the World, 1649-1815,* 1980.

Ronald H. Fritze

Dutch War, Second (1665-1667). A naval conflict between England under the recently restored Charles II* and the United Provinces of the Netherlands, brought about by colonial and commercial rivalries and resulting in a Dutch victory (see Colonization*; Navy*).

By the early 1660s English merchants were increasingly hard pressed by rival Dutch traders in India, West Africa, and the Americas. Although some diplomatic progress had been made toward alleviating problems, Charles II's government was in a warlike mood. Confidence was running high, and there was a surplus of aggressive men at court, particularly the king's own brother, the duke of York (see James II*) and his cousin Prince Rupert of the Rhine. James and Rupert also possessed substantial interests in the Royal Africa Company (see Trading Companies*), which sought to trade slaves with the Americas in competition with the Dutch. Furthermore, the war party sought hostilities with the Dutch as the best way to discredit the pacific policies of the king's chief minister, Edward Hyde*, earl of Clarendon.

Fighting began in October 1663 when English forces led by Sir Robert Holmes attacked the Dutch slave factories in West Africa. Next James ordered the capture of the Dutch colony of New Amsterdam, which took place on 7 September 1664. It was renamed New York. The English government thought that such shows of force would intimidate the Dutch, who in 1664 were suffering from a devastating outbreak of bubonic plague (see Epidemics and Plague*). The Dutch, however, were not so easily cowed, and they counterattacked. Their admiral, Michael de Ruyter, recaptured the West African bases and raided Barbados but failed to regain New Amsterdam. Meanwhile both sides readied themselves for all-out war. The English officially declared war on 4 March 1665, the Dutch in May.

Formal hostilities commenced with the bloody Battle of Lowestoft on 3 June 1665, involving close to 300 ships. A large Dutch fleet led by Jacob Opham attempted to intercept a convoy of English merchantmen returning from Hamburg. James, leading an equally large English fleet, arrived to challenge the Dutch. A fierce fight ensued in which James's flagship, the *Royal Charles,* sank the Dutch flagship, killing Opham. Although badly mauled, the Dutch withdrew in good order, and James failed to follow up his advantage. Meanwhile on 1 August English warships attempted to attack some Dutch merchantmen in the Danish harbor of Bergen. Fire from the Danish shore batteries drove the English off and resulted in England declaring war on Denmark.

France entered the war on the side of the Netherlands in January 1666, forcing the English fleet to cover both ends of the English Channel. The Dutch admiral de Ruyter returned to the offensive and engaged the English commander, George Monck*, duke of Albemarle, in the Four Days Battle (or Dover Strait), 1-4 June. On this occasion the Dutch ships outgunned the English, inflicting much heavier losses and forcing them to retreat. The Dutch fleet then blockaded the Thames estuary. Undaunted, the dogged Monck repaired his fleet and ventured out to break the Dutch blockade and on 25 July drove off de Ruyter at the Battle of North Foreland, sometimes known as the St. James's Day Fight. The English fleet followed to the coast of Holland and during August raided into the Zuyder Zee, sinking over 150 merchant ships at anchor. Militarily these successes marked the high point of the war for England.

The financial strains of the naval war were causing more and more problems for the English government. Since 1665 London* had been suffering from the same plague (London, Plague of*) that had struck the Dutch and was seriously hampering the war effort. The English began peace negotiations with France and the Netherlands in August. Meanwhile a final blow came with the Great Fire of London* in September 1666. As a result, and against the advice of Monck, Charles agreed to put his fleet into its bases if the Dutch would do the same. The Dutch made a token effort at compliance. Then early in the summer of 1667 de Ruyter raided into the Thames estuary, devastating commercial shipping and descending on the naval base at Chatham, where he burned four English warships and towed off the *Royal Charles* as a prize. The English were outraged but paralyzed.

Desperate for peace, Charles's government signed the Treaty of Breda on 21 July 1667. The treaty slightly favored the victorious Dutch, although England did not have to concede much since France and the Netherlands were equally anxious for peace. England was even allowed to keep New York, although it had to return Acadia (in Canada) to France and Surinam to the Dutch. The defeat showed the weak and fragile condition of the restored monarchy.

Bibliography: Ronald Hutton, *The Restoration: A Political and Religious History of England and Wales 1658-1667*, 1985; J. R. Jones, *Britain and the World, 1649-1815*, 1980.

Ronald H. Fritze

Dutch War, Third (1672-1674). A predominantly naval conflict in which England under Charles II* allied itself with the powerful Louis XIV of France to crush the United Provinces of the Netherlands. Clever defensive fighting by the Dutch allowed them to hold off a combined Anglo-French attack and forced Charles to make a separate peace.

Shortly after the end of the Second Dutch War* in 1667, England allied with the Netherlands and Sweden in the Triple Alliance* (13 January 1668), which was opposed to further French aggression in the Spanish Netherlands. It was a fragile alliance, and on 22 May 1670 Charles agreed with Louis XIV in the secret Treaty of Dover* to support a French war on the Netherlands. Preparations for the war began in England, and on 13 March 1672 English warships made an unsuccessful surprise attack on the Dutch Smyrna convoy as it passed through the English Channel. An English declaration of war on the Netherlands followed on 17 March.

The Anglo-French naval strategy basically consisted of combining their fleets and then attempting an amphibious invasion of the Dutch coast in support of the main French army's land attacks. Charles's government planned to destroy the Dutch navy in one campaign and had not thought beyond that point. Meanwhile as the Anglo-French fleet massed at Sole Bay, the Dutch admiral Michael de Ruyter launched a preemptive strike on 28 May 1672. Learning from the events of the First and Second Dutch Wars* (1652-1654, 1665-1667), de Ruyter had developed tactics that negated the superior size and armaments of the English warships. The Dutch attack so badly mauled the allied fleet that they had to suspend their invasion plans.

War with the Protestant Dutch in alliance with Catholic and absolutist France quickly proved unpopular with parliament* and the English people. Charles, however, continued the French alliance, although his brother, the duke of York (see James II*), was forced to resign as commander of the navy* because of his conversion to Catholicism*. Prince Rupert of the Rhine, his cousin, replaced him in command. Again Rupert's plan was to destroy the Dutch fleet and open the way for a naval invasion of Holland. The allied fleet sailed against the Dutch navy's anchorage, but de Ruyter was prepared and managed to drive off his enemies in the Battle of Schoonveldt Channel on 28 May 1673. He then forced the English fleet back to its bases on the Thames River and blockaded it. An outbreak of the plague (see Epidemics and Plague*) on their ships, however, quickly forced the Dutch to withdraw, and the Anglo-French fleet began to blockade the Dutch coast by August.

The approach of an important Dutch East Indies convoy caused William of Orange*, the leader of the Netherlands, to order de Ruyter to take his fleet out and protect the merchantmen. Proceeding to sea, de Ruyter maneuvered his ships in ways that cleverly nullified the superior numbers and armaments of the allied fleet. As earlier in the war, the English and French squadrons failed to coordinate their actions during the Battle of Texel that followed on 11 August 1673. As a result de Ruyter managed to escort the East Indies convoy safely home and inflicted enough damage on the allied fleet to make an amphibious invasion impossible for that year. Meanwhile Dutch forces had seized the colonies of New York and New Jersey in North America during August.

Opposition to the war was growing in England, along with increased fears of Catholicism and royal absolutism*. Faced with powerful political opposition at home and stalemated militarily by the Dutch navy, Charles made a separate peace with the Netherlands on 19 February 1674 with the Treaty of Westminster. The Dutch agreed to return the colonies they had captured and again agreed to salute the English navy in the Channel. Otherwise the war was a Dutch success, for they had staved off an invasion by the combined English and French fleets. For Charles, the Third Dutch War greatly increased the suspicions held by the British political nation toward his government.

Bibliography: Ronald Hutton, *Charles II*, 1989; J. R. Jones, *Britain and the World, 1649-1815*, 1980.

Ronald H. Fritze

E

East India Company. Often considered the greatest of English trading companies*, the East India Company was founded on 31 December 1599 and at its peak two centuries later achieved a level of financial and political power that few nations, let alone corporate enterprises, could equal.

Originally chartered to the earl of Cumberland and over 200 investors, the company (then known as The Governor and Company of Merchants of London* Trading to the East Indies) was granted the right of foreign trade* to all lands between the Cape of Good Hope and the Straits of Magellan not already in the possession of any "Christian potentate in amity with her Majesty" for a period of fifteen years. In the first year of James I's* reign, the company established its first factory in Surat, India, and immediately met harassment from the Dutch and Portuguese. As a result, the company developed a well-armed fleet, which by 1700 was second in size and power only to the royal navy*: So successful was the trading enterprise that the company was granted a permanent charter in 1610. Two years later it became a joint-stock company and the following year expanded its trade to Japan, with the trading station at Bantam, Java, the center of the Southeast Asian trade. By the 1620s the company, as a result of rendering naval assistance to several Indian states and the English Crown, was given unprecedented political power, including the right to negotiate treaties, mete out civil punishment to those under its jurisdiction, and generally function as a semi-autonomous political state.

During Charles I's* reign the company, which profited greatly from the luxury trade (satin, silks, velvet, cutlery, ceramics, and glassware), continued to experience a shortage of capital and now faced the rivalry of another eastern trading company chartered by Charles in 1635. This was short-lived, however, due to the rival's loss of shipping and Indian factories to the Dutch and of their African settlement to the East India Company (which, as a result of the Civil War*, defied both Charles and the new company's charter).

Under the Commonwealth* in 1651 the company took possession of the island of St. Helena as an Atlantic victualing station (lost to the Dutch in 1665 but regranted to the company in perpetuity in 1673). For the remainder of the Interregnum*, however, its fortunes were diminished under the onslaught of independent merchants on the lucrative eastern trade. But the company's persistent antagonism and the relentless attacks by pirates and rival European powers decimated these independents, while refortifying the English belief that successful foreign trade could be accomplished only through powerful corporate bodies capable of financially and militarily protecting theirs and English interests through monopolies*. As a result, a 1661 charter gave the company absolute proprietary rights over all possessions, governmental control over all facets of life in those territories, and full diplomatic power to negotiate with local (non-Christian) princes as a near-sovereign state. The only check was that as an English entity, the company was still subject to royal authority and could have its charter revoked upon three years' notice.

By the time of the Glorious Revolution*, the company had undergone several more changes, including six charters since the Restoration*, continued threats from the Great Moghul and his rajas, and renewed attacks at home by those (especially the Levant Company) who argued that the company's unbridled economic and political power caused a flood of Indian manufactures in England detrimental to domestic industry, while instituting an export trade that drained the country of its bullion reserves. Nonetheless, as early as 1670, it was observed by Sir Joshua Child that the company possessed a fleet of between thirty-five and forty armed merchant vessels with almost 4,000 seamen, an import and re-export business worth nearly £500,000 annually, and nearly a quarter of the total volume of English trade. Indeed the company's operations included three distinct theaters (a direct trade between Asia and England; re-export trade between Asia, England, and Europe; and "local" trade among various Asian ports), and all showed great profit.

By the turn of the century the company was challenged by yet another chartered company, but by Anne's* reign a merger of the two companies and the opening of its stock to the general populace created an even stronger entity. While struggles with the Dutch, Portuguese, and French persisted, by the mid-eighteenth century the company began to absorb vast tracts of land as well as dramatically increasing its profits by introducing the tea trade. Unquestionably the company's zenith came in the late eighteenth and early nineteenth centuries, but by the late Stuart period it had made its mark. Its development of a "factory system" to cut down the turnaround time and delivery of full cargoes, both going to and coming from England; its remarkable trading organization (both in terms of the volume of goods handled and its structural efficiency as a single joint-stock company); and the fact that the company both reflected the nature of the change in overseas trade in Stuart England and became an agent of that change, suggest reasons why it came to be recognized as a source of national pride and a boon to the English economy at a time when most other European economies were facing near collapse.

Bibliography: K. N. Chaudhuri, *The East India Company: A Study of an Early Joint-Stock Company, 1600-1640*, 1965; M. E. Wilbur, *The East India Company and the British Empire in the Far East*, 1945.

James I. Miklovich

Ecclesiastical Courts. Often referred to as the "bawdy courts" because of their focus on sexual and moral infringements, the ecclesiastical courts of the Tudor and Stuart periods administered a church law that had evolved from several sources. The most important of these sources was the *corpus juris canonici*, which was the common canon law of the Western church, modified according to local custom and with accretions made by English synods and councils. A second source was the *corpus juris civilis*, the codification of Roman law compiled by the Byzantine emperor Justinian in the sixth century A.D. A third source was the ecclesiastical common law, which was alleged to be older than the law contained in papal codes and derived from ancient usage.

The structure of the church courts that administered the composite ecclesiastical law formed a hierarchy of overlapping justice based around the diocese. At the top of the judicial order was the bishop's consistory court, subdivided into various branches to deal with different types of ecclesiastical matters. In a few dioceses, there was another episcopal court, a court of audience, to deal with the very important cases that required the bishop's personal oversight. Below the consistory court level in the diocese, there were usually two or more archidiaconal courts; the number of these courts in English dioceses ranged from one in Ely to six in Lincoln. The archdeacons who oversaw these courts were traditionally said to be *oculus episcopi* (the bishop's eye). In addition to the courts of the archdeacons, the administration of diocesan justice might be complicated by the "peculiars" within the ecclesiastical unit. By historical precedent, they were more or less independent of the authority of the bishop and/or the archdeacon.

Above the diocesan court system were the judicial systems of the two archdioceses or provinces in England, Canterbury and York. The archdiocese of Canterbury, which enjoyed precedence in English ecclesiastical affairs, held its courts in London*. Of the various London archdiocesan courts, the prerogative court of Canterbury heard primarily probate cases in which the deceased had substantial amounts of property in more than one diocese. The Canterbury courts of arches and of audience functioned primarily as appellate courts for cases heard in the system of diocesan courts within the archdiocese of Canterbury. The principal court of the province of York was the court of chancery. The courts of the archdiocese of York functioned very differently from those of Canterbury in that it was often difficult to distinguish between the court of the archdiocese and those of the diocese of York.

Historically, ecclesiastical appeals beyond the level of the archdiocese had presented certain problems. Despite the great medieval statutes of *praemunire* (1353, 1365, 1393) forbidding appeals outside England, prior to the Reformation such appeals did go to Rome. By the end of the sixteenth century, however, such appeals were being dealt with by a court of delegates, a royal tribunal appointed from the ranks of civil lawyers. Additionally, the courts of the commissioners for causes ecclesiastical, more commonly known as the courts of High Commission (see Prerogative Courts*), developed in the sixteenth century and began to exercise authority over ecclesiastical causes from 1559 on. Their authority derived from the king or queen as supreme governor of the Church of England (see Anglicanism*).

The courts of High Commission, which became notorious by mid-seventeenth century, were different in their *modus operandi* from the diocesan hierarchy of courts in that they had the power of coercion in forcing compliance to the court's summons. They were also able to fine, imprison, and take bonds of individuals to obtain performance of the court's edicts. Moreover, when the judge administered a formal list of articles or charges, the defendant was required to answer them on oath, swearing the infamous oath ex officio, which forced self-incrimination.

While the ex officio oath might be required even in regular diocesan judicial proceedings, by the late Tudor and Stuart period it was generally accepted that the penalties of the church courts did not extend to life, limb, or property. In the regular diocesan hierarchy of courts, the worst penalties one could receive were excommunication, suspension, admonition, and penance. By the same token, the ordinary church courts had no power to make an arrest. They issued citations to summon litigants to court, but if a defendant failed to appear, he or she was only held to be contumacious and subject to excommunication.

The areas of jurisdiction of the ecclesiastical courts fell into three main categories: instance cases, office cases, and record cases or non-contentious court business. Instance cases were approximately equivalent to what we now call civil justice; they were brought at the instance of an individual who thought that he or she had been wronged by another individual. Office cases, loosely equivalent to criminal cases, were corrective or disciplinary cases where the court prosecuted the cause for the "reformation of morals and the soul's health."

Cases came before the church courts in a variety of ways. The judge might be informed of suspicious circumstances in his jurisdiction by any ecclesiastical officer and then summon the suspected person for examination. More likely, however, was the case brought to the court's attention by local churchwardens elected annually in every parish. The reports they made at regular intervals led to bills of presentment for various offenses committed by parishioners. Supervision of the churchwardens was achieved by visitations made by the archdeacons, the bishops, or other ecclesiastical authorities. The archdeacons usually visited each parish twice a year, around Easter and Michaelmas, while the bishop customarily made a visitation following his accession and then triennially thereafter.

After the appointment of William Laud* as archbishop of Canterbury in 1633, the ecclesiastical courts became a focus for much parliamentary opposition to the entire system of episcopal administration of the English church. During the Civil War* period, all ecclesiastical courts were abolished, but they were reinstated in basically the same form at the Restoration*, with the notable exception of High Commission. The use of Latin in ecclesiastical court procedure was ended around 1735, and ecclesiastical court jurisdiction over the laity ceased by the end of the eighteenth century. The system of ecclesiastical courts in England continues to the present, although modern ecclesiastical court business deals mainly with administration of church officials and buildings.

Bibliography: Ralph Houlbrooke, "Church Courts," in Ronald H. Fritze, ed., *Historical Dictionary of Tudor England. 1485-1603*, 1991, and *Church Courts and the*

People During the English Reformation, 1979; Martin Ingram, *Church Courts, Sex, and Marriage in England,* 1987; R. Marchant, *The Church Under the Law: Justice, Administration and Discipline in the Diocese of York*, 1969.

Janet A. Thompson

Edgehill, Battle of (1642). On 23 October 1642 Charles I's* army* faced parliament's* army under Robert Devereux*, 3d earl of Essex in the first pitched battle of the Civil War*. Both anticipated a decisive victory.

On the eve of battle Charles's advisers debated the appropriate battle formation for the infantry. General of the Army Robert Bertie, earl of Lindsey, favored the Dutch formation, with pikemen flanked by musketeers. General of Horse Prince Rupert, the king's nephew, endorsed the Swedish formation, where pikemen formed an inverted wedge with musketeers on both wings and in the center. Although the latter provided great tactical flexibility, it required well-trained troops, which Charles lacked. Nevertheless, Charles overruled Lindsey, who resigned his commission, became a "simple colonel," and assumed a regimental command. Patrick Ruthven, later earl of Forth and of Brentford, replaced Lindsey.

The Cavalier* army deployed along a steep ridge at Edgehill, while the Roundheads* assumed positions about half a mile from its foot. The armies were equally matched, each with approximately 10,000 men. Essex was stronger in foot, Charles in horse. After the Roundheads initiated a brief but ineffective artillery duel, the Cavalier infantry advanced. As he prepared to advance, Sergeant Major General Sir Jacob Astley, who commanded the king's foot, prayed: "Lord I shall be verie busie this day. I may forget Thee but doe not Thou forget me." Facing the oncoming enemy, Essex's brigade of Roundhead infantry broke and ran, creating a hole in the center of the parliamentary line. Meanwhile, Rupert led a spirited cavalry charge against parliament's left wing. According to plan, Lieutenant Colonel Sir Faithfull Fortescue's troop of horse fired their pistols in the ground and defected to the king. This helped Rupert rout the left wing, his men chasing the Roundheads over two miles to Kineton before looting Essex's trains. Rupert was unable to rally his troops and return to the fight. Henry Lord Wilmot's cavalry charge broke parliament's right flank, and his men also pursued the broken Roundheads, likewise ceasing to be a factor in the battle.

Back in the center of the battlefield, Astley led the royal foot forward and came to "push of pike" with the Roundhead infantry. A bitter struggle ensued, with the Cavalier infantry eventually being attacked by Roundhead pike, horse, and musketeers. The parliamentary horse advanced and temporarily captured some of the king's guns, but without nails to spike the cannon, all they could do was cut the drag ropes, making the guns immobile. Under attack from seemingly all sides, the king's foot gave way. Two royal brigades remained intact and took a stand with cannon and a ditch before them. Rupert returned around twilight, but the exhaustion of his men and their horses and the lateness of the hour discouraged him from re-engaging the enemy. Both armies slept on the field in a bitterly cold night.

By the following day, Essex received reinforcements, but neither he nor the king was interested in continuing the fight. Charles dispatched Sir William Le Neve, Clarencieux king at arms, ostensibly to offer the king's pardon but in reality to investigate the condition of Essex's army. Edgehill was arguably a strategic victory for the king as the road to London* remained open, though with losses of 1,500 men equally split between the two sides, historians have generally considered it a draw. Although Charles could have marched on London, he captured Banbury Castle and returned to Oxford instead. Essex meanwhile marched toward Warwick and away from London. By the time the king eventually reached London in mid-November, he found that Essex had beaten him there and been reinforced by the London Trained Bands. Facing Essex's 24,000 men on Turnham Green, a greatly outnumbered Charles again retired toward Oxford.

Bibliography: H. C. B. Rogers, *Battles and Generals of the Civil War*, 1968; Peter Young, *Edgehill 1642: The Campaign and the Battle*, 1967; Peter Young and Richard Holmes, *The English Civil War: A Military History of the Three Civil Wars, 1642-1651*, 1974.

David B. Mock

Eliot, Sir John (1592-1632). A gentleman from Cornwall and an outspoken member of parliament*, Eliot sat in the House of Commons during five parliaments between 1614 and 1629. Historians once touted him as an oppositionist leading the Commons in a struggle with the Crown which during the 1620s led to the Commons's seizure of the legislative and after Eliot's death to the Civil War*. Recent historians by contrast have portrayed Eliot as a tortured figure epitomizing the dilemma of early Stuart gentry who served in the dual role of local governors and central legislators in a country functionally incapable of financing a foreign war. Eliot found it particularly difficult to reconcile royal service as vice admiral of Devon and clientage under the royal favorite, the 1st duke of Buckingham (George Villiers*), with the insistent local demands placed upon parliament men in wartime. His impassioned speeches gave voice not only to concerns regarding the state of the royal finances but also to anxieties about the future of parliaments, for it was becoming increasingly difficult during the 1620s to do both the king's and the country's business.

Having witnessed the pathetic sight of the soldiers returning from the failed Cadiz expedition*, Eliot turned against Buckingham during the winter of 1625-1626. His decision to attack Buckingham during the impeachment* proceedings in the parliament of 1626* was a crucial one made more significant by the absence of several of the most prominent speakers from the previous parliament of 1625*, who were excluded by Charles I's* decision to prick (appoint) them to be sheriffs*. Though imprisoned for his conduct in the 1626 session, Eliot was released before it concluded and subsequently played an important role in the parliament of 1628* in the debates concerning the Petition of Right*, which was designed to protect the king's subjects against taxation* levied without parliamentary consent and various abuses of wartime administration.

Finally in 1629, while other MPs held the speaker of the House of Commons in his chair to prevent the dissolution ordered by the king, Eliot read resolutions that condemned extraparliamentary taxation and recent appointments of Arminians* to positions of authority in the church. Such action was a deliberate appeal to the public and a challenge to royal authority, and it could not go unpunished. Afterward Eliot and his compatriots were imprisoned in the Tower and prosecuted, without careful regard to legal proprieties, in King's Bench (see Common Law and Courts*). While in prison Eliot wrote political tracts, including *The Monarchie of Man* and *Negotium Posterorum*, which show him to have been a loyal but aggrieved subject seeking to solve the contemporary crisis of counsel and willing to appeal to posterity to judge his conduct. But he neither requested nor received mercy from the king. Though his fellow miscreants were eventually freed, Eliot died in the Tower in 1632. Whether he was the martyr of an incipient parliamentarianism now seems doubtful, but his life certainly exemplifies the tensions that beset the ruling elite of early Stuart England.

Bibliography: J. N. Ball, "Sir John Eliot and Parliament, 1624-1629," in Kevin Sharpe, ed., *Faction and Parliament*, 1978, 173-207.

Myron C. Noonkester

Elizabeth, Electress of the Palatinate and Queen of Bohemia (1596-1662).
Elizabeth, born 19 August 1596 and named for the queen of England, was the eldest daughter of James VI of Scotland* (see James I*; Anne of Denmark*). In June 1603 she went with her mother from Scotland to England after her father ascended the throne there. From the time she was about twelve, Elizabeth was often at the royal court*. Court poets wrote about her beauty and charm, and Elizabeth was more popular with the English people than any others of the royal family except her brother Henry*. There were a number of marriage proposals, including one from Philip III of Spain; Prince Henry and other Protestants were horrified, and the idea was dropped. Around 1612 James wished to form an alliance with the princes of the German Protestant Union and so supported a marriage between Elizabeth and the Elector Palatine, Frederick V. Frederick came to London* in October 1612, but there was soon great sadness for Elizabeth. Her brother Henry, to whom she was very close, died 6 November. His final words were, "Where is my dear sister?" Soon after the funeral, Frederick and Elizabeth were married on 14 February 1613. For the first five years after their marriage, Elizabeth and Frederick lived in Heidelberg. Her first child, Frederick Henry, was born 2 January 1614. She and Frederick were to have twelve more. Yet except for her third son, Rupert, of whom she was truly fond and who fought to support his uncle Charles I* during the English Civil War*, she felt responsibility but little affection for many of her children. Her daughter Sophia once said of her mother that she preferred dogs and monkeys to young children.

In August 1619 the Bohemian estates elected Frederick king of Bohemia, but his reign was brief and ended in disaster amid the beginning of the Thirty Years War*.

Badly defeated in the Battle of White Mountain on 8 November 1620 by Catholic forces, Frederick and his family fled into exile, finally arriving at The Hague, where Maurice of Orange offered them refuge. Elizabeth's father and other German princes attempted to restore Frederick but were unsuccessful. Frederick died in 1632 in Mainz.

Elizabeth's position in Holland was perilous. She was dependent on the generosity of Holland's government. The English parliament* also voted her a pension, but this ended with Charles I's execution* in 1649. Though Elizabeth's son Charles Louis regained the Rhenish Palatinate in 1648 after the Peace of Westphalia, he refused to give her financial help and embarrassed Elizabeth with his support of the parliamentarians* during the Civil War. At the Restoration* of Charles II* in 1660, Elizabeth's situation improved. In 1661 she returned to England, and the government soon granted her a pension. But Elizabeth did not live long enough to enjoy it, dying 8 February 1662. The Hanoverian claim to the English throne came from Elizabeth through her daughter Sophia, wife of Ernst Augustus, elector of Hanover, and mother of George I.

Bibliography: Alice Buchan, *A Stuart Princess,* 1934; Jessica Gorst-Williams, *Elizabeth, the Winter Queen,* 1977; Carola Oman, *Elizabeth of Bohemia,* 2d ed., 1964.

                                                                              Carole Levin

Enclosure. See Agriculture; Fen Drainage.

Engagement and Engagers. On 26 December 1647 Charles I* and three Scottish nobles signed the Engagement at Carisbroke Castle, Isle of Wight. Representing the Hamiltonian royalists* and the conservative Covenanters*, the noblemen the earls of Lanark, Lauderdale (John Maitland*), and Loudoun had started negotiating with the king on 22 October. Within two months the king and nobles had hammered out yet another pact, which the king intended to repudiate once restored to power. For the Scots, faced with incompatible allies and an arrogant but captive monarch, the Engagement was as satisfactory an arrangement as could be achieved.

The document played to the Scots' concerns about their security and the king's desire to return to his role as supreme governor of the three kingdoms. Royal promises to adhere to the Solemn League and Covenant*, to guarantee Scotland's religious settlement of 1639, to give Presbyterianism* a three-year trial in England, and to suppress Protestant sects there ensured the Covenanters' position. The Scots agreed to provide an army to restore "the just rights of the Crown." The king also promised payment of any sums owed by England. Although one clause authorized "the Scots army to possess themselves of Berwick, Carlisle, Newcastle-upon-Tyne, Tynemouth, and Hartlepool" temporarily, some Englishmen claimed that a secret treaty granted England's four northern shires to Scotland*.

The Engagers began maneuvering to raise an army in Scotland. The committee of estates was the first scene of their activity. Securing the majority's adherence to the treaty, the Engagers worked to gain enough members in the estates. The Scottish parliament sat on 2 March and in mid-April accepted the Engagement. The Tailors' Hall (Edinburgh) petition, an attempt by leading army officers to oppose the treaty, was undermined by Major-General John Middleton. Protests from the commission of the general assembly were ignored as the country girded for war.

Raising the Engager army met substantial resistance south of the Tay River. The ministers refused to preach in favor of the levies; committees of estates in Haddington, Fife, Renfrew, Lanark, Kirkcudbright, and Wigton balked at raising troops, and numbers of senior officers resigned their commissions. Quartering troops on opponents of the levy, the Kirk party*, proved necessary to gain recruits and money. In July 1648, when the Engager army entered England, it was weak and poorly led.

The tardiness of the Engagers' military actions put any chance of success immediately into question as the New Model Army* crushed royalist risings in England and Wales*. James, duke of Hamilton, commander of the Engager army, proved to be a most inept adversary for Oliver Cromwell*. Military defeat at Preston (of Hamilton's English allies) and Winwick (of the Scots) was followed by the duke's capture at Uttoxeter. Within days the Kirk party rose to challenge Lanark's army in Scotland, now reinforced by troops retreating from the English debacle. The arrival in the Scots border counties of several thousand cavalry under Cromwell prompted the Engagers to agree to disband in the Treaty of Stirling signed with the Kirk party on 27 September. To implement an agreement with Cromwell to remove the Engagers from political power, the Scots estates passed the Act of Classes in January 1649. To reinforce their exclusion from public life, the Kirk* ordered the Engagers to undergo public repentance. Purging of Engagers from the army continued until Dunbar in September 1650. The Public Resolutions, passed on 14 December, rehabilitated this outcast party, whose members again took their places in the military and civilian bodies, only to lose all when the English conquered Scotland in 1651.

Bibliography: Walter Makey, *The Church of the Covenant, 1637-1651*, 1977; David Stevenson, *Revolution and Counter-Revolution in Scotland, 1644-1651*, 1977.

Edward M. Furgol

Engagement Controversy. The Rump Parliament* introduced an oath of loyalty or engagement for its chief officials. Later in October 1649 this requirement was broadened to include the military, ministry, magistrates, teachers at schools, and members of the universities*. Finally in February 1650 the engagement was made mandatory for all males. On 19 January 1654, early in the Protectorate*, the oath was abolished. A purpose of this oath was to expose enemies of the regime, who it was assumed would not risk perjury and falsely take the oath. Its second purpose was to provide a legal recognition of the Commonwealth's* de facto authority. Little official attempt was made to defend the Engagement, but a variety of unofficial pamphlets appeared to explain its reasonableness, legality, and necessity. A handful of opponents published critiques. The Engagement controversy was not recognized as significant by the great constitutional historian S. R. Gardiner; more recent historiography has remedied this somewhat, but considerable work has yet to be done.

Engagement theorists drew on the Bible*, history, natural law theory, and Providence to justify loyalty to the Commonwealth (see Historical Thought*; Political Thought*). Though proponents of the Engagement used providential arguments, there was a pervasive pragmatic theme. Romans XIII was the most cited germane text: "The powers that be are ordained by God." While the Commonwealth was a de facto regime of dubious legality, it made sense to engage to end political strife and avert further civil war. Essentially these arguments were directed at royalist*, Leveller*, and Presbyterian* subversion and calls for counterrevolution. The most persuasive and productive pro-government writers were Francis Rous, Anthony Ascham, John Dury, and Marchamont Nedham.

Early Engagement tracts, such as Rous's *The Lawfulness of Obeying the Present Government* (25 April 1649), had the difficult task of justifying the necessity of the new oath and the invalidity of the Solemn League and Covenant*. Salving the consciences of Presbyterians who felt excluded by the new government settlement was a priority. To some extent, Engagement theorists sought to remove barriers of conscience that prohibited Presbyterians and royalists from submission to the government. The expediency of stable government and the idea that former oaths were invalid were perhaps the least radical means of persuasion. Ascham extended the logic of loyalty to a regime by arguing in *Of the Confusions and Revolutions of Government* (November 1649) that good laws need not be exercised by a legitimate magistrate. These arguments led implicitly and openly to the notion of the Rump Parliament as a transitional regime, to be replaced by a permanent legal one.

The quintessential Engager, who personified the exigencies of the controversy, was Nedham, a political chameleon who became the most forceful and perhaps most influential theorist. Nedham was a parliamentarian* newspaper writer who converted to a royalist pamphleteer but who took the Engagement. His *The Case of the Common-wealth of England Stated* (8 May 1650) jettisoned much of the extraneous theory of Rous and Ascham and argued principally that the government was owed allegiance by right of conquest. Conquest as a sign of God's favor and Providence was not new to this dialogue. But Nedham did not seek to interpret Providence; rather, he attempted to show the necessity of submission to a government established by the sword and the futility of resistance.

Thomas Hobbes*, the royalist political theorist and author of *Leviathan,* did not participate in the controversy directly, but Ascham and others used his notions of conquest and submission. His *De Corpore Politico* (1650) contained arguments of profound influence for the Engagement theorists. Edward Gee's *An Exercitation* (December 1649) was the most forceful of the anti-Engagement tracts. He denied that a usurping power could exercise lawful authority without the consent of the people. By introducing the efficacy of consent, he debunked the argument that all existing powers drew legitimacy from God.

Echoes of the Engagement controversy reappeared before and after the 1688 Glorious Revolution*. Inevitably Nedham re-emerged to publish an anti-Whig* attack on the earl of Shaftesbury (Anthony Ashley Cooper*) and Charles II's* critics in the

Cavalier Parliament* in 1676. Unfortunately he died before applying his versatile pen to the changing political tides. This was left to other new-style Engagers.

Bibliography: P. A. Knackel, ed., *The Case of the Commonwealth of England, Stated*, 1974; J. Wallace, *The Engagement Controversy, 1649-1652, An Annotated List of Pamphlets*, New York Public Library Bulletin 68, 1964, 398-495.

John H. F. Hughes

Epidemics and Plagues. England experienced recurring crisis mortality due to plagues and epidemics in Stuart times. In fact the only periods when the country was plague free were 1612-1624 and 1654-1664, and it was never free of other contagion.

Plague was especially lethal, though by the seventeenth century confined principally to urban centers. In cases of bubonic plague sixty to eighty percent died from the bacillus-caused illness soon after infection; the incubation period was usually six days and the time of outbreak between July and October. The lymph nodes of victims would swell and suppurate, forming the eponymous buboes. Besides the black carbuncle that would form at the site of the flea bite, other boils and subcutaneous spots would appear. Its respiratory form, pneumonic plague, which produced gangrene in the lungs, was not dependent on infected fleas but on human proximity. Spread as easily as the common cold, the mortality rate in pneumonic plague was 100 percent. Outbreaks were in winter and in colder climates.

Though the plague of London* of 1665 is the most famous in the Stuart era, there were other years of epidemic disease. Nearly 3,000 residents of the city of London died in 1603, resulting in the introduction of bills of mortality to keep track of the dead. In 1625, the year following a plague-free period, 35,000 Londoners perished, necessitating a delay in the coronation of Charles I* until the following year. In 1630, 1,317 plague deaths in London were recorded; in 1636 10,400 died. In the year immediately preceding both of those plague years, not one fatality was attributed to plague. The unpredictability of these health calamities made for an uncertain existence.

Self-medication and professional treatment alike borrowed from some of the simple plague remedies found in printed literature. Paracelsian remedies were as acceptable as any others to readers of popular medical tracts. Treacle and mithridate, a compound antidote against poisons, were recommended as a prophylactic against plague in the 1618 *London Pharmacopoeia* of the Royal College of Physicians*; Oliver Cromwell* later discovered that the mixture cleared up his acne as well. Opiates, alcohol, and tobacco were popularly thought of as cures for plague. Above all, however, was the belief that all medicines worked only by the grace of God. Paracelsians, searching for answers beyond the laboratory, believed that there might be spiritual causes of the disease, and even the Corporation of London had suggested daily visits to church during an outbreak.

There were periodic outbreaks of other diseases like sweating sickness, likely an arborvirus infection, which killed its victims within twenty-four hours. Increases in other diseases and the appearance of new ones were noted by professionals. Some thought scurvy was a new disease, endemic to the malevolent air of London; others identified rickets as new, perhaps an offshoot of the "French pox," or what the English called syphilis. A morbid strain of fevers struck between 1638 and 1643, particularly virulent within populous communities. An illness that produced diarrhea killed thousands of babies between 1669 and 1671. Malarial fevers were a special problem along the east coast of England, most notably in Essex. Typhoid fever, "ordinary ague," killed many in 1612, including Henry, prince of Wales*. Typhus struck in 1636.

London was consumed with smallpox and fevers during the seventeenth century. In 1645, 1,354 deaths were recorded attributable to smallpox, 1,279 to fever. The year 1659 was another deadly one, with 2,303 fatalities blamed on fever and 1,523 on smallpox. A great fever raged in Hampshire in 1639; there were other fever epidemics in the country in 1651 and from 1657 to 1659.

Contemporaries noticed an increase in the incidence of leprosy, though any skin irritation, such as eczema, might be labeled leprous. There also seems to have been greater incidence of venereal disease, especially syphilis, which imitates the symptoms of many other ailments, including gout. Health caregivers and record keepers may have diagnosed ague, or fever, as a disease in itself rather than the symptom of another malady, making historical assumptions tenuous.

Bibliography: Leslie Clarkson, *Death, Disease and Famine in Pre-Industrial England*, 1975; Charles Creighton, *A History of Epidemics in Britain*, 2 vols., 2d ed., 1965; Paul Slack, *The Impact of Plague in Tudor and Stuart England*, 1985.

Elizabeth Lane Furdell

Evelyn, John (1620-1706). An important link between the aristocratic "virtuoso" culture of the early seventeenth century and the scientific culture of the Restoration* era. Evelyn is also important for his extensive and historically valuable *Diaries*, which cover personal and public events for most of the seventeenth century.

Evelyn was the second son in a prosperous family of Surrey gentry, recently risen on the strength of gunpowder manufacture. In 1637 he entered Balliol College, Oxford, and in 1640 he accompanied his elder brother, George, to the Middle Temple. In 1641, disturbed by the political situation and particularly by the execution of Thomas Wentworth*, earl of Strafford, whom he admired, Evelyn left England for the Continent, ostensibly to join the English volunteers in Dutch service. As a convinced Anglican* and royalist*, Evelyn found England in the 1640s uncongenial, and he spent most of the decade on the Continent, marrying Mary Browne, the thirteen-year-old daughter of Charles I's* ambassador to France, in 1647 and traveling extensively in the Low Countries, France, Italy, and Switzerland.

He returned to England for good in 1652, purchasing Sayes Court, a small estate, and living a secluded life, stirring to publish two pamphlets supporting Charles II* in the months preceding the Restoration. After the Restoration, Evelyn held a succession of minor posts in the new regime, although he disapproved strongly of Charles's licentious royal court*, and was one of the original members of the Royal Society*.

In 1664 he published the book for which he was best known during his lifetime, *Sylva, or a Discourse of Forest Trees*. This was prompted by an inquiry directed to the Royal Society concerning the navy's* timber needs. In a large folio dedicated to Charles II, Evelyn compiled much of the knowledge of forestry available at the time. The year 1664 also saw the publication of Evelyn's major work on gardening, *Kalendarium Hortense*. Through his writings and his garden at Sayes Court, Evelyn was one of the major influences introducing more open and spacious styles, in keeping with French and Italian examples, to English gardens.

Evelyn was one of the commissioners appointed for taking care of the sick, wounded, and prisoners during the Second and Third Dutch Wars* (1665-1667, 1672-1674) and exercised his duties with diligence, remaining in London* during the plague (see Epidemics and Plague*; London, Plague of*). In 1671 he was appointed to the council on foreign plantations*, and he reached the height of his political career under James II*, when he became one of the commissioners for the privy seal. Evelyn became increasingly concerned by James's measures promoting Catholicism* and gave grudging acceptance to the Glorious Revolution*.

After the revolution, Evelyn lived in retirement, eventually inheriting the family estate of Wotton on George Evelyn's death without direct heirs. He continued writing and publishing on subjects as varied as numismatics and salads into extreme old age, dying in 1706.

His extensive *Diaries* are the principal sources for Evelyn's life. While not as personally revealing as those of his close friend Samuel Pepys*, Evelyn's *Diaries* are an invaluable record of contemporary events and one devout and intelligent country gentleman's reactions to them.

Bibliography: John Bowle, *John Evelyn and his World*, 1981; E. S. De Beer, ed., *The Diaries of John Evelyn*, 6 vols., 1955.

William E. Burns

Exchequer. The Exchequer was a royal court that received and audited certain classes of royal revenue and heard cases concerning the king's financial rights. It enjoyed both a common law* and an equitable jurisdiction, but its most significant functions were fiscal in nature. The "Lower" Exchequer, or Exchequer of Receipt, received revenue from various accountants, including sheriffs* and collectors, and presented them with tallies—sticks with notches in them to indicate the amount paid. The accountants subsequently handed these tallies to the officials of the "Upper" Exchequer, or Audit, when their accounts were examined. If the accountant was cleared of all the charges laid to his account, he received a quietus, or discharge.

The Exchequer handled both receipts and disbursements from royal revenues. The kinds of revenue received in the Exchequer were various, comprehending both the ordinary and extraordinary revenue of the Crown and including items ranging from parliamentary grants of taxation* to issues charged upon jurors who failed to appear for cases in the common law courts*.

The collection of these revenues occupied many officials and created many classes of Exchequer records, all with their characteristic requirements for accountants to meet. In order to expend money, the Exchequer required a warrant from one of the king's officials designating the amount and person to be paid, though in many cases payments might be assigned by tally or treasury order to someone whom the Crown owed. In some cases, officials of the government made payments directly out of revenues they had collected. Such practices circumvented the slow procedures of the Exchequer, and mastering them was one of the challenges facing royal ministers as they sought to exert detailed control over the Crown's finances during the latter part of the seventeenth century. Such practices have also complicated the task of modern historians who wish to compare the yields of royal revenues with royal expenditures.

The Exchequer took its name from the custom of comparing counters on a checkered cloth, a ritualistic and mysterious relic of a preliterate, prenumerate past. The records of the Exchequer were similarly archaic, including huge parchment rolls inscribed primarily in Latin and bearing entries in clumsy Roman numerals, which were incapable of providing the information necessary for modern bookkeeping. The officers of the Exchequer included barons, the king's and lord treasurer's remembrancers, auditors, ushers, and several specialized officials, most of whom were dependent on fees for their livelihood. Though in 1554 it absorbed the courts that had managed the revenues of the monastic dissolution, the Exchequer continued to subject certain of its accountants, including sheriffs, to its "ancient course." Nevertheless, the simplified features characteristic of the new revenue courts were incorporated into some procedures at the Exchequer. Among these, the practice of allowing accountants to "declare" those revenues they had actually collected rather than answering customary "charges" offered the greatest relief from the rigors of the "ancient course."

As its methods would suggest, the Exchequer's main purpose as an institution was not to manage and exploit royal revenues but to see that the king's rights were honored and that he was not defrauded by his own officials. Despite the dislocations of the Civil War* and the promise afforded by a host of new auditing and revenue-collecting committees, the Exchequer was reinstated in 1654 as the chief agency of national finance. It continued so after the Restoration*, for in the words of Sir George Downing, "the Exchequer is one of the fundamental pillars of monarchy, the easiest and the cheapest." During the post-Restoration period it proved itself capable of absorbing various fiscal innovations into its routine. In the later seventeenth century, with the emergence of the guiding authority of treasury commissioners and the inauguration of new forms of revenue such as the excise and hearth money, the Exchequer retained an important share of fiscal responsibility. Even the measures adopted after the Glorious Revolution* of 1688, with their provisions for fiscal reform and a funded national debt, accorded the Exchequer a place of great significance as the kingdom made the transition from royal to public finance.

The customs of the Exchequer testify not only to the relentless administrative rhythm of English governance but also to its centralization, continuity, and adaptability. Some classes of Exchequer records such as the pipe rolls, which contain sheriff's accounts, run consecutively from the twelfth to the nineteenth centuries.

Though it has sometimes been viewed as a cumbersome and outdated institution, the Stuart Exchequer displayed the values of an aristocratic society unwilling to relinquish altogether the certainty of custom even as it began to recognize the efficiency and prosperity that fiscal innovation might afford.

Bibliography: C. D. Chandaman, *The English Public Revenue, 1660-1688*, 1975.

Myron C. Noonkester

Exchequer, Stop of. See Stop of the Exchequer.

Exclusion Crisis. The roots of Exclusion, the attempt to alter hereditary succession to the throne or limit the powers of a popish successor, lie in the years 1672-1673. In 1672 Charles II's* Declaration of Indulgence* lifted penalties against private Catholic* divine service, reviving fears about the Counter-Reformation. In 1673 fears intensified when his brother and heir apparent, the duke of York (see James II*), openly refused to attend Anglican* communion, married a Catholic, and resigned his position as lord admiral rather than receive the sacrament in the Church of England and declare against the Catholic doctrine of transubstantiation, as required by Test Act* of 1673 (25 Car. II, c. 2).

After parliament* rejected the indulgence, Charles again allied with "the old Cavaliers* and church party." His new lord treasurer, the earl of Danby (Thomas Osborne*), introduced a "Test Bill" in April 1675, requiring that members of parliament and officeholders declare resistance to the king unlawful and swear not to attempt any alteration of church or state. Opponents of the bill decried court corruption of parliament and the bishops' political activity. Anthony Ashley Cooper*, earl of Shaftesbury's *Letter from a Person of Quality* (1675) and Andrew Marvell's *An Account of the Growth of Popery and Arbitrary Government* (1677) claimed to detect a conspiracy to bring in absolutism.

Such hardening of sides doomed Danby's Test Bill and led to a prorogation from November 1675 to February 1677. When parliament reconvened, fear of French influence, popery, and evil counselors grew. Then in late summer 1678 revelations were made about a Popish Plot* to execute the king and return England to Rome.

Charles was unwilling to dismiss the sham plot revelations because he had indeed received secret payments from Louis XIV (see Treaty of Dover*). Parliament hunted for plotters and Jesuits. Edward Coleman, former secretary to York, was executed on the basis of his letters expressing hopes for Catholicism in England. On 9 November 1678 Charles offered "limitations" on the royal powers of any future Catholic king. But others wanted Exclusion. In voting on the Test Act* of 1678 (30 Car. II, st. 2, c. 1), excluding Catholics from parliament, a proviso excepting York passed by only two votes. When attention turned to Danby (privy to secret payments to the Crown), Charles prorogued and then dissolved the Cavalier Parliament* on 24 January 1679.

The height of the Exclusion Crisis came with three general elections and the three Exclusion Parliaments held between March 1679 and March 1681. In the first election, Danby's supporters were tarred as "pensioners" in the torrent of partisan pamphlets and newspapers printed after the Licensing Act* (14 Car. II, c. 33) lapsed in 1678. The first Exclusion Parliament, 6 March to 27 May, impeached Danby and sent him to the Tower. On 21 May the first Exclusion bill, excluding York from the succession in favor of his daughter Mary*, passed its second reading by a two-to-one margin in the House of Commons (one-third abstained). Antipathy to York was based on his Catholicism and his high-handed defense of royal prerogative*. To stymie the Exclusionists (the nucleus of the first Whigs*), Charles prorogued and then dissolved parliament on 12 July.

Elections for the second Exclusion Parliament in the autumn of 1679 strengthened the Exclusionists. Charles's successive prorogations of parliament (7 October 1679-21 October 1680) suggested arbitrary rule. Shaftesbury and the Exclusionists organized mass petitions to urge Charles to summon parliament, keeping alive popular partisanship. In the summer of 1680, Charles prosecuted for seditious libel journalists supporting Exclusion and petitioning. The Petitioners* of 1680 became the Whigs. Those organizing addresses from official bodies in "abhorrence" of petitions, the Abhorrers*, became the first Tories*.

When parliament finally met in October 1680, it refused to grant supply without Exclusion. The second Exclusion Bill passed the House of Commons unanimously, only to be rejected by the House of Lords on 15 November 1680. The bill would have excluded York not only from the succession but from England as well. Charles quickly summoned a new parliament to meet at Oxford, distant from London* Whig radicals. Despite a Tory challenge, mainly Whigs were returned. The third Exclusion Parliament, the Oxford Parliament*, met on 21 March 1681 and again considered Exclusion. But Charles dissolved parliament a week later; increasing customs revenue and secret supply from France freed him from needing it.

Exclusion Crisis partisanship continued after the dissolution through the *Quo Warranto* campaign and political trials. *Quo Warranto,* a legal device used by the Crown to revoke charters and remove Whigs from town councils (see Local Government, Towns*), bolstered local Tories. London defended their charter at law unsuccessfully, and though London juries dismissed evidence against Shaftesbury and individual Whigs, one radical, Stephen College, was executed in August. Whigs and Tories continued to gather at rival coffee houses* and feasts, buttressed by partisan oaths, healths, and sermons. But the Whig press wilted as prosecutions and Roger L'Estrange's vicious attacks on Whig principles in his *Observator* took their toll.

Whig and Tory ideological battles produced classic works of political theory. The Tories upheld divine right monarchy*, first printing Sir Robert Filmer's *Patriarcha* in 1680. A plethora of Tory tracts and sermons on the evils of resistance reinforced Filmer's arguments for subjection to the Crown. This "drum ecclesiastic" provoked Shaftesbury's assistant, John Locke*, to write *Two Treatises of Government* to justify the right of resistance, probably in the early 1680s. Algernon Sidney penned a line-by-line rebuttal of Filmer. Whigs discussed radical steps against arbitrary rule. Proposals circulated for an "Association," a paramilitia to resist any Catholic coup. And in 1681 Whigs claimed they had to bring armed supporters to Oxford.

In April 1681 Charles II's *Declaration* claimed that some members of parliament had planned to go beyond Exclusion and return to their "old Beloved Commonwealth Principles." This evocation of the Civil War* became a touchstone for loyal Tory addresses. Most Whigs had already turned or been purged from town councils and county benches (see Local Government, Counties*) when evidence was uncovered of radical Whig plans to kidnap and kill Charles and James. The Rye House Plot* of 1683 ended the Exclusion Crisis. Locke hid his papers and followed Shaftesbury abroad. Lord William Russell and Sidney died on the scaffold. Tory ideology, which equated Whiggism with fanaticism, was vindicated. In 1685 James II acceded to the throne with strong support.

Historians disagree about whether the first Whigs introduced partisan organization into English politics. J. R. Jones argues that Shaftesbury organized a parliamentary party committed solely to Exclusion. Jonathan Scott claims the first parties were ideological, not organizational, and that Exclusion was just one expedient to quell century-long fears of popery and absolutism*. In any case, 1678-1683 was a harbinger of the "exclusion crisis" of the Glorious Revolution*.

Bibliography: J. R. Jones, *The First Whigs: The Politics of the Exclusion Crisis, 1678-1683*, 1961; Jonathan Scott, *Algernon Sidney and the Restoration Crisis, 1677-1683*, 1991.

Newton E. Key

Exclusion Parliaments (1679-1681). See Exclusion Crisis and Oxford Parliament.

F

Fairfax, Thomas, Lord (1612-1671). General of the New Model Army*, Fairfax served as a cavalry commander under his father, Ferdinando, earning a reputation for bravery at Wakefield (1643). Marston Moor* (1644) established his military leadership. When the Self-Denying Ordinance* was proposed, the Long Parliament's* leaders identified Fairfax as the ranking officer of greatest distinction and the one least objectionable politically. In February 1645 they appointed him general.

On 14 June Fairfax triumphed at Naseby*. He then defeated Goring at Langport and in mid-September forced Prince Rupert's surrender at Bristol. In January 1646 he took Dartmouth, and in March he negotiated the disbanding of Goring's army and the surrender of Exeter. With the surrender of Oxford (25 June) and Raglan Castle (19 August), the First Civil War* ended.

In the ensuing conflict over disbanding, Fairfax mediated between the parliamentary Presbyterians* and the army*, standing with his troops regarding pay and indemnity. The conflict escalated with Cornet Joyce's seizure of Charles I* and the election of agitators*; Fairfax approved of neither. Always more comfortable as a soldier than as a statesman, he wanted to resign. Instead, through the next two years he kept the army under control as best he could, which sometimes meant seeming to lead where he knew the army would otherwise go without him.

On 13 March 1648, Ferdinando died, and Thomas became 3d Baron Fairfax. That spring the Second Civil War* began. Fairfax defeated royalist* forces at Maidstone, Kent, and then besieged Colchester. The war ended on 28 August when Colchester surrendered, the senior officers submitting to the victors' "mercy." Fairfax executed two, Sir Charles Lucas and Sir George Lisle, an act that dogged him the rest of his life.

The war brought the conflict between the army and the Presbyterians to a head, and when Pride's Purge* occurred on 6 December, Fairfax was in no position to oppose. He was appointed a commissioner for the trial of the king (see Charles I, Trial, Execution, and Cult of*), but when his name was called on the first day, 20 January 1649, his wife shouted from the gallery, "He has more wit than to be here." Behind the scenes he lobbied for putting off the king's execution and ever afterward felt guilt at complicity in his death.

In the new Commonwealth*, Fairfax was appointed to the council of state*. Exempted from signing the Engagement*, he nonetheless promised to defend parliament*. In the following months he suppressed the London* Levellers*, the Diggers*, and Leveller mutineers in the army, breaking their power at Burford in mid-May 1649. On 20 June 1650, when the council ordered a preemptive strike into Scotland*, Fairfax protested that it would violate the Solemn League and Covenant*, and he resigned his commission, retiring to Nunappleton, Yorkshire. For his daughter Mary's tutor, Fairfax hired Andrew Marvell, the poet and future member of parliament from Hull.

Under the Protectorate*, Fairfax was appointed to parliament but did not serve, and he was regarded with suspicion, especially after Mary's marriage in 1657 to the 2d duke of Buckingham (George Villiers*). Under Richard Cromwell*, Fairfax did take his parliamentary seat, and when the army deposed Richard and recalled the Rump Parliament*, Fairfax was named to the council of state but did not serve. When, at the beginning of 1660, General Monck* invaded from Scotland, Fairfax pacified York and pressed Monck successfully to declare for calling the Convention Parliament*. In May he served as a delegate to Charles II* to arrange the Restoration*, receiving a royal pardon. He later spoke against exceptions to a general amnesty.

Bibliography: Thomas Lord Fairfax, *Short Memorials*, and *A Short Memorial of the Northern Actions,* in C. H. Firth, ed., *Stuart Tracts, 1603-1693,* 1896; J. Wilson, *Fairfax,* 1985.

Mark Heumann

Family. See Social Structure and Ranks.

Fen Drainage. Draining the East Anglian fens (marshes), which Charles I* encouraged to improve agriculture* and increase royal revenue (see Taxation and Revenue*), challenged local property rights to commonable fenland and caused dozens of riots during the seventeenth century. Earlier carried out piecemeal by commissions of sewers, drainage (of about 1430 square miles) was entrusted to undertakers (who undertook to carry it out systematically): Sir Cornelius Vermuyden in the Hatfield Level in 1626; the earl of Bedford (after earlier efforts) in the Great Level and Deeping Level in 1631; Sir John Monson in the Ancholme Level in 1635; and various courtiers, headed by Sir Robert and Sir William Killigrew, in East, West, and Wildmore Fens, Holland Fen, and Lindsey Level.

Supporters, claiming the fens were barren and unproductive, argued that drainage would bring such benefits as reduced poverty and unemployment, better wages, increased arable, more productive pasturage, less flooding, and internal colonization*. Opponents, like Sir John Maynard, argued that the traditional fenland economy was already quite productive, noting the value of common pasture, winter fodder, fish, wild fowl, rabbits, turf, sedge, wood, reeds, hemp, flax, and so on. They contended that drainage actually made flooding worse in places and interfered with navigation, that drained land was inequitably distributed or illegally enclosed, and that undertakers imported Dutch and French labor. Opponents included gentry as well as commoners (perhaps Oliver Cromwell* in 1637), and justices of the peace, sewer commissioners, constables, and juries were frequently uncooperative (see Local Government*). However, the often unscrupulous undertakers had the support of the king, privy council*, Star Chamber (see Prerogative Courts*), Exchequer*, and Duchy of Lancaster courts.

Keith Lindley describes the riots as "defensive, conservative, and restrained," often occurring only when locals failed to obtain legal redress (e.g., through a trial of title). Frequently the rioters' goal was to break down fences, fill in ditches, or otherwise obstruct drainage and enclosure, and while threats of violence were common, serious injury was not. Opponents were more concerned with preserving traditional rights than with political and constitutional issues. However, the frequency, size, and organization of riots may have driven some nobility and gentry, wary of social upheaval, into the king's arms in the 1640s. Fenland riots were among the larger disturbances of the Stuart era, often numbering in the hundreds, and were carried out with considerable skill.

During Charles's reign, especially the Personal Rule* (1629-1640), riots were part of a pattern of resistance to central government interference (as with ship money*). With the Short Parliament* (1640) and Long Parliament* (1640-1649), opponents looked to the Commons for assistance, while Lords supported the undertakers. Fenland riots contributed to the disorder that brought the Civil War* (1642-1648), during which opponents of drainage tended to side with parliament* and undertakers with the king, though not always; commoners' alignment probably had less to do with supporting parliamentarians* against royalists* than with the opportunity to take back common lands. During the Interregnum* (1649-1660), however, drainage revived due, for example, to the Rump Parliament's* passage of the Great Level Act of 1649 to benefit a few powerful parliamentarians, backed by the council of state*. The Levellers* John Lilburne* and John Wildman helped lead resistance in the Hatfield Level, particularly the Isle of Axholme. But ultimately this hurt both the Levellers, whose enemies cited the riots to portray them as communist enemies of property like the Diggers*, and local commoners, whose affiliation with Lilburne and Wildman branded them as subversives and diverted attention from the question of title, where they had a strong case.

Following the Restoration* in 1660, parliamentary consent was necessary for drainage projects (e.g., the Great Level Act of 1663). But while parliament refused to consider schemes that lacked some local support, many that it did approve provoked disturbances. Ultimately the involvement of substantial local men allowed prewar undertakers or their descendants to revive some projects, notably Sir John Monson in Ancholme Level. But trouble did not end until the Riot Act (1 Geo. I, st. 2, c. 5) passed in 1715, and over half the land in the Isle of Axholme once in undertakers' hands was returned to commoners. Of course, in many fenland communities there was no rioting or little, and peaceful accommodation between undertakers and commoners occurred.

Bibliography: H. C. Darby, *The Changing Fenland*, 1983; Mark E. Kennedy, "Charles I and Local Government: The Draining of the East and West Fens," *Albion* 15 (1983): 19-31; Keith Lindley, *Fenland Riots and the English Revolution*, 1982.

William B. Robison

Fiennes, William, 1st Viscount Saye and Sele (1582-1662). One of the leaders of aristocratic opposition to Charles I*, he was born at Broughton Castle, Oxfordshire, on 28 May 1582, the son and heir of Richard Fiennes, 7th Lord Saye and Sele. Educated at Winchester and New College, Oxford, he married Elizabeth Temple (around 1602) and succeeded as 8th Lord Saye and Sele shortly before 6 February 1613. A zealous Protestant from his youth, he was strongly opposed to James I's* pro-Spanish foreign policy and an opponent of the Crown's attempts to assert its royal prerogative* rights over the subject's property without parliamentary consent. In 1622 he was imprisoned for refusing James's benevolence (a compulsory levy for the aid of the Palatinate), arguing that the subject should not be compelled to give to the Crown out of parliament* (see Taxation and Revenue*).

Saye's fortunes changed briefly in 1624, with George Villiers*, 1st duke of Buckingham's rapprochement with the anti-Spanish war party, and he was created a viscount through the duke's influence on 7 July 1624. But he broke with the court after the York House Conference (February 1626) when it became apparent that the duke and the new king, Charles I*, were intent upon the promotion of Arminian* clergy within the church. Saye refused Charles's forced loan* of 1626. During the parliaments of 1626* and 1628*, he emerged as a vigorous defender of the House of Lords' powers of judicature (which had been revived in 1621) and a fierce opponent of Buckingham.

Saye was profoundly alienated by the policies pursued during Charles I's Personal Rule*. During the 1630s he was actively involved in plans to create a godly commonwealth on Providence Island in the Caribbean. In 1637 he led the resistance to the imposition of ship money* in Oxfordshire and Gloucestershire and initiated a challenge to its legality (in which his counsel was Oliver St. John), later taken up by his friend and feoffee, John Hampden*. On the outbreak of war with Scotland* in 1639, he refused to support the king against the Covenanters* and was again briefly imprisoned. He voted against the provision of supply before redress of grievances in the Short Parliament* (April-May 1640) and was arrested, with John Pym* and Hampden, after its dissolution. In August 1640 he signed the Petition of the Twelve Peers (calling on Charles to summon a parliament) and was probably complicit in the Scottish invasion of that year.

With the earls of Bedford and Essex (Robert Devereux*), Saye was one of the peers Charles sought to conciliate at the beginning of the Long Parliament*, appointing him to the lucrative mastership of the court of wards (17 May 1641). After the outbreak of the Civil War*, Saye became one of the most influential members of

the Long Parliament, closely allied in politics with St. John and the younger Sir
Henry Vane in the Commons and with Lord Wharton and the earl of Northumberland
in the House of Lords. An advocate of a decisive victory over the king, he supported
a military alliance between the parliamentarians* and the Scots in 1643 and (with
Northumberland) introduced the legislation in February 1644 that led to the creation
of the Committee of Both Kingdoms*. Strongly critical of the management of the war
under the 3d earl of Essex, he was one of the principal architects of the military
reforms of 1644-1645 that led to the creation of the New Model Army* and secured
the passage of its officer list by the production of a proxy vote (17-18 March 1645).
Committed to the imposition of strict limitations on the king's personal authority,
Saye resisted Presbyterian* attempts to disband the New Model Army during the
spring of 1647, before a secure settlement had been established.   An Erastian
Independent* in religion, he vigorously opposed Scottish attempts to impose a
clerically controlled Presbyterian church in England during the 1640s, though he
supported the establishment of a lay-controlled Presbyterian state church provided this
allowed liberty of worship to Independent congregations.

In July 1647 he was one of a group of leading Independents who, with Oliver
Cromwell* and Henry Ireton*, devised the Heads of the Proposals*, a comprehensive
program for constitutional reform and limited religious toleration (published on 1
August 1647). The army's coup d'état and Charles I's execution* (January 1649)
moved Saye to boycott political life during the Commonwealth* and Protectorate*.
In 1657 he refused Cromwell's invitation to attend the protectoral "upper house"
created under the Humble Petition and Advice*.

Now in his late seventies, he resumed public life with the meeting of the
Convention Parliament* (25 April 1660), supporting the Restoration* of Charles II*
and being rewarded with appointment to the privy council* (by 6 June 1660). He died
at Broughton Castle on 14 April 1662, leaving an extensive library (valued for probate
at £500). His political and religious beliefs are most fully expounded in the *Vindiciae
Veritatis* (written during 1646 and 1648 and published anonymously in 1654).

Bibliography: J. S. A. Adamson, "The *Vindiciae Veritatis* and the Political Creed of
Viscount Saye and Sele," *Historical Research* 60 (1987): 45-63; M. L. Schwartz,
"Lord Saye and Sele's Objections to the Palatinate Benevolence of 1622," *Albion* 5
(1971): 12-22.

                                                                    John Adamson

Fifth Monarchy Men. A religious and political sect, the Fifth Monarchists believed
that Christ would return to earth after the saints had seized civil and military power;
the millennial kingdom they intended to establish would be external and visible and
would impose godly discipline on the unregenerate. The movement originated after
Oliver Cromwell's* dramatic victory at Worcester in September 1651, when some of
the godly met with him to urge that he press forward in the Good Old Cause*.
Cromwell soon proved unreceptive to their vision, but in December they gathered in
London* to formulate General Heads of Prayer, pledging to pull down anything that

stood in the way of Christ's kingdom, to remove ungodly ministers and magistrates, and to unite the godly. Their leaders on this occasion were the ministers Christopher Feake (1612-c.1683), John Simpson (d. 1662), and Henry Jessey (1601-1663). Following the dissolution of the Rump Parliament*, the most politically prominent of the Fifth Monarchists, Major-General Thomas Harrison (1616-1660), played a key role in establishing the Assembly of Saints (Barebone's Parliament*), of whose more than 140 members only twelve were Fifth Monarchy Men. With other radicals they shared a desire for sweeping law reform, the abolition of tithes, and complete freedom of preaching in public places. In all this they failed, though the cumulative strength of the radicals was sufficiently pronounced to persuade the moderates in the Assembly, who feared the security of property, to yield their power to Cromwell.

The collapse of this Nominated Assembly drove the Fifth Monarchists to increasingly strident hostility against the regime. Unwilling to accept the Protectorate*, Harrison lost his commission and underwent brief imprisonment in 1654 and 1655. Other Fifth Monarchists, including Simpson and Anna Trapnel (fl.1642-1660), proclaimed visions depicting Cromwell's imminent destruction and attacked the government in print. Vavasor Powell (1617-1670) tried to rally supporters in Wales*, raising fears of insurrection. A more serious threat were the negotiations between the Fifth Monarchists and the Commonwealthmen*, including Vice-Admiral John Lawson and Colonel John Okey, during the winter of 1655-1656; the state quelled this threat with a series of arrests. In late 1656 the Fifth Monarchy Men issued militant resolutions in which they reiterated their determination to overthrow nations, kings, corporations, and universities*, identified Cromwell as the little horn in Daniel's prophecy, and praised the work of John of Leyden, the notorious leader of the Münster Anabaptists.

The first attempt to topple the government came in 1657, when Thomas Venner (c. 1608-1661) and 124 followers in London planned an uprising. Most Fifth Monarchists, including Harrison and John Carew (1622-1660), refused to join them. The printed manifesto of the Vennerites called for the godly to rule through a sanhedrin, for laws derived from Scripture, and for the reform of land tenures. The army* suppressed the rebels before they could launch an attack, but Venner tried again in January 1661. This time approximately fifty men took up arms and occupied government troops for nearly four days. Venner and his principal supporters were executed; one of them, Roger Hodgkin, defiantly called for divine vengeance on Charles II*, the judges, and the City of London. Fifth Monarchists continued to oppose the Stuart regime in subsequent decades; indeed, Henry Danvers (c.1622-1687) was supposed to have led an uprising in London to support Monmouth's Rebellion* in the spring of 1685.

The Fifth Monarchists, the majority of whom were female, drew most of their strength from urban areas, particularly London. Before the Restoration, most of their adherents came from southern England and Wales, but after 1660 their strength shifted to Yorkshire, Durham, and Westmorland, as they won recruits among Baptists* and ex-soldiers. Socially the Fifth Monarchists came from the middling and lower social orders; the most prominent occupation involved the clothing industry, in which approximately a third of the saints participated. The leadership of the movement was provided by ministers and military officers.

Bibliography: B. S. Capp, *The Fifth Monarchy Men: A Study in Seventeenth-Century English Millenarianism,* 1972; P. G. Rogers, *The Fifth Monarchy Men,* 1966.

Richard L. Greaves

Five Articles of Perth. In 1615 James I* appointed as archbishop of St. Andrews John Spottiswoode, an administrator willing to accommodate his desire for the Scottish Kirk* to adopt practices compatible with those of the Anglican* church. This led to the Five Articles of Perth. Spottiswoode convened a general assembly in Aberdeen in 1616 that adopted a new confession of faith, a liturgy to be written with canons, and a confirmation ritual compatible with Anglican practices, except that ministers could administer it. English-style scholarships for divinity students and studies of parish record keeping and ministers' stipends were recommended. James was determined to have bishops alone administer confirmation and to append to the Aberdeen recommendations his views on the propriety of private baptism, justification for kneeling at communion, and guidelines for the celebration of five chief holidays, including Christmas and Easter. Together these reforms comprised the so-called Five Articles of Perth. They were accepted by Spottiswoode, who advised the king not to impose them.

In 1617 James made his final return to Scotland*. In the Scottish parliament a bill was debated that allowed the king to decide "all matters decent for the external policy of the Kirk." It was opposed so broadly that James prudently withdrew the bill but unwisely reasserted his royal prerogative* to decide all church issues. After the parliament adjourned, James punished protesters and reasserted to the bishops his determination to enforce the articles. The bishops assured James that a compliant general assembly could be convened. Unfortunately the November 1617 general assembly was so poorly attended that it was ended without a vote. James then imposed the celebration of religious holidays and threatened financial punishments. James's anger abated, but his resolve remained firm.

Good fortune and planning before the opening of the last general assembly of James's reign in Perth on 25 August 1618 helped the government. Spottiswoode managed to get the Five Articles approved by the Perth assembly. Enforcement proved impossible. While holiday celebrations were seriously encouraged, church attendance remained low, and few ministers were penalized. While proclamations urging obedience were issued in 1619 and 1620, little action was taken. In the parliament of 1621 the government secured passage of the bill enacting the Five Articles by a narrow margin. Still James pressed for enforcement. In September a proclamation required the Scottish council to obtain conformity to the articles from every public official on pain of dismissal. Some council members affirmed their obedience very belatedly, as did many judges and court officials. No effort was made to determine if they kept their word. Lesser officials were questioned only if complaints were lodged. While High Commission (see Ecclesiastical Courts*;

Prerogative Courts*) proceeded more diligently, few ministers were deprived, and all serious efforts to effect obedience were ended in 1622.

The campaign to implement the Five Articles of Perth was one of James's most counterproductive projects. His enactment of the Five Articles was a major blunder that marked the limitation of his ability to control the Scotland by pen. The experience showed the Scots that successful defiance could be organized, and James's intransigence reinforced their suspicions of efforts to reform the Kirk, which led to the Bishops' Wars* in the next decade.

Bibliography: Maurice Lee, *Government by Pen: Scotland under James VI and I*, 1980.

Sheldon Hanft

Five Knights Case (1627). This case arose out of the financial troubles of Charles I* during the first years of his reign and his attempts to resolve them partially through the expedient of a forced loan*. The case came before the King's Bench (see Common Law and Courts*) in 1627 and raised the question of whether the king's special command was sufficient cause for the arrest and imprisonment of his subjects when no statute of parliament* had been violated.

In 1626 Charles was desperate to finance his military adventures. England had been at war with Spain on and off for some years and renewed the conflict while James I* was still king (see Spanish War of 1625-1630*). Although popular with parliament at its beginning, support withered in 1625 after Charles became king. The parliament of 1625* granted the Crown the historic import duty, tonnage and poundage, for only one year instead of for life, as was customary when a new king ascended the throne (see Taxation and Revenue*). Parliament also granted a war subsidy that Charles thought insufficient. In disgust and frustration, Charles dissolved parliament in August 1625. The military situation worsened, and the Crown was near bankruptcy. Charles was forced to call a second parliament in 1626*, but the election was another humiliation for him. The House of Commons was more uncooperative, and the House of Lords for the first time joined forces with Commons against a Stuart king. The Lords were extremely upset with the Crown's mercenary sale of titles and with the crass promotion by the king's favorite, George Villiers*, 1st duke of Buckingham, of his many friends and relatives. Both houses proceeded to blame the national disgrace of the Cadiz expedition* (1625) on Buckingham and began work on his impeachment*. To save Buckingham, Charles had to dissolve his second parliament, but this left his financial situation worse. Parliament had not voted tonnage and poundage for a second year, or a new war subsidy.

Charles claimed a royal prerogative* right to tonnage and poundage and continued to collect it anyway. In September 1626 he also declared the largest forced loan in English history. While the revenue produced saved the Crown for the moment, the policy lost Charles the trust and support of the propertied and mercantile classes. Forced loans were not new to Englishmen, and individuals had refused in the past. This time, however, resistance was widespread. Charles imprisoned seventy-six gentlemen for refusing, including fifteen peers. The number of commoners imprisoned or impressed into the military has never been accurately counted. Not all chose to suffer their fate quietly. In 1627 five knights—Sir Thomas Darnel, Sir John Corbet, Sir Walter Earl, Sir John Heveningham, and Sir Edmund Hampden—sued for a writ of habeas corpus from the King's Bench. Their barristers based their case on Magna Carta and other ancient statutes of England's fundamental law and claimed that the forced loan was illegal and, therefore, that the arrests were arbitrary. The five knights had violated no statute of parliament, and argued that without cause in law being shown, they must be granted a writ of habeas corpus and released from prison. The Crown's position, based solely on legal precedent, was that the king's special command was sufficient cause. The king claimed the right to imprison any of his subjects without due process of law on the plea of national security. The court agreed with the Crown, sidestepping the question of whether the forced loans were legitimate.

Historically the court was correct. The King's Bench still operated on the principle that all justice flowed from the king, and the court's function was to dispense this justice. The argument presented by the five knights' barristers implied that the judiciary in England was independent of the executive and that subjects of the king had the right to be protected in their rights and privileges by the king, but that the courts should protect them from the king, when he or his agents acted contrary to law. English courts in general, and the King's Bench in particular, were not independent of the executive in 1627.

In the next parliament (of 1628-1629*), however, the interpretation of habeas corpus as presented during the Five Knights Case was included by Sir Edward Coke* as one of the major elements of the Petition of Right* of 1628. Although many other cases were part of its evolution, the Five Knights Case was a significant cause of the Habeas Corpus Act (31 Car. II, c. 2) of 1679. All those imprisoned for nonpayment of the forced loan were released by Charles on 2 January 1628, just three months before the new parliament was convened. Charles hoped this would be a conciliatory measure that would help produce a tractable parliament. Instead, twenty-seven of the released prisoners successfully stood for election and carried their fight into parliament.

Bibliography: William F. Duker, *A Constitutional History of Habeas Corpus,* 1980.

Richard L. Hillard

Five Members (1642). On 3 January 1642 Charles I* accused Lord Mandeville and five members of parliament* (MPs) of high treason for their role in the passage and proposed publication of the Grand Remonstrance*, which had been presented to the king on 1 December 1641. In early January 1642 rumors circulated around London* that parliament was considering articles of impeachment* against Queen Henrietta Maria*. This threat to his wife encouraged Charles to dispatch his attorney general with a warrant to arrest the Five Members for high treason and other high misdemeanors, including attempting to subvert the fundamental laws of the realm, to alienate the affections of the English people from their king, to make the army* disobedient, to encourage the Scots to invade England, to conspire to wage war against king and Parliament, and to subvert the power and authority of Parliament. The accused MPs were John Pym*, Denzil Holles, Sir Arthur Haselrig, John Hampden*, and William Strode as well as one peer, Edward Montague, 2d earl of Manchester, lord Kimbolton, viscount Mandeville. The Commons refused to surrender its members, however, citing privilege. The House of Lords also refused to act until an investigation could be held into the precedent for the arrest of members of parliament.

When Charles' attorney general returned without the Five Members, Henrietta Maria was furious, exclaiming: "Go, you coward, and pull these rogues out by their ears, or never see my face more." Stung by his wife's words, Charles promised to arrest the men within the hour and placed himself at the head of a force of approximately 400 armed men. Upon his arrival at Westminster, the king, accompanied by Prince Rupert, stepped uninvited into the hall. With his soldiers watching from the antechamber, the king asked Speaker of the House William Lenthall to identify the members he had accused of treason. Lenthall refused to do so, however, citing his responsibility as speaker to the Commons. In fact the accused MPs were not in the chamber; they had been forewarned of the king's approach and had sought the protection of London at Grocers' Hall. After looking around unsuccessfully for Pym and his associates, Charles admitted, "I see that the birds are flown." As he left, the chamber was filled with shouts of "Privilege! Privilege!"

The next day Charles approached the City of London in an effort to get the city officials to surrender the Five Members, but the Common Council refused the orders of both the king and the lord mayor to relinquish them. London also named Philip Skippon, a former sergeant-major general, as commander of the London Trained Bands. On 11 January the Five Members victoriously returned to parliament, the day after Charles had left for Hampton Court. Parliament officially responded to the king's attempt to arrest the Five Members in a resolution dated 17 January, which concerned Charles's recent breach of parliamentary privilege. The declaration of the House of Commons concerning the king's recent violation of its privileges criticized the king for a number of offenses, including placing himself in the speaker's chair, keeping the door to the hall open, and tolerating soldiers who gave "wicked oaths" and intimidated MPs. Commons further protested Charles's claim that the five sought refuge in London only to escape justice. Parliament strenuously objected to the issuance of warrants without charges or accusations and the threat of force to capture the Five Members. Finally parliament suggested that reconciliation was possible only if Charles would issue warrants for those who advised him to act illegally and would declare them public enemies. Parliament further demonstrated its opposition to the king by promising its protection to the protectors of the Five Members. Although Charles declared his willingness to cooperate with parliament on 20 January, his illegal attempt to arrest the Five Members swung public opinion to parliament's side.

Bibliography: J. Forester, *The Arrest of the Five Members by Charles I*, 1860; S. R. Gardiner, *Constitutional Documents of the Puritan Revolution, 1625-1660*, 3d ed., 1927.

David B. Mock

Flight of the Earls (1607). The Flight of the Earls was the departure of the chief leaders of Gaelic Ireland* into exile on 4 September 1607. An event of tremendous symbolic significance in Irish history, it marks the surrender of the leaders of Gaelic Ireland to the forces of Anglicization. Its impact on the affairs of Ulster was particularly significant, as the earls were subsequently attainted and their lands alienated to the Crown in 1612. This cleared the way for widespread plantation* of Ulster by English and Scottish settlers during the following decades. Further, it deprived Gaelic Ireland of its natural leadership in future resistance to English policy. Though it was primarily organized by Connaught Maguire, lord of Fermagh, to transport himself and Rory O'Donnell, earl of Tyrconnell, to the Continent, the most prominent figure involved was Hugh O'Neill, earl of Tyrone.

The flight is usually portrayed as the natural postscript to the O'Neill or Tyrone Rebellion (1594-1603), in which English forces defeated a Gaelic and Catholic* rebellion. Modern research, however, has found this assumption misleading. The main question is why O'Neill joined in this venture. Maguire and Tyrconnell had suffered severe reductions of their authority since the capitulation of 1603. Like many other young Irishmen, they hoped to build new fortunes serving the Spanish army in the Netherlands. O'Neill, however, was a mature man beyond such adventures. Further, in the previous four years, Tyrone had experienced success negotiating the English system and was repeatedly favored by James I*. He had recovered his fortune and a promising future by cooperation with the English Crown. His sudden decision in late August to join Tyrconnell and Maguire surprised his contemporaries and has intrigued historians as well.

O'Neill probably believed that his loyalty to James was compromised by Tyrconnell's negotiations with the Spanish. In a letter to James explaining the flight, O'Neill listed four reasons. The first was increasing government pressure upon Catholics to conform with the Church of England (see Anglicanism*). The second was an assertion that the king's officers in Dublin wished to deprive him of his rightful property. The third concerned the introduction of English common law* officials into Tyrone, where they contradicted his authority as the king's lieutenant. Finally he maintained that the officials in Dublin were both ambitious and hostile to him personally. This is a highly perceptive summary of the English policy regarding Ulster and reflects general "old Irish" fears in the early seventeenth century. Since Hugh O'Neill was fully cognizant of the bleak future of Gaelic Ireland, his flight into voluntary exile in 1607 was both reasonable and as symbolically important as Irish tradition has maintained. He remained on the Continent for the remainder of his life, a model for the community of Irish exiles that would be known as "the Wild Geese" throughout the seventeenth and eighteenth centuries.

Bibliography: N. P. Canny, "The Flight of the Earls, 1607," *Irish Historical Studies*, vol. 17, no. 67 (1971).

                                                                        John Nolan

Forced Loan (1626-1627). The forced loan (a term coined by later historians) was a tax levied by Charles I* to pay for the Spanish War of 1625-1630*. Unlike privy seal loans, which were personal requests from the king to individuals to lend him money with the expectation of repayment, the forced loan was imposed on all subsidy payers (see Taxation and Revenue*). It demanded the equivalent of five subsidies, and there was no mechanism for repayment. It was described as forced largely because the king used an unprecedented degree of coercion to collect the tax, imprisoning over a hundred leading gentry who refused to pay and threatening lesser taxpayers with impressment. Otherwise the forced loan stood in a long tradition of aids, loans, and benevolences that medieval and early modern monarchs had resorted to when they were unable to raise taxes through parliament*. These were justified by the argument that when the security of the realm was threatened, a king was entitled to demand aid from his subjects, provided that he consulted his council and refrained from the use of coercion. However, this view had been contested in a series of statutes against aids and benevolences, which declared that even in cases of emergency, national taxes could be taken only with the consent of parliament. Thus when Charles requested a benevolence in the summer of 1626, most taxpayers refused, stating explicitly that they would give only "in a parliamentarie manner."

The forced loan was launched in October 1626. Allowing for the writing off of debts that the Crown owed to various counties for billeting, coat and conduct, and purveyance, it raised a total of £267,064, close to the £275,000 that was raised on a grant of five subsidies from the parliament of 1628*. In financial terms it was a success. However, there was a considerable price to pay in terms of political opposition. Beginning with the stand taken by leading judges and peers in November 1626, this spread to the shires in the following January. In Northamptonshire, Lincolnshire, and Gloucestershire, groups of leading taxpayers openly refused to pay in the presence of privy councilors and loan commissioners, and in Essex there was long, drawn-out resistance from hundreds of ordinary subsidy payers. Between March 1627 and the end of the year, the struggle to collect the money became a process of attrition, with the privy council* gradually wearing down opposition through a mixture of encouragements to local commissioners and threats against those who resisted. In November 1627 five of the imprisoned gentry refusers secured a hearing from the judges in an attempt to test the legality of the action taken against them. This became known as the Five Knights Case*.

The controversy raised by the forced loan focused on three principal areas. First was the issue of whether the king could raise what was in effect a national tax without the consent of parliament. Opponents of the loan argued that it contravened the statutes against aids and benevolences and would threaten the very existence of parliaments in the future. Second, it brought into question the scope of the royal prerogative*. Clerical supporters of the loan, such as Robert Sibthorpe and Roger

Manwaring, had put forward absolutist* arguments to claim that the king's actions were not restricted by statute, that when he judged there to be a necessity for taxation his subjects must accept this and obey him, and that any defiance of the king's commands was tantamount to resistance and rebellion. These views were condemned in the 1628 parliament as a fundamental threat to the liberties and property rights of the subject. Third, the verdict in the Five Knights Case raised the threat of arbitrary imprisonment. The judges had failed to uphold the loan refusers' right to habeas corpus and had ruled instead that they should remain in prison without the king having to show cause for this or present them for a proper trial. This became the main cause of contention in the debates during the 1628 parliament that led to the passage of the Petition of Right*.

Bibliography: Richard Cust, *The Forced Loan and English Politics, 1626-1628*, 1987; J. P. Sommerville, *Politics and Ideology in England, 1603-1640*, 1986.

Richard Cust

Forest Laws. Charles I's* attempts to revive the full system of medieval forest laws and courts during the Personal Rule* of the 1630s was regarded as an attack upon the ancient constitution; along with extraparliamentary taxation* and the questionable jurisdiction of the prerogative courts*, it was a leading cause of conflict between king and parliament* that arose during the initial meetings of the Long Parliament*.

Under the Anglo-Norman and Angevin kings, nearly a third of England had been given over to a system of royal forests, which functioned as game reserves for breeding and protecting deer and boar for the king's recreation in hunting. The forests were legal franchises; the forest laws, which derived only from the royal prerogative*, superseded common law*, and severe punishments were provided for those who presumed to hunt the king's deer without his license. The forest laws were mitigated by Magna Carta of 1215 and the Charter of the Forest of 1217, and extensive areas of the royal hunting reserves were subsequently disafforested. In the minds of Sir Edward Coke* and other common lawyers, the ancient constitution had existed since time immemorial, and the laws that the ancient constitution embodied had been restored by Magna Carta and the Charter of the Forest. The forest laws did not exclude royal tenants from possessing and cultivating land within the royal forests as long as they did not enclose land, cut down timber, or impede the king's beasts when they sought food and cover. Many private owners of disafforested land sought and were granted hunting franchises called liberty of chase or free warren or were allowed to enclose their own private hunting reserves called deer parks. Following the Great Peasants' Revolt of 1381, parliament began to enact a series of game laws intended to punish those who were not entitled by estate or income to hunt or who poached on royal or aristocratic game reserves. Because deer had always been considered wild beasts in common law, the lawyers who drafted such legislation were placed in the legally absurd position of trying to make a crime of taking something that could not be stolen. Consequently the game laws could do no more than make the circumstances in which deer were taken illegal, but not the act itself. The game laws supplemented the forest laws in the punishment of unlawful hunting, but the forest laws remained in effect in an enfeebled form to protect the game, timber, and other natural resources of the royal forests from unauthorized exploitation.

Common lawyers and judges continued to recognize the existence of the forest laws into the early seventeenth century. The forest laws were enforceable only in royal forests where forest and game officers continued to be appointed, where forest courts continued to sit, and where forest boundaries were periodically identified by perambulation. A system of superior forest courts functioned under the jurisdiction of two chief justices in eyre, together with local forest courts called swanimotes.

Demographic expansion (see Population*) and a developing economy led to more intensive exploitation of forest resources in the sixteenth century, while Charles I's inability to levy taxes through parliamentary subsidies led him to turn to extraparliamentary financial expedients, generally described as "fiscal feudalism." One of these fiscal expedients was the enhancement of revenues from forest resources, which was bound to lead to conflict with landowners and dwellers within the royal forests. The plan to revive the forest laws and courts after three centuries of attenuation was conceived by the attorney general, Sir William Noy, a legal antiquarian who ransacked the past for profitable schemes. With the earl of Holland presiding as chief justice in eyre, eyre courts were convened first in Windsor, then Dean, and later Waltham forests. The first aroused little alarm because royal rights had always been maintained in Windsor Forest; the second exacerbated existing popular unrest; and the third outraged property owners throughout the realm by constituting nearly the whole of the county of Essex as a royal forest and imposing stiff fines for encroachment and illegal exploitation of forest resources upon landowners whose ancestors had dwelled there unmolested for three centuries. This had the effect of canceling all of the provisions of Magna Carta and the Charter of the Forest promising disafforestation. Landowners who thought that they were secure in the titles to lands and homes found themselves denied the opportunity to plead their cases according to the rules of English law. As Edward Hyde*, earl of Clarendon, observed in his *History of the Rebellion,* the forest eyre proceedings touched persons of high rank who thought that they were "above ordinary oppressions." Although the assessment of heavy fines upon these landowners did not necessarily turn them into parliamentarians*, by the Act for the Certainty of Forests of 1641 (16 Car. I, c. 16), the Long Parliament restored forest boundaries to what they had been in the twentieth year of the reign of James I* (excepting recent disafforestations) and declared illegal any forest courts that had been erected in the previous sixty years.

Bibliography: George Hammersley, "The Revival of the Forest Laws under Charles I," *History* 45 (1960): 85-102; Roger B. Manning, *Hunters and Poachers: A Social and Cultural History of Unlawful Hunting in England, 1485-1640,* 1993; Philip A. J. Pettit, *The Royal Forests of Northamptonshire: A Study in their Economy, 1558-1714,* 1968.

Roger B. Manning

Fox, George (1624-91). Founder of the Religious Society of Friends, the Quakers*, George Fox was born in July 1624 at Fenny Drayton, Leicestershire. His parents brought up their son in a religious household, and they originally wanted him to study for the ministry in the Anglican* church.   Instead he became apprenticed to a shoemaker. Fox, a serious and earnest youth, became disillusioned with the church and the frivolous state of English society. In 1643 he left home for nine months, searching for religious truth in the Bible* and in the company of Seekers*.

In 1646-1647 he received a revelation and came to rely on the "inner light of the living Christ," the divine truth within each person. In the tradition of the mystics, Fox saw no need for intermediaries in religion because of this divine presence in each soul.   Believing that formal education was unnecessary, Fox emphasized the priesthood of all believers. People should sit in silence and allow the spirit of Christ to speak to them.   He also ignored signs of class distinction and social and ecclesiastical conventions. Fox began to preach his message in 1647 and soon attracted followers. In 1649 he was jailed in Nottingham for disturbing a church service, the first of eight jail sentences. Fox received a vision in 1652 when he climbed Pendle Hill in Lancashire and saw a multitude waiting to be "gathered."

A charismatic preacher, Fox attracted many followers, such as Robert Barclay (1648-1690), William Penn (1644-1718), and Isaac Penington (1616-1679). In 1652 Fox's message impressed Margaret Fell of Swarthmore Hall near Ulverstone. Her husband, Judge Thomas Fell, vice-chancellor of the duchy of Lancaster, also fell under his influence, and Swarthmore Hall became the headquarters of Fox's activities. Margaret Fell raised money to finance Fox's activities and carried on correspondence with his missionaries, who were usually sent out in pairs. After the death of her husband, Fox married her in 1669.

Fox did not intend to start a new denomination, but it became apparent that some organization was needed. During the 1660s he initiated a system of local and county meetings to discuss issues and to conduct business, and in 1668 an annual meeting on the national level was established.   He also carried his message outside England, visiting Ireland* (1669), the West Indies and North America (1671-1672),and Holland (1677, 1684). Fox spent the last years of his life in London*, working for religious toleration. He died on 13 January 1691.

During his life Fox published several pamphlets dealing with theological and social questions, *The Great Mission* (1659) being his only lengthy theological treatise. His *Journal*, published posthumously in 1694, described his conversion and religious experiences. In addition to championing religious freedom, Fox preached against slavery, war, and violence; advocated prison reform; preached on the equality of all people; and promoted education. He also instituted a register of births, marriages, and deaths before a national system was adopted in the nineteenth century.

Bibliography: N. Penny, ed., *The Journal of George Fox*, 2 vols., 1973; Harry Emerson Wildes, *Voice of the Lord: A Biography of George Fox*, 1965.

René Kollar

French War of 1627-1629. This conflict grew out of the failure of the Anglo-French alliance of 1624 and the acute mistrust with which the British royal court* regarded French intentions. Britain had allied with France at James I's* insistence, to ensure the support of a major Catholic* power in any conflict with Habsburg Spain and Austria. Many British diplomats, however, feared the influence of ultra-Catholic and pro-Spanish *Devots* at the French court. Cardinal Richelieu, who had come to power with *Devot* support in 1624, was particularly mistrusted.

In September 1625 Richelieu employed ships borrowed from the English and Dutch to defeat a rebellious Huguenot fleet and blockade the Protestant port of La Rochelle, provoking consternation in London*. British naval intervention was avoided only when Louis XIII and the Huguenots reached an accord in February 1626. Shortly thereafter France secretly concluded a separate peace with Spain, which the British regarded as a betrayal of trust. Richelieu's attempt to construct a credible French navy added to the anxiety of the British council of war, which concluded in June that the buildup of French naval power must be opposed "for reasons of state." Tensions were further exacerbated by Charles I's* expulsion on 8 August of Queen Henrietta Maria's* French attendants, whom he blamed for fomenting marital discord, by English seizure of French ships suspected of carrying Spanish cargoes, and by the impounding in retaliation of England's Bordeaux wine fleet of more than 200 ships in November.

In August Louis XIII dispatched a new ambassador, the Maréchal Bassompierre, who successfully negotiated a compromise settlement of issues relating to Henrietta Maria's household, renewing hopes of Anglo-French cooperation. But in January 1627 Louis repudiated Bassompierre's treaty, convincing Charles and his favorite, the 1st duke of Buckingham (George Villiers*), that amicable relations would be impossible so long as Richelieu held power. They embarked on war in an effort to topple the cardinal and force a change in French policy.

Britain hoped to exploit discontent with Richelieu among the French aristocracy. Buckingham's client Walter Montagu had been sent to France in June 1626 to contact dissident noblemen and returned in March 1627 to encourage and coordinate a French rebellion. A plan was developed for a Huguenot rising in the south under the duke of Rohan, which Savoy, a member of the anti-Habsburg coalition outraged by Richelieu's peace with Spain, promised to support with troops. Meanwhile, a British force would attack France's west coast, encouraging a new rebellion by La Rochelle and perhaps ultimately striking at Bordeaux.

A fleet carrying 100 horse soldiers and 6,000 foot left England under Buckingham's command on 27 June and arrived at the Ile de Ré off La Rochelle on 10 July (see Navy*). Buckingham landed on the island against opposition and laid siege to the citadel of St. Martin, hoping that its capitulation would precipitate the anticipated rebellion. Success depended on starving the garrison out before the French gathered a relief force or upon the arrival of sufficient additional British troops to hold the island against a counterattack. On 27 September St. Martin offered to surrender. Before terms were negotiated, however, a flotilla of boats managed to slip through the English blockade in the middle of the night, resupplying the fortress.

Against the advice of his council of war, Buckingham elected to continue the siege, encouraged by news that the promised Huguenot rebellion had begun and the expectation that long-awaited reinforcements from England were at last on their way. These had been repeatedly delayed over the summer by administrative problems and acute shortages of funds. They were finally on ship by 18 October, but unfavorable winds prevented them from sailing. By then the French had gathered a relief force, and Buckingham decided, after failing to take St. Martin by storm, to abandon the siege. The French, however, had already landed sufficient troops on the island to attack the retreating British troops from the rear as they attempted to cross a narrow causeway, linking Ré to an adjacent island from which Buckingham planned to disembark. The duke lost an estimated 1,000 men, including over half his officers, in a humiliating defeat, which greatly reinforced his unpopularity.

A French army now laid siege to La Rochelle in retaliation for the support it had reluctantly given Buckingham's expedition. The British government resolved to mount a relief expedition the next summer. The critical need for money to support this force helped persuade Charles to summon the parliament (of 1628-1629*) in March and to accept the Petition of Right* in June in return for five subsidies (see Taxation and Revenue*).

After Buckingham's assassination on 14 August 1628 while overseeing preparations, the expedition embarked under the earl of Lindsey but failed to break the siege. La Rochelle capitulated on 18 October. Peace negotiations began shortly thereafter, leading to the formal conclusion of peace in April.

Bibliography: S. R. Gardiner, *A History of England from the Accession of James I to the Outbreak of the Civil War, 1603-1642*, vol. 6, 1886; Roger Lockyer, *Buckingham: The Life and Political Career of George Villiers, Duke of Buckingham, 1592-1628*, 1981.

Malcolm Smuts

G

Gentry Controversy. The gentry controversy was an extended scholarly debate concerning the social origins of the English Civil War* and Revolution of the 1640s. It occurred at a point in historiographical development when Whiggish interpretations, which placed emphasis on aspirations for political liberty and religious freedom as causes of the revolution, were coming under assault from rival socioeconomic explanations. The controversy began in the pages of the *Economic History Review*, but eventually generated both heat and light in a variety of articles, essays, and monographs. Disagreement initially centered upon R. H. Tawney's thesis, outlined in his Raleigh Lecture of 1941 and in an article of the same year in the *Economic History Review*, that the period between 1558 and 1640 witnessed "the rise of the gentry" and that this social transformation was one of the causes of the revolution (see Social Structure and Ranks*). With its suggestion of economic determinism and its Marxist overtones (Tawney was in fact a Christian Socialist), such a thesis was perhaps bound to cause controversy. Yet the dispute focused in its early stages on the methodology of counting manors, which Tawney used to substantiate his thesis.

Lawrence Stone precipitated the controversy by publishing "The Anatomy of the Elizabethan Aristocracy" in the *Economic History Review* in 1948. In that article he deployed economic statistics to support his argument that much of the Elizabethan aristocracy was poised on the brink of financial disaster. The reply of Hugh Trevor-Roper, published in 1951, was entitled "The Elizabethan Aristocracy: An Anatomy Anatomized," though the last word of the title might have more appropriately captured its author's intentions had it read "atomized." Stone's thesis complemented Tawney's, and his analysis incorporated Tawney's ill-fated methodology of counting manors. Thus Trevor-Roper's attack on Stone led inevitably to criticism of the interpretation that had previously marked the period from 1540 to 1640 as "Tawney's Century." Having dismissed the methodology employed by Tawney and Stone, Trevor-Roper inverted their arguments in "The Gentry, 1540-1640," offering his own interpretation that the Civil War was precipitated by the grievances of declining gentry who faced the prospect of exclusion from the royal court*. According to Trevor-Roper, these declining gentry, with their "country-house" radicalism, ultimately occupied the front ranks of both the Civil War and revolution, leading the parliamentary cause and the New Model Army* to victory. This interpretation eventually inspired other work emphasizing that the Civil War was the consequence of a split between "the court and the country" (see Court versus Country*). Though Stone and Tawney quickly replied to Trevor-Roper, Stone himself later admitted that Trevor-Roper's argument had at first carried all before it. Eventually, however, it came under scrutiny not only from Christopher Hill and Perez Zagorin, who sought either to qualify or refine it, but also from subsequent revisionist historians who denied that any polarity between court and country existed, since many supposed leaders of the "country" such as John Pym* already held local office under the Crown and were usually within prospect of securing a place at court.

In succeeding years new contributions to the controversy issued from various quarters. In 1956 J. P. Cooper criticized the counting of manors from a quantitative historian's perspective. J. H. Hexter brilliantly summarized the debate in a 1958 article, "Storm Over the Gentry," but eschewed the economic determinism on which the contributions of all of the previous participants had apparently rested. Hexter insisted that the revolution was irreducibly political and that it reflected the decline in the military control of the aristocracy over the gentry, allowing the House of Commons to assume primacy over the House of Lords (see Parliament*). Paraphrasing Patrick Henry, Hexter justified his conclusion with a phrase that was at once humorous, defiant, memorable, and evocatively American: "If this be whiggery, make the most of it."

The gentry controversy produced insight as well as scholarly virtuosity. It displayed in high relief the promise and the difficulties involved in the manipulation of statistical data to produce a quantitative history of the early modern period. Even some of the exasperating features of the controversy, such as the propensity of historians to introduce countless examples of rising and declining gentry and rising and declining peers, produced a backlash against the impressionistic methodology of earlier social history, which often extrapolated ambitiously from a chance comment made by a prominent figure of the period. Accordingly, several important studies painstakingly examined the financial accounts of the gentry and nobility. At the other extreme, given additional evidence and time to reconsider opposing arguments, several participants retreated from any imputation of doctrinaire economic determinism. The result was an increased sensitivity to the necessity of employing appropriate historical methodologies and asking appropriate historical questions. A case in point was the increased awareness among historians of the problem of determining which "revolution" they were seeking to explain—that of 1640, 1642, or 1649—and whether a truly social revolution had occurred at all. The controversy thus indirectly encouraged recent revisionist treatments of the period, which have questioned earlier attempts to locate a "high road to civil war." The controversy also stimulated research regarding local history and the fortunes of the gentry during the early modern period, with the somewhat ironic outcome of the localist or "county community" school of historiography that emerged during the 1960s and 1970s. For several of the participants, restatements of their position in the controversy became major works in their own right. Of no one was this more true than Lawrence Stone, whose works on the aristocracy, education, the family, social structure, sexuality, and divorce have formed pioneering contributions to the social history of the period. Like Tawney, Stone has never allowed criticism to deter him from asking provocative historical questions and answering them with equally provocative conclusions. He also possesses a quality rare among historians: the willingness to adjust or even re-orient his work in response to criticism. Trevor-Roper, meanwhile, has continued to write prodigiously and elegantly, earning a barony and a Regius Professorship as rewards for his labors.

The historical achievements that resulted from the controversy, however, could not salve the wounds suffered by many of the participants. "An erring colleague," wrote Tawney, in a metaphor that captured the Biblical proportions of the event, "is not an Amalekite to be smitten hip and thigh." Meanwhile, as recently as 1992, Stone, writing in the *Times Literary Supplement,* obliquely lampooned Trevor-Roper's inability to pronounce an accurate judgment on the forged Hitler diaries. Despite an animus that will likely perish only when its participants do, the gentry controversy cannot be reduced to the truism that the acrimony of scholarly debate is directly proportional to its insignificance. It was and remains a seminal debate worthy of one of the most controversial and fascinating of all historical periods.

Bibliography: R. C. Richardson, *The Debate on the English Revolution,* 1977.

Myron C. Noonkester

Glorious Revolution (1688-1689). The series of events that led to the deposition of the Catholic* James II* from the throne of England and his replacement by the joint monarchy of his daughter Mary II* and her husband William III*, thereby ensuring a line of Protestant succession.

Despite his Catholicism, James II acceded smoothly to the throne on 6 February 1685, following the death of his brother Charles II*. The years of Charles's reign had been marked by outbreaks of anti-Catholic feeling, most notably in 1673-1674, when James' second marriage to the Catholic princess Mary of Modena* had fueled fears of a possible Catholic dynasty. The result was the Test Act* (25 Car. II, c. 2) of 1673, which required officeholders to be in communion with the Anglican* church, and James himself was forced to resign his post as lord admiral of the navy*. Following the Popish Plot* of 1678, a further Test Act* (30 Car. II, st. 2, c. 1) was passed. Between 1679 and 1681 parliament* made three attempts to exclude James from the throne on the basis of his religion, the so-called Exclusion Crisis*; Charles thought it prudent to exile James from England during these years for his own safety. Between 1682 and 1685, however, James was able to consolidate his power with the aid of the Tories*, who supported the monarchy and its heir, and he was able to succeed to the throne without trouble.

Upon becoming king, James began to consider ways in which to soften the treatment meted out to his co-religionists. He wished to repeal the Test Acts, which kept Catholics out of office and barred them from parliament, and the penal laws, which essentially forbade the practice of Catholicism. However, he did not consider that the majority of his country was opposed to any relaxation of these laws, a majority that included his own base of support among the Tories. With the rest of the population*, the Tories believed rightly or wrongly that there was a link between Catholicism and absolutist* rule. James's attempts to rehabilitate the Catholics therefore made him suspect in the eyes of many of his subjects.

In the aftermath of the Monmouth Rebellion* in 1685, James increased the size of his army* and commissioned a number of Catholic officers, in violation of the Test Acts. This standing army alarmed the parliament of 1685*, but James dismissed their concerns and promptly prorogued them. He did not call them again. James then decided to appeal to the Protestant Dissenters*, who were in much the same position as the Catholics insofar as the practice of their religion was concerned. In order to gain their cooperation, he first had to remove their legal disabilities. He did this through the use of his dispensing power*, a power that was meant to be used individually and selectively but that he used to dispense the entire nation from compliance with the penal laws under a Declaration of Indulgence* (1687). He then moved to the suspension of other laws (see Suspending Power*) and began a campaign to pack parliament with enough Dissenters to ensure parliamentary approbation of the repeal of the laws with which James had dispensed. But the Dissenters, although they favored toleration, would not support a repeal of the Test Acts, leaving James with no possibility for a favorable parliament.

James jailed seven recalcitrant bishops (see Seven Bishops Case*) for refusing to order the declaration read in the churches; their acquittal, to the acclaims of the people, proved James's unpopularity. However, the discontented subjects were unable to protest the inequities effectively, due to James's large standing army, which remained loyal to him. To force James to honor his responsibilities, a foreign challenge was necessary. This challenge came from the Dutch Republic in the form of James's son-in-law, William of Orange.

William, who had been fighting a continuous war with the French for some years, regarded England as the source of fresh support for his cause. But not until the general unrest of 1688 did he begin to see that he might secure that support by aiding the oppressed citizenry of England. Initial plans for invasion did not encompass the deposition of James; William expected to impose restrictions on James and strike a close bargain for financial aid. France turned its attentions to Germany, leaving William free to proceed with plans for invasion. Following the announcement of the English queen's pregnancy in late 1687, seven men sent William an "invitation" in April 1688, asking him to come to England to preserve the nation and the Protestant religion. The suspect birth of a son to James in June only confirmed William in his decision to invade (it was rumored that the infant was not really James's).

William landed at Torbay on 5 November. Alarmed by the actual invasion, James turned to the Tories for help, but they only offered the suggestion that James call a free parliament. James refused to do so, believing that his army would be sufficient to repel the invasion. He marched west to engage William, but defections on the way convinced him that it would be best to return to London* and stall for time over negotiations. He sent his wife and infant son to France and tried to escape to the Continent himself on 10 December, but he was picked up and returned to London on

15 December. His cowardly retreat threw the government into chaos, and only William's arrival arrested the process. William, by now determined on taking the throne himself, made it possible for James to escape a second time, which he did on 22 December. William was now free to take over the government.

William called for a general election to a Convention Parliament*, which convened on 22 January 1689. The most immediate and pressing concern was how to fill the throne vacated so abruptly by James. Various proposals were put forward, but it soon became clear that the only solution acceptable to all elements of the convention was to offer the Crown jointly to William and Mary, with William having the responsibility for governmental affairs. On 28 January the Commons of the Convention declared that James had abdicated the throne, leaving it vacant. William and Mary agreed that failing issue of their own, Mary's sister, Anne*, and her children would inherit the throne after them.

The issue of the throne was settled as part of the Declaration of Rights*, which laid out under two sections and thirty-two headings conditions under which the throne would be offered; these conditions were to be binding on the person chosen to take the throne. In consultations between the Commons, the Lords, and William and Mary, the package was refined and presented to William and Mary on 13 February. They accepted the declaration and the offer of the throne but did not specifically bind themselves to the provisions contained in the declaration. It was not until the declaration was enacted as a statute in the form of the Bill of Rights* (1 Gul. III & Mar., sess. 2, c. 2) on 16 December 1689 that the king and queen bound themselves formally to its terms. The bill further refined the declaration in that it contained only thirteen articles dealing with grievances that had led to the revolution. The succession of the Crown was detailed, including a prohibition against any Catholic or any person married to a Catholic inheriting the throne. The monarch's dispensing power was defined (but not abolished), and the monarch was forbidden to maintain a standing army without the consent of parliament. Many of the articles, however, were vague and were obviously meant as suggestions for further legislation. In the event, only about half of the issues mentioned in the articles were dealt with by subsequent legislation.

The revolution also encompassed a financial and religious settlement. The Commons established a distinction between the civil and military portion of the Crown budget; the monarch's personal needs would be met by a grant voted by parliament, while extraordinary expenditure such as that required for war would be considered by parliament on a case-by-case basis. The principle of the Civil List was thus established, making royal revenue dependent upon parliament (see Taxation and Revenue*).

In dealing with religion, a Toleration Act (1 Gul. III & Mar., c. 18) was passed in 1689, which exempted Protestant Dissenters (not Catholics) from the penalties of the nonconforming laws, provided they take an oath of allegiance and declaration against Catholic beliefs. Dissenting preachers and gatherings were permitted provided that the authorities where notified and the preachers subscribed to thirty-six of the Thirty-nine Articles of the Anglican church.

While the events of the Glorious Revolution were not in and of themselves unique, the revolution itself proved innovative, particularly in its constitutional influence on subsequent rebellions, most notably that of the American Revolution in the late eighteenth century. Its intrinsic importance can be found in its legacies.

Bibliography: J. R. Jones, *The Revolution of 1688 in England*, 1972; John Miller, *The Glorious Revolution*, 1983.

Connie S. Evans

Godolphin, Sidney, 1st Earl of (1645-1712). The third son of Sir Francis Godolphin, Sidney was born on the family estate in Cornwall. He graduated with an M.A. from Oxford in 1663 and was appointed page of honor to Charles II* in 1662, groom of the bedchamber in 1672, and master of the robes in 1678 (see Court, Royal*). From 1668 to 1681 he sat as member for Helston in the House of Commons. Between 1669 and 1678 he served in a secondary position during several diplomatic missions, but he showed no particular genius in this field. In the military he had received a commission in 1667 as cornet in Lord Sunderland's troop, but he showed no enthusiasm for this service, and a leg injury resulting in a fall from a horse ended his military career.

Godolphin secretly married Margaret Blagge on 16 May 1675 after a nine-year engagement. They revealed their marriage and lived together the next year. In 1678 Margaret died shortly after the birth of her first child, Francis. There were some contemporary rumors that Godolphin remarried but no evidence.

Godolphin's genius was in the field of government finance. Charles II first appointed him one of the treasury lords in 1679 and first lord in 1684. In 1687 James II* appointed him a treasury lord. In 1690 William III* made him head of the treasury commission. Godolphin accomplished his most significant work financing the wars of William and Queen Anne*, while maintaining the financial stability of the government.

In politics Godolphin was considered a moderate Tory*, but he accepted a nonparty philosophy of government. Godolphin opposed Charles II's policy in the Exclusion Crisis* and was removed from the treasury board. Nevertheless James II liked and trusted him. In 1685 Godolphin was made chamberlain to Queen Mary (of Modena*). He had a personal relationship with the queen that some contemporaries thought had romantic overtones. James hoped to convert him to Catholicism*, and masses were said every day in the king's chapel for his conversion.

In the Glorious Revolution* of 1688, Godolphin supported James. He was appointed one of a council of five to operate the government in London* while James and his army advanced to Salisbury. He accompanied the earls of Halifax and Nottingham to negotiate with William at Hungerford. Then he opposed William's succession in favor of a regency.

However, Godolphin had contacted William as early as 1681, indicating his zeal for service to the Dutch ruler, and when William became king, Godolphin served him for all but five years of his reign. When Queen Anne succeeded William in 1702,

Godolphin became lord treasurer and first minister. He was made earl of Godolphin in 1706. He advised the queen, controlled the cabinet* and the committee, managed parliament*, helped devise military strategy, and provided the funds for the War of the Spanish Succession (1702-1713). One can make a strong case that he should be considered the first prime minister. He served until he was dismissed after the Tory takeover in 1710.

Godolphin's character was dominated by the qualities of efficiency and caution. He was personally honest and conscientious about demanding honesty, frugality, and accurate accounts.

Bibliography: William Calvin Dickinson, *Sidney Godolphin, Lord Treasurer, 1702-1710*, 1990.

W. Calvin Dickinson

Good Old Cause. This was first used as a republican rallying cry in opposition to the establishment of the Protectorate* in December 1653. Originally it referred to republicans opposed to the constitutional principles of the Protectorate's founding document, the Instrument of Government* (16 December 1653). After the fall of the Protectorate in April 1659, Commonwealthmen*, pamphleteers, and political theorists (see Political Thought*) debated the merit of various government models, using the fulfillment of the cause as a necessary goal. Interpretations of what this meant were myriad.

In its early appearances, the Good Old Cause was used by republican pamphleteers for nostalgic effect, to conjure the halcyon days of the 1648 revolution and the establishment of the Commonwealth*. Their writings were premised on the notion that the 1648 revolution was a movement toward an ideal government, which was interrupted by the establishment of the Barebone's Parliament* (1653) and later the Protectorate. This is evident in *A Copy of a Letter from an Officer of the Army in Ireland* (June 1656?), which argued that the Protectorate was a betrayal of republican principles. An ambiguous alternative to the regime was offered, called a free state or free representative. This virtually secular argument was juxtaposed to Sir Henry Vane's *A Healing Question* (May 1656), which called for sectarian and army* radicals to overthrow the Protectorate and establish an oligarchic government of saints. After 1656 the cause resurfaced in February 1658, when the Lord Protector Oliver Cromwell* was accused by disaffected officers of straying from its principles.

Elements of radical thought associated with the cause can be found among both republican and conservative members of parliament* in Richard Cromwell's* parliament (January-April 1659). Radical and conservative MPs were hostile to the army's role in government, to the "Other House" or Cromwellian Lords, and to the prerogatives of the lord protector. Conservatives, however, separated themselves from radicals by wanting a more intolerant religious settlement. This anti-sectarian, anti-army conservatism encouraged an alliance of Commonwealthmen and chief officers (the Wallingford House party), which overthrew Richard Cromwell and closed the conservative-dominated parliament. These uneasy confederates acted in the name of the cause.

Achieving this ideal remained elusive for the restored Rump Parliament* (May 1659-February 1660), which was viewed by many radicals and army republicans as an interim regime mandated to produce a definitive constitution quickly. Proponents of the cause like John Streater, an officer-pamphleteer, argued against a modified Protectorate and a so-called single person as head of state. Throughout the summer of 1659, while the Rump debated constitutional reform, pamphleteers chorused the views of Streater, James Harrington*, and others. Their principal concern was that neither the Protectorate be restored nor a non-elected or select senate be installed. Several anonymous pamphlets from as early as March 1659 identified the cause as popular power or the public interest versus the private. Government models were proposed to secure the principles of the cause, but few provided comprehensive definitions. A disciple of Vane, Henry Stubbe wrote in his *An Essay in Defense of the Good Cause* (September 1659), "That liberty civil and spiritual were the good old cause," yet he did not define them—as arguably all efforts for the period failed to do.

The most coherent statement on the cause by a contemporary was in *A Negative Voyce* (20 November 1659). After the 13 October army coup and the closure of the Rump, both the ousted Commonwealthmen and republican army leaders claimed to be the true advocates. This writer argued that the army was attempting to secure the cause by means incompatible with its principles. Past attempts to embody the preservation of the cause in a protector and constitutions had failed because no single person could be trusted with the public interest. Nor, the author argued, could a senate that was not directly answerable to the people. In essence the principles of the cause were religious toleration for Protestants and an elected, possibly bicameral, government free of army interference but united in purpose with the army.

In general, however, these principles remained ill defined and provided fodder for the critics of the republicans. William Prynne*, the prolific Presbyterian* pamphleteer, in *The Republicans and Others of the Spurious Good Old Cause* (February 1660), saw all adherents as incapable of creating stable constitutional government. Historians have perhaps, too, generalized when associating the cause with the broad republican movement. Instead it appears principally to have been used by the Commonwealthmen to describe their constitutional agenda, which by no means included all republicans.

Bibliography: John Hughes, "The Commonwealthmen Divided: Edmund Ludlowe, Sir Henry Vane and the Good Old Cause 1654-60," *The Journal of the Seventeenth Century* (1990): 116-36; A. H. Woolrych, "The Good Old Cause and the Fall of the Protectorate," *Cambridge Historical Journal* 13 (1957), pp. 133-61.

John H. F. Hughes

Goodwin's Case (1604). On the first day of business in James I's* initial parliament (of 1604*), Sir William Fleetwood and Sir Thomas Wentworth* made the disputed Buckinghamshire election the first issue to be addressed in the session. On the surface

the issue seemed simple. Sir Francis Goodwin, a local gentleman with Puritan*
connections, defeated a member of the privy council*, Sir John Fortescue, in the
county election. Partly out of a desire to have a third privy councilor to represent its
interests in the House of Commons, the government examined the election,
discovered a technicality by which Goodwin could be outlawed, and used it to void
the election results. Another election was conducted, for which better preparations
were taken by the council, and the desired result was achieved.

Goodwin's Case has also been seen as a reflection of local political maneuvering
between the two families and their allies, who had contested county elections for
nearly three decades. From this perspective the parliamentary fracas can be construed
as a national manifestation of the growing political awareness and assertiveness
exercised by the gentry on the local level from the late Elizabethan period.

Accounts of the government's unusual behavior in Goodwin's Case stirred the
members of the Commons to rally to the defense of their privilege. They examined
the warrants, declared Goodwin the victor, and quickly had him sworn and seated.
These events initiated a significant debate over where the power to decide disputed
elections resided. The Commons compiled a list of cases showing its exercise of this
power well before 1406, while the government's claim was based on fifteenth-century
precedents in which the court of Chancery had resolved electoral discrepancies. Two
late Elizabethan elections wherein returns were questioned were found but they
provided little guidance. In the 1586 election, both Chancery and the Commons
reached the same conclusion, and in 1593 the house dropped its challenge at the
urging of its speaker.

For many members of Commons the dispute entailed important issues touching
their independence. One observed that if a person were elected who offended the
council or a lord chancellor, new elections could be held and the house "burdened"
or "packed" with people who depended on the government for their seats. While care
was taken not to insult the privy council or the lord chancellor, the House
demonstrated that it felt as strongly as did the government about the importance of this
case as a precedent for settling future disputes. Their resolve was strengthened by
James's admonition that the House's privilege was dependent on his grace, and his
remarks did little to encourage the trust that had developed between James's
predecessor and her parliaments.

Implicit in this aspect of the debate was a key question about the character of early
Stuart government. The Commons, by its lists of precedents and its rejection of
James's claims, asserted its emergence as an essential and autonomous element of
accepted government. It neither challenged the king's sovereignty nor claimed such
for itself. But in this case, as in no previous incident, the Commons began to assert
the existence of political power that had long been ceded to it and that it had no desire
to diminish or relinquish, even if it not been exercised in recent times.

In the end, James's government gave way. It allowed the house to quash
Fortescue's writ and hold a new election. Both men found other seats quickly. An
important consequence of this case was the tacit acceptance after 1604 that the
Commons was the sole judge of its own electoral affairs unless it sought advice from
the judges.

Bibliography: J. P. Kenyon, ed., *The Stuart Constitution: Documents and Commentary*, 1966; J. R. Tanner, *English Constitutional Conflicts of the Seventeenth Century, 1603-1689*, 1928.

Sheldon Hanft

Grand Remonstrance (1641). On 1 December 1641 Charles I* received a petition and an extensive list of grievances from the Long Parliament*. Encompassing some 204 points, this Grand Remonstrance was not a quick reaction to any particular event. John Pym*, an opposition leader in the House of Commons, established a committee as early as 10 November 1640 to examine Charles's misgovernment. On 23 July 1641 parliament ordered the committee to draft a remonstrance on the state of the kingdom, which it debated and approved by a close vote in November.

The remonstrance clearly stated parliament's numerous grievances against Charles and his advisers. The accompanying petition demanded that bishops be deprived of their seats in the House of Lords in order to reduce the clergy's power and hamper their efforts to undermine England's religion and laws. In addition, parliament insisted that the king remove those privy councilors (see Privy Council*) who had advocated policies contrary to the best interests of the English people and required parliamentary approval of all future councilors. Finally the petition asked the king to use lands confiscated in Ireland* to subsidize suppression of the Irish Rebellion* and to reward his English supporters. Parliament advised Charles that if he adopted the proposed policies, it would fund his Irish war.

In the Grand Remonstrance itself, parliament claimed that Jesuit priests and evil advisers had attempted to alienate Charles from his people's affections and undermine the fundamental laws of the realm by showing Charles ways to raise extraparliamentary revenue (see Taxation and Revenue*) and increase his expectations concerning the royal prerogative*. The various grievances date from James I's* reign. Among the issues cited were the dissolution of parliament at Oxford, the dismal Cadiz expedition*, England's desertion of the Palatinate in the Thirty Years War*, the dissolution of the parliament of 1628* after it had pledged five subsidies, and Charles's failure to abide by the Petition of Right*. The remonstrance also noted the king's visit to the parliament of 1629*, which led to the arrest of several parliamentary leaders, and the continued collection of tonnage and poundage, the book of rates, forest laws*, excessive fees for wardship, and fees for distraint of knighthood*. The document also raised nonmonetary issues, such as the destruction of the Forest of Dean and confiscation of lands that fell between the low- and high-water marks, depopulating enclosures, and the commissioners of sewers' confiscation of commons. There were complaints about the legal system, where judges were replaced for refusing to violate their oaths of office and for loss of royal pleasure rather than for malfeasance of office. Parliament lamented the heavy fines, imprisonment, and whippings that Star Chamber imposed (see Prerogative Courts*) and claimed that the faction surrounding the king wished to ignore the legal protection of property and the individual. Parliament also criticized the king's efforts to force the English Book of Common Prayer on the Scots. Parliament advised Charles that if he accepted the document, it would relinquish the armory at Hull to men whom Charles named and whom it approved.

The Grand Remonstrance passed the House of Commons on 22 November 1641 by a vote of 159 to 148. A furor immediately erupted concerning its possible publication. The threat of appealing to public opinion was a serious breach of protocol, which infuriated most members and even led some to draw their swords. But despite the debate in Westminster, the Grand Remonstrance was published before Charles had an opportunity to respond.

On 23 December Charles presented the "King's Answer to the Petition Accompanying the Grand Remonstrance" to parliament. He promised to protect England from papists but added that it would be unconstitutional for him to prevent the bishops from sitting in the Lords. He further suggested that eliminating the court of High Commission (see Ecclesiastical Courts*) would eliminate the "inordinate power" that parliament believed the clergy wielded. Although he believed the Church of England (see Anglicanism*) to be the "most perfect of religions," Charles suggested that if parliament convened a national synod to examine illegal ceremonies, he would consider its findings. He encouraged parliament to levy specific charges against his councilors instead of general statements, promising to surrender the guilty to parliament. The king, however, retained the right to name his own councilors. On the distribution of the Irish lands, he suggested that any decision would be improper while fighting continued.

On the same day Charles attempted to increase his control of London* by making Colonel Thomas Lunsford lieutenant of the Tower. Although the common council of London protested and the Commons conferred with the Lords, the latter would not agree to remove Lunsford. The king himself replaced Lunsford on 26 December with the loyal but less controversial Sir John Byron. Parliamentary leaders' insistence on publishing the Grand Remonstrance angered Charles and encouraged his unsuccessful attempt to seize the Five Members* in early January 1642. This further undermined his popularity and pushed the country closer to the Civil War*.

Bibliography: W. H. Coates, "Some Observations on the Grand Remonstrance," *Journal of Modern History* 4 (1932), pp. 1-17; S. R. Gardiner, *Constitutional Documents of the Puritan Revolution, 1603-1688,* 3d ed. rev., 1927; H. L. Schoolcraft, *The Genesis of the Grand Remonstrance,* 1902.

David B. Mock

Great Contract (1610). An abortive agreement in the parliament of 1610* involving an attempt to establish royal finance on a new basis. In February 1610 the lord treasurer, Robert Cecil*, earl of Salisbury, approached parliament* with a novel and far-reaching appeal to remedy the king's financial difficulties. He proposed that parliament (specifically the House of Commons, which always originated supply) grant the king the large sum of £600,000 to pay his debts and—something that was entirely unprecedented—an annual revenue of £200,000 to eliminate his annual deficits. (Subsidies and fifteenths, the usual parliamentary grants since the reign of Henry VIII, were one-time levies; recurrent direct taxation* was unknown in England.)

The House of Commons, either failing to understand Salisbury's appeal or unwilling to agree to it, turned his proposal into a contract to purchase the abolition of wardship—the king's right to control the estates and marriages of his tenants-in-chief in cases where those tenants were minors—which was a great complaint of the English aristocracy and gentry. (Wardship had an important purpose in classical feudalism, ensuring that the military service for which land was granted was performed; by the seventeenth century, when feudalism had long since ceased to be the basis of military service, wardship had become a fiscal device, with individual wardships sold for hard cash or given as rewards.)

Negotiations proceeded very slowly and were frequently interrupted, notably by a prolonged dispute over impositions*, additional customs duties introduced by Salisbury in 1608 that the Commons loudly protested were illegal. Not until July was a tentative agreement reached. As embodied in a "memorial," the Great Contract (as it was already being called) provided for the abolition of wardship as well as of purveyance (the king's right to buy provisions and carriage at prices below those current in the markets) and also for relief of a host of other grievances. In return the king would receive an annual revenue of £200,000, although since wardship and purveyance between them were worth perhaps as much as £100,000 per annum to the king, his actual gain would be considerably less.

Parliament was prorogued on 23 July and was to meet again in October to conclude the agreement. During the recess some doubts about the contract were expressed at the royal court*, notably by the chancellor of the Exchequer*, although these objections apparently did not dissuade Salisbury and the king from continuing to pursue the agreement. However, they came to see that it would be necessary to insist on certain conditions not stipulated in the "memorial"—including the grant of a large supply—in order to ensure that the agreement really would be valuable to the king. These conditions were not new, although they had been lost sight of. However, when the Commons assembled again in October, such enthusiasm as they had felt for the Great Contract in July had largely dissipated, and they withdrew their assent as soon as the king presented his additional conditions.

It was once assumed that the Commons's great objection was a fear that an increased revenue would make the king independent of parliament. However, this apprehension was mentioned only once by a single member and does not seem to have been widely shared. Rather, the Great Contract apparently fell victim to the Commons's fiscal conservatism, something that was to be a recurrent problem for the Crown throughout the period. Permanent direct taxation of any size, let alone the large sum of £200,000 per annum, was, after all, too great an innovation for them to accept.

Bibliography: Eric Lindquist, "The Failure of the Great Contract," *Journal of Modern History* 57 (1985): 617-651; Alan G. R. Smith, "Crown, Parliament and Finance: The Great Contract of 1610," in Peter Clark, Alan G. R. Smith and

Nicholas Tyacke, eds., *The English Commonwealth, 1547-1640: Essays in Politics and Society*, 1979.

Eric N. Lindquist

Gunpowder Plot (1605). A conspiracy of English Catholics* to blow up parliament* and James I* on 5 November 1605. A Roman Catholic zealot, Robert Catesby, led the plot; he and his co-conspirators Thomas Winter, Thomas Percy, John Wright, and Guy Fawkes were angry that James had failed to relax penal laws against English Catholics. Upon his accession in 1603, James suspended recusancy* fines, and Catholics had hopes of greater religious toleration. James's ministers, however, particularly his secretary of state, Robert Cecil*, feared that the Catholics were a potential threat to the security of the kingdom; an abortive Catholic plot against James in 1603 only increased anti-Catholic sentiment. Thus, under pressure from his counselors, James re-established recusancy penalties, greatly disappointing many Catholics.

Catesby's plan was to place barrels of gunpowder underneath the parliament building and ignite them on the day of opening session, killing the king and queen (Anne of Denmark*), Prince Henry*, the privy council*, and both houses. In the ensuing confusion, they hoped that the Catholic rebels could take over the government and place Princess Elizabeth* or Prince Charles* on the throne.

In May 1604 the conspirators rented a house adjoining parliament and began to dig a tunnel from the cellar to a chamber below the House of Lords, where the gunpowder would be placed. The passage proved very difficult to dig, but in March 1605 they were able to rent a house with a cellar immediately underneath the Lords, which Guy Fawkes filled with approximately twenty barrels of gunpowder, topped with iron bars to increase the explosive impact.

In the meantime Catesby was organizing a group of Catholics in the Midlands. He invited several Catholic gentlemen on a large hunting party in Warwickshire on the opening day of parliament so they would be able to help the rebels seize control of the country after the explosion occurred. Meanwhile, eight more men entered the conspiracy. Some of the plotters were worried about the fate of the Catholic members of parliament, but the group decided that any warnings would endanger the plan. One of them, however, Francis Tresham, sent an ambiguous letter to his brother-in-law, Lord Monteagle, urging him to stay away from parliament on 5 November. Monteagle, immediately suspicious, showed the letter to Cecil, who informed James.

On 4 November, the day before the opening of the session, search parties discovered Guy Fawkes, who had been guarding the gunpowder mine. Under torture Fawkes confessed and revealed the names of the other conspirators. Catesby, Percy, and two other members of the plot died resisting arrest, and the others were captured. Tresham died in the Tower. But the remaining members of the conspiracy were tried before Sir Edward Coke* and executed on 31 January 1606. An act of parliament established 5 November as a national day of thanksgiving; popularly known as Guy Fawkes Day, the anniversary is still celebrated with bonfires and fireworks.

The plot confirmed Protestant fears about the dangers of popish rebellions, and the parliament of 1606* passed more regulations against Catholics. In this sense the plot was a boon to Protestant leaders, and it has been suggested that Cecil and his protégés may have encouraged the conspiracy in order to ruin the Catholic cause. There is not sufficient evidence to support such a theory, but there are questions about Cecil's role in discovering the plot.

Bibliography: Hugh Ross Williamson, *The Gunpowder Plot*, 1951; Oswald Tesimond, *The Gunpowder Plot*, 1973.

Jo Eldridge Carney

Gwynne, Nell (1650-1687). An actress and Charles II's* mistress, born Eleanor Gwynne (called variously Hellen Gwynn, Ellen Gwynn, and Elinor Gwyn) on 2 February 1650. Her father, who died when she was an infant, was Thomas Gwynne, a ruined royalist* soldier from an old Hereford family; her mother was Eleanor Smith. As a girl Nell served drinks in a local brothel, hawked fish, then sold oranges at the Theatre Royal. She appeared on stage as early as 1664, but her first important role was in 1665 as Cydaria in *The Indian Emperor* by John Dryden*, who wrote her other suitable parts, such as Florimel in *Secret Love,* considered her most successful performance. "A bold merry slut" and "pretty witty Nell" (Samuel Pepys's* descriptions), she was an excellent comedienne. Charles II first met Nell in 1668, attracted by her saucy wit and her urchin looks. She became his mistress in 1669 and bore him two sons, Charles (born in 1670 and created duke of St. Albans in 1684) and James (born in 1671).

Stories about Nell's wit abound, but the most familiar highlights a lively incident concerning her great rival, the duchess of Portsmouth, Charles's French mistress, during the general discontent caused by the Popish Plot*. It also reveals her enduring popularity with the English populace. As the mob jostled her coach in Oxford, thinking she was the Catholic* Portsmouth, Nell stuck her head out the window and delighted the crowd with her famous riposte, "Pray, good people, be civil; I am the Protestant whore." The relationship and Charles's affection continued until his death, and his last words to his brother James included, "Let not poor Nellie starve," a paraphrase of his actual thoughts, which also included concern for his other mistresses. His intention to create Nell countess of Greenwich, a title she coveted, was frustrated by his death. James II* paid off her debts and gave her a pension.

Nell died of apoplexy on 14 November 1687 in London* and was buried in the chancel of St. Martin-in-the-Fields; Thomas Tenison, later archbishop of Canterbury, preached her funeral sermon. The tradition that she inspired Charles to establish the Royal Hospital at Chelsea has no documented evidence to support it. During her life, both praise and criticism were forthcoming. Both Aphra Behn* (*The Feigned Courtezans*) and Thomas Duffet (*Spanish Rogue*) dedicated plays to her, and Robert Whitcomb praised her highly in *Janna Divorum*, a study of gods and goddesses, comparing Nell to some of them. However, the Tories* thought her "puddle Nell," "hare-brained whore," and "darling strumpet of the crowd."

Bibliography: B. Bevan, *Nell Gwynn,* 1969; R. MacGregor-Hastie, *Nell Gwyn,* 1987; R. Sumner, *Mistress of the Streets,* 1974.

Martin J. Manning

H

Habeas Corpus Parliament (1679). See Exclusion Crisis.

Hale Commission. The Hale Commission, known by the name of its first chairman, Sir Matthew Hale, was an extraparliamentary committee on legal reorganization that assembled for the first time on 30 January 1652. The Rump Parliament* instituted the commission and ordered it to recommend measures by which the irregularities, delays, and expenses of existing legal procedures might be reformed. Because the commission's membership contained a mixture of radicals and lawyers, many of its proposals were the result of compromise or a coincidence of interests.

Contemporary newspapers reported many actions of the commission, which met three times a week until 23 July 1652. The commission's proposals included the integration of reformed county courts into a central court system, the abolition of imprisonment for debt, and the reform of appeal procedure to promote affordability, reduce delays, and emphasize the facts of the case while diminishing the import of technicalities. The commission also recommended that the appeal of a judgment need not be deemed an accusation against the judge who rendered it, as the common law* had required. At the insistence of radical members, who wished to simplify and cheapen procedure, and of Hale, who wished to restore the competitiveness of the court of Common Pleas with respect to other central courts, the commission urged the abolition of fines on original writs that initiated process in the Common Pleas. In other piecemeal reforms the commission proposed that copyhold land be liable for debt and that probate jurisdiction be removed from the civil law, which was associated with foreign influences and Catholicism* and placed under the jurisdiction of the common law.

In January 1653 parliament* spent two days considering "the Book containing the whole system of law" that the Hale Commission had prepared. Though none of the commission's proposals became law during the Rump Parliament, Barebone's (or the Nominated) Parliament*, which succeeded the Rump, passed two measures recommended by the commission: one removed fines on bills, declarations, and original writs, and the other established procedures for civil marriage. Both subjects had been addressed by the commission during the early months of its existence, before legal work had prevented Hale's attendance. Proposed structural changes, such as establishing local courts of judicature that were to be courts of record and a court of appeal, did not become law, partly because of the social conservatism of those gentry whose cooperation was necessary to make the regimes of the Commonwealth* and Protectorate* viable.

The Hale Commission responded primarily to the aspirations of lawyers for reform rather than the insistence of radicals that many features of the law, such as the cumbersome court of Chancery and professional pleading, be abolished. Its inability to implement most of its proposals meant that it would be judged in succeeding centuries upon the basis of what it foreshadowed rather than what it accomplished. On many points it anticipated nineteenth-century legal reforms, which were designed to promote reason and equity in what had remained until then an esoteric tradition. In the meantime the Hale Commission had demonstrated the plausibility of thorough reform of the law, a precedent that could not be taken lightly by either those who favored such reform or those who opposed it.

Bibliography: Mary Cotterell, "Interregnum Law Reform: The Hale Commission of 1652," *English Historical Review* 83 (1968): 689-704.

Myron C. Noonkester

Hampden, John (1594-1643). Descended from an old English family whose ancestral home was at Great Hampden in Buckinghamshire, Hampden graduated from Magdalen College, Oxford, in 1610, married Elizabeth Symeon of Oxfordshire (his first wife) in 1619, and fathered nine children. He was elected to the parliament of 1621* from the borough of Grampound and to the parliaments of 1625*, 1626*, and 1628-1629* from Wendover. Hampden was not a great speaker but was widely respected for his attention to parliamentary duties. He served on most important committees and was a valued confidant of other leaders, including Sir John Eliot* and John Pym*. His sage counsel and knowledge of parliamentary law and precedents made him invaluable in the struggle between parliament* and Charles I*.

The ship money* case propelled Hampden into national prominence. In 1634, without parliament's approval, Charles invoked traditional privilege to levy funds from maritime counties and towns to bolster the navy*. Charles viewed the Franco-Spanish war as a threat in the English Channel; Anglo-Dutch disputes over fishing rights in the North Sea were another cause. However, in 1635, when Charles called for another levy that was extended to inland counties and towns, he met opposition. Hampden, along with Lord Saye and Sele (William Fiennes*), refused to pay, arguing that the money was not to be spent to thwart a naval threat, but to support an unpopular detente with Catholic* Spain and defray expenses involved in the king's dispute with the Scots. Hampden also contended that Charles intended to make this nonparliamentary taxation* permanent rather than a voluntary levy in times of crisis. In 1637 the case went before the court of the Exchequer*, which on 12 June 1638 ruled in Charles's favor. But five of twelve judges sided with Hampden, indicating increasing dissatisfaction with Charles's financial policies.

In spring 1640 Hampden sat in the Short Parliament*, which Charles dissolved when it attempted to abolish ship money and refused to grant him subsidies to replace it. Hampden was arrested with other parliamentary leaders. Released, he spent several months with Pym in London* before sitting for Buckinghamshire in the Long Parliament*, which Charles convened in November 1640.

Hampden's reputation for integrity and forthrightness gave him great influence. He helped draft impeachment* proceedings against the earl of Strafford (Thomas Wentworth*). Hampden at this point did not advocate abolishing monarchy as some radical members of parliament* did but wanted to rid the monarchy of unscrupulous and self-serving advisers. He did align himself with the Puritans* against the king and the episcopate, represented by Archbishop Laud*, and in the dispute between the Crown and the Scots church. Charles, angered by parliament's refusal to support the First Bishops' War* and its renewed attempts to abolish ship money, ordered impeachment* proceedings against Hampden, Pym, Denzil Holles, William Strode, and Sir Arthur Hasilrig, and personally led a force to parliament to arrest them on 3 January 1642. But the Five Members* escaped and returned in triumph several days later.

Hampden now adopted a less conciliatory attitude toward the king, and when on 4 July 1642 the final break came between Crown and parliament, Hampden was the leading member of the committee of safety, which raised troops to protect parliament and forced Charles to leave London. Hampden formed his own regiment, primarily from Buckinghamshire, to fight under the earl of Essex (Robert Devereux*). He served with distinction from July 1642, advocating strong military action against the king, and was one of several major figures who rejected reconciliation.

Hampden suffered a shoulder wound on 18 June 1643 in a skirmish with royal troops under Prince Rupert at Chamlgrove Field. He died a week later at Thame on 25 June and was buried at Great Hampden. His death caused consternation in the parliamentarian* ranks, at the time heavily beset by royalist* forces. But Hampden also enjoyed the respect and admiration of the royalists at the time of his death, not for his politics but for unwavering devotion to his cause.

Bibliography: G. E. Aylmer, *Rebellion or Revolution? England, 1640-1660*, 1986; Derek Hirst, *Authority and Conflict: England, 1603-1658*, 1986.

									Kenneth Postan

Hampton Court Conference (1604). A debate between the Anglican* establishment and Puritans* chaired by James I*. Puritans were encouraged at the accession of a new king who wooed them in his revised preface to *Basilikon Doron*. They therefore presented James with the Millenary Petition* in 1603, claiming the support of 1,000 ministers therein. Their petition requested the abolition of such "papistical" survivals in the church as the sign of the cross in baptism. It sought a well-educated, preaching, and resident ministry. Expensive, dilatory ecclesiastical courts* and the ex officio oath were attacked. All Puritans favored such basic reforms. Some wished to move far closer to the Genevan model, but their ideas were not yet emphasized, which strengthened the position of the moderate petitioners.

James agreed to meet the moderate Puritans. He wanted some reform, unity, and a debate in which he could demonstrate learning and leadership. A conference in which Puritan critics apparently faced defenders of the established church as equals was significant. Such conferences usually preceded religious change on the Continent. Elizabeth had given no such recognition to critics, and this conference alarmed supporters of her settlement led by the ailing Archbishop John Whitgift and Bishop Richard Bancroft* of London*. Orchestrated Puritan petitions worried James, who issued a proclamation on 24 October 1603 against extremists who "seditiously seek reformation" of a church whose constitution and doctrine were "agreeable to God's word."

The conference met at Hampton Court. The chief Puritan speakers were probably government nominees: John Reynolds was friendly with Whitgift, while Thomas Sparks later defended jure divino episcopacy. Over thirty Puritans were in attendance nearby, some far more extreme than these speakers. Significantly, no Puritans were allowed at the first session on 14 January, attended by king, privy council*, primate, nine bishops, and several deans. James asked what reforms were needed. Whitgift and Bancroft begged that church government and liturgy remain the same and that Puritan charges not be heard. James wanted to hear them, doubting the perfection of the prayer book, ecclesiastical courts, and clergy. King and bishops agreed on possible reforms and the agenda for the second session.

On 16 January Puritan representatives led by Reynolds met Bancroft and other leading ecclesiastics before the king and his councilors. James said he wanted the amendment of abuses, uniformity of practice, and unity against "enemies to religion." Puritan requests included better ministers, changes in the Thirty-nine Articles and church services, the restoration of "prophesyings," and individual clerical powers of censure over the laity. Bishops were not to proceed against clerical Nonconformists without royal and parliamentary assent. Bancroft's attempts to silence their complaints were ignored. James joined in their attacks on inadequate ministers and seemed amenable to more Calvinistic* modifications of the prayer book and Thirty-nine Articles but denied that the sign of the cross in baptism and the surplice were contrary to Scripture. When Reynolds mentioned "presbyteri" assisting bishops, James erupted, probably glad of the opportunity to reject Scottish-style Presbyterianism* publicly. "No bishop, no king," he said. No doubt this was what he referred to when he privately claimed that he had trounced the Puritans. He might have threatened to "harry" some "out of the land," but James and the Puritans probably parted quite amicably at Hampton Court.

The third and plenary session on 18 January was attended by leading ecclesiastics and thirty-two Puritan ministers. James urged unity, asking all to show greater toleration. He gave Puritans some concessions—for example, bishops alone could not deprive ministers, and those with ticklish consciences were not to be forced into conformity too fast. He denounced pluralism and nonresidence and called for learned ministers.

The conference had achieved something. Some problems within the church had at last received public recognition and promises of action by the king. James had listened to the moderate Puritans and possibly pleased some with his decisions and sympathy, for example, toward Puritan ministers in recusant*-ridden Lancashire. Perhaps he raised, then dashed the hopes of more extreme Puritans, some of whom believed the establishment stage-managed the conference. Extremists lacked political importance, however, and if the conference precipitated their degeneration into fragmented sectarianism, that surely weakened them and benefited the establishment. It may be that James's inability (even unwillingness) to follow up fully the proposed reforms was a greater error, although, as James and Bancroft knew, reform was difficult (even impossible) while the laity held impropriations*. Whitgift and his supporters were no doubt relieved that their new king had in effect publicly approved the organization and doctrine of the established church (not that these had been really challenged at Hampton Court). The conference might have increased Bancroft's determination to monitor and improve diocesan activities insofar as practicalities allowed. Apart from the new version of the Bible* to be produced, the conference did not dramatically alter, improve, or harm the established church, although judgments of its significance remain varied and controversial. Perhaps James's aims were essentially political. Compared to the reign of his son, his reign was characterized by unity, possibly a tribute to the willingness to appear to compromise that he displayed at Hampton Court.

Bibliography: Patrick McGrath, *Papists and Puritans Under Elizabeth I*, 1967; F. Shriver, "Hampton Court Revisited: James and the Puritans," *Journal of Ecclesiastical History* 32 (1982): 48-71.

Vivienne C. Sanders

Harrington, James (1611-1677). Born to Sir Sapcote Harrington and his wife, James was a member of the prominent Harrington family of Rutlandshire, a family reputed to hold one of the largest landed fortunes in England. James lived his entire life on his inheritance from his father. He was philosophically opposed to primogeniture, and he partially supported three brothers and four sisters with his legacy.

Harrington's formal education consisted of only two or three years at Trinity College, Cambridge. He enrolled in 1629 but left without earning a degree. In 1631 he enrolled in the Middle Temple, a law school, but he abandoned this after only a few weeks. Harrington embarked upon the customary grand tour of Europe in 1632, visiting the Netherlands, Denmark, France, and Italy. He observed closely the government of each country, admiring the Venetian republic the most. He acquired an imperfect knowledge of Venice's government, using it as a model for his Oceana government.

Harrington assumed no military role in the Civil Wars* of the 1640s, but he did sympathize with the parliament*. He loaned money to the government in 1641 and 1642, and in 1645 he raised money for the parliamentary armies. During Charles I's* captivity in 1647, Harrington was made groom of the bedchamber, a position that made him a frequent companion to the captive king. He reportedly tried to convert the king to his developing republican ideas. Charles's execution* in 1649 grieved Harrington, and he withdrew from society and started composing *Oceana* in 1654.

Harrington's ideal republic, which he called Oceana, was based on his agrarian law: 5,000 landowners, each controlling land worth not more than £2,000. The national government consisted of a popular assembly that proposed legislation and a senate that approved proposals. Deputies were elected for three-year terms, and one-third were automatically rotated out each year. Various officers of state were elected out of the senate. Harrington published *Oceana* in 1656, dedicating it to Oliver Cromwell*. Cromwell's government seized the printed copies, and only a personal appeal by Harrington to Cromwell's daughter brought about release of the publication.

After Cromwell's death, Harrington launched a full-scale campaign to popularize his ideas and have them accepted. He wrote a number of additional publications explaining his ideas, including *Aphorisms Political* (1659), *The Art of Lawgiving* (1659), *Brief Directions* (1659), and *The Rota* (1660). The Rota Club was organized in 1659 to promote Harrington's ideas. Meeting in London* coffee houses*, the debate club was open to all, and it sometimes drew large crowds. After the Restoration* Harrington's popularity declined. He was arrested and committed to the Tower of London in 1661 because of his republican ideas. Released after a few months because of his deteriorating health, Harrington later married at age sixty-four.

Harrington had little influence on seventeenth-century England, but several of his ideas—religious toleration, extension of the franchise, state-financed education, and the secret ballot—later became part of the English government. Harrington's *Oceana* was more important in influencing the United States; at least thirteen of his ideas were incorporated into America's new government in the eighteenth century.

Bibliography: W. Calvin Dickinson, *James Harrington's Republic*, 1983; James Harrington, *The Political Works of James Harrington*, ed. by J. G. A. Pocock, 1977.

W. Calvin Dickinson

Heads of the Proposals (1647). Detailed guidelines for a proposed settlement between the army* and Charles I*, drafted in July 1647. Henry Ireton* and John Lambert had seized Charles in June with the collaboration of Oliver Cromwell* and the general council of the army. Through the Heads of the Proposals, Cromwell and his allies sought a peaceful, workable agreement among Charles, parliament*, and the army. The Heads were an expanded constitutional restatement of demands in the council of the army's Declaration of the Army of 15 June. Also included were additional proposals for law reforms to appease growing Leveller* discontent.

The first statements of the Heads, like the basic terms of the declaration, demanded the dissolution of the Long Parliament*. Future parliaments were to be called on a regular biennial basis, and no parliament was to remain in session longer than 240 days or to be dissolved without its consent until it had lasted at least 120 days. The king had to seek approval of the council of state*, whose authority was strengthened by this document, before calling any extraordinary parliament. Proposed electoral reforms would establish more proportional parliamentary representation, taking seats away from dying towns and adding representatives from growing counties. The number of seats in the House of Commons allotted to an area was to be determined by the total taxation* assessed there. New provisions for the indirect election of county sheriffs* and justices of the peace (see Local Government*) were also included. The Heads called for an act to place the army, navy*, and appointment of the great officers of state under parliamentary control for ten years. Demands for the payment of arrears to the army, as well as all other public debts, were stated. Furthermore, an Act of Oblivion was to be passed to absolve all persons of "trespasses" that had been committed through their participation in the war. In an attempt to gain Charles's acceptance, more lenient terms were offered to his royalist* supporters: only five were to be denied pardon, while others were to be reprimanded, suffer monetary penalties, and be excluded from public office for five years.

The Heads suggested no definite plan for church government. Instead it repeated measures that would expand the scope of religious toleration, proposed acts to eliminate the coercive powers of the bishops and clergy, stated that forced use of the Book of Common Prayer should be curtailed, called for the repeal of acts that imposed penalties for not attending church or for attending religious services elsewhere, and suggested that no one should be compelled to take the Covenant* or receive punishment for refusing. Finally, the Heads requested action on public grievances, especially in the area of trade and law reform. Such actions were to be directed against monopolies*, unfair restrictions on free trade, unjust tithes, unequal excises, and inadequate poor laws*. In general the Heads of the Proposals represented more generous and pragmatic terms for Charles. In return for his agreement, the document clearly stated that he, his queen, and his heirs would be restored to "regal power" without further limitations.

The Heads of the Proposals were debated by the council of the army on 16-17 July and unofficially submitted to Charles on 23 July. However, rioting erupted in London* on 26 July, and the mob, in possible cooperation with Political Presbyterians*, forced the withdrawal of the speaker and the Independent* minority in the House of Commons. Cromwell, hoping to avoid the use of military force in London, officially published the Heads of the Proposals on 1 August. By 8 August, though, the army had been ordered to secure and occupy London.

Despite the tense situation Cromwell, Ireton, and Sir Thomas Fairfax* continued to pursue a peaceful settlement with Charles through the terms of the Heads. Charles never officially responded, yet his outright rejection of the revised Propositions of Newcastle* (known as the Hampton Proposals) in September seemed to indicate that he preferred the Heads of the Proposals. However, he continued to negotiate secretly for an alliance with the Scottish nobility.

Opposition to the Heads as a peace settlement with Charles grew among John Lilburne* and the Levellers. By 28 October the Levellers and their supporters in the army had produced a constitutional document, the first Agreement of the People*, which called for major parliamentary reform but made no mention of the role of kingship. Cromwell, in an effort to reunite all elements of the army, called a special meeting of the council of the army at Putney, which lasted from 28 October to 1 November. After the Putney Debates*, Cromwell's group was less enthusiastic in negotiations with Charles. In November the king escaped to the Isle of Wight, where he continued to move toward agreement with the Scots. On 26 December he signed an Engagement*, allying himself to the Scottish nobility in return for military support and thus altering the course of any further agreement with either the army or parliament.

Bibliography: S. R. Gardiner, *History of the Great Civil War, 1642-1649*, 1893. J. P. Kenyon, *The Stuart Constitution, 1603-1688*, 1966.

Nancy Vannett

Henrietta Maria (1609-69). Charles I's* wife, Henrietta Maria, unwittingly provided impetus for the Civil War*, her Catholicism* making her a scapegoat for the king's poor decisions. She was born 26 November 1609, the youngest child of Marie de Medici and Henri IV of France. Her father was assassinated in 1610, her brother became Louis XIII, and her mother queen regent. The other royal children grew up in a relaxed atmosphere at Saint-Germain, but their education was inadequate, and Marie rarely visited, concerning herself only with politically advantageous marriages for them. She planned to marry Henrietta Maria to the comte de Soissons, but Marie and Soissons' rebellion in 1620 ended that prospect. Negotiations with James I* for her marriage to the prince of Wales were initially impeded by English pursuit of a Spanish match*, but Cardinal Richelieu—anxious to prevent the English from entering the Thirty Years War* on the Protestant side and seeking concessions for English Catholics—eventually succeeded. Henrietta Maria married Charles I by proxy in Paris on 11 May 1625, shortly after his accession.

The English were impressed with Henrietta Maria but feared she would convert Charles to Catholicism. She did not get along with Charles's favorite, the 1st duke of Buckingham (George Villiers*), which strained her relationship with Charles. Parliament* linked her with William Laud's* policies, and her youth, French attendants (eventually dismissed), and expensive masques (produced by Inigo Jones) also gave offense. Charles and Henrietta Maria grew closer after Buckingham's assassination in 1628 and were happy despite tensions in England during the Personal Rule* (1629-1640). She gave birth to a son who died within hours in 1629, and then the future Charles II* in 1630, followed by Mary in 1631, the future James II* in 1633, Elizabeth in 1636, Henry in 1640, and Henrietta (Minette) in 1644.

Their peace was broken when Laud imposed the Book of Common Prayer on Scotland* in 1637, which led to rebellion (see Bishops Wars*; Covenant*). Many attributed Charles's decision to send an army* against the rebels to Henrietta Maria. Charles was forced to summon parliament but dissolved the Short Parliament* in 1640 for refusing supply and attacking Laud, Henrietta Maria, and Catholics. Opposition to Charles increased, the rebels sent an army across the border, and Charles had to sign a humiliating truce, involving monetary payment to the Scots. He then called the Long Parliament* to seek supply. Meanwhile Henrietta Maria tried to get money from Rome, and a marriage was arranged between Mary and William of Orange (the parents of William III*) primarily for monetary reasons.

John Pym* and parliament focused their attacks on the earl of Strafford (Thomas Wentworth*) and Henrietta Maria. Strafford was executed in 1641, and the queen fled to Holland in hopes of relieving the pressure on Charles. Parliament wanted to impeach her (see Impeachment*) but let her go, believing they could better deal with Charles with her away. However, the Civil War erupted in August 1642. The queen remained devoted to Charles and did everything in her power to help the royalist* cause. She sold some of the Crown jewels to buy weapons and attempted to persuade other heads of state to support her husband. The prince of Orange was the main contributor, sending men and supporting her in Holland. Royalists controlled much of the north by 1643, so the queen returned to England. Charles was confident and parliamentarian* forces temporarily in disarray, but Oliver Cromwell's* New Model Army* soon turned royalist confidence into despair, and the royalist defeat at Naseby* in 1645 virtually destroyed Charles's hopes of victory.

Meanwhile Henrietta Maria was forced to travel to France after giving birth to Minette in 1644. Though extremely ill, she continued to help Charles from France. He surrendered to the Covenanters* in Scotland in 1646 but was returned to the English after refusing to make religious concessions. Following the failed Engagement* and the Second Civil War* in 1648 came Charles's trial and execution* in 1649. Henrietta Maria was initially in a state of shock but realized that her children needed her. Charles II attempted to recover the throne in the Third Civil War* but was defeated at Worcester in 1651. During the Interregnum* Henrietta Maria and Minette lived outside Paris, while her sons enjoyed French society and fought as mercenaries. Her relationship with her children worsened because they refused her control.

The Restoration* of Charles II in 1660 elated Henrietta Maria. She promised not to meddle in politics because that would jeopardize her son's reign. She believed Catholicism would have a better chance of surviving if it remained in the background. She resided in London* for several years, and people learned that she was not as fanatical as they had thought. The Great Plague of London drove her back to France in 1665 (see Epidemics and Plague*). She died in 1669 in the convent she had established at Chaillot.

Bibliography: Elizabeth Hamilton, *Henrietta Maria*, 1976.

Paul Miller

Henry Frederick, Prince of Wales (1594-1612). The first son of James VI of Scotland (later James I* of England), Henry was born 19 February 1594. Within a year James had him removed from his mother's care and placed under the guardianship of Alexander Erskin, earl of Mar, because of James's fear that Henry would be influenced by Anne of Denmark's* tendency toward Catholicism*. James gave Mar a warrant that Anne could not have control of Henry until the prince was eighteen. When Elizabeth I died and James went to England to ascend the throne there, James ordered that Henry stay at Stirling and told Anne when she came to join him not to bring their son. Anne disregarded James's order, however, and brought Henry with her, arriving at Windsor at the end of June 1603.

The English immediately adored Henry. He was witty, athletic, and outgoing and carried himself like a prince. As part of the peace negotiations with Spain, there was discussion of a marriage between Henry and Anne, the eldest daughter of Philip III of Spain. But the negotiations foundered over the Spanish demand that Henry be educated in Spain so he could adopt the Catholic faith. Proposals for Henry's marriage to a French princess also came to nothing.

In 1605 Henry entered Magdalen College, Oxford, where he enjoyed athletic pursuits. Henry was popular at Oxford, and his national popularity also continued to grow. People saw him as a welcome relief from his father. He was interested in naval and military issues, and his opinions on national issues were often in conflict with James. Henry admired Sir Walter Raleigh* and wished him freed from the Tower of London. He also disliked his father's favorite, Robert Carr*, and disapproved of how his father conducted his royal court*.

Despite these conflicts Henry was invested as prince of Wales in 1610, and many of the English people had high hopes for a future when Henry would eventually become king. But in 1612 Henry became ill, suffering from violent headaches and fever. He died 6 November 1612 of typhoid fever at the age of eighteen. Given the dissatisfaction with James's reign and the conflicts with which Charles I* had to deal, Henry was not only deeply mourned at the time of his death, but was later seen as the last chance for positive change in the early Stuart age.

Bibliography: Roy Strong, *Henry Prince of Wales and the Lost Renaissance*, 1986; E. C. Wilson, *Prince Henry and English Literature*, 1946.

Carole Levin

High Church Party. Term used to describe a group in the Church of England (see Anglicanism*) that supports a great or "high" emphasis on the episcopal and ceremonial aspects of the church and stresses their historical continuity with medieval Catholicism*. The term *High Church party* was first applied to the nonjurors, who opposed William III* of Orange, and the Tory* clergy who followed them in the early eighteenth century. Later it was revived and used to refer to the party of that same name that arose within the Church of England at the time of the Tractarian movement of the nineteenth century. Any references to a High Church party before the Glorious Revolution* are anachronistic. Historians during the late nineteenth and early twentieth centuries, however, frequently used the term *High Church* to describe the positions of late Elizabethan and Jacobean clerics such as John Whitgift, Richard Bancroft*, and Richard Hooker; William Laud* and the Arminians* in Caroline England; and Gilbert Sheldon*, William Sancroft*, and their supporters during the Restoration* era. Obviously these groups held certain beliefs and assumptions in common about the nature of the Church of England, but to lump them together in a continuous tradition of a so-called High Church party is both simplistic and inaccurate.

Bibliography: George Every, *The High Church Party, 1688-1718*, 1956; John Spurr, *The Restoration Church of England, 1646-1689*, 1991.

Ronald H. Fritze

High Commission, Court of. See Ecclesiastical Courts; Prerogative Courts.

Historical Thought and Writing. The seventeenth century elaborated on the great achievements of Tudor chroniclers and antiquaries, while adding contributions to historiography that had not been anticipated previously. Perhaps the most obvious change from earlier times was the rapid disappearance of the chronicle. Although the medieval annalistic (year-by-year) format had been ignored by humanist historians like Polydore Vergil (1470-1555) at the beginning of the sixteenth century, it had remained the dominant model for historical writing in Elizabeth's reign. Early seventeenth-century historians largely eschewed the chronicle, though annalistic writing remained popular among readers of history, who often composed chronologies for their private use, and among townsmen, some of whom continued to record urban events under the dates of mayors and sheriffs* well into the Hanoverian period. A few highly successful Stuart histories continued to appear, somewhat misleadingly, under the title of "chronicles"—for instance, the immensely popular and often reprinted *Chronicle of the Kings of England* (1643) by Sir Richard Baker (1568-1645). But such works bear scant resemblance to the chronicles of an Elizabethan writer like Raphael Holinshed (d. 1580) or John Stow (d. 1605) and are really cast in a humanist mold, in the sense that they are organized primarily by reigns rather than years and generally tell a continuous story rather than listing disconnected events. Medieval chronicles, of course, continued to be edited and published from manuscript by antiquaries such as Thomas Habington (1560-1647), Sir Henry Savile (1549-1622), John Selden* (1584-1654), Sir Roger Twysden (1597-1622), and Thomas Gale (1635-1702).

Another change, less obvious at a glance but just as important, came early in the century and involved the understood meaning of the word *history*. Elizabethan and early Jacobean authors had accepted a conventional Renaissance definition of history as a narrative prose genre that ought to teach by example from the past. In this regard, it was formally distinguishable from other works concerned with the past, notably the antiquarian "discourses" produced by the Elizabethan Society of Antiquaries (a group that revived briefly under James I* until being dissolved in 1614) and the county survey or "chorography." Increasing attention to non-narrative records by antiquaries and historians alike and more widespread familiarity with languages such as Anglo-Saxon and Welsh contributed to the breaking down of this barrier, and in 1618 Selden published an antiquarian study, *The History of Tithes*, which he termed a history. The boundaries between the genres become much fuzzier from this point on, and many antiquaries began to consider themselves as historians, although they did not write didactic political narratives.

Political history, of course, remained a central concern. Among early Stuart political historians, several names stand out. Sir Walter Raleigh's* incomplete *History of the World* (1614), written during his long captivity in the Tower, is the only example of its kind from the early seventeenth century, though it would inspire many imitators, especially among mid- and late-century chronologers. Several authors wrote or translated histories of foreign countries, such as Richard Knolles's (1550?-1610) often-reprinted *General History of the Turks* (1604), and even the classical period found a few historians, though ancient historians like Tacitus and Sallust continued their dominance of this field. English history was surveyed by several authors, of whom the best was Samuel Daniel (1562-1619), a former poet in whose works were combined a keen sense of historical development and cultural change, together with a scholarly approach to sources. Most authors opted for shorter periods than Daniel and wrote histories of particular reigns. Thus Sir John Hayward (1564?-1627) wrote lives of the first three post-conquest kings, Edward Lord Herbert of Cherbury (1583-1648) a sympathetic life of Henry VIII, Bishop Francis Godwin (1562-1633) lives of Henry VIII and his first two children, and the great antiquary William Camden (1551-1623) a large and important book, the *Annales* of Queen Elizabeth's reign (1615). This last was easily the most scholarly of the early Stuart histories, in both the breadth of its coverage of events and the depth of its sources. Camden was granted privileged access to state papers, and like the other historians of his day, he enjoyed the use of the immense private library of his former student Sir Robert Cotton* (1571-1631). Camden also contributed to a growing interest in history at the universities* by founding his still-enduring chair in ancient history in the early 1620s. Francis Bacon's* *History of the Life and Reign of King Henry VII* (1622) also deserves mention, less for its scholarship, which was not deep, than for its sustained use of a historical figure as a model for the future Charles I*; it was thus one of the last English examples of a familiar Renaissance genre, the humanist history written explicitly as an advice book to a prince.

A striking point about most early Stuart historiography was the lack of controversy about the past that it reveals, in sharp contrast to historical thought outside the pages of formal historical writing, where issues such as the relative antiquity of Oxford or Cambridge, the origins of the English church, and the nature of the Norman Conquest continued to inspire debate throughout the century. Most Jacobean historians were not oblivious to problems of interpretation and ambiguities of fact, but they preferred to gloss over them rather than to engage in a polemic that threatened to subvert the "dignity" of history and to undermine confidence in its reliability as the custodian of the past. This attitude would change sharply and irrevocably with the advent of the Civil War*, the emergence into the open of competing religious and political ideologies, and the virtual collapse for a time of censorship. Historians soon began to line up behind one side or another and to write highly partisan histories, both explaining the causes of the war and in some instances gazing back on more remote times to paint a picture of ancient and medieval Britain, its customs, politics, and religion. Such histories were either sharply royalist* and Anglican* as in the writings of the most notorious of royalist historians, the Laudian Peter Heylyn (1600-1662) or they voiced a variety of anti-royalist, anti-prelatical opinions that are in turn

distinguishable according to degrees of radicalism. The former court poet Thomas
May (1595-1650), among the earliest to write a history from the parliamentarian*
perspective, penned a history of the Long Parliament* highly favorable to that body
in the middle years of the war, and a number of others published histories of the early
seventeenth century that were unsympathetic to Charles I or his father.

Divisions within the two principal camps led to further controversies, with Heylyn
attacking not only parliamentarian historians but also moderate royalists like the
church historian Thomas Fuller (1608-1661); Presbyterians* like Clement Walker (d.
1651) heaped more venom on their Independent* rivals than they did on the defeated
royalist foe; and the great poet John Milton* began his own unfinished *History of
Britain* in the late 1640s in large measure to criticize the failings of the republican
regime that he so passionately supported. A few authors, such as the parliamentarian
Bulstrode Whitelocke (1605-1675) and the moderate royalist, Edward Hyde*, earl of
Clarendon, would attempt to write relatively impartial and balanced accounts of the
war and the Interregnum*, but even they could not rise above a sense of the recent
past colored by partisan politics and religious difference. Others, like the former
parliamentary clerk John Rushworth (1612-1690), assembled and published useful
volumes of documents that became fodder for further controversy; the republican
theorist James Harrington* (1611-1677) cast his own account of English history in the
form of an allegory, *The Commonwealth of Oceana* (1656). But the more or less
univocal, royalist, and nonpolemical tone of Elizabethan and early Stuart history
writing had vanished for good, and Restoration* historians remained seriously divided
over the causes of the war and indeed over the entire course of English history.

The issue of whether William I had really conquered England in 1066 or had
simply won by battle his rightful Crown and then confirmed the laws of the Anglo-
Saxons had been latent in much pre-war political discourse. The scholarship of Sir
Henry Spelman (1564-1641), Selden, and Cotton on the character of medieval
feudalism suggested a stronger break at the conquest than many common lawyers
(most famously Sir Edward Coke*) were willing to accept. Mid-century radical
groups such as the Levellers* and Diggers* went further than the royalists in this
regard and suggested that 1066 had indeed been a conquest, one that had enslaved the
free Anglo-Saxons under a "Norman Yoke" and should now, in the revolutionary
context of the late 1640s and 1650s, be reversed. The topic continued to be important
during the Restoration, emerging during the Exclusion Crisis* (1679-1681) and again
before and after the Glorious Revolution* of 1688, as historians such as the Whig*
William Petyt (1636-1707) and the Tory* Robert Brady (d. 1700) presented alternative
accounts of the ancient common law* and the effect on it of the conquest; the works
of earlier scholars like Selden and Spelman were also reprinted and translated for
polemical purpose.

Biographical writing also deserves mention. Though this remained in many ways
a genre distinct from history, it maintained and developed the Renaissance emphasis
on the individual as historical actor. Just as English artists had established themselves
as masters of the miniature, so a series of authors such as Izaak Walton (1593-1683),
Anthony Wood (1632-1695), Fuller, and John Aubrey* (1626-1697) wrote outstanding
examples of collected lives of worthies of their own times. Although these now have

to be used by modern biographers with some caution, they remain important sources and are among the most robust and charming examples of later Stuart prose; in particular Aubrey's *Brief Lives* (written 1669-1696, published 1813), the work of a wide-ranging antiquarian mind, has proved especially enduring. Building on the religious diary tradition of the early Stuart era, some dissenting and sectarian authors wrote lives either of notable godly figures or in some instances of themselves—the "autobiographies" of the Quaker* George Fox* and the Presbyterian Richard Baxter provide two examples of the latter.

Aside from political history and biography, the second half of the century witnessed a resurgence of interest in ecclesiastical history, largely ignored by the Jacobeans. This occurred at the very time that the continued existence of an established church came into question in the face of the Puritan* assault that was not entirely reversed in 1660. In addition to many works on the more arcane aspects of biblical chronology (establishing the dates of major events recounted in the Bible* and the precise age of the earth) by prominent ecclesiastics such as Archbishop James Ussher (1581-1656), local gentry began investigating the physical features of their parochial churches, including funeral monuments; scholars also continued to recover and publish more and more records of the so-called primitive or early Christian church in Britain. Throughout the Middle Ages historical writing had been largely a clerical preserve, and it is often overlooked that the clergy regained some of this preeminence toward the end of the seventeenth century and into the early eighteenth, with many of the outstanding scholars and historians holding some position within the established church or one of the dissenting groups: two famous instances are the non-juring bishop George Hickes (1642-1715), the outstanding medieval linguist of the last years of the century, and the Whig bishop Gilbert Burnet*, whose *History of the Reformation* (1679-1715) and *History of His Own Times* (1724-1734) are among the most commonplace items in early eighteenth-century private library catalogs.

Any account of the historical thought of the seventeenth century would be incomplete were it to leave out the antiquaries. Although their activities were frequently satirized as irrelevant, pedantic, and dull, it was scholars such as Spelman and Camden—with their willingness to travel about the countryside in search of documents, archaeological sites, and architectural survivals—who above all made the seventeenth century a profoundly historical age, in a way that the sixteenth century, for all its important historical writing, had not been. The actual works by leading scholars were important in themselves as good models of how to deal with difficult sources in many different languages. Their greatest influence came in inspiring an interest in the study of the past that went well beyond publishing for scholars to encompass the elites of various towns and shires. Little work has been done thus far on the hundreds of minor local antiquaries and collectors active in the shires from the late sixteenth to the early eighteenth centuries, or on the assembly of private and public libraries of which a significant proportion of the books could be said to be historical. Recent research reveals a number of facts about the broader "sense of the past" that was developing in the seventeenth century beyond the confines of formal historical writing. First, it reveals the existence in the localities of hundreds of little-known folk beliefs and oral traditions about the past. Educated readers, already distrustful of more famous legends such as those surrounding King Arthur, were increasingly inclined to discount as "vulgar error" the hundreds of rural and civic oral traditions recorded by traveling antiquaries from the mouths of the middling and poorer (and generally illiterate) sort of people that they encountered. Second, a degree of popular awareness of history as a whole and of English history in particular can be said to have been achieved by 1700, which encouraged such phenomena as gentry tours to historic sites and recreational digs for old coins and other artifacts; the sentiments behind this are well captured in such works as the diaries of John Evelyn* (1620-1706), Elias Ashmole (1617-1692), and Wood, and in occasional works such as the moving *Hydriotaphia: Urn-burial* (1658) by Sir Thomas Browne (1605-1682). These interests spilled over into the development of a kind of Baconian "natural history," wherein antiquary-topographers like Robert Plot (1640-1696), broadening the chorographic tradition of Elizabethans such as Camden, surveyed particular counties systematically for their flora and fauna, as well as for their archaeological remains. It was their discovery of increasing numbers of animal fossils that helped open the biblical account of the Creation and the Flood to criticism and would eventually subvert some long-accepted Renaissance notions of the limited age of the world (commonly believed to be only five or six millennia) and of its inevitable decay. Finally, much evidence in local archives and in the writings of the antiquaries themselves suggests that national historical episodes (the conquest, Magna Carta, the Armada, and the Civil War itself) were beginning to displace or to distort local, orally transmitted beliefs about the history of particular places, creating in the early eighteenth century a common currency for discussions of history that has survived to the present day.

Bibliography: David C. Douglas, *English Scholars, 1660-1730*, 1951; J. G. A. Pocock, *The Ancient Constitution and the Feudal Law*, 1987; D. R. Woolf, *The Idea of History in Early Stuart England*, 1990.

Daniel R. Woolf

Hobbes, Thomas (1588-1679). The foremost political philosopher of the seventeenth century, Hobbes was born near Malmesbury in Wiltshire. His father was an undistinguished cleric, but Hobbes had a rich uncle who financed his education at Oxford. After graduating in 1608, he took service with the Cavendish family, acting as a tutor and secretary in the household of successive earls of Devonshire and maintaining a close connection with the earl (and later marquis and duke) of Newcastle. Hobbes displayed an early interest in classical literature, and in 1629 his translation of Thucydides was published. His duties as a tutor took him to the continent, and there in the 1630s he made the acquaintance of Mersenne and other French scientists and philosophers. During the 1630s he acquired a growing reputation as a philosopher and scientist. He formulated a plan to write a trilogy covering the whole field of philosophy. The first part was to deal with body or matter in general, the second with man, and the third with the citizen or politics. He produced the third part first, completing *De Cive* (*On the Citizen*) in 1641 and publishing it in the following year. By May 1640 he already had written an English treatise, *The Elements of Law*, which sketched out various aspects of his philosophy but paid particular attention to politics, anticipating *De Cive* on many points.

The reason Hobbes finished the political part of his enterprise first was that he believed it was desperately urgent to resolve the disagreements dividing Englishmen. In his opinion, previous writers on ethical and political theory had failed to construct a rigorously argued system of thought and had instead been content to purvey their own prejudices, wrapped up in fine language. Hobbes was an extremely elegant writer, but he was highly suspicious of rhetoric, which he regarded as a mask for ambition. He thought that England's political dissensions resulted largely from the circulation of misguided and seditious ideas couched in eloquent language by ambitious men. Hobbes's Cavendish allies were royalists*. In 1640 the earl of Devonshire unsuccessfully attempted to secure a seat for Hobbes in the Short Parliament*. At the time of that assembly, manuscript copies of *The Elements of Law* circulated, and according to Hobbes's later testimony he would have been in danger if the king had not suddenly dissolved the parliament*. The dedicatee of the *Elements* was Newcastle, who spent large sums in raising forces for Charles I* during the Civil War*. The *Elements* was a trenchantly absolutist* work which argued that vigorous measures should be taken to stamp out such seditious ideas as that kings are bound by law or that subjects hold rights of property against their sovereigns. When the Long Parliament* met, some people who had taken a high view of the royal prerogative* were called in question. Fearing that parliament would punish him for his political opinions, Hobbes fled to France.

In Paris, Hobbes brought out *De Cive* and resumed work on the first two parts of his trilogy but found that new commitments slowed his progress. These included teaching mathematics to the prince of Wales (see Charles II*), who arrived in the French capital in 1646. The man who secured this appointment for him was Henry Lord Jermyn, a close associate of Queen Henrietta Maria*. Other friends of Hobbes who were connected with Jermyn and the queen included Sir William Davenant and Henry Lord Percy. It was on the advice of this group and of Newcastle that Charles went to Scotland* in 1650, agreeing to abandon episcopacy in order to gain the Scottish military support that enabled him to make a bid for the English throne. The queen's group and Newcastle were noted for their willingness to sacrifice the bishops to political ends and for their lack of concern about constitutional propriety. Among the royalists they were opposed by Edward Hyde* and his allies, who wanted to preserve episcopacy and to ensure that the king abided by settled constitutional norms. Hyde was an advocate of mixed and limited monarchy; he strongly disliked Hobbes's political philosophy. While Charles was in Scotland, Hobbes completed *Leviathan* (1651), which attacked ideas of mixed monarchy and castigated the pretensions of all clerics, including bishops. After the failure of Charles's Scottish adventure, Hobbes's friends were replaced in royal favor by Hyde and his associates, and Hobbes himself was dismissed from the royal court*. He then returned to England, where he made his peace with the government of the Rump Parliament*. After the Restoration* he resumed his association with Charles, who protected him from his critics. The latter included bishops who resented his criticisms of the clergy and suspected that his materialism and various odd theological doctrines amounted to atheism. They also included Hyde, whose political ideas Hobbes once more attacked in a history of the Civil War entitled *Behemoth*, which was first published in 1679—the year of Hobbes's death—but written several years earlier.

The *Elements* claimed that human nature is such that outside the state, people would live in the gravest danger of imminent death. The same basic case was repeated in *De Cive* and *Leviathan*. Hobbes asserted that to set up the state, it is necessary for individuals to lay down their rights in favor of a sovereign, though he argued that there are a few rights with which they could not part (especially the right of self-defense). The details of the account of the origins of government that Hobbes presented in the three versions of his political philosophy show interesting variations, but the broad thrust of his argument remained the same, and throughout he insisted that absolute sovereignty was necessary to preserve the state from destruction. In *De Cive,* Hobbes expanded his comments on religion considerably, and in *Leviathan* he took the process still further, devoting half the book to questions of religion and church-state relations. One reason he spent so much space on these questions is that he believed that the self-interested and groundless claims of clerics were largely responsible for civil strife throughout contemporary Europe. It is sometimes supposed that his close analysis of biblical passages indicates that he was a sincere Christian, but this claim is far from convincing. First, even if he did not believe the scriptural message, he was well aware that most of his contemporaries treated the Bible* as gospel; if he was to persuade them, it was useful to prove that Scripture taught a Hobbesian message. Second, he strongly hinted that there are no good grounds for believing anyone who claims to have had a revelation from the Almighty and therefore no good grounds for holding that the revelations recorded in Scripture are true. Third, there is a dry humor about much of his discussion of the Bible. Nowadays Hobbes is sometimes seen as a Protestant Christian of a slightly unorthodox variety. There is more truth in the common contemporary notion that he was an atheist or something close to one.

The first two parts of Hobbes's trilogy were published in 1655 (*De Corpore*, or *On Body*) and 1658 (*De Homine*, or *On Man*). He also wrote a number of works on geometrical questions and was involved in a debate with the eminent mathematician John Wallis; Wallis won. In his later years Hobbes feared that he would be tried for heresy and so wrote on the connected themes of heresy, the usurpation of powers by clerics, and the nature of the common law* (which, he said, did not warrant the burning of heretics). In 1679 Hobbes died.

Bibliography: Thomas Hobbes, *Leviathan*, ed. by Richard Tuck, 1991; Hobbes, *English Works*, ed. by William Molesworth, 11 vols., 1839-1845; Hobbes, *Opera Philosophica*, ed. Molesworth, 5 vols., 1839-1845; there is an ongoing Oxford edition of Hobbes's philosophical works, the first of which is *De Cive*, ed. by Howard Warrender, 1983; Johann P. Sommerville, *Thomas Hobbes: Political Ideas in Historical Context*, 1991.

Johann P. Sommerville

Humble Petition and Advice (1657). The first part of a conservative constitution, completed with the Additional Humble Petition and Advice (26 June 1657), which established the governing institutions of the late Protectorate*. The Humble Petition and Advice replaced the Instrument of Government* of December 1653. Superficially it leaned more toward the traditional trinity of king, Lords, and Commons than its predecessor. Nevertheless, in its final form it was a republican constitution.

The document was drawn up in early 1657 by a shady cabal of courtiers led by Richard Boyle, Lord Broghill, a member of Lord Protector Oliver Cromwell's* council of state*. On 23 February Sir Charles Pack, member of parliament* (MP), presented the original version to parliament, including the clause asking Cromwell to accept the title of king. A spirited debate began, with the opposition to kingship led by John Lambert, author of the Instrument. The introduction of what was first called the "Remonstrance" was not entirely unexpected. In January there was a debate on the merits of the "ancient constitution," and it was obvious that some MPs wanted to revive aspects of the monarchy. On 5 March parliament resolved to include a clause for the creation of the Other House, or Lords. On 7 March it was decided that the protector could nominate his successor. Then, before addressing the issue of kingship, the house voted that it would confirm and the protector nominate members of the Other House. Finally on 23 March the house voted 123 to 62 to offer Cromwell the Crown.

The proposal of monarchy alarmed republicans in the army*, who, no doubt encouraged by John Lambert, sent a petition to Cromwell signed by 100 officers, declaring against monarchy. Cromwell pacified their concerns in a conciliatory speech on 5 March. To what extent Cromwell was engaged in duplicity or whether he was the aloof object of his councilors' and courtiers' spontaneous efforts is impossible to determine. His attitude during the debates on monarchy was indecisive. On 16 April he received a deputation from the monarchists but would not commit himself. His final decision came only after another petition from the army on 8 May, appealing for him to refuse the Crown. On the same day, in his speech to parliament, Cromwell refused to consider kingship but recommended the substance of the new constitution. On 3 June the Humble Petition and Advice was approved by the House. Modifications were later made in the Additional Humble Petition and Advice. Three weeks later, on 26 June, Cromwell was confirmed in his new powers in a ritual with all the pomp of a royal coronation.

For Lambert and the republicans, even the semblance of monarchy was dangerous. Unable to block the constitution, Lambert on 24 June argued against the proposed oath for the protector, which included references to "former Chief Magistrates" (kings). This suggested that the protector derived his authority from royal predecessors. By having this clause in the oath removed, Lambert ensured that the new constitution remained decidedly republican in content and in spirit, even though most MPs did not support him.

After Cromwell's rejection of monarchy, the Humble Petition and Advice remained a flawed, poorly written, ambiguous, conservative republican constitution. Ironically the preamble thanked God for the Commonwealth's deliverance from monarchy. The unsettling matter of the succession was resolved, and the protector could nominate his heir. Parliament would consist of two houses, a conspicuous departure from the Instrument, but the role of the Other House and the relationship of the protector to both houses was not clarified. Members of the Other House were to be nominated by the protector and approved by the Commons. By the Additional Humble Petition and Advice, a document of even more enigmatic origins, the Commons lost all role in the selection of the new "Lords." Another prerogative lost to the Commons, from the original to the final amendments in the Additional Humble Petition and Advice, was their right to vet all new members. The parliament was to provide money for an armed force of 30,000, but by the amended version, the monies raised by parliament could be spent as the council and protector saw fit. In fact, like the Instrument, the new constitution placed considerable power in a council of twenty-one members, presided over by the protector. The religious clauses were overtly reactionary, calling for punishment of extreme sectarians and suggesting a new article of faith and a purge of the Independent* church. Anglicans*, Roman Catholics*, "Irish Papists," and royalists* were excluded from political institutions and denied freedom to practice their religions. The Humble Petition and Advice ceased to function as the basis of government in May 1659, when the Rump Parliament* was restored by the Commonwealthmen* and the Wallingford House party.

Bibliography: S. R. Gardiner, *Constitutional Documents of the Puritan Revolution*, 1906; J. P. Kenyon, *The Stuart Constitution: Documents and Commentary*, 1966.

John H. F. Hughes

Hyde, Anne, Duchess of York (1637-1671). First wife of Charles II's* brother, the duke of York the future James II* (1685-1688)—and mother of Mary II* (1689-1694) and Anne* (1702-1714). She was born on 12 March 1637 in Windsor Park, the oldest daughter of Edward Hyde*, later earl of Clarendon, and his wife, Frances. In 1649 she traveled with her mother and siblings to the Netherlands, where in 1654, contrary to her father and Queen Henrietta Maria's* wishes, she was named a maid of honor to Mary, princess of Orange, daughter of Charles I*, wife of William of Orange, and mother of Anne's future son-in-law, William III* (1689-1702). She was also the favorite of Elizabeth*, daughter of James I* and widow of Elector Frederick of the Palatinate. She first met York in Paris in 1656; after a long interval they met again in Breda, where they were engaged on 24 November 1659. Both returned to England at the Restoration* and over the strenuous objections of Charles II, Henrietta Maria, Clarendon, and many of York's friends were privately married on 3 September 1660.

The duke and duchess had eight children, but only Mary and Anne survived much past infancy. The duchess was unpopular, and many at the royal court* regarded her as an upstart and as too extravagant, though Henrietta Maria was won over to her side. She was thought to have too much influence over her husband, though this did not prevent him from having a series of mistresses. She was herself rumored to have had lovers, notably Henry Sidney, and was lampooned by Andrew Marvell, but there is little evidence of any affairs. Clarendon blamed his daughter's marriage for his fall from power in 1667, which left her and York isolated at court. Thereafter, during the ascendancy of the Cabal*, she and James may have worked against the earl of Arlington (Henry Bennet*) and the 2d duke of Buckingham (George Villiers*). In 1670 she secretly converted to Catholicism*. She died on 31 March 1671 of breast cancer.

Bibliography: Leslie Stephen and Sidney Lee, eds., *Dictionary of National Biography*, 32 vols., 1908-1909.

William B. Robison

Hyde, Edward, Earl of Clarendon (1609-1674). By turns a moderate opponent of Charles I*, adviser in exile to Charles II*, lord chancellor and leading minister, and a perceptive historian of his times. Born into the gentry, Hyde practiced as a barrister and in the 1630s figured among the intellectuals forming the humanist Great Tew Circle. After serving in the Short Parliament*, he was a leader in the Long Parliament*, where he criticized Charles I's Personal Rule* and helped to devise the legislation that dismantled prerogative government (see Royal Prerogative*) and asserted common law's* supremacy. Calls for further change, however, disturbed Hyde, who by autumn 1641 was more trusting than fearful of the king and who helped to create a moderate party in parliament*. He rejected proposals to abolish episcopacy and opposed the Grand Remonstrance*, which he claimed was divisive and, because of recent reforms, unnecessary. While working for moderation in parliament, Hyde simultaneously advised the king to pursue compromise. In May 1642, after Charles had fled London*, Hyde ceased his labors for conciliation and joined the king at York. As an adviser during this period, he developed his concept of a regulated monarchy, a potent though not unfettered partner with parliament but not its servant. This vision of limited but preeminent monarchy informed his service to Charles I and Charles II thereafter.

In March 1645 Hyde's career took its decisive turn with appointment to the prince of Wales's council. Four years later Hyde accompanied the prince, now Charles II, into exile, where he guided and tried to mold the young man into a responsible monarch. Despite efforts to displace him as the king's principal counselor, Hyde dominated Charles's council. Yet while he restrained the rashest plans for reclaiming the throne, he could not make Charles attend to business or regulate his personal life: the king had a will of his own. Still, Charles recognized both Hyde's abilities and his devotion to the monarchy.

After years of waiting, Hyde returned to England in triumph at the Restoration* and received reward for his service, becoming lord chancellor and earl of Clarendon. During his years of ascendancy Clarendon directed the Crown's daily business and as much as any other figure shaped royal policy. His conservative principles of government, founded on the rule of law, had been conceived in the 1640s, defined in exile, and were now applied. He worked to erect a government in which monarch and ministers ruled by law, employing as partners the landed elite that had traditionally held public office. As a result Clarendon was hostile to further reform in government, whether at court, in government departments like the treasury, or in allowing parliament a role in foreign policy.

Ironically Clarendon's respect for monarchy made him ineffective in the end, because he both deferred to Charles and yet censured royal behavior that was insufficiently regal. The censure garnered him the resentment of royal companions and ultimately of Charles, who tired of Clarendon's disapproving presence. The deference and Clarendon's difficulty in managing the Cavalier Parliament* meant that little legislation of the 1660s bore his distinctive stamp, although he was the architect in foreign affairs of Charles's marriage and the sale of Dunkirk to the French. Clarendon personally favored a moderate religious settlement but could not prevent passage of the intolerant legislation inaccurately termed the Clarendon Code*. Unable to build a following because of his jealousy of others and his failure to take consistent positions, Clarendon also lost the energy to control parliamentary affairs as he grew older.

The victim of court plots even in the 1650s, Clarendon was charged with treason in 1663 by the earl of Bristol, a charge lacking substance and against which Charles defended him but significant because it revealed Clarendon's unpopularity outside court circles. His daughter Anne's* marriage in 1660 to the duke of York (see James II*), forced by her pregnancy and unwelcome to Clarendon, York, and the king, was nonetheless widely considered evidence of the earl's ambition. This tie to the royal family caused great resentment against Clarendon and made his natural aloofness intolerable. He increasingly received the blame, moreover, for policies he lobbied against, especially the disastrous Second Dutch War* (1665-1667), and he was implausibly held accountable for natural catastrophes like the plague (see Epidemics and Plague*; London, Plague of*), the Great Fire of London*, and even the harsh winter of 1666-1667. Clarendon thus made an excellent scapegoat for the king, who dismissed him from office in August 1667. Charles did not impede the impeachment* that followed, and Clarendon, unwilling to test the king's loyalty, fled again into exile in November. He spent his last seven years in France until his death in December 1674, finishing work on an account of his own life and his *History of the Rebellion*, masterpieces of historical writing and invaluable for their insight into Stuart politics (see Historical Thought*).

Bibliography: R. W. Harris, *Clarendon and the English Revolution*, 1983; Ronald Hutton, *Charles II*, 1989.

James Rosenheim

I

Impeachment. The process of impeachment arose in the fourteenth century as a means of bringing royal officers to account judicially before the houses of parliament*. In its mature form it was first used against Edward III's chamberlain, William Latimer, who was accused of having "notoriously accroached royal power" in the Good Parliament of 1376 and was removed from office upon judgment in the House of Lords. Some eighteen officials and judges were impeached between 1376 and 1397, all of whom were condemned by the Lords. Most commonly the procedure involved an accusation by the House of Commons based on petition or clamor, followed by hearing and judgment in the Lords. By interposing themselves between petitioners and the Lords, the Commons thus transmuted private complaints into public charges brought on behalf of the entire realm. The last significant medieval impeachment was brought against the duke of Suffolk in 1450. After that the process was gradually replaced by attainder, essentially a private bill of condemnation that did not require judicial proceeding.

Under the Tudors parliament was at most an accessory in the deposition of unpopular ministers. Richard Empson and Edmund Dudley were executed under royal warrant rather than the bill of attainder that had been introduced against them, and the Lords merely petitioned Henry VIII against Cardinal Wolsey without taking judicial action. Complaints against other ministers in 1536 and 1569 amounted to no more than grumbling, and in 1589 Elizabeth I's assertion that she would punish her own servants met with apparent satisfaction. James I* successfully challenged the Commons's attempt to proceed against two courtiers in 1610, but in the debates the impeachment of Latimer was cited, and in 1614 the starker precedent of the Merciless Parliament of 1388 was raised, when Richard II's judges had been executed for ruling on behalf of the royal prerogative* at the subject's expense.

The actual revival of impeachment occurred in the parliament of 1621*, when the House of Commons presented an indictment against the monopolist Sir Giles Mompesson and the Lords condemned him. Only days later an accusation of bribery was lodged against the lord chancellor, Sir Francis Bacon*, who had also been implicated in the monopoly* scandal. James tried to head off the impeachment of his chief minister by offering to appoint a commission of six lords and six members of parliament to investigate the charges against Bacon, but the Commons declined the gambit and proceeded to an impeachment that resulted in Bacon's resignation and, briefly, his imprisonment. With this, parliament had forged a weapon against Crown officials and judges that it would use repeatedly over the next century and continue to exercise occasionally as late as 1805.

The revival of impeachment and with it of parliamentary judicature was principally the work of Sir Edward Coke*, who, assisted by John Selden* and others, cobbled together a procedure from the uncertain precedents of the Tower rolls and persuaded the initially dubious Lords to act upon it. Coke's maneuver enabled parliament to resurrect itself as the high court of the realm at a time when its legislative powers were largely frustrated and its influence on royal policy blunted. The process of impeachment was refined in use against Lord Treasurer Cranfield* in the parliament of 1624*, the 1st duke of Buckingham (George Villiers*) in the parliament of 1626*, and Charles I's* chaplain, Roger Manwaring, in the parliament of 1628*, with the Commons preferring more specifically framed charges and expanding the scope of its jurisdiction to persons outside parliament.

The Long Parliament* commenced its work in November 1640 by impeaching the earl of Strafford (Thomas Wentworth*), Charles I's chief minister, as well as several lesser figures. The parliamentary leadership had to resort to attainder against Strafford when judicial process failed to produce the desired result, but by this time the struggle for control of the government had largely swept aside legal nicety. Strafford was followed to the block in 1645 by Archbishop Laud*, also by way of attainder when impeachment failed to prove treason against him. The trial and execution of Charles I* himself in 1649, although in no sense an impeachment, may be justly viewed as the final outcome of a process that had begun with the actions against Mompesson and Bacon in 1621.

With the Restoration* of government by king, Lords, and Commons in 1660, a second round began in the process of negotiating the terms of constitutional monarchy in England. In this process impeachment again played a critical role. The earl of Clarendon (Edward Hyde*) was driven into exile by an impeachment proceeding in 1667, and the earl of Danby (Thomas Osborne*), impeached for treason in 1678, spent five years in the Tower. With parliament's constitutional primacy established after the Glorious Revolution*, impeachment lost its function as a means of coercing royal policy and compelling ministerial accountability. It lingered into the eighteenth century, now the instrument of party government; the last major prosecutions were carried out against the earl of Oxford and other Tory* lords in 1715.

However clothed in judicial form, impeachment in the Stuart era, no less than in that of the Plantagenets, was essentially an act of political negotiation and, when negotiation failed, of struggle. It bequeathed its most important legacy to the United States, where, in the absence of a system of ministerial responsibility, impeachment remains the final instrument of control over the executive branch of government.

Bibliography: E. R. Foster, *The House of Lords, 1603-1649: Structure, Procedure, and the Nature of Its Business*, 1983; Clayton Roberts, *The Growth of Responsible*

Government in Stuart England, 1966; C. G. C. Tite, *Impeachment and Parliamentary Judicature in Early Stuart England*, 1974.

Robert Zaller

Impositions. Impositions were taxes on imports and sometimes exports levied by royal decree, or in some cases by monopolies* such as the Merchant Adventurers (see Trading Companies*) rather than by parliamentary sanction. Their constitutionality had not been questioned prior to the reign of James I* when a merchant named John Bate was arrested for refusing to pay the imposition on currants imported from the Mediterranean. Because the court of the Exchequer* argued that regulation of commerce was an extension of the royal prerogative* over foreign policy, in Bate's Case* (1606) it upheld the right of the Crown to regulate trade* by using impositions. Nonetheless, Chief Baron Sir Thomas Fleming did not extend the arbitrary taxing power of the Crown beyond the realm of regulating foreign commerce (see Taxation and Revenue*).

Quick to recognize any vehicle for increasing revenues, Lord Treasurer Robert Cecil* issued a new Book of Rates (1608) to extend impositions to a variety of, though not all, imports, which he calculated would raise perhaps £70,000. Cecil used the "new" impositions not as a means of regulating trade but to raise revenue, a function not comprehended by the ruling in Bate's Case.

When the parliament of 1610* met, the subject of impositions became foremost among the concerns of the House of Commons. The question about impositions was mingled with other grievances: monopolies and abuses of purveyance and wardship. Parliament's arguments ultimately focused on the limitation of the royal prerogative. When James I forbade the Commons to discuss his prerogative rights, the members adopted a petition arguing that parliament had the right to debate any question that affected the nation. James retreated so far as to allow parliament to discuss impositions. In the debate that ensued, members of parliament postulated that the Crown had no constitutional authority to levy new impositions for revenue purposes.

In 1614 the Addled Parliament* returned to the issue of impositions, which Sir Edwin Sandys equated with tyranny. A bill drawn up in the Commons to end impositions was narrowly defeated in the House of Lords. The Commons also attempted to establish control over new books of rates, which placed new values on taxable goods. Acrimonious charges between the two houses over impositions and additional questions about royal conduct led James to dissolve the Addled Parliament without obtaining the much-sought revenues.

During the 1620s parliament's dismay about impositions was overshadowed by other issues such as monopolies, forced loans*, and foreign policy questions. Sir John Eliot* argued that the trade depression derived primarily from impositions. Only after the Petition of Right* (1628) condemned impositions again did the issue regain its former prominence. When London* merchant Samuel Vassall refused to pay the imposition on currants in 1630, the Exchequer* ordered him imprisoned. By the reign of Charles I*, impositions had become intertwined with questions about parliament's approval of tonnage and poundage, the major portion of the customs duties. The

Crown boldly resumed collections of impositions and tonnage and poundage in defiance of the Petition of Right. Following the refusal of some merchants to pay the taxes, the House of Commons denounced the arbitrary collections, and Charles dissolved the parliament of 1629* to begin his experiment of governing without it (see Personal Rule*).

Impositions continued to increase under the first two Stuarts. By the 1630s, the impositions produced as much as £218,000 in one year. Indeed the increases in revenues from impositions exceeded the amounts returned by ship money*. The greater receipts from the new impositions were due in large part to the emerging importance of the colonial trade. Yet parliament had the last word on impositions. The Long Parliament* voted to prohibit new impositions in 1641, concurrent with the abolition of ship money and monopolies.

Bibliography: Frederick C. Dietz, *English Public Finance, 1558-1641*, 1932; G. D. G. Hall, "Impositions and the Courts, 1554-1606," *Law Quarterly Review* 69 (1953): 200-218.

Daniel W. Hollis III

Impropriations, Feoffees for (1626-1633). A group of Calvinist* clergy and lay people who bought impropriations (church property that came into lay hands) and advowsons (the right to nominate the next minister of a parish) to advance reform of the Church of England (see Anglicanism*). They aroused the ire of Archbishop William Laud* and were suppressed by Charles I's* government.

The Church of England lost considerable wealth as a result of the Protestant Reformation. Meanwhile, many ministers suffered from inadequate stipends, a problem aggravated both by the inequitable distribution of the church's revenue among the clergy and by lay people's receiving church revenues. By the beginning of the seventeenth century, many people of varying religious opinions proposed buying back the impropriated properties and returning them to the support of the parish clergy. The Puritan* William Stoughton suggested such a plan in 1604, as did Richard Bancroft*, the conservative archbishop of Canterbury in 1610. The Arminian* bishop Richard Montagu approved such schemes in 1621. So the Feoffees for Impropriations were not unique.

The feoffees formally organized on 15 February 1626, although some individual members may have been engaged in similar activities as early as 1612 or 1613. The feoffees consisted of four clerics, four lawyers, and four lay members. As old members died or resigned, they were replaced by new members selected by the remaining feoffees. The group worked as a trust, buying impropriated property to support godly preachers as vicars or lecturers. Thus they hoped to improve the quality of life for selected ministers who favored purification of the church and the maintenance of the Calvinist theological consensus.

During six years the feoffees collected £6,361 6s. 1d., which they used to buy seventeen impropriated properties and thirty-three advowsons. These were located in eighteen counties, and the feoffees appointed eighteen vicars, curates, or lecturers in eleven counties, with at least six in London*. Also among their assets was the endowment for the lectures at St. Antholm's Parish in London, a training ground for Puritan preachers. All of these acquisitions remained under the feoffees' control and were used to support godly ministers rather than being simply given back to the individual churches.

All of the feoffees were Londoners, although their charter stated that in the future only eight of the twelve were required to be residents of London. Among the original members were the minister John Davenport of St. Stephen's Coleman Street in London; Richard Sibbs, preacher for Gray's Inn and master of St. Catherine's Hall, Cambridge; and John White of the Middle Temple, lawyer of the Puritan Winthrop family. Several feoffees participated in the Massachusetts Bay and Providence Island companies (see Colonization*). In 1626 they added a thirteenth member to serve as the deciding vote, choosing Rowland Heylyn, an alderman and sheriff* of London. When Heylyn died in 1632, he was replaced by Nicholas Rainton, lord mayor of London from 1632 to 1633. Another unofficial member was the stalwart Puritan preacher Hugh Peter. Basically the feoffees consisted of well-to-do Londoners with strong commitments to the godly or Puritan branch of English Protestantism.

Although the feoffees' activities were popular with many Protestants, they drew unfriendly attention from the Arminians and the central government. Laud began to view them with suspicion in 1629. His follower Peter Heylyn (a nephew of Rowland Heylyn) even preached a sermon against their activities on 11 July 1630 at Oxford University. Ultimately Laud complained directly to Charles I, who referred him to Attorney General William Noy. Laud opposed the feoffees because they supported the establishment of a radically different Church of England from the one he envisioned. Not only did Charles sympathize with Laud's position, but Noy noted that the feoffees had never received proper incorporation by the king or the parliament* and that their activities appeared to concentrate on parliamentary boroughs, which seemed to subvert the Crown's efforts to secure the election of a compliant parliament. Although the feoffees vigorously denied the charge, the suspicion lingered.

During Easter term 1632, Noy brought suit against the feoffees in the equity side of the Exchequer*. He asked for the suppression of the organization, with the Crown taking control of its assets and employing them for proper purposes. After several months of pretrial maneuvers, the judges or barons of the Exchequer heard the case on 31 January, 7 February, and 11 February 1633. On the last day, Noy declared that the king had ordered him not to proceed with criminal charges against individual feoffees. Still, on 13 February the Exchequer found against the feoffees and abolished them, while making arrangements for the Crown to administer their properties. Almost a year later, on 17 January 1634, Charles I's government again considered criminal charges against the feoffees, but the matter was allowed to fade.

The feoffees did not forget this unfair treatment. On 31 December 1640 the Long Parliament* considered reversing the Exchequer's decree. Finally, on 10 March 1648, the House of Lords canceled the Exchequer decree and on 28 March ordered restoration of the confiscated properties to surviving feoffees. Nothing, however, came of the second order because the House of Commons failed to act on it. The feoffees' work no longer seemed so urgent to the triumphant godly members of the Long Parliament. The return of Charles II* in 1660 also saw the restoration of the Exchequer decree against the feoffees.

The Feoffees for Impropriations existed for only a brief time and acquired a relatively small amount of property and patronage. It seems likely that Laud and Peter Heylyn feared and disliked them more for the ideas they represented than because of any immediate threat they presented to the growing Arminian control over the Church of England.

Bibliography: Isabel M. Calder, "A Seventeenth Century Attempt to Purify the Anglican Church," *American Historical Review* 53 (July 1948): 760-775; Christopher Hill, *Economic Problems of the Church*, 1956; Paul S. Seaver, *The Puritan Lectureships: The Politics of Religious Dissent, 1560-1662*, 1970.

Ronald H. Fritze

Indemnity and Oblivion, Act of (12 Car. II, c. 11, 1660). In his Declaration of Breda*, Charles II* granted England a general pardon for all wrongs done against him or his father during the Interregnum*, and he shrewdly left to the Convention Parliament* the task of deciding who should be punished. That body quickly began work on a bill to settle the troubling problem. It was generally known that the king wanted only his father's judges, the regicides*, excepted from leniency, yet when the Bill for Indemnity and Oblivion was introduced in the House of Commons, it became obvious that few wanted all of those men exposed to a possible death sentence.

While the Commons and Lords eventually agreed on a general amnesty for England, the Commons originally singled out only seven of the sixty-seven men who had sat on the court that tried and sentenced Charles I*. This number later increased when several regicides refused to turn themselves in as ordered by proclamation. The remaining regicides were to be punished, if convicted, by a sentence less than death. The bill as eventually passed also identified twenty men who had been prominent in Interregnum governments and who could be subject to a punishment less than death. These men became symbolic sacrifices to atone for England's sin of deviating from monarchy.

The House of Lords was far more vengeful than the Commons. It wanted all regicides excepted from the pardon, and it sought to exact punishment on others who had injured its honor. The Commons flatly rejected this latter motive, and after repeated urging from the king for quick passage, the two houses agreed to what was essentially the Commons's bill in late August 1660. It was the key piece of legislation for the Convention, serving to quiet the fears of the nation in general and the army* in particular. The few regicides excepted and the small number of others specifically named who would be subjected to punishment adequately atoned for England's sins. Charles II, not particularly bent on revenge, readily accepted the bill, wanting a secure England rather than one wracked with purges.

Bibliography: Ronald Hutton, *The Restoration: A Political and Religious History of*

England and Wales, 1658-1667, 1985; James R. Jones, *Charles II: Royal Politician,* 1987.

David A. Davis

Independents, Political. An unstable association of differing political factions in the Long Parliament* that arose in the aftermath of the First Civil War* and that was generally in favor of a harsh settlement with Charles I*. They supported terms that would have prevented the king from behaving tyrannically in the future even if they had to encroach heavily on the royal prerogative*. A small segment of the Political Independents went much further and supported the establishment of a republic. Most Political Independents favored religious toleration for the various Protestant sects and opposed the establishment of any coercive national church. Political Independents, however, frequently were not Religious Independents*.

Although many parliamentarians* were deeply troubled about taking up arms against Charles I, others saw military victory as the surest way to secure a satisfactory settlement of their problems with the king. These people became known as the War Party. Although they did not possess anything approaching a majority in the Long Parliament, they were able to ally themselves with John Pym* and the pragmatists known as the Middle Group, a faction in the Long Parliament that was willing to seek a negotiated settlement with Charles I but only if it secured stringent concessions. Meanwhile, they were willing to prosecute the war vigorously. It was this War Party-Middle Group alliance that pursued the Scottish alliance in 1643, created the New Model Army*, and formulated the Self-Denying Ordinance* in 1645, all policies that made the parliamentary victory possible.

Military victory in 1646 left the parliamentarians with a number of difficult or insoluble problems. They still needed to suppress the Irish Rebellion* as well as reduce the state's crushing financial commitments by disbanding the large numbers of now unneeded troops, most of whom were owed substantial amounts of back wages, an awesome financial obligation. Furthermore, the Long Parliament needed to pay off the army of their Scots allies and deliver on their promise in the Solemn League and Covenant* to establish a Presbyterian* national church. Unfortunately many members of the Long Parliament opposed a strict Presbyterian church settlement or else held the Scots army in contempt for its largely ineffectual and half-hearted role in the ultimate defeat of royalist* forces. Finally there was a need to reach a reasonably amicable settlement with the captive Charles I. The king, however, showed no inclination to cooperate or to compromise with his victorious subjects.

The core of the Political Independents derived from the old War Party. They were joined by Oliver St. John and those members of the Middle Group who maintained a deep suspicion of Charles I's promises to rule constitutionally. Others supported the Political Independents because they opposed the Presbyterian religious settlement of the Scots and supported religious toleration for most of the Protestant sects. Hence the Scots were actually the first to label this party as the Independent party, even though many Political Independents were not religious Independents. Also included among the Political Independents were a small group led by Henry Marten who clandestinely advocated the establishment of a republic in England. Most Political Independents, even if they were also Religious Independents, tended to give priority to political reform rather than any particular religious considerations. Sir Arthur Haselrig and Edmund Ludlow were good examples of that sort of behavior. Thanks to the pragmatism and political skills of the Middle Group, the Political Independents managed on occasion to attract significant support from the uncommitted members of the Long Parliament. They also found natural allies among many of the officers and troops of the New Model Army. The Political Independents supported a policy of treating the army* fairly during the process of demobilization. In contrast, the opposing party of the Political Presbyterians* was overly hasty and stingy in its dealings with the soldiers and attempted to use demobilization as an opportunity to purge Independents and sectaries from all ranks of the army. As a result, it alienated the army, drove it into an alliance with the Political Independents, and ultimately politicized and radicalized it into seizing control of the government.

By the spring of 1647 the Political Independents in the Long Parliament found themselves completely overmatched by the voting strength of the Political Presbyterians, who were led by Denzil Holles. When a mob of London* apprentices rioted at the Houses of Parliament in support of the Political Presbyterians on 26 July, a frightened speaker of the house and a group of Political Independents fled to the protection of the army on 30 July. In response the army entered London on 6 and 7 August and restored control to the Political Independents by arresting or driving off the leaders of the Political Presbyterians. The problem for the Political Independents was that the English people were largely drifting in a conservative direction that favored the Political Presbyterians because most people longed for the restoration of stability and traditional government under the king, with or without the imposition of safeguards against the reoccurrence of tyranny. While the Second Civil War* (March-August 1648) served to radicalize the army even further, it actually strengthened support for the Political Presbyterians in the Long Parliament.

The Middle Group within the Political Independent party still pinned their hopes on the successful formulation of a tough settlement with the king. Unfortunately for them, the willingness of negotiators for the Treaty of Newport* (September-November 1648) to capitulate to the king's stubbornness left that settlement thoroughly discredited with the army and the radical republicans. To them it appeared that the Middle Group was selling out to the Political Presbyterians. Therefore, the disgruntled army, with the assistance of radicals in the Long Parliament, bypassed normal constitutional procedures and seized power by forcibly blocking its opponents from entering the House of Commons on 6 December 1648, an event commonly known as Pride's Purge*. That action created the Rump Parliament*, which initially had a Political Independent majority. These supposedly reforming politicians were closely associated with Oliver Cromwell* and the army. Unfortunately the Rumpers had achieved little reform by the time a disgruntled Cromwell dissolved them by force on 20 April 1653, also bringing an end to the last vestige of the Political Independents.

Bibliography: David Underdown, *Pride's Purge: Politics in the Puritan Revolution*, 1971; George Yule, *The Independents in the English Civil War*, 1958.

Ronald H. Fritze

Independents, Religious. The radical wing of the mainstream Puritan* movement during the Civil War*, as distinct from Presbyterians*. Independents were generally orthodox Calvinists* in theology, though they rejected not only episcopacy but the system of hierarchical classes or synods advocated by the Presbyterians and outlined by the Westminster Assembly*. Instead they favored control by individual congregations. Some Independent ministers tried to work within the parochial system, while others gathered their own churches of followers. They also went beyond Presbyterians in promoting not only war against the king in 1642 but the revolution of 1648-1649.

The origins of Independency go back at least to the Separatist* churches of Robert Brown and Henry Barrow and the "semi-separatist" congregations of Henry Jessey and Henry Jacob. Of more immediate importance for the Independency of the revolutionary period was the experience that many Puritans had of exile in the Low Countries during the persecutions of the 1630s. There they were able to create covenanted congregations of saints, independent of any comprehensive national church and with little interference from political authorities. These closely knit communities often returned entire to England after 1640, where they became cells of religious and political radicalism. Similarly, the experience of the New England exiles, especially as articulated by John Cotton in his *Keys to the Kingdom of Heaven* (1644), also provided a major inspiration to English Independency, since there too Independent congregations could flourish without incurring the charge of Separatism or of breaking ranks with the larger reforming movement.

Upon returning to England, Independency was at first more of a tendency than a distinct party, and for a time the Independents kept a low profile, working in alliance with the Presbyterians in the cause of national reform. The existence of early Independent activity is indicated by the appearance of Katherine Chidley's *The Justification of the Independent Churches of Christ* (1641). (As with Puritanism generally, women participated in large numbers within Independent congregations, though there is little indication, apart from Chidley's tract, that they extolled women's rights as such, beyond the general egalitarianism of the congregation.) The most notorious early pamphlet was Henry Burton's *The Protestation Protested*, which appeared in the summer of 1641 and scandalized London* by expressing impatience with parliamentary reform and appearing to advocate outright separation from the national church. However, Burton's tract was not representative of other Independents, who disavowed it. He had no experience with either exile or gathered congregations and, despite his immoderate language, eventually fell into line. Most prominent Independents urged restraint and signed *Certain Considerations to Dissuade Men from Further Gathering Churches* in December 1643. The real split occurred early in 1644 when the five dissenting brethren of the Westminster Assembly—

Thomas Goodwin, Philip Nye, Sidrach Simpson, William Bridge, and Jeremiah Burroughs—set out some of their ecclesiological principles in the moderately worded *Apologetical Narration.*

Independency was sometimes lumped together with more extreme sectarianism and denounced by conservative Puritans such as Thomas Edwards in his *Gangraena* (1646) and the Scot Robert Baillie in *A Dissuasive from the Errors of the Time* (1645). They accused the Independents of separation from the Church of England (see Anglicanism*) and of breaching Calvinist principle by attempting to gather churches exclusively of the elect, making the visible church correspond as nearly as possible to the invisible. How far Independents intended separation from the parish system is unclear; they were accused of deliberately obscuring their intentions, but in the expectant atmosphere of the 1640s, they were probably uncertain in their own minds, and when much was changing within the national reform, the notion of Separatism was of limited validity.

The practice of conversion relations among some Independent churches (especially in New England), whereby prospective members were required to describe to the congregation the sincerity of their spiritual convictions as reflected in the ordeal of their conversion, does indicate a more selective attitude toward church fellowship. Yet the dissenting brethren explicitly eschewed "Brownism" in favor of a not always clearly defined "middle way," and this was not entirely disingenuous. They consistently advocated preaching and themselves preached to the wider audience of the parishes, as well as taking in (though not necessarily communicating with) apparently unregenerate members. They adhered in theory to the Calvinist principle that elect and reprobate could never be perfectly known or separated in this life, and the fact that they continued to practice infant baptism indicates that they still accepted the principle of the church as a mixed multitude. The essential point may be that for the Independents, regeneration was not so much a prerequisite for individual membership as something that took place within the overall context of a communal congregational life. The purification and exercise of public worship were themselves the means of regenerating the participants and even, in some sense, the entire congregation together, transforming it into a holy community comprising Christ's kingdom on earth. Their ecclesiology therefore blended consistently into their eschatology.

The brethren continued to participate actively in the reform of the national church within the Westminster Assembly (at least until they found themselves hopelessly outvoted). There they made common cause with the Presbyterians on the need to suspend those of "scandalous" behavior from the sacrament of the Lord's supper against the "Erastians," who favored open admission. Though this latter group had few adherents among the clergy, they had considerable sympathy in parliament*, which had final say in any church settlement. Independents were also disproportionately active in political reform and encouraged the war effort by preaching to parliament and the army* and producing resistance tracts.

Independency therefore was more than simply a method of church organization. Independents were more militant both religiously and politically than other Puritans (see Independents, Political*). Their preaching was more frequently characterized by violent millenarian* and apocalyptic images, upon which they were more likely to act. They generally urged a harder line in the war against the king, and as a rule Independents supported Pride's Purge* and the regicide*, while Presbyterians did not. Most notable among these republicans are Hugh Peter, who was considered effectively a regicide for his strong advocacy of Charles I's trial and execution*, and John Owen*, whose political sermons of the late 1640s and early 1650s expressed the militant line and who became the leading clerical Independent during the 1650s, serving the Commonwealth* government in a number of capacities.

Some Independent ministers attacked the radical sects beyond the mainstream of respectable Puritanism, such as Baptists*, Ranters*, Seekers*, and Quakers*, though others had connections with these groups. Independents were once seen as the principled champions of "religious toleration"; in fact they eloquently defended toleration for their own way within the Presbyterian system but seldom set it forth as a blanket principle for others. Experience in New England would seem to indicate that their commitment to toleration was limited in practice. On the other hand, by rejecting a clerical system of synods in favor of congregational government, Independency allowed a greater role for the laity in church government. In fact their contribution to modern democracy, however repressive and authoritarian at times, is their theory and practice of participation in the congregation, and Independent preachers and propagandists often described the ideal of congregational life by analogy with participatory democracy.

In New England and in England after the Restoration*, Independency eventually lost much of its political fervor and became Congregationalism*. Its principles are set forth in the Savoy Declaration (1658).

Bibliography: G. Nuttall, *Visible Saints,* 1957; M. Tolmie, *The Triumph of the Saints*, 1977.

Stephen Baskerville

Indulgence, Declaration of (1672). With the Restoration* of Charles II* to the throne of England in 1660 came the return of the old order of worship to the Church of England (see Anglicanism*). Due to the Civil War* and Interregnum*, parliament* had attained sufficient strength relative to the Crown that it was able virtually to dictate religious policy. Therefore, despite Charles's promise of religious toleration in his Declaration of Breda* (1660), the Cavalier Parliament* (1661-1679) in 1662 passed the Act of Uniformity* (14 Car. II, c. 4), part of what became known as the Clarendon Code*. The act enforced the use of a revised version of the Book of Common Prayer and thus basically alienated Protestant Dissenters* and Roman Catholics* from ecclesiastical affairs. The king requested that the act contain provisions allowing him to use the dispensing power* to exempt all persons who were not clergymen and to excuse loyal clergy from some ceremonial requirements, but parliament rejected these in March and April, respectively, thereby limiting the royal prerogative* in religious matters.

Charles, who was sympathetic to Catholicism, made several attempts to suspend the Act of Uniformity. The first came in May, but opposition from the judges and bishops in June dissuaded him from this use of the suspending power*. In December he issued a "declaration to all his loving subjects" (his first "Declaration of Indulgence"), in which he denied undue favoritism to Catholics, refuted charges that he was planning to set up a military government, and called for parliament to pass an act enlarging his dispensing power ostensibly on behalf of Dissenters, though it was clear that Catholics would benefit as well. Parliament rejected this suggestion in February 1663.

Charles's most serious attempt came in March 1672, when he issued his second Declaration of Indulgence. This followed his signing in 1670 of the secret Treaty of Dover* with Louis XIV, in which he promised to convert publicly to Catholicism. The indulgence suspended all penal laws against nonconformists and recusants*, requiring only that Protestant ministers have a license and that Catholics not practice their faith in public. However, this again met with judicial hostility, and in 1673 parliament reasserted its power and rescinded the indulgence, the Commons stating that "penal statutes in matters ecclesiastical cannot be suspended but by an act of parliament." Charles, therefore, withdrew the declaration, and parliament in the same year passed the first Test Act* (25 Car. II, c. 2), which barred Catholics and most Dissenters from Crown offices. Charles made no further attempt to suspend the Act of Uniformity, though the Catholic issue continued to trouble him with the Popish Plot* (1678) and the Exclusion Crisis* (1678-1681). His brother James II* would revive the controversy with his own Declaration of Indulgence* in 1687-1688.

Bibliography: J. P. Kenyon, *The Stuart Constitution, 1603-1688: Documents and Commentary*, 1966; J. R. Tanner, *English Constitutional Conflicts of the Seventeenth Century: 1603-1689*, 1966.

                                                                        Paul Miller

Indulgence, Declaration of (1687, 1688). Following the Popish Plot of 1678*, anti-Catholic forces in parliament* attempted to exclude Charles II's* brother, the openly Catholic* duke of York (see James II*) from the throne. This Exclusion Crisis* led Charles to dissolve four successive parliaments between 1679 and 1681 and to rule without parliament, in defiance of the Triennial Act of 1664* (16 Car. II, c. 1), for the last four years of his reign (see Cavalier Parliament*; Oxford Parliament*).

James II succeeded his brother in 1685 and soon aroused opposition by dispensing Catholic army* officers from the provisions of the Test Act* of 1673 (25 Car. II, st. 2, c. 2, supplemented in 1678 by 30 Car. II, st. 2, c. 1). The parliament of 1685* refused his request to repeal it, and in November James prorogued the body, never to recall it. In 1686, in the case of Godden v. Hales, the court of King's Bench (see Common Law and Courts*) ruled that the king could use the dispensing power* to exempt appointees from the act. James thereafter used that power to dispense Catholics and appoint them to positions in the army, on the privy council*, in local government*, and at the universities*. James aroused much opposition, which escalated when he began to appoint Catholics to church offices.

In an attempt to protect Catholics further and to win over the large number of Protestant Dissenters*, James II produced his first Declaration of Indulgence in April 1687. The indulgence suspended the penal laws against Dissenters as well as Catholics and granted both groups freedom of public worship, though it was not as broad as Charles II's Declaration of Indulgence* of 1672, which had attempted to suspend the 1662 Act of Uniformity* (14 Car. II, c. 4). As far as the 1673 Test Act was concerned, James's first declaration simply suspended the requirements that officeholders take the oaths of allegiance and supremacy and affirm that they were receiving the Anglican* sacrament. However, public opinion was strongly against James, and it became obvious that parliament, if called, would not support his recent measures.

James then issued a second Declaration of Indulgence in April 1688. The provisions were essentially unchanged; the difference was that in May the clergy were ordered to read the second indulgence from their pulpits. Many clergy, including Dissenters, refused to read it and sent a petition to James asking him not to force them to do so. The Anglican clergy thus formally broke their policy of nonresistance* and joined the rest of the nation against James. Archbishop William Sancroft* and six other bishops, who denied the legality of the suspending power*, were charged with seditious libel for refusing to read the declaration but were acquitted in June (see Seven Bishops, Trial of*). Shortly after, opposition to James reached a critical point with the birth of a male heir to the throne, leading to the Glorious Revolution* of 1688. The threats of Catholicism and Crown intervention in religious matters were thus eliminated. The Act of Toleration of 1689 (1 Gul. III & Mar., c. 18) allowed Dissenters to worship freely, but the Test Acts remained in effect until 1829. The Bill of Rights* (1 Gul. III & Mar., sess. 2, c. 2) abolished the suspending power and limited the dispensing power.

Bibliography: J. P. Kenyon, *The Stuart Constitution, 1603-1688: Documents and Commentary*, 1966; J. R. Tanner, *English Constitutional Conflicts of the Seventeenth Century: 1603-1689*,1966.

Paul Miller

Inflation of Honors. A term used by Lawrence Stone to describe the substantial increase in the number of knights and peers under the early Stuarts, a phenomenon that he thought had grave consequences.

Queen Elizabeth was notoriously sparing in bestowing rewards, including honors and titles. When she came to the throne in 1558, there were fifty-seven peers; when she died in 1603, there were fifty-five. Similarly, at the end of her reign there were about 600 knights, no more than there had been at the beginning, and many of those had received their knighthoods not from the queen herself but rather from the 2d earl of Essex while on campaign (the queen was not pleased by Essex's generosity).

This situation changed radically under Elizabeth's successor. James I* himself called the first years of his reign a "Christmas"; he was extraordinarily generous and open-handed with all kinds of rewards, including titles and honors. In just his first four months in England, he made 906 knights, more than Elizabeth had made in forty-five years. Later he even created a new order of hereditary knights, the baronets.

Similarly, James enlarged the peerage considerably. In the first three years of his reign, he created or restored twenty-seven peers, increasing the total number by about fifty percent, a remarkable expansion after nearly a century of stable size. There was a further increase toward the end of his reign, mainly due to the 1st duke of Buckingham (George Villiers*), the powerful favorite who saw to it that his family and followers were well rewarded.

Buckingham retained his position as favorite under James's son and successor, Charles I*, and the stream of rewards, including new titles, continued to flow bountifully. All told, between 1615 and 1628, the number of peers grew from eighty-one to 126, which meant that the peerage had more than doubled in size in the quarter-century since the death of Queen Elizabeth. Charles became more sparing after Buckingham's assassination in 1628 but opened his hand again in the early 1640s, when he was trying to assemble a party to oppose parliament* and needed to reward his supporters.

In many cases, according to Stone, James and Charles in bestowing knighthoods and peerages were recognizing legitimate claims to increased status that had been ignored by Elizabeth. However, Stone argues, overall the inflation of honors was severely damaging to the aristocracy (and to the Crown as well). As with any other kind of inflation, there was a reduction in value. As knights and lords became more plentiful, they commanded less respect. Moreover, especially during Buckingham's reign as favorite, a traffic in honors developed, and peerages were openly sold, sometimes to unworthy candidates, which brought at least a portion of the aristocracy into contempt. The inflation of honors was one aspect of a general "crisis of the aristocracy" identified by Stone, a crisis that, he argued, created the conditions that made the upheavals of the mid-seventeenth century possible. (See Gentry Controversy*; Social Structure and Ranks*).

Bibliography: Lawrence Stone, *The Crisis of the Aristocracy, 1558-1641*, 1965.

Eric N. Lindquist

Instrument of Government (1653). This was the first republican constitution of an Interregnum* regime and the founding document of the Protectorate*. It vested executive power in a chief of state (the Lord Protector) and a council of state* and the legislative authority in an elected parliament*.

The Instrument came into being because of the failure of the Barebone's Parliament* (July-December 1653) to provide a permanent constitutional settlement. Oliver Cromwell*, lord general of the army*, regarded Barebone's Parliament as an interim assembly with the explicit purpose of devising a new constitution. Like the Rump Parliament*, which Cromwell and the army overthrew, Barebone's Parliament became unacceptable to the army by assuming the role of a permanent governing body. Exasperated by sectarian radicals, moderates who backed Cromwell voted to dissolve the parliament on 10 December 1653. Shortly before this, the council of officers, council of state, and Cromwell had shown interest in a new constitution drafted by the flamboyant cavalry officer John Lambert. Lambert had been a close associate of Cromwell during the Civil Wars* but had retired from politics with the establishment of Barebone's Parliament. Apparently Lambert proposed a constitution with Cromwell as a monarch, which the lord general rejected. Later this was modified, and the chief of state called the lord protector. On 16 December the Instrument of Government was proclaimed, and Cromwell took his oath of office. The origins of this document are mysterious. Its seems likely that Lambert had attempted to resurrect the Levellers'* proposed constitution, the Agreement of the People*, and Henry Ireton's* Heads of the Proposals* (1647).

By the Instrument, the powers of the protector were greatly limited; by no means did he rule England. He was obliged to call parliaments at regular intervals, the first by September 1654. His command of the militia, army, and navy* was by parliamentary consent. Foreign policy, including questions of war and peace, was to be conducted in partnership with parliament. Perhaps most important, parliament's legislative authority was preserved. The protector could not enact or repeal laws except, under a special proviso, when they conflicted with the Instrument. Lambert used the distribution of members of parliament suggested in the Agreement of the People, 400 in England and thirty each from Wales* and Scotland*. To ensure government continued between parliaments, the protector was to have a council of state. Even the franchise was determined. All males other than Catholics*, royalists, and Irish rebels (see Irish Rebellion*) with £200 per annum could vote. A state-supported church was to be created and tithes preserved. Protestant Dissenters*, except the Anglican* hierarchy, were granted toleration. From Cromwell's speeches it is apparent that he thought the Instrument could be modified, as it was dramatically by the Humble Petition and Advice* in 1657.

Historians have often characterized this as a reactionary document. In essence, however, it established a moderate republican regime. The republican Commonwealthmen*, who opposed the regime, denounced the powers of the protector as quasimonarchical and a military dictatorship. Article XXVII, which allowed a standing army to be supported by £200,000 per annum, was seen as creating a mercenary force to control parliament and suppress opposition. The Instrument, however, provided more consensus, political stability, and continuity than either the Rump or Barebone's Parliament achieved.

Bibliography: S. R. Gardiner, *Constitutional Documents of the Puritan Revolution*, 1906; A. H. Woolrych, *Commonwealth to Protectorate*, 1986.

John H. F. Hughes

Interregnum. As a general political term describing the interval between periods of established government, the word *interregnum* was used by contemporaries in the mid-seventeenth century (see the *Oxford English Dictionary* for examples). In the more precise technical sense in which it is employed today, *Interregnum* refers to the period between Charles I's execution* and the Restoration* of the monarchy in 1660, and it was these years that Charles II* later reclaimed by backdating his reign to 1649. In reality, however, the effective loss of royal control under Charles I came earlier, a fact recognized in G. E. Aylmer's collection of essays on the Interregnum, which chose 1646 as its starting point.

Historiographically the Interregnum was relatively neglected until comparatively recently, despite the heroic efforts of such nineteenth-century historians as William Godwin and S. R. Gardiner. The neglect was no doubt the product of a predisposition to view these years as a period of political deceleration, a decade in which religious fervor was extinguished and predictably concluded with turning back the clock at the Restoration. The 1640s captured the imagination of historians in a way that the 1650s did not. This neglect was unwarranted and is in the process of being rectified. Of the 107 items listed in the bibliography in Ronald Hutton's *The British Republic, 1649-1660* (1990), no fewer than forty came out in the 1980s and only twenty-four were published before 1970.

Charles I's execution, which ushered in the Interregnum, was the result of an army* coup and was for many, perhaps for most, an unintended and unwanted solution. Convinced republicans in 1649 and later were few in number. As a result the supporting base beneath the successive regimes of the 1650s was too narrow for comfort. The continuing presence of a standing army, its uneasy relations with the parliament* that had first called it into being, its intrusions into local politics, and its self-evidently heavy cost explain why the label "military dictatorship" has sometimes been applied to the 1650s. In 1657 parliament offered Oliver Cromwell* the Crown, convinced that this was the only way for him to break free of the army and its power-hungry officers (army opposition to the move demonstrated their awareness of this very fact). The initial welcome given to Richard Cromwell* a civilian who did not have his father's links with the military is explained to large extent by expectations that he would establish a different style of government in which army influence would be reduced.

Notwithstanding the army, the Cromwellian Protectorate*, like the Commonwealth* before it, was a constitutional experiment, and Cromwell's powers in some ways became more, not less, prescribed as time went on. In the lord protector's council there were twice as many civilians as soldiers, and Cromwell struggled, not very successfully, it is true, to find a proper place for a parliament or assembly. Such a body, however, could hardly have been representative, since under the Instrument of Government* the size of the House of Commons was reduced to four-fifths of what the Long Parliament* had been, the proportion of county members was increased by about forty-five percent at the expense of towns (see Local Government, Towns*), and the franchise was restricted to those with real or personal property worth £200.

The structures and modes of working of Interregnum government and administration were a mixture of inheritance and improvisation. The council of state* in the 1650s had its own special characteristics. Cromwell's court was distinctively his own—though in the end its austere Puritan* simplicity gave way to greater pomp and ceremony. Barebone's Parliament* of 1653, by virtue of the way in which it was nominated and the godly brief it was given, was a unique venture, and its failure deeply grieved Cromwell. The Instrument of Government and the Humble Petition and Advice* broke new constitutional ground. In local government* the actual machinery remained the same in most respects, but its social composition to some extent changed. The justices of the peace continued to provide the normal, routine administration. The experiment with the major-generals*, the chief representatives of the central government, in the years 1655-1657 complemented their work since they acted as mediators rather than French-style intendants. Underpinning Interregnum government was a new kind of civil service: a salaried, career-conscious, streamlined, efficient, and less corrupt bureaucracy. The careers of William Clarke (c.1623-1666), William Petty (1623-1687), John Thurloe* (1616-1665), Benjamin Worsley (1618-1678), and John Milton* (1608-1674) are indicative of the high caliber of men upon whom the republic called.

In religion, theory and practice diverged in these years. Though constitutionally nonexistent, in practice the Anglican* church was never extinguished. Prayer book services continued to take place even in London*. Conversely the Presbyterian* experiment intended for the whole country scarcely got off the ground. There was much continuity among the clergy, despite natural wastage and purges carried out by the triers and ejectors*. In the mid-1650s almost half of the clergymen who had been in post in 1642 were still serving. Tithes were never abolished, despite a radical pressure for such a move.

New stirrings in radical religion in the Interregnum are unmistakable and are bound up with groups such as the Muggletonians, Ranters*, and Quakers*. The success story of the Quakers is extraordinary. In the space of a decade, they mushroomed from negligible origins to a formidable total of about 60,000. It seems highly likely that the nervous paranoia that Quakers provoked helped facilitate the Restoration.

No single label, it is clear, will suffice to describe the complexity of events, circumstances, and cross-currents of the Interregnum. There was, certainly on the part of the political elite, a search for stability and settlement. But equally noticeable was the resistance to such a development and the profound sense of loss, frustration, and defeat that many 1640s radicals experienced as they moved into the different world of the next decade. But moderate Puritans were in power in the Interregnum, and though the millennium that had once been hoped for did not arise in the 1650s, reform still had a place in the decade, and schemes for university* expansion, commercial and colonial reorganization and growth, and currency reform (see Coinage and Monetary Policy*) were all rehearsed. Foreign intellectuals like Samuel Hartlib, John Dury, and John Comenius—resident in England at this time—urged on this "Great Instauration." There was much healing of old wounds, as former royalists* and parliamentarians* learned to live with each other again. For Scotland* and Ireland* the impact of the Interregnum was decisive and long-lasting—Cromwell insured that—and was an integral part of what has come to be termed the "British Revolution." The Restoration of 1660 could not sweep aside this complex, ill-assorted, and insistent legacy.

Bibliography: G. E. Aylmer, ed., *The Interregnum: The Quest for Settlement, 1646-1660*, 1972; Christopher Hill, *The Experience of Defeat: Milton and Some Contemporaries*, 1984; Ronald Hutton, *The British Republic, 1649-1660*, 1990.

R. C. Richardson

Ireland, 1603-1688. Ireland was the third of the three kingdoms of Britain during the years of the Stuart kings. The relationship between it and the kingdoms of England and Scotland*, as well as the role of the king as overlord in Ireland, were subjects of great debate in the seventeenth century. This struggle played an important part in the politics of all three. By the same token, the degree to which this kingdom would be assimilated into the British Empire was a central theme of Irish history during these years. The politics, legal system, culture, religion, language, economy, and even population* of Ireland underwent tremendous changes between 1603 and 1688 as a result. In many ways it could be argued that Ireland was permanently altered by the years of Stuart rule and that the seventeenth century was the formative century for modern Ireland.

The Stuart years began in defeat with the submission of Hugh O'Neill, earl of Tyrone at Mellifont, only six days after the death of Elizabeth I and the beginning of Stuart rule. The O'Neill Rebellion (1595-1603) had resulted in the near total subjugation of Ireland by English forces, and acceptance of English rule by its leader was symbolic of the status of the island. Ireland lay open to whatever changes the Stuart rulers wished to impose on it. Though O'Neill and other native Irish leaders were pardoned by James I*, it was quickly made clear that the first Stuart king intended to incorporate Ireland fully into his realm. Late in 1603 Sir John Davies arrived in Dublin as solicitor general. In that position and later as attorney general, he was charged with imposing English common law* and English-style land tenure on Ireland in place of its ancient system of Brehon law. It was a task he and his successors would continue aggressively throughout the seventeenth century. Their success significantly disrupted the traditional pastoral economy of the native Irish and paved the way for agricultural practices similar to those used in Britain (see Agriculture*).

In 1605 James mandated that all his subjects in Ireland should conform with the Church of England (see Anglicanism*) and ordered the expulsion of all priests. Those who refused to take the oath of supremacy and attend "official" services were barred from public service, as well as limited in other civil rights. This attack on the Catholic* faith was paralleled throughout the century by the gradual development of a Protestant church of Ireland modeled on that of England. This included the establishment of a school system administered by the Protestant church, the construction of a Protestant cathedral, and the expansion of Trinity College in Dublin. The attempt to establish religious conformity was considered a vital part of the kingdom's assimilation and would remain one of the major bones of contention between the Stuart monarchs and their Irish subjects.

The major changes approaching in Ireland were further signaled in September 1607, when O'Neill, Hugh O'Donnell, earl of Tyrconnell, and other leading magnates of the native Irish abandoned the country in the Flight of the Earls*. Unable or unwilling to adjust to life under English law, they instead chose to join a growing community of Irish exiles on the Continent. By 1630 this community included the Franciscan College of St. Anthony at Louvain, an Irish regiment in the Spanish Army of Flanders, St. Isidore's Franciscan College in Rome, and an Irish Franciscan House in Prague. Such exile institutions did much to preserve native Irish culture, religion, and literature throughout the century but also removed the most talented native Irish leadership from the island.

The effect of this can be seen in the aftermath of the flight. Less than two months later, the earls' lands (comprising most of Ulster) were declared forfeit to the Crown. Following several extensive surveys of the region, the Ulster plantation* was begun in 1610. Granting land to "undertakers" willing to plant Protestant subjects there, James hoped to replace the native Irish population with subjects whose interests coincided with those of the Crown. Nevertheless a majority of settlers in Ulster were Scottish Calvinists*. Corporate groups such as the City of London* also played a major role in this plantation. Though a vast amount of land changed hands legally, the number of settlers remained relatively small. They lived surrounded by native Irish in a frontier situation similar to the contemporaneous settlements in Virginia, Massachusetts, Bermuda, and Maryland. During the same years, the plantation of Munster was reestablished and parts of Leinster opened for settlement as well, but even these relatively civilized regions of Ireland did not attract a large English population. Nevertheless, attempts to replace the native Irish populace remained a constant in the struggle for seventeenth-century Ireland.

Plantation, the establishment of Protestant religion, and the institution of English law remained the primary themes of government throughout the remainder of James I's rule. To one degree or another, this program would remain the focus of efforts to assimilate Ireland throughout the remainder of the century. James attempted to confirm his actions in three successive Irish parliaments but failed to produce a satisfactory parliament due to the nation's insistence on returning Catholic representatives. The composition and role of the Irish parliament remained a constitutional question of debate for many years. Thus Ireland became an area in which the king's authority to rule by royal prerogative* was tested and became entangled in the growing constitutional crisis of England.

During the early years of Charles I's* reign, his Irish policy was lenient, largely because the new king needed the support of Ireland. Desperate for help in his ill-advised continental wars (see French War*; Spanish War*; Thirty Years War*), Charles granted twenty-six concessions known as "graces" to Irish Catholics, guaranteeing them free exercise of conscience in religion and limited political participation. These mainly benefited the "Old English," who in return agreed to finance expansion of the Irish army for Charles's use. While this attracted some criticism in England, it remained in effect for six years.

In 1632 Charles decided to enhance the value of his Irish support by tightening his rule there. Thomas Wentworth* (later earl of Strafford) was sent to take charge of Irish affairs as lord deputy. The program he implemented, known as "thorough"*, was widely viewed as a prototype for the absolutist* rule that Charles aspired to build in England. A serious attempt was made to make Ireland more productive economically and, through control of its parliament, more responsive to royal will. Though this program worked initially, Wentworth's high-handed manner, his refusal to guarantee the "graces," and his contemplation of renewed plantation projects gradually eroded Charles's support in Ireland. At the same time Wentworth's continued toleration of Catholicism and mobilization of the Irish army to support the king during the Bishops' Wars* of 1638-1640 raised suspicion in England, where it was rumored that Charles planned to use the Irish to help restore Catholicism. Wentworth was sacrificed in 1641 as part of the growing political crisis in England, and subsequent Irish policy was left unresolved.

The fear of renewed plantation, the religious insecurity of Irish Catholics, and the power vacuum in England were major factors in the Irish Rebellion*, which broke out in October 1641, claiming to support the interests of the king. Exaggerated tales of massacres of Protestant settlers by Irish Catholics became standard parliamentarian* propaganda, but no evidence exists of atrocities taking place on a wide scale. Initially a native revolt against plantation limited to Ulster, this rebellion spread to the Anglo-Irish nobility as well. Despite its failure to seize Dublin, the rebellion controlled most of the island, and little was done to put it down. Money was raised by parliament* by the sale of speculative shares in Irish land, to be confiscated after the rebellion, but most of the funds raised were subsequently used in the English Civil War*, which broke out the next year (see Adventurers*).

For over a decade the island remained in turmoil. A Confederation of native Irish and Old English, convened at Killkenny, attempted to establish a single Catholic rule throughout the island. The Confederation, however, was severely divided between those who put priority on the interests of religion (the native Irish) and those willing to compromise religiously to remain loyal to the monarchy (the Old English). This split was exacerbated by the presence of a papal nuncio, Giovanni Rinuccini, on the island from 1646 through 1649. The Confederation was opposed by the Scots of Ulster, who brought over a large army from Scotland, and the Protestant "New" English of the east coast, who equivocated between king and parliament. As the royalist* cause in England collapsed, the "New" English gradually all joined the parliamentary cause, with a few hard-core royalists such as the earl of Ormonde (James Butler*) joining the Confederation. All through this conflict, Ireland was subjected to the ravages of seventeenth-century warfare, with its attendant pillage, massacre, and economic devastation.

This era of confusion was brought to an end by the Cromwellian conquest of 1649-1653. Though Oliver Cromwell* himself was in Ireland for less than a year (1649-1650), the arrival of the New Model Army* tilted the military balance in favor of the Protestant New English. Massacres at Drogheda and Wexford were intended to instill fear in the populace, and the countryside was systematically devastated so that it could not support guerrilla fighters. By 1653 most resistance ended, though small bands of outlaws known as "tories" continued to be a problem in Ireland. As the rebellion was put down, parliament began legal actions that would define the future status of Ireland. The 1652 Act of Settlement* asserted the guilt of the entire Irish nation, defined categories of Irishmen liable to be dispossessed, and established the legal right to "transplant" the holdings of all other Irish. The "Act of Satisfaction" in 1653 allocated lands to those who had invested in the war effort and to parliamentary soldiers in compensation for back pay owed them. All surviving native Irish landowners were transplanted to the province of Connaught, west of the Shannon River. The remainder of the decade saw bribery, speculation, litigation, and resurvey on a scale to be expected from one of the greatest land transfers in history. By 1658 the vast majority of Ireland was owned by English Protestant landowners, while the native population was largely dispossessed laborers.

This change in the legal status of the land did not dramatically alter the population, since the hoped-for immigration of large numbers of English to their new holdings did not follow. In all, probably fewer than 20,000 English resettled in Ireland as a result of the Cromwellian settlement. Many others who received lands remained absentee landlords over vast estates populated by Irish Catholics. The Restoration* of Charles II* did not significantly alter this situation. While Ormonde returned as lord deputy and a few land cases were concluded favoring the restoration of influential or notably loyal Catholics, in general the land situation was not changed. Charles II's Irish parliaments remained exclusively Protestant, reflecting this Protestant ascendancy. Similarly the religious situation saw little change in Charles's reign. The Protestant church of Ireland made accommodation for the consciences of the Ulster Scots but failed to make any inroads on the Catholic population and a small but active population of Quakers*. Perhaps the most notable features of the Restoration period were the economic recovery of the island and the emergence of several vibrant, exclusively Protestant, urban areas. Nevertheless the long-term prospects for Irish development of the Irish economy were limited by the mercantilist* policies of the English government.

The anti-Catholic mania that swept England in the last years of Charles II's reign also had an impact in Ireland, where Protestant landowners were acutely aware of the dissatisfied Catholic populace. Their fears that the land and religious situation would be altered were realized in the reign of James II*, whose own Catholicism naturally raised the hopes of Irish Catholics. Though James talked publicly of religious toleration, his actions implied a threat against Protestant interests in Ireland, and particularly against the Ulster Presbyterians of Scottish descent.

James II's Irish policy was largely influenced by Richard Talbot, earl of Tyrconnell, who used his high position in the Irish army to install Roman Catholic officers throughout it. Many of these units were called to England to support James in October 1688, where their presence served as a stimulus to the Glorious Revolution*. Appointed lord deputy in 1687, Tyrconnell introduced toleration of Catholicism and took steps to alter town charters to allow Catholics a role in them. He was preparing to alter the land settlement when news of William of Orange's* landing in England and James's flight to the Continent altered the situation. In January 1689 the Ulster Scots rose against James's rule, accepting William and Mary* as their rightful monarchs. The rest of the island, however, remained in Tyrconnell's hands, and James came there in March, accompanied by French troops, to direct continued resistance. James convened an Irish parliament, which repealed the land settlement and provided him financial support. The city of Derry was besieged by

James's forces, but its resistance denied access to Ulster and allowed William time to build up an army for the conquest of Ireland. In the subsequent conflict James's army was decisively beaten at the Battle of the Boyne on 1 July 1690, and three days later James sailed for France. By 1691 the entire island lay prostrate at William's feet. Just as in 1603, Ireland in 1691 once again awaited the will of the victors.

Bibliography: Margaret MacCurtin, *Tudor and Stuart Ireland*, 1972.

John Nolan

Ireton, Henry (1611-1651). Soldier and political leader, Henry Ireton was one of Oliver Cromwell's* closest associates in winning the Civil War*. When the war broke out he joined the parliamentarian* forces as a cavalry officer, rising swiftly in the ranks. He fought at Edgehill*, the second Battle of Newbury, Naseby* (where, at Cromwell's insistence, he commanded the left wing as the youngest regimental commander in the New Model Army*), and the siege of Bristol. In 1646 Ireton married Cromwell's daughter, Bridget, which sealed their close personal relationship.

At the war's end, with the army* on the verge of mutiny, Ireton frequently became the spokesman for the senior officers, most notably in the Putney Debates*, as they wrestled against the political and social radicalism of the Levellers* and tried to hold the fragile victorious coalition together. The objectives were a "godly reformation" and a relatively moderate political arrangement to restrain the king, who, though a prisoner, still enjoyed wide support.

Ireton was the most eloquent and determined defender of the Cromwellian position, combining social conservatism with an openness to religious radicalism. After acting vigorously to put down the royalist attempt at a counter-revolution in the Second Civil War*, he was one of the principal organizers of Pride's Purge*. When the negotiation for an agreed settlement with the king finally failed, Ireton was one of the stalwarts of who pressed for his trial and later signed the death warrant (see Charles I, Trial, Execution, and Cult of*). Under the republican council of state*, he went with Cromwell to pacify Ireland* and succeeded to command of the campaign to complete the island's subjugation. He died of fever in November 1651 while besieging Limerick.

Cromwell relied on Ireton for his courage, incorruptibility, and political judgment. More than anyone else in Cromwell's close circle, he understood Cromwell. No one else could articulate Cromwell's position with as much clarity, persuasiveness, or vigor.

Bibliography: R. W. Ramsey, *Henry Ireton*, 1949.

S. J. Stearns

Irish Rebellion (1641-1653). The first revolt of Ireland* after the Protestant plantations* of the early seventeenth century. During its course, an attempt at unified government for Catholic* Ireland, the Confederation of Killkenny, failed. The rebellion and its suppression were major issues contributing to the commencement of the First Civil War* in England in 1642 and complicated British affairs throughout the 1640s.

The immediate cause of the rebellion was the "thorough"* rule imposed on Ireland by Thomas Wentworth* as lord lieutenant (1632-1641). His haughty manner and refusal to grant special "graces" to Catholics alienated both native Irish and the Anglo-Irish nobility known as "Old English." Upon his removal and execution in early 1641, they saw an opportunity to break the Protestant "New English" ascendancy. During the summer of 1641 Charles I* plotted the takeover of Dublin with these elements, in hopes of securing Ireland against parliament*. When this plan was canceled, native Irish leaders decided to take matters into their own hands.

The rebellion began on 22 October. Led by Sir Phelim O'Neill, it claimed royal sanction, but documents supporting this are dubious. Its stated goals were the establishment of tolerance for Irish Catholics and confirmation of their rights to participate in the Irish parliament. Native Irish also hoped to regain lands lost during the plantation of Ulster. The first weeks were marked with occasional acts of brutality against Protestant settlers, which were sensationalized by the English press and magnified into the premeditated massacre of thousands. The religious hysteria that subsequently swept the British Isles was an important component in the break between Charles I and the Long Parliament*.

The rebellion initially consisted of native Irish, but in late 1641 the Catholic Old English joined in. By January 1642 most of the island was in rebel hands, with the exception of Dublin, Cork, and Carrickfergus. Failure to seize these ports doomed the rebellion, as they became gateways for attempts to restore the English/Protestant ascendancy. In 1642 parliament refused to give Charles I an army* to suppress the rebellion, fearing he would use it against them, perhaps in coalition with the rebels. It was agreed, however, to provide funds for an army of Scottish Covenanters* to aid Protestant settlers in Ulster. This army remained a force in Irish affairs until 1649, in constant opposition to the rebellion.

The first Killkenny Assembly, which was to act as the Irish Confederation government, convened in late 1642. The Old English dominated this group, though native Irish constituted most of the Confederation's armies. They looked to Owen Roe O'Neill, a professional soldier, for leadership. The First Civil War* in England (1642-1646) delayed royal efforts to end the rebellion, though the earl of Ormonde continued to hold Dublin in the king's name. By 1643 Charles desperately needed Ormonde's troops in England, and he entered negotiations with the Confederates. In September 1643 a truce was settled. It held for two years while Charles tried to negotiate for Confederate support, and the Confederates concentrated their military activity against the Scots in Ulster. The decline of the royal cause in 1644 and 1645 was reflected in Ireland, and many English garrisons declared for parliament.

Meanwhile the Killkenny Assembly developed serious rifts. The Old English wanted to make peace with Charles on easy terms and join him against the English parliament. The native Irish, supported by the Catholic clergy, wanted to hold out for full recognition of Catholic rights. Some even called for full sovereignty under the leadership of O'Neill. The arrival of the papal envoy Giovanni Rinuccini in October 1645 widened this division. His insistence on full recognition of the Catholic faith strengthened the native Irish, as did O'Neill's victory over the Scots at Benburb on 5 June 1646. Subsequently O'Neill and Rinuccini staged a takeover of the Killkenny government. While this provided a temporary advantage for the native Irish, it permanently divided the Confederacy. In 1647 the royalist* cause completely collapsed, and Ormonde turned Dublin over to a parliamentary garrison in June. The new threat temporarily pulled the Killkenny Assembly together, but by 1648 it was again falling apart. The Old English joined with Ormonde, still trying to generate support for the king. Rinuccini withdrew from Killkenny with O'Neill's army and excommunicated those who opposed him. Disillusioned, he returned to Rome in February 1649.

With the papal legate's departure, the rebellion entered its final phase, Oliver Cromwell's* conquest of the island. Cromwell landed at Dublin on 15 August 1649, following the parliamentary army's victory over Ormonde at Rathmines on 2 August. Cromwell's subsequent campaign was short but ferocious. On 11 September he captured Drogheda, massacring the garrison and townspeople in retaliation for the 1641 "massacres" and as a warning against resistance. A second massacre occurred at Wexford, though this was spontaneous. In the following months Confederation forces retreated west, despite an alliance between Ormonde and Owen Roe O'Neill. The death of the latter in November 1649 left the native Irish leaderless. In the same month the Scottish army evacuated Ulster. On 27 March 1650 Cromwell took Killkenny, the center of Confederation, and on 26 May returned to England.

The rebellion was not quite over. Resistance continued for two and a half years west of the Shannon River, while Cromwell's son-in-law, Henry Ireton*, took over the campaign. In August 1650 Charles II* repudiated the rebels, and in December Ormonde, with the Old English leaders, took his cue and departed from Ireland. Only isolated pockets of native Irish continued to resist. Ireton died in November 1651 and was replaced by Charles Fleetwood, who rounded up the last of the rebels, including Phelim O'Neill, who was executed on 10 March 1653.

The Rebellion of 1641-1653 was incredibly destructive. Estimates of lives lost range as high as 600,000, including deaths from starvation, exposure, and plague (see Epidemics and Plague*), which swept the island in 1649. Massive regions were denuded in scorched-earth policies or by the simple foraging of armies. In 1652-1653 wolves were reported coming from the hills and dragging people out of their homes. By the rebellion's official end, the "Act of Satisfaction" on 26 September 1653, the entire island was open to the imposition of the Cromwellian settlement (see Act of Settlement*).

Bibliography: Patrick Corish, "The Rising of 1641 and the Catholic Confederacy," "Ormonde, Rinuccini and the Confederates," and "The Cromwellian Conquest," in T. W. Moody, F. X. Martin, and F. J. Byrne, eds., *A New History of Ireland*, vol. III: *Early Modern Ireland*, 1976.

John Nolan

J

James VI and I (1566-1625). In 1603, an old dream of the English monarchy became reality. England had successfully united unto itself Ireland* and Wales*, but three centuries of intermittently strenuous and brutal attempts to bring the remaining part of the British Isles, Scotland*, into the English hegemony had failed. Tudor dynastic failure, not English imperial might, finally resolved the problem. A king from Scotland came south to take over the rest of Britain. He came with his own dream, a united kingdom of Great Britain. But English relief at the peaceful succession of an adult Protestant male with a family, after fifty years of female government and doubts about the future, was not enough to outweigh intense and xenophobic hostility to a king who saw his role as much greater than being king of England. The early years of the reign were dominated by James's plans for an incorporating union*, opposition to it in England, and growing resentment to that opposition in Scotland. The king who had in 1598-1599 produced an extreme defense of divine right* in his *Trew Law of Free Monarchies* and a manual of kingship, *Basilikon Doron,* now compounded fears about his ideology of monarchy when he trumped parliamentary refusal to sanction the kingdom of Britain in 1604 by creating it, and the flag that would give it visual expression, by proclamation. But the ace was held by the parliament of 1607*, which killed the incorporating union, leaving only minor concessions like the repeal of hostile laws and the naturalization of the *post-nati* and a deal of mutual distrust and alienation.

The issue of union was intertwined with a wider tension. James, as he said himself, was a "cradle-king": James VI from the age of one. The thirty-six year old who became James I had a long and successful reign behind him, ruling a kingdom with much less institutional sophistication but with plenty of political complexity. It was also a very pushy kingdom, outward looking and intensely conscious of its place in Europe. And it was a high-morale kingdom, not least because it had fought off its more powerful neighbor for centuries and then given it a king. None of this was ideal preparation (from the English point of view) for ruling England, with its profoundly different tradition of intense pride in its law and government institutions and its habitual if somewhat artificial feelings of superiority, grounded in almost a thousand years of belief in being God's chosen people. It was not a happy situation when the king's English subjects regarded it as their right and duty to tell a king of long experience how to be king of England, as Nicholas Fuller said in the Commons in 1610. Conversely, a king whose experience of a different kingdom led him to criticize English inefficiency as in his repeated complaints about the time members of the Commons spent in talking rather than in enacting and about their sterile obsession with their privileges was a constant reminder of unwelcome foreign ideas and rule.

The result was that genuine problems of English government could be swept under the carpet and explained wholly in terms of a Scottish king. The channels of patronage, already clogged up by importunate English suitors, now seemed to be blocked by even more importunate Scots, to whom the king of England lent an all too willing ear. James's new council promptly had five Scotsmen added to it, which undermined the impact of the intelligent widening of the English composition of a council that had become far too narrow in Elizabeth's last years (see privy council*). Scotsmen got office; Sir George Hume as chancellor of the Exchequer* and master of the wardrobe, Sir Thomas Erskine (displacing Sir Walter Raleigh*) as captain of the guard, the duke of Lennox as steward of the household, and so on. Even after James had accepted how unpopular this was, this spendthrift king continued to provoke perennial complaints by handing out far too much money to the Scots, while the bedchamber remained a Scottish enclave for most of the reign. In terms of relations between his two kingdoms, this was a problem in its own right but beyond it lay a much deeper English problem. The financial difficulties of the monarchy, in part inherited from Elizabeth's running down of Crown revenue and land (see Crown Lands*; Taxation and Revenue*), were not going to be resolved by the mere insistence that a Scottish king spend less on the Scots. The extravagance of the king would die with him; the underlying problem would not. But it was all too easy to assume that James's resorts to extraparliamentary sources of money, such as the notorious imposition* on currants that led to Bate's Case* in 1606 and starkly raised the issue of the royal prerogative*, or Sir Robert Cecil's* radical Great Contract* of 1610, were necessary only because of James's extravagance, and that somewhat simplistic point of view was compounded by the fact that the particular beneficiaries were not English. Similarly, the huge pressure on royal court* and government place, already evident before 1603 and relieved only by the hopelessly inadequate practice of granting offices in reversion, could readily be attributed to what was at most a superficial problem, the existence of the Scots. In the scale of unsatisfactory answers, Sir Robert Walpole's eighteenth-century placemen would in the long run be a better one than reversions and anti-Scottish moaning.

Yet the extraordinary thing is that this reign, as historians are now beginning to realize, was not one of unrelieved problems, let alone failure. The vain pedantic favorite-dominated buffoon of tradition is no longer the prevailing image of James I; the question of why James VI succeeded in Scotland while James I failed in England is no longer posed in that unreconcilable form. As king of England, James made many mistakes, not least in the way he presented himself, by pen rather than by portraits and processions. But his great strength was his ability to diffuse rather than confront issues. Laziness it has been called, but it was a laziness that normally worked.   James was an infinitely less paranoid creature than his predecessor; Puritans*, Catholics* (despite the Gunpowder Plot*), and Spain, were not nightmare threats to him. The Hampton Court Conference* did something to reassure the first group that the new king was at least accessible, and all but the most extreme found themselves at home in the Jacobean church. Catholic appeals to the son of Mary, queen of Scots, were met with the wrong response, but it was a negative rather than threatening response. And James's foreign policy involved immediate peace with Spain and prolonged efforts to maintain stability in Europe by Anglo-Spanish diplomacy. This ended in disaster at the very end of the reign, when his foolish son-in-law Frederick Elector Palatine's acceptance of the Bohemian throne led to the outbreak of the Thirty Years War* (see Elizabeth*), and pressure on the king of England to head the Protestant cause in resistance to the Catholic Habsburgs. The failure of the Spanish match* for his son Charles* in 1623 left James with no viable policy and allowed the English war party, led in 1624 by Charles and the 1st duke of Buckingham (George Villiers*), to push England into the humiliating war which, as James forecast, it was unable to sustain (see Spanish War of 1625-1630*).

But for almost a quarter of a century, England was at peace and domestic tensions reduced; to that extent, James's reign provided a welcome breathing space between the last years of Elizabeth and the increasingly problem-ridden reign of Charles I. Moreover, incorporating union there might not be, but the English and the Scots learned that coexistence was possible and that there was no particular reason to depart from it. The Anglo-Scottish union was one of the least fraught and most long-lived of the dynastic unions of early modern Europe. That was James's real success and the one closest to his political heart.

Bibliography: Bruce Galloway, *The Union of England and Scotland, 1603-1608*, 1986; Maurice Lee, Jr., *Government by Pen*, 1980 and *Great Britain's Solomon*, 1990; Kevin Sharpe, ed., *Faction and Parliament: Essays on Early Stuart History*, 1978; A. G. R. Smith, ed., *The Reign of James VI and I*, 1973; Jenny Wormald, "James VI and I: Two Kings or One?" *History* 68 (1983): 187-209.

Jenny Wormald

James VII and II (1633-1701). The second son of Charles I*, James became king on 6 February 1685 at the death of his older brother, Charles II*, and ruled until 23 December 1688.

Born on 14 October 1633, James grew up in a protective environment. He and Charles were extremely loyal to their father and family. James's education was in the "school of experience," and he evinced an early and abiding interest in warfare. When the Civil War* began in 1642, the royal family's ordered existence was disrupted. James was held under virtual house arrest from July 1646 through April 1648, when he escaped to France, beginning twelve years of exile. In 1649 Charles I's trial and execution* left Charles II as king in exile and James the heir to a throne that existed only technically.

The years of exile were characterized by poverty, futility, and despondency for the royalists*, who to no avail sought foreign backing for their quest to regain the throne. European states were unwilling to commit themselves to the Stuart cause; factionalism among the exiles created additional problems. But despite the relative poverty of the English court in exile, James pursued an active social life; it was during this period that he developed his propensity for the charms of the opposite sex. As late as 1659, James had virtually abandoned hope that he would ever return to England. Despite Oliver Cromwell's* death in 1658, the Interregnum* government continued under his son, Richard Cromwell*, and royalist plots to overturn it came to nothing. However, Richard was powerless to control the faction-ridden parliamentary army, the Scottish army under General Monck* took London* in February 1660, Charles was formally invited to return in May 1660, and he landed at Dover on 26 May to much acclaim.

James disliked life at the Restoration* royal court* and continued a hedonistic lifestyle. In spring 1660, Anne Hyde* daughter of Charles's lord chancellor, Edward Hyde*, earl of Clarendon became pregnant by James, and Charles reluctantly agreed to their secret marriage in September. Surviving its rocky start, the marriage produced eight children, of whom only two daughters survived: Mary* (born 1662) and Anne* (born 1665).

A political challenge following Clarendon's fall probably spurred James's private conversion to Catholicism* in 1669, although he was not baptized until 1672. His wife also converted, and James was an acknowledged Catholic long before 1676, when he stopped attending Anglican* service. Charles, despite his personal preference, would not convert and would not permit James to raise his daughters as Catholics.

After 1673, when the widowed James married the Catholic Mary of Modena*, fears of a Catholic succession and French control of the Netherlands produced the first informal efforts to bar James from the throne. The Test Act* (25 Car. I, c. 2) of 1673 required all officeholders to take Anglican communion within three months of appointment, and James was obliged to resign as lord admiral. Charles's minister, the earl of Danby*, held the line until 1678, when the Popish Plot* led to an outburst of anti-Catholic feeling in Parliament*, resulting in a second Test Act (30 Car. II, st. 2, c. 1) and Charles's decision to send his brother to Holland. James was the subject of three exclusion bills filed during the Exclusion Crisis* between 1679 and 1681. The country party or "Whigs"* supported exclusion, while the court party or "Tories"* supported the monarchy (see Court versus Country*). Charles prorogued the Oxford Parliament* of March 1681 after one week and resolved not to call another. James returned home sporadically but was not allowed to return permanently until May 1682. Thereafter he and Charles looked for support to the Tories, whose anti-Whig policies culminated in 1683, when Whig leadership was decimated as a result of the Rye House Plot*. James grew stronger then and succeeded to the throne peacefully when Charles died in 1685.

James's parliament of 1685* was overall a success, but the same year he faced his first challenge with Monmouth's Rebellion*, mounted by Charles's illegitimate son. It was summarily put down and the rebels ferociously punished, earning James a reputation for mercilessness. Parliament reacted against his excesses in November, but James prorogued it after two weeks. Clearly James was estranged now even from his Tory supporters. He issued a series of arbitrary pro-Catholic measures, among them his Declarations of Indulgence* (1687 and 1688) providing toleration for Catholics, but this and the trial of the Seven Bishops* in 1688 increased alienation from all sides. The birth of James's son in June 1688 was held suspect and prompted a Dutch invasion led by his son-in-law William of Orange* in November. James half-heartedly attempted to repulse the attack but eventually fled to France on 23 December. William called a Convention Parliament*, which bestowed the Crown upon him and Mary. These events came to be called the Glorious Revolution*.

James made several poorly mounted attempts to regain his throne, most notably in the Irish venture, which led to the infamous loss at the Battle of the Boyne in 1690. For the most part, however, James resigned himself to the loss of his throne, seeing it as punishment for his early dissolution; this theme was to dominate the rest of his life. He died on 5 September 1701, leaving his son James Edward as the king in exile. Some historians have viewed James as an absolutist* monarch in the style of his father, others as a king who wanted only toleration for his co-religionists. Perhaps the truth lies somewhere between.

Bibliography: John Miller, *James II, A Study in Kingship,* 1977.

Connie S. Evans

Jews in England, Efforts for Readmission and Toleration. Edward I expelled the Jews from England in 1290, although a minuscule number, mostly foreign merchants in residence, remained in England during the centuries that followed. As a result, English society contained virtually no Jewish presence and therefore possessed no first-hand experience of Jewish customs and culture. Various negative stereotypes about Jews, however, continued to persist throughout the later Middle Ages and the Tudor era.

The early seventeenth century witnessed the growth and appearance of philo-Semitism among various English people, which culminated in an unsuccessful effort to get the Jews formally readmitted into England. Protestantism's and Calvinism's* emphasis on the Bible* and Bible reading, particularly the Old Testament, was a preliminary source for this positive interest in the Jews and their history and culture among many scholars and reformers. Within Protestant England specifically, three groups in particular contributed further to the growth of philo-Semitism under the early Stuarts. The first group were the so-called Judaizers, who had concluded that Mosaic law was still binding on Christians as well as Jews in spite of the coming of Jesus Christ. John Traske (1585-1636) began his judaizing, or advocating a return to Jewish religious practices, including a Saturday Sabbath, during 1617. Although his teachings aroused the opposition of clerical authorities, those teachings also presented Judaism in a favorable light. A second group of philo-Semites were scholars who attributed mystical properties to the Hebrew language and considered it a vehicle for the discovery of a universal, perfect language. Finally, millenarian* Protestants considered the Jews to be an integral part of the supposedly approaching Apocalypse, or end of the world. Many Protestant millennialists considered the destruction of popery and the conversion of the Jews to be the prelude to the Second Coming of Christ. Furthermore, many English millenarians saw Protestant England as the instrument for accomplishing both of those conditions. All three of these groups contributed to the growth of philo-Semitism in early seventeenth-century England.

The era of the English Civil Wars* and the establishment of the Commonwealth* experienced an increase in philo-Semitism, particularly as evidenced by the growth of support for the readmission of the Jews into England. A few English favored the readmission of the Jews as part of a generalized program of religious toleration and out of a sense of sympathy to a persecuted race. More frequently, those English who favored the readmission of the Jews did so in order to convert them to Christianity and so fulfill a condition for the arrival of the anticipated millennium. Such millenarian considerations continued to exert influence under Oliver Cromwell* and the Protectorate*. Besides having sympathy for religious toleration and millenarian aspirations, Cromwell also favored allowing the Jews to settle in England for the purpose of their helping to promote England's foreign trade*. Seventeenth-century Englishmen widely but mistakenly believed that all Jews were rich and astute at business, so it naturally followed that they, including Cromwell, also believed that the Jewish community in Amsterdam was responsible for the coveted Dutch prosperity. That belief was not totally mistaken; the Jews of Amsterdam formed an important component in the Dutch network of international trade.

British academics, such as John Dury, also respected the scholarship of Jews from the Netherlands and had established contacts with the leading rabbi of Amsterdam, Menasseh ben Israel (1604-1657) during the 1640s. Menasseh further aroused the expectations of the millenarians in 1650 by publishing his *The Hope of Israel*, which included an account of the supposed recent discovery of the Ten Lost Tribes of Israel in South America. Meanwhile, the English Navigation Acts of 1650 and 1651 were hurting the trade of Amsterdam's Jewish merchants. That circumstance prompted Menasseh to plan a mission to England to seek relief. Before he could depart, the First Dutch War* (1652-1654) broke out and disrupted contacts between the English philo-Semites and the Jews of Amsterdam. Once peace was reestablished, Menasseh resumed his plans and journeyed to England in September 1655. The following November he published his *Humble Address*, which presented both economic and millenarian arguments for the readmission of the Jews into England. A further petition to the council of state* requested the formal repeal of the expulsion of the Jews and the granting of full religious toleration to them. Cromwell responded in December by convening a committee at Whitehall to study the possibility of readmitting the Jews. The committee found that there were actually no laws barring Jews from resettling in England or practicing their religion. At the same time, various clergy and merchants of London* led by the controversialist William Prynne* opposed the issuing of a formal invitation for the Jews to return to England. Somewhat disgusted by the spectacle of such squabbling, Cromwell adjourned the Whitehall Conference on 18 December. Under the circumstances Cromwell could not bring himself to issue a formal invitation for Jewish resettlement in England on his own authority. He did, however, grant toleration to the small existing Jewish community in England and gave Menasseh ben Israel a pension of £100 a year. It was a small compensation for the disappointed Menasseh, who had nurtured high hopes for his people's return to England. He died soon after in 1657. After the Restoration*, Charles II* continued the Protectorate's policy of granting informal toleration to Jews resident in England. Thanks to that policy, the Jewish community in England experienced a slow but steady growth after 1660, while it also made a significant contribution to England's rise as a world trading power during the late seventeenth century.

Bibliography: W. K. Jordan, *The Development of Religious Toleration in England from the Convention of the Long Parliament to the Restoration, 1640-1660*, 1938; David Katz, *Philo-Semitism and the Readmission of the Jews to England, 1603-1655*, 1982.

                                                              Ronald H. Fritze

Jonson, Ben (1572-1637). After William Shakespeare*, the greatest playwright of the English Renaissance. His comedies command respect for their sharply etched characterizations, vigorous theatrical prose, incisive social satire, and masterful construction. Jonson's work advances the value of self-knowledge, the importance of social harmony established through high ideals and individual integrity, the destructive effects of a slavish devotion to money, power, or status, the vital example that the ancients provided, and the necessary task of the writer to function as social conscience. Evidence suggests that Jonson was born on 11 June 1572 in London*, the son of a minister and stepson of a bricklayer, to whom he was apprenticed after studying with the antiquary William Camden at Westminster School from 1583 to 1588.

By 1597, having completed Thomas Nashe's *Isle of Dogs,* he had married, soldiered in the Low Countries, and acted. In 1598 *The Case Is Altered* and *Every Man in His Humour*, the first of his comical satires, were staged. He was also imprisoned in Newgate briefly for the murder of an actor. His remaining comical satires appeared shortly thereafter: *Every Man Out of His Humour* (1599), *Cynthia's Revels* (1600), and *Poetaster* (1601). With the accession of James I* in 1603, Jonson wrote a Roman play, *Sejanus*, and began composition of his twenty masques and entertainments, many done in troubled collaboration with the great stage designer Inigo Jones (see Art*). In 1605 he wrote *Eastward Ho!* with John Marston and George Chapman, and in 1606 his most famous comedy, *Volpone*, was staged, followed by *Epicoene* (1609), *The Alchemist* (1610), *Catiline* (1611)—his second Roman play—and *Bartholomew Fair* (1614).

Two years later appeared *The Devil Is an Ass,* along with the first folio of his works, an anthology of nine plays, two collections of poetry (*Epigrams* and *The Forest*), and several masques (semi-theatrical entertainments with allegorical plots and mythological, fantastic characters). The quality of Jonson's dramas declined in his last decade, though to call his later plays "dotages" as John Dryden* did is probably too harsh. His career ended with *The Staple of News* (1626), *The New Inn* (1629),

The Magnetic Lady (1632), and *A Tale of a Tub* (1633, based on an earlier version). Jonson died on 6 August 6 1637 and was buried in Westminster Abbey, his tombstone reading "O rare Ben Jonson."

Jonson's comical satires, an innovative dramatic form influenced by the poetic satires then current, developed "humor comedy," Jonson appropriating the term humor from contemporary psychology and reinterpreting it as any affected behavior deserving of mockery. From his one-dimensional humor characters spring the more rounded figures of his greatest comedies; such tricksters as Volpone or Subtle and Face (in *The Alchemist*) compel our interest and amazement, while their rejection of orthodox social morality prompts our laughing condemnation, at times even disgust, as with Volpone's repulsive innuendoes to Celia. Volpone's "hymn" to his gold is a masterful monologue of perverted prayer, a revelation of his monomaniacal character, and a caricature of Jacobean acquisitiveness and self-aggrandizement. These comedies and *Epicoene* reveal Jonson's skill at tight plot construction inherited from classical dramatists who were, as he stated in his critical work *Timber, or Discoveries*, his "guides, not commanders."

Jonson's poetry and masques praise those virtues whose absence is pilloried in the plays. Many poems celebrate members of nobility as living symbols of a code seen as central to the English social fabric. In "To Penshurst" he epitomizes this idealistic code in the Sidneys' family home, a structure against which other houses are mere symbols of wealth rather than expressions of "the mysteries of manners, arms and arts." His epigrams indict fops and buffoons, his epitaph "On My First Son" is a moving remembrance of "his best piece of poetry," and the songs from the plays combine graceful diction and careful rhythm, which counterpoint the dramatic prose and blank verse. Jonson's spare disciplined lines, controlled emotional tone, and balanced phrasing place him within the neoclassical tradition. His masques depicted for courtly audiences the interplay of allegorical figures representing what he termed in *Hymenaei* (1606) "the more remov'd mysteries" or exalted ideals of the true nobility: statesmanship, service, devotion to the monarch, marital fidelity, beneficence, and the well-ordered, rational life. He also developed the anti-masque, an antic scene of grotesque and debased characters.

Jonson's criticism, the largest body of literary commentary by a Tudor dramatist, records his measured respect for classical models, rejection of an easy imitation of their work, and his belief in literature* as an agent of moral and social improvement. His comments praise writing as a disciplined, scholarly craft, not mere hack work for the ill educated and unappreciative. His criticism again reveals his neoclassical outlook by stressing the virtues to be found in Greek and Roman masters, yet he blends their influence with a strong respect for native English tradition and individual originality.

Bibliography: Alexander Leggatt, *Ben Jonson: His Vision and His Art*, 1981; Rosalind Miles, *Ben Jonson: His Life and Work*, 1986.

Christopher Baker

Justices of the Peace. See Local Government, Counties, and Local Government, Towns.

Juxon, William (1582-1663). Archbishop of Canterbury and lord treasurer, this moderate Arminian* and protégé of William Laud* was born in Chichester, Sussex. Admitted as a scholar of St. John's College, Oxford, in 1598, he graduated with a bachelor of civil law degree in 1603. Shortly after his ordination, he served as vicar of St. Giles, Oxford, from 1609 to 1616. In 1615 he became rector of the parish of Somerton in Oxfordshire. Several years later the fellows of St. John's College unanimously elected him as their president upon the recommendation of William Laud, the previous holder of that office. Juxon served as the president of St. John's until 1633, when further patronage from Laud took him away to higher offices.

Juxon initially received nomination to the bishopric of Hereford in late 1632, but Laud's promotion to be archbishop left the important diocese of London* vacant, so he secured the appointment of the trusted Juxon, and on 27 October 1633 Juxon was consecrated. Juxon's close association with the controversial Laud must have caused apprehension among many Londoners, but his moderation and pleasing personality soon won the admiration of all the contending religious parties in London.

On 6 March 1636 Laud helped Juxon to advance once again by securing his appointment as lord treasurer of England, making Juxon the first cleric to serve in that office since 1469. During his tenure, Juxon proved to be honest and competent. Although he continued the sensible policies of limiting the government's spending while expanding its revenues, he could not muster support for any general reform of royal finances (see Taxation and Revenue*). His efforts to increase revenues were aided by the expansion of trade in the 1630s, which caused a growth in customs revenues that was largely mirrored by increases in revenues from impositions* and wardships. Unfortunately the crisis of the Bishops' Wars* during 1639-1640 and the accompanying increased expenditures ultimately brought his efforts to naught.

Juxon was a firm royalist*, and like the other Arminian bishops, he abstained from voting on the attainder of Thomas Wentworth*, the earl of Strafford. He also urged Charles I* not to sign the bill of attainder and resigned as lord treasurer on 21 May 1641 a few days after Strafford's execution. Juxon continued to advise Charles I during the 1640s, even during the king's trial. He ministered to the king prior to his execution (see Charles I, Trial, Execution, and Cult of*) and accompanied him to the scaffold on 30 January 1649. Afterward he saw to the embalming of Charles I's body and its burial on 7 February at St. George's Chapel, Windsor. During the Interregnum*, Juxon retired to the manor of Little Compton, Gloucestershire, which was his personal property. He appears to have considered resistance to parliament* and its army* to be futile, although he did aid other persecuted Arminians and royalists.

The Restoration* of Charles II* saw Juxon's fortunes improve once again, and on 13 September 1660 he became archbishop of Canterbury. By that time the aged Juxon's health was declining steadily, while his king Charles II held him in slight personal regard, so that he was able to accomplish little as archbishop before his death on 4 June 1663. He was the last cleric to hold the office of lord treasurer.

Bibliography: Thomas A. Mason, *Serving God and Mammon: William Juxon, 1582-1663*, 1985.

Ronald H. Fritze

K

King's Evil. The popular name for scrofula, a form of tuberculosis characterized by enlarged lymphatic glands, especially in the neck. From Edward the Confessor's time, English monarchs participated in a ritual that fostered belief in the legitimate king's sacerdotal powers, laying hands on the afflicted to cure them of this malady. Elizabeth I was particularly enthusiastic, preparing herself by prayer and fasting. James I* "touched" but did not like the practice. Despite widespread application of more scientific medicine* in the later Stuart era, it was still widely held that the king's evil was curable only by the monarch's touch. Stuart sovereigns, especially Charles II* and Anne*, touched thousands, adding to the mystique of divinely chosen kingship.

Many scientists such as Robert Boyle and trained medical men like sergeant-surgeon Richard Wiseman believed in the practice's efficacy (see Science and Scientific Revolution*). Wiseman, who was with Charles II in France and witnessed the touching-in-exile of multitudes, reported inexplicable cures, enhancing the Stuarts' reputation. Among charges brought against the leader of Monmouth's Rebellion* in 1685 was touching for the king's evil. James II* began the ceremonies almost as soon as his predecessor was buried. William III*, foreign born and king by virtue of parliamentary support rather than inheritance, disdained touching, undermining his popularity.

No sooner had William died in 1702 than crowds gathered at the house of Queen Anne's sergeant-surgeon, awaiting resumption of the ceremonies. Recognizing the practice's value, the speaker of the House of Commons, Robert Harley, insisted that the privy council* publish the times and places of the queen's appearances. Accordingly, in a notice printed in the *London Gazette*, Anne asked her ill subjects who wished to be touched to come to Whitehall on 22 March. She also touched frequently at the Banqueting House. Though her own health was fragile, Anne would touch 200-300 subjects in an afternoon. Samuel Johnson reported that in 1712 his mother brought him at the age of three to be touched by Anne, but the disease stayed, permanently scarring his features. Anne was the last English sovereign to administer the royal touch. Sir Richard Blackmore, her physician-in-ordinary, was not as impressed with the magical side of monarchy as Wiseman. In 1726 he published a treatise on the king's evil, recommending surgery for excisable tumors and purgatives for young victims.

Monarchs did not always relish close personal contact with contagious, scrofulous subjects. Touch-pieces, coins sometimes called "angels" that had been fingered by the sovereign, were occasionally distributed instead. During one month of Anne's reign, nearly 2,000 pieces of "healing gold" were distributed in lieu of the actual ceremony.

Bibliography: Marc Bloch, *The Royal Touch*, 1973; Raymund Crawfurd, *The King's Evil*, 1911.

Elizabeth Lane Furdell

Kirk (Church of Scotland). The Church of Scotland's history during the seventeenth century was determined more by politics than theology, though doctrine was not a negligible concern. Protestantism, following closely to Calvinist* teachings, was the accepted religion in Scotland*. The controversy that caused turmoil within the Kirk concerned the type of structure that it should adopt. The Stuart monarchs preferred episcopacy, while many ministers and people favored a Presbyterian* form of church government.

Episcopacy was the established church structure in pre-Reformation Scotland and remained so after the introduction of Protestantism. In the 1560s, when the queen, Mary Stuart, was a Catholic*, a general assembly was created to govern the reformed Kirk. It included both spiritual and temporal elements: the "godly baronage" (peers and commissioners of shires), commissioners of burghs selected by town councils, and bishops, commissioners, superintendents, and ministers. But because of the influence in Scotland of John Calvin's ideas and the preaching of his disciple John Knox, support grew for a Presbyterian structure.

When James VI* was placed on the Scottish throne as an infant in 1567, Scotland had an episcopal form of church government that presided over a largely Protestant Kirk; the general assembly was retained. But a strong case for Presbyterianism was made in John Knox's very influential First Book of Discipline (1560) and Andrew Melville's more radical Second Book of Discipline (1581), and presbyteries were adopted, though not implemented, by the general assembly in 1578. James, an admitted Protestant by way of the anti-Catholic Negative Confession of 1581, realized the political importance of episcopacy. Bishops represented Crown votes in parliament and made for more efficient control of the realm. Furthermore, James held to the Erastian belief that a Christian prince had the divine right* to rule in all religious matters. Therefore the Black Acts in 1584 denounced presbyteries, emphasized the Crown's supremacy regarding all aspects of the church, and solidified the episcopate, which now answered to the king rather than the general assembly.

However, Melville's faction continued to object to royal control of the Kirk, and James, still threatened politically by Catholicism and ultra-Protestantism, agreed in 1586 to a compromise allowing the creation of presbyteries. The episcopate withered, and in 1592 the Presbyterian system became statutory, though the office of bishop was not abolished altogether. But by 1596 the king was free of the aforementioned threat and began to turn against the Presbyterians. In 1600 he began appointing "parliamentary bishops," for whom he soon found a place in ecclesiastical administration. His position was strengthened by his survival of the allegedly ultra-Protestant Gowrie conspiracy in 1600, his accession to the English throne in 1603, and the Gunpowder Plot* of 1605, which enhanced his anti-Catholic credentials.

The Anglican* church appealed to James because it adhered to episcopacy and believed in the supreme authority of the king, and he attempted to unite the English and Scottish churches, both of which were reformed in doctrine. But the Presbyterians in Scotland continued to oppose episcopacy because of its association with popery and corruption. They were joined by the Scottish nobility, primarily because the latter were threatened by the increasing power of the bishops, who were gradually gaining both religious and political supremacy through James's policies. In 1606 he forced a convention of ministers to approve "constant moderators of presbyteries," then also appointed "constant moderators of synods," creating what looked suspiciously like diocesan episcopacy; he also had parliament pass an act restoring "the estate of bishops." At the Glasgow general assembly in 1610, James pronounced his religious superiority and pushed through a canonical law stating that ministers must swear obedience to bishops. Consecration of bishops also began. This was a severe defeat for Presbyterians, but it increased unity within their movement.

James continued his plan for uniting the English and Scottish churches. After he appointed the sympathetic Archbishop Spottiswoode in 1615, an Aberdeen general assembly the next year produced a new confession of faith and formulated what became known as the Five Articles of Perth*, though Spottiswoode advised James not to impose them. Adopted by the Perth assembly in 1618, they included kneeling at communion, the Christian calendar (with Christmas, Good Friday, Easter, Ascension Day, and Whitsunday as holidays), private communion, private baptism, and episcopal confirmation. The assembly also adopted a new liturgy and canons compatible with Anglican practice. Believing in his spiritual supremacy, James did not expect the great opposition that followed. Presbyterians believed the articles were popish and fervently attacked the episcopate. The bishops were forced to defend the articles, and their popularity and James's began to decline.

Charles I's* accession only made matters worse for the church. He attempted to further impose the structure of the "popish" Anglican church upon Scotland. Arminianism* and the anti-Calvinist preachings of the archbishop of Canterbury, William Laud*, made the acceptance of Anglican episcopacy virtually impossible for Presbyterians. Charles and Laud made an enormous mistake by attempting to introduce a Scottish Book of Common Prayer, closely resembling the English prayer book, into the church in 1637. This measure symbolized the two things that Presbyterians opposed the most: royal interference in religious matters and liturgical changes.

The newly proposed liturgy sparked a riot at St. Giles in Edinburgh and caused many ministers and nobles to unite in rebellion. Those opposed to the present form of episcopacy, called Supplicants, favored a reduction in the power and influence of bishops. They were not necessarily anti-episcopal, but they were definitely pro-Presbyterian. The Supplicants developed a new state government called the Tables, which was composed of nobles, barons, burgesses, and ministers. They also wanted to place all of the bishops on trial for abuse of office. Charles responded by defending his right to change the liturgy, which forced the Supplicants into revolution.

Early in 1638 the Supplicants, led by Alexander Henderson and Archibald Johnston of Wariston, produced the National Covenant*. It was a moderate document that basically restated the Negative Confession of 1581 and placed the blame for problems on the king's advisers and the bishops. The episcopate and the king were not attacked. Charles sent his representative, the marquis of Hamilton, to threaten the Covenanters*, but the situation proved to be more serious than Charles had imagined. An assembly without Crown representatives attending was held in Glasgow late in 1638. It voted to abjure and remove all bishops and repeal all prior legislation that was favorable to the bishops. The episcopacy was replaced with a Presbyterian polity, and Charles, having no success in the Bishops' Wars* and receiving no help from the Short Parliament*, reluctantly accepted the situation.

The achievement of the long-desired goal of establishing an independent church under a Presbyterian government eventually caused more harm than good to the Church of Scotland. The much-needed cooperation of the nobility against the bishops allowed the former to influence church policy. Led by the 8th earl of Argyll (Archibald Campbell*), their influence continued to grow throughout the 1640s. The nobility were represented by laymen who entered the church hierarchy in the form of ruling elders. Although ministers held a majority in assemblies and committees, ruling elders proved to be an obstacle in the unification of the Kirk.

At the outbreak of the English Civil War* in 1642, Scotland positioned itself as a mediator, but through the persuasion of the radical Wariston, the Scots soon sided with the English parliament*. Wariston produced the Solemn League and Covenant*, which promised military aid to the parliamentarians* in return for a promise to reform the Anglican church along Presbyterianism lines. The Long Parliament* agreed, but only for military purposes. When the New Model Army* gained the upper hand in 1646, parliament did move toward Presbyterianism; however, they also adhered to Erastianism and began to dictate church policy themselves. The Presbyterians deeply resented being used by the English parliament.

Tension continued to mount between the Presbyterian ministers and the nobility over supremacy in church policy. A severe blow was dealt to the nobility in 1647 when several nobles—Lauderdale (John Maitland*), Lanark, and Loudoun—approached Charles I, who had been in Scottish custody since 1646, and promised to help restore him to the throne in return for his acceptance of the Covenant. This agreement between Charles I and the nobility, called the Engagement*, was accepted by the noble-dominated Scottish parliament in 1648. However, the majority of the ministers opposed the Engagement and did everything in their power to hinder the raising of an army. When the Engager force finally entered England, Oliver Cromwell's* forces crushed it at Preston. A new Act of Classes prevented Engagers from holding national office, and the once dominant nobility gave way to the newly powerful ministers.

However, the power of the ministers was soon threatened after Charles I's execution* in 1649. The Kirk divided into Resolutioners and Protesters. The former, who were in the majority, accepted Charles II* and welcomed the Engagers back into society. The Protesters, or Remonstrants, did not believe that Charles would work in the Scots' best interests regarding Presbyterianism and also opposed the Engagers. Resolutioners were conservatives who believed that royal authority, combined with Presbyterian church government, was the only way to restore order in the Kirk, while the Protesters lobbied for an independent church, free of secular control. Thus the main argument focused on the relationship between church and state.

By 1652 Cromwell placed Scotland under military rule because Scottish support for Charles II posed a threat to the Commonwealth*. Cromwell mistrusted both factions, but was concerned with their loyalty only during the Interregnum*. In 1653 Cromwell attempted to unify the Kirk, but Resolutioners and Protesters were unwilling to compromise. The debate between the two factions lasted throughout the Interregnum, with the Protesters gradually losing ground as it became apparent that Charles would be restored to the throne.

In 1660 Charles II was placed on the English throne, and immediately the two most prominent Resolutioners, James Sharp (later archbishop of St. Andrews) and the earl of Lauderdale, attempted to persuade him to follow their plan of church government. However, the Scottish nobility convinced Charles that the monarchy and presbytery could not peacefully co-exist, and the king assigned the earl of Middleton to take charge of the Restoration* in Scotland.

Middleton formally reestablished episcopacy in 1661 and made Presbyterian church government illegal. Sharp and Lauderdale decided not to oppose him but instead to get as many Resolutioners as possible nominated to bishoprics in hopes of producing a moderate episcopacy. They failed; Sharp was the only one who became a bishop. Middleton aroused much opposition when he began removing from office those Presbyterians who threatened his authority. By 1663 he lost all influence over Scottish affairs and was replaced by the earl of Rothes.

A growing problem for the Kirk was the growth of conventicles, or religious gatherings outside the established church. Rothes, Sharp, and Lauderdale's advocacy of the use of force in collecting fines from conventiclers caused a great deal of opposition, and the conventicles began to arm themselves. The Pentland Rising* in 1666 was evidence of the people's dislike of Kirk policy. Lauderdale was then given control of Scottish policy in 1667 and became more tolerant toward Dissenters*. The first of several indulgences was granted to dissenting ministers in 1669, giving them the chance to return to the established church. However, these angered both Dissenters and the established church, and conventicling continued to increase.

Lauderdale continued to search for a moderate policy that would keep Scotland peaceful, but the growth of conventicles constantly threatened the episcopacy. After 1672 he turned to a policy of severity concerning Dissenters. His opponents were pleased because of the disorder that they had created by promoting conventicles. Through the Clanking Act, he imprisoned and fined many Dissenters, which only increased the opposition. Lauderdale failed to limit conventicling by force, but after the assassination of Sharp in 1678, repression continued.

Richard Cameron and radical conventiclers associated with the assassination of Sharp planned a rebellion against the government. Rebel forces in the Covenanter Rebellion* (1679) won a battle at Drumclog but were defeated at Bothwell Bridge. Charles II then removed Lauderdale in 1679 and placed his brother, the duke of York (see James II*), in control of Scottish policy.

York, a known papist, surprised many by initially following a policy of moderation. However, the emergence of radical sects, most notably the Cameronians, caused him to reinstate the policy of severity. James eliminated the possibility of rebellion by using violent measures against Dissenters between 1684 and 1687, a period known as the "killing times." The Glorious Revolution* of 1688 brought religious toleration to Scotland and ended the conflict between church and state.

With respect to official doctrine, the seventeenth-century Kirk inherited the Confession of 1560, which included the idea of election but was ambiguous about predestination and limited atonement (the notion that Christ died only for the elect). This was supplemented by the Negative Confession of 1581, with its rejection of popery. The general assembly formulated a new Confession of Faith in 1616, which was more explicit about predestination (however, despite the Synod of Dort's* condemnation of Arminianism* in 1619, the "Aberdeen Doctors" contended that Christ had died for all). In the 1640s the general assembly accepted the Westminster Assembly's* Confession of Faith and Catechisms, which were even more thoroughly predestinarian. This continued to be used, though without legal foundation, after the rejection of Covenanter reforms in 1661 and the incorporation of the Confession of 1560 in the Scottish Test Act of 1681. At no time did official doctrine necessarily represent the beliefs of all Scottish Christians.

Bibliography: Julia Buckroyd, *Church and State in Scotland, 1660-1681*, 1980; Ian B. Cowan, *The Scottish Covenanters, 1660-1688*, 1976; Gordon Donaldson, *The Faith of the Scots*, 1990, and *Scotland, James V to James VII*, 1965; Walter Makey, *The Church of the Covenant, 1637-1651: Revolution and Social Change in Scotland*, 1979; David George Mullan, *Episcopacy in Scotland: The History of an Idea, 1560-1638*, 1986.

Paul Miller

Kirk Party (1647-51). The immediate origins of the Kirk party lay with the commission of the general assembly's refusal to espouse the Engagement* in 1648. The commission viewed the document as derogatory to the Solemn League and Covenant* of 1643. That committee's previous intervention in political affairs—the most dramatic being its work in favor of that same Covenant— legitimized the concept that the ecclesiastical nation possessed a right of consultation on anything affecting Presbyterianism* in the three kingdoms. The National Covenant* (1638), with its pledge of allegiance to reformed Kirk* and rightful king, provided authority for those presuming to speak for the Covenanters* regarding the former.

The Kirk party included Covenanters from numerous backgrounds; however, it was conspicuous in appealing only to a minority of nobles like the 8th earl of Argyll

(Archibald Campbell*) or great lairds (untitled heads of kin). Its support among the lairds of the shires from Angus in the east and Argyll in the west to the English border was extensive. (For instance, it controlled the shire committees of Haddington, Fife, Renfrew, Lanark, Wigton, and Kirkcudbright, which refused to levy troops for the Engager army.) Equally strong was the adherence of burgesses in the same area. The clergy heavily favored the Kirk party, except in the northeast and northern Lowlands, as well in parts of the Highlands. The Kirk party included the radical Covenanters, such as Archibald Johnston of Wariston and the Reverend Samuel Rutherford, who wanted to establish not only a church free from noble interference but a nation led by the godly headed by a weak monarch. In spring 1648 such plans lay dormant as the Engagers imposed their will on Scotland*.

With control of the estates lost, shire committees cooperating with the Engagers, and the Engager army quartering on recalcitrant burghs, only rebellion held out any possibility of changing the situation. Argyll and nobles such as the earls of Eglinton and Cassillis abandoned plans for a rising out of fear of the Engager army. However, in June a gathering of peasants and deserters at Mauchline Moor, Ayrshire (under clerical leaders), turned rebellious, but was quickly dispersed by Major General John Middleton. In August Colonel Robert Montgomery, Eglinton's son, started a rebellion that spread as news of the defeat of the Engager army flew north. Within weeks, the whole southwest Lowlands, Argyll, Fife, and the Scots were in the field. Backed by Oliver Cromwell's* arrival in the Borders with thousands of cavalry, the Kirk party rising, known as the Whiggamore Raid, triumphed in the Treaty of Stirling on 27 September. The Engagers disbanded; the Whiggamores remained in arms, ushering in the Kirk party regime.

Spending the remainder of 1648 solidifying control by purging Engagers, the Kirk party worked to secure an estates amenable to its policies. Meeting in Edinburgh in January 1649 the parliament (with only sixteen nobles attending) passed an Act of Classes (in accordance with a promise to Cromwell) to purge Scotland's ruling bodies of Engagers and profane men. Despite a number of rebellions (Pluscardine's and Ogilvie's) and Montrose's invasion of the mainland in spring 1650 (defeated at Carbisdale), the Kirk party remained solidly in control of Scotland until suffering military defeat at Dunbar on 3 September 1650.

The Kirk party implemented policies that ensured independence from the nobility and a leading role for the radical Covenanters. Lairds received the right to purchase the nobles' feudal superiorities (as tenants-in-chief of the Crown), freeing them from service obligations. Backed by a Kirk party committee of estates, shire committees, and burgh councils of similar mien, the presbyteries and Kirk sessions forced members of the social hierarchy to endure public repentance in the Kirks (instead of private penance before the session). Swinging the weapon of excommunication, which had civil (no officeholding allowed) as well as religious penalties, the Kirk party took revenge on the Engagers.

With the death of Charles I* the Kirk party immediately declared his son Charles II*. After prolonged negotiations (culminating in the Treaty of Breda), the new king reached Scotland in June 1650. Initially the Kirk party maintained strict control over his movements and associates. With the arrival of Cromwell's army imminent, the regime began levying troops. To ensure the army provided no basis for a revival of the Engagers, the Kirk party purged questionable recruits despite objections from Argyll and Lieutenant General David Leslie. Military defeat at Dunbar opened the way for debilitating divisions within the Kirk party. A separate army, led by Colonels Gilbert Kerr and Archibald Strachan (the latter one of the few republican Covenanters) and minor lairds, sprang up in the southwest. Their clerical counterparts issued the Remonstrance, which argued against acceptance of purged Scots. (The English removed Kerr's force from the scene at the Battle of Hamilton, just as Kirk party troops from Stirling approached to coerce its obedience.) Engager-royalist* stirrings (the Start and Middleton's Rising in October) proved the power of Scotland's conservative leaders could barely be held in check. On 14 December the commission of the general assembly passed the Public Resolutions, which allowed those previously purged to return to public life. The Remonstrants protested (hence their new name of Protesters), took control of the church in the southwest, and obstructed the new levies. During the winter and spring the Resolutioners and Protesters waged a war of words, as the conservatives received civil and military positions. When the general assembly met in July, the estates had already rehabilitated the Engagers. Within days the assembly split on Resolutioner-Protester lines, and the Church of Scotland experienced its first schism. The Kirk party remained as partners in the government with their enemies until the defeats of Alyth, Worcester, and Dundee. Despite attempts by Kirk partymen, national fortunes failed to revive. The Kirk party disappeared under the imposition of English rule.

Bibliography: Walter Makey, *The Church of the Covenants, 1637-1651*, 1977; David Stevenson, *Revolution and Counter-Revolution in Scotland, 1644-1651*, 1977.

Edward M. Furgol

L

Latitudinarians. A party that appeared in the Church of England after 1660, which advocated the use of reason and moderation in church affairs. The Latitudinarians rejected the necessity of strict and detailed adherence to any specific system of ecclesiastical organization, ceremonies, or dogmas. As their name implies, they allowed for a wide latitude in what Protestants could believe.

Latitudinarianism developed out of the teaching of the Cambridge Platonists. These scholars held the neo-Platonic and somewhat mystical view that reason could be used to analyze both natural and revealed religious beliefs because an indwelling God guided human reason toward correct conclusions. They sought to reconcile first the feuding Calvinists* and Arminians* of the Church of England and later the Anglicans* and the Dissenters*. Both before and after the Glorious Revolution*, their students, who rose to high positions in the church, also hoped to gather all the English Protestants into one comprehensive church. They rejected superstition (Roman Catholic* ceremonialism) and any intolerant, fanatical attitudes about religion (uncompromising Puritans* or followers of William Laud*). These attitudes made them the natural political allies of the Whigs* and the Dissenters and the hated enemies of the Tories* and their clerical supporters.

The Latitudinarians achieved the highest offices in the Church of England only after the Glorious Revolution, when they enjoyed the patronage and support of William III of Orange*. Gilbert Burnet*, bishop of Salisbury (1689-1715); Edward Stillingfleet, bishop of Worcester (1689-1699); Thomas Tenison, bishop of London (1692-1695) and archbishop of Canterbury (1695-1715); and John Tillotson, archbishop of Canterbury (1691-1694) were all prominent Latitudinarian scholars and divines appointed by William of Orange. The enemies of the Latitudinarians portrayed them as being without firm principles, which was not true. The Latitudinarians placed great emphasis on the maintenance of traditional moral and ethical behavior. They also believed that Protestant Christianity could survive only by adapting to and incorporating social changes such as the new scientific discoveries (see Science and the Scientific Revolution*).

Bibliography: G. R. Cragg, *The Church and the Age of Reason*, 1960; John Marshall, "The Ecclesiology of the Latitude-Men 1660-1689: Stillingfleet, Tillotson, and 'Hobbism,'" *Journal of Ecclesiastical History* 36 (1985): 407-427; John Spurr, "'Latitudinarianism' and the Restoration Church," *Historical Journal* 31 (1988): 612-682; Norman Sykes, *From Sheldon to Secker: Aspects of English Church History, 1660-1768*, 1959.

Ronald H. Fritze

Laud, William (1573-1645). As archbishop of Canterbury and one of the principal governmental ministers of Charles I*, William Laud played a major role in the events leading to the Civil War*. Historians have differed widely in their appraisal of him. Although highly acclaimed during the Restoration* period and by the proponents of the Oxford Movement, he has also been viewed as the person most responsible for the Civil War, and the breakdown of the religious consensus in early seventeenth-century England has been blamed primarily on his ecclesiastical policies.

The son of a clothier, William Laud was born at Reading on 7 October 1573. He was educated at Reading Free School and St. John's College, Oxford. He became a fellow of St. John's in 1593 and received his B.A. in 1594, his M.A. in 1598, and a D.D. in 1608. He was ordained in 1601 and became vicar of Stanford in 1607. After being appointed chaplain to Richard Neile in 1608, he was made president of St. John's in 1611. Neile was the political leader of a small but growing anti-Calvinist party in the Church of England (see Anglicanism*), and at Oxford Laud had clearly identified with that position. In 1603 he opposed the Millenary Petition* presented to James I* by his Puritan* subjects, and in the same year he engaged in controversy with the staunchly Calvinist* vice-chancellor of the university*, George Abbot*. Even after Abbot become archbishop of Canterbury, Laud continued to win preferment in the church and to pursue policies that alienated committed Calvinists. In 1616 he was made dean of Gloucester, where he came into conflict with the bishop for moving the communion table to the east end of the choir. As a member of the royal delegation to Scotland* in 1617, he angered the Scots by wearing a surplice to a funeral. His career advanced rapidly when he came to the attention of the king's favorite, the 1st duke of Buckingham (George Villiers*). Although Archbishop Abbot, believing him to be "unsound in religion," opposed his promotion, and the king was concerned about his "restless spirit," which "loves to toss and change," Laud was appointed bishop of St. David's in 1621. At the king's behest, he engaged in a dispute with the Jesuit John Fisher after the conversion of the countess of Buckingham to Roman Catholicism*.

After the death of James in 1625, Laud became the chief architect of Charles I's religious policy. In 1625 Charles made him dean of the Chapel Royal. In 1626 he was translated to Bath and Wells and two years later to London*. In 1629 he became chancellor of the University of Oxford and in 1633 archbishop of Canterbury. He also took a leading part in the administration of the country, serving as one of the king's principal advisers. Although Laud is accused of destroying the Elizabethan and Jacobean religious compromise by introducing new doctrines, his opposition to the

Calvinist doctrine of absolute predestination does not necessarily indicate that he held to the Arminian* alternative. At his trial he denied he was an Arminian, and throughout his career he was opposed to public theological controversy, suppressing both Puritan and Arminian doctrinal polemics. He was, however, committed to an anti-Puritan policy, providing Charles with a list of clerics labeled "O" for orthodox and "P" for Puritan to be used in appointments. He was equally committed to the restoration of the clerical estate to the rightful place he believed had been undermined by the Reformation. He alienated the already hostile Puritans, as well as other churchmen, by imposing uniformity and severely punishing those who dissented. Although he believed that men might hold their own opinions in private, he insisted that public obedience was essential and that a "uniform and decent order" be maintained throughout the Church of England.

In 1637 Laud attempted to impose the same uniformity on Scotland. A new liturgy based on the Book of Common Prayer was drawn up by Scottish bishops in collaboration with Laud; when it was introduced in Scotland, the result was the signing of the National Covenant* and the Bishops' Wars*, which forced Charles to reconvene parliament* in 1640. In convocation Laud introduced new canons*, proclaiming the divine right* of kings and requiring the swearing of an oath never to "consent to alter the government of this church by archbishops, deans, and archdeacons, etc." The so-called et cetera oath made Laud even more unpopular, and he was attacked on all sides as being responsible for Charles's most hated policies. On 18 December 1640, Laud was impeached by the Long Parliament* for high treason (see Impeachment*), and in 1641 he was confined to the Tower. After a grossly unfair trial in March 1644, he was eventually sentenced to death by an act of attainder. On 10 January 1645 he was beheaded on Tower Hill. (See also Personal Rule*; Thorough*.)

Bibliography: Charles Carlton, *Archbishop William Laud*, 1987; Kevin Sharpe, "Archbishop Laud," *History Today* 33 (August 1983): 26-30; H. R. Trevor-Roper, *Archbishop Laud, 1573-1645*, 3d ed., 1988.

Rudolph W. Heinze

Lauderdale, Earl of. See Maitland, John.

Law Enforcement. The subject of law enforcement consists of three components: the criminal law as enacted by parliament* and the local communities, the criminal courts and their prosecutorial system (see Common Law and Courts*; Ecclesiastical Courts*; Prerogative Courts*), and the officials whose duties included law enforcement—the attorney and solicitor-general of England, the justices of the peace (JPs) of the counties and councilors of boroughs, and the constables of hundreds, boroughs, and villages (see Local Government*). The criminal law was originally in the hands of the communities in Anglo-Saxon England, upon which the Normans imposed the role of the king for capital crimes (felonies for which the sanction was the death penalty). By the 1590s the role of king and parliament had become supreme in the definition of the criminal law, the privy council* and the judges of Assize in its central administration, and JPs and councilors in its local administration. Enforcement was in the hands of the constables, who were appointed annually for each parish of the country. All of these officials served without pay, as the law enforcement system was an amateur one based on honorary service.

The seventeenth century witnessed several important developments in law enforcement. These included the growing importance of parliament in setting the agenda of defining crime at both the capital and non-capital levels, the declining role of the monarch as the fountain of criminal justice, the declining role of the established church (see Anglicanism*) in identifying criminous behavior, the increasing burdens placed on JPs for administering the system, and the increased workload placed upon parish constables for its enforcement. Many of these developments dated from the mid- and late 1500s, and most of them had been completed by the 1690s. They were occasioned, moreover, by several significant changes. These included the rise and fall of the concept of hereditary divine right* monarchy, by which the king made law as the servant of God in England—a concept that was achieved by James I*, lost by Charles I*, and ended by the Glorious Revolution* of 1688-1689; the abolition of the prerogative courts in 1641, especially the court of Star Chamber, which had been used so successfully in the sixteenth century for the prosecution of overmighty subjects who had used their position to influence JPs, jurors, and local inhabitants; the rise of the Puritan* ethic between 1600 and the 1640s, which broadened the definition of crime to include offenses against morality and public sensibilities; and the rise of the nonpartisan state, where the Whig* philosophy of government abdicated intervention, leaving the subject of law enforcement almost entirely in the hands of the county and city communities.

While the king, privy council, and parliament could be considered the authors of law enforcement, the JPs and constables were its dispensers. The key to the system was the JP. Appointed by the lord chancellor upon recommendation of the lord lieutenant* of each county, the JP was authorized to issue warrants for the arrest of any suspect to a crime. These powers were increased by legislation under James I and Charles II*. Since law enforcement was a private act, the responsibility of arrest was solely in the hands of the victim or next of kin, as no warrant for an arrest could be made without a person to serve as private prosecutor—one who would be willing to swear out a warrant and post a bond to appear in court and testify against the accused. There is some evidence to suggest that in the course of the seventeenth century, victims increasingly sought arbitration, mediation, or restitution of goods to satisfy a crime rather than to seek redress through the courts. The physicality of arrest and detention was in the hands of the parish constables. These officers, who were often merely poor laborers, were appointed without pay. There is some evidence to suggest, however, that by the 1680s men of higher socioeconomic status were being appointed and serving in that capacity. Research into the policing function in the seventeenth century, however, is still in its infancy.

Once an alleged culprit was informed upon, arrested, gaoled, and held in custody with or without bail, the culprit was tried. While many manorial and liberty courts had criminal jurisdiction by the 1500s, most of them lost their jurisdiction (usually by default) to assizes and quarter (for borough and county) sessions in the course of the seventeenth century. These were the courts on which the law enforcement system was wholly dependent, especially after 1660. While there was an appeal process to King's Bench, rarely was it used. Evidence collected to date suggests that at some point in the late 1500s or early 1600s, the JP, acting with the clerk of the peace, made the decision to have the culprit tried at either assizes or quarter sessions. By the 1620s it was clear that almost all cases of capital personal crimes went to assizes and that capital property crimes were split between assizes and quarter sessions, with the more difficult cases at sessions. Misdemeanors became heard almost exclusively before quarter sessions by the early 1600s, and then by quarter and petty sessions by the early 1700s. Due largely to an increase in regulatory offenses and administrative responsibilities, legislation in the seventeenth and early eighteenth centuries enabled JPs to defer trial of an ever-increasing number of regulatory offenses from quarter to petty sessions (meetings of two to three JPs), especially from the 1670s through the 1690s.

Law enforcement is often judged not only by the ability of the criminal justice system to procure arrests and convictions but also by its sanctions. The seventeenth century is particularly pivotal with respect to the history of capital punishment. The execution rate, which was 0.03 per 100,000 by 1900, was twenty in the 1580s, thirty in 1605, ten by the 1630s, and five by 1700. It has been suggested that more people were hung between 1580 and 1630 than in the 360 years since then. Thus the long-term secular decline in executions had its most dramatic origins between the 1630s and the 1690s. Alternative punishments, restitution of goods stolen, and changes in public and private sensitivities and in socio-economic conditions have been attributed as possible explanations of the decline. What has not been adequately addressed as yet is the huge number of executions that occurred in the earlier part of the century.

Violent crime is often used as a measurement of the degree of violence in society because the law of homicide has been relatively consistent over the centuries from late medieval to modern times. The major sources for examining the prosecution of those persons causing violent deaths are the coroners' reports and indictments preferred before the circuit courts of assize. Calculated as rates per 100,000 of population*, the prosecutions for homicide were approximately twenty in the early 1400s, declining gradually to the early 1500s and then more rapidly until it reached only ten by 1600. The decline then continued at a more rapid rate, reaching five by 1650 and 1.5 by 1720. This long-term trend was interrupted by a "crime wave" in reported homicides in the late sixteenth and early seventeenth centuries. Since homicides are the crimes that are most frequently reported once committed, the evidence collected to date suggests that violent crime was in a long-term secular decline from the 1500s to the 1700s and that the law enforcement system that has been so badly mauled by critics of the common law* criminal justice system may not have been as inept as it has been portrayed.

The evidence for all capital felonies that has been collected to date follows a similar pattern. Overall there is a drop from the fifteenth to the eighteenth centuries, with a major rise between the 1560s and the 1620s, peaking around 1600. A considerable historical literature has developed on this subject, which is based on regional and short-term fluctuations, parliamentary legislation, and the role of local authorities, juries, and judges in the prosecutorial system. In addition, there is the view that high crime rates do not necessarily reflect a criminous or violent society. Changes in the rates of recorded crime may reflect changes in prosecutorial energy at the level of the local community or the national state, socioeconomic factors, mentality, or external influences such as a country at war. In the end, scholarly studies of crime will be increasingly important for the light they provide into the history of law enforcement.

Bibliography: J. M. Beattie, *Crime and the Courts in England, 1660-1800*, 1986; J. S. Cockburn, *Calendar of Assize Records. Home Circuit Indictments, Elizabeth I and James I. Introduction*, 1985; J. A. Sharpe, *Crime in Early Modern England, 1550-1750*, 1984.

Louis A. Knafla

Levellers. A radical political party that arose during the First Civil War*, enjoying its greatest influence from 1646 to 1649 in London* and the New Model Army*. The name, first used in 1647, was an insult hurled by enemies. Members of the party were neither "levellers" in the traditional sense—riotous destroyers of enclosures—nor did they favor economic "levelling" like the communistic Diggers*; indeed, they were vigorous defenders of property.

The Levellers' roots lay in Puritanism*, which included egalitarian, anti-hierarchical elements; in social and economic pressures on urban artisans and shopkeepers and rural copyholders and leaseholders; and in the political idea that popular sovereignty, justified by natural law, had been effaced by the Norman Yoke in 1066 (somewhat contradictorily, they also cited Magna Carta as a guarantee of liberties). More immediate impetus came from the split between Presbyterians* and Independents* in the Long Parliament* and the Westminster Assembly of Divines* and the hostility between parliament* and the New Model Army. The Levellers advocated a host of political, social, economic, and legal reforms, spelled out in many pamphlets and in the three versions of the Agreement of the People*.

The movement had four main leaders. John Lilburne* (1615-1657), son of a gentleman, was a popular Puritan pamphleteer, an officer in the parliamentary army* until 1645, and a self-made "martyr." Richard Overton (c.1600-after 1663), a Baptist*, operated an illegal printing* press, espoused the heretical idea of the death of the soul in *Man's Mortality* (1644), and ridiculed Presbyterians in his Martin Marpriest tracts (1645). William Walwyn (1600-1680), a bishop's grandson and member of the Merchant Adventurers Company (see Trading Companies*), was a deeply religious intellectual and exponent of social reform. John Wildman (1623-1693), a shadowy figure and possible agnostic, had a briefer association with the Levellers but a long career as a conspirator, culminating with the Glorious Revolution*.

Lilburne, Overton, and Walwyn came together in summer 1645 in the battle for religious freedom against the Presbyterian-dominated parliament, but they soon embraced political, social, and economic reform, as shown by Lilburne's *England's*

Birth-Right Justified, written while he was gaoled in Newgate. Later Overton published *The Ordinance for Tithes Dismounted*, antagonizing both Presbyterians and lay impropriators. In 1646 Walwyn defended toleration in a pamphlet war with Thomas Edwards, author of *Gangraena*. Lilburne, after offending the Lords, was back in Newgate that summer, where he wrote *The Free-man's Freedom Vindicated*, denying the house's jurisdiction over commoners. He was fined £2000 and put in the Tower.

In *A Remonstrance of Many Thousand Citizens* Overton and Walwyn defended Lilburne and called for abolishing the monarchy and the House of Lords, dissolving the Long Parliament, annual elections, toleration, and eliminating impressment and imprisonment for debt. Lilburne followed with London's *Liberty in Chains Discovered* and in 1647 *Regal Tyranny Discovered*, denouncing London's government and the monarchy. Leveller opposition to Presbyterian plans to disband the army and negotiate the king's return culminated in March with the Large Petition (probably by Walwyn), which reiterated their entire platform. By this time the army was on the verge of mutiny over disbandment and parliament's failure to pay arrears of wages or indemnify soldiers for acts committed during the war. In April and May the cavalry and infantry regiments elected agitators*—some, like Edward Sexby, with Leveller ties—who formed a council to speak for them. Overton, in A *New Found Stratagem*, called for the army to lead the struggle for liberty, and Lilburne remained in contact with the agitators from prison.

The officers or Grandees, including General Fairfax*, Oliver Cromwell*, and Henry Ireton*, temporarily stood with the rank and file. In June Ireton's Leveller-influenced A *Solemn Engagement of the Army* rejected disbandment before redress of grievances and established a council of the army including officers and agitators. But the Levellers wanted no disbandment or accommodation with the king and opposed the Grandees' moderate Heads of the Proposals* in July. Eventually the king rejected the Heads, and the army seized London to protect Independent members of parliament. Though Cromwell visited Lilburne in prison, distrust grew between officers and men. In October the agitators of five regiments signed *The Case of the Army Truly Stated*, the basis of the first Agreement of the People*, which demanded biennial parliaments, proportional representation, popular sovereignty, toleration, freedom from impressment, and equality before the law. The Grandees rejected this at the Putney Debates* in late October and early November, partly because the Levellers wanted to enfranchise all men except servants and recipients of alms. Cromwell broke up the Ware "mutiny"—actually just a meeting of soldiers and agitators—which followed on 15 November. Meanwhile, Lilburne had been released, and Charles I had fled to the Isle of Wight, claiming the Levellers planned to kill him.

The king's recalcitrance drove the Grandees back toward the Levellers in December, but Wildman denounced them in *Putney Projects* and Lilburne in *England's Freedom, Soldiers' Rights*. The Levellers now had an excellent organization in London and a newspaper, *The Moderate*. In January 1648 Lilburne's Earnest Petition made new demands for local elections and abolition of the excise (see Taxation and Revenue*). The Commons soon put him back in the Tower and Wildman in the Fleet, where they remained during the Second Civil War*. Though

Lilburne attacked Cromwell and Ireton as tyrants, he was quiet during the war, and when the Presbyterian-controlled Commons released him in August, he supported Cromwell. After the war, parliamentary Independents' plans to negotiate with Charles again led Grandees to seek Leveller aid. The resulting September Petition reprised the Agreement but omitted mentioning the monarchy or Lords, ignored the franchise, and condemned economic levelling. Regrettably, Colonel Thomas Rainsborough, the best Leveller spokesman in the army, died in the war.

Cromwell consulted the Levellers about the king's fate. Lilburne, among the first to call for Charles's death earlier, now wanted to delay it until a constitutional settlement was arranged. In November Lilburne and Wildman met with Ireton, and though the meeting ended badly, Colonel Thomas Harrison persuaded them, plus Walwyn and Maximillian Petty, to serve on a committee with representatives of the army, London, and parliamentary Independents to revise the Agreement. But in early December the army seized the king, Fairfax occupied London, and Pride's Purge* removed the Presbyterians from parliament; the Grandees no longer needed the Levellers. The second Agreement excluded wage earners from the franchise and allowed for a council of state*, but at the Whitehall debates, the Grandees refused complete religious toleration, and the Levellers withdrew and published their Agreement. The Grandees' version, sent to the Commons in January, was lost in the uproar over Charles's trial and execution*.

The Leveller party, the Grandees and the Rump Parliament* united, appeared dead. But Lilburne returned to the fray in February and March, denouncing the trial without jury of the king and of five peers, the Grandees' suppression of petitions, and the council of state, calling for the Rump's dissolution, annual parliaments, and a democratic council of the army in *England's New Chains Discovered*. Overton also attacked the officers in *The Hunting of the Foxes*. Late in March Lilburne, Overton, Walwyn, and Thomas Prince were arrested. In April the funeral of Roger Lockyer, an ex-agitator executed for mutiny, occasioned a mass pro-Leveller demonstration, and on 1 May the Leveller leaders produced the third Agreement, which made even more radical demands. But in May Fairfax and Cromwell easily suppressed Leveller-inspired mutinies, and the party leaders were subjected to stricter confinement. During the summer Lilburne published *An Impeachment of High Treason Against Oliver Cromwell . . . and Henry Ireton* and in October was charged under the new Treason Act. He was acquitted in a spectacular trial in London's Guildhall, which led to wild demonstrations of joy in the city, and the four leaders were released in November upon taking the oath of loyalty to the government. But this was a final hurrah; the Leveller party was essentially dead.

The Levellers were largely forgotten until the rediscovery of seventeenth-century pamphlet literature in the nineteenth century and the publication of the army debates in the 1890s. Since then, they have been the subject of much research and historiographical controversy, the complexity of which is only hinted at here. The Marxist C. B. Macpherson argues that the Levellers wanted to deny the vote to all wage-earners and believed in the theory of possessive individualism: that a man who alienated his labor (a wage earner) forfeited his birthright and with it his right to vote. Keith Thomas rejects this interpretation, and a number of historians believe that when the Levellers excluded "servants" from the franchise, they meant only those living in their masters' homes. Christopher Hill, following the Soviet historian M. A. Barg, suggests that there was a fundamental split between "Levellers" and "True Levellers," the latter more socially radical group belonging with the Diggers and their like; however, G. E. Aylmer and others question this. Brian Manning notes that the Levellers distrusted both the rich and the poor. The enormous influence on the "English Revolution" accorded the Levellers by Hill and H. N. Brailsford has been toned down in more recent accounts. Mark Kishlansky downplays the extent to which the Levellers directed the radical activity of the New Model Army and denies that all agitators were Levellers. David Underdown suggests that probably only a few Levellers were deeply committed. However, the Levellers remain integral to understanding seventeenth-century political thought*, as R. B. Seaberg points out. And whatever the exact nature of their role, it is clear that from 1646 to 1649 it was an important one.

Bibliography: G. E. Aylmer, ed., *The Levellers in the English Revolution*, 1975; F. D. Dow, *Radicalism in the English Revolution, 1640-1660*, 1985; Howard Shaw, *The Levellers*, 1968.

William B. Robison

Licensing Act (14 Car. II, c. 33, 1662). With the Restoration* the press again came under control of the royal prerogative*. In May 1662 the Licensing Act, following upon the Act of Uniformity (14 Car. II, c. 4), was passed "for preventing the frequent abuses in printing* seditious, treasonable and unlicensed books and pamphlets, and for regulating of printing and printing-presses." It established censorship on the basis of parliamentary authority but also enforced conformity with "the doctrine or discipline of the Church of England" (see Anglicanism*). The number of master printers, other than for the king and the universities*, was reduced to twenty, with none to be admitted except by approval of the archbishop of Canterbury and the bishop of London. No book could be published without a license from a censor appointed, according to subject, by the appropriate civil or ecclesiastical authority, and all were to be registered by the Company of Stationers of London, except acts of parliament, proclamations, and books and papers printed by a warrant under the king's majesty sign manual or from one of the secretaries of state. Printing was restricted to London*, York, Oxford, and Cambridge, and a copy of every new book had to be delivered to the king's library, with copies sent to the vice-chancellors of the two universities. The act was originally only for two years, but renewals carried it to 1679, and it was renewed in 1685 to last until 1695.

It was strictly enforced. However, men still printed pamphlets that the censor would never have passed, and one, John Twynn, was executed for treason. This came about after Roger L'Estrange, surveyor of the imprimery and printing presses, became licenser of the press, took power to search and seize unlicensed printing from the Stationers, and was granted a monopoly of news publications. A few months later

Twynn was arrested for printing *A Treatise of the Execution of Justice Is as Well the People's as the Magistrates*, which allegedly advocated killing the king and overthrowing the government. Twynn had two illegal presses, which he operated secretly at night; he was hung, drawn, and quartered. Soon after, a printer, a bookseller, and a bookbinder were indicted for printing and publishing two books critical of the king and the government, but all were fined and remained in prison during the king's pleasure. By 1666 L'Estrange was out of favor, and his publications were superseded by the *Oxford Gazette*, which was authorized by the lord chamberlain.

Whether censorship succeeded in restraining dissident thought can scarcely be judged, but the system was rigid and enforced by frequent persecutions. When William III* landed in England, his secretary noted that in Exeter, the capital of the west, there was not a press on which he could print a manifesto. The Licensing Act ran out in 1695 and was not renewed. Parliamentary opinion had ceased to regard censorship as a guarantee of public peace. Now authors and publishers had nothing to fear from the censor before publication, but after publication they were exposed to an oppressive libel law. In religious literature this no longer mattered, but political writers were still at the mercy of the government and the judges, without much protection by juries. Soon there were new, if minor, restrictions on liberty of expression (e.g., a 1698 law against denying the divinity of Christ by writing or speaking). Not long afterward, for political reasons, new restrictions were placed on journalists, though not on writers of books, who were subject to a severe libel law. (See also Literature*.)

Bibliography: C. Clair, *A History of Printing in Britain*, 1965; *English Historical Documents, 1660-1714*, 1953.

                                                                     Martin J. Manning

Lilburne, John (1615-1657). Leveller* leader, author of eighty pamphlets, and a master at dramatizing his encounters with "martyrdom." Born at Sunderland, second son of Durham gentleman Richard Lilburne and his wife, Margaret, he was apprenticed in 1630 to a London* cloth dealer. An avid reader of Scripture, theology, history, and law, Lilburne embraced Puritanism, opposed Archbishop William Laud's* Arminianism*, and became acquainted with John Bastwick, Henry Burton, and William Prynne*. Arrested in 1637 for smuggling a Bastwick pamphlet into England, he refused the ex officio oath in Star Chamber (see Prerogative Courts*) and was flogged, pilloried, and imprisoned in the Fleet. In 1638 he began writing pamphlets and by 1639 advocated separation from the Anglican* church.

Oliver Cromwell* persuaded the Long Parliament* to release him in 1640; he became a brewer and married Elizabeth Dewell, with whom he had ten children. Already a popular hero, he demonstrated at Westminster in 1641, served as a parliamentarian* captain at Edgehill* (1642), was captured at Brentford, refused a royalist* bribe to defect, and was exchanged in 1643. Cromwell procured him a major's commission in the Eastern Association, where he quarreled with Colonel

Edward King and the earl of Manchester. A lieutenant-colonel at Marston Moor* (1644), he resigned in 1645, refusing the Solemn League and Covenant*.

Lilburne began illegally printing* anti-Presbyterian pamphlets and, for accusing Commons Speaker William Lenthall of supporting the king, was gaoled in August-October 1645 at Newgate. There he wrote *England's Birth-Right Justified*, hinting at popular sovereignty, insisting on the rule of law, and denouncing lawyers, tithes, and monopolies. Demands that parliament* pay arrears in army* wages and compensate him for injuries, plus criticism of Lords' Speaker Manchester, landed him in Newgate in June-August 1646. His *The Free-man's Freedom Vindicated* denied Lords' jurisdiction, but he was fined £2,000 and moved to the Tower.

There Lilburne denounced London's oligarchy in *London's Liberty in Chains Discovered* (1646), condemned monarchy in *Regal Tyranny Discovered* (1647), criticized parliament's plans for disbanding the New Model Army*, and kept in touch with increasingly mutinous soldiers. He contributed to the first Agreement of the People*, a radical republican constitution published in November 1647 during the Putney Debates*. Bailed, he went to Ware, where Cromwell crushed mutiny in mid-November; afterwards he wrote *England's Freedom, Soldiers' Rights*, claiming the court-martial of mutineers was illegal.

In January 1648 Lilburne's *Earnest Petition* made new demands for election of local officials and abolition of the excise (see Taxation and Revenue*). The Commons returned him to the Tower, where he remained during the Second Civil War*, attacking Cromwell and Henry Ireton* as tyrants. But when the Presbyterian*-controlled Commons released him in August, hoping that he would make trouble for the officers (Commons granted him reparations; Lords dropped its sentence), he pledged to support Cromwell, who consulted the Levellers in November about the constitution. Lilburne, an early proponent of Charles's execution*, now wanted to postpone it until a constitutional settlement could prevent military dictatorship. He and John Wildman failed to reach agreement with Ireton at Windsor but were persuaded by Colonel Thomas Harrison to serve, with William Walwyn and Maximillian Petty, on the committee that produced the second Agreement in December. Unwilling to exclude Catholics* and atheists from toleration, they withdrew on 15 December.

Lilburne refused to sit on the High Court that tried Charles in January 1649 and in February described the trial of five royalist noblemen as illegal. *England's New Chains Discovered* condemned the officers for suppressing petitions, criticized the council of state*, called for annual parliaments, advocated social and economic reform, demanded payment of arrears, and condemned censorship and trials without juries. By March he was urging nonpayment of taxes and, in *The Second Part of England's New Chains Discovered*, called for the Rump Parliament's* dissolution and restoration of a democratic council of the army. Refusing a position in the government, he was charged with high treason and arrested with Overton, Walwyn, and Thomas Prince; at his hearing he denied the council of state's jurisdiction. Lilburne helped draft the third Agreement in May and was subjected to stricter confinement. That summer he wrote *An Impeachment of High Treason Against Oliver Cromwell . . . and Henry Ireton*, following the suppression of mutiny at Burford, and a pamphlet that helped incite a failed insurrection at Oxford. Tried in London's Guildhall in October under a new Treason Act, he was found not guilty, provoking wild celebration. Released, he became a soap boiler.

Lilburne took the Engagement*, the loyalty oath to the new republic, but though legally elected to the London Common Council, was not allowed to take his seat. In 1651 he and Wildman helped organize opposition to fen drainage* at Epworth. In 1652, he was fined £7,000 for defaming Sir Arthur Haselrig and banished under pain of death. In the Netherlands he befriended royalists and was suspected of plotting. In 1653 he returned home, was arrested, tried at the Old Bailey, found not guilty, but kept in prison in the Tower, on Jersey (1654-1655), and at Dover, where he was able to visit his family. After 1653 he produced only one pamphlet. Around 1656 he became a Quaker*. He died on 29 August 1657.

Bibliography: G. E. Aylmer, ed., *The Levellers in the English Revolution*, 1975; Pauline Gregg, *Free-born John: A Biography of John Lilburne*, 1961; Howard Shaw, *The Levellers*, 1968.

William B. Robison

Literature. Between the death of Elizabeth I in 1603 and the accession of William* and Mary* in 1689, England moved unmistakably from the ancient to the modern world. The writing of this period is a rich amalgam of trends and schools, earlier works revisiting social and spiritual themes of the Tudor Renaissance, while later ones consciously imitated classical models and became decidedly topical and political. By 1660, aided in part by the "new science" or empirical study of physical nature championed by Francis Bacon* (1561-1626) and the newly founded Royal Society*, English literature was ready to eschew John Donne's* (1573-1631) self-dramatized struggle for faith in favor of the political engagement and more rational, Latitudinarian* belief conveyed in John Dryden's* (1573-1631) heroic couplets. Poetry of the era began with the Metaphysical school and its devotional adherents, who flourished alongside the more classical Cavalier* (royalist*) poets; Andrew Marvell's (1621-1678) poems later blend both these styles. John Milton* (1608-1673) is the last example of an author proving himself in almost every literary genre popular in the sixteenth century; his prolific tracts on political and religious governance mark him as one of the most skilled of Puritan* propagandists. Jacobean dramatic comedy, especially Ben Jonson's* (1572-1637) masterpieces, satirized city life, and tragedy of this period was an intense exploration of the bizarre and sensational in human nature. After 1660 the comedy confined itself exclusively to social mores and manners, while tragedy depicted heroic figures caught between love and honor. Seventeenth-century prose is among the greatest in the literature, not only in the graphic diaries of Samuel Pepys* (1633-1703) and John Evelyn* (1620-1706) but especially in the stylistically impressive sermons and religious essays of Donne and Thomas Browne (1605-1682) and in John Bunyan's* (1628-1688) fiction.

John Donne's work defined the features of Metaphysical verse. This label, first applied to poetry by Samuel Johnson, conveys its tendency for learned allusions and a tone ranging from the meditative to the argumentative. Donne's "school" rejected Petrarchan conventions of idealized love in favor of a franker sensuality, used conceits (closely reasoned and often arresting metaphors), and favored a colloquially emotional poetic voice. The result is usually more intellectually challenging than lyrically appealing. George Herbert's (1593-1633) devotional poetry (*The Temple*) flows from his quiet life as a selfless parson and lacks Donne's self-consciousness, chronicling the experience of one who believes rather than one who sometimes doubts that he does. Yet he approaches Donne's wittiness in the ingenious structure of "The Pulley" and the metaphors of "Prayer (I)." Henry Vaughan's (1621-1695) verse (*Silex Scintillans*; *Olor Iscanus*) is mystical and abstract, influenced by Herbert and by alchemical and hermetic lore. He strives to capture abstractions normally beyond the reach of words, as in "The World": "I saw eternity the other night/ Like a great ring of pure and endless light." More grotesquely daring than these was Richard Crashaw (c.1613-1649), a Catholic* whose extreme images link him to the European Baroque. His works (*Steps to the Temple*; *Carmen Deo Nostro*) brim with the overcharged language of intense mystical union: "Live here, great heart: and love and die and kill,/And bleed and wound" ("The Flaming Heart").

Unlike the Metaphysicals, the Cavalier poets aimed more for a disciplined clarity than intellectual agility. In keeping with the neoclassical goals and models outlined by Jonson, the "Sons of Ben" fashioned poetry of formal design, regular rhythms and rhyme, restrained and decorous imagery, and a deceptively "artless" tone of urbane, intelligent wit. Robert Herrick (1591-1674) published his *Hesperides* and *Noble Numbers* in 1648, the first a collection of secular lyrics, the second religious. His fusion of nature themes, rural and pagan ritual, and the pastoral mode lend his secular lyrics a delightful blend of indulgence and innocence. His "To the Virgins, to Make Much of Time" is probably the finest *carpe diem* poem in the language. Edmund Waller (1606-1687), Sir John Suckling (1609-1642), and Richard Lovelace (1618-1657) rank at the top of numerous minor lyric poets writing in the Cavalier vein, the last two having died in the king's service. Lovelace's "To Lucasta, Going to the Wars" captures in eleven lines the dilemma of the lover and warrior: "I could not love thee, Dear, so much,/ Loved I not honor more."

Bridging both major poetic currents of the era, Thomas Carew (1595-1640) and Andrew Marvell combined the cognitive richness of the Metaphysicals with the Cavaliers' polished form. Carew, in personal life a wastrel, praised Jonson's dramatic indictment of society ("To Ben Jonson") and composed a prescient appreciation in his "Elegy on the Death of Doctor Donne": Donne "committed holy rapes upon our will" and "ruled as he thought fit/ The universal monarchy of wit." Of greater stature is the Puritan political functionary Marvell, who wrote, notes R. M. Adams, "the most major minor verse in English." His "To His Coy Mistress" is at once a *carpe diem* celebration, syllogistic argument, invitation to love, and meditation on death and time. The "Horatian Ode Upon Cromwell's* Return from Ireland*" praises the lord protector, while crediting Charles I* for meeting death nobly. Marvell's rural poems recall those of Herrick earlier yet possess a richer ambiguity; viewing his garden, the poet's mind keenly appreciates its beauty, "Annihilating all that's made/ To a green thought in a green shade" ("The Garden").

Jacobean and Caroline theater was an extension of the Elizabethan but with a shift of focus and an innovation; traditional comedy became more realistic, tragedy melodramatically macabre, and tragicomedy achieved marked popularity. The growth of more demanding and worldly spectators at such indoor theaters as Blackfriars (in contrast to the rather more heterogeneous audiences at William Shakespeare's* Globe) influenced the drama's new direction. *Michaelmas Term* and *A Trick to Catch the Old One* by Thomas Middleton (c.1570-1627) are boisterous comedies of trickery and connivance, the latter later rewritten adeptly by Philip Massinger (1583-1640) as *A New Way to Pay Old Debts*. Jonson's comedies developed the realism of "city comedies" to a high art. Tragedy evolved into a more unconventional, at times *outré*, form that often indulged in sensationalism for its own sake. The revenge plays (*The Revenger's Tragedy* and *The Atheist's Tragedy*) of Cyril Tourneur (c.1580-1626) portray a world of corruption and vengeance exceeding that of Elsinore. John Webster (c.1580-c.1625) wrote *The White Devil* and *The Duchess of Malfi*, tragedies featuring strong female protagonists enmeshed in historically based plots of intrigue and grisly mayhem, including a severed hand and a poisoned picture that kills when kissed. The plays of John Ford (1586-c.1640) are similarly gruesome; *'Tis a Pity She's a Whore* centers on incest, *The Broken Heart* features a love triangle and suicide, *The Witch of Edmonton* treats of witchcraft and presents a bleeding corpse. Less bizarre in their efforts to hold the interest of audiences, Francis Beaumont (1584-1616) and John Fletcher (1579-1625) developed the romantic tragicomedy. In their *Philaster* and *A King and No King*, and in Fletcher's *Faithful Shepherdess,* fanciful characters set in mythical locales and contrived plots are miraculously rescued at the brink of disaster. Still performed is Beaumont's *Knight of the Burning Pestle*, an entertaining burlesque of the London* bourgeoisie.

The professional stages were closed by order of the Long Parliament* in 1642; when they reopened after the Restoration*, they had lost the rich variety of the Tudor-early Stuart period and gained in its place a comedy focused on the manners of aristocrats and a tragedy that depicted (in formal speeches of heroic couplets) the struggles of heroic personages in both love and war, strongly influenced by the popular operas (such as *The Siege of Rhodes*) of William Davenant (1606-1668). Dryden was a master of the heroic tragedy and discussed it in the essay "Of Historic Plays" (preface to *The Conquest of Granada*, 1672), in which he credits *Henry V* by Roger Boyle, earl of Orrery (1621-1679), with being the first exemplar of the type. The best of Dryden's heroic plays was *All for Love*, a reworking in blank verse of the story of Antony and Cleopatra. Other classical tragedies were Thomas Otway's (1652-1685) *Venice Preserved*, Nat Lee's (c.1653-1692) *Rival Queens*, and *The Rehearsal* by George Villiers*, 2d duke of Buckingham (1628-1687). Restoration comedy, the more highly developed genre, was a witty, cynical satire of those who violated accepted norms of aristocratic social intercourse or who, aspiring to a status beyond their station or an ill-fated romantic liaison, incurred the mockery of others who could as likely be potential gulls. This dramatic art imitated the life of the Restoration court, at which a fascination with sexual intrigue replaced marital fidelity and moral integrity. Chief examples of this comedy of manners were: *The Man of Mode* by Sir George Etherege (c.1631-1694); *The Country Wife* and *The Plain Dealer* by William Wycherley (c.1640-1716); *The Relapse* and *The Provok'd Wife* by Sir John Vanbrugh (1664-1726); *The Way of the World* by William Congreve (1670-1729); and *The Beaux' Stratagem* by George Farquhar (c.1677-1707).

Science* and religion fueled the growth of seventeenth-century prose style. With the works of Francis Bacon, English prose acquired a spare and utilitarian style, adapted to the needs of Bacon's own projected revitalization of knowledge based on empirical principles. In his *Essays*, Bacon achieved a compressed, aphoristic, and memorable vehicle for the expression of trenchant observations: "Reading maketh a full man, conference a ready man, and writing an exact man" ("Of Studies"). This style became the basis for a modern prose whose aim, as summarized in Thomas Sprat's (1635-1713) *History of the Royal Society* (1667), was to deliver "so many *things*, almost in an equal number of *words*." The clarity of later essayists such as Joseph Addison (1672-1719) and Richard Steele (1672-1729) owes much to Baconian prose. However, the very style rejected by the Baconians, displaying what Sprat termed "amplifications, digressions and swellings," was key to the Latinate fullness of the great religious authors of the time. Donne's prose was an early example of this so-called baroque style, marked by elaborate sentence structure, gripping imagery, and frequent rhetorical devices. A more mellifluous baroque prose was that of Thomas Browne, whose *Religio Medici* recorded his personal religious belief and whose *Hydriotaphia, Urn-Burial* ends with a moving disquisition on death: "But man is a noble animal, splendid in ashes, and pompous in the grave, solemnizing nativities and deaths with equal luster, nor omitting ceremonies of bravery in the infamy of his nature." The era held other noteworthy achievements of religious or philosophical prose, such as the devotional tracts *Holy Living* and *Holy Dying* by Jeremy Taylor (1613-1667).

The Authorized or King James version of the Bible* (1611) stands as a monument of influential English prose and a rare tribute to effective committee work. *The Anatomy of Melancholy* of Robert Burton (1577-1640) is a bewilderingly thorough discussion of a condition that fascinated the late Renaissance. *Pilgrim's Progress* by John Bunyan, a mainstay of evangelical piety since its appearance in 1678, charts the allegorical progress of Christian, the Protestant Everyman, through a life of temptation and struggle until he finally reaches the Celestial City.

The diaries of John Evelyn and Samuel Pepys are invaluable eyewitness records of seventeenth-century life. Evelyn's is the more stylistically polished and, though not fully published until 1955, has a formal and precise quality that assumes a wider audience than the diarist himself. Equally as perceptive, yet conveying a much greater sense of his own personality, is Pepys, whose prose is more unpredictable, spontaneous, and honest. Pepys is an observer on whom nothing is lost, who can render the apparently trivial with fascinating detail and the apparently imposing with brutal frankness: "The Queen [Charles I's widow], a very little, plain old woman, and nothing more in her presence in any respect nor garb than any ordinary woman" (22 November 1659) (see Henrietta Maria*). Both diarists left memorable accounts of the Great Fire of London * of 1666.

It is the variety of themes and forms which make seventeenth-century literature so absorbing to a modern reader. The uneasy transition from old world to new, with its concomitant debates on the nature of authority both ancient and modern, raises issues of contemporary relevance on the kinds and validity of knowledge. The greater willingness of writers to reveal the processes of their own inquiries (as in Donne, Browne, or Pepys) opens a way to a key element of postmodern literary theory, the subjectivity of authorship. What Dryden said of Geoffrey Chaucer applies to the seventeenth century as well: "Here is God's plenty."

Bibliography: Douglas Bush, *English Literature in the Earlier Seventeeth Century (1600-1660)*, vol. 5 of *The Oxford History of English Literature*, 1962; James Sutherland, *English Literature of the Late Seventeeth Century*, vol. 6 of *The Oxford History of English Literature*, 1969.

Christopher Baker

Local Government, Counties. The justices of the peace (JPs), magistrates exercising royal authority delegated to them by letters patent, were the very foundation of local government in the counties of Stuart England. Members of the county commission of the peace were chosen by the lord chancellor from among members of the peerage and the armigerous gentry resident in the shire. Except for a handful of clerics who were joined with them in the commission, these knights and esquires were invariably lords of manors and owners of considerable estates. They regarded themselves as the natural leaders of society and constituted an officeholding elite, from which were also drawn the deputy lieutenants, sheriffs*, and higher militia officers, as well as the many other royal commissioners who were appointed from time to time to survey lands, take depositions for Crown courts, oversee sewers, and search out and disarm recusants*. Although JPs were voluntary, unpaid magistrates and often labored under a heavy burden of duties imposed by the privy council*, it was a matter of great pride and not inconsiderable power to be a member of the commission of the peace and an even greater badge of respect to be "of the quorum." The latter had originally been designated by the lord chancellor because of their specialized legal knowledge, but by the seventeenth century the distinction had become purely honorific. Conversely, a gentleman's status was much diminished if he was left out of or dropped from the commission of the peace. The JPs were the heads of what came to be called "county families," and only those who belonged to these local elites might aspire to represent their county communities in parliament*.

Although the source of their legal authority derived from commissions periodically issued by the Crown, the power of the JPs derived from their standing in the local community and their great wealth, together with their affinities and alliances. Consequently there was always the danger that the JPs might grow too independent. They were supervised in their judicial capacities by assize judges who rode out on circuit twice a year (see Common Law and Courts*). The lord chancellor or sometimes the king, being present in the court of Star Chamber (see Prerogative Courts*), would deliver charges to the assembled JPs, which would be repeated at the quarter sessions, county courts convened under royal authority four times a year in the principal county towns. Although appointed by the lord chancellor, the JPs were initially nominated by a local magnate who was usually the lord lieutenant* or a member of the privy council. By regulating the flow of patronage through these officials, the Crown could exercise a degree of control over county magistrates, but a person of standing could not be permanently excluded from the commission of the peace. Indeed an uneven or interrupted flow of patronage could hamper county government by promoting factionalism.

The issuance of the Book of Orders* in January 1631 marked an attempt by Charles I's* government to increase the regulation of local government by the privy council. Although the Book of Orders codified practices and procedures that had been followed in matters of Poor Law* administration, punishment of vagrancy, and regulation of food distribution since the late Elizabethan period, the degree of supervision of the work of the JPs that resulted increasingly standardized magisterial practice and multiplied the administrative duties of the justices. This reform of the magistracy and the tightening of centralized control over local government was prompted by the fear of widespread popular disorder—an official view to some extent justified by the food riots, forest uprisings, and fen disturbances that clustered around the crises of 1629-1630 and the agricultural improvements of that period (see Agriculture*; Fen Drainage*; Forest Laws*).

The Book of Orders was one of a number of privy council directives and parliamentary statutes that transformed the JPs into administrators as well as judges. Originally most of the collective work of the justices was done in the quarter sessions, which by law were required to meet for a minimum of three days at each session. The Book of Orders obliged the JPs in each hundred or other division of the county to meet monthly in petty sessions to deal with Poor Law matters, vagrancy, and the like, in addition to the quarterly meetings. Thereafter the quarter sessions dealt mostly with judicial matters—primarily misdemeanors and simple felonies such as grand larceny, with the more complicated felonies reserved for the assizes. At the assizes, the county jails were delivered of felons for trial, and appeals were heard from the quarter sessions. Here the work of the JPs was subjected to supervisory review by the justices of assize, who instructed the JPs in legal matters. At both the quarter sessions and the assizes, the grand jury presented offenses and returned indictments, and petty juries were impaneled for trials.

The role of the lord lieutenant was at first primarily military. Under the Tudors this official attended to the raising, training, and command of the county-trained bands. He was also empowered to appoint provost marshals in order to preserve discipline during county musters and to sweep up vagrants. During the seventeenth century, the lord lieutenant also came to exercise an important supervisory role as the king's personal representative and a member of the privy council, although most of the actual work was performed by deputy lieutenants since the lieutenant was often absent from the county. At the Restoration* the lords lieutenant, who were drawn from courtier circles, reemerged with greatly enhanced powers.

The Civil War* dissolved much of this centralized control, and the Militia Ordinance of 1642 (see Army*) enabled parliamentarians* to take over the lieutenancy and the command of the militia. County committees emerged from the deputy lieutenancies in areas controlled by parliament to oversee the work of JPs, to levy taxes, and to coordinate the war effort (see County Associations*). The war years severely disrupted local government, and in many counties the assizes, quarter, and petty sessions did not sit for several years. Purges of royalists or their refusal to serve the new regime left the county commissions short of magistrates. One important change in local government was the presence on county committees of small gentry, who had not been part of the officeholding elite before the war. These men had proved their worth during the war years, but their presence greatly offended the old elites. Although the Protectorate* government made an effort to reconcile political opponents to the new regime, the presence of troops and revenue officers in the localities, together with more interference from Westminster than the late king had ever contemplated, sabotaged attempts at reconciliation. Altogether the Civil War and Interregnum* had a very divisive effect upon county government.

At the Restoration of Charles II*, the Crown purged the commissions of the peace once again, but the reconstitution of the commissions did not simply restore the elites of prewar years, since some of the newer magistrates were retained. During the Exclusion Crisis* (1678-1681) and the reign of James II*, the key to retention of local office was undoubted loyalty to the regime, and frequent purges of the commission of the peace signified an unprecedented degree of royal interference and promoted party strife. The government reconstituted the corporations of parliamentary boroughs and appointed sheriffs, an office that had been declining in importance, with a view to manipulating parliamentary elections and the selection of juries. James II carried out further purges and appointed Catholics* to the lieutenancy and the commission of the peace. In some areas Charles II and James II also commissioned military and naval officers as JPs (see Navy*). The continuity of local government was disrupted to the point where it began to break down, and this royal interference was a major cause of the Glorious Revolution* of 1688. The revolution settlement left the local oligarchies once again in control of county government and free to pursue their own interests in matters such as the enforcement of the game laws and the Poor Law.

Bibliography: Thomas G. Barnes, *Somerset, 1625-1640: A County's Government during the "Personal Rule,"* 1961; Andrew M. Coleby, *Central Government and the Localities: Hampshire, 1649-1689,* 1987.

Roger B. Manning

Local Government, Towns. In contrast to the continental pattern, the vast majority of the 650 to 700 towns in Stuart England were very small, and only London*, England's one true metropolis, ranked with Europe's great cities. A handful of regional centers, including Norwich, Bristol, York, Exeter, and Newcastle, formed a second rank, none of which boasted as much as a tenth of London's 200,000 population at the turn of the seventeenth century. The vast majority of the rest were literally of the common market variety, with anywhere from 700 to 3,500 inhabitants and governed by relatively few officials and institutions.

England's towns experienced far less uniformity in governing structures than did its shires. Indeed one might almost say that no two were governed exactly alike, although the vast majority fit more or less into one of a few common patterns. Save for London, which was unique in many respects, almost all Stuart towns were governed by a charter of incorporation granted on petition by the Crown, the authority of a manorial government, or a combination of the two. In addition to their essential format, however, virtually all town governments were enhanced by myriad local customs. Furthermore, the form of government seems to have had no necessary correlation with the size or influence of the community (London itself, for example, remained unincorporated at the turn of the century) or with its possession of a parliamentary franchise.

Incorporation conferred on the town the legal status of a corporate body. It conveyed the rights to have a common seal, to hold land in mortmain, to implead and be impleaded against in the courts of law, to make bylaws, and to enjoy perpetual succession. In addition it usually described a governing structure, addressed the question of selection for office, defined the town's relationship with external authorities, and recognized a variety of privileges, which could run from holding fairs and markets to sending members to parliament*. Many such charters were largely descriptive rather than prescriptive: they confirmed and formalized existing conditions more than they created new ones.

Atop the political structure of most corporate towns sat the mayor. Though he served for but a year's term and could rarely succeed himself immediately, his powers had often become considerable at the turn of the century. They commonly included, inter alia, the roles of coroner, clerk of the market, and magistrate in the town courts; the power to appoint many other officials; and the responsibility to carry out the law of the land in his own jurisdiction without interference from officials of the manor or shire. In that handful of cases in which particularly important towns received the status of counties, the mayor's role grew even weightier, assuming the functions of, for example, justice of the peace and sheriff* (see Local Government, Counties*).

Assisting the mayor were a smallish inner council (variously styled "the aldermanic bench," "the capital burgesses," "the twelve," etc.), a larger outer council ("the common council," "the twenty-four," etc.), two chamberlains, a town clerk, a recorder, and numerous lesser officials ranging from the constables on down to the town scavenger. The councils were advisory and legislative bodies that usually held some electoral role as well. Their ranks were replenished by election or (with increasing frequency) by co-option from the membership of the lesser council or the freemanry at large, and increasingly they came to enjoy the nomination and even the selection of the mayoral incumbent.

The town clerk, who could serve indefinitely, presided over the paperwork of local government. His efforts in keeping minutes of the town courts and assemblies, where these have survived, tell us much of what we may discover about the governance of specific towns. The chamberlains, selected yearly, bore responsibility for the town's finances, kept accounts (another very valuable archival source), and gave annual reckonings. The recorder served as legal counsel and often represented the town's interests in the shire, the central courts, or the royal court. Among all town officials, the recorder alone required some formal legal training and often resided outside the community.

Even by about 1700 nonincorporated communities remained in the slight majority of all English towns. They were, at least in theory, governed by the lord of the manor, usually through his bailiff. The central institution here was usually the leet court, in which matters relating to the government of the town and the lord's interest in that government were heard, determined, and recorded.

In reality most towns by about 1600 had long since established detailed customs and at least some institutions and officials that derived from the community itself. These shared a degree of governing authority with the manorial officials. They could consist merely of a jury of townsmen in the leet court who spoke for the interests of the townsmen, though they might be rooted as well in institutions, which were altogether separate. The gild merchant, which exercised authority over numerous economic functions; the parish vestry, which came to exercise authority over poor relief (see Poor Laws and Poverty*) and other social issues; and the charitable trust, whose authority over social or educational institutions often extended into more general aspects of local government, all exemplify such institutions.

Such was the overlap in functions between manorial and community-based institutions that (as had long been the case) conflict often arose between them. Frequently the petition by local citizens for incorporation arose precisely from such conflict, though litigation provided an alternative recourse.

Despite such conflict many communities seemed content not to incorporate. Lewes, for example, proceeded quite happily with an unincorporated body of local leaders called "the Twelve," and the government of Peterborough long functioned with a similar combination of manorial authority and the leadership of a local trust. Such bodies may have lacked the full rights of a corporate charter, but in practical terms they could be just as well run and could leave scope for considerable self-direction.

If we look at the governance of Stuart towns as a whole, some general tendencies stand out. One was the growth of more oligarchic rule, which was especially pronounced in corporate towns. Indeed incorporation itself seems often to have facilitated the tendency toward oligarchy. Many charters even named the first officials of the new corporation. These were almost always the leading townsmen who would have petitioned for the incorporation to begin with, and incorporation considerably enhanced their authority over their fellows.

We should not assume that oligarchy was necessarily an unwelcome characteristic of government. Especially in the early years of the century, townsmen often appreciated the willingness of the wealthy few to undertake the growing expenses of government and to apply their influence and expertise to the solution of local problems. For its part the Crown, always interested in authority and order in local society, had long found this an attractive reason to grant such authority.

Yet in practical terms, the growth of oligarchy often meant the growth of self-selection among higher officials, the declining electoral role of the freemanry, and a diminished sense of responsibility by the governors toward the governed. In time, these trends grew commonly to be resented by the lesser freemen of many towns and formed the basis of factional strife, contested elections, and occasional violence. During the unrest and instability of the Civil War* and Interregnum* many towns saw such strife linked to regional and national allegiances. Yet though freemen successfully broadened popular participation in some communities, few town governments witnessed particularly sweeping or enduring revolutions in structure, and in many communities oligarchy remained undiminished in 1660.

This strength of this authority and the threat it continued to represent to the Crown led the later Stuarts to try to clip the wings of the numerous urban corporations. It did so principally by reviving the writ of *quo warranto*, challenging the authority of recipient towns and causing them to surrender their charters. These were then replaced with instruments of government providing less autonomy and a greater opportunity for royal influence in local affairs by 1688.

Bibliography: Peter Clark and Paul Slack, eds., *Crisis and Order in English Towns*, 1972; Peter Clark and Paul Slack, *English Towns in Transition*, 1976.

Robert Tittler

Locke, John (1632-1704). Locke's father was a landowner and attorney. His religious beliefs were Puritan*, and he fought with the army* of parliament* during the Civil Wars*. John Locke was educated at Christ Church, Oxford, beginning in 1652; he took his Master's degree in 1658. Not satisfied with his education, he read much on his own, particularly enjoying the ideas of Descartes. Locke became a lecturer at Oxford after finishing his degree. He had a love affair at Oxford, which took away "the use of my reason," but he lost the lady and never married.

Locke took up the practice of medicine* and worked with Robert Boyle (see Science and the Scientific Revolution*). In the 1660s he became the personal physician to Anthony Ashley Cooper*, first earl of Shaftesbury, saving Cooper's life in 1668 with surgery on a tumor. He also acted as tutor to Cooper's son and grandson. In 1683 he fled to Holland as a political exile because of his liberal ideas and his association with Cooper. After Monmouth's Rebellion* in 1685, Locke was one of eighty-five men whom James II* named as conspirators in the revolt; the king offered him a pardon the next year. In 1689 he returned to England with Queen Mary II* and held some government positions during the reign of William III*. The most important of these was commissioner with the board of trade* and plantations* from 1696 to 1700. Retiring from this post because of sickness, Locke died in October 1704.

Locke's significant writings were in three general areas: psychology, religion, and government. He dealt with the doctrine of the mind and free will in *An Essay Concerning Human Understanding* (1690 and 1700). The human mind is empty or blank (*tabula rasa*) at birth, and all knowledge comes from the senses. Sensations are stored in the memory, and ideas are generated out of this memory. Man's mind does not possess free will in the simple and broad meaning of the term, but Locke believed that reason determines the will.

Religion was important in Locke's life, and he considered entering that profession. He was not orthodox, however, preferring a simple faith without the decoration of church doctrine. He wrote three versions of *The Reasonableness of Christianity as*

Delivered in the Scriptures (1695 and 1697), and he wrote several other religious discourses, which were published after his death. In his four *Letters Concerning Toleration* (1689-1706), he advocated religious freedom for the Protestant denominations. No church should be allowed to compel adherence, and religious persecution should not be allowed.

Locke's major philosophical contribution was in the field of government. The rather short *Two Treatises of Government* outlined his philosophy of government, and *The Fundamental Constitutions of Carolina* (1720) institutionalized the principles. Early commentators believed that the treatises were written after the Glorious Revolution* of 1688, but actually they were written in or before 1683 and published with some additions in 1690. The first treatise was an attack on Sir Robert Filmer's *Patriarcha* (1680), and the second was an attack on Thomas Hobbes's* *Leviathan* (1651).

The first premise of Locke's theory of government was an ideal "state of nature," which may or may not have actually existed. In this state, man possessed the natural rights of life, liberty, and property, but each individual had to protect his own rights. For better protection Locke thought that citizens, by unanimous consent, formed government, whose sole purpose was to protect natural rights. The legislative power in the government was the strongest, and it was the only organ that could make law. It was to make law only for the public good of society, and legislation must conform to the laws of nature. The executive power was to execute the laws made by the legislative. Thus Locke proffered the idea of separation of powers. He did not demand that the executive be a king, but he preferred and presumed that. Citizens' ultimate protection of themselves and their natural rights was laid out in Locke's right of revolution. If the government did not carry out its obligation of protecting individuals' natural rights or if government violated natural rights, then citizens would exercise their right of revolution.

Although currently Locke's philosophy is assumed to justify the revolution of 1688 and the American Revolution in the eighteenth century, it was not accepted by the contemporary supporters of 1688. The unhistorical approach of the two treatises made them suspect and irrelevant to the seventeenth-century situation, and some of Locke's ideas alarmed thinkers and leaders of the time. During Queen Anne's* reign, Locke was particularly out of favor. (See also Historical Thought*; Political Thought*).

Bibliography: Maurice W. Cranston, *John Locke, A Biography*, 1957.

W. Calvin Dickinson

London. Throughout the seventeenth century, London stood apart from all other urban communities of the realm in virtually every respect. Not only was it the only true metropolis in the British Isles, but its size made it unique in type and function. Already ten times the size of the next largest English community in about 1600 with about 200,000 inhabitants, London grew to very nearly half a million souls in the course of the seventeenth century. By about 1700 it surpassed the size of its nearest

English rival by some fifteen times and had pulled to a tie with Paris for second place (behind Constantinople) among European cities.

In topographical terms, the opening of the century saw most of London still largely contained within or immediately to the north of the old City wall, with some developments farther to the west toward Westminster and Holborn; to the east, especially along the river front and main roads to Essex; and across the Thames to the south from Bermondsey to Lambeth.

The early decades of the century saw the aristocracy and others of the better sort beginning to develop residential areas to the north and west, especially around Lincoln's Inn Fields, Long Acre, Covent Garden, and other approaches to Westminster. These years saw the introduction of Italianate style, chiefly by Inigo Jones, in such projects as the Whitehall Banqueting House (1619-1622) and both Covent Garden and Lindsey House on Lincoln's Inn Fields (c.1630s).

While these innovations came to a halt during the turmoil of the Civil War* and Interregnum*, they resumed quickly at the Restoration*. Supported again by aristocratic patronage and royal encouragement, developers in this era perfected the residential square, which so typifies the grace and refinement of the West End. Beginning with Bloomsbury Square (from 1661) this activity continued after the Great Fire of London* with St. James and King (now Soho) Square, among others, by the end of the century.

On the opposite ends of both the metropolis and the social scale, the pre-fire years saw substantial development of workers' housing in the East End districts of, for example, Shadwell, Spitalfields, Wapping, Limehouse, and—across the River Thames—Southwark and Bermondsey. Additional development in Spitalfields (especially by Huguenot refugees after 1685) and new development in such areas as Whitechapel, Mile End, Bethnal Green, and Stepney followed in the latter decades of the century.

The most pivotal topographical event was the Great Fire of 1666. Starting at the end of a hot, dry summer in Pudding Lane near the Tower, it spread west and north for four days, destroying in its wake the vast majority of medieval and Tudor London: St. Paul's Cathedral, the Guildhall, eighty-nine churches, and some 13,200 houses. The difficult task of rebuilding, supervised by Charles II* and guided by the brilliant hand of Christopher Wren, respected ancient property lines and proceeded so swiftly as to replace almost all housing by 1677. Churches and other public buildings, many designed by Wren himself in an essentially Palladian mode, took longer.

Much of London's staggering growth and functional importance derived from the almost unique circumstance of serving as both the national center for commercial activities and in effect the center of the national government. London's commercial foundations lay with its overwhelming and historic dominance of the English wool and woolen cloth trade*. By the seventeenth century, it had become the center for finance, luxury items, professional services, foreign trade*, dramatic and other entertainments, shipbuilding, and a myriad of small, workshop-focused industries. These activities made it an unrivaled magnet for those seeking jobs, training, spouses, entertainment, consumer goods, and professional services and also for those seeking refuge from persecution abroad.

London's political importance contributed greatly to its economic life. As the residential base for those involved at Westminster, it catered to a great many highly trained, wealthy, and influential people. Many of them took second residences in the area, and most consumed specialized goods and services. In this way, the profits of government office wound up in the City's economy.

London's population also included many who were destitute. The problems of London's poor were frequently compounded by the epidemic diseases, plague, and influenza (see Epidemics and Plague*) among them, which spread so easily in such a densely settled area. Plagues of 1603, 1625, and 1665 were especially acute, though the 1665 epidemic proved London's last (see London, Plague of*). London's response to poverty and disease consisted of a vigorous and complex effort by agencies both public and private. Nevertheless, the problem of poverty remained chronic throughout the period, resulting in poor health and housing and a constantly high mortality rate (see Poor Law and Poverty*).

By 1600 London's governing structure had evolved to such complexity as to be fully described only in our own time, most notably by Valerie Pearl. Its three most puissant bodies: the court of the lord mayor and aldermen, the court of common council, and the court of common hall, lay in sometimes uneasy interaction at the topmost echelon. The first served roughly as an executive, the second as a consultative and legislative assembly, and the third as an electoral body. Together they formed a porous sort of oligarchy, dominated by senior members of the twelve great livery companies, guilds, and especially by the great merchants of the Levant trade. In addition those companies and guilds themselves enjoyed particular jurisdictions over some activities and areas. The governing structure extended down to the level of the parish, neighborhood, and ward, theoretically providing both an abundant opportunity and an established sequence for holding office.

The political tensions of the nation expressed after the calling of the Long Parliament* were keenly felt in London. The traditional hegemony of the livery companies and greater guilds, and especially of the Levant merchants, came under sustained attack by merchants of somewhat lesser standing and more radical politics. In the winter of 1641-1642 these challengers, led especially by those in the colonial trades, broke the grip of the standing aldermanic oligarchy. They created a committee of public safety, significantly curtailed the powers of the mayor and alderman, and vied for control of the City with other nontraditional factions, chiefly on the parliamentary side, throughout the Civil War period. In so doing they opened the door to a variety of more popular and radical groups, including Levellers* and numerous religious sects. Some of these remained active throughout the period and in some cases well beyond the Interregnum and Restoration. During the Commonwealth* the emphasis of London's merchant leadership on an active government support for trade proved a compelling influence on national policy, both foreign and domestic.

Though the Restoration effectively restored to power many greater merchants of the sort who had governed prior to 1641, it also recognized a far wider participation in City government than had applied before that time. The electoral franchise for shrieval, aldermanic, and other offices, as well as for parliament, broadened considerably, while the general and often radically inclined citizenry remained more politically aware and active than ever before. This may be seen in the wide support for radical, pro-Exclusionist candidates in City elections of 1679 and 1680 (see Exclusion Crisis*), in the formation of more than two dozen broadly based political clubs by about 1685, and in the popular activism of "the crowd," which numbered in the tens of thousands by 1689.

Though Charles II's vigorous counterattack on London's popular radicalism succeeded in regaining considerable royalist* control in 1682, his measures were rescinded early in 1689. London thus quickly regained its considerable political autonomy and with it the tradition of popular radicalism that had been forged in mid-century.

For all these apparent threats to its stability, the century's end found London the greatest city of Europe west of Constantinople. Largely rebuilt, graced on its west side with residential squares, an abundance of churches, and a considerably uniform architectural elegance, it also held the busiest dockland, handled an unrivaled volume of trade, hosted the national government, and lay poised to assume its role as the center of the British Empire.

Bibliography: A. L. Beier and R. Finlay, eds., *London, 1500-1700: The Making of the Metropolis*, 1986; Valerie Pearl, *London and the Outbreak of the Puritan Revolution*, 1961; Lawrence Stone, "The Residential Development of the West End of London in the Seventeenth Century," in B. Malament, ed., *After the Reformation*, 1980.

Robert Tittler

London, Fire of (1666). Pre-fire London* was a disaster waiting to happen. Buildings were of timber-frame construction on stone or brick foundations. Walls were of wooden laths and plaster. The steep-gabled, red-tile roofs were waterproofed with pitch. Upper stories jutted out beyond the foundations, overhanging the narrow streets. Party walls were supposed to be made of stone or brick but seldom were. Although earlier legislation promoted brick construction, brick was little used within the City walls, where older law and custom favored rebuilding from salvaged materials.

The Great Fire broke out early Sunday morning, 2 September 1666, in Farriner's baking shop, Pudding Lane (modern EC3). It was seriously out of control by daybreak. Some proposed pulling down houses lying beyond the flames to confine the fire but the lord mayor resisted because by City law, the person who destroyed another's house was required to rebuild it. It was past noon when houses started being pulled down by royal decree. Seamen proposed blowing up houses with gunpowder, but that was not done until Tuesday, when Charles II* and the duke of York (see James II*) rode the fire's perimeter, ordering the houses blown and watching to see it done. By then half the City was already destroyed.

Ultimately 373 acres out of the 458 acres within the walls was consumed, along with sixty-three acres outside the walls. From the Tower of London on the east to

Temple Bar, from the Barbican north to the Thames and London Bridge, Shakespeare's* London was destroyed. The surveyors estimated 13,200 houses destroyed and eighty-nine parish churches burned, along with St. Paul's Cathedral and all the stationers' book stocks. The overall loss to householders was estimated at roughly £6 million. Popular opinion blamed foreigners and Catholics* for the fire; a Frenchman, Robert Hubert, confessed to setting it and was hanged.

The Joiners, Masons, Plasterers, Plumbers, and Turners all lost their guildhalls; the Bricklayers and the Carpenters were spared. The Royal Exchange was destroyed, as was Lombard Street, the center of London finance. But the Exchange regrouped at Gresham College, as did the city government, and the Lombard Street merchants managed to remove their money and securities, so there was no financial panic. Within a week the city government was directing the cleanup.

On 13 September a royal proclamation called for an overall plan for rebuilding, prescribing brick or stone construction. Christopher Wren, John Evelyn*, and Robert Hooke all drew up plans; however, none was adopted, and rebuilding proceeded slowly. Wren, eventually appointed surveyor-general of His Majesty's works, designed the Custom House, Temple Bar, and many churches, including the new St. Paul's with its famous dome.

In February 1667 parliament* instituted the court of fire judges to adjudicate landlord-tenant disputes. The fire court overruled all contracts and substituted an equitable settlement between the parties that would get the destroyed buildings rebuilt as soon as possible. The landlord who was capable of rebuilding was allowed increased rents; the tenant who rebuilt received a longer lease and reduced rents. The extraordinary powers of the fire court encouraged negotiated settlements.

Accompanying this statute was the Rebuilding Act. Intended to make another Great Fire impossible, it instituted London's first comprehensive building code. It also abrogated the craft guilds' labor and contracting monopolies, inviting building craft workers into the City to work under the same conditions as freemen for seven years. Judges of the King's Bench (see Common Law and Courts*) were empowered to fix wages for the building trades and prices for building materials and their transport; this was done in conference with the guildsmen. In May 1667 the city surveyors, headed by Robert Hooke, staked out the first plots for house building under the act.

Bibliography: Walter George Bell, *The Great Fire of London in 1666*, 1920; T. F. Reddaway, *The Rebuilding of London After the Great Fire*, 1951.

Mark Heumann

London, Plague of (1665). Bubonic plague was a fact of seventeenth-century life (see Epidemics and Plague*). Over 33,000 died in London* in 1603, over 41,000 in 1625. However, since 1647 plague deaths had been very few, and the old pesthouses, where the infected were "hospitalized," had been converted to other uses. In 1664 there were many doctors who had never seen a case of plague, with its characteristic bubo, the hard, dark, swollen lymphatic node in the groin, armpit, or neck.

The plague proper began in March 1665 in the parish St. Giles-in-the-Fields. The London outparishes, St. Giles included, housed the poor, four to six families per tenement building, and sanitation was primitive. By mid-May the epidemic was fully recognized. Neglected sanitation regulations started being enforced and houses were fumigated, but to little effect. Houses suspected of plague were quarantined, the inhabitants locked inside, and a red cross painted on the door. The practice was much resented and sometimes provoked riots.

The Royal College of Physicians* issued directions for compounding medicines, and it recommended public health measures: fumigation, sanitation and waste disposal, removal of slaughterhouses, relief and work for the poor, the use of quicklime in burials, and restrictions on travel, assemblies, begging, and the sale of tainted food. The college also paid to dispense medicines to poor people sequestered in infected houses. As the plague worsened, the physicians were commissioned to find a cure (see Medicine*).

Five pesthouses were erected, over the protests of local residents in some cases. The "plague-nurses," ill paid by the parish to care for the stricken, were universally feared and suspected of murdering and plundering their charges. Plague orders issued on 5 July evicted lodgers; banned street vendors, vagrants, and beggars; limited public recreation; closed schools and law courts; and required the killing of dogs and cats and the removal of their bodies.

From mid-June the well-to-do generally began evacuating. Parliament* had been prorogued since March. The Royal Society* suspended its meetings at Gresham College at the end of June. On 6 July the king proclaimed a day of fast and humiliation and called for collections to relieve sufferers. Then he removed to Hampton Court, where the privy council*—headed by George Monck*, duke of Albemarle—appointed nine justices of the peace to govern the outparishes. Three of them actually stayed the course of the plague, as did the lord mayor, the earl of Craven, who opened his townhouse to plague victims, and the former general Monck, who supervised the western outparishes purely through his personal authority. Many Nonconformist ministers stayed to care for the sick, and some physicians stayed to treat the poor free of charge.

As the plague worked its way west to east across the city, Samuel Pepys* observed corpses lying unburied and "night-bearers" carrying away the dead in daylight. At the peak in mid-September, the weekly death toll was officially above 7,000; however, the bills of mortality, issued weekly since 1603, consistently underreported plague deaths, and the actual toll may have been twice that. As the plague declined in October, merchants and tradesmen reoccupied empty houses; this caused an increase in deaths during the first week of November. With the sharp frost in late November, the plague waned rapidly and was over by the end of December.

Out of a population of 460,000 to 480,000, as many as 110,000 Londoners died, one quarter or more of the permanent resident population. Roughly forty percent of the victims were in the outparishes. The poor suffered most.

Bibliography: Walter George Bell, *The Great Plague in London in 1665*, 1924; J. D. F. Shrewsbury, *A History of the Bubonic Plague in the British Isles*, 1970.

Mark Heumann

London, Treaty of (1604). The hostilities that had begun between Spain and England as long ago as 1568 when the Spanish, largely for religious reasons, had expelled Dr. John Man from his embassy at Madrid came to an end in 1604. For England, with a new king and an already straitened budget, at least some rapprochement was highly desirable.

The preceding war had been largely a war by proxies. The Spanish succored the rebellious Irish, and the English were unabashed in their support for the Dutch rebels of Spain. When direct confrontation occurred, as with the 1588 Armada or on the Spanish Main, it was a remote naval contest. For the English this evolved into a reasonable lucrative piratical tradition that left the nonconfrontational Elizabeth secure in her illusions of staying above the fray.

James I* dreamed other dreams. He saw himself as the Solomon of Europe, who would midwife lasting peace throughout the Continent. It had to begin with the throne that he had just inherited. Thus after a substantial foreign policy brawl in England, the pro-Spanish advocates led by Robert Cecil* bested the pro-French forces led by Lord Cobham and Sir Walter Raleigh*. It was not so much that Cecil loved the Spanish; rather, he pragmatically realized that a bankrupt England and increasingly untrustworthy Dutch allies left England remarkably little choice.

The first contacts came through the Count d'Aremberg, minister in the Spanish Netherlands, who arrived to congratulate the new king of England on his accession. At first his proposals were checked by French schemes, but largely through Cecil's machinations, Aremberg subsequently had timely contact with James. Combined with the liberal and official distribution of the Spanish gold among James's counselors, this led to peace.

The Treaty of London took effect on 8 August 1604. Some of the sorest points between the two nations were circumvented, such as access to the Spanish colonies in the New World, English involvement in the Low Countries, and the English treatment of domestic Catholics*. But much was gained. For example, hostilities ceased. Moreover, Spain opened the Spanish Netherlands and the Iberian peninsula to English commerce, and—de facto—the British trade* became much easier into the Mediterranean besides. English traders were not to be molested for their religion, provided they maintained a certain discretion. James had already suspended the letters of marque authorizing privateering raids—in fact this was the signal that negotiations were possible—and promised as well to resist aiding the Dutch rebels. But the English-held cautionary towns (Flushing, Brille, and Rammekens) were not surrendered, and a complete abandonment of the Dutch cause was not promised (the Dutch could still recruit "volunteers" for service in the Low Countries, and a similar promise to Spain meant little).

It was the duke de Frias, constable of Castille, who finally brought the ratification to England. After a duly magnificent signing in James's private chapel in London* and continuing notable Spanish liberality (over 200,000 crowns in jewels alone were distributed), James reciprocated the gesture. His choice to lead the return embassy was the lord high admiral, Charles Howard, the earl of Nottingham. The entourage was large, the generosity was comparable to the Spaniard's own, and Nottingham effected the oath taking on 27 May 1605 in Madrid. For the first time in thirty-five years, the two counties exchanged resident ambassadors. In fact relations became so immediately improved that the earliest discussions of a possible Stuart-Habsburg marriage alliance began (see Spanish Match*).

Bibliography: P. M. Handover, *The Second Cecil, 1563-1604*, 1959; Robert W. Kenny, "Peace with Spain, 1605," *History Today* 20 (1970): 198-208; J. D. Mackie, "James VI and I and the Peace with Spain, 1604," *The Scottish Historical Review* 23 (1925-1926): 241-249

Gary M. Bell

Long Parliament. Convened at Westminster on 3 November 1640 in the aftermath of Charles I's* military defeat by the Covenanters* at Newbury (30 August 1640), which had left a Scottish army in occupation of the north of England. The king had been reluctant to call a new parliament* and did so only when oppositional groups in England (particularly the reformist aristocratic circle centered on the earls of Bedford and Warwick and John Pym*) had forced his hand. From the outset, the reformists took the lead, initiating an attack on the leading "evil counselors" of the years of the king's Personal Rule* (1629-1640) and seeking thorough changes in secular and ecclesiastical policy. Coordinating their attack in both houses, their prime targets (who became in turn the scapegoats for the unpopular polices of the Personal Rule) were the archbishop of Canterbury, William Laud*, and the lord lieutenant of Ireland*, Thomas Wentworth*, the earl of Strafford, who was attainted of treason and executed (12 May 1641).

The first session of the parliament (November 1640-September 1641) effected a major redefinition of the relation between the royal prerogative* and the liberties of the subject. Regular parliaments were provided for the future by the Triennial Act of 16 February 1641 (16 Car. I, c. 1); the prerogative courts* of Star Chamber and High Commission were abolished (16 Car. I, c. 10 and 11); liturgical and doctrinal innovations favored during the 1630s were proscribed. But the "reformation of counsel" around the king proved far more intractable. Token appointments by the king of oppositional figures in May 1641—including Viscount Saye and Sele (William Fiennes*) and Oliver St John—did not disguise Charles's continuing distrust of the reformist party. In parliament doubts that the king would ever be reconciled to reform were exacerbated by his complicity in the series of army plots* against the parliament (March-July 1641).

The king, however, was not without friends. During the first session (November 1640-September 1641) the evident collusion between the reformers and the Scottish Covenanter leadership (still maintaining its army of occupation in the north) made them vulnerable to the charge that they were the cat's paws of the Scots, and the spring and summer of 1641 saw the gradual emergence of a "king's party" in the two houses—an alliance of constitutional royalists* (principal among them Sir John Culpeper and Edward Hyde*) apprehensive that the triumph of "Pym's junto" would install in power a doctrinaire Puritan* clique. The king's position was greatly strengthened by the completion of a treaty with the Scots (the Treaty of London, August 1641), and the subsequent withdrawal of the Covenanter army. By the end of August, there was a widespread expectation that the king would dissolve the parliament, notwithstanding an act of May 1641 prohibiting its dissolution without its own consent (16 Car. I, c. 7).

But the possibility of a dissolution was foreclosed in October by news of the outbreak of a Catholic* Irish Rebellion* (provoked in part by the Westminster parliament's assertion of legislative supremacy over Ireland), necessitating the continuance of the parliament to sanction taxation* and the raising of troops to suppress the revolt. Against a background of sharp dissension as to whether a commander nominated by the king or by parliament should have control of the forces raised for service in Ireland and increasing disorder in the capital (largely directed against the bishops who had been the mainstay of the king's party in the Lords), Charles attempted to cow his parliamentary opponents by the arrest of five members* of the Commons and Viscount Mandeville from the Lords (4 January 1642). This "violence against the parliament" further polarized relations between king and legislature, forcing Charles to leave London* (10 January), and provoking parliament to issue its Militia Ordinance, by which it nominated its own lords lieutenants* for the counties and empowered them to raise forces in defiance of the king. Protesting that the person of the king was now in the custody of "evil counselors," in May 1642 the houses took the decision to raise an army for the defense of parliament and the Protestant religion, naming the 3d earl of Essex (Robert Devereux*) as their commander-in-chief. The king's rejection of the Nineteen Propositions* (June 1642), effectively parliament's ultimatum to the king, made war almost inevitable. While the parliamentary leadership was an alliance of leading members of both houses, in the Commons it was Pym who served as the most articulate spokesman of parliamentary policy and (until his death in September 1643) the principal draftsman of parliament's public declarations.

On the outbreak of the Civil War*, the composition of the two houses had changed markedly. Bishops had been expelled from the Lords (13 February 1642), and by May many members of both houses had heeded the king's summons to York. During the war roughly one-third of the pre-1640 Protestant peerage sided with parliament; a slightly larger proportion sided with the king. The Commons were similarly divided, with a large group of "neuters" in both Houses seeking not to be drawn into the conflict. Executive functions were concentrated in a series of committees, the most powerful of which, the committee of safety, assumed day-to-day management of the war (superseded by the Committee of Both Kingdoms* in February 1644). Financial management was delegated to a series of powerful administrative committees dealing with advance of money, sequestrations, compounding (fines on royalist* "delinquents"), and revenue (with control of the Exchequer*). One of the innovative aspects of the parliamentary experience of the 1640s was the frequency with which peers and members of the Commons were brought into day-to-day collaboration through the proliferation of bicameral committees.

The inconclusive outcome of the first battle of the Civil War, at Edgehill* (23 October 1642), brought into the open the differences that existed at Westminster as to what parliament's war aims should be and how they should be attained. While a war party, centered around Henry Marten and the younger Sir Henry Vane, advocated a vigorous campaign to effect an "absolute victory" over the king, Essex's objectives were limited to the attainment of a strategic superiority whereby parliament could initiate negotiations from a position of strength. The equally explosive question of church reform was defused for the time being by referring the matter to the Westminster Assembly of Divines* (June 1643).

Management of the war effort remained a major source of parliamentary dissension throughout 1643-1645. Doubts that English forces alone could achieve a victory over the royalists led to the negotiation of the Solemn League and Covenant* with the Scots (July-September 1643), guaranteeing the intervention of a Scottish army on the parliamentarian* side in return for the establishment of a Presbyterian* church settlement in England. Overall conduct of the war was now referred to the Committee of Both Kingdoms, an action that further compromised Essex's supremacy of command (February-May 1644). Victory in July 1644 at Marston Moor*, crushing the major royalist north field army, was quickly offset by Essex's disastrous campaign in the west country (July-August). Investigations into the circumstances of Essex's surrender resulted in a scheme for the amalgamation of the three southern field armies (of Essex, the earl of Manchester, and Sir William Waller) and a controversial series of military reforms, which included the Self-Denying Ordinance* (removing members of both houses from civil and military office), the creation of a New Model Army*, and the appointment of Sir Thomas Fairfax* as the new commander-in-chief (December 1644-March 1645), with Oliver Cromwell* as his lieutenant-general (June 1645). In the Lords, where the proposals had faced their strongest opposition, the military changes marked the emergence of a coalition of peers committed to securing an absolute victory over the king and centered on the 10th earl of Northumberland and Viscount Saye and Sele.

With the New Model Army's victory at Naseby* (14 June 1645), which effectively marked the end of the royalist cause as a military challenge to parliament, three questions dominated debate at Westminster. How was the church to be settled? On what terms was a peace to be concluded with the king? And how was Ireland to be reduced once again to Protestant rule? In these deliberations, organized factions and "parties" came to exercise increasing influence on the outcome of parliamentary business, though these interests remained loose coalitions of like-minded men rather than parties in any modern sense. From the end of 1645, the labels "Presbyterian" and "Independent"* came into common usage to designate the two major parliamentary groupings. A bicameral group within parliament dominated by Essex, Denzell Holles, and Sir Philip Stapilton, the Presbyterians were an alliance of members of the wartime peace party, the Scots commissioners, and conservative City merchants, and strongly backed by the London High Presbyterian clergy. The congeries of parliamentary interests opposing them were misleadingly labeled

"Independents" because they opposed the imposition of a disciplinarian Presbyterian settlement and advocated limited toleration to "tender consciences" within an Erastian Presbyterian church (very few members of this group were in fact Independents in ecclesiology). Where "Presbyterians" favored lenient terms and returning executive powers to the king within all three kingdoms, the "Independents" remained in general far more suspicious of royal authority and looked to the New Model Army as the bulwark against an agreement with the king that betrayed "the Cause" of 1642. Political groupings were, however, far more fluid and complicated than this terminology suggests, and factional alignments were further complicated by the increase in the size of the Commons between 1645 and 1647 as a result of by-elections for the seats of dead or disabled members of parliament (MPs), which gradually restored the membership of the house to its pre-1642 level.

With the king's surrender to the Scottish army in May 1646, the Presbyterian interest rode high, strongly influencing the legislation for the church settlement. Although Essex's death in September 1646 robbed them of their most effective parliamentary leader and the withdrawal of the Scottish army in December weakened their military power base, the "Presbyterians" remained strong enough in the two houses to obstruct the pay of the New Model Army over the winter of 1646-1647 and in early April to wrest control of the imminent campaign in Ireland from the Independent-dominated Derby House Committee* (active from October 1646 as the principal Irish affairs committee). Between April and July 1647, the Presbyterian interest dominated parliamentary business in the two houses and at Derby House. But their inept and partisan attempt in the spring of 1647 to dispatch part of the New Model Army to Ireland and to disband the rest provoked widespread apprehensions that the dissolution of the army was to be the prelude to a Presbyterian-backed restoration of the king. The resulting confrontation (June-July 1647) between the Presbyterian-dominated parliament and the New Model Army (now refusing to disband before its grievances were met) broke the power of the Presbyterian junto. Eleven leading Presbyterian MPs (including Stapilton and Holles) were impeached by the army and withdrew from the Commons. A botched attempt to restore Presbyterian dominance at Westminster with the support of the London mob between 26 July and 4 August provided the New Model with the pretext for intervening in Westminster. With the collapse of the attempted Presbyterian coup and the flight or impeachment* of many leading Presbyterians, the Independent leadership in the two houses introduced a series of proposals for a new settlement with the king (largely based on the army-endorsed settlement, the Heads of the Proposals*), only to see their hopes dashed in November 1647 by the king's decision to break off negotiations and escape from army custody to the Isle of Wight. There he concluded an "Engagement"* for a new Scottish invasion of England under the duke of Hamilton (26 December). Under strong pressure from the army, the parliament passed a vote forbidding any further negotiation with the king (3 January 1648) and thereby splitting the Independent interest between those who sought to appease the army and those who now thought that the only hope for political stability lay in a speedy settlement with the king.

The outbreak of the Second Civil War* in England in the spring of 1648 and the advance of Hamilton's army from Scotland in July served to strengthen most MPs' resolve for a settlement with Charles I. During April and May 1648, many of those who had been impeached or who had ceased attending parliament after the botched Presbyterian coup of July 1647 now returned to their seats, thus shifting the balance of power—decisively in the Lords, less markedly in the Commons—toward those anxious for an agreement with the king on almost any terms. On the motion of the Lords, a new series of negotiations was begun with Charles I at Newport, Isle of Wight (18 September-5 December). By 1648, however, the parliament's reputation was at its nadir. The county committee structure by which it governed the localities was widely hated; accusations that members of both Houses were guilty of venality and peculation were rife; Leveller* critics demanded electoral reform; and parliament's decisions to renew negotiation with the king had further outraged opinion in the army. By November, Henry Ireton* and other leading officers were openly canvassing with the civilian allies the possibility of a coup d'état.

Parliament's decision on 5 December 1648 that the king's responses to the Isle of Wight proposals constituted a secure basis for a peace provided the army with the occasion to act. Westminster was occupied by troops, and the Commons purged by Colonel Thomas Pride on 6-7 December (see Pride's Purge*). At the insistence of Ireton and other radical officer-MPs, the king was brought to trial and executed on 30 January 1649 (see Charles I, Trial, Execution, and Cult of*). By a narrow vote of the Commons, the House of Lords was abolished (Oliver Cromwell being among the dissenters). From February 1649, the purged House of Commons constituted itself as a unicameral parliament, soon known opprobriously as the "Rump Parliament."

Following the demise of the Protectorate* in 1659, army leaders reassembled the Rump Parliament. When General George Monck* entered England in 1660, intent upon effecting the Restoration* of Charles II*, he ordered the Rump to readmit those members still living who had been expelled by Pride's Purge. The Long Parliament resumed sitting on 21 February 1660 with a new council of state*. After attempting (unsuccessfully) to ensure that royalists would not be elected to the new parliament that would be elected following Charles II's return, it dissolved itself on 16 March.

The foundations of the modern study of the Long Parliament were laid by Samuel Rawson Gardiner in the final two volumes of his *History of England* and in his *History of the Great Civil War, 1642-49*. His work remains the best general history of the parliament, though his account is deeply flawed by its Whiggish concentration on the House of Commons, to the virtual exclusion of the upper house and the bicameral committee structures through which much of the parliament's business was transacted. A number of monographs have dealt with particular episodes. Conrad Russell provides a brilliant analysis of the opening years of the parliament and of the events that led to war. The City's influence on parliamentary politics is most effectively considered by Valerie Pearl and Robert Brenner. The events leading up to and immediately following the purge of 1648 are canvassed by David Underdown.

Bibliography: Robert Brenner, *Merchants and Revolution*, 1993; Samuel Rawson Gardiner, *History of England*, 10 vols., 1887-91, and *History of the Great Civil War,*

1642-49, 1893, rprt. 1987; Valerie Pearl, *London and the Outbreak of the Puritan Revolution*, 1961; Conrad Russell, *The Fall of the British Monarchies, 1637-42*, 1991; David Underdown, *Pride's Purge: Politics in the Puritan Revolution*, 1971.

John Adamson

Lords Lieutenant. First appointed by the duke of Northumberland as an ad hoc response to the political turmoil of the late 1540s, lords lieutenant had become a permanent feature of local government* by the accession of James I*. The office was acknowledged in the Militia Act of 1558, and though the statute itself lapsed in 1604, lords lieutenant remained in place, their authority resting upon the royal prerogative*. The formal duties of the lieutenants were military. Their commissions required them to act as the commander of the militia within their lieutenancy. They were responsible for repelling invasions, putting down riot and rebellion, assisting in the arduous business of raising and supplying the king's forces in times of war, and training and securing equipment for the militia. Stuart lieutenants performed these tasks with varying degrees of success throughout the century; lords lieutenant put down the Midland Rising* of 1607, organized housing and supply for the king's army* during the wars of the 1620s, and stood to arms against foreign invasion in the 1660s, 1680s, and 1690s. These duties remained constant throughout the Stuart period, even after the passage of new Militia Acts under Charles II* (the first was in 1661, 13 Car. II, c. 6).

Beyond these formal responsibilities, lords lieutenant were often charged with the execution of other administrative chores and played an important informal role in the provinces. The nature of these duties and the office itself changed dramatically over the course of the seventeenth century, reflecting broader changes in English politics. Before the Civil Wars* lieutenants were called on to perform a wide range of miscellaneous duties, among which were the sale of mulberry trees and Virginia Company lottery tickets. Though the duty was an unwelcome one, lieutenants also played an important part in raising money for an impecunious Crown through loans and benevolences (see Taxation and Revenue*). The privy council* often called on lords lieutenant to adjudicate local disputes, settle potentially dangerous feuds among local gentlemen, and report on local economic and social conditions. Informally, lieutenants often acted as consensus builders, organizing parliamentary selections and acting as peacemakers when the demands of central government met local opposition. Despite their position as royal appointees, lieutenants typically preferred to champion the interests of the provinces over Whitehall.

The lieutenants' utility for king and council in the prewar period lay in the fact that they were by and large local magnates who commanded the respect of the locality. Under James I and Charles I* lieutenants were chosen from among the higher nobility; nearly all of them ranked as earls or higher, and typically they held substantial interests within the county entrusted to them. Though in theory a lieutenant served at the king's pleasure, in practice early Stuart lieutenants served for life. Moreover, in some counties, such as Lancashire and Cheshire, the office was routinely passed from father to son. A lord lieutenant named his own deputies from among the most prominent local gentry. A deputy's place was at times burdensome, for they often carried out much of the work entrusted to their masters, but it was also a highly prized honor, which recognized a gentleman's place among the county's inner circle. These appointments, along with sought-after commissions in the militia, were exclusively in the lieutenant's gift, and conscientious peers used them to promote harmony in their shire.

The importance of consensus building and the local orientation of the lords lieutenant made them ill suited to cope with the political stresses placed on local society under Charles I. Lieutenants and their deputies were not enthusiastic about raising the men and money necessary to fight the king's wars against France and Spain (see French War of 1627-1629*; Spanish War of 1625-1630*, Thirty Years War*), especially when their recompense proved to be complaints in parliament* about their lack of statutory authority.   The run-up to the Civil Wars left the lieutenants bewildered and increasingly ineffective. Most took their stand with the king, but some made an effort to remain neutral or joined parliament. In the spring of 1642 parliament seized control of the lieutenancy, naming its own supporters to office. The lieutenancy was overtaken by events as the kingdom descended into war; in many areas, the parliament's nominees never acted, and in others their efforts were largely fruitless. Newer forms of administration, such as the county committee (see County Associations*), eclipsed the lieutenancy, which was finally abolished along with the monarchy and the House of Lords in 1649.

The Restoration* saw a return to older methods, and new lords lieutenant were among the first officers appointed after Charles II* returned to claim his throne. The experience of the Civil Wars and the Interregnum* had changed the political landscape, however. Although initially the government did its best to recreate the pre-war institution, bringing the few remaining prewar veterans out of retirement, from early in the 1660s a new spirit animated the lieutenancy. Many of the newly commissioned lieutenants were of lower rank than their predecessors, and for the first time politics rather than birth informed most of the king's choices. New lieutenants were overwhelmingly Cavalier* in their background, and their choices for deputy lieutenancies were carefully scrutinized by the Crown for political orthodoxy.

Lords lieutenant during the Restoration were among the principal guardians of the Cavalier regime. The days of particularist consensus building were over; lieutenants organized the persecution of former republicans and religious radicals, and later, during the Exclusion Crisis*, they became the principal local leaders of the royalist cause. Lieutenants took responsibility for the nomination of sound justices of the peace and the purge from local government of all of those who were unreliable. They also organized election contests and sponsored loyal addresses to the throne. The hard work of politically minded lieutenants, such as the first earl of Yarmouth and the duke of Newcastle among others, resulted in the creation of what in 1685 appeared to be an unshakable royalist Anglican* edifice in the country.

Despite the lackluster performance of the militia in Monmouth's Rebellion* in 1685, the lieutenants were unanimously behind the accession of James II*. They continued to be the executors of the one-party state until the king's radical Catholicizing policies began. Reluctant lieutenants were sacked in unprecedented numbers in 1687 as James attempted to refashion English politics. The new lieutenants, many of whom were obscure Catholics*, found that they were powerless to impose their will on their subordinates; the lieutenancy, so effective in fastening royalist Anglican rule on the kingdom, failed as an instrument of James's policies. Deputy lieutenants resigned by the score, and some who remained in commission resisted from within; some lieutenants themselves dragged their feet. The invasion of William of Orange* was assisted by the defection of several key lords lieutenant, most notably the earl of Bath in the west and the duke of Norfolk in East Anglia.

William's triumph in the Glorious Revolution* ratified the politicization of the lieutenancy, as James's men were turned out and replaced by new appointees, some of whom had been vocal supporters of exclusion. While they continued their important military duties, politically the position of the lords lieutenant had changed dramatically by 1690. From its origins as an institution whose principal political aim was to create and enforce consensus, the lieutenancy had come to be the guarantor of single-party dominance in the state.

Bibliography: Lindsay Boynton, *The Elizabethan Militia, 1558-1638*, 1967; Victor L. Stater, *Noble Government: The Stuart Lord Lieutenancy and the Transformation of English Politics*, 1994; J. R. Western, *The English Militia in the Eighteenth Century*, 1965.

                                                            Victor L. Stater

M

Main and Bye Plots (1603). The rejoicing that surrounded the accession of James I* in 1603 was marred by two things: the unrest and unease provoked by the fact that a foreigner had become king of England (seen in the wild speaking that landed a number of small fry in court throughout the summer) and attempted preemptive strikes before James had fully established his regime, in two intertwined and remarkably ill-conceived plots. Indeed, the idiocy of both makes them difficult to explain.

The Bye Plot was masterminded (if that is the appropriate word) by Father William Watson, pamphleteer and member of the group of Appellant priests who had emerged at the end of Elizabeth's reign, deeply hostile to the Jesuits and to any idea of papal intervention, committed to non-resistance, and loyal to Elizabeth. This last makes Watson's outbreak distinctly paradoxical, although it appears that his idea—borrowed from a Scottish *motif*—was to kidnap rather than kill the new king. He was not the only person to be taken in by the romantic aura surrounding James's mother, Mary, Queen of Scots—from one point of view a martyr—although this time it was James rather than Mary who was seen to disappoint the Catholics*. James did in fact intend to reduce the savage Elizabethan recusancy* fines but not surprisingly failed to do so within the first three months of his reign. This was not fast enough for Watson, who did not stop to think. He planned an illusory uprising in June 1603 and died for it. Meanwhile, the Jesuits alerted the government. Such evidence of loyalty was to do them no good in the aftermath of the Gunpowder Plot* (1605), but more immediately, it seems to have persuaded James not to change his mind about his intended remission of the recusancy fines.

The other plot, the Main Plot, was a Protestant conspiracy. The link, tenuous though it is, came in the involvement of George Brook, brother of Lord Cobham, in the Bye Plot. In the summer of 1603 Lord Cobham tried to draw the ambassador from the Spanish Netherlands, Count d'Aremberg, into a plot to replace James with his cousin Arabella Stuart*, with Spanish backing, and probably to kill him and his children. Each group of plotters had some awareness of the other, though how much cannot now be discovered. But the Main Plot brought in a very big fish, Sir Walter Raleigh*. This posthumously most charismatic figure of the period was in fact desperate for recognition and office in 1603; frustrated by Elizabeth, he had deeply worried Sir Robert Cecil* by his haste to reach the new king on his journey from Scotland*. His ambition was again frustrated; indeed, he now lost some of what he had, including Durham House and his monopoly* of wine licenses. The loss of his monopoly of sweet wines had been the final straw that provoked the 2d earl of Essex into rebellion in 1601; it may be that Raleigh was similarly provoked. Yet it was Cobham's evidence that convicted him, and it is by no means certain that the verdict was correct. Nevertheless, this crazy plot was in conception infinitely more dangerous than the Bye Plot. The plotters survived, after the grisly piece of theater in which they were brought to the scaffold and then pardoned. James had shown a macabre mercy not extended to Watson and Brooke. Raleigh went into the Tower, established his credit with posterity, and lived until 1618, when his disastrous expedition to Guiana stirred up Spanish fury and ensured that this time there was no reprieve.

Bibliography: S. R. Gardiner, *History of England from the Accession of James I to the Outbreak of the Civil War, 1603-1642,* 10 vols., 1883-1884, vol. 1; P. Holmes, *Resistance and Compromise*, 1982; Linda Levy Peck, *Northampton*, 1982.

Jenny Wormald

Maitland, John, 2d Earl and 1st Duke of Lauderdale (1616-1682). Lauderdale was the scion of an East Lothian family that had risen to prominence as royal servants. Educated at the University of St. Andrews, Lord Maitland (courtesy title of the Lauderdale heir) was an intelligent, articulate young man when he entered public life in 1640. Following his father's lead he became a Covenanter* and committed Presbyterian*. During the Second Bishops' War* he commanded a regiment and later accompanied the Scottish negotiators to London*. Over the next three years, Maitland served on Scottish civil and religious commissions and British committees.

Despite his youth the Covenanters appreciated Maitland's talents. In August 1643 he became a Scottish representative to the English parliament*. Although receiving command of the East Lothian foot, Maitland concentrated on London politics, serving on the Committee of Both Kingdoms* and at the Westminster Assembly of Divines*. In November 1644 and January 1645 he negotiated with the English royalists at Oxford and Uxbridge.

Fearful of the English Independents* as political revolutionaries, the new earl began intriguing with royalists* in 1646. Lauderdale initiated negotiations with Charles I* for a treaty with Scotland* in June 1647. In company with the earls of Lanark and Loudoun, he signed the Engagement* with the king on 26 December. Lauderdale proved vital in securing the estates' approval of the treaty in March 1648. During the summer he served as the Engager ambassador to Charles, duke of Rothesay (the future Charles II*, prince of Wales in the other two kingdoms) and the Dutch. The earl joined the royal court* in exile, where he became friendly with Charles II*. Lauderdale persuaded the new king to accept a Covenanter alliance, returning home with Charles in June 1650. Following public repentance in December as an Engager, Lauderdale returned to public office in March 1651. He served on the Worcester campaign and was taken prisoner after the battle.

Imprisoned until March 1660, Lauderdale was forfeited by the English. During his confinement, the earl studied theology and corresponded with the English Presbyterian minister Richard Baxter. Degradation led Lauderdale to become a convinced royalist, albeit still sympathetic to Presbyterians. In April 1660 Charles II wrote to the earl asking him to organize a royalist party in Scotland.

The Restoration* brought a revival of Lauderdale's fortunes. He received his lands back, but the earl of Middleton's Episcopalian-royalist party dominated the Scottish government. Present at Charles's court as one of the king's secretaries, Lauderdale schemed for Middleton's fall, which he achieved in March 1663. The earl, having abandoned the principles of his youth, tried to remain in power by any policy that might serve. His allies in Scotland, the earls of Tweeddale and Rothes and Archbishop James Sharp of St. Andrews, persecuted the Presbyterians, which led to the Pentland Rising* in 1666. With repression discredited, Lauderdale, now royal commissioner to Scotland, began a policy of toleration in 1667. Two years later an indulgence provided further evidence of conciliation with the Presbyterians. Lauderdale's regime was characterized by corruption (exemplified by his brother Charles of Haltoun), reliance on royal prerogative*, and disrespect for parliamentary opposition. Despite the equivocal nature of his regime, the earl's policies had the support of moderates, such as the earl of Kincardine.

A reversal of Lauderdale's tolerant religious policies followed his marriage to the relentlessly ambitious countess of Dysart in 1672, the same year that he was created duke. Between 1673 and 1677, the estates passed a series of repressive acts against Presbyterians. The earl's moderate supporters left the privy council*, which relied even more on Lauderdale's toadies. The military occupation of the covenanting southwest in 1678, followed by Sharp's assassination, and the Covenanter Rebellion* in May 1679, ended the earl's career. Although royal commissioner until 1681, he was effectively superseded by the dukes of Monmouth and York (see Monmouth's Rebellion*; James II*). Retiring to English spas, Lauderdale experienced the indignity of losing his Scottish pension. Lauderdale's last political act was an attempt to save the life and estates of the condemned 9th earl of Argyll (Archibald Campbell*). The duke, one of Scotland's most talented politicians, died on 24 August 1682, a man rejected by his king and country.

Bibliography: Julia Buckroyd, *Church and State in Scotland, 1660-1681*, 1981; W. C. Mackenzie, *The Life and Times of John Maitland, Duke of Lauderdale (1616-1682)*, 1923.

Edward M. Furgol

Major Generals. In the summer of 1655, in the wake of several abortive royalist* attempts to overthrow the Cromwellian regime, Penruddock's Rising* in Wiltshire, and an almost simultaneous effort in Yorkshire, the Lord Protector Oliver Cromwell* divided the kingdom into twelve regions, putting over each a major general to guarantee military security. While the challenges to his regime had been put down with ease, Cromwell was perhaps overly alarmed. He had been kept thoroughly informed about a wide range of activity subversive to the stability of his rule and believed in acting firmly to preempt resistance. On this occasion he went beyond defending the Protectorate* and invested in the major generals' power to override the local civil authorities, not only to prevent counterrevolution but to reform the manners of society—that is, to impose the social discipline of a godly society, a project dear to his heart. When this experiment in the military's direction of local government* had run its course by the winter of 1656-1657, and the generals had made themselves odious by their various impositions—supressing alehouses, horseracing, cockfights, theaters, and brothels; punishing swearing, blaspheming, and the like—the arrangement was allowed to wither away, to widespread satisfaction.

But this was not before the Cromwellian regime had established its reputation for being obsessively "puritanical." The modern notion of Puritanism* as the ideology of those who were against pleasure on principle and of Cromwell himself as a rather heavy-handed and sanctimonious dictator owes much to this period of his rule. Though Cromwell's reputation for governing tyrannically gained considerable credibility in this rather brief period and the royalist propagandists at the time made much of it, for most of his time in power he made repeated efforts to reconstitute something like the ancient constitution of king and parliament* rather than rule by force. Very solidly backed as he was by the army*, Cromwell could hardly have been overthrown by enemies from within or without, by royalists or republicans, so the entire exercise in military government now seems to have been an unnecessary overreaction.

Dissatisfied with the workings of the political system under the Instrument of Government*, the Protectorate's* formal "constitution," Cromwell might have settled for ruling through the army permanently. He chose rather to renew the pursuit of legitmacy and summoned a new parliament (see Protectorate Paliaments*). When in January 1657 that parliament, full of resentment, voted clearly against the taxation* required to support his experiment, he bowed to their wishes and allowed it to come to an end. He was not forced to govern by consent but believed that he ought to, for his common sense ultimately told him that he could hardly create a good and godly society by force. The episode of the rule of the major generals, while not genuinely characteristic of the Cromwellian regime, is nevertheless the pivotal one in the British tradition of civil-military relations, the example invariably cited whenever the case is being made against militarism and military rule over civilians and for the civil control of military power. It may be seen as an interlude in Cromwell's intermittent but continuing struggle to find a broadly acceptable constitutional form to govern England. He had not fought against Stuart absolutism*, as he saw it, to make himself an absolute master.

There seems to be a general consensus among modern historians that the role of the major generals was unpopular and that this was not an invention of royalist propagandists, but there is disagreement about the depth and extent of feeling against military rule, as there is about the significance of this episode for understanding the character of Cromwell's rule.

Bibliography: W. C. Abbott, *The Writings and Speeches of Oliver Cromwell*, 4 vols., 1937-1947.

S. J. Stearns

Malignants. The term *malignant* was a derogatory political nickname, commonly applied by supporters of the parliament* to those who favored Charles I* and the future Charles II* during the English Civil Wars*. The word first seems to have come into general use in London* during 1641, when it was employed by John Pym* and other parliamentarian* leaders to denote those whom they regarded as ill affected to the authority of the state. In the autumn of 1641 Pym denounced "the abounding malignity" of those who had opposed the proceedings of the House of Commons, and over the succeeding months the term was increasingly applied to hardline supporters of the king. From the very beginning, malignancy was intimately associated with popery. Malignants were regarded as "bad Protestants"—men and women who, whether through a misguided sense of loyalty to the king or a secret desire to subvert the established constitution, had entered into a tacit alliance with the adherents of the Catholic* church. By November 1641 the existence of a "popish and malignant party," busily working to undermine England's ancient laws and liberties, had become an article of faith among many of the Long Parliament's* most committed supporters.

Like many other terms of political abuse—*Cavalier** and *Roundhead**, for example— the word *malignant* gradually spread from the capital, where it had first been coined, to the provinces. During early 1642, parliamentary supporters all over England genuinely came to believe that those whom they had previously regarded as harmless, if politically misguided neighbors, were in fact dangerous malignants. The passing of this particular word into common parlance thus represents a crucial milestone along the road to the Civil War, marking the point at which the inveterate mistrust and suspicion that had so long been evident at the political center finally came to be reflected in the country as a whole.

Following the outbreak of hostilities, the term *malignant* was often used simply as another word for *royalist**, as an alternative to other popular pejoratives like *delinquent* and *Cavalier*. Whereas these latter terms were usually applied to those who were quite open in their support for the king, however, *malignancy* frequently retained its original and particularly sinister sense of concealed disaffection.

Bibliography: Anthony Fletcher, *The Outbreak of the English Civil War*, 1981.

Mark Stoyle

Marston Moor, Battle of (1644). The biggest battle of the English Civil Wars*, resulting in the destruction of the royalist* army in the north. In late April 1644 York, garrisoned by the marquis of Newcastle, came under siege by the parliamentarian* forces of Ferdinando, Lord Fairfax, and the Scots under Lord Leven. The king, pressed by the earl of Essex (Robert Devereux*) and Sir William

Waller in the south, wrote to Prince Rupert on 14 June directing him to relieve York and, in ambiguous terms, to engage the enemy in battle immediately thereafter.

On 1 July Rupert's cavalry faced the allied parliamentary and Scots forces on Marston Moor, six miles due west of York. As Rupert intended, the allies expected his infantry to arrive shortly. Instead it descended on York from the northwest and relieved the city. Once there Rupert disregarded Newcastle's authority and assumed command of all royalist troops without conferring with him.

Early on 2 July Rupert began massing his troops at Marston Moor. The allies, having expected a movement south, were strung out between Long Marston and Tadcaster. At midmorning the rear guard, Sir Thomas Fairfax's* cavalry, sighted the enemy. But Rupert was not yet prepared for all-out battle because Newcastle and Lord Eythin were reluctant to deploy their infantry, and the allied troops were recalled short of Tadcaster.

To prepare for the York infantry's arrival, Rupert deployed musketeers behind the hedgerow marking the south edge of the Tockwith-Marston road and dividing the moor, north, from Marston Field. The allied infantry under Manchester, Ferdinando Fairfax, and Leven faced them along a slight ridge. On the east side, north and west of Long Marston, royalist cavalry under George Goring and Charles Lucas faced Thomas Fairfax's cavalry. On the west Rupert's cavalry came under allied artillery fire in the early afternoon and gave up some ground to Oliver Cromwell's* cavalry. At midafternoon Newcastle's infantry, the Whitecoats, and Eythin's began taking up their positions on the moor.

Toward evening the battle began, roughly 18,000 royalist soldiers confronting 28,000 allied. Taking advantage of the disarray in the royalist command, Leven attacked downslope under the cover of a thunderstorm. Thomas Fairfax attacked Goring but was repulsed at a narrow lane, most of his raw troops fleeing. Lucas attacked Leven, who lacked reserves, but was himself captured by pikemen.

Meanwhile Cromwell broke part of Rupert's right wing, commanded by John Byron. Rupert committed his reserves and held Cromwell's cavalry, while Newcastle's Whitecoats attacked the allied center under Ferdinando Fairfax. The Scots reserve cavalry under David Leslie routed the remains of Byron's forces. Defeating Rupert, Leslie and Cromwell swept north and east.

Manchester's foot attacked Goring's cavalry from the front, Leslie and Cromwell from the rear, defeating him. The allied cavalry then turned against the Whitecoats, who were pinned against a hedgerow, and slaughtered them. The battle was over by 9 PM. The remains of the royalist army retreated to York, pursued by Cromwell's cavalry.

Of the three allied generals, only Manchester saw the battle to the end; Leven and Ferdinando Fairfax, thinking their side defeated, had left the field early. Thomas Fairfax gained respect for having ridden back alone through the royalist lines, disguised as a royalist officer, to join Manchester. Cromwell's performance confirmed him as the parliament's* greatest field commander.

The battle ended the king's effective power in the north. York surrendered on 16 July. Rupert, his reputation badly damaged, retreated into Lancashire with 6,000 horse. Newcastle soon left for Holland. But the allies failed to follow up on the opportunity created by Marston Moor. While Ferdinando Fairfax reduced royalist strongholds in Yorkshire and the Scots besieged Newcastle, Manchester did nothing, and on 2 September the king forced Essex to surrender at Lostwithiel.

Bibliography: P. Newman, *Marston Moor, 2 July 1644: The Sources and the Site*, 1978; Austin Woolrych, *Battles of the English Civil War*, 1961; P. Young, *Marston Moor 1644*, 1970.

Mark Heumann

Mary II (1662-1694). The eldest surviving child of the duke of York—subsequently James II*—and his first wife, Anne Hyde*, Mary ascended the throne of England jointly with her husband William III* on 13 February 1689, following the deposition of her father in the Glorious Revolution* of 1688.

Born on 30 April 1662, Mary led a rather uneventful life as a child, despite her position as second in line to the throne of her uncle Charles II*. Emotionally estranged from her parents, she cared deeply for her younger sister, Anne*. Her parents' secret conversion to Roman Catholicism* was kept from her by her Protestant overseers, and she was little affected by her mother's early death in 1671. Mary thus became a "child of the state," growing to young womanhood at Richmond Palace. In 1673 her father married the Catholic Mary of Modena*. The marriage was highly unpopular with the members of the House of Commons, who feared a Catholic dynasty; it was this marriage that laid the foundation for Mary's eventual ascent to the throne.

Mary was soon to become a pawn in her uncle's political scheming. William of Orange, Charles's nephew and stadholder of the Netherlands, was anxious for English backing in his war against the French. To that end William broached the possibility of a marriage between himself and his first cousin Mary. Charles, wishing to conciliate the French, held out the marriage as a reward for concluding a peace, but William adamantly refused. In the event Charles settled for an Anglo-Dutch alliance, personified by the marriage between William and Mary, which took place on 4 November 1677.

Mary, now princess of Orange, returned with William to Holland. Initially opposed to the marriage, Mary grew to love William and settled happily into a life of domesticity, though the couple remained childless. After James's accession to the throne following his brother's death in 1685, Charles's illegitimate son mounted Monmouth's Rebellion*, which ended in his execution. With Anglo-Dutch relations deteriorating on both the diplomatic and personal levels, Mary and William became the acknowledged leaders of the Protestant cause in Europe.

As king, James alienated his Protestant subjects with his growing Catholicism; the suspect birth of a son in June 1688 confirmed the Commons's fears of a Catholic succession. William responded to an "invitation" to invade England to rescue the country and the Protestant religion. James fled the country in the face of the invasion; the Commons of the Convention Parliament* then determined that the king had abandoned his throne and offered it, with certain parliamentary safeguards, to William and Mary as joint monarchs. This event came to be known as the Glorious Revolution*.

Crowned on 11 April 1689, Mary was content for William to be the dominant partner in the joint monarchy but proved to be quite capable of managing the affairs of government during his sojourns on the Continent. Preferring the role of queen consort, however, the ever self-effacing Mary continued to look to William for guidance until her untimely death on 28 December 1694.

Bibliography: H. W. Chapman, *Mary II, Queen of England,* 1953.

Connie S. Evans

Mary Beatrice of Modena (1658-1718). Mary Beatrice, second wife of James II* and mother of James Francis Edward Stuart, the "old Pretender," was the only daughter of Alfonso IV, duke of Modena, who had her brought up as a strict Catholic. In part due to French diplomacy, a marriage was arranged for Mary with the widowed duke of York (see James II*), brother and heir of Charles II*, in 1673. He was then forty; she was fifteen. They had five children between 1675 and 1682, all of whom died.

Because of her religion, Mary Beatrice was very unpopular in England. She had a great deal of influence over James, however, and encouraged his practice of Catholicism*. James became king in 1685 and quickly dissipated the goodwill many people initially felt by his high-handed actions. But many people were content that if they could tolerate James, the next heir was his elder daughter, Mary*, a good Protestant. A crisis came when Mary Beatrice gave birth to a son in 1688. There was such dismay that people began whispering that the baby boy was smuggled into the royal apartments in a warming pan. In fact, there is no doubt that the birth was genuine.

With such great upset over James, Mary Beatrice and the baby prince fled to France. James himself soon followed, and his daughter Mary and her husband, William of Orange*, were acclaimed as co-monarchs in the Glorious Revolution*. James, Mary Beatrice, and their son lived at the palace of St. Germain. Mary Beatrice strongly supported schemes to restore James to the throne. Louis XIV gave the couple a pension of 50,000 crowns a month. The dignified Mary Beatrice was much better received at the French court than James, who became increasingly feeble-minded. After James's death in 1701 Mary Beatrice spent more and more time at a nunnery at Chaillot, where she died in 1718.

Bibliography: Mary Hopkirk, *Queen over the Water,* 1953; Carola Oman, *Mary of Modena,* 1962.

Carole Levin

Meal Tub Plot (1679). Also known as the Presbyterian Plot, it was an attempt by Roman Catholics* to implicate the Whigs* and their Dissenter* allies in a fictitious conspiracy to exclude Charles II's* brother and heir, the duke of York (the future James II*), from the royal succession by force.

The Meal Tub Plot occurred in the midst of the anti-Catholic hysteria associated with the supposed Popish Plot* (1678) against Charles II. Catholics retaliated by making similar accusations concerning a counterplot by Whigs and Dissenters against the Catholic York. Elizabeth Cellier, also known as the "Popish Midwife," had close associations with the countess of Powis, the earl of Peterborough, and other Catholic aristocrats. She had even attended the duchess of York, the royal heir apparent's wife.

Early in 1679 Mrs. Cellier obtained the release of the petty criminal Thomas Dangerfield from Newgate Prison. Soon after, he informed his benefactor and her Catholic friends of a plot by the Presbyterians* to bar James from the throne on Charles's death. The exultant Catholics quickly brought Dangerfield's tale to the attention of first James and then Charles II. Tory* leaders quickly seized on the plot as evidence of the treasonous and subversive nature of the Whigs and Dissenters. They called for action. The royal brothers, however, proceeded with caution and skepticism since the only evidence for the existence of the plot that they possessed was the dubious word of Dangerfield. To bolster his credibility, Dangerfield planted faked evidence of the plot on a Whig official, Roderick Mansell. The ploy was so transparent that instead of incriminating Mansell, Dangerfield triggered a search of his patroness Mrs. Cellier's house. There the authorities discovered more fabricated evidence of a Presbyterian plot in Mrs. Cellier's meal tub, which thus gave its name to the whole incident.

The Meal Tub Plot was obviously a sham and one that discredited the Tory allies of the royal brothers, not their Whig enemies. Dangerfield was arrested and testified that Mrs. Cellier and her friends had conspired with him to accuse falsely their Protestant enemies of planning a rebellion against James's succession. Those whom they attempted to implicate included such Whig greats as Anthony Ashley Cooper*, the earl of Shaftesbury, and George Villiers*, the 2d duke of Buckingham, along with George Savile, the marquis of Halifax. In fact Shaftesbury emerged as an even greater hero of Protestantism than he already was. A renewed frenzy of anti-Catholicism followed and included massive processions in which the pope was burned in effigy. Meanwhile within the royal household, Charles II and James both strongly suspected that Dangerfield had actually been an *agent provocateur* employed by the Whigs to set up the Catholic aristocracy in an embarrassing sham plot.

Unfortunately the true nature of the Meal Tub Plot has evaded both its contemporaries and subsequent historians. Some historians agree with the opinion of Charles II that Dangerfield was actually a Whig double agent. Others believe Dangerfield's story that Mrs. Cellier and her aristocratic friends did truly engage in a conspiracy to create the appearance of a Presbyterian plot against James. Another theory suggests that Dangerfield, as a denizen of London's* underworld, heard rumors of vague treasons and plots by Protestants. He used that shadowy information to curry favor with his Catholic benefactors, but when the attempt to frame Mansell for the Presbyterian plot failed, Dangerfield turned on Mrs. Cellier and the others to save himself. Whichever was the case, the fictitious Meal Tub Plot fizzled into an ignominious end and provided yet another example of the paranoid style and hysterical nature of politics during the last years of Charles II.

Bibliography: J. R. Jones, *The First Whigs: The Politics of the Exclusion Crisis, 1678-1683*, 1961; Maurice Petherick, *Restoration Rogues*, 1951.

Ronald H. Fritze

Medicine. Medicine and medical science in the seventeenth century were in dramatic transition from an elite-controlled Galenic-educated base to a profession stimulated by competition, new prescriptives, and theoretical challenge. During this era of unprecedented change in medicine, practitioners ranged from the traditional university-schooled physician, through practically trained surgeons and apothecaries, to unprincipled quacks and charlatans. In the medical marketplace of Stuart England, there was room for them all.

English doctors were still associated with the more contemplative aspects of healing rather than with the treatment of patients. Medical students at Oxford were required by the Caroline Code of 1636 to study the humoral theories of Galen advanced during the Roman Empire; similar requirements for students at Cambridge dated from Elizabethan statutes of 1570 (see Universities*). Four humors in the human body were thought to be responsible for sickness, health, and temperament. A surfeit or deficit of any of these humors needed adjusting by the physician, usually through bleeding, purging, or ingestion of salubrious concoctions. Continentally trained doctors, many schooled at Leyden, and graduates of the twenty-five Dissenting Academies founded after the Restoration*, had been exposed to a new experimental curriculum. Their studies, based on the teachings of Paracelsus and van Helmont, advocated a search for application of specific organic and inorganic materials to cure specific diseases. Such physicians also tended to support anatomical studies, previously left to the province of surgeons, whose increasing numbers and hands-on style of practice threatened the doctors' domination of health care. By the beginning of the eighteenth century, even the apothecaries were awarded the right by the lords justice to prescribe as well as to prepare medicaments for the sick. There were plenty of physicians and surgeons practicing in the provinces.

The debate over theory and jurisdiction was heightened by scientific empiricism, which reached its peak after the Restoration. Experimentation was the mode, and ironically many charlatans were licensed and accorded respectability in the name of science*. Besides the mountebanks, foreign and domestic, who occasionally traveled with entertaining medicine shows, innumerable midwives and other "wise women" plied their inexpensive cures to a public that could not afford a physician even if it could find one.

Since obstetrics was virtually ignored by physicians, midwives licensed by the bishop for their moral character rather than their skill more than compensated. Besides, many physicians thought that sexual intercourse was the best medicine for all women's ailments. Midwives, organized by the Chamberlen family of man-midwives and inventors of the obstetrical forceps, petitioned the Crown in 1616 and again in 1634 for self-governance. Elizabeth Cellier (fl. 1680) suggested in 1687 that midwives be required to undergo professional examinations and staff a royal birthing hospital. Though municipal licensing of midwives was introduced in Edinburgh in 1694, episcopal licensing remained the norm throughout England. Many of the medical "irregulars" were sincere in their intentions and as competent as some of their professional counterparts. That most members of the Royal College of Physicians*, the institution charged with policing the practice of medicine, chose to abandon London* to those irregulars during the 1665 Plague of London* (see also Epidemics and Plague*) did the elite no credit.

Magic and mystery still held powerful sway in the healing arts, particularly outside London. Dead pigeons were tied to the patient's feet for the pox, and eagle stones were placed under the pillow of a woman in difficult labor. Prescribed cordials included "unicorn" horn, distillations from the skulls of hanged men, or powdered centipedes for sore throat. Most dramatically, Stuart monarchs, especially Charles II* and Anne*, "touched" thousands of their subjects suffering from the king's evil*, a form of tuberculosis, testimony to persistent belief in thaumaturgy.

Among the diseases that needed treatment were plague, smallpox, scarlet fever, rickets, venereal disease, sweating sickness, malarial fevers, and leprosy. In addition accidents and physical deformities required surgical intervention in an age before anesthesia or antiseptics. New medicines prescribed included cinchona, ipecac, tobacco, and metals such as mercury. Many of the more controversial "specifics" like cinchona (quinine) came from the Western Hemisphere. The search for a universal specific obsessed many scientists and further split the medical community. Patients faced both the blessings and the traumas of medical care buffeted by winds of change that blew at hurricane force. Many sick people, of course, treated themselves with cures that reflected folk culture. Apothecary Nicholas Culpeper (1616-1654) translated the *London Pharmacopoeia* from the Latin into English so that any man might know its secrets. He also published a popular recipe book of 369 herbal remedies.

Among the celebrated Stuart era doctors were William Harvey (1578-1657), royal physician and discoverer of the circulation of the blood; Thomas Sydenham (1624-1689), called the "English Hippocrates" for his multiple contributions to medicine; Thomas Willis (1621-1675), an anatomist known for his work on the brain; Francis Glisson (1597-1677), pioneer in the study of rickets; Richard Lower (1631-1691), a physiologist who performed the first blood transfusion in 1665; and Richard Wiseman (1622-1676), premier Caroline surgeon. Many more dedicated men and women remain unsung.

Bibliography: Lucinda M. Beier, *Sufferers and Healers, the Experience of Illness in Seventeenth Century England*, 1987; Roy Porter, *Disease, Medicine and Society in England, 1550-1860*, 1987.

Elizabeth Lane Furdell

Mercantilism. Since the advent of classical liberal economic theory, best exemplified by Adam Smith's *Wealth of Nations* (1776), mercantilism has been a staple item in discussions of seventeenth-century economic history. The traditional textbook account of mercantilist theory begins with the concept of limited wealth. Thus, a nation's wealth was measured entirely in terms of the amount of gold and silver bullion and specie that it possessed. Since there was a finite quantity of gold and silver in the world, a nation could increase its share only at the expense of other nations—through war, by establishing a more favorable balance of trade, or some combination thereof. Starting with a predominantly agricultural economic base, nations following a mercantilist policy sought to improve their balance of trade by promoting domestic industries, to produce exportable goods and reduce the need for imports; establishing trading companies* to gain a larger share of world trade, including the carrying trade; and founding colonies, which would serve as a source of cheap raw materials and a market for finished goods (see Colonization*). The agents of this process were supposedly merchants and manufacturers seeking monopolies*. The Dutch, the French in the age of Louis XIV's minister Colbert, and the English are all said to have exemplified such practices. The English Navigation Acts* are seen as the fruit of mercantilist policy, as are the Dutch Wars*, which they are said to have caused.

Recent studies suggest that this is too neat a picture; some even question whether mercantilist theory or coherent, consciously mercantilist policies ever existed in the seventeenth century.   Though D. C. Coleman acknowledges that the term *mercantilism* is a useful shorthand for various early modern economic ideas and practices, he also approves A. V. Judges's description of it as "an imaginary system" and contends that Adam Smith "invented the concept of the 'mercantilist system'" in order to destroy it in favor of what is usually called *laissez-faire*. He and others have noted that "mercantilist" legislation, regulation, taxation, and so on often stemmed more from the government's immediate fiscal needs than from any overarching policy. This becomes clear when the traditional elements in the history of mercantilism are considered in their proper political, social, and economic context.

In seventeenth-century England, what Smith later identified as "mercantile policy" resulted from the interaction of state and individual interests, and Charles Wilson argues that the former were paramount. The early Stuarts believed that regulating the economy was part of the royal prerogative*. The privy council* handled it until 1622, when it began appointing commissions of trade; from 1630 to 1640 there was a permanent commission, including merchants. Parliament* assumed responsibility during the early Interregnum*; the first Board of Trade was established in 1650, but the council of state* soon took over. Oliver Cromwell* set up a trade committee in 1655. During this period, mercantile interests petitioned the government, which consulted them about policy, but it never merely operated at their behest. And it was guided more by notions about the common weal than by mercantilist theory.

In 1622, with England in the midst of economic depression, the government had called upon various experts for assistance, including Gerald Malynes, Edward Misselden, and Thomas Mun. All three agreed that the problem was that too much specie was leaving the country, though they differed about solutions. Malynes said that English currency was undervalued and that the government needed to control the rate of exchange. Misselden claimed that English coin specifically was undervalued, while other nations' coin was valued higher, and that the value of England's silver coins needed to be raised. In what was to be a guiding principle well into the eighteenth century, Mun argued that the problem was not monetary in origin but the result of an unfavorable balance of trade, a notion later elaborated in his best known-work, *England's Treasure By Foreign Trade* (1664). However, as Wilson notes, Mun was responding to a particular problem, not attempting to create a universal theory.

English policymakers did indeed become obsessed by the balance of trade (rather ironically, since foreign trade* formed only a small part of the seventeenth-century economy). But "mercantilist" proposals and resulting legislation, proclamations, and the like tended to arise from crisis rather than preconceived policy. The depression of the cloth trade* led to government tinkering and, because the economy was too dependent upon this one industry, to efforts at diversification. Mun and others recommended reducing dependence on cloth, cutting out the Dutch middleman in foreign trade, and developing colonies, the fishing industry, and the merchant marine. Such thinking helped produce the Navigation Act of 1651, but the critical impetus came from a crisis: the depression that began in 1649, combined with the refusal of the Dutch to accept an alliance including restrictions on their part of the Anglo-Dutch trade. The act alone did not cause the First Dutch War* (1652-1652), which was a product of decades of tension (the Cockayne project*, the Amboina massacre*, fishing disputes, competition for African trade), triggered by the Dutch refusal to lower the flag in deference to English ships.

The weaknesses of the 1651 act led to renewed legislation after the Restoration*, producing the Navigation Act of 1660, the Frauds Act of 1662, and the Staple Act of 1663. Though supplemented by further acts in 1673 and 1696, these were essentially the basis for regulation of foreign trade until the early nineteenth century. Merchants influenced the passage of this legislation, as they did the disastrous Second Dutch War* (1665-1667), and they often served as advisers on various government boards from the 1660s on. But mercantile interests were too diverse to operate as a monolithic bloc and lacked access to what Wilson calls the "innermost counsels of state." Besides, the government had its own reasons for such measures, including the need to maintain national security, the fact that increased trade led to greater tax revenue (see Taxation and Revenue*), and the desire to avert the social disorder occasioned by economic hard times. The Board of Trade, reestablished in 1695, included not only businessmen like Sir Josiah Child, but also intellectuals like the economist Charles Davenant, the philosopher John Locke*, the scientist Sir Isaac Newton, and the architect Christopher Wren, hardly the puppets of mercantile interests. Seventeenth-century "mercantilist policy," though certainly influenced by concern about the balance of trade, arose piecemeal from a variety of causes.

Bibliography: D. C. Coleman, "Mercantilism Revisited," *Historical Journal* 23 (1980): 773-791; Charles Wilson, *England's Apprenticeship, 1603-1763*, 2d ed., 1984.

William B. Robison

Middlesex, Earl of. See Cranfield, Lionel.

Midland Rising (1607). The Midland Revolt was a popular rebellion that began as a series of large-scale anti-enclosure riots on the last day of April 1607 and ended in a pitched battle at Newton, Northamptonshire on 8 June. Originating in the northern part of Northamptonshire, the disturbances spread into the adjoining counties of Leicestershire and Warwickshire, where some of the protesters called themselves "levellers" and "diggers," names that later applied to movements of popular protest during the social upheaval that accompanied the English Revolution (see Diggers*; Levellers*). The rebels were outraged by what they perceived as the conversion of arable land to grassland during a period of dearth or high grain prices (see Agriculture*). The Midland Rising also elicited sympathetic demonstrations in other parts of the Midlands. Many of the protesters were cottagers and artisans who lived within Rockingham Forest and were dependent on grain grown in the arable villages to the south and southwest of the forest. The Northamptonshire trained bands were regarded as being unreliable for use against the protesters, so Sir Edward Montagu, a deputy lieutenant, and other gentry of the county raised an irregular force of servants and retainers to disperse the crowd of levellers gathered at Newton. The leader of the rebels was John Reynolds, a peddler or tinker by trade, who was known as "Captain Pouch" because of the supposedly magical contents of the leather bag he carried by his side. Reynolds declared that the enclosures were illegal and that he and his followers were casting them down in the king's name. The chronicler Edmund Howes testified that Captain Pouch maintained good discipline, and the levellers offered violence to no person. Reynolds and the leaders were executed for high treason, but the remainder of the surviving participants were tried on changes of felony-riot and misdemeanor-riot.

The government attempted to depict the Midland Rising as a bloody-minded conspiracy against gentlemen and tried to link it to other, unrelated enclosure riots. Although the Midland Revolt of 1607 was an agrarian rising comparable to the riots and rebellions of 1549 and expressed generalized hostility toward the gentry and aristocracy, the Northamptonshire demonstrations were almost exclusively directed at enclosures on the estates of two recusant* families, the Treshams of Rushton and Newton and the Vauxes of Harrowden. There is some indication that religious factionalism may have exacerbated the hostility toward Sir Thomas Tresham of Rushton, who was regarded as a harsh landlord by tenants in certain Puritan* villages. Although the government attempted to discredit the motives and behavior of the participants in the Midland Revolt, the grievances of the rebels led to the prosecution in the court of Star Chamber (see Prerogative Courts*) of Sir Thomas Tresham and a number of Midland peers and gentry for making depopulating enclosures in violation of the Tillage Act of 1597 (39 Eliz. I c. 2).

Bibliography: Edwin F. Gay, "The Midland Revolt and the Inquisitions of Depopulation, 1607," *Transactions of the Royal Historical Society* 18 (1904), pp. 195-

244; Roger B. Manning, *Village Revolts: Social Protest and Popular Disturbances in England, 1509-1640*, 1988.

Roger B. Manning

Millenarianism. A view focusing on the imminent Second Coming of Christ. Millenarianism predicted Christ's triumphant return to establish an earthly kingdom and rule with his saints either for a literal one thousand years or an indeterminate period. Millenarian views were inspired by a focus on biblical prophesies. Ruling saints would labor without pain or oppression, premature death, famine, or disease. The return would be preceded by extraordinary events such as the conversion of the Jews*, defeat of the Turks, and fall of Rome. Millenarianism developed throughout the Middle Ages. The hope of an imminent heaven on earth combined with the abject poverty of European peasantry to produce a surge of militant religiosity. Its popularity increased, spurred on by Reformation strife and an increasingly literal exegesis of prophetic biblical texts such as Revelation 20:4 and Daniel 7:18, 27. Early Reformation proponents such as Thomas Muntzer declared Münster the New Jerusalem and prepared to pave the way for Christ by annihilating the godless. Later in the sixteenth century John Foxe's *Acts and Monuments* placed England and other European nations within a historic framework determined by apocalyptic prophesies. He did not, however, consider England to be an elect nation. Thomas Brightman (d. 1607) predicted a gradual Godly transformation of society for one thousand years. Brightman believed that the millennium had already started with Marsilius of Padua's challenge to the papacy in the fourteenth century and would climax with the conversion of the Jews and Turks. Johannes Alsted (d. 1638) differed with Brightman, positing a sudden transformation of the world. His millennium would be a period of universal peace and harmony. Joseph Mede (d. 1668) extended millenarianism to government, postulating the theory of the elect nation. He also took Daniel's prophesy of the seventy weeks, extending its completion from the older view of the death of Christ to the advent of a future millennium.

Millenarian ideas, diffused throughout society, were championed and legitimized by Puritan* ministers calling for a determined overthrow of the Stuart monarchy during the English Civil War*. The death of Charles I* was considered preparation for the triumphant return of King Jesus. English millenarian literature* proliferated throughout the seventeenth century, with eighty titles produced by 1649. The idea that the millennium was to be a future event grew throughout the 1640s and 1650s. Prophets particularly focused on 1656 (which equaled the number of years between Creation and the Flood) and 1666 (from 666 as the biblical mark of the Beast).

Biblical prophets referred to the historic succession of four monarchies: Babylon, Persia, Greece, and Rome. These would also be succeeded by a fifth, the rule of Jesus and his saints. English millennial enthusiasts, the Fifth Monarchy Men*, prepared the way for the triumphant return of the Messiah throughout the 1650s with an aggressive political campaign and some violence. Their movement faded after the Restoration* with the cautious and often confused policies of the Stuarts.

Diggers*, founded by Gerrard Winstanley, sought a return to the purity of the Garden of Eden, where private property, the class system, and government fulfilled no purpose. Other radical English expressions such as Ranters*, Seekers*, and Levellers* all emerged from millennial roots exposed by the trauma of the Civil War and Interregnum*.

Most millenarians were not politically radicalized. These tended to see either spiritual rather than physical fulfillments or peaceful long-term answers to prophesy.

Bibliography: Bernard S. Capp, *The Fifth Monarchy Men*, 1972; Norman Cohn, *The Pursuit of the Millennium*, 1957; K. Firth, *The Apocalyptic Tradition in Reformation Britain*, 1979; Keith Thomas, *Religion and the Decline of Magic*, 1971.

William Nikides

Millenary Petition (1603). James I*, on his journey to London* after his accession to the throne, was presented this petition by Puritan* ministers in April 1603. It received its name from the fact that it had a thousand ministers' signatures. Essentially it directed the king to remove, amend, or qualify various rituals and ceremonies in accordance with Puritan theology. People were not to bow at the name of Jesus. Only the canonical Scriptures were to be read in the church. The cap and surplice would no longer be mandatory. Ministers were to be capable of preaching; if they were not, they could be removed. The legality of a minister's marriage was to be revived, and all abuses by duplication or impropriations* of the tithe were to be abandoned. Excommunication could be done only with consent of the pastor and not over trivial matters. Ecclesiastical courts* would have to restrain their use of fines and fees, but especially to correct the long delays. James promised a conference to address these matters. A year later at the Hampton Court Conference*, Puritan representatives not only pressed for the reforms noted, but went somewhat further in advancing a rigid form of Calvinism*. Some minor concessions were achieved, but generally the Puritans' position was not eased.

Bibliography: Henry Bettenson, ed., *Documents of the Christian Church*, 1963; Godfrey Davies, *The Early Stuarts, 1603-1660*, 1959.

John S. Erwin

Milton, John (1608-1674). Now known as the greatest epic poet in English, Milton was best known in his own day for his briefer poetic works and his vigorous Puritan prose; by his death the popularity of both the epic form and political Puritanism* had faded, but his reputation as poet and apologist had been set. A native of London*, he was born in Bread Street, Cheapside. He attended St. Paul's School and later Cambridge, earning his B.A. in 1629, M.A. in 1632, and for his disciplined life and auburn hair the nickname "Lady." After Cambridge Milton's devotion to scholarship led to a six-year retreat at Horton, his father's rural home, where he taught himself what the university* had not in history, literature*, philosophy, and languages. This period was capped by a trip to Italy in 1639. The next twenty years were an immersion in Puritan politics; he emerged as a pamphleteer and Latin secretary (1649-1659) for Oliver Cromwell*. Milton went blind toward the end of 1651, an infirmity surely aggravated by his unremitting studies since grammar school. With the Restoration* Milton found himself a marked man for his anti-monarchical sentiments and allegedly was spared from execution by the intervention of the poet Andrew Marvell. His latter years were quietly spent at home, dictating his epic and final works. He died on 8 November 1674.

Milton's career is noteworthy for its adherence to a set of clearly articulated political and poetic values, which remained consistent throughout his life; it is easy to disagree with him but hard to fault his integrity. In his prose he set for himself a characteristically Puritan task of attempting to foster a New Jerusalem in England by his anti-Catholic and anti-monarchical views, his fierce individualism grounded in a learned reliance on Christian truth, and the embodiment of these values in a strong parliamentary government. As a poet he cast himself in the role of divinely appointed seer, able to mingle both classical and Christian myths with poetic practice to "justify the ways of God to man" (*Paradise Lost*, I). His blindness he took as a sign of divine election for these tasks.

Milton's nonpolitical writings began with youthful Latin poetry and prose prolusions (academic exercises). His first significant English poem, "On the Morning of Christ's Nativity" (1628), displays a command of Christian humanist ideas, mingling classical and Christian allusions. Three years later appeared "L'Allegro" and "Il Penseroso," a pair of lyrics celebrating the active and contemplative attitudes, Milton favoring the latter. Composed on his twenty-fourth birthday in 1632, his sonnet "How Soon Hath Time" reveals the urgency of his poetic calling as well as the divine will he felt directing it. His masque *Comus* (1634) is a semi-theatrical rendition of the triumph of virtue over temptation and reveals him grappling with a lifelong artistic problem: recreating spiritual struggle in dramatic terms. In 1637 he composed "Lycidas," an elegy on the death of his friend Edward King. The poem, criticized by Samuel Johnson for its artificiality of feeling, has since been praised for its complex interweaving of themes and images of life, death, rebirth, youth, and poetic aspiration.

Between 1640 and 1660 Milton turned to Puritan prose. In 1641-1642 he composed five "antiprelatical tracts" against the Anglican* tradition of hierarchical structure and episcopal church rule; chief among these were *Of Reformation Touching Church-Discipline in England* (1641), *The Reason of Church Government* (1642), and *An Apology for Smectymnuus* (1642) ("Smectymnuus" being an anagram for the names of several Presbyterian* clerics). In 1644 he wrote *Of Education* and *Areopagitica*. The first critiques the traditional curriculum he had received, arguing for an expansion of subjects especially in "modern" fields such as languages and science*. The other, ostensibly a defense of freedom of the press (see Printing and Book Trade*), is in fact an argument for intellectual inquiry in all its forms (any restriction of the quest for truth created "a fugitive and cloistered virtue") and also one of the finest examples of Latinate English prose.

The liberal views of the divorce tracts, *The Doctrine and Discipline of Divorce* (1643) and *The Judgement of Martin Bucer Concerning Divorce* (1644), are related to, but not solely prompted by, his troubled first marriage to Mary Powell in 1642. She returned to her father after only several months of marriage but rejoined Milton in 1645. Their children were Anne, Mary, John (who died in childhood), and Deborah. Mary Powell died in 1652; Milton married Katherine Woodcock in 1656. After her death two years later, he married Elizabeth Minshull.

Milton began writing political pamphlets in 1649, openly criticizing the monarchy in *The Tenure of Kings and Magistrates*. That year he also became Latin secretary to Cromwell and composed *Eikonoklastes* ("the icon-breaker"), a response to *Eikon Basilike*, a laudatory work on the recently executed Charles I*. *The Defence of the English People* (1651) and the *Second Defence* (1654) defended the Puritan regime before a continental audience. His last political tract, *The Ready and Easy Way to Establish a Free Commonwealth*, appeared two months before the Restoration* of Charles II*, when any hope for the English republic was gone. At about this time he also completed *De Doctrina Christina*, his idiosyncratic treatise on Christian theology marked by an Arminian* liberalism that distanced him from Puritan orthodoxy.

Composition of *Paradise Lost* began during the 1650s. Aging, blind, and politically disaffected, Milton turned to the epic to promulgate his final vision of "God's ways to man." His poem is at once a defiant statement of personal faith, a defense of biblical authority, the repository of a lifetime of esoteric learning, and the culmination of a self-stated artistic goal to compose a work "so written to aftertimes, as they should not willingly let it die" (*Reason of Church Government*). That both poetic fashion and political power had passed him by mattered little; the poem triumphs over its own anachronism. Satan's grand but doomed rebellion, God's inexorable victory, and the troubled fall into knowledge of Adam and Eve retell the Christian myth with compelling power and design as well as—to some critics of Eve—telling implications about the author himself.

Three years before his death, Milton published *Paradise Regained* and *Samson Agonistes*. *Paradise Regained* retells Christ's redemption of fallen man, though in keeping with Milton's deemphasis on Christ's humanity in favor of God's primacy, he omits the crucifixion. Once again, Satan is defeated, this time as Jesus defeats his tempter in the desert and exemplifies patient obedience to divine will. Samson, Milton's rendering of the Greek tragic hero, is a type of the "warfaring Christian" praised in *Areopagitica*: strong yet flawed, although beset by enemies without and doubts within, he struggles to attain a new sense of devotion to God. Notwithstanding his respect for historic and literary tradition, the authority of Scripture, and the sovereignty of God, Milton's focus on the plight and potential of the individual, whether in the wrong (Satan) or in the right (Jesus, Samson, Milton himself), marks him as one of the greatest Renaissance authors.

Bibliography: W. B. Hunter, *A Milton Encyclopedia*, 1983; J. H. Summer, *The Muse's Method: An Introduction to Paradise Lost*, 1962.

Christopher Baker

Monck, George, 1st Duke of Albemarle (1608-1670). A professional soldier, Monck was a key figure in restoring Charles II* to the throne in 1660. He began his military career as a volunteer in the expeditions to Cadiz in 1625 and the Isle de Rhe in 1627 (see Cadiz Expedition*; Spanish War of 1625-1630*), before serving in the Low Countries in the Dutch army in the 1630s, distinguishing himself at the siege of Breda in 1637. He fought in the First Bishops' War* in 1639, then against the Irish Rebellion* in 1641, before returning to England on the outbreak of the Civil War* in 1642, with Irish troops to help the royalist* cause. He was captured by Sir Thomas Fairfax* at Nantwich in 1644 and imprisoned in the Tower of London, where he occupied his time writing his *Military Observations* (not published until 1670). At war's end parliament* offered him a command in Ireland* in return for his allegiance. He accepted and was made governor of Ulster in 1647. He had only modest military success, capturing Robert Monro, commander of the royalist Scots in Ireland, in 1648. But he was forced first to make a truce and then, because of mutiny among his troops, to surrender Dundalk, which raised suspicion about his loyalty and earned his recall to England and parliamentary censure. Oliver Cromwell*, however, continued to have confidence in him and, having successfully quashed the Irish revolt, took Monck with him when he turned his attention next to Scotland*. After Cromwell had defeated the Covenanters* equally decisively, he left Monck in charge of the parliamentary forces in Scotland. Monck held this command intermittently until the Restoration*, interrupted by his successful service as an admiral in the First Dutch War* (1652-1654). In his Scottish command, which included broad civil powers, Monck was unswervingly loyal to the Cromwellian regime, but he was also quite firmly opposed to political activity within his army*, either by senior officers or the rank and file. Therefore, following Cromwell's death in September 1658, as the Protectorate* began to crumble and a power struggle ensued, Monck's force was quiet and obedient to his firm orders, something that could not be taken for granted in the other armies.

In 1659 Monck was wooed by the restored Rump Parliament* and by his military colleagues in England, whose men were far more restless. Keeping his own counsel, he finally intervened early in 1660, marching his effective and disciplined force to London* and obliging the Rump to restore all of its surviving excluded members. In secret correspondence with Charles he advised a moderate course, which was quickly adopted and embodied in the Declaration of Breda*. Monck was then able to see the king restored. Charles rewarded him with the command of all his forces and a dukedom. The king also relied on his military advice, though not his views on politics or religion. In the Second Dutch War* (1665-1667), a naval contest like the first, Monck was much less successful, the war ending with a humiliating Dutch triumph over the English fleet in the Medway, though this was not directly his fault. Despite his record of victory in the First Dutch War, Monck had little naval experience and was no match for the veteran Dutch sea commanders (see Navy*). He gave up his military command, served briefly as first lord of the treasury, and chose to retire in 1668. Ironically, although he prided himself on military professionalism in his determination to remain aloof from politics, his place in history depends largely on his very political success in restoring the Stuart monarchy to power rather than his brilliance as a commander in the field.

Bibliography: J. D. G. Davies, *Honest George Monck*, 1936.

S. J. Stearns

Monmouth's Rebellion (1685). A failed rebellion centered in southwest England and spearheaded by James Scott, duke of Monmouth and Buccleuch, the illegitimate son of Charles II*, which was mounted to wrest the English throne from Monmouth's Catholic* uncle, James II*.

Born in 1649, Monmouth was the product of a questionable relationship between Charles and Lucy Walters; there was and still is speculation that the couple had been legally married, thereby making Monmouth legitimate. In any case, the young duke was quite popular, making his mark in the navy* and the army* and receiving early acclaim on a tour of the western counties in 1679-1680. Charles's minister, the earl of Shaftesbury (Anthony Ashley Cooper*), promoted Monmouth's recognition as heir in order to guarantee a Protestant succession, and other Whigs* took up the issue. Rumors culminated in the Rye House Plot* of 1683, which forced Monmouth into exile in Holland. While awaiting recall Monmouth heard the news of Charles's death and James's accession to the throne. At first unwilling to challenge his uncle, Monmouth was reluctantly persuaded by fellow exiles and English conspirators that the overthrow of James would be welcomed by the country at large.

A small invasion force was mustered, departed for Lyme Regis on 30 May 1685, and landed there on 11 June. The men of the West Country who rallied to Monmouth did so primarily in order to defend the Protestant religion, and the question of Monmouth's legitimate right to the throne mattered little. After reaching Taunton, Monmouth was declared king on 20 June; the rebel army marched successfully to Bristol, but Monmouth declined, on the advice of his war council, to capture it and bypassed a great opportunity to solidify his successes. Minor battles ensued as the army marched to Warminster, and royal troops under the command of Lord Feversham began to turn the tide. As rebel desertions mounted and promised troops failed to materialize, Monmouth broached the possibility of escape but was dissuaded from this course. In an attempt to obtain additional men, Monmouth marched to Wells and then turned toward Bridgwater, while the king's army settled in the village of Weston Zoyland in the area known as Sedgemoor. Monmouth and his advisers decided on a surprise night attack late on 5 July, but an alarm was raised and battle quickly enjoined. The rebel forces fought valiantly, but as dawn approached, it became clear that the king's army was in control of the battle. As Monmouth's troops fled the field, they were pursued by the royal forces and wholesale slaughter ensued; approximately 700 rebels were estimated to have been killed, against a loss of only twenty-seven for the king.

In the aftermath of the Battle of Sedgemoor, Monmouth escaped with several others, but he was captured on 7 July and transported with his fellow prisoners to the

Tower of London on 13 July. Previously attainted by parliament*, Monmouth begged for and obtained an interview with James, but his uncle was determined on the duke's death. Monmouth signed a statement attesting to his illegitimacy and James's right to the Crown, but he refused to characterize his invasion as a rebellion and would not repent a long-standing extramarital liaison. Denied the sacrament, Monmouth went to the scaffold on 15 July and died bravely despite a botched execution, which required five blows of the axe. The rebels who supported his cause were dealt with in the infamous Bloody Assizes* six weeks after Monmouth's death. The rebellion proved to be only the first of the series of events that would eventually deprive James II of his throne in the Glorious Revolution* of 1688.

Bibliography: Robert Dunning, *The Monmouth Rebellion*, 1984; W. MacDonald Wigfield, *The Monmouth Rebellion*, 1980.

Connie S. Evans

Monopolies. Monopolies afforded their holders exclusive control over the disposition of certain goods, laws, fines, or fees. Royal grants of patents of monopoly stirred cross-currents of sentiment among various economic interests, particularly during periods of economic depression, and raised questions regarding the extent to which the power to execute royal prerogatives* could be vested in those other than the sovereign. Monopolies granted in Stuart Britain included the sale of gold and silver thread, the collection of greenwax fines, and the sale of soap, the last being a monopoly, which Charles I* bestowed upon several court Catholics* during the 1630s.

Patents for monopoly had become a parliamentary grievance during the reign of Elizabeth I, and in 1603 in the case of *Darcy v. Allen* the judges declared monopoly grants illegal. In a proclamation issued in 1610, James I* declared that he would no longer grant monopolies that conferred the power to execute the penal laws, to dispense with the law, or to compound for forfeitures. Despite this resolve, the Crown continued to issue grants not only for such relatively noncontroversial endeavors as new inventions and industries, the printing* of books, and the production of saltpeter, but also for those authorizing individuals to enforce the penal laws and to dispense with statutes (see Dispensing Power*). As the parliament of 1621* opened, the worries of the House of Commons over this unrelieved grievance were evident. Speakers decried monopolies as illegal and suggested that the king had received misinformation regarding them. Patents that gave individuals authority to enforce penal laws caused the greatest consternation. Facing a wave of anger, James shrewdly allowed the Commons to attack the conduct of the patentees.

Because they comprehended the range of early modern administrative and economic activities, monopolies prompted varying reactions. The monopoly held by the king's boatmen of lampreys caught in the Thames was not very controversial since it was obviously an attempt to reward the king's servants and did not affect the general population. Some monopolies, such as the ones for lighthouses and fines on weights and measures before the clerk of the market, while occasionally controversial, filled gaps in existing administration. Other monopolies attracted little favor with anyone other than the patentee of the moment. Sir Giles Mompesson, commonly known as "the lord of hosts," held grants for the licensing of inns, for concealed Crown lands*, and for gold and silver thread. His prosecution before the House of Lords in 1621 led to attacks upon referees, those who had prepared patents or recommended that the Crown grant them, and ultimately to a 1624 statute that prohibited certain monopolies (21-22 Jac. I, c. 3). Nevertheless several patents, such as those for glassmaking, were exempted from the statute's provisions and remained legal.

The Crown's response to complaints regarding monopolies generally involved condemnation of the practice and punishment of the monopolists where it could be shown that there were abuses. But new grants were usually forthcoming. Despite the statute of 1624, for example, the Crown entertained various projects and monopolies during the 1630s, including those pertaining to soap and fen drainage*. The Crown found monopolies appealing for two reasons: they raised revenue expeditiously (see Taxation and Revenue*) and circumvented the inefficiency associated with amateur local government*. Gentry disliked monopolies because they contradicted the social values of the local community. Monopolists driven by the profit motive to enforce laws literally showed little flexibility or awareness of local circumstances.

Monopolies may, nevertheless, represent a pathway to modernity that was not taken. They suggested that royal authority was divisible and might be the agency of centralization and administrative rationalization. Until the later part of the seventeenth century, projectors and customs farmers continued to be of value in meeting the financial requirements of the Crown. As such, monopolies and the patents that furthered them deserve consideration that transcends not only the complaints of the gentry and the self-serving denials of the monopolists themselves but the confines of British history, for as the activities of the *arbitristas* in Spain indicate, monopolies were a European phenomenon inextricably associated with the operation of the royal state. In the case of England, it is arguable that certain of the principles on which monopolies operated were institutionalized in the fiscal arrangements that produced a funded national debt near the end of the seventeenth century. Indeed it had never been a question of whether projectors should formulate prospective policies or whether monopolies should regulate certain public services but merely who should benefit from such ventures and at whose expense.

Bibliography: E. R. Foster, "The Procedure of the House of Commons against Patents and Monopolies, 1621-4," in W. Aiken and B. D. Henning, eds., *Conflict in Stuart England*, 1960, pp. 57-85.

                                                                    Myron C. Noonkester

Music. As in earlier times, musical trends during the Stuart period were shaped by two major factors: the tastes of the royal court* and the vicissitudes of the economy.

Slowly but surely over the course of the century, private collections of music manuscripts became less normative in the face of technological improvements in music printing*. The refinement of music engraving especially nourished the nascent music publishing industry as psalters, songbooks, and broadside ballads proliferated. Songbook publishers promoted tavern singing clubs to enlarge their markets, although many songbooks still printed only texts with instructions that they be "sung to the tune of . . . ." Scholars are divided as to the effect of the various music printing monopolies* but agree that their real purpose was quality control rather than economic protection.

During the early Stuart years, Elizabethan styles remained popular. Indeed, although signs of change were discernible much earlier, for music the Elizabethan period is considered to close only in 1623 with the death of William Byrd. Madrigals, part songs usually for five or six voices, continued in favor throughout the reign of James I*, and instrumental music retained its vocal character. However, James I did put his own stamp on music fashions by much Italianate borrowing. This included music for solo performer and continuo (the later being an instrument or group of instruments that played an accompanying bass line), along with the increased popularity of bowed string instruments.

Rising commercial opportunities for virtuoso solo performers helped doom the madrigal, even as such madrigalisms as text painting influenced English art song. (Text painting is the affective use of music to portray a text.) This is not surprising as madrigals were an imported style; the concurrent English native style was, as it had always been, rooted firmly in solo song even when rendered in polyphony.

The English verse anthem also rested in this tradition. Verse anthems were sacred works that combined sections for solo voices and instruments with others employing full, unaccompanied chorus. The full anthem was for chorus alone. Later various hybrids would develop, such as the full verse anthem, the cantata anthem, and the ode.

With this emphasis on song, it might be expected that solo keyboard music would remain secondary to or at least dependent on song. One exception was the fancy, a highly improvisatory work, usually for organ or virginals. Even these were often based on a preexisting melody, most often secular, although sacred melodies and even plainsong tunes were used for organ works in this and similar genres. Other popular solo keyboard forms derived from popular masque and dance tunes. These ranged from richly embellished virtuoso works, frequently variation sets, to simpler pieces intended to accompany actual dancing. They bore such titles as "Lord Zouche's Fancy," "My Ladye Neville's Domp," and "Spill No Beere."

In 1649 the Puritan* Interregnum* ushered in a new set of musical priorities. Far from opposing music per se, the Puritans merely railed against what they considered to be music's abuses. These included the performance of non-sacred music on the Sabbath, elaborate music in church, and music on the commercial stage (as an extension of their prohibition of for-profit theatrical life in general). The last stemmed from its prevailing taste for texts overtly designed to titillate.

As a result of the Interregnum hibernation of professional liturgical and theatrical music, their practitioners turned to secular chamber music and to teaching, often at the country estates of former Cavaliers*. Music and drama (see Literature*) both thrived in schools and private homes, albeit with subject matter and language accommodating to Puritan ideals, "for many chose rather to fiddle at home, then to go out and be knockt on the head abroad." The Commonwealth* emphasis on education combined with the large number of former cathedral musicians turned teachers to encourage this development of a dilettante tradition. The violin, recorder, oboe, and flute were popular amateur instruments, gathered together in small ensembles called consorts. The viol consort gave way to the violin, with the bass viol surviving as a continuo instrument. The guitar, in use much earlier, began to replace the lute as the plucked string instrument of choice. Church organs frequently found new lives as chamber instruments in the homes of the gentry. Oliver Cromwell* himself, an ardent music lover, took the organ from Lambeth Palace to his residence "for safekeeping." As in earlier times, household servants were often hired for their ability to double as musicians, and master, servant, and professional musician often whiled away a musical evening together. Women* especially benefited from these new dilettante opportunities.

Juxtaposed on the musical dilettante tradition was another in musical drama. Matthew Locke, Christopher Gibbons (son of Orlando Gibbons), and William Davenant were among the academic composers of masques. Even proto opera might be acceptable if performed in an educational setting and marketed as a "Moral Representation in Recitative Music" or "in the manner of the ancients." Musical plays were a convenient way around Puritan officials who, somewhat inexplicably, tended to be much more lenient with sung texts than spoken ones.

In the area of sacred music, the metrical Psalm continued to prosper. The Puritan ideal for church music coincided with declining parish incomes and an increased desire for congregational participation in worship. Combined with the improved musical education of the worshipers, improvised congregational harmony became an attainable goal for many parishes. In 1645 the Long Parliament* ordered that "everyone that can read is to have a Psalm book, and all others, not disabled by age or otherwise, are to be exhorted to learn to read. But for the present, where many in the Congregation cannot read, it is convenient that the Minister or some fit person appointed by him and the Ruling Officers, do read the Psalm line by line before the singing thereof." The "lining-out" method offered an affordable alternative: a leader would sing or speak the text a line at a time, to be repeated by the congregation. Unfortunately this method was conducive to neither enthusiasm nor creativity and so served only to hasten the eventual decline of congregational singing until the arrival of cheap hymnals in the eighteenth century.

With the Restoration* of the monarchy and the ascent of Charles II* in 1660, the English citizenry, wearied of Puritanical prohibitions, eagerly patronized the reopened theaters and music establishments both commercial and ecclesiastical. Public concerts in halls and churches reflected the new commercialization of music, but there still was no polarization between professionals and amateurs; indeed, they often made music together. Playbills and newspapers advertised concerts, almost all of which were a mixture of genres both vocal and instrumental, with little regard for programmatic coherence or unity. Lord North was to write that "flourishing upon a key at the entrance of a consort is common." In 1672 John Bannister produced the first regular public concerts at Whitefriars. From 1678 Thomas Britton held concerts above his coal shop in a series called the "Kit-cat Club." By 1691 weekly concerts were held in at least two locations, the Vendu and York buildings. The season went from October to May or June with both single and series concerts. Patrons, mostly from the upper and middle classes, paid at the end of a concert. By leaving early one could often avoid paying at all. Theaters, guild halls, school halls, and churches were favorite concert venues. All of this was memorialized in *A Compleat and Humourous Account of All the Remarkable Clubs and Societies in the Cities of London and Westminster Compil'd from the Original Papers of a Gentleman Who Frequented Those Places upwards of Twenty Years* by Edward Ward (1667-1731).

Continental-style opera was not supported by seventeenth-century English audiences, who retained their preference for primarily dramatic works laced with large amounts of incidental music. Henry Purcell's *Dido and Aeneas* stands as the sole major exception.

Music was an integral part of Restoration drama both within the play and as incidental music before and after performances and between acts. This included all drama, even tragedy. As Charles II did not encourage extravagant court masques, stage plays with music increased in number. Theater songs, especially masque tunes, took pride of place in the flourishing songbook industry. Music was used in drama to a variety of purposes: to move the plot, to convey intense emotion, to display a musician's virtuosity, to communicate the passing of time or a change of locus. Stage musicians were expected to memorize all music, be it solo or accompaniment.

Restoration church music took much from the early Stuart period, adding to it a wider use of instruments and a taste for ever larger and grander works. Within three weeks after Charles II's return to London*, Samuel Pepys* noted that he heard the organ played in the chapel at Whitehall Palace. This was the first time Pepys had heard an English organ service or seen an English vested choir. Barnard's *First Book of Selected Church Music* was reprinted and with available manuscripts helped reestablish the earlier repertory. The later Stuart reigns saw a polarization of sacred musical styles: congregational psalm singing in most parishes and sacred art music in such places as wealthy urban parishes, cathedrals, and college chapels. In the latter locations, sacred music became increasingly a spectator form. Sunday afternoon concerts in cathedrals and important parishes became fashionable places to see and be seen.

During the reign of Charles II, the ode—a vocal offering in celebration of royal events, holidays, and the like—evoked memories of earlier motets and anthems to the same purpose. Some bore religious texts, others secular; all were blatant glorifications of the dedicatee. John Blow (1649-1708), organist at Westminster Abbey and composer to the Chapel Royal, and his student Henry Purcell (1659-1695), holder of several royal musical appointments, were notable composers in this genre (and several others).

Continental influences were soon adopted, the court as usual leading the way. Charles II imitated the French court with its "twenty-four violins," even to inviting the presence of a string orchestra in the Chapel Royal on Sundays and festivals. English musical expatriates returned from sojourns in France and Italy, and Italian virtuosi were welcomed and patronized. As a result French and Italian styles greatly affected the sacred music of England in general and of such composers as Henry Purcell, Pelham Humfrey (1647-1674), and John Blow (1648-1708) in particular.

Another characteristic of seventeenth-century British music was the decline of art music in Scotland*, as the Scottish royal patrons took their patronage to London. Scottish music increasingly being left to amateurs, metrical Psalm singing flourished, borrowing Lutheran and French chorale tunes, and amateur song schools arose in many towns. As usual in such situations, folk song prospered. By mid-century the Scottish folk song tradition was valued enough for its tunes to be written down.

In Wales* the bardic harpists of the sixteenth century gave way to the balladeers of the seventeenth. Printed ballads—long, free-verse poems—were published in pamphlet form "to be sung to" a well-known tune. These balladeers served an important social purpose, as there were no vernacular newspapers in Wales until the nineteenth century. Religion in Wales remaining quite conservative, the metrical psalm tradition did not develop there until 1621, with the publication of the first Welsh Book of Common Prayer.

Bibliography: D. W. Krummel, *English Music Printing, 1553-1700*, 1975; Paul Lang, *Music in Western Civilization*, 1941; S. Sadie, ed., *The New Grove Dictionary of Music and Musicians*, 6th ed., 20 vols., 1980; *Musica Britannica*, 1951-.

Ann E. Faulkner

N

Naseby, Battle of (1645). On 9 May 1645 Charles I* left Oxford in what would prove to be his last military campaign. Early 1645 saw intense political and military activity as parliament* appointed Lord General Sir Thomas Fairfax* as its new commander-in-chief, passed the Self-Denying Ordinance*, fielded the New Model Army*, and saw its new army march and counter-march between Taunton and Oxford once the campaign season began. Charles I's army*, on the other hand, won victories over the Scots, besieged Taunton, and captured Leicester. As the king attempted to unite his forces in the west in early June, Fairfax was able to strike the Cavaliers* at Naseby before they were able to do so. Charles learned of Fairfax's approach on 13 June and quickly convened a council of war at Market Harborough. Because Fairfax was moving so quickly, Charles decided—against the advice of Prince Rupert, who was now captain-general of the army—to stand and fight. This was a surprising decision, particularly since the king's 7,000 to 8,000 men were greatly outnumbered by the 13,000 to 14,000 Roundheads*. Still the Cavaliers had little respect for the untried "New Noodle Army."

The Battle of Naseby began early on 14 June. Around 3:00 A.M. Fairfax roused his troops and had them in place within two hours. On the advice of Oliver Cromwell*, his new lieutenant general of horse, Fairfax had his men redeploy along the reverse slope in order to reduce their visibility and to encourage the Cavalier horse to charge uphill. Rupert and a scouting party saw this maneuver, but he impetuously and erroneously assumed that the troops were withdrawing rather than repositioning themselves for battle. Based upon Rupert's advice, Charles descended from his position atop Dust Hill. The Cavaliers deployed with Rupert commanding the cavalry on the king's right flank, Sir Marmaduke Langdale the horse on the left, and the seasoned Sir Jacob Astley the foot in the middle. On the other side of the battle lines Fairfax sent Commissary-General Henry Ireton* to lead the cavalry on his left flank, Cromwell to command the cavalry on the right, and Major General Philip Skippon to direct the infantry in the center. Around ten o'clock the battle began with a general advance by the royalist* army. The cavalry charge that Rupert led was largely successful, but as at Edgehill* he lost control of his men as they chased the fleeing parliamentarian* horse miles away from the fighting. Meanwhile Cromwell routed Langdale on the other flank. Astley and the royalist foot were initially successful in pushing back the parliamentary infantry, but effective attacks by Cromwell's horse and remnants of Ireton's on the flanks and the timely intervention of Fairfax in leading the reserve foot gradually drove the king's infantry back. Watching Astley under attack from all sides, Charles decided to lead his reserve into the fray. As he prepared to do so, however, Robert Dalyell (or Dalzell), earl of Carnwath, grabbed the reins of the king's horse and convinced him not to jeopardize his life. The reserve, misunderstanding the king's intentions, marched away from Astley and thus failed to reinforce him. By the time Rupert's cavalry returned, the king's foot were being overwhelmed. Rather than committing his horse to assist the infantry, Rupert watched Astley's men fight valiantly before throwing down their weapons and asking for quarter. After three hours of fighting, some 1,000 royalists lay dead along with some 200 Roundheads. Fairfax also took 4,500 to 5,000 prisoners and a large quantity of weapons and cannon. Less tangibly, the morale and the confidence of the New Model Army grew.

The significance of the Battle of Naseby extends beyond its martial aspects. After the battle, Fairfax seized the king's correspondence, which provided clear evidence of Charles's desire to secure help from the French, the Irish, and the pope. Furthermore, parliament now believed that it could defeat Charles without the support of the Scots, a sentiment that would have important political and religious implications. Despite his stinging defeat and the substantial loss of life and materiel, Charles I withdrew toward Wales*, continuing the fight for another year.

Bibliography: H. C. B. Rogers, *Battles and Generals of the Civil War*, 1968; Peter Young, *Naseby, 1645: The Campaign and the Battle*, 1985; Peter Young and Richard Holmes, *The English Civil War: A Military History of the Three Civil Wars, 1642-1651*, 1974.

David B. Mock

Navigation Acts (1651, 1660, 1662, 1663, 1670-1671, 1673). The Navigation Act of 9 October 1651 resulted from competition for markets between England and the United Provinces of the Netherlands, the dominant maritime commercial powers of the mid-seventeenth century. The act established an imperial monopoly over seaborne trade and is an example of mercantilist* policy. The Book of Rates (1642) had called for a protectionist trade policy, but the outbreak of the Civil War* prevented effective implementation.

The Hispano-Dutch peace treaty of 1648 ended the commercial advantage enjoyed in the 1620s and 1630s by English maritime interests, which as neutrals reached markets from which the Dutch were excluded. The disruptions in trade* caused by the Civil War crippled English commerce, as aggressive Dutch merchants established dominance over the East Indies spice trade and markets in Spain, the Mediterranean, the Baltic, and the West Indies. They established a virtual monopoly over the English carrying trade and excluded English interests from Dutch colonial markets. The English responded with ship seizures, which amounted to outright piracy. The Commonwealth* government joined in the piracy, even allowing warships to take part. Dutch losses mounted (140 vessels in 1651 alone).

The Navigation Act of 1651 prohibited the carrying of any product grown or manufactured in Asia, Africa, Europe, or America for importation into England, Wales*, or Ireland* in any but English vessels. Parliament* offered to rescind the act in exchange for a large indemnity, which the Dutch refused. By May 1652, tensions reached the point of war as English and Dutch warships opened fire on one another in the English Channel and the North Sea.

The First Dutch War* of 1652-1654 proved the vitality and combat effectiveness of the new English navy*. Under commanders such as George Monck* and Robert Blake, using new battle line and squadron tactics, English warships handily defeated the hitherto dominant Dutch. But despite battle attrition, the resilient Dutch shipbuilding industry replaced losses, enabling them to disrupt trade in distant areas that the English navy could not patrol effectively.

The act and the Dutch War enjoyed support from London* merchants and radicals in Barebone's Parliament* but proved unpopular among other trading interests and became difficult to enforce, particularly during the Spanish War of 1655-1659*, when much of England's commerce traveled in Dutch bottoms to avoid Spanish privateers.

The Treaty of London (April 1654) ceded the spice island of Pula Run to England and provided compensation for losses in the Baltic and the East Indies. A Dutch promise of no support for Charles II* and the exclusion of the house of Orange, with no compensation for Dutch losses, seemed an English victory. Despite this appearance, the Navigation Act remained in force. In 1655 the English confiscated sixty Dutch ships for violating the act.

The Restoration* in 1660 brought a confirmation of the act. The Navigation Act of 1660 (12 Car. II, c. xviii) mandated that (1) all commodities exported from or imported to the colonies must be hauled in English or colonial-owned vessels; (2) the master and three-fourths of each crew must be English; (3) goods imported in foreign ships must originate in that country; (4) colonial merchants must be British natives; and (5) certain commodities such as sugar, tobacco, cotton, wool, indigo, and ginger could be exported only to England or an English colony. The Navigation Acts of 1651 and 1660, with subsequent modifications, became a cornerstone of early imperial commercial, maritime, foreign, and trade policy as the British colonial empire took shape.

The 1662 modification (14 Car. II, c. xi) required that ships be built within the empire to avoid paying alien duties. The 1663 (15 Car. II, c. vii) modification required that all products of European origin destined for the colonies first pass through England or Wales for transfer to ships meeting the nationality requirement. An act of 1670-1671 (22-23 Car. II, c. xxvi) forbade landing enumerated goods in Ireland (which had been allowed under the 1660 act). The 1673 change (25 Car. II, c. vii) imposed duties on commodities shipped between colonies.

For Scotland* the enforcement of the Navigation Acts meant economic disaster. Scottish ships were considered alien and paid twice the English duty. A 1668 commission to resolve the problems of Scottish free trade to the plantations* and high tariffs (see Taxation and Revenue*) failed to resolve the dispute, which remained problematic until the 1707 Act of Union. (See Trading Companies*; East India Company*.)

Bibliography: Ephraim Lipson, *The Economic History of England*, vol. III: *The Age of Mercantilism*, 1931.

Stanley D. M. Carpenter

Navy. The seventeenth century was a period of major but erratic development in naval history. After the Elizabethan triumphs, the early Stuart period saw a dismal decline. In the reign of James I*, a period of peace, the navy was bedeviled by neglect, waste, corruption, and incompetence. The aging earl of Nottingham, lord admiral until 1618, did nothing to tackle these problems. The marquis (later 1st duke) of Buckingham (George Villiers*) succeeded him and launched an energetic drive to cut costs and strengthen the fleet. But when the navy was put to the test in Charles I's* French War of 1627-1629* and Spanish War of 1625-1630*, the results were not encouraging. The Cadiz expedition* in 1625 was frustrated by poor leadership, ships, seamen, and victuals. Buckingham's own expedition to the Ile de Re in 1627 had at least some temporary success, but the earl of Denbigh's expedition to La Rochelle in 1628 turned back feebly without even attempting to engage the enemy. Most contemporaries, including the large crowds of unpaid and mutinous seamen, blamed Buckingham for these failures. Many of the problems were in fact outside his control, for parliament* refused to fund the wars adequately, and there was little he could do about the shortage of money and supplies. Nor should we forget that the Elizabethan navy too had death and disease on a horrific scale among unpaid, ill-fed mariners.

Buckingham was well aware that the ships too were often unsatisfactory. Large warships were useless against fast privateers, and hired merchantmen were of little value because the owners were unwilling to put them at risk. In 1627 he called for a navy of seventy large ships, plus thirty pinnaces for service against privateers. Though this was far beyond the king's resources, the 1630s did see an energetic program of building. From 1635 Charles put out a large fleet each summer, paid for by his new ship money* levies. With England still at peace, there was no opportunity for them to achieve anything notable, and they are often dismissed as an expensive irrelevance. This verdict is probably too harsh. Charles's main aim was to assert his claim to the sovereignty of the seas and to deter the French and Dutch by a display of force; in this he had some success for several years, though it was limited by the fact that he could not afford to go to war. The ship money fleets also marked a step forward in the professionalization of the navy. They consisted increasingly of warships rather than hired merchant vessels, and they provided a degree of continuity in naval service.

Charles was less successful in paying his seamen, which helps to explain why the naval forces in the Downs revolted with the Long Parliament* on the outbreak of the

Civil War* in 1642; another decisive factor was the popularity of the earl of Warwick, the commander-in-chief. Those captains who remained loyal to the king were ignominiously packed ashore. Under the energetic leadership of Warwick, lord admiral from 1643, the navy played a significant part in the Civil War. Inevitably the war was decided on land, but the navy prevented foreign aid from reaching the king and protected maritime trade, which allowed customs revenues to flow into parliament's coffers. The navy also enabled parliament to hold on to Hull, a valuable northern outpost, and prevented the fall of Plymouth in 1644, after the defeat at Lostwithiel. Charles's gentleman-captains quickly vanished from the scene after 1642; the parliamentary officers were mainly former merchant commanders. Even so they were alarmed by the growing political radicalism in the New Model Army*, and at Westminster Warwick was ousted in 1645 by the Self-Denying Ordinance*; by the winter of 1646-47 his successor, William Batten, was negotiating with the Scots on a compromise peace with the king. He resigned in 1647 and was replaced by Colonel Thomas Rainsborough, an Independent*, who was intended to bring the navy into line with parliament's wishes. The plan backfired. In May 1648 a mutiny broke out in the Downs, triggered by personal and political grievances rather than the usual complaints over pay and conditions. Rainsborough was bundled ashore, and the squadron declared for the king. The mutineers sailed to Helvoetsluys, and the prince of Wales (the future Charles II*) arrived to take command. In July he brought the ships back to the Downs, hoping to capitalize on the Second Civil War*, but with the collapse of royalist* forces on land, he had little choice but to return to Holland. Warwick was despatched with a parliamentarian* force to reduce the rebels, and for many weeks the two fleets lay close together under the watchful eyes of the Dutch. Warwick did secure some of the ships, but he returned to England when winter closed in, his mission only half accomplished.

The republican regime established early in 1649 felt little confidence in Warwick and his captains and judged it essential to put the navy into safer hands. In February 1649 Warwick was replaced by three generals-at-sea, among them Robert Blake, who was to be the key figure in naval affairs until his death in 1657. The generals and the admiralty commissioners ashore pushed through a drastic purge and remodeling of the officer corps. Parliament also embarked on a rapid buildup of the navy, for the new republic knew it had no friends abroad. Over the next decade, the navy trebled in size, the most rapid expansion England had ever seen. The sudden emergence of English naval power and assertiveness greatly alarmed neighboring powers, and in 1652 a fierce naval war erupted between the English and Dutch (see First Dutch War*, 1652-1654). Dutch trading preeminence and English claims to the sovereignty of the seas were at stake; domestic concerns were equally important, for the Dutch were the most formidable supporters of the exiled Stuarts. The year 1653 saw three major actions in the Narrow Seas, ending in decisive victory for the English, but the Dutch were able to drive English shipping from the Mediterranean and Baltic. The peace of 1654 brought England only limited commercial gains but was far more successful politically. By now Oliver Cromwell* was installed as lord protector. Cromwell knew his regime depended in part on naval power and believed the fleet would cost no more to maintain in war than peace. After some debate he decided that war with Spain was most likely to bring riches and undermine the power of international Catholicism* (see Spanish War of 1655-1659*). Blake was sent on two major expeditions to Spain and the Mediterranean. Though the Spanish navy declined to fight, he scored a notable success against the North African corsairs by attacking their base at Porto Farina, near Tunis, and in 1657 he destroyed a Spanish plate fleet in the Canaries. William Penn's expedition of 1654-1655 against Hispaniola, designed as a first step toward overrunning the Spanish-American empire, proved an expensive failure; the English had to console themselves with Jamaica, which offered no treasure and little else of value. Overall the Cromwellian period of naval history is more significant in terms of its scope and enterprising spirit than its lasting achievements. It looks toward the age of gunboat diplomacy, with an aggressive navy actively advancing England's imperial and commercial expansion.

The navy could do nothing to prevent the Restoration* in 1660. Edward Montague, Blake's successor, reached an understanding with Charles II*, and many of the captains followed his lead, some reluctantly; hard-line opponents were purged. The seamen were more enthusiastic; government finances had collapsed in 1659, leaving them angry and unpaid, and they welcomed Charles as the best hope for securing their arrears. In May Montague's fleet brought the king home in triumph.

Naval operations under the Restoration navy were usually on a smaller scale, for Charles followed a policy of peace. Understandably most new commands went to former Cavaliers*, but the Second Dutch War* (1665-1667) saw large numbers of old Cromwellians recalled to service, including Montague, now earl of Sandwich. Despite initial confidence, this war was much less successful than its predecessor. There were fierce disputes between the main commanders Sandwich, Prince James (see James II*), and George Monck*, and the Dutch were better led and had a far stronger fleet than ten years earlier. The war ended with a humiliating Dutch raid on the Medway in 1667, when several English warships were towed away or burned at anchor. The Third Dutch War* (1672-1674) proved equally disappointing.

Traditionally the Restoration navy has been seen as incompetent and corrupt, saved from disaster only by the heroic efforts of Samuel Pepys*, a key naval administrator for part of the period. That picture owes much to Pepys himself and is suspect. The small forces set out in times of peace proved sufficient for the demands made of them. The main effort was directed at protecting merchant shipping in the Mediterranean from Barbary corsairs; an elaborate convoy system proved generally successful. The period also saw increasing professionalism among the officer corps; old divisions between gentleman-captain and "tarpaulin" diminished as a new breed came to the fore, "gentle" by birth but bred to the sea from an early age, usually in the navy itself. Growing professionalism did not breed a sense of common purpose, however; the Restoration navy was marred by bitter faction fighting.

The navy's part in the Revolution of 1688 was far from glorious (see Glorious Revolution*). There was widespread discontent at James II's policies, and by 1688 he commanded no more than lukewarm support in the navy, as elsewhere. In the event the "Protestant wind" trapped the fleet in the Thames, and William of Orange* was able to land unchallenged. He inherited a powerful navy that had already overhauled the Dutch and was able to contain the rising strength of the French. The fleet consisted of 119 ships, far stronger than in 1660 and sufficiently disciplined to employ the new "line astern" formation in battle. Hired merchantmen had been largely phased out. The development of the navy from the 1630s through the Commonwealth* to the later Stuarts was in many ways evolutionary. By 1689 it stood poised to play a central role in England's development as a great power.

Bibliography: K. R. Andrews, *Ships, Money, and Politics: Seafaring and Naval Enterprise in the Reign of Charles I*, 1991; Bernard Capp, *Cromwell's Navy: The Fleet and the English Revolution, 1648-1660*, 1989; J. D. Davies, *Gentlemen and Tarpaulins: The Officers and Men of the Restoration Navy*, 1991; M. Oppenheim, *A History of the Administration of the Royal Navy from 1509 to 1660*, 1896, reissued 1988; J. R. Powell, *The Navy in the English Civil War*, 1962.

Bernard S. Capp

Neutralism. Neutrals or "neuters," those individuals who were either unwilling or unable to espouse any single religio-political cause, were a familiar feature of the seventeenth century. Whatever the great political question of the day, a number of people could usually be found sitting on the fence—afraid of offending either camp perhaps, genuinely unable to decide where the merits of the case lay, or simply waiting to see which side would come out on top before making the decision to commit themselves. The more closely one was involved in politics, of course, the more likely it was that one would find oneself compelled to adopt such strategies from time to time. At the political center, therefore, neutralism whether of the genuine or the purely tactical variety was a state through which many of the "better sort" must regularly have passed. However, ordinary Englishmen and women, especially those who lived outside the larger towns, were rarely confronted with such stark political choices. This being the case, neutralism as opposed to simple indifference can hardly be said to have existed at the popular level before 1642. With the outbreak of the Civil War*, however, ordinary people suddenly found that their political opinions had become important and they were being pressured into taking sides. Predictably enough, some were unwilling to do so.

That the war was unpopular can hardly be doubted. The anguished hand-wringing of contemporaries and the countless pleas for peace amply confirm this. The frequency with which individuals changed sides, moreover, and the exasperated comments that so many military commanders made about the difficulty of raising men must surely bear witness to a widespread lack of commitment. Drawing on such evidence, many historians have come to see the Civil War as a conflict fought amid a sea of passivity and political indifference. The conflict was both initiated and sustained, it is argued, by two small groups of committed partisans, men whose politico-religious opinions were wholly unrepresentative of majority opinion. The great mass of the English people, meanwhile, tried desperately to remain uninvolved in a war that few among them could understand or care about. In support of this view historians cite a number of occasions upon which clear demonstrations of neutralist sentiment were made, most notably in 1642 and in 1645-1646.

During the summer of 1642 many provincial communities made determined efforts to keep the approaching conflict at arm's length. In counties controlled by especially tightly-knit gentry elites, these efforts were often surprisingly successful. By forbearing to quarrel with each other and by refusing to let "foreign" military forces establish themselves within the county boundaries, a few unified gentry groups managed to keep their own particular localities in a trembling quiet, while other less fortunate shires descended into chaos. As Anthony Fletcher has shown, neutralist initiatives of this kind achieved considerable success in Derbyshire, Norfolk, Suffolk, Staffordshire, and the Isle of Wight. Yet such localist responses could not delay the spread of the war forever. Sooner or later all the counties mentioned above were dragged into the conflict, either as a result of outside intervention or because divisions had emerged among the local gentry themselves.

Following the collapse of these initial "war-free zones," neutralism as a significant force became temporarily submerged. Admittedly a number of counties entered into truces or pacts during late 1642 and early 1643, but these short-lived cessations should probably be seen as tactical moves, designed to give each side a chance to reorganize and regroup, rather than as genuinely neutralist initiatives. From early 1643 onward, genuine neutralism became extremely hard to find. That this was so probably reflected the war's increasing bitterness. As the conflict dragged on, as outrage succeeded outrage, and propagandists vied with each other to produce ever more alarming conspiracy theories, the political nation became increasingly polarized. This polarization emerged in an increasing willingness to perpetrate atrocities, in an increasing disregard for the social niceties, and in an increasing inability to contemplate any peace that was not an absolute conquest. Significantly enough, when neutralism finally reemerged on the political scene in 1645-1646, it did so as a result of the activities of the Clubmen*, most of whom emanated from levels of society well below that of the hopelessly fragmented elite.

How genuinely neutral were the neutrals? To the military commanders and propagandists who provide us with so much of our information about the Civil War, protestations of neutrality were regarded as a cloak for disaffection and nothing more. "Those who are not with me are against me," Sir Richard Grenville told the countrymen of southeast Cornwall in 1645, subsequently proceeding to arrest, plunder, and even hang those who had refused to turn out for the king. Contemporary pamphleteers evinced little more sympathy for those who tried to keep out of the conflict. "Base neuters" were frequently castigated by the diurnalists of both sides, who portrayed them as concealed enemies, simply awaiting the right opportunity to declare themselves.

For modern scholars wholeheartedly to endorse this view would be unfair. Clearly there were a number of genuine neutrals, equally hostile to either side. Nevertheless it is tempting to conclude that such persons were in the minority. True impartiality is very hard to sustain in a country torn apart by civil war, and this was especially so in an age when religion was deeply embedded in the fabric of day-to-day life and religion and politics were so inextricably intertwined. Among the aristocracy and the greater gentry, few were either able or willing to perform the balancing act of neutrality for long. And even among the common people, the extent of political indifference has probably been exaggerated.

Bibliography: G. E. Aylmer, "Collective Mentalities in Seventeenth Century England: IV. Cross Currents: Neutrals, Trimmers and Others," *Transactions of the Royal Historical Society*, 5th series, 39 (1989): 1-22; Anthony Fletcher, *The Outbreak of the English Civil War*, 1981; and J. S. Morrill, *The Revolt of the Provinces*, 1976.

Mark Stoyle

New Model Army. The Long Parliament* created the New Model Army in early 1645 as a response to the nearly disastrous loss of momentum in its war against Charles I*. With the aim of ending the recriminations that were crippling its military effort, the House of Commons adopted a motion to remove members of both houses from all offices, military or civil, for the duration of the war. The Self-Denying Ordinance*, as it would later be known, was blocked by the Lords for four months. In the meantime, the Commons set about to outflank the Lords' opposition by creating a new army* with new leaders, none of whom were members of either house. The existing armies of the earls of Essex (Robert Devereux*) and Manchester and Sir William Waller were starved of money, while their members were recruited into the new army. Composed two-thirds of infantry, largely conscripted, and one-third of cavalry, all volunteers, the new army numbered 22,000 men and 2,300 officers. In a sense the New Model Army did not represent a radical departure from past practice. It was an amalgamation of three existing armies, financed along similar lines. However, its creation marked a victory for the war party over the peace party led by Essex.

Sir Thomas Fairfax* was named commander-in-chief of the new army, apparently on account of his excellent military record in the north and his lack of involvement in the political infighting that had plagued the southern armies. But when he submitted his list of officers for parliament's* approval, Essex's followers in the Lords tried to alter a third of the names. They demoted or excluded known radicals and promoted or reintroduced Presbyterians* and Scots who had been left off the list. Only after the Commons threatened to go ahead without them did the Lords reluctantly approve Fairfax's nominations. They did not, however, swallow their hatred of Oliver Cromwell*. When in June 1645 the Commons overrode the Self-Denying Ordinance by naming him to the vacant lieutenant generalship of the cavalry, the Lords balked. Only the stunning victory at Naseby* a few days later forced them to approve Cromwell's appointment, and then only for a few months at a time.

The New Model's crushing victory at Naseby owed not a little to the king's great blunder in attacking a force nearly twice as large as his own. For all Fairfax's numerical superiority the battle was in fact a close call. The rest of the First Civil War* was essentially a mopping-up operation. By June 1646 royalist* headquarters at Oxford had surrendered, and the king had given himself up to the Scots at Newark. In the first fifteen months of its existence, the New Model had not lost so much as a skirmish; indeed, it would lose no important engagement throughout the subsequent Second Civil War* (1648) and the invasions of Ireland* (1649-1653) and Scotland* (1650-1651).

How are we to explain this formidable battlefield record? A major reason was that the New Model was more generously financed than any of the royalist or other parliamentarian* armies. A second reason was that it had unobstructed access to a great economic powerhouse: the metropolis of London*. Vast quantities of clothing, gunpowder, pikes, halberds, swords, and muskets poured out of London workshops. The quality of military leadership was a lesser factor, since the New Model generals were not noticeably superior to their royalist counterparts.

Religion provides another important reason for the New Model's success. It explains why men were ready to risk their lives in battle and why they were confident of victory. The four leading generals (Fairfax, Cromwell, Philip Skippon, and Henry Ireton*) were all devout Puritans*. So were a high proportion of the lower-ranking officers. These men stamped the army with the imprint of their own piety and zeal. They shared a conviction that they were the instruments of divine providence, frequently expressing a thirst for the destruction of Antichrist and the coming of the millennium. It is true that many of the rank and file, who included a high proportion of conscripts and former royalist prisoners of war, were not noted for their piety. But others were. The widespread habits of Bible* reading, extemporaneous prayer, and lay preaching earned the New Model the reputation of the "praying army." Religious fervor had practical results. The soldiers' conviction that they were fighting the warfare of heaven bred in them the courage to perform acts of daring and improvisation not only on the battlefield but in the political arena.

In the spring of 1647, responding to popular war weariness and resentment of taxation*, the New Model's enemies in parliament seized the initiative by moving for the army's virtual disbandment and a negotiated peace with the king. To defend themselves from destruction, the rank and file organized resistance to parliament's order and persuaded the officers to throw in their lot with them. The result was the seizure of the king, a collective rendezvous of the army, and the creation of the general council of the army to oversee political affairs. With the officers' blessing, representatives or "agitators"* were chosen from each troop and company. It was this body that debated the Levellers'* proposed constitution for England, the Agreement of the People*, in the fall of 1647. Alarmed at the attraction exerted by this democratic document, Cromwell and Ireton eventually cut off the debate and sent the agitators back to their regiments. Further argument was foreclosed by the eruption of the Second Civil War.

The royalist uprisings of 1648 were easily snuffed out by the veteran regiments of the New Model, culminating in the devastating defeat of a combined English and Scottish royalist army at Preston in August. With steadily mounting impatience, the army now denounced Charles Stuart as "that man of blood" who must be brought to account for his crimes against the English people. Parliament's stubborn refusal to act on this advice led to the arrest and expulsion of moderate members of parliament (see Pride's Purge*), the creation of an army-dominated high court of justice to try the king for treason, and the establishment of the English republic. Having put down a Leveller-inspired mutiny at Burford in May 1649, the army officers then set about to organize the invasion of Ireland in the summer of the same year.   To the accompaniment of savage massacres at Drogheda and Wexford, the Irish rebels were beaten into submission, though their final surrender took another three years of bloody fighting and a continually increasing commitment of troops from England (see Irish Rebellion*).

Meanwhile, Cromwell had left Ireland in May 1649 to deal with a resurgent royalist threat from Scotland.   Under his leadership at Dunbar (1650) and Worcester (1651), the battle-seasoned troops of the New Model clinched their military mastery of the three kingdoms.   Their last challenge was a political one.   The Rump Parliament*, as the purged Long Parliament was coming to be called, showed little inclination to usher in the godly republic for which the council of officers so fervently yearned.   So another political intervention was undertaken: the Rump was expelled and a hand-picked or Nominated Assembly, also known as Barebone's Parliament*, was summoned. This body also proved a disappointment to the army grandees, who engineered its dissolution at the end of 1653. From that point on the army fought no more battles on British soil.   The collapse of its unity and morale after Oliver Cromwell's death in 1658 paved the way for the return of monarchy in 1660. Ironically the army, which had overseen the execution of one king in 1649, was instrumental (through the agency of General George Monck*) in the Restoration* of his son Charles II* in 1660. The revolutionary experiment had come full circle.

Bibliography: C. H. Firth, *Cromwell's Army*, 1902; Ian Gentles, *The New Model Army in England, Ireland and Scotland, 1645-1653*, 1992; Mark A. Kishlansky, *The Rise of the New Model Army*, 1979.

Ian Gentles

Newcastle, Propositions of (1646).   A set of comprehensive demands proposed by parliament* in an attempt to reach a definitive peace settlement with Charles I* after his army* was defeated by parliamentary forces.   By the spring of 1646 Charles's royalist* forces had been effectively subdued by the New Model Army*.   When subsequent attempts to raise any sizable new army failed, Charles fled cross-country to surrender to the Scots at Newark in May 1646.   Charles was then placed at Newcastle-upon-Tyne, which had been secured by the Scots after his surrender. Quickly the parliamentary majority proposed a new postwar settlement, which it presented to Charles at Newcastle in July 1646.   The Propositions of Newcastle basically restated in more severe and restrictive terms the parliamentary peace proposals made at Oxford in the winter of 1642-1643 and Uxbridge in 1644-1645. The Propositions of Oxford had in part called for the abolition of episcopacy and had denied pardons for some of Charles's closest supporters.   The Propositions of Uxbridge included terms that diminished Charles's executive power and also demanded that he sign the Solemn League and Covenant*.   The Newcastle proposals repeated these same demands, as well as insisting that Charles relinquish royal control of the militia for twenty years.   An added condition within the Newcastle Propositions increased the list of royalist estates that were to be seized as a source of money for the debt-ridden Long Parliament*.

Despite its victorious status and the rigidity of its new proposal, parliament realized that some type of compromise with Charles was imperative if it was ever to establish a realistic and lasting government. In February 1646 parliament managed to gather enough funds to secure Charles's release from the Scots. Soon Charles was returned to English control and placed in Holdenby House in Northamptonshire. The public's positive reaction proved that Charles, despite his military defeats and the publishing of his treacherous communications with the Irish, which had been uncovered at the Battle of Naseby*, retained strong support from the general public. Parliament, on the other hand, was confronted by continuing critical problems. The army had not received pay from parliament for many months, and parliament failed to secure an ordinance that would have protected the troops from war crime charges. Parliament could not, now that a temporary peace had been established, ask for an increase in taxation* to settle the army's arrears. Such a tax would have created greater public animosity and protest. In an unsuccessful attempt to alleviate the army's payment situation, parliament tried to demobilize some units without pay and arranged for other troops to be sent to Ireland*. These feeble measures caused angry reactions throughout the New Model Army and added to its growing hostility toward parliament.

As parliament's problems mounted, its public stance weakened. Charles then was in a good position to stall and moderate his response to the Propositions of Newcastle. In May 1647 Charles presented his third and most temperate answer to parliament. Charles countered parliament's demand concerning the militia by agreeing to surrender his control for only ten years. He in essence acceded to parliament's call for an authoritarian church, and he stated that such reforms should be handled by the Westminster Assembly of Divines*. However, Charles stipulated that twenty clergymen of his own choice were to be added to the reforming assembly. Lastly, Charles firmly repeated that he would not permit parliament to punish any of his loyal supporters.

As parliament's power to deal effectively with Charles waned, the New Model Army began to assert a more active role in the negotiations. A council of the army was formed, which ordered Charles to be seized at Holdenby House and brought to their headquarters. Discussions of settlement with Charles now centered around Oliver Cromwell*, Henry Ireton*, and the council of officers. Despite its diminished status, parliament continued to support the Propositions of Newcastle. The Four Bills issued by parliament in December 1647 reconfirmed the basic terms of the Newcastle proposals.

Bibliography: S. R. Gardiner, *History of the Great Civil War 1642-1649*, 1965; J. P. Kenyon, *The Stuart Constitution, 1603-1688*, 1966.

Nancy Vannett

Newport, Treaty of (1648). The defeat of royalist* forces at Preston in August 1648 heralded the end of the Second Civil War*. Parliamentary efforts were again focused on securing a political settlement with Charles I*. The Long Parliament* repealed the Vote of No Addresses* on 24 August, making possible renewed negotiations. Spurred by the London Levellers'* Humble Petition and Advice* of 11 September which called for the House of Commons to wield supreme political power and for the abolition of both the monarchy and the House of Lords and mindful of pressure from the army* to reach a settlement quickly, parliament* sent peace commissioners to negotiate with the king.

Charles agreed to meet with the commissioners at an inn in Newport, Isle of Wight. The negotiations commenced on 18 September with the stipulation that they would be concluded within forty days.

William Fiennes*, viscount Saye and Sele, an early and staunch opponent of Charles, led the Lords' delegation. Saye and Sele understood the implications of failure to reach a settlement. Neither side, though, seemed willing to moderate its basic position. Parliament offered essentially the terms of the Newcastle Propositions* of 13 July 1646, which had demanded that (1) Charles take the Solemn League and Covenant* and impose it on all his subjects; (2) the king make the Church of England (see Anglicanism*) a Presbyterian* institution; (3) the armed forces remain under parliamentary control for ten years and under indirect control thereafter; and (4) proscribed royalist officers and officials be excluded from pardons and public office.

Charles agreed only to allow a three-year Presbyterian experiment and parliamentary control of the armed forces for ten years. No basis for compromise appeared likely, and the Treaty of Newport became a dead issue.

Faced with Charles's intransigence, parliament's own lack of a compromise position, and pressure from the more radical army factions, the commissioners ceased negotiations on 27 October 1648. The unwillingness of Charles to compromise at Newport contributed to his trial and execution* three months later. He anticipated the result of the failure at Newport by writing to the prince of Wales (the future Charles II*): "the commissioners are gone; the corn is in the ground; we expect the harvest."

Bibliography: John Kenyon, *The Civil Wars of England*, 1988.

Stanley D. M. Carpenter

Nineteen Propositions (1642). The second document that the Long Parliament* sent Charles I* after his departure from London* in January 1642, the Nineteen Propositions clarify parliament's* political position as of June 1642. The Nineteen Propositions were an extreme attack upon royal prerogative* as it proposed to transfer much of the king's political and military authority to parliament and to eliminate the abuses it saw in Charles's government. Insisting that the king's ministers be appointed by vote of both its houses, parliament denied the king the right to choose his own ministers, privy councilors, and judges. It also required royal officials to take an oath to maintain the provisions of the Petition of Right* and to inquire into suspected breaches of the law. Once in office, these officials would retain their seats during good behavior rather than during the pleasure of the king. Parliament also claimed the right to remove a chief minister of state, insisting that private men were not to conduct the business of state. Instead parliament was to debate and resolve "great affairs of state." The privy council*, on the other hand, would resolve other so-called appropriate matters. Parliament further limited royal authority by requiring the king to secure the approval of a majority of the privy councilors prior to taking action. It also declared the right to approve those who were selected to educate and care for royal children and to approve the marriage partners of royal children. It insisted that the king accept the Militia Ordinance and reform the church in accordance with the teachings of a Christian synod.   Parliament demanded that the laws against Jesuits and recusants* be rigidly enforced and that Catholic* lords lose their votes in the House of Lords. The Nineteen Propositions additionally required Charles to restore those members of parliament who had been deposed from office. It encouraged Charles to engage in a stricter alliance with the United Provinces (Netherlands) and other Protestant states against the pope and to work to reestablish Frederick to his throne in the Palatinate (see Elizabeth*; Thirty Years War*).

Parliament offered to turn Hull over to someone Charles named and it approved once the king accepted the Nineteen Propositions. Parliament also promised to regulate the king's revenue to his "best advantage" and to provide for an "ordinary and constant" increase in his income (see Taxation and Revenue*).

In essence the Nineteen Propositions involved a complete revision of English government whereby power was transferred from the king to parliament and a privy council whose membership parliament approved. The judicial system (see Common Law and Courts*) and the militia would also fall under parliamentary control.

Sir John Culpepper and Lucius Carey, Viscount Falkland, drafted Charles's reply, which was dispatched to parliament on 8 June. The king argued that the provisions of the Nineteen Propositions were unacceptable because they would erode the real political power of the king and subvert the fundamental laws of the realm. The king proposed instead that the proper government was a "mixed government" wherein the king shared power with the House of Lords and the House of Commons.

The Nineteen Propositions led to a propaganda battle with the king. Historians C. C. Weston and J. R. Greenberg suggest that the king's opponents in parliament used his answer to the Nineteen Propositions to justify their resistance. John Sanderson, on the other hand, suggests that John Filmer's notion of resistance was already popular by the summer of 1642 (see Political Thought*).

The Nineteen Propositions intensified the mutual suspicion and animosity between Charles and his opponents. In July 1642 Parliament placed the command of the army* in the hands of the earl of Essex (Robert Devereux*) and the navy* under the earl of Warwick. Within a month, Charles I would declare war on parliament.

Bibliography: J. P. Kenyon, *Stuart Constitution,* 2nd rev. ed., 1986; John Sanderson, "The Answer to the Nineteen Propositions Revisited," *Political Studies* 32 (December

1984): 627-636; C. C. Weston and J. R. Greenberg, *Subjects and Sovereigns: The Grand Controversy over Legal Sovereignty in Stuart England*, 1981.

David B. Mock

Nonresistance. The doctrine that subjects, owing an unconditional allegiance to their ruler, had no right actively to resist him was a central belief of absolutism*, divine right monarchy*, and (for most) of royalism*. The doctrine of nonresistance, however, needs to be distinguished carefully from these other theoretical positions. Nonresistance implies less than absolutism, for an absolute monarch is not just irresistible but also free of constitutional limitation. While most divine right theorists were believers in the doctrine of nonresistance, there were believers in nonresistance who were not divine right theorists. Again royalists were mostly defenders of the principle of nonresistance, but there are exceptions to the rule.

Before the Civil War* almost everyone accepted in public the idea of the irresistibility of the king. They were aware that resistance had been defended in sixteenth-century Britain and on the Continent, but few thought these doctrines had much application in their own political community. The general view was that kings were appointed by, and therefore accountable only to, God. Subjects had a duty to refuse obedience to commands from the king that ran counter to the commands of God, but this refusal should remain passive. The subject should never actively resist the king's will and indeed should maintain his passivity even when being punished for it. One of the finest spokesmen for this view was James VI and I*.

It is important to remember, with regard to both the period before the Civil War and Tory* thought, that belief in nonresistance did not automatically commit a person to the belief that rulers were unlimited. The alternatives to active resistance, such as persuasion, prayer, or even passive resistance, were thought by many to be sufficient to restrain an erring ruler. Many in England also believed that their own "ancient constitution" functioned so well that misgovernment could not occur. Resistance was therefore unnecessary as well as unlawful.

An alternative view of nonresistance, associated with Hugo Grotius, John Selden*, Dudley Digges, and (to a limited degree) Thomas Hobbes*, was that before the development of political societies, individuals possessed a natural right to defend themselves, but on entering into society these individual rights had been totally abandoned in return for the protection provided by government. It followed, therefore, that individuals had given away whatever right of resistance they might have had.

Both of these arguments for nonresistance, one based on divine right and the other on consent, were used by royalists in the 1640s. By this time, of course, the doctrine was facing challenge, initially from the Scots Covenanters*, later (and with more hesitation) from the English parliamentarians*. In response to the arguments of these groups, royalists exhaustively explored the arguments in favor of nonresistance. One of the fullest statements of them is in John Maxwell's *Sacro-sancta Regum Majestas* (1644).

With the Restoration* the doctrine of nonresistance once again became dominant, though it never again achieved its virtually unchallenged position of the period before 1640.   Nonresistance became particularly closely associated with the political teachings of the Church of England (see Anglicanism*) and after the Exclusion Crisis* (1678-1681) of its Tory supporters. Indeed so firmly attached were Tories to the principle that in 1688-1689 their support for William of Orange* was made possible only by resort to fictions that covered over any idea that resistance to James II* had occurred. He was deemed to have abdicated the throne, not to have been pushed off it. Even so, many Tories carried their adherence to the doctrine of nonresistance to the point of becoming Jacobites. (See also Political Thought*.)

Bibliography: Mark Goldie, "The Political Thought of the Anglican Revolution," in Robert Beddard, ed., *The Revolutions of 1688: The Andrew Browning Lectures 1988*, 1991; J. P. Sommerville, *Politics and Ideology in England, 1603-40*, 1986; Perez Zagorin, *A History of Political Thought in the English Revolution*, 1954.

Glenn Burgess

O

Ormonde, Duke of. See Butler, James.

Osborne, Thomas, 1st Earl of Danby, Marquis of Carmarthen, Duke of Leeds (1631-1712). Born in Yorkshire and raised in the country, Osborne in 1647 succeeded to his father's baronetcy and in 1653 married Lady Bridget Bertie, by whom he had five daughters and three sons. A protégé of the 2d duke of Buckingham (George Villiers*), he became high sheriff* of Yorkshire in 1661 and was elected to parliament* in 1665. Buckingham rewarded his assistance in attacking the earl of Clarendon (Edward Hyde*) by arranging his appointment in 1668 as one of two treasurers of the navy*, and by 1671 Osborne had secured the dismissal of his coordinate and held the position alone.

Ambitious, greedy, parsimonious, and incapable of true loyalty, Osborne surrounded himself with nonentities for fear of competition. For all that, he was a competent financial administrator whose efforts secured recognition. His *annus mirabilis* came in 1673, when he was made a viscount in the Scottish peerage and appointed to the privy council*. When Baron Clifford* had to resign in June, Osborne bought preference by bribing him with a pension and became the lord high treasurer of England and chief minister to Charles II*. He finished the year by becoming Viscount Latimer and less than a year later was awarded the earldom of Danby. Now his own man, he broke with Buckingham and succeeded him as lord lieutenant* of the West Riding of Yorkshire.

The five years as chief minister were the apogee of Danby's career. In support of Charles's absolutist* pretensions, he managed parliament by adroit bribes, defended the cause of Protestantism, sought English diplomatic leverage at French expense, and showed special concern for the realm's fiscal stability and credit. Though he made peace with the Dutch and championed the marriage of Charles's niece Mary* to William of Orange*, he was drawn into colluding in Charles's receipt of secret bribes from the French. Early in 1678 he wrote on Charles's behalf to Ralph Montagu, the English ambassador in Paris, demanding three annual payments of six million livres to the king, this while he was guiding through parliament legislation to appropriate money for a war with France. When he declined to use his influence to make Montagu secretary of state, Montagu turned against him, the letters were read in Commons, and Danby was impeached. Because of his personal unpopularity, he was also accused of complicity in the mythical Popish Plot* (1678) invented by Titus Oates and in the murder of Sir Edmund Berry Godfrey. The dissolution of the Cavalier Parliament* in January 1679 saved him momentarily, but the new parliament (see Exclusion Crisis*) that met in March contained even more of his opponents, and he was forced to resign. The impeachment* was revived and he was sent to the Tower, where he remained for five years despite having received a pardon from Charles at the time of his resignation.

In 1685 James II's* first parliament annulled the impeachment and Danby returned to Lords, where he soon found himself in opposition to James's religious policy. He intrigued against James on behalf of William and Mary and in 1688 signed the letter inviting William to assume the throne of England. He also seized York on William's behalf during the Glorious Revolution*. As reward he was created marquis of Carmarthen in 1689 and made president of the council. Over the next three years, he became lord lieutenant of the three ridings of Yorkshire while serving as virtual prime minister. He was not as powerful as during his earlier chief ministry, for his enemies were numerous and weakened him with rumors that he favored the return of James. Though he was created duke of Leeds in 1694, Commons impeached him in the following year for taking a bribe from the East India Company*. The impeachment was not pursued due to the lack of key testimony from a servant who had fled the country, but Leeds had lost all influence even as he retained his position. In 1699 he had to resign that and the lord lieutenancy as well.

Leeds's last years were spent in parliamentary activity and in preparing two volumes of vindication that he published in 1710. These had little effect, as his argument amounted to little more than that he had been pardoned by Charles II and was no worse than the run of officials in his time, and as his editing of documents was characterized by shameless omissions and alterations. He died in Easton Neston, Northamptonshire, on 26 July 1712 and was succeeded in his dukedom by Peregrine Osborne, his only surviving son.

Bibliography: Andrew Browning, *Thomas Osborne, Earl of Danby and Duke of Leeds, 1632-1712*, 3 vols., 1944-1951.

Joseph M. McCarthy

Overbury, Sir Thomas (1581-1613), Murder of. Overbury was a courtier and writer who achieved his greatest fame as the victim of a scandalous murder plot in 1613. Educated at Queen's College, Oxford, and the Middle Temple, Overbury became particularly powerful as the friend and adviser of James I's* favorite, Robert Carr*, whom he had met in Scotland* in 1601. Although Carr advanced rapidly at the royal court*, he depended heavily on Overbury's abilities and intelligence; indeed, Queen Anne (of Denmark*) dubbed Overbury Carr's governor. As the indispensable "man behind the favorite," Overbury's wealth and power grew along with Carr's, though his arrogance earned him many enemies.

Overbury's brilliant career ended when Carr began having an affair with Frances Howard, countess of Essex (see Robert Devereux*). Overbury initially condoned the liaison; he even composed many of Carr's love letters. However, when the countess decided to apply for divorce in order to marry Carr, Overbury opposed the match, fearing his influence over Carr would be lost to the powerful Howard faction. Overbury tried to dissuade Carr from the marriage, warning him against Frances Howard's tarnished reputation. This opposition aroused the anger of Carr and the Howards. The king and queen were also annoyed with Overbury's growing impudence. In order to remove Overbury from the scene, James offered him a diplomatic appointment abroad; when Overbury refused, he was sent to the Tower.

Although the imprisonment was to be temporary, while the divorce proceedings took place, Frances Howard had other plans. She immediately arranged to have Overbury poisoned, enlisting the help of several others, including an apothecary, James Franklin; a confidante, Anne Turner, who dabbled in aphrodisiacs and poisons and kept a house of assignation; and a jailer, Richard Weston, who served as Overbury's person attendant and mixed the various poisons into the prisoner's food.

None of the poisons worked immediately, but Overbury's extreme suffering steadily increased. Overbury had been in the Tower over three months when Frances Howard became impatient of the delay; under her orders, an apothecary's assistant, William Reeve, administered a mercury-tainted enema to Overbury. He died the next morning, 15 September 1613. Soon after, Carr married Frances Howard, and James created him earl of Somerset.

Suspicious rumors followed Overbury's death, but nearly two years passed before the truth was revealed. Reeve, who had been sent to Flushing, confessed his role in the murder. Sir Ralph Winwood, the secretary of state, then extricated a confession from Sir Gervase Helwys, lieutenant of the Tower, who knew of the plot. James was shocked and saddened at the revelations involving his favorite, but he ordered an immediate investigation. Franklin, Turner, and Weston were convicted and executed. The Somersets were tried in May 1616; although Somerset was only aware of his wife's crime after the fact, they were both found guilty and sentenced to death. James reduced their conviction to imprisonment, first in the Tower, then to retirement in the country.

The scandal severely damaged the reputation of James's court, but it enhanced the reputation of Overbury's literary works. His character sketches and his poem, "The Wife," which, ironically, describes the ideal virtues for a prospective bride, became enormously popular after his death.

Bibliography: M. A. DeFord, *The Overbury Affair*, 1960; William McElwee, *The Murder of Sir Thomas Overbury*, 1952.

Jo Eldridge Carney

Owen, John (1616-1683). Calvinist* theologian and leader of the Independents*. Probably born at Stadham in Oxfordshire, where his father was a Nonconformist vicar, Owen entered Queen's College, Oxford in 1628, receiving the B.A. in 1632 and M.A. in 1635. He left Oxford in 1637 as Laudianism (see William Laud*) increased and became chaplain to Sir Robert Dormer of Ascot and later to John Lord Lovelace of Hurley, Berkshire. When Lovelace joined the king's army* in 1642, Owen removed to London*. There he heard leading preachers and experienced an assurance of grace. After he published *A Display of Arminianism* (1643), the Long Parliament* preferred (appointed) him to the parish of All Saints at Fordham in Essex. There he adhered to the Solemn League and Covenant*. He became vicar of St. Peter's in Coggeshall in 1646, where he adopted Congregationalism* and became acquainted with General Thomas Fairfax* during the siege of Colchester.

Owen first preached to parliament* in 1646 and was its preacher on 31 January 1649, the day after the execution of Charles I*, placing recent events in a millennial framework. In 1649 he accompanied Oliver Cromwell* to Ireland* and the next year to Scotland*. In 1650 Owen was appointed a preacher to the council of state* and given lodgings in Whitehall. In 1651 he was made dean of Christ Church, Oxford; in 1653 he was awarded the D.D. by the university* and named by Cromwell its vice-chancellor, a post he held until October 1658. Owen was a leading adviser to Cromwell on religious affairs.

Meanwhile he emerged as the leader of the conservative Religious Independents*, a group that included Thomas Goodwin, Philip Nye, Joseph Caryl, and Nicholas Lockyer. He led the Savoy Synod of 1658, which produced a Congregationalist version of the Westminster Confession (see Westminster Assembly of Divines*).

Owen opposed making Oliver Cromwell king and participated in the steps that led to the downfall of Richard Cromwell*. In London he gathered a church of army leaders including Charles Fleetwood and John Desborough. The reconvened Long Parliament remove him from his deanery in 1660, and he retired to Stadham.

Owen was invited both to New England and to take up an academic post in the Netherlands, but returned to London to lead an Independent meeting that continued his earlier ministry there to Cromwellians. When Joseph Caryl died in 1673, his congregation merged with Owen's, leaving Owen pastor to the leading London Independents. Owen also became an important spokesman for the Dissenters*, conferring both with Charles II* and the duke of York (see James II*), advocating toleration, opposing Presbyterian* schemes for comprehension, and defending Dissent. Connected to anti-government plotters, he was questioned in the wake of the Rye House Plot* in 1683. He died that year and was buried in Bunhill Fields. His numerous works constituted a sustained defense of high Calvinism and the piety of supernatural grace against Arminians* and Socinians and gained him a European-wide reputation as a theologian.

Bibliography: Peter Toon, *God's Statesman: The Life and Work of John Owen*, 1971.

Dewey D. Wallace, Jr.

Oxford Parliament (1681). When Charles II* dissolved the second Exclusion Parliament on 18 January 1681, he thwarted the second attempt in two years to exclude his brother, the duke of York (see James II*) from the succession (see Exclusion Crisis*). But the king immediately offered a third opportunity by summoning a new parliament to meet on 21 March 1681 at Oxford. He apparently intended to break his opponents and planned for a brief session, just long enough to allow the Whigs* to display their similarity to Civil War* parliamentarians* and thus justify their repression. If parliament met at Westminster, members could have met dissolution or prorogation with an appeal to popular opinion or a physical retreat into the City of London*. Meeting at Oxford made the Whigs vulnerable; those who took armed retainers with them did so not to use against the king but for self-defense.

The fate of recent parliaments and the choice of Oxford made it clear that exclusion could not be achieved by persuading but only by pressuring the king. This fact determined the character of the election and the short session that ensued. Elections occurred in as divisive a context as any since the 1640. Opponents of the royal court* (see Court versus Country*) were being ruthlessly purged from offices, and volumes of propaganda inflamed opinion. Whigs attacked pensioners and Catholics*, demanding exclusion (and other measures) to preserve subjects' liberties, while Tories* excoriated exclusionists for attempting to alter the constitution and threatening renewed revolution. Moreover, recent petitioning campaigns by Whigs (see Petitioners*) urging Charles to meet the long-delayed second Exclusion Parliament and by court supporters "abhorring" such petitions (see Abhorrers*) provided organizational foundations for conducting the election. Still, this was not the most contested of the three elections held in 1679-1681, because few Tories would stand where Whigs were certain victors.

Of members who took their seats before the dissolution on 28 March, the opposition dominated court adherents by 309 to 193. Newcomers to parliament constituted only twelve percent of the whole, below the norm for Charles's parliaments and indicative of incumbent members' party commitment. After the election, partisans on both sides indulged the new practice of sending instructions to members. Those to Whigs called for exclusion, even if in general terms and without identifying James's successor. They further demanded that parliament vote no money until liberties had been secured. As for the Tories, their addresses stressed the need to preserve church and royal prerogative* and to provide immediate supply.

Charles's speech opening parliament hinted at compromise, but Whigs had no interest in a proposed regency for William* and Mary* and rapidly introduced a new bill for exclusion. They tried to guarantee a long session by impeaching an informer, Edward Fitzharris, whom they hoped would implicate James, Queen Catherine*, and leading Tories in a papist conspiracy, a charge demanding parliamentary investigation. The Lords, however, refused to accept the impeachment* since sufficient remedy was provided by Fitzharris's indictment at common law*. Thus obstructed, the Commons proceeded with exclusion, leading the king to dissolve parliament without warning. Most expected another election soon, and it appeared only slowly that no new parliament would be held.

Far from constituting a royal triumph, the Oxford Parliament's demise revealed Charles's inability to work with his national assembly or to obtain the money he needed for an active foreign policy. Dissolution also deprived Whigs of the best forum for their arguments, leading the most extreme partisans to consider overt resistance. Only the Tories benefited from the parliament, which highlighted their loyalty to the Crown and fed a growing reaction against perceived Whig extremism. (See also Parliament*.)

Bibliography: Ronald Hutton, *Charles II*, 1989; J. R. Jones, *The First Whigs,* rev. ed., 1970.

James Rosenheim

P

Parliament. The early seventeenth-century parliament was an institution of enormous prestige, both because its role in bringing together representatives from all parts of the kingdom to consult with the king endowed it with an almost mystical status and because it possessed the only power in the kingdom to make binding law. In practice, the meetings of parliament commonly left its reputation tarnished and its effectiveness doubtful. Parliaments met briefly and infrequently and were only one element and not often the dominant one in the political life of the country. All too frequently their actual achievements were negligible.

Parliament's function was a combination of the administrative and the political. The sixteenth century had seen it firmly established as the supreme legislative authority; its statutes were binding on all subjects, overrode all other law, and could be altered only by another statute. Some challenged parliament's ability to alter what they called the "fundamental laws," while others denied its right to legislate contrary to the laws of God; but these were moral and political arguments, not legal ones (see Political Thought*). The Crown's right to exempt individuals from the operation of individual laws—its dispensing power*—was generally acknowledged but narrowly confined to particular cases in which no subject's rights or interests were infringed. Most significant, only an act of parliament could authorize direct taxation* and the collection of the main customs duties (tonnage and poundage). While the Crown's right in an emergency to raise money by "forced loans"* and "benevolences" was usually accepted, these were either repaid or levied by persuasion, not by compulsion.

Legally and administratively, parliament's role was the making of law. Politically it had a wider significance. Parliament, as the place in which—in constitutional theory, if not in fact—all the voices in the kingdom could be heard, offered an unrivaled forum for gauging the temper, opinions, and grievances of the country; to governments it provided a useful, if at times unpredictable, means of demonstrating the unanimity of the country behind some currently favored project or policy. As a result monarchs allowed debate to range widely over all manner of subjects. Sixteenth-century parliaments had freely debated foreign affairs, religion, even such touchy subjects as the succession and the marital status of Queen Elizabeth I. But while the Commons in particular claimed to defend their privilege of free speech, in practice the liberty depended to a large extent on the tolerance of the monarch. James I* learned tolerance slowly; Charles I* barely learned it at all. Both sought to suppress debate, when it suited them, on what they regarded as matters of royal prerogative*. Members were arrested for words spoken during the parliaments of 1626* and 1629* and were arrested more frequently after the lapse of parliamentary privilege following the dismissal of a parliament.

Parliament's medieval origins lay in the king's court, and much of its early development was on judicial lines, with the Commons acting as petitioners and the Lords as judges. In the sixteenth century, the evolution of the other courts (see Common Law and Courts*) rendered parliamentary judicature less important. By the early seventeenth century, each house claimed and exercised a right to judge matters pertaining to its privileges and membership, a right that the Commons defended in 1604 in Goodwin's Case*. The House of Lords in addition still exercised very occasionally its power to hear appeals from other courts (though only on points of law). But during the 1620s the appellate jurisdiction of the House of Lords was considerably expanded, so that judicial hearings came to occupy a large proportion of the time of a session. Most dramatic was the revival of the fifteenth-century practice of impeachment* by the Lords on complaint by the Commons—used against Sir Giles Mompesson in 1621, Francis Bacon*, Viscount St. Albans, and Lionel Cranfield*, earl of Middlesex, in 1624.

Parliament was composed of the three elements—the king, the House of Lords, and the House of Commons—whose agreement was necessary to make law. Clear enough in practice, some theoretical confusion resulted from the common usage of the medieval concept of the three estates— nobility, clergy, and Commons. Whenever parliament was equated with the three estates, it could appear that the king stood outside rather than as part of it. Until the Civil War*, however, the distinction was practically irrelevant. What was clear, and fundamental to the operation of seventeenth-century parliaments, was that they existed by the authority and at the behest of the king. Parliament met and was either suspended by prorogation or dismissed by dissolution at the king's pleasure. Some did argue that ancient precedent and a thirteenth-century statute meant that parliament should be held at least every year, but neither possessed any force in face of the practice of centuries.

Formally, the king's own role in parliament was limited. He could withhold his assent from the bills passed by the two houses, but he could not amend them. In fact the royal power of veto was used sparingly; Charles I rejected only one bill. Only occasionally did the king intervene, usually in an attempt to overcome some impasse, either by message—normally sent by a member of the privy council*—or else by summoning one or both houses to attend him. Informally, however, the influence of the Crown was pervasive.

The House of Lords was composed of the peers of the realm and the bishops. The fact that the king summoned them not collectively but individually seemed to imply that he had the right to summon some and not others, as indeed had been the case in the Middle Ages. By the seventeenth century, however, peers and bishops expected to receive a summons as of right. Twenty-six bishops were summoned; the number of lay lords fluctuated with the extinction and creation of titles and the succession of minors. In 1601 fifty-two lay lords were summoned; by 1682 there were 158 claiming the right to be summoned. The representative body, the Commons, possessed the sole right to initiate grants of supply; its tendency to greater turbulence made it more often the focus of attention. But in many respects the Lords were the weightier house. In the Lords sat the greatest and many of the wealthiest men in the kingdom. Some of them, through their ability to secure election to the lower house for their clients, could exercise a considerable influence over it.

Members were elected to the House of Commons either as representatives of counties (the more prestigious knights of the shire) or of boroughs (burgesses). Each county and each borough sent two members, except for those in Wales*, which sent only one each. In 1601 there were 467 members. The king's right to confer parliamentary representation on new boroughs resulted in a steady growth; by 1660 there were 507 members. Thereafter the growth slowed; Durham, enfranchised in 1675 by act of parliament, was the last new parliamentary borough to be created until the Reform Act of 1832. In the counties, electors were qualified by virtue of holding an annual income from freehold land of forty shillings or more, a fifteenth-century qualification that created an enormous range of anomalies but made the county franchise surprisingly inclusive. A variety of franchises was used in the boroughs. Those in which all members of the borough corporation, or all freemen, could vote were the commonest; in a number, most notoriously Westminster, all inhabitants held the right to vote. But the significance of the right to vote is disputable. Contested elections were relatively uncommon, at least in the early part of the century; the governing elites of counties or boroughs preferred to avoid the expense and contention of an actual election, often making their "selection" of candidates less formally. Members by and large were no longer paid "expenses" by their constituencies, as they had been in the Middle Ages, and tended to regard any formal attempt to instruct them on how to behave in parliament as an impertinence. But if the formal means of making members accountable were weak, informally they were in close touch with the opinions and concerns of the country at large and highly susceptible to pressure.

Parliaments were presented with a vast amount of business, both public and private. The demand for private bills—measures to protect individuals or corporations against litigious rivals, competitors, and the vagaries of the courts—placed huge pressure on parliamentary time. Ensuring the precedence and success of government projects was a constant preoccupation for the government. In each house the presiding officer could assist by ordering business, delaying or hastening certain items as required. In the Lords, the lord chancellor or lord keeper of the great seal normally presided ex officio; the Commons elected their own speaker, although frequently on nomination from the royal court* and subject to the king's approval (which was withheld by Charles II* in 1679). In the Lords, privy councilors could promote government business; in the Commons, where few councilors sat, government management was generally in the hands of the able clients of individual ministers—the "men of business"—or minor government officials. Management was a difficult and sensitive art. The rumor that there were "undertakings" to deliver a planned program of business poisoned the Addled Parliament* of 1614.

Despite the pervasive rhetoric of harmony and unity, conflict in parliament was natural and inevitable. It was a place where conflicting interests met, clashed, and (it was hoped) resolved. Well before even the sixteenth century, the meetings of a parliament had often been lively affairs. But because of the revolutions of the seventeenth century, the conflicts within parliament during the period have seemed particularly significant, a series of battles that added up in the end to a war. Much recent work has rejected such a view. "Revisionists" have emphasized the basic agreement that existed on the nature of England's monarchical constitution; they have stressed the absence of any formed opposition in parliaments, where conflicts were most frequently stimulated by divisions between factions within government; and they have shown how rarely or reluctantly parliament attempted to enter into confrontation with or to "seize the initiative" from the court. Procedural changes, previously identified as attempts by the early seventeenth-century Commons to enhance their power or effectiveness, now appear in a different light. The development of the committee of the whole house, once seen as a means of escaping from the chairmanship of a speaker too close to the court, is now regarded as designed for more practical and immediate purposes and often encouraged by the government. The appointment of the standing "grand committees" for grievances, religion, courts of justice, and trade* became a routine means of satisfying the demand for redress of grievances in a relatively harmless manner, away from the floor of the house.

For all that, it is clear that the issue of parliamentary power and privilege was a peculiarly sensitive one throughout the seventeenth century. Why this was so is still a little obscure, but three points stand out. First, a crisis in royal finance placed a strain on the relationship between Crown and parliament. The government could address the problem either through parliamentary taxation or by an attempt to expand and further exploit revenues to which the king was entitled by royal prerogative. Although the convention that parliamentary taxation was intended only for "extraordinary" purposes, normally war, was rarely respected and almost ignored, there was still resistance to moves to establish regular parliamentary taxes, as the earl of Salisbury (Robert Cecil*) found when proposing to exchange some of the king's prerogative sources of finance for them in the Great Contract* of 1610. In any case the standard parliamentary tax, the subsidy, had seen a considerable reduction in its value over a long period. On the other hand, attempts to exploit the prerogative revenues aroused the hostility of members concerned that success could lead to an abandonment of parliaments altogether. Certainly this formed an element in the argument over the extension of the impositions*—nonparliamentary customs revenue in the parliaments of 1610* and 1614.

These problems were bad enough in peacetime; England's involvement in European war from 1624 made them far worse (see French War*, Spanish War of 1625-1630*, Thirty Years War*). When they were compounded by the accidental failure in 1625 to pass the bill authorizing the collection of tonnage and poundage, Charles I's government collected the duties anyway. The argument over its right to do so continued to 1629. On parliament's failure to vote subsidies in 1625 and 1626, the government sought to fill the gap with a benevolence in 1626 and forced loans* in

1626 and 1627; similarly, these attracted considerable opposition and condemnation in the 1628 Petition of Right*.

Second, disagreement—or at least differences in emphasis—over the nature of the relationship between Crown and parliament helped to sour the atmosphere of parliamentary debates. James I could belittle and patronize parliament but seemed to share his subjects' broad understanding of its constitutional and legal role. But in the reign of Charles I, members became concerned at the tone and nature of comments from the king and people appearing to have his confidence (such as Roger Manwaring and Robert Sibthorpe), which painfully stretched the argument that parliaments existed by the king's permission and not by the subjects' right. In any case the turbulence in parliament simply reflected the turbulence outside it. The tensions of the 1620s over religion found expression in parliament, particularly in the parliament of 1628-1629*, culminating in the arguments over Arminianism* that led to a bitter dissolution. The political strain became too great to be accommodated within parliament. The 1629 session had ended with Sir John Eliot* appealing beyond parliament to the people; the parliaments that met in the wake of the Scottish rebellion in 1640 resulted in a more direct appeal.

The Long Parliament*, which opened in November 1640, inaugurated a constitutional revolution. The Triennial Act of 1641 (16 Car. I, c. 1) ended the king's power to summon parliament at will and provided for regular meetings; a second act (16 Car. I, c. 7) prevented the dissolution of parliament except by its own consent; a third of 1642 (17 Car. I, c. 27) excluded the bishops from the Lords. With the breakdown of relations between king and parliament over the militia, the two houses claimed validity for legislation—their "ordinances"—that had not received the royal assent. The army's* purge of parliament in 1648 (Pride's Purge*) and the Commons's abolition of the House of Lords and the monarchy in 1649 finally demolished the "ancient constitution."

The debate of the early 1640s on the legitimacy of parliament's actions in resisting the king and in effect claiming a sovereignty excluding him was extended to a wider one over the decade. The claim that the three estates comprehended the king was used by Presbyterian* writers such as Philip Hunton and William Prynne* to argue for a radically reduced account of his importance and role, while Henry Parker's *Observations upon Some of His Majesties Late Answers and Expresses* stressed the representative nature of the House of Commons. The problem with the latter point was that it could invite the response from its opponents that parliament's claim to represent the people was belied by its members' patent pursuit of their own (or their factions') interests. The Putney Debates* between the army factions in 1647 discussed Leveller* proposals for a broader franchise (even for universal manhood suffrage) and for a redistribution of parliamentary constituencies. After the expulsion of the Rump Parliament* in 1653, subsequent parliaments were summoned on a different basis. Barebone's Parliament* was a nominated assembly of a single chamber, although it was geographically based. The Instrument of Government* of December 1653 reformed the franchise in the counties and radically reduced the numbers of boroughs, and this arrangement governed the Commons in the parliaments of Oliver Cromwell*, although the Humble Petition and Advice* of May 1657 added an "Other House" of forty members. The parliament of 1659, however, was based on the old franchise, and the Lords were restored in the Convention Parliament* of 1660.

The Restoration* government reconstructed parliament largely as it had existed before 1641. The ordinances were ignored; the Triennial Act and the exclusion of the bishops, which had passed with the royal assent, were repealed. There is little indication that the events of mid-century had in any sense increased the stature of parliament: royalists'* argument that parliament had been perverted from its proper courses was largely accepted. The financial settlement of the ordinary revenues of the Crown in 1661-1662 was designed to satisfy the Crown's long-felt need for an adequate annual revenue that would obviate frequent recourse to parliament. A return to occasional parliaments was not unlikely.

In fact between 1660 and 1681 parliaments were far more frequent than they had been during the first half of the century. Only in 1672 and 1676 was there no meeting of a parliament at some point during the year. That frequency is attributable to a number of factors. As in the 1620s, the government became embroiled in a number of costly European wars; there were the Second and Third Dutch Wars* in 1665-1667 and 1672-1674, respectively, and preparations were made for war with France in 1678. However, for one reason and another, the revenue settlement of 1661-1662 failed to raise the sums expected, leaving a growing deficit. At the same time parliament's reluctant acceptance of the replacement of the more effective assessment (introduced during the Civil War) and a remodeling of the subsidy rendered parliamentary taxation more attractive than it had been in the first half of the century, and the practice of routinely appropriating such grants to the repayment of loans, first used in 1665, added to their value.

In short, it was largely the realities of government after 1660, rather than any shift in constitutional doctrine, that led to such frequent meetings. Indeed legal and constitutional argument about the role of parliament continued, most notoriously over the royal power of dispensing* with statute or suspending* it altogether. The primacy of statute was in one sense acknowledged. When additional customs duties were levied, it was with parliamentary approval, and in 1661 the government sought to clear up the controversial area of the power to levy the militia with a statute declaring the power to rest in the king (13 Car. II, c. 6). The removal of a major area of royal power from the prerogative to statute (although how much it had belonged to the prerogative in the first place was arguable) seemed to confirm parliament's legislative importance. Yet government seemed rather more willing than it had been before 1640 to claim a power to dispense with statutes or even suspend them. Charles II claimed in 1672 a power to suspend all the penal laws against Nonconformists and Catholics*; James II did the same in 1687. At the same time, however, the government machine was beginning to adapt to regular parliaments. In part this was simply a consequence of the importance parliamentary finance assumed in the 1660s and 1670s. A number of ministers, particularly Thomas Osborne*, earl of Danby, gave growing attention to the arts of parliamentary management, raising the value of conformity to the court through more sophisticated exploitation of the court's patronage.

Despite the almost universal condemnation of the activities of the Long Parliament, and the court's more blatant attempts at manipulation (which earned the Cavalier Parliament* of 1661-1679 the alternative sobriquet of the "Pensionary Parliament"), parliaments continued to reflect current political controversies, and the events of the 1640s were still seen as a reference point for politics. Techniques used then were frequently turned to at times of tension (such as the Exclusion Crisis*) for inspiration, above all in the tendency to appeal to a wider opinion outside Westminster (printing an official record of Commons proceedings became regular from 1680). During the 1680s it became the practice to identify members with party labels—"Whigs"* and "Tories"*. Claims that this represented a new type of parliamentary behavior may be questioned; the existence of pressure groups was not new, and there is little reason to believe that Whigs and Tories represented anything much more elaborate in terms of organization or discipline. One legacy of the Civil War seems to have been a tendency for the Lords and Commons to become locked in disputes concerning their privilege—over the case of *Skinner v. the East India Company* in 1668-1670 and the case of *Shirley v. Fagg* in 1675. In part these were synthetic disputes, raised for political reasons to delay or disrupt other business, but they struck a note of genuine concern in each house concerning privilege.

Parliament was little more securely entrenched in 1688 than it had been in 1603; indeed, the success of the government for most of the 1680s in doing without it showed that its survival could be held to be genuinely in doubt. A sense of this contributed to the increasingly shrill debate over the antiquity of parliament. Early seventeenth-century historians (see Historical Thought*) had assumed that parliament had survived barely altered from Saxon times. Challenges to this orthodoxy, most notably by Sir Robert Filmer in *The Freeholders' Grand Inquest* (1648), aimed particularly at the alleged antiquity of the House of Commons; its defenders (especially William Petyt) feared that conceding this point might even jeopardize the survival of the Commons as an effective part of the legislative trinity.

The Glorious Revolution* of 1688 largely dispelled these fears (although the concern that parliament was to become simply a legislative organ of government became more acute over the following century). The Bill of Rights*, passed by the Convention Parliament* of 1689, declared the illegality of the king's suspension of statutes, the illegality of the power of dispensing "as it hath been assumed and exercised of late," the illegality of levying money "by pretense of Prerogative without grant of Parliament," and so on; but it was practice, rather than theory or law, that was to cement parliament's position in the 1690s and beyond.

Bibliography: Mark Kishlansky, *Parliamentary Selection: Social and Political Choice in Early Stuart England*, 1986; Sheila Lambert, "Committees, Religion, and Parliamentary Encroachment on Royal Authority in Early Stuart England," *English Historical Review* 105 (1990): 60-95; Conrad Russell, *Parliaments and English Politics, 1621-29*, 1979.

Paul Seaward

Parliament of 1604-1610. The first parliament* of James I* met five times before it was finally dissolved on 9 February 1611 (having actually sat for the last time in December 1610). The king first summoned the parliament on 19 March 1604, about a year after his accession. His main legislative goal was progress toward an Anglo-Scottish union*, perhaps his most cherished ambition. When the House of Commons was slow to respond to his appeal, he was quick to display his exasperation. There were other disputes and controversies between the king and the lower house, notably Goodwin's Case* (1604) and the events that led to the famous protest known as the "Apology." (In the end the Apology was never adopted by the house.) Notwithstanding these controversies, the session was extremely productive of legislation; the thirty-three public and thirty-nine private acts signed by the king were substantially more than had passed in any session of parliament in Elizabeth's reign. Perhaps the most significant (certainly to the king) was an act authorizing English commissioners to discuss with their Scottish counterparts an Anglo-Scottish union. (The power to conclude, however, was reserved to parliament.) This apparently satisfied the king as a reasonable first step toward his great goal.

Parliament was prorogued on 7 July 1604 and was scheduled to meet again in November 1605 to consider the commissioners' report, but the meeting was postponed because of the Gunpowder Plot*. When it finally met on 21 January 1606 (continuing until 27 May), further discussion of the union was put off by mutual consent. In the wake of the plot, the parliament passed new penal statutes, including one that required suspected recusants* to take an oath of allegiance* to the king (3 Jac. I, c. 4). A subsidy bill also passed, giving the king three subsidies and six fifteenths, an unprecedentedly generous grant in time of peace. In all, the session yielded twenty-seven public and twenty-nine private acts. However, a bill to outlaw purveyance (the king's right to purchase provisions and carriage at below-market prices), a measure zealously pursued by the House of Commons, was twice stopped in the House of Lords (see Prerogative, Royal*).

The union was the chief business of the third session (18 November 1606-5 July 1607), though the parliament also found time to produce another substantial body of legislation: thirteen public and twenty private acts in all. An act repealing hostile laws against Scotland*, one of the thirteen public acts, represented another step toward the king's goal, though it was much less than he had hoped for. The House of Commons (perhaps discreetly encouraged by the Lords) strongly resisted the commissioners' recommendations regarding naturalization and free trade. As a result of his experiences in this session, the king seems to have despaired of further substantial progress toward his union, and he never again spoke of it to parliament.

By the time parliament met again on 9 February 1610, another pressing matter had come to the fore: the king's increasingly unhappy fiscal situation. The earl of Salisbury (Robert Cecil*), lord treasurer and the king's chief minister, appealed for a large supply to discharge the king's debts and an annual revenue to eliminate his large annual deficits. The latter was an unprecedented demand. The House of Commons demanded certain favors in return, notably the abolition of wardship, the king's right to control the estates and marriages of his tenants in chief when they were minors. Negotiations went slowly, and a tentative agreement was not reached until

July. As summarized in a "memorial," the Great Contract*, as the agreement came to be called, provided an annual revenue of £200,000 for the king and abolished wardship and purveyance and remedied other grievances for his subjects. The session, which ended 23 July, also produced another large body of legislation: twenty-three public and forty-three private acts. On the other hand, it was greatly troubled by the issue of impositions*, extraparliamentary customs introduced by Salisbury in 1608, which the House of Commons regarded as illegal.

In the fifth session (16 October-6 December 1610) the relative harmony that had prevailed through most of the parliament's history disappeared. The Great Contract collapsed, largely, it appears, because of second thoughts in the House of Commons about permanent direct taxation*, a radical innovation, that the agreement would have entailed. The king appealed for ordinary subsidies, but his appeal was doomed by his refusal to withdraw the impositions. In the ensuing stalemate, some members of the House of Commons made speeches critical of the king, who became increasingly exasperated. At last he prorogued the parliament until February 1611, but before the end of December he decided, with the advice of the privy council*, to dissolve it. Not a single statute was passed in the last session.

The unhappy ending of the first Stuart parliament has perhaps made it seem a greater failure than it was. In its first four sessions, the parliament passed a vast quantity of legislation, which was some proof that all three components of parliament—king, Lords, and Commons—were in basic agreement on a wide range of matters and also that parliament was still a very useful institution. On the other hand, in matters promoted by the king involving substantial change, such as the union and the Great Contract, the House of Commons played a very conservative (the king would have said obstructive) role. There were limits to the usefulness of parliament to the Crown in the early seventeenth century.

Bibliography: Elizabeth Read Foster, ed., *Proceedings in Parliament 1610*, 2 vols., 1966; Bruce Galloway, *The Union of England and Scotland, 1603-1608*, 1986; Wallace Notestein, *The House of Commons, 1604-1610*, 1971.

                                                                Eric N. Lindquist

Parliament of 1614. See Addled Parliament.

Parliament of 1621. James I's* third parliament*, called seven years after its predecessor (the Addled Parliament*), convened on 30 January 1621 in an atmosphere of crisis. The immediate occasion for its summoning was the Spanish invasion of the Rhenish or Lower Palatinate, the patrimony of James's son-in-law, the Elector Palatine Frederick V (see Thirty Years War*). This attack coincided with the rout of Frederick's army at White Mountain in Bohemia, where the elector had assumed command of a revolt against Habsburg Austria. As Frederick was the leader of Protestant Germany as well as a kinsman, James had little choice but to assist him and little way to make such assistance credible without calling a parliament to provide funds for military support.

James's opening speech to parliament called for supply (see Taxation*), and the House of Commons, urged on by the privy council*, quickly voted half the sum suggested. This gesture was partly tactical, for it freed the Commons to launch an attack against the patents of monopoly* that were detested by tradesmen and consumers alike and—through peers jealous of his influence—against the marquis (later 1st duke) of Buckingham (George Villiers*), who controlled royal patronage. This attack soon focused on a member of parliament (MP), Sir Giles Mompesson, who had obtained particularly obnoxious patents for licensing inns and alehouses. Technically Mompesson could be punished only for offenses against the house, but led on by Sir Edward Coke*, the former jurist, the Commons revived its long-dormant power of impeachment* against him and persuaded the House of Lords to exercise its ancient jurisdiction as a court.

Mompesson was duly condemned, but he was merely a means of getting at his patron, and James himself had to intervene on Buckingham's behalf before the Lords on 10 March. He permitted his chancellor Sir Francis Bacon* to be sacrificed instead when Bacon was not only implicated in having certified monopolies but accused of taking bribes. Neither of these acts would normally have attracted attention; the former was a routine legal function, and the acceptance of gratuities was common practice on the bench. In the atmosphere of the moment, however, they proved fatal. Bacon was tried and condemned by the Lords, forced to resign the great seal, and banished from office.

The Commons consolidated their victory by drafting a comprehensive bill against monopolies, a revised version of which finally became law in the parliament of 1624* (the Monopolies Act, 21 Jac. 1, c. 3). The remainder of the first session was largely taken up with bills to promote trade*, which had been severely depressed by the outbreak of the war on the Continent, and with proposals to tighten the disabilities against recusants. The simmering anti-Habsburg sentiment in the Commons led to an ill-judged attempt to punish a Catholic* barrister, Edward Floyd, for disparaging the Elector Frederick and James's daughter, Elizabeth*. The house was forced to beat an embarrassed retreat when the king challenged its jurisdiction, while a further attempt to implicate Buckingham in the monopoly scandal failed in the Lords. The session closed on 4 June with an emotional declaration of support for the recovery of the Palatinate.

During the recess James canceled a number of monopolies, but he also detained the earl of Southampton, a leader in the opposition to Buckingham, and Sir Edwin Sandys, an MP. When parliament reconvened on 20 November, the diplomatic situation was much worsened. The Lower Palatinate hung by a thread, while the Upper Palatinate, situated athwart Austria, had been occupied by Bavaria. Lord Digby, James's special envoy to Vienna, detailed the failure of his summer peace mission. The king asked for more money to support the war.

The Commons were still skeptical about James's resolve to fight, but when, after an unprecedented three-day debate on foreign policy, Sir George Goring, a courtier attached to Buckingham, moved a bellicose petition against Spain, the house unanimously adopted it. Whether the petition was a deliberate effort to sabotage the parliament cannot be proved, but it was taken for one when James, at Newmarket, refused to receive it. A standoff between the king and the Commons ensued, with James denouncing the petition as a breach of the royal prerogative* and the house insisting on its right to tender counsel. The issue of Spain now receded before that of privilege, and the Commons, facing adjournment for Christmas and the likelihood of dissolution, hastily drafted and approved a Protestation of its liberties on 18 December. The Commons Protestation of 1621*, a key document in the seventeenth-century constitutional debate, declared that the privileges of parliament, including the right to debate and advise on the affairs of church and commonwealth, were "the ancient and undoubted Birthright and inheritance of the Subjects of England."

Parliament was adjourned the following day, and on 28 December the king personally tore the Protestation from the *Commons's Journal* and ordered parliament dissolved. A public proclamation followed on 6 January 1622, and several MPs, including Coke, were imprisoned or sent abroad. The struggle joined between parliament and Buckingham was terminated only by the latter's assassination in 1628, and Sir Edward Coke, sitting in his last parliament that year, recalled the Protestation with pride. A no less lasting achievement was the revival of impeachment, which, repeatedly invoked against royal officials in the seventeenth century, helped shape both the theory and practice of ministerial responsibility.

Bibliography: Conrad Russell, *Parliaments and English Politics, 1621-1629*, 1979; S. D. White, *Sir Edward Coke and the "Grievances of the Commonwealth," 1621-1628*, 1978; Robert Zaller, *The Parliament of 1621*, 1971.

Robert Zaller

Parliament of 1624. The last parliament* of James I* (19 February-29 May) was called for two ancient and customary reasons: money and advice. During its lifespan the Spanish treaties were annulled, taxation* voted, and seventy-three statutes enacted. Pressure to call parliament came from royal advisers who opposed the proposed marriage of Prince Charles (see Charles I*) to the Spanish Infanta (see Spanish Match*) and wished to see England go to war with Spain in order to assist James's son-in-law Elector Frederick in recovering the Palatinate of the Rhine (see Elizabeth*; Thirty Years War*). To this end Charles and George Villiers*, 1st duke of Buckingham, the king's favorite, organized a loose grouping of privy councilors (see Privy Council*), members of parliament, peers, and courtiers into the "patriot coalition," which set the agenda. The elections were marked by Charles's active role in securing the election of clients, councilors, and members of his household; he was the dominant electoral patron of 1624.

At the opening ceremonies, James invited parliament to fulfill the wording of the writ of summons to debate foreign affairs and present advice to him. The Commons's speaker, Sir Thomas Crew, was duly elected, while John Williams, lord keeper and bishop of Lincoln, presided over the Lords. The discussion on foreign policy initially focused on Buckingham's "Relation," an account of his and Charles's visit to Spain, which spoke of Spanish perfidy and the humiliation to which Charles had been subjected. Naturally the subsidy bill was also directly related to foreign policy. The Commons saw the subsidy as going toward the projected war, while James wished to use it to pay his debts and the administrative costs of government. He requested an unprecedented six subsidies and twelve fifteenths, with part to be appropriated for war. In addition, he was willing to allow the appointment of a Commons committee for appropriation of war supply. However, after negotiation James accepted three subsidies and three fifteenths and a breaking of the treaties but with no guarantee of war.

In 1624 the public acts had their origins in either the Great Contract* (1610) or the Grace Bills (1614). Furthermore, the legislation of the two Jacobean parliaments of the 1620s was inextricably linked. Over 100 bills introduced in the parliament of 1621* were reintroduced three years later, and only one public act of 1624 had not been examined three years earlier. This led to an unusual procedural anomaly: public bills thoroughly examined and accepted by the Commons in 1621 were not committed at the second reading stage in 1624. The important bills were the Monopolies Act (21 Jac. I, c. 3) and the Informers Act (21 Jac. I, c. 4). The former had its origins in 1621 and was an attempt by the Commons to remedy the worst aspects of monopoly* patents and *non obstante* grants. It received royal support but met substantial opposition in an upper house concerned, for example, about loss of patronage and a misplaced belief that the bill limited the royal prerogative*. But despite the ease with which Charles I later circumvented the bill, it was a major advance in regulation. The Informers Act also received James's imprimatur, and it did substantially rectify a major legal, social, and economic grievance.

Apart from the anti-Catholicism evident in debates on breaking the treaties, religion was relatively unimportant in 1624. But the issue of Arminianism* was briefly debated. The subject arose after the publication of *A Gagg for the New Gospel* by Richard Montague, a member of the Durham House group of Arminians. The tract was a response to a Catholic* pamphlet, *The Gagg of the Reformed Gospel.* Montague stated that the Catholic church was still a true church, that the pope was not necessarily the Antichrist, and that the elect could lose God's grace. The Commons debated the publication on the floor of the house and in committee. They drafted a petition against Montague but referred the matter to Archbishop George Abbot* to examine because they were "not willing to become judges in soe deepe points of religion."

Again, following the example of 1621, the ancient process of impeachment* was activated during the session. The lord treasurer, Lionel Cranfield*, earl of Middlesex, was the victim of a campaign by Buckingham to strip him of power, office, and influence over the king. Middlesex was isolated and exposed as one of the few prominent Lords and privy councilors who opposed not only a war with Spain but the breaking of the Spanish match negotiations. He initially came under attack from the committee for trade* in the Commons. Led by Edwin Sandys, a client of Buckingham and long-term enemy of the lord treasurer, the committee alleged that Middlesex had taken bribes, increased impositions*, and made innovations in the court of wards. The charges were brought to the Lords by Sir Edward Coke* and Sandys, and a long inquiry into Middlesex's conduct took place. He was found guilty by the Lords, fined £50,000, deprived of his offices, and imprisoned in the Tower. James mitigated the fine, and Middlesex was released shortly after parliament ended.

Charles and Buckingham's attempt to control the parliament met with only limited success. They achieved the breaking of the Spanish treaties, but not England's direct involvement in the war. In the end the aged but politically astute James held the upper hand. However, satisfied members of parliament could return to their counties with substantial legislative reforms and secure in the knowledge that the Spanish match was no longer viable.

Bibliography: Thomas Cogswell, *The Blessed Revolution,* 1989; Robert Ruigh, *The Parliament of 1624,* 1971; Conrad Russell, *Parliaments and English Politics, 1621-1629,* 1979.

Chris R. Kyle

Parliament of 1625. The parliament of 1625 was convened by Charles I* less than three months after the death of his father, James I*. The session opened in Westminster on 18 June, sat through 11 July, adjourned, reconvened in Oxford on 1 August, and sat until the dissolution on 12 August.

Business in 1625 focused on issues of religion and finance connected to England's policy regarding the Habsburgs and the restitution of the Palatinate to Frederick, Count Palatine, husband of James's daughter and Charles's sister Elizabeth* (see Thirty Years War*). A major speech relating to Crown policy and finance was delivered by Sir John Coke, secretary of state, on 4 August, following a short speech by the king charging parliament with the financial responsibility for that policy. Loan of money to Christian IV of Denmark and support of Count Mansfeld's troops in Germany necessitated parliamentary supply.

Domestic policy was also debated. Many members of Parliament perceived a new leniency toward recusants* in England connected with the king's recent marriage to the Catholic princess Henrietta Maria*, sister to Louis XIII of France. A petition concerning religion, focusing on the spread of Catholicism* and the enforcement of laws against recusants, was drafted in the House of Commons in June and sent to the Lords on 1 July for amendment. It was engrossed by 6 July and two days later presented to the king at Hampton Court. Charles promised a speedy answer, which was delivered in Oxford on 8 August by George Villiers*, 1st duke of Buckingham and lord high admiral. Lord Treasurer James Ley followed the answer with an analysis of the king's financial estate: debts, anticipations, and engagements.

The Commons, dissatisfied with the position taken by the Crown servants, Coke on 4 August and Buckingham and Ley on the 8th, presented a protestation to the king before the dissolution on 12 August. Thanking him for his answer to the petition, they then promised "to discover and reform the abuses and grievances of the realm and state," refusing to pass another subsidy bill until those grievances were redressed. During the final days of the session, debate centered on Buckingham's growing personal power. Rumors were abroad of a pending naval action, but parliament was not consulted about the Cadiz expedition* that would sail in October. The secrecy regarding that campaign would become an issue in 1626.

Leadership in the lower house included John Pym* (in religious issues), Sir Edward Coke*, Sir Francis Seymour, Sir Robert Phelips, Sir Thomas Wentworth*, Sir Edwin Sandys, and John Glanville. All but Sandys and Pym were pricked (appointed) as sheriffs* following the dissolution in order to prevent their election to the next parliament. Glanville, for his leadership in drafting the protestation, was pressed into service by Buckingham as secretary to the Cadiz expedition.

In 1625 the House of Lords sat for sixteen days in Westminster and ten in Oxford. Twenty-three spiritual Lords and seventy-four temporal Lords attended one or more days of the session. The House of Commons sat for nineteen days in Westminster and ten in Oxford. There were 487 men returned to seats in the Lower House.

Daily attendance was low. Division figures in the Commons reveal that on 22 June there were 367 voting members present and four tellers. By 5 July the number had dropped to 227 voting members and four tellers. Attendance figures sharply decreased in the upper house for the same period: on 22 June seventeen bishops and thirty-two temporal peers were present; on 5 July the numbers had decreased to fourteen bishops and twenty-three lords. The decline in parliamentary attendance was related to the increase in plague mortality in the city (see Epidemics and Plague*).

Seventeen bills were introduced in the upper house and fifty-three in the lower. Out of the total of seventy, two private bills and seven public bills passed into statutory law in this session, including those for two temporal subsidies and three clerical subsidies (see Taxation and Revenue*).

Accounts of the parliament of 1625 are sparse, probably because of the dislocation from the city and the decline in attendance. All of the extant proceedings of the business in both houses are published, although no private diaries of peers have been discovered.

Bibliography: Maija Jansson and William B. Bidwell, eds., *Proceedings in Parliament 1625*, 1987. This edition includes the *Journals* from both houses and Sir John Eliot's *Negotium Posterorum*.

Maija Jansson

Parliament of 1626. The second parliament of Charles I* convened on 6 February 1626 and was dissolved on 15 June the same year. It met in an atmosphere of tension exacerbated by the secrecy of the planning for the Cadiz expedition* coupled with its tragic failure (see Spanish War of 1625-1630*). Many Englishmen turned against the new king's policies, blaming his adviser and favorite, George Villiers*, 1st duke of Buckingham. During the session relations between parliament and king were further strained when impeachment* proceedings were brought against Buckingham, and the king charged John Digby, earl of Bristol, with high treason.

On 17 February the lower house began examining particulars of the staying of a French ship taken for prize by the English admiral. Without due process of law, its cargo was confiscated by Buckingham. French reprisals were swift and severe, with the taking of English merchant ships on the high seas and the sale of their freight in the markets of Paris. In the lower house this case and the matter of the duke's loan of ships to Louis XIII opened the way for a general debate about Crown policy and Buckingham's part in it.

Through a series of subcommittees and committees of the whole house, debate in the Commons focused on matters that ultimately served as the basis for thirteen articles of impeachment exhibited against the duke. Members of parliament (MPs) addressed issues of plurality of office, corruption and self-aggrandizement through the buying and selling of offices (statutorily prohibited by 5 and 6 Edw. VI, c. 16), extortion, bribery, and ultimately treason.

Buckingham was first charged with holding more offices than he could effectively perform. Furthermore, it was charged, he not only bought offices for his relatives but also for himself, as that of the lord high admiral's place (see Navy*) and the wardenship of the Cinque Ports. It was particularly with regard to those offices, critical to the defense of the realm, that Buckingham was accused of neglecting his duty in not guarding the seas, which as a result were infested with pirates. Article 5 concerned the unjust stay of the *St. Peter* and the taking for personal use of the gold, silver, jewels, and other items on board.

Article 7, the most legally specific charge, was that he lent a royal naval ship to the French king as well as six merchant ships commandeered without security or assurance for redelivery. The taking of the merchant vessels by threats and without orders or consent of the masters raised constitutional issues regarding personal property and the rights of free subjects. Furthermore, the discovery that these ships had been procured for use against the Protestants in La Rochelle touched on the formulation of foreign policy and the place of parliament in those decisions. The matter of selling places of judicature struck at bribery and rewards. Compelling Lord Robartes to buy his title brought renewed questioning of the practice of buying and selling honor first raised in the Addled Parliament* of 1614 with regard to the baronetcies.

Parliamentary committees were unable to discover all of the means of Buckingham's wealth. Although he was selling lands given to him by James I* and keeping the rents in reversion, that policy alone did not explain the growth of his fortune. Ultimately parliament concluded that through "unusual clauses" and sloppy bookkeeping, the duke had so confused treasury accounts that they could not be cleared. On that point he was charged with exhausting, intercepting, and misemploying the king's revenue. Lastly, Article 13 spelled out Buckingham's "transcendent presumption" in administering medicine to James I without license and without consultation with the royal physicians, the implication being that the administering of the posset had a direct effect on the king's death and consequently could be interpreted as an act of treason.

In a celebrated privilege case, two MPs, Sir John Eliot* and Sir Dudley Digges, were imprisoned for treasonous remarks made during the debates relating to Buckingham. Both were released before the end of the session.

The articles were drafted in the lower house and presented to the Lords in a joint conference 8 and 10 May. They were reported in the upper house on 13 and 15 May;

the duke gave his response on 8 June. On 14 June the Commons engrossed a remonstrance to the king calling for Buckingham's removal. Fearing further embarrassment, Charles hastily dissolved the parliament without allowing time for the passage of a subsidy bill.

During the time the lower house was occupied with drafting charges against the duke, the king was prosecuting a case in the upper house against the earl of Bristol. The attorney general, Sir Robert Heath, charging him among other things with protracting the treaty negotiations in 1623-1624, presented the Crown case on 1 May and formally charged Bristol with treason on 6 May. Procedural matters regarding his not having received a summons to the session and concerning witnesses in parliament raised issues related to the nature of parliament as a high court and as such to the jurisdiction of the law courts (see Common Law and Courts*).

Further tensions between Crown and parliament after the dissolution of 1626 became evident in the parliament of 1628*. Charles, now without subsidy monies, sought to fill his coffers with revenues from a loan demanded of taxpayers without security for repayment. This "forced loan"*, which called for the imprisonment of refusers, raised legal issues that would be addressed in the Petition of Right* in 1628 (see Taxation and Revenue*).

The House of Lords sat for seventy-five days in 1626. Twenty-one spiritual lords attended the session at least once. The earl of Bristol did not receive a writ of summons.

The Commons sat for ninety-seven days. During the session, eight returns in disputed elections were voided and new writs issued, although the results of the by-elections in Camelford and Liskeard are not known. Four persons died during the session and five members were elevated to the peerage (Sir Dudley Carleton*, William Lord Cavendish, Sir Henry Ley, Edward Montagu, and Algernon Lord Percy). Membership in the lower house was around 484 at the end of the session.

During the parliament, 119 bills were introduced in the lower house and twenty-three in the upper. The house was dissolved before the passage of any of the 142 bills.

Bibliography: William Bidwell and Maija Jansson, eds., *Proceedings in Parliament 1626*, 4 vols., 1991; Elizabeth Read Foster, *The House of Lords, 1603-1649*, 1983.

                                                                    Maija Jansson

Parliament of 1628-1629. The third parliament* of Charles I* convened at Westminster on 17 March 1628 and sat through 26 June, when it was prorogued until 20 October; it was again prorogued until 20 January 1629, when the second session convened. On 10 March 1629 the king dissolved the parliament, beginning the eleven years of Personal Rule* that lasted until the meeting of the Short Parliament* in April 1640.

In his opening speech Charles focused on the European situation and the strength of the Catholic* alliances on the Continent in an effort to underline the necessity for supply. Concerns of both houses, however, were closer to home and connected to the domestic ramifications of an increasingly arbitrary royal policy exercised in governing both church and state. The experience of members of parliament (MPs) recently imprisoned for refusing to pay the forced loan* epitomized complaints against the Crown. Continuing recusancy* and the growth of Arminianism*, reflected in the works of Roger Manwaring and others, were also matters of issue.

On 24 March Lord Montagu proposed that the Lords take the initiative in drawing a petition to the king requiring that laws against recusants be observed. He was seconded by William Fiennes*, Lord Saye and Sele, and John Holles, Lord Clare. A petition was drafted, largely the work of Samuel Harsnet, bishop of Norwich, and presented to Charles on 31 March. He responded on 7 April to the satisfaction of both houses.

Immediately following opening procedural business, MPs in the Commons addressed the issue of the fundamental rights of free Englishmen. On 22 March Robert Goodwin spoke passionately about liberty, followed by some of those who together with John Selden* and Edward Littleton would provide the leadership of the session: Sir John Eliot*, Sir Francis Seymour, Sir Benjamin Rudyard, Sir Robert Phelips, and Sir Thomas Wentworth*.

In the arguments that unfolded through the rest of March, the idea of freedom was examined and analyzed with regard to the policies of the Crown. Four points later to be addressed in the Petition of Right* were studied from every perspective. Forced loans and coercive taxation*, imprisonment or detention without cause shown, billeting of soldiers on private families, and the commissions for proceeding according to martial law during peacetime were proved to be contrary to the laws of England.

The committee system, honed and shaped in earlier parliaments, provided the structure for effective debate based on facts and precedents garnered by an elaborate system of subcommittees. The Commons passed three resolutions: (1) that no free man ought to be committed, detained in prison or otherwise constrained by the king or privy council* unless some cause be expressed for the commitment; (2) that a writ of habeas corpus may not be denied to any man committed or detained in prison even if the imprisonment is by command of the king; and (3) that if a free man be committed or detained and no cause is expressed and he is granted a habeas corpus, then he ought to be delivered or bailed. The resolutions, with an additional one acknowledging that a free man's property in his goods and estate was such that no tax or other charge could be levied on them without assent of parliament, passed on 3 April.

On 7 April both houses met in what was arguably the most organized joint conference of the early Stuart parliaments. In it the groundwork was laid for drafting the Petition of Right. Sir Dudley Digges gave the introduction, followed by Edward Littleton, who presented the legal precedents in charters and statutory law for the rights of free Englishmen. John Selden analyzed some thirty-four court cases, and Sir Edward Coke* closed by proving that the resolutions of 3 April were but declarations of the fundamental laws of the kingdom.

Both houses conferred again on 16 and 17 April. The Petition of Right passed in Commons on 8 May and was sent up to the Lords, who proposed several alterations and an addition. Accommodation was reached following a conference on 17 May, and on 28 May the petition was presented to Charles I. The king's brief response of 2 June was found unsatisfactory and ambiguous by parliament, which requested a new "clear and satisfactory answer." The second answer, delivered on 7 June, was accepted, and immediately procedures were begun to enroll and print the Petition.

The lower house then renewed its attack on the 1st duke of Buckingham (George Villiers*), drawing a remonstrance against him. In response Charles dissolved the session on 26 June. After the dissolution, the king ordered the printer to publish the first answer to the Petition rather than the agreed-upon second. Charles continued to collect customs duties on tonnage and poundage without parliamentary consent and to confiscate the goods of merchants who refused to pay.

When parliament reconvened on 20 January 1629, the first order of business in the Commons was the case of Mr. Rolless, an MP whose goods had been confiscated. Debate then turned to the Crown's interference with the printing of the Petition and then to matters of religion, sparked by the appointment of William Laud* to the bishopric of London* during parliament's prorogation. The Commons quickly adopted a resolution supporting the Articles of the Church of England (see Anglicanism*) and rejecting "the sense of the Jesuits and Arminians"*.

In February debate in the Commons again focused on the Crown's power to tax, culminating in the passage of a resolution that a man should have privilege for his goods as well as his person. Charles confronted parliament by declaring that the confiscation of goods had been at his own instance and not that of the customs officers. He then adjourned the session on 25 February to let tempers cool. When the house reconvened on 2 March, Speaker Sir John Finch declared the king's pleasure was that they adjourn again until the 10th of the month. Sir John Eliot, however, demanded the reading of a further resolution on religion. Finch refused and was held in his chair by MPs who called for the resolution, which named Arminians "capital enemies" to the king and commonwealth. The resolution was read, and the house adjourned itself. On 10 March Charles dissolved the parliament and subsequently published his reasons for so doing (Rushworth, I, App., 7-11). The Lords had engaged in little more than routine business for the brief second session.

The upper house sat for eighty days in the first session, twenty-one in the second. Sixteen spiritual lords and ninety-nine temporal lords attended at least one day of proceedings.

The Commons met for eighty-five days in the first session, thirty in the second. The exact membership of the lower house is not known. At the outset, 507 men were returned; at the close of the first session membership was 488, including twenty-three MPs who had been committed or confined for refusing the forced loan.

Of ninety bills introduced in the first session, eight passed into statutory law as public acts (including bills for five temporal and five clerical subsidies) and nineteen as private acts. No legislation passed during the second session of the parliament of 1628.

Bibliography: Robert C. Johnson et al., eds., *Proceedings in Parliament 1628*, 6 vols., 1977; Richard L. Greaves and Robert Zaller, eds., *Dictionary of British Radicals in the Seventeenth Century*, 3 vols., 1982.

Maija Jansson

Parliament of 1640. See Short Parliament.

Parliament of 1640-1653. See Long Parliament; Rump Parliament.

Parliament of 1653. See Barebone's Parliament.

Parliaments of 1654-1655, 1656, 1659. See Protectorate Parliaments.

Parliament of 1660. See Convention Parliament (1660).

Parliament of 1661-1679. See Cavalier Parliament.

Parliaments of 1679, 1680. See Exclusion Crisis.

Parliament of 1681. See Exclusion Crisis; Oxford Parliament.

Parliament of 1685. James II* succeeded to the English throne upon Charles II's* death on 6 February 1685 and shortly thereafter summoned his first and only parliament* in order to obtain revenue. He did not dictate the outcome of elections, but his ministers did supervise their conduct. In the counties the lords lieutenant* largely succeeded in achieving consensus and avoiding contested elections, occasionally assisted by returning officers who refused to conduct polls. The boroughs, ninety-eight of which had new charters as the result of Charles and James's *quo warranto* proceedings since 1681, could be counted upon to return reliable members of parliament (MPs). Despite James's concern about a replay of the elections during the Exclusion Crisis* (1678-1681), there was little organized Whig* activity, and an overwhelming Tory* majority—mostly country gentry—was returned to parliament. Though there were an unprecedented sixty-six petitions protesting the conduct of county elections, all but one were ignored. A great many Tory MPs were new, making them much easier for their leaders to manage.

Parliament convened on 19 May. The Commons initially startled James by asking him to prosecute all Nonconformists but quickly explained that they did not mean to include Catholics*, only Dissenters*. Without questioning James's previous unauthorized collection of revenues, parliament renewed those given to Charles for life and passed additional indirect taxation* (impositions* on sugar, tobacco, vinegar, and wine) to pay off the old king's debts and for resupply of ordnance and the navy* (James used much of this to maintain a standing army*). They balked only at his request to repeal the 1673 Test Act* (25 Car. II, c. 2). On the outbreak of Monmouth's Rebellion* and the related revolt of the 9th earl of Argyll (Archibald

Campbell*) in Scotland*, parliament voted additional funds and on 15 June hurriedly passed a bill of attainder against Monmouth, allowing him to be executed without trial. When Speaker Edward Seymour protested the use of new borough charters to retain MPs favorable to the royal court* and suggested that they be suspended, he was ignored by members concerned about the prospect of inciting another civil war.

Monmouth attempted to appeal to Whigs, and during the rebellion Tories strongly supported James in parliament and in the field. They rejoiced at the suppression of "Whig rebellion"; the trials of Henry Cornish and John Hampden (for the 1683 Rye House Plot*) and of Brandon, Delamere, and Stamford (exclusionists charged with supporting Monmouth); and the king's dismissal of the marquess of Halifax on 21 October (for refusing to support repeal of the Test Act). But when parliament reconvened in November, James alarmed Tories by announcing that since the militia had proved ineffective, he planned to maintain a standing army, which had tripled in size to 14,000 during the rebellion. More provocatively, he noted that he had commissioned numerous Catholic officers, whom he exempted from the Test Act through the dispensing power*. He also requested additional funds for the army.

James's criticism of the militia insulted the very Tory gentry who had opposed his exclusion from the throne and supported him in the preceding months. After a narrow vote (183 to 182) to consider the issue of Catholic officers before proceeding to supply, the Commons addressed the king, warning that Catholics could be dispensed from the Test Act only by statute, offering to indemnify those already serving from penalties, and asking that James offer no further illegal commissions to Catholics. Though Commons then turned to supply, James was incensed; he was even angrier at the Lords, who declared that commissioning Catholic officers was illegal, called for the judges to be consulted, and sought to coordinate its efforts with the Commons. Therefore, the king prorogued parliament on 20 November, initially until February, but in fact it never met again, though it was not formally dissolved until July 1687.

Having alienated the Tories, who now occupied a position analogous to the country opposition in the Cavalier Parliament* (1661-1685), James was forced to turn to the Whigs for support, but that had little chance of success. Furthermore, he had revived the fears of popery and suspicions of Jesuit political machinations earlier associated with the Popish Plot* (1678) and the Exclusion Crisis. Inflamed by his further appointment of Catholics in the army, privy council*, local government*, universities*, and the church, his Declarations of Indulgence* (1687-1688), the arrest of the Seven Bishops*, and the birth of a Catholic male heir in 1688, these fears would lead to his ouster in the Glorious Revolution*.

Bibliography: J. R. Jones, *Country and Court: England, 1658-1714*, 1978; J. P. Kenyon, *The Stuart Constitution: Documents and Commentary*, 1966; J. R. Tanner, *English Constitutional Conflicts of the Seventeenth Century, 1603-1689*, 1928.

                                                                                William B. Robison

Parliament of 1689. See Convention Parliament (1689).

Parliamentarian. *Parliamentarian* is a term initially applied to those members of the English parliament* between 1628 and 1642 who opposed Charles I's* use of personal power to rule England between 1629 and 1640. Most were concentrated in the House of Commons, although there were some in the House of Lords. Parliamentarians were committed Protestants—in large part Puritans*—opposed to Archbishop William Laud* and his Arminian* policy (see also High Church*) regarding operation of the Church of England (see Anglicanism*). Parliamentarians also tended to believe in an international papist conspiracy that was encouraged, either directly or indirectly, by Charles.

More important than the religious aspects of parliamentarianism, however, was the parliamentarians' belief that the king's Personal Rule* constituted a grave threat to English constitutional government. According to such prominent parliamentarians as Sir John Eliot*, John Hampden*, and John Pym*, Charles's failure to call parliament during that eleven-year period abrogated that body's unique role of bringing ruler and subjects together to consider each party's needs and the resolution of any conflicts that existed between them. Under the absolutist* policies pursued by Charles and such councilors as George Villiers*, 1st duke of Buckingham (until 1628), Laud, and Sir Thomas Wentworth*, the people of the British realm were not participants in government but mere observers.

Parliamentarians tended to gravitate into two camps: conservative and radical. The radical wing was dominated by the militant Puritan minority, who fed on the growing fear of popery, as well as the abuses of power by Charles and his advisers, to call for the overthrow of Anglican episcopacy and severe curtailment of the traditional powers of monarchy. The conservatives—moderates like Viscount Falkland, Edward Hyde*, and Sir John Culpepper—resisted innovations despite the common bond of Protestantism between themselves and the Puritans. The conservatives saw the need only to redress abuses of the traditional institutions, not eliminate them. The philosophical differences between the two elements of the parliamentarians eventually led to a rift. When Charles, under increasing financial pressure, finally called the Long Parliament* into session in November 1640, the members drew up the Grand Remonstrance*, which detailed grievances—real or imagined—from the time of the last parliament of 1628-1629* up to and including the Short Parliament* in the spring of 1640. The Grand Remonstrance passed by only eleven votes and led to conservative parliamentarians' being dubbed "royalists*," those being members who favored traditionalist compromise between king and parliament. Also, for the first time, a social division between the two factions became evident, the royalists being more aristocratic.

The Militia Ordinance of 1641 illustrates the difference between them. It was proposed to allow parliament to organize its own army* to fight the Scottish rebels, who had already defeated royal forces in the Bishops' Wars*, conflicts resulting from Laud's imposition of the Book of Common Prayer and changes in structure in the Scottish Kirk*. A vote for or against the ordinance established the difference between a royalist and a parliamentarian. The royalists could not go along with abandoning the monarchy to complete domination by a parliament that had its own army, while the parliamentarians feared a popish king's gaining dictatorial powers in matters of finance and defense and obstructing further political reforms, such as the establishment of regular parliamentary sessions.

The Militia Ordinance did pass and led to formation of a parliamentary army commanded by Robert Devereux*, 3d earl of Essex, which soon engaged royal forces at the start of the Civil War* in the summer of 1642. The term *parliamentarian* became synonymous with the term *Roundhead** between then and 1653, when the Rump Parliament* was dissolved by Oliver Cromwell*.

Bibliography: Douglas Brunton and D. H. Pennington, *Members of the Long Parliament*, 1968; Esther S. Cope, *Politics Without Parliament,* 1987; Kevin Sharpe, *Politics and Ideas in Early Stuart England: Essays and Studies,* 1989.

                                                                Kenneth Postan

Penruddock's Rising (1655). Led by the royalist* conspirator Sir Joseph Wagstaff and two Wiltshire gentlemen, Colonel John Penruddock and Hugh Grove, the rising's objective was to seize Salisbury, declare Charles II*, and march west to recruit more royalists. The conspirators hoped this would lead to a general insurgency against the Protectorate* of Oliver Cromwell*.   But the rising was hampered by a lack of coordination with other royalists outside the county, the support that rallied to the government, and the vigilance of informers within conspiratorial circles.

In January 1655 agents of the state secretary John Thurloe* uncovered a royalist plot to distribute arms in northern Wales* and the Midlands. This embarrassment shook the royalist faction known as the "Action Party," and to recover confidence at Charles II's exiled court, a representative was sent to Cologne. At this point, Henry Wilmot, earl of Rochester, became involved, for it was he who was sent to Cologne and recommended that the Action Party be given further support.   The other prominent royalist faction in England, the Sealed Knot, denounced the Action Party as reckless incompetents. To mediate these divisions, James Butler*, marquess of Ormonde, and Daniel O'Neill were sent to England in early February. Their mission failed to resolve the dispute. On 23 February the earl of Rochester and the royalist conspirator Sir Joseph Wagstaff arrived in London*. A murky compromise was reached whereby Rochester was made overall head of operations to coordinate the rival factions.

In late February or early March, Rochester was contacted by royalists from a disparate organization called the Western Association. They requested that Wagstaff lead a rising planned for early March. This was to occur simultaneously with royalist uprisings in Yorkshire and at Chester, Shrewsbury, and elsewhere, which either failed to happen or were of no consequence. Throughout these disturbances, members of the Sealed Knot remained generally aloof.

In Wiltshire, Penruddock and Grove were the most prominent local gentry involved in the rising. Accounts differ in details, but the events unfolded rapidly toward disaster for the conspirators. Originally the plan was to seize the Wiltshire assize judges at Winchester on 8 March. This was abandoned, and instead on 11 March Penruddock, Grove, Wagstaff, and their followers (numbering close to 200) rallied at Clarendon Park near Salisbury. They captured the city and seized two judges and a sheriff*. These men refused to declare Charles II. The next day, the royalists marched west to Blanford, where Penruddock proclaimed the king. It is possible that by 13 March their numbers reached 400, but 200 appears more likely.

The government was not idle. Thousands of militia rallied to the government in Somerset, and on 14 March Major General John Desborough left Newbury to intercept the insurgents. The actual demise of the royalist effort occurred, though, when a cavalry force from Yeovil surrounded them at South Molton on 15 March. About sixty royalists were captured, including Penruddock and Grove; Wagstaff escaped. Although there had been verbal promises of quarter, Penruddock and Grove were beheaded after a trial at Exeter on 18 April. The total number executed was not more than twelve after trials at Salisbury, Exeter, and Chard.

Bibliography: S. R. Gardiner, *History of the Commonwealth and Protectorate*, vol. 3, 1901; A. H. Woolrych, *Penruddock's Rising*, 1980.

John H. F. Hughes

Pentland Rising (1666). From 1639 to 1692 organized political violence formed part of the political process in Scotland*. During the Restoration* period the adherents of the Covenants* twice rose in rebellion to alter government policy. The first and more serious revolt in 1666 occurred against the background of political, religious, economic, and international changes caused by the policies of Charles II* and his Scottish ministers of state.

The restoration of the monarchy brought expectations and anxieties to Scottish Presbyterians*, who formed the majority south of the Tay River. Their hopes for a repeal of the hated parliamentary union* with England were quickly realized. However, in 1661 the earl of Middleton's royalist* regime overturned all the constitutional advances secured by the Covenanters*, save the abolition of the committee of articles. Many who had served on Covenanter political bodies were now excluded from civil affairs and fined for their past anti-royalism. Hopes for separate religious settlements in Scotland and England were dashed with the reestablishment of episcopalian church government, the deprivation of Presbyterian ministers, and a repressive policy against Presbyterian church services. These innovations infuriated many lairds, burgesses, and farmers in the southern Lowlands. The Scots government, under Middleton and later the earl of Rothes and Archbishop James Sharp of St. Andrews, copied Edward Hyde*, the earl of Clarendon's harsh policies against Dissenters*.

These grievances were compounded by other acts of the Restoration regimes. High customs and excise duties (see Taxation and Revenue*), levied to pay for governing Scotland (and enriching royalists), stirred up the population*. The English declaration of war against the Dutch in 1665 (see Second Dutch War*, 1665-1667) provided the penultimate cause for rebellion. The Scots' close economic ties with the Dutch (exemplified by their coal and salt exports), their tradition of sending students to universities in the Netherlands, the presence of Scots in the Dutch army, Dutch support for the Covenanters from 1638, and most significant a shared Presbyterian perspective meant that the Scots, unlike the English, viewed the war with disapprobation.

Fearing rebellion in Fife and the southwest, the government chose a policy of massive repression to maintain order. Consequently it deployed the Scots army to those disaffected areas. In response to the rapacious behavior of troops in the southwest, the local Presbyterians (who had a reputation for fanaticism) took the field in November 1666. They captured the area commander, Major James Turner, in Dumfries. As the Whigs marched north through Ayrshire and Lanarkshire, their force increased to 3,000 men (the name of these "Whiggamores" was later applied to the English parliamentary Whigs*, initially as an insult, by their opponents). Fortunately for the government, a planned conjunction between the Dutch and Fife Presbyterians failed to transpire. The Whigs doggedly marched to Colinton, west of Edinburgh. Lacking united leadership or common goals, plagued by bad weather, demoralized by lack of succor in Lothian, and harried by the army under Sir Thomas Dalziel, they retreated to Rullion Green in the Pentland Hills. On 28 November Dalziel attacked and destroyed the Covenanting horde. Thirty prisoners who refused to swear fealty to the regime were hanged; others were exiled to Barbados to work on the plantations*. The Presbyterians' most serious rebellion of the Restoration discredited violence as an instrument of opposition until the Covenanter Rebellion* of 1679.

Except for the recalcitrant prisoners, the Pentland Rising had positive results for the Presbyterians. Rothes and Sharp received blame for the rising, allowing the earl of Lauderdale (John Maitland*) to establish his own Scottish regime in 1667. He initiated a policy of toleration for Presbyterians, culminating in the Indulgence of 1679. Lauderdale's conciliatory moves secured a degree of peace and stability by splitting the moderate Presbyterians (acceptors of the Indulgence) from the radicals (who refused to countenance any aid from government).

Bibliography: Julia Buckroyd, *Church and State in Scotland, 1660-1681*, 1981; I. Cowan, *The Covenanters*, 1973.

Edward M. Furgol

Pepys, Samuel (1633-1703). Samuel Pepys was born on 23 February 1633 in St. Bride's Parish, London*, the fifth son of a tailor. He attended a Huntington school for two years beginning 15 March 1644, St. Paul's School in London, and Cambridge University. At Cambridge, Pepys first resided in Trinity Hall (21 June 1650), later transferring to Magdalene College, which offered him a scholarship (5 March 1651). He received a B.A. in 1653 and an M.A. in 1660.

Pepys entered the household of his cousin Sir Edward Montagu in 1656. Montagu's military prowess, albeit in the service of Oliver Cromwell* during the Interregnum*, nevertheless earned him the respect of the restored Charles II*, who made him general of the fleet and earl of Sandwich. Montagu's young cousin Pepys entered the king's naval service (see Navy*) as well, rising at his mentor's side.

From 1660 Pepys served as a member of the Naval Board, clerk of the acts of the navy, and a clerk of the privy seal.

As an Admiralty secretary (1673-1679, 1684-1688), Pepys reformed English naval administration, often against powerful opposition. His changes included the reorganization of officers' ranks, promotion opportunities for career officers, development of the convoy strategy, and a control system for naval contracts. His political activities increased apace, leading to a seat in the House of Commons for Castle Rising in 1673.

His battles over reform of the Admiralty and being falsely accused of popery in 1673 and 1679 took their toll, the latter resulting in his imprisonment in the Tower of London in 1679. By 1688 the former innovator preferred the status quo and remained loyal to James II*, going quietly into retirement in Clapham rather than serving William* and Mary*. He resigned as secretary of the Admiralty on 20 February 1689 and set about writing his *Memoirs Relating to the State of the Royal Navy of England for Ten Years Determined December 1668,* which he published in 1690. Samuel Pepys died at Clapham on 26 May 1703 and was buried at St. Olav's on 5 June.

Pepys' noted *Diary,* invaluable to social historians as a picture of Restoration* London, was begun on 1 January 1660. He used a shorthand devised by John Skelton, further disguising those entries he considered "unfit for publication" by writing them in French, Latin, Greek, or Spanish. The project ended on 31 May 1669 when Pepys, fearing imminent blindness, decided to rest his eyes. For the same reason, at the age of thirty-seven, he took leave of his naval administrative duties and traveled to France and Holland to collect information on foreign navies. Although his eyesight improved, he never resumed the *Diary.*

Pepys's library of over 3,000 volumes went first to a nephew, John Jackson, son of his sister Paulina, then to the Magdalene College Library. Sizeable manuscript collections remain in the Rawlinson collection of Oxford's Bodleian Library and in the Library of the Inner Temple.

Bibliography: V. Brome, *The Other Pepys,* 1992; Robert C. Latham and William Matthews, *The Diary of Samuel Pepys,* 11 vols., 1970-; I. E. Taylor, *Samuel Pepys,* 1989.

Ann E. Faulkner

Personal Rule (1629-1640). Charles I* ruled England for eleven years without summoning a parliament*. On 27 March 1629, shortly after he had dissolved his third (the parliament of 1628-1629*), he publicly proclaimed that the abuse of parliaments had "driven" him from meeting them, that he would call another only when he had evidence that the English people were more docile, and that he would punish severely anyone who spread rumors about parliaments. He abandoned his Personal Rule in April 1640 not because his conditions had been met, but because he wanted parliamentary support to continue the Bishops' Wars*.

Charles's statements in 1629, the interval before he next issued writs for parliament, and the complaints about the "intermission of parliaments" that arose in

1640, prompted some to refer to the Personal Rule as the "eleven years' tyranny." Although few scholars today would describe the period in those terms, there is continuing disagreement about its nature and ongoing debate about how to interpret the evidence from a host of local studies that shows varied conditions and reactions. Were the English people primarily concerned with their personal and local affairs and resentful of any interference in their lives by the Crown, or did they see their situation in terms of a larger political or religious conflict? Does the absence of major revolts prior to the Bishops' Wars signify that all was well and that up to that point Charles was moving successfully toward establishing absolutism* in England, if not in Britain? Tradition held that the summoning and dissolving of parliaments was a royal prerogative*, and despite the fourteenth-century statutes that called for annual parliaments, it was the need to deal with particular kinds of business, such as financing war, rather than the calendar that determined when parliaments met. Between 1610 and 1621, parliament had sat only in 1614 and only for six weeks (see Addled Parliament*). No statutes had been enacted between 1610 and 1624.

The king accompanied his forceful adjournment of parliament on 2 March 1629 with the arrest of nine members of parliament, including Sir John Eliot* and John Selden*. These "parliament prisoners" became a symbol of the infringement of liberties, but after a year or so all but three had made peace with Charles. Eliot died in the Tower of London in 1632; the other two remained imprisoned until 1640. However much rhetoric their cause aroused in 1640, it brought them relatively little support during the 1630s.

Charles I ruled without parliament by concluding his wars with Spain and France (see French War of 1627-1629* and Spanish War of 1625-1630*) and by refraining from intervening in the Thirty Years War* in Germany. He financed his government by supplementing his ordinary income by various means, including the collection of tonnage and poundage (see Taxation and Revenue*), the levying of ship money*, the distraint of knighthood*, and enforcing the forest laws*. Although his fiscal measures aroused complaints, Charles was able to win widespread compliance with them; few persisted in resistance when faced with prosecution. The courts repeatedly upheld royal authority. Although divided, the judges ruled for the Crown and against John Hampden* in the much publicized case of 1638 concerning the legality of ship money.

Religion was the focus of some of the most bitter controversy during the personal rule, and the polemics over Puritanism*, popery (see Catholics*), and Arminianism* that raged in sermons and pamphlets have continued in the works of historians. Official vigilance reduced but did not eliminate criticism of ecclesiastical policies and practices. William Prynne*, Henry Burton, and Dr. John Bastwick won notoriety for their outspoken statements about religion and their determination to defend their views at their trial in the Star Chamber in 1637 (see Prerogative Courts*).

Grievances concerning religion had so concerned the House of Commons in 1629 that they had voted to give them priority. In one of the three resolutions they passed in the stormy scene on 2 March when the king tried to end the parliament, the Commons declared as public enemies those who made or supported innovations in religion. Charles's appointment in 1633 of the bishop of London, William Laud*, who had been a principal target of parliamentary criticism in 1629, to succeed George

Abbot* as archbishop of Canterbury seemed particularly ominous to people worried that the Protestantism of the Church of England (see Anglicanism*) was in danger. The authority of bishops itself became an issue, as some claimed that bishops derived their power *jure divino* (from God) rather than from the Crown or statute. While some bishops exercised only loose oversight of their dioceses, others aroused opposition with their active attempts to enforce uniformity.

Episcopal attitudes were one of the factors that determined whether parishes became scenes of religious conflict; the stance of the parish clergy and the degree of unity in the community itself also played a part. Episcopal efforts to insist that parish churches have altars instead of communion tables, that ministers refuse to administer the sacrament to parishioners who would not come up to the rail and kneel, and that other ceremonies be observed stirred controversy that sometimes reached the point of violence; so did the 1633 declaration requiring clergy to read the Book of Sports*, which explicitly sanctioned recreations on Sunday rather than insisting on observation of the Sabbath (see Sabbatarianism*). Charles's Catholic wife, the French princess Henrietta Maria*, made people especially anxious that popery would supplant Protestantism in England. The conversions of some courtiers and the arrival in London* of an ambassador from Rome added to the fears of a Popish Plot* to overthrow religion, law, and liberty. Prosecutions of both clergy and laity who challenged ecclesiastical policies and practices drove some opposition underground and contributed to the "Great Migration" to New England (see Colonization*).

Archbishop Laud and the lord deputy of Ireland*, Thomas Wentworth*, who became first earl of Strafford in 1639, used the term *thorough** in their correspondence to describe the well-governed realm that they wanted to help the king establish. While subsequent parliamentary complaints focused on these two as the king's chief advisers during the Personal Rule, neither they nor anyone else held a role comparable to that of the 1st duke of Buckingham (George Villiers*) prior to his assassination in 1628. During much of the 1630s, personal rivalry and conflicting agenda divided Charles's councilors. Nevertheless the privy council* handled both routine and extraordinary business. Its efforts to ensure the success of revenue-raising measures and see that the county militia see were prepared (see Army*) were important. In 1630 the council issued a Book of Orders* for use by justices of the peace (JPs) in overseeing relief of the poor, administration of justice, and suppression of disorder (see Local Government*; Poor Laws and Poverty*). Although procedures for reports from the JPs were modified in the course of time, the Book of Orders exemplifies a concern about good governance that court and country shared. Supplementing the work of the privy council and the JPs in enforcing order were the judges, who brought royal messages and authority to the counties at the semi-annual assizes.

The character of the Personal Rule owes much to the king himself. By 1629 Charles had exhausted his patience with parliament. Obtaining advice and assistance from men he thought would respect his authority in church and state, he attempted to govern on his own. He misjudged how deeply entrenched was the notion that parliament should meet if the kingdom went to war. His decision to go to war against Scotland* in 1639 stirred people from discontent into thought of resistance. After he had summoned and then dissolved his fourth parliament in May 1640 (see Short Parliament*), that resistance challenged his Personal Rule.

Bibliography: Esther Cope, *Politics without Parliaments, 1629-1640*, 1986; Kevin Sharpe, "The Personal Rule of Charles I," in Howard Tomlinson, ed., *Before the English Civil War*, and *The Personal Rule of Charles I*, 1992.

Esther S. Cope

Petition of Right (1628). In 1628, desperate for money, Charles I* called his third parliament (of 1628-1629*). Many members, however, had become deeply angered in recent years by various practices of the Crown, which had convinced them that the Stuart monarchs were intent on establishing a divine right* absolutism*. The House of Commons, with support from the House of Lords, took the bold action of refusing to grant any money until Charles agreed to a Petition of Right that contained remedies for these abuses of royal authority.

England was at war with Spain and France in 1628, and Charles had suffered major disasters in both conflicts (see French War of 1627-1629*; Spanish War of 1625-1630*). His first parliament (of 1625*), already suspicious of him, had been niggardly in its financial support, and his second (parliament of 1626*) voted no money at all. Charles was now desperate. Claiming his royal prerogative* was sufficient authority, he ordered the collection of the import duties parliament had just failed to approve (see Taxation and Revenue*) and initiated the largest forced loan* in English history. Resistance to the loans was widespread. The legitimacy of the loans and imprisonment for refusing to pay was challenged in the Five Knights Case* of 1627. Although the knights lost, the issues remained alive and were added to the growing collection of claims of abuse of power that faced the Crown during the next parliament.

The monies collected were not sufficient for the Crown's needs, and in January 1628 Charles had to call for the election of a third parliament. He did his best to influence the elections and garner a cooperative parliament, partly by releasing all those who had refused to pay the forced loan. The election results, however, were against him. This parliament, one of the more celebrated in English history, had an impressive roster of names, including Sir Edward Coke*, England's most distinguished jurist and legal scholar and an opponent of Stuart absolutism.

Early in the session Coke presented Commons with a set of proposals to remedy the abuses of power by the Crown, which immediately received considerable support. After several false starts and much negotiating with Lords, and with the inspired leadership of John Pym* and Sir John Eliot*, the proposals received the unanimous consent of both houses and became the Petition of Right. The Petition contained four major prohibitions. First, no one should be forced to make a loan, gift, or benevolence or pay a tax that did not have the consent of parliament. Parliament was claiming once again, and not for the last time, that its consent was required before any monies could be collected by the Crown. Without this right, parliament understood clearly that it had no real power. The second prohibition, building on Magna Carta and a direct response to the Five Knights Case, stated that no one could have their liberties, properties, or life taken except by the lawful judgment of their peers or the law of the land. Cause in law always had to be shown for the king to imprison anyone. The third and fourth prohibitions concerned the manner in which the king had been cutting fiscal corners to maintain the troops he needed for his wars. Charles had forced civilians to put military men up in their homes and had used martial law to enforce the practice. The Petition forbade the billeting of troops in civilian homes or the use of martial law in times of peace.

Commons claimed the Petition made no new law but only reaffirmed existing statutes, although there was some significant evolution in meaning of the old statutes. Commons insisted on calling the proposals a Petition of Right rather than one of "grace" to give it a stronger standing in the courts. Parliament also requested that Charles give his consent in public before both houses. Charles used such evasive language on 2 June that parliament, amid much wringing of hands and emotional displays of despair, held out and refused to pass any money bills. Finally on 7 June, confronted by an aroused and unified parliament, Charles gave in, came again to parliament, and spoke the formal words, "*Soit droit fait comme il est désiré*," ("Let right be done as is desired"). A great shout went up in parliament, and the passage of the Petition of Right was celebrated in the streets.

In less than a year it became clear Charles had no intention of observing the prohibitions of the Petition. He was forced to dismiss the parliament of 1629 because of the members' rage about this and other matters. He made an expedient peace with Spain and France and for the next eleven years lived off what income he could squeeze from his subjects without having to call another parliament (see Personal Rule*). The issues raised in the Petition of Right did not disappear, and Charles's failure to face them contributed significantly to England's Civil War* that came once parliament met again.

Bibliography: Frances Helen Relf, *The Petition of Right*, 1917; J. R. Tanner, *English Constitutional Conflicts of the Seventeenth Century*, 1948.

Richard L. Hillard

Petitioners. Term given to those who were later called Whigs* during the Exclusion Crisis* (1679-1681). Led by Anthony Ashley Cooper*, earl of Shaftesbury, they organized a campaign of popular petitions to apply pressure on Charles II* to agree to the exclusion of the duke of York (see James II*) from the succession. They also organized a campaign of pamphlets and popular demonstrations involving large numbers of London* citizens.

After passage of the first Exclusion Bill in May 1679, the Whigs in London organized petitions thanking the House of Commons for prosecution of the Popish Plot* (1678), and the signers pledged their support. This petition drive hastened Charles's decision to prorogue parliament* until August 1679. In June 1679 a second petition drive occurred in London, coinciding with the Scottish Covenanter Rebellion*. A huge petition was to be signed by lords, gentlemen, and important citizens of London. It called for settling matters in Scotland*, for parliament to meet in August, and for bringing Thomas Osborne*, earl of Danby to trial. There were plans to send the petition to grand juries in the counties if enough signatures were obtained in London. The defeat of the Scottish rebellion by the duke of Monmouth ended this petition drive.

In December 1679-January 1680 the Whigs launched another petition drive calling for parliament to meet to provide security for Charles and Protestantism. The Whigs used printed petition forms, provided tables with pen and ink, and canvassed door to door for signatures. Charles rejected a Whig petition signed by sixteen peers and attempted to suppress these petitions by using the lord mayor of London. In January 1680, two Whig-generated petitions, which contained 30,000 and 50,000 signatures, were rejected by Charles, who likened these "petitioners" to those who had opposed his father in 1641. These Whig petitions inspired counterpetitions or "abhorrences" from Tories* protesting the pressure being put on Charles (see Abhorrers*). Whigs countered that such abhorrences interfered with subjects' rights to petition. Such petitions and counterpetitions involved the country in political excitement, which usually existed only in and around London.

Throughout 1680 the Whigs produced more petitions, which were rejected. After dissolution of the second Exclusion Parliament in January 1681, Whigs circulated petitions in the western portions of England that represented parliament as the best means of preserving king and nation. After Charles announced that parliament was to meet at Oxford instead of Westminster, a petition signed by sixteen peers calling for parliament to sit in its usual place to protect it from Catholics* was presented to him in January 1681; he rejected it as he had all the others. After dissolution of the Oxford Parliament*, Charles received addresses of thanks from the Tories. During the struggle over the election of sheriffs* in London in autumn 1682, both the Whigs and Tories presented petitions in support of their candidates. Prosecution of Shaftesbury for treason and his flight into exile ended the petitioning campaign in late 1682.

Bibliography: K. H. D. Haley, *The First Earl of Shaftesbury*, 1968; J. R. Jones, *The First Whigs*, 1961.

Mark C. Herman

Plague. See Epidemics and Plague; London, Plague of.

Plantation. A social and economic unit usually based on agriculture, designed to function in unstable or remote colonial areas. This expanded metaphor originated in the late Tudor era. It added social, economic, and religious facets to what had earlier been an agricultural term. Fact and mythology gave support to the dream of colonization* in popular English imagination. Thereafter one begins to see usage indicative of broadened meaning such as the "plantation of [a] commonwealth" (J. Hooker, 1586) and "plantation of the faith" (Francis Bacon*, 1605). From the outset of the Stuart period, the word begins to become synonymous with *transplantation*.

An idea emerged that self-sustaining and semi-autonomous groups, representative of English society, would be the ideal unit to be uprooted and transplanted to the wilds of Ireland* or the New World. This approach to building an overseas empire is uniquely English.

The concept of the plantation has roots in medieval monastic organizational structure and in Thomas More's *Utopia* (1516). The increased knowledge of the primitive Christian church that resulted from the writings of Reformation historians also made a contribution. At the most basic level, an assumption is made that logic can produce a reasonably perfect and harmonious society. The growing interest in the yet ill-defined idea of commonwealth added a distinctly socialistic tone to several schemes of plantation, particularly in their early stages. The models for plantation societies were based on the institutions of Stuart England. These were perceived as so strong and formative that Sir John Davies, attorney general for Ireland early in the reign of James I*, believed that contact with them would civilize the Irish, causing them to "become English." The models were, like England, fundamentally based on an agricultural economy.

As change occurred at home, plantations were expected to replicate the current ideals of English society. They seldom did. From the beginning, detailed proscriptive charters, constitutions, and by-laws tried to strike a balance between individual, corporate, and royal interests. As mercantilism* became institutionalized, the plantations were increasingly expected to sacrifice self-interest to that of the nation. The charter or compact was designed to enforce God's law, as well as common law* and statute. It was recognized that unregulated greed, selfishness, and the indulgence of other base impulses could cripple or bring about the failure of a colony. Financial success at the expense of public order was not condoned. Writing to Governor John Lord Vaughn in 1676, Secretary of State Henry Coventry related "in plain terms, the King intendeth to make a plantation of Jamaica and not a Christian Algiers." This element of the concept was often a failure. Corrupt administrators prevented Ireland from reaching the ideal. Beyond the line of amity in the New World, distance demanded and provided independence beyond that granted by charter. Charles II* later tried to provide greater control by appointing and recalling royal governors.

The plantation concept ignored indigenous people as a source of labor. Their conversion to Christianity was encouraged, but their incorporation into society was not addressed. In 1609 the committee reporting on the plan for the plantation of Ireland included a provision that no planters should have the use of their land until the natives had been removed. In part this position stems from the popular perception that England was overpopulated. The Crown could relieve the nation of potentially unemployed troublemakers by pursuing a policy that demanded that planters take their own retainers and laborers. The hope was that these servants, in an environment of unlimited fertile land, would become loyal yeoman farmers of England's new shires. Many plans and charters provided for the equitable treatment of colonists with minimal holdings.

In summary, the concept of plantation was a hodgepodge of untried and unproved theory inherited by James I from his Tudor predecessors. It was based largely on More's utopianism, Sir Francis Drake's adventures, and the vision of the New Eden promoted by Richard Hakluyt, propagandist of New World colonization, and his Stuart successor, Samuel Purchas. Its salvation was contained within the scope of its narrow-minded insularity. Popular belief accurately predicted that successful colonies would not be dominated by soldiers, clerics, or appointed courtiers but would draw on England's great strengths: the yeomanry, the petty nobility, the merchants, and English laborers.

Bibliography: R. S. Dunn, *Sugar and Slaves*, 1972; T. W. Moody, et. al., eds., *A New History of Ireland*, 1976.

Thomas R. Reid

Political Thought. The seventeenth century was a period of great activity in political theorizing. Two of the most famous texts in the history of political thought were written during the Stuart period: Thomas Hobbes's* *Leviathan* (1651) and John Locke's* *Two Treatises of Government* (1689), both systematic philosophical discussions of the origins and nature of political authority. Commonly Stuart political writings were rather less systematic, and frequently they took the form of controversial pamphlets aimed at establishing or refuting particular claims.

Perhaps the most important controversy to engage the attention of English political thinkers in the early years of James I's* reign was the dispute over the oath of allegiance* of 1606. This oath rejected papal claims to be able to depose heretical kings. Pope Paul V condemned the oath, and a number of leading Catholics* (including Cardinal Robert Bellarmine, the major Spanish theorist Francisco Suarez, and the English Jesuit Robert Parsons) wrote against it. James I himself defended the oath and attacked the papal deposing power in three works, and a number of writers including John Donne*, Lancelot Andrewes*, and the Catholic priest Thomas Preston (alias Roger Widdrington) supported his position. The central contentions of the papalist case were that kings derive their power from the people and are limited by whatever conditions were imposed upon them when they were granted power, and that the spiritual power of the pope is superior to the mere temporal power of monarchs; the pope may therefore intervene in the secular affairs of states (for instance, by deposing kings) when he judges this to be in the spiritual interest of Christendom. The main claims of James I and his supporters were that monarchs derive their powers from God alone and not from the people and that the temporal authority of the state and the spiritual authority of the clergy are both equally derived from God; clerics are therefore not superior to secular magistrates, and popes may not depose kings. James and his Protestant adherents argued further that though kings could not themselves employ spiritual powers (for example, the power to ordain or to excommunicate), they could use coercive means to ensure that clerics performed their spiritual functions properly; kings, they said, were the supreme governors of the church in their realms.

The assertion that monarchs derive their powers from God alone was the central plank of the famous theory of the divine right* of kings, a theory with a long history predating the seventeenth century, which James had already publicly adopted in his

Trew Law of Free Monarchies (1598). Implications drawn from the direct divine origins of royal authority included that kings are not accountable to their subjects and that no one may actively resist the monarch. Proponents of the theory did *not* claim that kings could sinlessly flout the law of the land whenever they pleased. Indeed they recommended that monarchs ordinarily abide by the law and that they rule by extra-legal means only in emergencies. The same recommendations were made by such continental absolutists as Jean Bodin, William Barclay, and Jacques-Bénigne Bossuet.

The notion that monarchs draw their authority immediately from God was often used to rebut the claims of papalists such as Bellarmine and Suarez. It could also be employed to underpin high views on the place of the royal prerogative* within the English constitution. Often writers who adopted the theory refrained from spelling out its constitutional implications in too great detail. Voicing absolutist* sentiments could be dangerous. In 1610 the civil lawyer John Cowell was attacked by the House of Commons for his absolutist views, and in the same year one member brought in a bill providing that clerics who preached against subjects' liberties should be deprived of their livings.   In 1628 the cleric Roger Manwaring was impeached (see Impeachment*) for using ideas similar to Cowell's in order to justify Charles I's* recent forced loan*. Nevertheless, a number of trenchantly absolutist treatises were penned in the years before 1641. They include works not only by clerics, but also by civil lawyers (such as Sir John Hayward and Alberico Gentili) and laymen (the best known being Sir Robert Filmer and Thomas Hobbes).

Filmer's *Patriarcha*, which dates from the early 1630s, combined an attack on the ideas of Bellarmine and Suarez with a vigorously absolutist analysis of the English constitution. It is notable for its patriarchalist account of the origins of government, equating the state with the family and arguing that the power of a king is essentially the same as the power of the father in an independent family. Earlier English writers had voiced patriarchalist political ideas but not in as thoroughgoing a fashion as Filmer. Hobbes's *Elements of Law* (completed in 1640) reached conclusions that were just as absolutist as Filmer's, but based its case on very different premises. Heavily influenced by science and the Scientific Revolution* and by geometry, Hobbes tried to build a rigorously reasoned political philosophy upon what he took to be the fundamental principles of human nature, in particular the principle of self-preservation.

Some early seventeenth-century thinkers adopted divine right notions of the origins of government but combined them with a very strong concept of custom to reach outspokenly anti-absolutist conclusions. The most famous of these theorists was the common lawyer Sir Edward Coke*, who argued that the English common law* was the ultimate guide on questions of royal authority and the subject's liberty. Coke's idea of an ancient constitution that had remained virtually unchanged since the earliest times was not widely accepted, but the notion that English customs (even if they did not date back to the most ancient times) were the definitive rule on what political arrangements suited the English was often expressed and was frequently employed in parliament* to challenge royal policies.

A different way of arguing that royal power in England was limited was to claim that the king derived his authority not from God alone but from the people, and that he was subject to the conditions which had been imposed when they transferred their authority to a monarch. The idea of an original contract between king and people was expressed long before the Civil War* by Sir Robert Phelips and others. During the war it became a staple item in the thinking of parliamentarians* and was used to justify resistance to the king or his evil advisers. Royalists* almost invariably rejected the notion of an original contract, though a few (including Hobbes) employed ideas of contract to generate anti-parliamentarian conclusions. Many royalists stressed the moderation of the king's cause, and in 1642 Charles's answer to the Nineteen Propositions* went as far as to affirm that England was a mixed monarchy in which the king ruled in coordination with the other two estates, the Lords and the Commons. Though this position was soon abandoned in favor of the idea that the king was above the three estates of Lords spiritual, Lords temporal, and Commons, much royalist propaganda emphasized Charles's devotion to the law and contrasted it with parliament's willingness to break legal norms. Some royalists, however, continued to express absolutist notions; among them were Hobbes, Filmer, and Michael Hudson. Leading parliamentarian pamphleteers such as Henry Parker and Charles Herle argued that power lay fundamentally in the people but equated parliament with the people. In the early years of the war, some thinkers took a rather different line, claiming that a corrupt parliament could itself be called to account by the population* at large. The idea that parliament is accountable for its misdeeds was important in the thinking of the Levellers* from the mid-1640s and in army* propaganda from 1647. The Levellers advocated major constitutional reforms which tended in a strongly democratic direction, but the army leadership claimed that such proposals threatened property. Ideas more radical than those of the Levellers were expressed by the Digger* Gerard Winstanley and others but never acquired a mass following. In 1656 James Harrington* published *Oceana,* in which he combined Machiavellian republicanism with the contention that the structure of power in any society is closely linked to the distribution of wealth. Harrington's ideas for constitutional reform were much discussed in the years preceding the Restoration*.

After 1660 theories of absolute monarchy circulated once more, and Filmer's *Patriarcha* was first printed in 1680. Opponents of such notions ranged from Edward Hyde* (an advocate of mixed and limited monarchy who denied rights of resistance) to radicals including Algernon Sidney. Sidney attacked Filmer's claims, and in 1683 he was executed. In the same year Oxford University condemned a number of writings that had asserted the contractual origins of royal power and the right of resistance to tyrants. But the Glorious Revolution* made possible the reassertion of ideas of this kind—for instance, in Locke's *Two Treatises of Government.* This is a convenient place to end a brief account of seventeenth-century political thinking, but that should by no means be taken to imply that Locke had the final word or that his views were immediately victorious.

Bibliography: J. G. A. Pocock, *The Ancient Constitution and the Feudal Law*, 2d ed., 1987; J. P. Sommerville, *Politics and Ideology in England, 1603-1640*, 1986.

                                                                        Johann P. Sommerville

Poor Law and Poverty.   Poor laws were instituted by many sixteenth-century European governments: Catholic* and Protestant, urban, provincial, and national. The legislation had two main focuses: first, regulating the supply of relief by reforms of medieval hospitals and almshouses, and by statutory provision for the "worthy" poor (usually the very young, very old, diseased, and disabled); second, controlling demand for relief by punitive measures against the "unworthy," especially the able-bodied who begged, who were defined as "vagabonds." The attitudes behind these developments were not wholly new. Thirteenth-century canon lawyers were critical of some kinds of voluntary poverty; a century later John Wyclif and the Lollards attacked clerical mendicants. Late medieval governments also took a dim view of mendicancy. To control wages and the labor supply, fourteenth-century legislation sought to ban begging by the able-bodied; in the fifteenth century royal proclamations* pilloried beggars for sowing sedition.

These early criticisms of voluntary poverty were not brought together into a coherent body of policy until the sixteenth century. In England between 1531 and 1601, a series of acts of parliament* required local authorities to relieve deserving paupers and arrest vagrants. This crystallization of policies occurred for several reasons. Between 1500 and 1650, population* growth caused poverty to increase by depressing wage levels and stimulating subsistence migration and price inflation (including rents and food stuffs). Towns were particularly affected, because they attracted penurious immigrants and suffered from London* trade* monopolies*. But the rural sector also experienced upheavals: the engrossing of smallholdings, enclosure of common lands, and the replacement of customary tenancies by leaseholds. In addition the Protestant Reformation brought increased hostility to voluntary poverty, which was manifested in parliament's dissolutions of the monasteries. A further factor is that Tudor governments were interventionist in dealing with social and economic problems, partly because the authorities subscribed to theories of paternalistic or "commonwealth" government and partly because they feared disorder and rebellion.

It was one thing to pass legislation but quite another to enforce it. In early modern Europe successful poor law systems were often established in smaller-scale states such as Holland, Venice, and Zurich. The larger kingdoms such as France and Spain appear to have lacked the political ability or the will to enforce such policies. Among the larger states England alone ran counter to this pattern, for by 1700 it had something resembling a national poor law in place.

The English legislation included several components, including Settlement Acts* and vagrancy regulations, as well as poor relief provisions. There is considerable evidence of the enforcement of the poor laws under the early Stuarts. The Book of Orders* of 1630 was the most comprehensive attempt to date to enforce the legislation. Large numbers of vagrants were arrested—about 25,000 between 1631 and 1639, according to reports by county officials to the privy council*. There is also considerable evidence of the implementation of poor relief in the 1630s. Of course, the orders of 1630 were not unprecedented. Similar action was taken after four poor harvests between 1594 and 1597 and following Elizabethan legislation in 1598 and 1601, but it was not sustained much beyond 1610. It was in the 1620s that widespread enforcement began, which suggests that the orders of 1630 were building on established foundations. By 1660 a third, perhaps even a majority, of English parishes were levying poor rates; by 1700 a large majority were doing so, and possibly one in twenty of England's population were receiving statutory aid.

If the Stuart enforcement of poor relief suggests classic "Whig"* progression, the same was not true of the vagrancy clauses of the poor laws. The Stuart peak for arrests probably occurred in the 1630s; after that vagrants were increasingly granted local relief (partly through the provisions of the Settlement Act of 1662), and obdurate cases were farmed out to private contractors. Arresting vagrants and relieving the worthy were not, however, the only options in dealing with the poor. Statutes also specified that vagabonds could be imprisoned in bridewells or "houses of correction," transported overseas, and conscripted into the armed forces; all of these alternatives were employed under the Stuarts. The seventeenth century also saw the development of workhouses, where non-offenders were to receive training and to work. The workhouses were designed to prevent poverty and to keep relief costs down.

Although Whitehall initiatives were important, there was a good deal of local experimentation and private effort. For instance, the towns of Dorchester and Salisbury established municipal breweries, whose profits were employed to support the local poor. In some towns schools and workhouses were created to train and employ non-offenders. Private charity remained important, probably equaling poor rates before 1650, but remaining stationary thereafter compared with rate-based relief. Bequests often included provision for the poor of the deceased's parish but also ambitious projects such as hospitals, almshouses, and loans for dowries and for setting up in a trade. Probate records do not record charity among the living, which probably continued to be considerable. Some parishes resisted the levying of statutory poor rates on the grounds that voluntary giving was morally superior.

What impact had the implementation of the poor laws in Stuart England? Although difficult to prove, enforcing the legislation probably helped to check poverty and disorder, especially when vagrants were banished overseas. Despite the high ideals of the first bridewells, it is doubtful that inmates received much real training in trades, since most of the work was penal in nature. Greater success was possibly experienced by the workhouses and schools established for nonoffenders. But all indoor facilities, penal or not, did remove the poor from the streets and highways, albeit often temporarily. Parish relief undoubtedly helped mitigate short-term disasters such as epidemics*, poor harvests (see Agriculture*), and trade slumps. During hard times, expenditure by parish overseers tended to rise to meet the heightened demand. It is impossible to demonstrate that English political stability increased as a result of the enforcement of the poor laws, but it is noteworthy how limited a role, compared with France, the poor played in political upheavals under the Stuarts. Socially, parish relief tended to highlight the differences between ratepayers and the dependent poor, though it may also have softened divisions by emphasizing the interdependence of the better-off and the needy. When rates continued to rise after 1650, the cost of poor relief became the focus of a national debate involving practitioners of the new "political arithmetic."

Why did England develop a national poor law system when other states did not? Indeed Stuart England's success in this area might seem paradoxical, given that the country experienced civil wars, revolutions, and counterrevolutions in the period. Politically, if there was a "sick man of Europe" in the seventeenth century, England might be considered a strong candidate. One set of explanations is political. Despite its internal upheavals, England was a compact, centralized state by contemporary standards. It was smaller in area and population than France and Spain and did not contain provinces with autonomous institutions. Again by contemporary standards, England had a quite centralized administration and judiciary. Through privy council* orders and assize judges, the government maintained contact with county officials. In the parishes, constables, churchwardens, and overseers of the poor had statutory responsibilities for the poor. Of course, these officials did not always pliantly and efficiently follow the commands of central government. Loyalty to one's locality remained strong, and where it conflicted with the demands of Westminster, the latter could be ignored, even sabotaged. Corruption and incompetence can be found at all levels of administration, and political conflicts did upset local administration, particularly during the First Civil War* (1642-1646). In general, however, local government* seems to have performed remarkably well under the Stuarts, especially in poor law administration.

Another important difference with many European powers was that England took a limited part in the massive land wars of the seventeenth century, which drained resources and disrupted administration. It is also important that England's elites were comparatively united in their views of the poor. Whatever differences existed between Anglicans* and Puritans*, with few exceptions they were critical of voluntary poverty and accepted the secular community's obligation to support the worthy poor. In Catholic Europe these positions were not wholly embraced, because the church defended the principles of monastic poverty and mendicancy and retained its own institutions of poor relief.

England's enforcement of its poor laws also had demographic and economic origins. It was no coincidence that efforts to control vagrancy and relieve the needy were so widespread between 1620 and 1650. This was a period of great hardship in the country, when population growth, food prices, and subsistence migration peaked, unemployment rose because of depressions in the chief export industry of woolen cloth (see Cloth Trade*), and wage levels for the employed were falling. Life expectancy at birth declined for several decades during the seventeenth century, which suggests that living standards were being pressed downward. After 1650 these disastrous conditions gradually eased, and the country enjoyed considerable economic progress as population levels held steady, real wages rose, exports were diversified, and agricultural output expanded. Parish relief was continued, however, because in this preindustrial economy there remained significant numbers of needy people. Admittedly the better-off ratepayers represented the large majority of the population, even during the hard years from 1620 to 1650, and so the poor were needy in part because of their "relative deprivation." But the social problems were also unquestionably there to be relieved in later Stuart England. In part need was connected with the life cycle. Ratepayers could (and did) end up as relief recipients in their old age or because of disability or widowhood. Family formation could also form a poverty trap because wages and productivity remained low. Poor relief probably helped to foster England's industrialization by providing a supplement to the low incomes of workers.

Bibliography: A. L. Beier, *The Problem of the Poor in Tudor and Early Stuart England,* 1983; Paul Slack, *Poverty and Policy in Tudor and Stuart England,* 1988.

                                                                                          A. L. Beier

Popish Plot (1636-1642). John Pym's* antipapist rhetoric preceding the Civil War* was credible because of Catholic* influence at the royal court* between 1636 and 1642. Suspicion about a "popish plot" to establish Catholic tyranny—related to fear of Spain—dated to Charles I's* marriage to Henrietta Maria* in 1625, strengthened in 1628-1629 during the controversy over the Petition of Right*, and worsened during the Personal Rule* (1629-1640) with the rise of the architects of "thorough"*, the Arminian* Archbishop William Laud* and Sir Thomas Wentworth*. Hitherto vague rumors appeared to gain substance in 1636, when papal agents George Con and Gregorio Panzani arrived at court, where they had great influence over the queen.

Motivated by papal policy and the Thirty Years War*, the Catholic camp's conspiratorial activities ranged from attempts to alleviate penalties and restrictions against Catholics (e.g., the oath of allegiance*) to plans for converting the king and realigning England as a Catholic nation. Charles's complicity in the latter is doubtful, but his actions contributed to English fears. The arrival in 1637 of his mother-in-law, Marie de Medici (Cardinal Richelieu's enemy), coincided with his rejection of a pro-French (and thus anti-Spanish) policy, and he refused to ban either Con or Marie from court or to stop public Catholic activities there. Suspicion also stemmed from Wentworth's actions as lord deputy of Ireland* and royal tampering with the Scottish Kirk*, culminating with Laud's introduction of the Anglican* prayer book and the resulting rebellion in Scotland*.

The signers of the Scottish Covenant* in 1638 suspected popery at court; many Scots there were Catholic, among them Henrietta Maria's confessor. This seemed to be confirmed by Charles's "Antrim Plot" (1638) to destroy the Campbells, using their Catholic clan enemies, which drove the 8th earl of Argyll (Archibald Campbell*) into Covenanter* ranks; the queen's raising money among English Catholics to fight Calvinist* Scots; the spectacle of the earl of Arundel, the inept English commander in the First Bishops War*, riding in Con's coach in 1639; and Charles's decision to let Spanish troops march across England to avoid Dutch ships. In 1640 English troops marching north destroyed altars and lynched two Catholic officers.

The plot poisoned Charles's relations with London* and helped wreck the Short Parliament* in 1640. Laud's notorious "etcetera oath" seemed proof of his popery (clergy and graduates had to swear that the ecclesiastical hierarchy, a listing of which was followed by "etc.", accorded with God's word). Rumors of plots poured into the Long Parliament* from its inception. Apparent confirmation came from the army plots* in May and July 1641; the king's suspicious travels in the north; a plan for

Scottish royalists* to seize the earls of Argyll and Hamilton in October; the king's appearance in the Scottish parliament accompanied by hundreds of armed retainers; and the Irish Rebellion* in November, in which Catholic rebels professed loyalty to Charles and committed atrocities against Protestants, which were exaggerated and spawned new rumors in England and Wales*.

Fear of the plot led to the impeachment* and eventual execution of Wentworth—accused of planning to bring an Irish army into England—and of Laud; the Root and Branch Petition* against episcopacy (1640); the Ten Propositions, which called for a purge of court papists (June 1641); parliamentary orders to destroy Laudian relics and establish a committee to deal with popish disorders (September); and Pym's controversial "additional instruction" (5 November, the anniversary of the Gunpowder Plot*), calling for parliament to act alone regarding Ireland if Charles kept his "evil" councilors. On 22 November the Commons narrowly passed Grand Remonstrance*, blaming Jesuits and evil counsel for Charles's policies and demanding the ouster of bishops from the House of Lords, removal of suspect members of the privy council*, and abolition of the court of High Commission (see Ecclesiastical Courts*; Prerogative Courts*). Charles rejected it on 23 December. Rumors that parliament might impeach Henrietta Maria led to Charles's attempt to arrest the Five Members* in January 1642 and to the queen's departure in February. With the queen's absence, the "Catholic court" collapsed, but continued anxiety contributed to increased presentations of recusants*, numerous petitions, the rise of millenarianism*, the Commons's "declaration of fears and jealousies" in March, the passage of the Nineteen Propositions*, which reiterated earlier concerns, in June, and the outbreak of the Civil War in August.

Bibliography: Caroline M. Hibbard, *Charles I and the Popish Plot*, 1983; Derek Hirst, *Authority and Conflict: England, 1603-1658*, 1986.

William T. Walker

Popish Plot (1678). Fear of popery was a recurrent theme in Restoration* England. By 1678 it had inspired the Clarendon Code*, opposition to Charles II's* Declaration of Indulgence* in 1672, and the first Test Act* (25 Car. II, c. 2) in 1673. The country opposition led by the earl of Shaftesbury (Anthony Ashley Cooper*) suspected the earl of Danby (Thomas Osborne*) of a conspiracy to establish absolutism* during his ministry from 1673 to 1678. Danby heightened such apprehensions by keeping the army* in existence during the summer of 1678 despite the end of Louis XIV's war in the Netherlands and by using money voted by parliament* for its disbandment to instead maintain it. Meanwhile, the French, with whom Charles and Danby were negotiating secretly for a subsidy, were also cultivating the opposition through Ralph Montagu, former English ambassador to France, in an effort to topple Danby, whom they did not trust. Moreover, Andrew Marvell had accused Danby (wrongly) of popery in his *Account of the Growth of Popery and Arbitrary Government* (1677), and the latter had recently entered into a political alliance with the king's openly Catholic brother, the future James II*.

Thus Danby was already in a difficult position when in August the fallen clergyman Titus Oates and the lunatic Israel Tonge "revealed" a Jesuit plot to murder Charles, burn London, raise a Catholic army, procure a foreign invasion, massacre Protestants, restore Catholicism, and put James on the throne (many of these elements were familiar; e.g., see Popish Plot of 1636-1642*). Though the story received support from a collection of disreputable characters—including William Bedloe, Robert Bolron, Thomas Dangerfield, and Dugdale—examination of the informers by the privy council* and courts (see Common Law and Courts*) revealed many inconsistencies. However, news of the "plot" created an immediate sensation among English Protestants, who equated Catholicism* with foreign tyranny, feared widespread infiltration of the government by clandestine papists, and believed English Catholics in general to be influenced by unscrupulous Jesuit fanatics. To make matters worse, it was discovered that many army officers were Catholics who had recently served the French king.

Charles was skeptical, except concerning the threat against himself, and he suspected the opposition of inventing the story, which is doubtful. Further developments increased hysteria in England, however. Oates denounced several priests and named as the plot's mastermind the Catholic Edward Coleman, an agent of James and Mary of Modena*. His correspondence was seized and revealed that he had been in contact with high-ranking French Catholics, including Louis XIV's Jesuit confessor. Then Sir Edmund Berry Godfrey, a magistrate who took Oates's testimony on 28 September and warned Coleman that he was implicated, disappeared and was subsequently found murdered on 17 October. This caused panic, especially in London.

Trials began in November and were conducted in shoddy fashion, with judges admitting hearsay evidence and openly demonstrating bias against the defendants. Thirteen were executed for treason (plotting against the king) or murder (of Godfrey), and three others for acting as priests. Despite their flawed evidence, it was not until July 1679 that Oates and the others were discredited, in proceedings that led to the acquittal of three Benedictines and the queen's ex-physician, Sir George Wakeman. Meanwhile parliament conducted an investigation in the fall of 1678, questioning Oates and others. Coleman refused to implicate James, whom Shaftesbury accused of obstructing justice and whom the earl's followers suggested should be banned from the royal presence and council.

In November members of parliament introduced a Test Bill (enacted as 30 Car. II, st. 2, c. 1) banning Catholics from parliament and wanted to arrest Catholic peers, increase security in London, and take other precautions. Charles retaliated by calling for investigation of Coleman's payments (French money) to members of the opposition, offering his own proposal for "limitations" on the succession, vetoing a militia bill that would have deprived him of control, and having Danby get James exempted from the Test Bill. However, in December the Commons used Montagu's papers as the basis for impeaching Danby, whom they labeled "traitorous" and "popishly affected." Though Charles prorogued the Cavalier Parliament* on 30 December and dissolved it on 24 January, Danby's ministry was finished. Charles was able to salvage his own image by sending James out of the country, abolishing the privy council, and creating a new, smaller council that included members of the opposition.

It was widely feared that the Popish Plot would lead to rebellion and civil war, but such worries proved groundless. Nevertheless, the opposition found itself stronger afterward, and the plot led inexorably to the Exclusion Crisis* (1678-1681), which was to dominate the affairs of the next three parliaments (see Oxford Parliament*).

Bibliography: J. R. Jones, *Country and Court: England, 1658-1714*, 1978; J. P. Kenyon, *The Popish Plot*, 1972.

William B. Robison

Popular Culture. Seventeenth-century England did not possess a single, unified popular culture so much as a series of interacting popular cultures of different regions, classes, trades, and ethnicities. In parts of Wales*, Welsh-speaking culture lingered on among a people dominated by an English-speaking or bilingual gentry. In some areas of the north, a Catholic* folk culture stubbornly held on, particularly where protected by Catholic gentry. Throughout the kingdom many aspects of popular culture varied along with socioeconomic structure on a regional basis. Areas that followed open field agriculture* tended to emphasize community and ritual and were more conservative in religion. Their dominant sport was often some form of football, a team game sometimes involving the entire male population of a village. Areas of woodland and pasture were more individualist and antiritualist in ethos and tended more to Puritanism* in religion. They often favored the various ancestors of cricket, games emphasizing individual skill and one-to-one confrontation. Areas of rural industry tended even more to Puritanism; clothiers in particular were commonly Puritans (see Cloth Trade*). The most culturally and politically radical group on the whole were "masterless" men and women—poor and itinerant workers and beggars largely isolated or hostile to their social superiors (see Poor Law and Poverty*). Cities had their own ritual calendars of festival and pageantry, but within the city populace some tradespeople, such as shoemakers, were identified with radicalism.

Many elements of what we now term popular culture were far from limited to the lower ranks of society. Civic and religious festivals and processions, such as the rich pageantry of the civic government of London*, were enjoyed by the populace and the social elite alike. Chapbook tales and ballads were enjoyed by upper-class people, particularly women and schoolboys, as well as by the lower classes. Political and religious holidays such as 5 November, commemorating deliverance from the Gunpowder Plot*; 17 November, commemorating Queen Elizabeth's accession; and 29 May, commemorating the Restoration* were invented and imposed by statesmen and divines, but were taken up as festivals by the common people.

The principal forces transforming the cultural life of the English people in the Stuart era were the growth of literacy, particularly male literacy, and printing*, and religiously inspired efforts to purify popular culture of offensive elements and the government's response to these efforts. Literacy expanded greatly under Elizabeth and the early Stuarts, with some studies showing as much as thirty percent of the male population able to sign their names, a figure implying a much greater proportion able to read. This expansion of literacy was accompanied by a vast increase in printed material, particularly in the forms of broadsheet ballads and chapbooks, small, cheaply made books selling for two or three pennies and aimed at a broad audience. These were circulated all over England by petty traders, of whom the most famous literary example is Shakespeare's* Autolycus.

Ballads covered many topics, including news and current events, as well as sensational stories of murders and monstrous births and traditional tales. Much popular literature* had descended to the popular level from elite culture, as had, for example, the chivalrous romance *Bevis of Hampton*, a perennial bestseller in chapbook form. Other popular stories reflected a hope for upward social mobility, such as the tales of the clothier Jack of Newbury and the merchant Dick Whittington, characters who rose from poverty to positions of wealth and status. Indeed England was unique in Europe in having entrepreneurs as folk-heroes. Generally the goal of rising within the system was more common in popular literature than that of overthrowing it, although nostalgia for an allegedly more egalitarian England before the Norman Conquest was sometimes expressed. Noble knights were presented as admirable figures, although clergymen usually were not. Popular anticlerical tales about monks and friars survived the Reformation by centuries.

Written popular literature also dealt with sex and love, reflecting a variety of attitudes toward marriage, but usually emphasizing love and compatibility between the two parties rather than social status or parental consent. Joke books and comic stories, often with women or outsiders such as Welshmen as butts, were also common, as were collections of songs. Religion was another popular theme, with chapbooks emphasizing its terrifying aspects, such as death, judgment, and hell. Another extremely widespread form of popular printed literature was the almanac, which in addition to calendrical and astrological information often included miscellaneous data such as lists of historical dates or fairs and markets, and sometimes political propaganda.

Many traditional rites, customs, and festivals highly offended the Puritan or godly elements in English society. Puritans found many aspects of popular culture doubly offensive, both as survivals from the time of popery and idolatry and as conducive to licentiousness, social disorder, and Sabbath profanation (see Sabbatarianism*). Puritans and others at the parish level also had solid economic reasons for opposing popular customs that catered to sexual licentiousness, because an illegitimate pregnancy could produce a bastard chargeable to the parish.

Puritan efforts to eradicate customs of which they disapproved were both continuous with efforts to Protestantize the country going back to the Reformation and comparable to what was going on all over both Protestant and Catholic Europe, as elites, particularly religious elites, were attempting to purify popular culture of what they regarded as un-Christian and disorderly. Puritanism was not limited to the socio-economic elite, and many Puritan artisans and yeomen partook of the urge to reform the habits of their neighbors. The godly themselves formed a distinct cultural group, with their own distinctive rituals such as sermon-going and their own popular literature.

In the Stuart era, popular culture became a battleground between these reforming Puritans on one hand and, on the other, both the royal government and people defending their traditional customs. James I* expressed in his writings a belief in the role of popular festivity in fostering social harmony and loyalty to the throne, going so far as to donate a hat, feather, and ruff worn by himself to Robert Dover, who had initiated and continued to preside over the Cotswold games, a festival of traditional pastimes. Dover, wearing the king's old clothes, thus embodied the king's approval of these recreations. James's 1618 Book of Sports* attempted to give royal sanction to popular sports and pastimes such as archery as Sunday recreation. This horrified Puritans, who saw it as rank Sabbath profanation.

Paradoxically, the reign of Charles I*, a man of outstanding taste in the visual arts but one much less involved in popular culture than his father, James, had been, saw an intensification of attempts to incorporate popular traditions into the established regime in church and state. Archbishop William Laud*, against strong Puritan opposition, actively promoted such popular customs as church ales. Laud's "beauty of holiness" movement, which reversed a policy of iconoclasm dating back to the Reformation, also garnered some popular support as well as opposition. The reissue of the Book of Sports in 1633 was part of this policy.

These initiatives were highly offensive to the godly portion of the community, and the Civil War* and Interregnum* were, culturally speaking, a revolt of the godly against the officially sanctioned culture, on both the high and popular levels, of Charles I's royal court* and regime. A vigorous program of iconoclasm and the suppression of all customs deemed Roman Catholic or licentious was carried out in the areas controlled by parliament*. Parliament's triumph throughout the land meant the suppression of maypoles (idolatrous), morris dancing (licentious), and Christmas (popish). Royalists* responded by identifying their cause with these suppressed traditions; keeping Christmas was one way of declaring one's support for the exiled king. Traditional communal events such as football matches sometimes served as cover for clandestine royalist gatherings. Riots against the government in the period immediately preceding the Restoration incorporated elements of festive culture such as football matches and stoning hens in mockery of the government's prohibition of stoning cocks.

Many elements of popular culture that the Interregnum Puritans had sought to suppress returned with a vengeance at the Restoration, which saw widespread morris dancing as well as the first maypole openly erected in London in twenty years. Restoration propaganda capitalized on this phenomenon to present the king as the restorer of "Merry England." Although many popular customs suppressed by the Puritans never returned, such as the bonfires for St. John's Eve, in many places enough did to give substance to this claim. The godly, making their compromises with the regime or withdrawing into communities of Dissenters*, abandoned their attempts to purify and reform the culture of the English people. Their political heirs, the Whigs*, rather than trying to suppress popular rituals, tried to manipulate them, particularly in London, where during the Popish Plot* (1678) the Whigs organized massive pope burnings.

The Restoration era was a silver age of traditional popular customs. In the ensuing century, economic trends such as enclosure and urbanization would disrupt village communities and weaken long-standing communal traditions, while efforts to purify popular culture would resume under the aegis of new religious movements.

Bibliography: B. Reay, ed., *Popular Culture in Seventeenth Century England*, 1985; Margaret Spufford, *Small Books and Pleasant Histories*, 1981; David Underdown, *Revel, Riot, and Rebellion*, 1985.

William E. Burns

Population. The rate of population growth in Stuart England was about 0.5 percent per annum, rather slow by modern standards but vigorous by preindustrial ones. From 1603 to 1714 the population of England grew from approximately four million to over five million, but there were dramatic fluctuations from year to year and a thirty-year period of significant decline after the Restoration*. In fact the decline was so marked that although the English had nearly doubled between 1541 and 1656 (2.77 million to 5.28 million), doubling did not actually occur until 1741 (5.5 million). In 1661 alone the decline was nearly three percent.

Migration had some impact on growth rates, particularly in years when movement in and out of England was dramatic. There was a large influx of foreigners in 1651 and a notable exodus in the years 1620 and 1680. But the real factors affecting population were fertility and mortality. The curve of fertility had been high during the sixteenth century, falling slowly until it sagged between 1650 and 1680. A sharp recovery in fertility followed this trough. One explanation of low fertility is the surprisingly late average age of first marriages for males and females. Between 1600 and 1649 first-time grooms averaged twenty-eight years, first-time brides twenty-six; between 1649 and 1699 the age for men had fallen to 27.8, but for women* it had risen to 26.5.

The population of England in the seventeenth century was also remarkably youthful juxtaposed with today's figures, comparable in some ways to an underdeveloped nation in the twentieth century. The percentage of the population younger than twenty-five consistently hovered around fifty-eight percent, with those under fifteen constituting an astounding thirty-eight percent of the nation, emphasizing the serious shortage of mature adults in the work force. Infant mortality rates were relatively low, averaging around 120 per 1,000, but probably fifty percent of pregnancies failed. Children under age ten accounted for thirty-four percent of all deaths, the majority of them under two years. There was a sharp rise in child mortality in the early seventeenth century, attributable to almost incessant waves of disease. In 1669-1671 thousands of babies died from a virulent strain of diarrhea, made more deadly by the swaddling and confinement of newborns. If one lived past childhood, surviving into middle age was likely, though only about ten percent lived to be sixty years old. Life expectancy rates at birth never varied from between thirty-two to thirty-four years. This was high compared to the rest of Europe, but when combined with the percentage of children in the population, it helps to explain the low productivity of a preindustrial state. Rates of death for women in childbirth were alarming, and incessant epidemics* and plagues cut a deadly swath into the people. Families tended to be nuclear, unlike those in today's Third World, so the deaths were especially disruptive.

Population was scattered somewhat unevenly throughout the country, with especially heavy concentrations in the south, where perhaps three-quarters resided. Large portions of the north were virtually uninhabited, and although the nation was still overwhelmingly rural, towns had begun to absorb the unemployed from the countryside. London* continued its population domination of England, the number of its residents rising from 200,000 inhabitants in 1600 to approximately 600,000 by 1700, making it the largest city in western Europe and twenty times larger than its nearest English competitors, Norwich and Bristol. Nevertheless, port towns like Liverpool and Glasgow grew at an even faster pace.

Dependable death rates owe much to the introduction of bills of mortality in 1603 when plague killed nearly 3,000 Londoners in a week. By mid-century the political arithmetic of John Graunt (1620-1674), a draper by trade, was based on the bills and provided such insight into population (more boys born than girls), growth patterns, and disease that Charles II* ordered he be made a member of the Royal Society*. Later Stuart demographers have been aided by more systematic tax-record keeping (see Taxation and Revenue*) and piqued by the compilations, however dubious, of pioneer statistician Gregory King (1648-1712).

Bibliography: C. W. Chalkin and M. A. Havender, eds., *Rural Change and Population Growth, 1500-1800*, 1974; E. A. Wrigley and Roger S. Schofield, *Population History of England, 1541-1871*, 1981.

Elizabeth Lane Furdell

Prayer Book Rebellion. See Bishops' Wars; Covenant; Scotland.

Prerogative (Royal). Throughout the seventeenth century there was a continued debate over the extent and use of the royal prerogative. The political dispute between the Crown and parliament* was explored by theorists (see Political Thought*). Sir Robert Filmer argued "for the superiority of princes above laws," while John Locke* later contended that the power to act with "dispatch" for the "public good" should not be used as an "arbitrary power." The political contest was decided at various times on battlefields such as Naseby* and in the courts with the Ship Money* Case (1637) and *Godden v. Hales* (1686). These great constitutional issues were framed by documents* such as the Petition of Right* in 1628 and the Bill of Rights* in 1689.

The areas of dispute can be broadly categorized into four areas: the controversy over taxation* and finance; the disputes over the king's dispensing* and suspending* powers; control over judges and juries and the limitations on the power of imprisonment; and the controversy over the succession of the monarchy.

During the initial third of the seventeenth century, James I* and Charles I* were faced with growing governmental expenditures and decreasing traditional revenue sources, such as those from Crown lands*. As a result, the parliaments of James I and Charles I focused primarily on the raising of revenue, from both direct and indirect taxation. Charles I's increasing dependence on parliament for revenue led to his attempts to raise money through other means, such as forced loans*. The resulting tensions and grievances led to the Petition of Right, in which Charles I acknowledged as "old liberties" that there could be no taxation or forced loan without the consent of parliament, as well as not imprisoning his subjects without cause, billeting soldiers without consent, and subjecting civilians to martial law. The dispute then arose as to whether the king could collect tonnage and poundage without an act of parliament. In the famous Ship Money Case of 1637, the court ruled that acts of parliament seeking to take away the king's "royal power" to defend the kingdom were void. The Long Parliament* responded in 1641 by forbidding tonnage and poundage without parliamentary consent, declaring illegal the judgment in the Ship Money Case, as well as the other taxes implemented by the king without the consent of parliament.

The middle portion of the century, 1640-1660, saw great constitutional, political, religious and social turmoil with Charles I's execution*, the Commonwealth*, the Protectorate*, and the Restoration*. Parliament at the Restoration recognized the king as the "sole supreme" commander of the army* and militia (13 Car. II, st. I, c. 6) and his power to license and control the press (Licensing Act*, 14 Car. II, c. 33) (see Printing and Book Trade*). There was, however, no return to the king of any of the powers to levy taxation without the consent of parliament.

Many of the other key issues concerning the royal prerogative remained unresolved. Perhaps nowhere else is this better illustrated than by the dispensing power. The religious settlement of 1661-1662 was a cause of continued friction between Charles II* and parliament. During the passage of the Act of Uniformity (14 Car. II, c. 4), Charles had sought unsuccessfully to reserve the power to dispense with the act in certain situations. Although Charles seriously considered suspending the Act of Uniformity shortly after its passage, it was not until 1672 that he issued his Declaration of Indulgence* suspending the penal laws. When parliament met, Charles was forced to withdraw the declaration in order to get revenue. Parliament then passed the first Test Act* (25 Car. II, c. 2), which was directed toward Catholics* but also applied to Dissenters*, excluding both groups from public office. In 1678 parliament passed the second Test Act (30 Car. II, st. 2, c.1), which excluded these groups from parliament.

As soon as James II's* parliament objected in the fall of 1685 to his commissioning of Catholic army officers in violation of the Test Act, James prorogued it. In 1686 Sir Edward Hales had his servant bring a collusive action against him, which led to the judgment in *Godden v. Hales* (1686). Eleven of the twelve judges agreed that there was "an inseparable prerogative in the kings of England to dispense with Penal laws." James, relying on this precedent, sought to apply the dispensing power broadly. His Declaration of Indulgence*, which led to the Seven Bishops'* famous petition challenging the dispensing power and subsequent acquittal on the charge of libel, acted as one of the catalysts for the Glorious Revolution* of 1688. The king's use of dispensing and suspending powers without the consent of parliament was declared illegal by the Bill of Rights* of 1689.

The Crown's prerogative over the courts was a continuous source of conflict (see Common Law and Courts*; Prerogative Courts*). In 1667 the House of Commons passed a resolution declaring illegal the government's fining or imprisoning jurors who returned an adverse verdict and in Bushell's Case* (1670) the practice was denounced as absurd. The Habeas Corpus Act of 1679 (31 Car. II, c. 2), adopted after the Popish Plot* of 1678 (and passed through the House of Lords only by the artifice of one of the tellers' falsifying the count) helped establish a procedure to prevent illegal detention, though it was temporarily suspended by parliament during William III's* reign. In response to the persecution arising out of the Rye House Plot* (1683) and the trials after Monmouth's Rebellion* (1685), the Treason Trial Act of 1696 (7 & 8 Gul. III, c. 3) confirmed the requirement for two witnesses for proof of the treason and that the accused be given a copy of the indictment and services of counsel. The act also provided for trial by jury, except for peers, who would be tried before the complete House of Lords, rather than a special jury of peers chosen by the king when parliament was not sitting. Finally the Act of Settlement of 1701 (12 & 13 Gul. III, c. 2) established a degree of judicial independence from the Crown.

The unpopular tendency of the later Stuarts to tolerate or convert to Catholicism and Charles II's failure to produce a legitimate heir, combined with the Popish Plot* and the resulting Exclusion Crisis* (1678-1681), led to a fundamental dispute over the succession to the Crown. The Popish Plot, with the alleged Jesuit plans to murder the king and put his Catholic brother on the throne, led to direct challenges to the hereditary monarchy. In succeeding parliaments three successive Exclusion Bills were introduced that would have removed James, duke of York, from the succession. Various compromises were proposed, including one by Charles II to limit the powers of any Catholic successor, which the Whigs* rejected, proposing to pass the royal prerogative without limitation to a Protestant successor. There was a division, however, on who that successor would be, with some proposing that the Crown pass to Mary*, princess of Orange, as though James were legally dead, while others put forth Charles II's illegitimate son, James, duke of Monmouth. Ultimately Charles, after negotiating a generous French subsidy, dissolved the last of the Exclusion Parliaments (see Oxford Parliament*) and, with the persecutions following the discovery of the Rye House Plot, ruled the remainder of his reign without calling a parliament, contrary to the Triennial Act* of 1664 (16 Car. II, c. 1).

After Charles II's death and James II's accession to the throne, the duke of Monmouth in the summer of 1685 unsuccessfully attempted to seize the Crown during Monmouth's Rebellion in the west. Monmouth sought to justify his action as being in the "defense and vindication of the Protestant Religion" and to deliver the nation from James's "usurpation and tyranny." Three years later, on the day the seven bishops were acquitted of the charges of seditious libel, William, prince of Orange, was "invited" by the famous seven to England because of James II's invasion of the people's "religion, liberties and properties." After James II's "abdication," as his disposition was described in the Bill of Rights, the principle of strict hereditary monarchy was effectively abandoned. The passage of the Act of Settlement (12 & 13 Gul. III, c. 2) and the Regency Act (6 Annae, c. 41) excluded Catholics from the succession, and provision was made for the peaceful succession of George I.

Bibliography: J. P. Kenyon, ed., *The Stuart Constitution, 1603-1688*, 1966; Goldwin Smith, *A Constitutional and Legal History of England*, 1990.

John Harrison Rains III

Prerogative Courts. The term *prerogative courts* was applied in a pejorative sense by Whig* historians to the courts of Star Chamber and High Commission, which were abolished by the Long Parliament* in 1641 (by 16 Car. I, cc. 10, 11). The Whig historians thought that these courts were extralegal tribunals because they depended upon the royal prerogative* rather than common law. Such an explanation owes more to myth and fancy than to fact or logic. The court of High Commission or Ecclesiastical Commission, a tribunal that exercised powers of the royal ecclesiastical supremacy, derived in part from the Act of Supremacy of 1559 (1 Eliz. I, c. 1), as the statute abolishing that court was obliged to acknowledge when it recognized the legal necessity of repealing the relevant section of 1 Eliz. I, c. 1. To call the court of Star Chamber a prerogative court only confuses the issue because all of the ancient courts, whether common law* or equity, had derived their authority from the king's judicial prerogative. The subject who feared that he might suffer a miscarriage of justice because someone had exploited procedural rules or intimidated judges or juries to frustrate the course of justice could always appeal to the king and his council to exercise this prerogative and grant him relief. Nor did the court of Star Chamber enforce the royal prerogative any more than did the courts of Common Pleas or King's Bench, with the possible exceptions of the enforcement of proclamations and the royal game prerogative. Sir Edward Coke*, the great defender of the common law, had voiced an objection to Star Chamber on very narrow technical grounds, but he had not scrupled to practice as a barrister in that court and as attorney general had played a leading role in shaping the doctrine of seditious libel.

The court of Star Chamber was one of a number of equity or English-bill courts, the others being the courts of Chancery, Requests, Exchequer Chamber, and Duchy of Lancaster Chamber. Courts of equity were less constrained by the rules and procedures that could be employed in the common law courts to frustrate a plaintiff's attempt to secure justice. These courts dispensed justice that accorded more with conscience than rigid rules of law. They employed the procedures of the Roman civil law, which depended on written evidence in the form of complaints and answers, interrogatories, and depositions. Whereas one had to know Latin and legal French in order to penetrate the indictments and pleadings at common law, the fact that all evidence and proceedings in Star Chamber and the other English-bill courts were in the vernacular made those courts much more accessible. The concept of equity as corrective of the law was an old one, and the rules of equity, which had been worked out in the late medieval Chancery, were applied in the court of Star Chamber and other English-bill courts in the sixteenth century.

The court of Star Chamber consisted of the members of the royal council, presided over by the lord chancellor and joined by the chief justices of the courts of Common Pleas and King's Bench. Its name came from the chamber in the old Palace of Westminster where it sat during the four legal terms. During the chancellorship of

Thomas Wolsey (1515-1529), Star Chamber became more distinct from the royal council and concerned itself with cases of both a civil and criminal nature, applying statute law and the principles of common law as well as equity. Since neither grand juries nor trial juries were involved in Star Chamber proceedings, the court effectively exercised a summary jurisdiction, as the Long Parliament was later to complain, although the court's penalties, unlike those of the common law courts, could not touch life or limb. The inquisitorial procedure used in Star Chamber resembled that used in High Commission and other ecclesiastical courts, but its origin was found in the older equity courts such as Chancery. This procedure, which required written answers to written complaints and which could extract sworn depositions from defendants as well as witnesses, was certainly devised to elicit fuller evidence and to get at the truth in a case. However, since Star Chamber complaints were often filed as cross-suits involving litigation in other courts, defendants and witnesses compelled to make full disclosure in Star Chamber or High Commission complained that their written evidence could be used to incriminate them in those other courts where litigation was pending.

The civil jurisdiction of the conciliar courts receded as the common lawyers, led by Sir Edward Coke, attacked the Star Chamber with writs of prohibition whenever it threatened to impinge on the jurisdiction of the common law courts. Star Chamber became primarily a court of criminal jurisdiction and increasingly concerned itself with punishing crimes against public order: riot, unlawful assembly, tumultuous hunting, and sedition. The crimes of perjury, subornation, maintenance, forgery, fraud, extortion, and conspiracy were also developed or refined in Star Chamber, which recognized that misdemeanors frequently posed a greater threat to public order than treasons and felonies, especially cunning crimes that were characteristic of the more sophisticated social and economic practices of the early modern world. Because the matters heard were misdemeanors, both sides to a dispute were entitled to and indeed required to have legal counsel. The court applied statute law and common law principles when they were available but did not hesitate to find a remedy for a wrong in defining the misdemeanors prosecuted in the court, and the judges of the common law courts were always at hand to lend their legal expertise. This corpus of law concerning misdemeanors was taken over by the common law courts not just at the point of abolition of Star Chamber but also during the heyday of the court in the sixteenth and early seventeenth centuries.

During the early seventeenth century the attorney general began to play a more prominent part in the court's proceedings by intervening *pro rege* (in the king's interest) and prosecuting matters that closely touched the interests of church and state. In the reign of Charles I*, bishops also sat upon the bench and participated in the prosecution of Puritans* for libeling prelates. In a very few cases such dissidents were subjected to the corporal penalties of having their ears cropped and their noses slit, but such punishments were not typical of those inflicted by the court and certainly were not more cruel or unusual than punishments routinely meted out at the assizes.

Much of the criticism directed against the court of High Commission is attributable to critics who confounded it with Star Chamber, but it can also be fairly objected that the two courts became too close during the Caroline period and shared many of the

same personnel.   The term "High Commission" is applied to the court of
Ecclesiastical Commission of the province of Canterbury, which sat from 1559 until
its abolition (see Ecclesiastical Courts*).   It was the most important of a number of
ecclesiastical commission courts, which were also established by letters patent in the
province of York and various dioceses in order to shore up sagging episcopal
jurisdictions. These ecclesiastical commissions, upon which sat lay as well as clerical
judges, existed alongside the ordinary church courts but exercised a jurisdiction
analogous to the criminal jurisdiction of Star Chamber.   These ecclesiastical
commissions enjoyed popularity when they were used to deprive Catholic* priests but
incurred odium when they began harassing Puritan ministers. The High Commission
especially looked as if it might turn into a heresy court when it began to inquire into
the beliefs of defendants employing the hated ex officio oath in order to elicit answers
that could incriminate a defendant; the common law judges fought the court with writs
of prohibition, while parliament* in 1607 unsuccessfully attempted to make the ex
officio oath illegal (see Parliament of 1604-1610*).   In actuality only a small
percentage of cases prosecuted in the court dealt with Puritanism*; a much higher
proportion concerned matrimonial causes and attempts to collect alimony or
accusations of immorality among the aristocracy.

The act abolishing the court of Star Chamber in 1641 also abolished the courts of
the Duchy of Lancaster and the County Palatine of Chester, as well as the Councils
of the Marches and Principality of Wales and in the North Parts, which had also
exercised equity jurisdictions, but, oddly, it left intact the far more unpopular court
of Wards.

Bibliography: Thomas G. Barnes, "Star Chamber and the Sophistication of the
Criminal Law," *Criminal Law Review*, 1977, pp. 316-326; H. E. I. Phillips, "The
Last Days of the Court of Star Chamber," *Transactions of the Royal Historical
Society*, 4th ser., 21 (1938), pp. 103-131; Roland G. Usher, *The Rise and Fall of the
High Commission*, 1968 repr. ed.

Roger B. Manning

Presbyterians, Political. A loose political grouping or party that appeared in the
Long Parliament* in the aftermath of the First Civil War*.   The Political
Presbyterians were led by Denzil Holles (1599-1680), a clever and ruthless
parliamentary politician, and they favored giving easy terms to Charles I* in order to
bring about the settlement of England's government.   They also supported the
establishment of a national church organized along loose Presbyterian lines, although
many Political Presbyterians were not adherents of Religious Presbyterianism*.

When the English Civil War broke out, the parliamentarian* side contained many
people who harbored the gravest doubts about the propriety of resisting their lawful
king.   One group went so far as to favor a negotiated peace, which would have
included extremely generous terms for the king and would not have required any
safeguards against future abuses of the royal prerogative*.   That group, which was
known as the Peace Party, was led by Robert Devereux*, 3d earl of Essex.   The

Peace Party opposed efforts to gain an outright military victory over Charles I and his royalist* supporters, but they did not command a majority in the Long Parliament. As a result, the so-called Middle Group and the War Party, which favored seeking a clear-cut military victory, in 1645 managed to pass the Self-Denying Ordinance* and to establish the New Model Army*. By early 1646 these reforms had assisted parliamentary forces in triumphing over the royalist armies.

Military victory over the king presented parliament* with the problems of how to reach an acceptable and permanent settlement with the recalcitrant Charles and also satisfy the demands of their Scots allies for the establishment of a national church in England constituted along strict Presbyterian lines. It was a situation fraught with political peril as Charles was not inclined to cooperate, the Scots were uncompromising, and most English parliamentarians did not support the religious demands of the Scots. It was under these circumstances that the so-called Political Presbyterian party arose in the Long Parliament during 1646. It attracted the members of the old Peace Party to it, along with conservative members of the Middle Group, people disgruntled by the Self-Denying Ordinance, those opposed to the continuing existence of the expensive standing armies, and anyone who favored soft terms for the settlement with Charles. Many religious conservatives, Presbyterians, Independents*, and Anglicans*, also tended to support the Political Presbyterians in an effort to combat the growth of radical and heretical religious sects such as the Baptists*, Quakers*, and the Fifth Monarchy Men*. Holles emerged as the leader of the Political Presbyterian party.

The Political Presbyterians were also allied with the Scots, who first gave their English allies the name "Presbyterian party." Few of the Political Presbyterians, however, favored the full Scottish demand for the establishment of a Presbyterian national church based on *iure divino*, or divine right*. Many Political Presbyterians were actually adherents of moderate episcopacy, of mild or extreme Erastian views, of a moderate Presbyterianism established by the state, or of Independency or Separatism*. Basically the Political Presbyterians were conservatives who wanted to return England to its traditional condition of being a society dominated by the aristocracy and gentry and ruled over by a law-abiding king. Their greatest fear was that a continued disruption of normal government would open the way to further social upheaval, anarchy, and the proliferation of sectarian heresy.

The Political Presbyterians were more a loose association or coalition of factions rather than a formally organized and disciplined political party of the type found in modern Britain. Votes shifted from individual issue to individual issue because many members of the Long Parliament were not deeply committed to either the Political Presbyterians or their opponents, the Political Independents*. Holles proved to be an extremely effective leader, who managed to line up big majorities behind most of his proposals, much to the frustration of the opposition. War weariness made the Long Parliament very responsive to programs for reducing the size of the military, for paying off the army of the Scots allies, and for reaching a settlement with Charles I. Protestant enthusiasm, ethnic animosity, and national security made proposals to suppress the Irish Rebellion* equally popular. Fear of sectarian anarchy also caused many Political Presbyterians to support the establishment of a Presbyterian national church.

Unfortunately for Holles and his allies, their commanding position in parliament allowed them to ignore their various opponents within the parliament, but it did not provide them with the strength to suppress opposition outside parliament, particularly in the New Model Army. Relations between the Political Presbyterians and the Political Independents and the army* deteriorated through the spring and early summer of 1647. In June the army began to call for the removal of the Eleven Members: Holles and ten other leading Political Presbyterians in the House of Commons. Tensions intensified when London* apprentices descended on the parliament and rioted in support of the Political Presbyterians on 26 July. This violence caused the speaker of the House of Commons and some of the Political Independents to flee on 30 July to the protection of the army. In response the army marched on London on 6-7 August, ousted the Political Presbyterians, and placed the Political Independents in control of both the parliament and the government of London.

Unfortunately for the Political Independents and the army, the financial problems of equitably disbanding the army and reconquering Ireland*, along with the continuing but unsuccessful negotiations with Charles I, were creating a growing conservative reaction in England. Such a development favored the Political Presbyterians but also prompted the outbreak of the Second Civil War* (March-August 1648). The rebellious conservatives were crushed, while the army was further radicalized against the king and the revolutionary republicans among the Political Independents gained new support.

By the autumn of 1648 the Political Presbyterians represented the wishes of the great majority of the traditional political elite of England, both conservative parliamentarians and crypto-royalists. These conservative forces possessed political power by virtue of their majority in the parliament, but the army and its Political Independent allies possessed the crucial military power. When the Political Presbyterians, who dominated negotiations with Charles I over the Treaty of Newport* (September-November 1648), appeared to be virtually surrendering to the king's demands, they also produced a final radicalization of the army. In an effort to avert such a betrayal of the sacrifices of the First and Second Civil Wars, the army decided to remove the Political Presbyterians from the parliament. That action, known as Pride's Purge*, occurred on 6 December 1648. New Model Army troops blocked various Political Presbyterians from entering the parliament and thus left the remaining Political Independents in control of the so-called Rump Parliament*. In the countryside, support for the conservative program of the Political Presbyterians remained strong throughout the Commonwealth* and Protectorate* eras and eventually helped to bring about the Restoration* of Charles II*.

Bibliography: David Underdown, *Pride's Purge: Politics in the Puritan Revolution*, 1971.

Ronald H. Fritze

Presbyterians, Religious. The distinguishing features of Presbyterianism in England throughout most of the seventeenth century were an adherence to the cardinal tenets of Calvinist* theology (the sovereignty and providence of God, the divine act of predestination upon which the salvation of the elect is dependent, the importance of preaching and the sacraments of baptism and the Lord's supper, and the importance of discipline in upholding godly precepts), the parity of ministers and congregations, a hierarchy of representative synods and assemblies, and the enforcement of discipline at the congregational level through a consistory comprised of the pastor and popularly elected elders. In contrast to Scottish Presbyterians, most of their English counterparts severely limited the power of synods, preferring to stress the role of individual congregations. Unlike the Independents* (Congregationalists*), the Presbyterians adhered to the notion of a parish rather than a "gathered" church, even after 1662, when Presbyterian clergy lost their livings in the established church.

Although the government had crushed Presbyterian organizations at the end of Elizabeth's reign, the movement did not perish, but for the first four decades of the seventeenth century the focal point of English Presbyterian activity was in the Netherlands. The most important Presbyterian minister early in the century was John Paget, who not only ministered to a Reformed congregation in Amsterdam but also refuted the Separatists* in works such as his *Arrow Against the Separation* (1618). From its founding in 1607, the Amsterdam congregation belonged to the classis of Amsterdam, but other English Presbyterian churches in the Netherlands shunned membership for years, underscoring the relative independence of English Presbyterian congregations; Utrecht joined the classis in 1629, Middelburg and Flushing in 1645, Dort in 1646, and Leiden in 1655.

The Long Parliament's* reform efforts opened the way for Presbyterian advances in England, notably through the work of the Westminster Assembly of Divines* (1643-1649). Called into existence by parliament*, it produced a confession of faith, a larger and a shorter catechism, a form of church government, and a directory for public worship. Debate was often heated, for some delegates championed modified episcopacy, others hierarchical Presbyterianism as in Scotland*, and yet others Independent polity. In the end the crucial issue for the country was the extent to which the power of presbyteries and synods would be subject to civil magistrates. The majority in the assembly believed that church officers by divine power had the right to bar scandalous persons from the Lord's supper. In parliament, however, Erastianism was triumphant; in October 1645 the House of Commons determined that Presbyterian elders could exclude offenders from the sacrament only for offenses specified by parliament. When the assembly criticized the parliamentary settlement of the church in 1646, parliament responded by declaring the protest a breach of parliamentary privilege. Whatever the merits of the theological documents of the assembly, which subsequently influenced not only later Presbyterians but also Congregationalists and Particular Baptists*, its efforts to alter the established church had only minimal success. Provincial assemblies were established only in London* and Lancashire, and no national assembly ever convened. Any hope of effectively implementing Presbyterian polity was dashed by Pride's Purge* in December 1648. English religion in the 1650s was very nearly a matter of consumer's choice.

For the Presbyterians the most significant ecclesiastical development of the 1650s was the emergence of voluntary associations, of which the best known is the Worcester Association founded under the leadership of Richard Baxter* in 1653. Intended to foster unity among Episcopalian, Presbyterian, and Independent parish ministers, the associations primarily attracted clerics more concerned with pastoral responsibilities than issues of polity. Among Independent ministers, for whom the ideal of the gathered church was paramount, there was little interest in the associations.

At the Restoration* the ecumenical spirit embodied in the voluntary associations spurred efforts to accommodate Presbyterians in the state church. Moderate Presbyterians (or Reconcilers) such as Edmund Calamy, Sr., and Richard Baxter expressed their willingness to accept a modified episcopacy of the sort previously suggested by Bishop James Ussher. Charles II* responded by sponsoring a conference at Worcester House in October 1660 involving bishops and Presbyterian clergy. The conference came to naught when the Presbyterians failed to persuade the bishops to accept their plea for ministers to operate freely within their parishes. Charles did, however, honor his promise to convene a conference of bishops and Presbyterians at the Savoy to consider revisions in the Book of Common Prayer. The Presbyterians enjoyed modest success in this endeavor, though Baxter's attempt to replace the Book of Common Prayer with a Reformed liturgy of his own devising was expectedly rebuffed.

The Savoy Conference* was still in progress when the Commons began considering the bill that ultimately became the Act of Uniformity (14 Car. II, c. 4) in May 1662. It went into force three months later on St. Bartholomew's Day. Presbyterians found four principles in the act objectionable: reordination for any minister not ordained by a bishop; full assent to everything in the Book of Common Prayer; the right of bishops to review all cases of scandalous persons barred from communion; and the requirement that all clergy declare the Solemn League and Covenant* unlawful. Between 1660 and 1662 nearly 2,000 clergy, approximately ninety percent of them Presbyterians, were ejected from their livings. The Cavalier Parliament* imposed further penalties in the Conventicle Act in 1664 (16 Car. II., c. 4), which prohibited religious services not conducted with the Book of Common Prayer, and the Five Mile Act in 1665 (17 Car. II, c. 2), which required Nonconformist ministers to take an oath not to seek changes in church or state or not to live within five miles of any place where they had formerly ministered (see Clarendon Code*). Presbyterians who took the oath, such as William Bates and Thomas Manton, became known as "dons"; those who refused, such as Nathaniel Vincent and James Janeway, were dubbed "ducks" for their willingness to take to the water by defying the law and holding conventicles. Throughout the reign of Charles II, a relatively small number of Presbyterians, such as Thomas Blood and William Lecky, went even further and engaged in assorted plots against the government. Many Presbyterians of this period were hardly as quiescent as traditional historiography has depicted them.

The Declaration of Indulgence* that Charles issued in March 1672 was of enormous value to the Presbyterians, 923 of whom obtained licenses to preach; altogether 1,339 licenses were issued, making the Presbyterians the largest group of

Nonconformists, roughly three times the size of their nearest competitor, the Congregationalists. Devonshire and London were the centers of Presbyterian strength. (By the 1710s there were 179,350 Presbyterians in England.) Like other Nonconformists, the Presbyterians were subjected to sporadic persecution in the 1680s, especially after the disclosure of the Rye House Plot* in 1683.

In the period following the passage of the Act of Toleration (1 Gul. & Mar., c. 18) in 1689, two significant developments occurred in Presbyterian circles. The first involved efforts to unite with the Congregationalists. Out of this came the establishment of the Common Fund (1690) to assist ministers and ministerial students and to coordinate charitable activity. This in turn led to the Happy Union (1691), linking Presbyterian and Congregationalist clergy. Although the union was short-lived in London, elsewhere it lasted nearly a century. The second development was a bitter theological controversy sparked by Samuel Crisp's publication of the Antinomian works of his father, Tobias; of the twelve clerics who endorsed their publication, six were Presbyterians. When Baxter, a moderate Calvinist, refuted Tobias's views, Samuel Crisp attacked Baxter. Supported by sixteen fellow Presbyterian ministers, Daniel Williams came to Baxter's defense, whereupon six Congregationalists, viewing this as a partisan attack on their denomination, castigated Williams. The debate continued, undermining the unity so recently achieved, focusing efforts of both groups on theological issues, and testifying to the breakup of the once-dominant Calvinism that had characterized Presbyterianism.

Bibliography: G. R. Abernathy, Jr., "The English Presbyterians and the Stuart Restoration, 1648-1663," *Transactions of the American Philosophical Society*, new ser., 55, pt. 2 (1965); C. G. Bolam, J. Goring, H. L. Short, and R. Thomas, *The English Presbyterians: From Elizabethan Puritanism to Modern Unitarianism*, 1968; R. S. Paul, *Assembly of the Lord: Politics and Religion in the Westminster Assembly and the Grand Debate*, 1985.

Richard L. Greaves

Pride's Purge (1648). On 6 December 1648 Colonel Thomas Pride arrested or turned away a majority of the members of the House of Commons. This purge of the Long Parliament* left a Rump Parliament* which could now proceed with the execution of Charles I*, the abolition of the monarchy and the House of Lords, and the establishment of a Puritan* commonwealth.

The majority of the parliamentarian* gentry had fought the war for moderate reform in both church and state but did not wish to destroy the essential framework of the government or society. There were some, however, who had fought for a complete reconstruction of both church and state, and to achieve this goal any action, even revolutionary, was justified. Given that few of the original leaders wanted revolution, their removal in 1648 was necessary before radical change could be achieved. David Underdown argues that religion was not the determining issue in the split within parliament* that produced Pride's Purge, though he suggests it was certainly of great importance. He observes that the revolutionaries in parliament and most of their supporters were not motivated so much by a difference in theology as by a Puritan determination to achieve the reformation of society and to see Puritan idealism triumph over constitutional conservatism. Conflict over what to do with the king led to the revolutionaries' excluding the majority from Commons.

Henry Ireton's* *Remonstrance* set out Charles I's conduct in the two Civil Wars* and analyzed the role of the king in modern society. Ireton demanded that Charles be brought to justice and the monarchy be abolished. Thomas Fairfax* found this proposal to be too radical, but after some failed negotiations with the captive Charles, the *Remonstrance* was approved by the council of officers and sent to the House of Commons on 20 November. The Commons postponed any discussion of the *Remonstrance* for a week and then on 27 November postponed it again until 1 December. On 27 November Fairfax ordered that Charles be brought strictly guarded from the Isle of Wight to Hurst Castle in Hampshire. Ireton wanted to dissolve parliament forcibly, but Fairfax overruled him. Fairfax did, however, on 30 November announce he would reoccupy London*, a move that took place on 2 December. In response some leading Presbyterian* members of parliament (MPs) fled. Fairfax also sent word to Oliver Cromwell* that he should return from the siege of Pontefract. On 5 December, after an all-night session, the Commons voted that Charles's removal to Hurst Castle had not been legal. The council of officers met with some of the leading Independent* MPs, but they could not agree with Ireton, who again argued for a forcible dissolution of parliament. Later in the day, apparently without Fairfax's knowledge, Ireton and some of the Independent MPs decided that at least a purge of the House of Commons was necessary.

The next morning, 6 December 1648, Colonel Thomas Pride stood at the top of the stairs leading to the House of Commons and with the help of Lord Grey of Groby, who pointed out to him the offending members, turned away about 186 MPs; a further forty-one were arrested, while eighty-six more subsequently stayed away in protest. The purged parliament or Rump (with about 154 members) could now begin the formation of a Puritan commonwealth. Fairfax was furious about the purge but did not intervene. That evening Cromwell finally returned, saying that while he had had no knowledge of the purge, he did give it his approval.

Pride's Purge led the way for Charles I's trial and execution* and the abolition of the monarchy. It was not, however, the end of the parliamentary career of those members who had been excluded. In February 1660, as part of the plan to restore the monarchy, General George Monck* exacted pledges from the excluded members and returned them to parliament. They then voted to dissolve themselves and called for a new election, finally ending the Long Parliament.

Bibliography: David Underdown, *Pride's Purge: Politics in the Puritan Revolution*, 1971.

Carole Levin

Printing and Book Trade. Compared with the best French work, most European printing deteriorated during the seventeenth century. In England it declined, especially compared to Tudor printing, due to government restrictions resulting from religious and political strife, a monopoly* that prevented beneficial competition, and a hatred of foreigners that kept out technical innovations.

Much early Stuart output consisted of tracts disseminated by rival political factions and religious denominations; workmanship was shoddy and typography poor. James I* recalled patents granted to John and Richard Day (primers and psalters) and James Roberts and Richard Watkins (almanacs and prognostications) and for £9,000 granted the London* Stationers Company a monopoly (excepting the royal printer) that allowed no printing outside the city save at Cambridge and Oxford. The number of presses and employees was restricted, and all printing required official approval. This formed the legal basis of the "English Stock," printing grants made not to an individual or partnership (as previously) but to the company as a whole. The Stationers bought out all profitable copy on the market and printed only what would sell. With no competition, workmanship deteriorated; the many editions of the Psalms with music were among the worst. The Stock was controlled by a master and wardens, who decided what to print, who printed it, and what he was paid. To prevent extra copies, the printer was issued just enough paper for the job. Patents were usually leased by the company to wealthy members with more capital and better presses. As privileges accrued, the "stocks" were divided (e.g., into English, Bible, Irish, Latin, ballad).

Melchisedec Bradwood of Eliot's Court Press printed The *Works of St. John Chrysostom* in eight folio volumes in 1610-1613, a fine example of Greek printing and an exception to inferior works. In 1611 the king's printer, Robert Barker, printed the King James's Bible* with financial help from London stationers John and Bonham Norton and John Bill, who shared the profits. The text was a great primer black-letter, with chapter headings and marginal references in Roman and alternative readings in italic. A quarto Roman-type edition followed in 1612. The first music book printed from copper plates in England was *Parthenia* (undated), an anthology for virginals with works by John Bull, William Byrd, and Orlando Gibbons (see Music*), engraved by William Houle, published by John Clarke, and issued 1612-1613 to celebrate the betrothal of James I's daughter Elizabeth* to Frederick of the Palatinate. By 1620 the English Stock consisted of law books (fifty-eight), school books (thirty-two), alphabet primers (five), psalms and psalters in all volumes, almanacs, calendars, prayer books (thirteen), and general works (eight). The Bible Stock, whose partners shared the right to issue the Scriptures with the king's printer, required eight auditors to keep accounts. The first collected edition of thirty-six of Shakespeare's plays was produced in 1623 by printer Isaac Jaggard and bookseller-publisher Edward Blount, poorly printed like most others. Jaggard's father, William, had printed an edition of *Nobilitas Politica vel Civilis* (1608), one of the period's handsomest books. Though Dutch printer William Janszoon Blaeu (1571-1638) introduced an improved hand press in 1620, which prevented slurred print, it was not generally adopted in England.

Charles I's* accession brought more restriction and persecution, partly due to Archbishop William Laud*. This culminated in Star Chamber's Decree Concerning Printing in 1637, which repeated a 1615 prohibition against printing seditious and schismatical books and ordered all books and pamphlets to be registered at Stationers'

Hall, with severe penalties for noncompliance (a milestone in publisher claims to copyright). Authors who challenged authority were treated harshly; William Prynne*, author of *Histrio-Mastix* (1633), was brought before Star Chamber, fined heavily, degraded from the bar, pilloried, had an ear cropped, and was sentenced to life imprisonment. His chief offense was opposition to Laud, who felt he had insulted Queen Henrietta Maria*.

Robert Young, king's printer for Scotland*, printed the first Authorized Version to appear there in 1633; his most important publication was Laud's Prayer Book (1637), a handsome work apart from dissimilar woodcut initials. Four great polyglot Bibles were printed during this period; the six-volume *Biblia Sacra Polyglotta* edited by Brian Walton and printed by Thomas Roycroft (1633-1657) exemplifies seventeenth-century English printing at its best. It was the second book in England to be published by subscription; the first was John Minsheu's *Guide into Tongues* (1617), a dictionary in eleven languages. Oxford benefited from the chancellorship of Laud (1630-1641), who obtained royal charters for the university to print "all manner of books," a privilege Cambridge had enjoyed since 1534.

Perhaps the most significant development in early Stuart printing involved newspapers. "News books" appeared as early as 1513 and were published infrequently until 1590. For the next twenty years, some 450 appeared, dealing mainly with foreign news. They were usually eight to twelve pages, inelegant, and crowded. The first phase of the "modern" newspaper, under James I, was the single relation, an account written long after the occurrence, often mentioning only the year (e.g., Nathaniel Newberry's "Newes out of Holland: Concerning Barnevelt and his fellow-prisoners their conspiracy against their native country, with the enemies thereof," 1619). The full title provided a detailed summary and covered the entire frontispiece.

The second stage was a series of relations called a coranto. The earliest known in English was a translation of a Dutch coranto published in 1620 in Amsterdam by Pieter van den Keere. The "Weekly Newes from Italy, Germanyie, Hungarie, Spaine and France" appeared in 1621, probably published by Nathaniel Butter. He, Thomas Archer, and Nicholas Bourne dominated this genre, bringing out numerous examples until Star Chamber suspended publication of foreign news in 1632. In 1638 Bourne and Butter received letters patent to print news from abroad, promising to publish nothing dishonorable to the king's allies, and continued publishing until 1642. The coranto appeared weekly, with gaps, providing information from the countries on the title page, which changed weekly and often described itself as a "continuation" of the previous week. Early corantos printed only foreign news since the Crown allowed printing of only trivial domestic news items. Some issued in English were printed in Amsterdam by Jan van Hilten.

The third stage was the diurnall, a weekly account of occurrences over successive days. Robert Cole and Samuel Pecke were the most important practitioners in England. Their copy was largely drawn from parliament's affairs, especially in the 1640s. Publication frequency was dictated by daily events. The fourth stage was the mercury, a book with a title page and an imprint. This word first appeared in the *Mercurius Gallo-Belgius*, a Latin publication from the late 1580s, which provided a continuous account of central European affairs. Copies penetrated into England but were mainly distributed at continental trade fairs.

The Civil War and Interregnum* witnessed the flowering of English journalism. At the end of the 1630s, most London printing offices were controlled by the Stationers; the rest were in the hands of John Haviland, Miles Flesher, and Robert Young, partners who bought several established houses. But the Long Parliament* rescinded the Stationers' privileges and in 1641 abolished Star Chamber (see Prerogative Courts*), so that the repressive 1637 decree lost its force. For a brief period, printers took advantage of the uncertain political situation to print and sell books without license or entry, and patents were openly infringed. With opposing armies on the move, presses operated in numerous places. Even before Charles I moved to Oxford, printing speeches and accounts of the turmoil in parliament became more frequent despite legal prohibitions. Hundreds, sometimes thousands, of handwritten copies of speeches circulated at the beginning of the 1640s. With so much to record, space became valuable and the newsbook format gave way to something resembling today's newspaper. Archer, Butter, and Bourne found their publications outmoded, since they did not include domestic news, and they went out of business.

Between 1640 and the Restoration*, 30,000 news publications and pamphlets appeared in London; all forms developed since the 1580s survived (*Compleat Angler*, "a discourse on fish and fishing" published in 1653, became a classic). The number of printers grew to about sixty, with increasing demand for cheap books, an unceasing flow of political pamphlets, and a rapidly growing periodical trade. Civil War journalists were more guarded since reports of battles and other affairs were not always reliable. Both Lords and Commons tried to reassert control over the London presses, appointing censors and licensers of printed books, though effective control did not return until Charles II* was restored. For the time being, journalists published as much as they dared. Printers, writers, and licensers had to balance truthfulness, impartiality, loyalty to causes, and service to the reader with the need for profit and to joust constantly with authority. Almost every writer and printer during this period spent time in prison for overstepping constantly changing boundaries.

In 1643 parliament reinvested the Stationers with the search and seizure powers of the 1637 act. In protest John Milton* published *Doctrine and Discipline of Divorce* without license or entry; when the Stationers took unsuccessful action against him in parliament, he wrote without license his famous advocacy for a free press, *Areopagitica, A Speech for the Liberty of Unlicensed Printing* (1644). Further decrees to control printing would come in 1647 and 1649. Many publications calling themselves "A Continuation of . . ." were actually outright piratings. Plagiarism and counterfeiting increased; journalists, subservient to political partisans, earned little respect; and pamphlet warfare increased so much that a 1649 act, a virtual revival of Star Chamber's decrees, imposed a forty shilling fine on anyone carrying or mailing seditious books or pamphlets. The act was renewed in 1652, but "disorderly" printing flourished.

Each side had propaganda organs. Sir John Berkenhead, a skillful Laudian controversialist, ran the king's from Oriel College, Oxford. His journal, *Mercurius*

Aulicus, reached 118 editions despite continual sieges and royalist* defeats. Published with a Sunday dateline to anger Puritans*, its insulting wit provoked continual ripostes from the parliamentary presses. Regularly smuggled into London, it was the royalists' voice, produced to raise morale by attacking parliament and Oliver Cromwell*. As the king's cause became hopeless, it exaggerated stalemates into victories and skirmishes into great battles. With the monarchy's collapse, Berkenhead became a secret agent on the Continent; at the Restoration* he returned to royal service in journalism.

Marchamont Nedham's *Mercurius Britanicus*, denounced by Berkenhead as all "lies," favored Puritans, attacked lords who defected to Oxford, insulted Henrietta Maria, and accused Charles I of becoming Catholic*. During the Commonwealth* parliament allowed only two news publications, one edited and written by Nedham. The Stationers' Company was reorganized under a new licensing system but with little more independence than a government department. Nedham concentrated on political news, even noting the future Charles II's* affairs. Three commissioners were appointed in 1655 to root out every publication except Nedham's *Politicus* and his *Publick Intelligencer*, which summarized the former twice weekly. During the Protectorate* Nedham defended Cromwell and the major generals*, attacking all other parties (royalists, republicans, Presbyterians*, Quakers*, Fifth Monarchy Men*). At its collapse he was criticized for his position as official propagandist, fired by the Commons, restored after writing a pamphlet explaining his position, and wrote inaccurate descriptions of the power struggle following Cromwell's death.

The Restoration was a bleak period for English journalism, with the press again controlled by royal prerogative*, though a new professionalism emerged in news journalism. Berkenhead was made licenser and Henry Muddiman, a schoolteacher, published *Mercurius Publius*, which set the tone for Charles II's return. Nedham fled to Holland, received a royal pardon, and continued to publish pamphlets, but he never returned to news journalism and lived in fear of recognition. Charles II and James II* encouraged a tight media policy with traditional government machinery and such innovations as a surveyor of the imprimery and printing presses with extensive powers of search and supervision by secretaries of state of incoming political information.

In May 1662 the Licensing Act* (14 Car. II, c. 33) established press censorship under which no "doctrine or opinion shall be asserted or maintained which is contrary to the Christian faith or the doctrine or discipline of the Church of England" (see Anglicanism*). The number of master printers was again reduced to twenty (excepting the king's and university printers); no more were admitted without approval of the archbishop of Canterbury and the bishop of London. All books had to be registered with the Stationers except acts of parliament, proclamations, and books or papers warranted by the king or his secretaries of state. Printing was restricted to Cambridge, London, Oxford, and York, and copies of new books had to be deposited with the keeper of the king's library and vice-chancellors of the universities. Originally for two years, the act was renewed until 1679, when it expired after the king prorogued parliament to prevent passage of the exclusion bill (see Exclusion Crisis*). Then Charles obtained legal authority to keep licensing going until 1695.

Shortly after the Restoration, Roger L'Estrange, who supported strong central control over publishing, was created surveyor of the press and given a monopoly to print "all Narratives of relacions not exceeding two sheets of paper and all advertisements." L'Estrange vested power to search and seize unlicensed printing in himself. However, some men still printed pamphlets without approval, and one, John Twynn, was executed for treason. Muddiman, pioneer of the gazette form in England and one of the period's foremost news writers, printed neatly summarized versions of newsletters from all over Europe with privileged information obtained from secretaries of state in whose Whitehall offices he worked, as well as from other contacts.

When the court shifted to Oxford due to the Plague of London* in 1665, L'Estrange stayed behind to edit his *Public Intelligencer*; he was compensated with a royal pension but remained as surveyor. Muddiman was summoned by the lord chamberlain's authority to edit the *Oxford Gazette*, printed by the university printer in the same format as his Bible. It continued as the *London Gazette*, published along with some advertising papers—*City Mercury*, *Weekly Advertisements*—commercial works licensed by L'Estrange solely for that purpose. After 1680 a penny post operated at hourly intervals within London, so printed materials could be quickly transported between the city and the suburbs.

The plague killed about eighty master printers, and the Great Fire of London* in 1666 destroyed presses, materials, premises, and stock of the booksellers, whose main base was in and around St. Paul's churchyard. Most were ruined; over 150,000 pounds of books were burned. It took all the Stationers' efforts to revive the industry. However, the system was still rigidly enforced by frequent persecutions. When William of Orange* landed in England, his secretary noted that in Exeter there was not a press on which he could print a manifesto.

Periodicals began to appear in 1665, when the Royal Society* started publishing *Philosophical Transactions*. *Gentleman's Journal*, the first miscellany, appeared monthly after January 1692. John Fell, dean of Christ Church and vice-chancellor of Oxford, restarted the "Learned Press," based on Laud's original plan. He set up a partnership in 1671, rented the university press (1672-1690), and equipped it with a foundry, matrices, punches, and type ("Fell Types"). He gave it to Oxford University in his will (1686).

During the Restoration the numerous obscure presses that had poured out partisan broadsides and pamphlets during the Civil War and Interregnum began publishing chapbooks. Popular stories, legendary tales, quips, and jests were printed by wandering chapmen ("Walking Stationers") on poor-quality paper sheets folded to make a small stitched book of eight pages and popular in towns and at country fairs, especially in northern England. Ballads and stories were illustrated by crude cuts, often having nothing to do with the subject.

The best-known music publishers during the second half of the seventeenth century were the Playfords. John, an Inner Temple bookseller, is best known for *The English Dancing Master* (eighteen editions, 1651-1728), an invaluable record of English popular melodies. Although the bulk of Playford's publications were printed from movable type, some of his later music books were engraved, such as the two-volume *Musick's Handmaid* (1678) and Henry Purcell's *Sonnatas of III Parts* (1683), the earliest known music engraved by Thomas Cross, who popularized music engraving in England. Playford's business was continued by his son Henry.

After James II fled England with the Glorious Revolution* of 1688, there was less reason for enforcing a licensing system, although attempts were made under William and Mary*. Royal power over the press, essential to divine right* theory, declined. By Anne's* reign (1702-1714) the Stationers' Company could not control clandestine domestic printing and importation of pirated copies. The booksellers appealed to parliament, which passed the groundbreaking Copyright Act in 1709. However, it also passed the Stamp Act in 1712, which taxed every printed sheet of paper used for books, newspapers, pamphlets, periodicals, or advertisements; it remained in effect until 1855.

Bibliography: C. Clair, *A History of Printing in Britain*, 1965; J. Feather, *A History of British Publishing*, 1988; A. Smith, *The Newspaper*, 1979.

Martin J. Manning

Privy Council. The Stuart privy council was a formally constituted body of the monarch's chief officials and advisers with its origins in early sixteenth-century administrative reforms. The privy council should not be confused with the king's counsel learned in the law, the Great Council, or the independent privy councils in Scotland* and Ireland*.

The privy council counseled the monarch and issued orders on his behalf. Parliamentary statutes, privy council orders, and royal proclamations formed the core of English law, which the council executed and enforced. The council's authority was derived from the king's, allowing it to act in matters of state, the public interest, and private legal cases. No matter was too small or too great for its consideration, but the Stuart council's fundamental duty was protecting England from foreign attack or domestic rebellion. The council accomplished this task by ordering the lord lieutenants'* maintenance of fortifications and regulation of the militia. The council also supervised the navy*, and councils of war were privy council subcommittees. Privy councilors and the chief English legal officials made up the court of Star Chamber (see Prerogative Courts*) until it was abolished by the Long Parliament* in 1641.

The council implemented taxes granted by parliament*—including subsidies, tonnage, and poundage—and punished defaulters. The council itself authorized and collected impositions*, forced loans*, and feudal dues such as ship money* to generate revenue when necessitated by war or the absence of parliament*. Peacekeeping duties of sheriffs* and justices of the peace (see Local Government*) were directed by the council. An example of this is the Book of Orders* (1631), intended to standardize local administration of existing poor relief legislation (see Poor Laws and Poverty*). The council also mandated corporate maintenance of highways and sanitation standards. The council called out the militia or sent serjeants-at-arms and messengers of the chamber to help local and corporate authorities suppress serious or widespread disorders. The council adjudicated petitions from individuals seeking pensions, restitution, or relief from oppression, including kidnapping and riots. Persons unable to pursue justice in the law courts (see Common Law and Courts*) because of hardship were also heard by the council.

Many of the early Stuart council's powers, appropriated by parliament during the Civil Wars* and Interregnum*, were not revived with the Restoration* of the monarchy in 1660. Most of the later Stuart council's business was colonial administration (see Colonization*). Charles II's* council could not impose taxation*, for example, without the consent of parliament, which also managed the navy and the new standing army*. The council's local regulatory and judicial roles were reduced as well.

The Stuart privy council was composed of the great officers of state (including the archbishop of Canterbury), the chief officers of the royal household, and other nobles appointed on the basis of social status, intimacy with the king, or political expediency. New monarchs customarily retained their predecessor's councilors, and all councilors were sworn to office by oath and served at the king's pleasure. James I* doubled the size of the council he inherited from Elizabeth I, and his son and grandsons redoubled it. A parliamentary initiative to limit council membership and add commoners to Charles II's council during the Exclusion Crisis* (1679-1681) failed.

A small, specialized bureaucracy assisted the Stuart council. The lord president's sole duty was that of moderator, but the office was usually vacant. Four clerks on a quarterly schedule took minutes of meetings, wrote council orders, and kept a register of council business. The keeper of the chamber served as doorkeeper and supplied writing materials and fuel. The keeper of the chest arranged for storage and transportation of council documents.

Because of its wide mandate, the early Stuart council met twice weekly, more often if necessary. This frequency declined to weekly under Charles II and monthly under James II*, corresponding to the council's declining power. Only councilors living in and around the royal court* were expected to attend on a regular basis. All four Stuart kings followed a pattern of attending all or almost all council meetings in times of crisis and far fewer meetings in times of calm. The council met most often in its chamber at the palace of Whitehall, traveling occasionally with or to the king for meetings outside London*.

James I's council began appointing ad hoc specialized committees to handle specific matters quickly and efficiently. These committees had a fixed number of members, usually some of the most active councilors. Committees drew up reports and were dissolved when the council approved the report. Eventually standing committees proved more efficient for addressing perennial problems such as trade* issues. Charles I* used committees to circumvent the body of the council for reasons of secrecy and expediency, thereby isolating himself and a small group of advisers from the rest of the country. As part of the Nineteen Propositions* (1642), the Long Parliament advocated strict rules to force the king to consult the whole council. Charles I refused these restrictions, and Charles II continued sidestepping the restored council by working primarily with a single powerful committee. During the Exclusion Crisis, parliament again objected to this exclusive use of committees and demanded that no business be considered by a council committee unless first considered by the whole council. Charles II adhered to those reforms for only a short time, and the later Stuarts continued conducting most council business in autonomous committees. Their council was viewed increasingly as a pro forma body and membership in it as an honor rather than a position of power. These developments paved the way for the emergence of formalized cabinet government* in the eighteenth century.

Bibliography: J. P. Kenyon, ed., *The Stuart Constitution, 1603-1688*, 2d ed., 1986; Edward Raymond Turner, *The Privy Council of England in the Seventeenth and Eighteenth Centuries, 1603-1784*, 2 vols., 1927.

Sabrina Alcorn Baron

Proclamations, Royal. The power to issue proclamations was one of the customary common law* prerogatives of the English Crown (see Prerogative, Royal*). Proclamations were royal edicts or ordinances. They could be seen as acts of legislation issued by the king alone or, more usually, with the advice of his council (see Privy Council*), though very few Stuart thinkers saw the matter in these terms. To state the legislative nature of proclamations too clearly was to risk suggesting that they could make laws of the same force as common law or statute law, and this no one seems to have believed.

Henry VIII's Act of Proclamations (31 Hen. VIII, c. 28) had attempted to give statutory definition to the authority of proclamations, but it was repealed in 1547. Thus in the early Stuart period, proclamations rested on the common law for their authority. There seems to have been a broad consensus with regard to what this meant. The judges in fact gave a ruling on the matter in 1610, which was reported by Sir Edward Coke* (12 Co. Rep. 74). The judges declared that a proclamation could not alter common law, statute law, or the customs of the realm. Nor could it make illegal what was hitherto legal. The only punishments that could be employed for transgression of a proclamation were fines and imprisonment. No proclamation could touch body or member, nor could they be used to confiscate property or interfere in any way with common law property rights. Proclamations were normally enforced in the Star Chamber (see Prerogative Courts*). It seems that Coke's report was incomplete, however. The judges also recognized that the king could issue proclamations relating to certain prerogative powers (the making of war and peace, control of the coinage*, pardoning), which were enforceable in the ordinary courts, and that in situations of necessity, a proclamation might be the vehicle for declaring that necessity had made something an offense that had not been an offense before.

Although the judge's resolutions of 1610 had little impact, they are important in delineating a position that most people accepted. The jurist Sir Matthew Hale (1609-1676), after the Restoration*, gave a very similar account of the power of proclamation, emphasizing the same limitations and functions, though he also mentions that the king was given power by statute to issue proclamations on some specific points. The situation after 1660 was different, however, in one crucial respect: the abolition of the court of Star Chamber in 1641 meant that proclamations not enforceable in the ordinary courts could not be enforced at all.

Throughout the Stuart period, any conflict over the matter of proclamations tended to take place at the practical rather than the theoretical level. The frequent use of proclamations early in James I's* reign, coupled with their use in unpopular matters, was complained about in the parliament of 1610*. There were fears that proclamations would achieve the force of (common or statute) law. But James accepted much the same constitutional theory on the subject as his subjects did and acted quickly to remedy the abuses. He nevertheless maintained, with his judges it would seem, that the power to issue proclamations was a necessary supplement to the law, for it enabled a rapid and flexible response to new problems. The events of 1610 reveal, more than anything else, a consensus on the subject of proclamations. It persisted throughout the century. Discussion of proclamations in the 1620s, for example, usually challenged particular proclamations, not the general principle behind them. Sometimes, too, the question of proclamations could become entangled with other issues, as in the debates on monopolies* in the parliament of 1621*.

The range of subjects dealt with in proclamations was broad throughout the Stuart period. Before the Civil War*, proclamations were used, for example, to regulate the coinage, foreign trade*, the army* and navy*, religious observance, prices and other commercial practices, weights and measures, and building in London*. They were also used in the control of the printing* press, being used to condemn such controversial works as Dr. John Cowell's *Interpreter* (1610), and Roger Manwaring's *Religion and Allegiance* (1628). After the Restoration (and therefore after the abolition of Star Chamber) the function of proclamations seems to have narrowed a little. Many now served simply to reinforce the provisions of statute or common law, but they were also used extensively in naval, military, and foreign affairs, to promote trade and industry, and to regulate the press. Most controversial, proclamations were still a major vehicle for the exercise of royal authority in ecclesiastical affairs.

Bibliography: Rudolph W. Heinze, "Proclamations and Parliamentary Protest, 1539-1610," in DeLloyd J. Guth and John W. McKenna, eds., *Tudor Rule and Revolution: Essays for G. R. Elton from his American Friends*, 1982; William Holdsworth, *A History of English Law*, 13 vols., 1922-1952: vols. 4 and 6.

Glenn Burgess

Protectorate (1653-1659). Oliver Cromwell's* Protectorate began in December 1653 with the adoption of the Instrument of Government*. This second experiment in governance within six months was part of a series of attempts in the 1650s to achieve the impossible: to clothe the rule of the sword in some sort of constitutional form and to achieve consensus about the fundamental nature of government. When the army* ousted the Rump Parliament* in April 1653, constitutional links with the past were severed. The army was the power behind the governments of the 1650s. A group of army officers, including Cromwell, wrote the Instrument.

Britain was governed by the Instrument until 1657, when it was replaced by the Humble Petition and Advice*. Cromwell, like the Stuarts, did not get on well with his Protectorate Parliaments*, which were so badly divided that they could not agree on the nature of government. Unlike the Stuarts, he used the army on three occasions to exclude undesirable members or to dissolve parliament*. Cromwell and the council of state* ruled more by ordinance than by parliament.

Because of the danger of being overthrown by his opponents, Cromwell established military rule in 1655 by dividing the country into military districts headed by major generals*. His resort to the military was a blunder, for he brought the army to everyone's doorstep and thus intensified civilian hatred of the military. The major generals interfered in the elections of 1656 and vigorously enforced the reformation of manners in their districts. They were reminiscent of Charles I's* policy of "thorough"* in the 1630s. Because of parliamentary pressure, military rule was ended within twenty-two months. Government under the Instrument became increasingly unsatisfactory, and in June 1657 yet another change in governance occurred with the adoption of the Humble Petition and Advice. The Petition marks another step in the movement toward more traditional political institutions. Although Cromwell was offered the Crown, he refused it after considerable hesitation because of army opposition. Yet when he was installed as lord protector in June 1657, he had the symbolic trappings of monarchy except for the Crown. Consensus was still impossible. The Petition was immediately attacked in parliament and was in danger of being rejected. Cromwell in anger dissolved what was to be his last parliament. At his death in September 1658, there was no more agreement on the issue of governance than in 1653.

Cromwell was also seriously threatened by attempts to assassinate or overthrow him. Royalists*, at home and in exile, constantly plotted to overturn the government and posed the added danger of an alliance with a continental power. Anabaptists, such as the Fifth Monarchy Men*, hoped to hasten the arrival of the millennium by killing Cromwell (see Millenarianism*). A vicious and widely circulated pamphlet, *Killing No Murder,* suggested that Cromwell's death would be good for the country. In response to these threats, the definition of treason was broadened in 1654.

Secretary John Thurloe* of necessity organized an intelligence system that was legendary in Europe for the rest of the century. He permeated anti-government groups at home and abroad and, acting on advanced information, squashed every plot against Cromwell. Though there were several close calls, Thurloe's reputation as "the master spy" was well deserved.

As an Independent*, Cromwell believed in religious toleration, which he practiced as lord protector. Except for the limitations in the Instrument excluding popery and prelacy and in the Humble Petition requiring a belief in the Trinity and the sacredness of the Scriptures, the triers* licensed preachers from various sects if they were persons of godliness, integrity, and good conversation and fit to preach the gospel. He tolerated Catholics* and effected the readmission of the Jews* extralegally in 1656. During the Protectorate, more than one form of worship could legally be practiced for the first time in English history.

Cromwell is perhaps best known for his "reformation of manners." Theaters, which were closed in 1642, remained illegal, though plays were surreptitiously performed. Dueling, cockfighting, horse racing, and superfluous alehouses were outlawed. Cromwell did not disapprove of all of these practices; rather, his goal was to reduce crowds and opportunities for his opponents to meet. The major generals, however, were enthusiastic "moral inquisitors" and vigorously enforced the ordinances. Local officials disliked their meddling, and the populace hated their interference with their pleasures. Evidence indicates that they had little long-term impact (see Popular Culture*).

Cromwell pursued the most aggressive foreign policy since Elizabeth I's reign. He quickly ended the unpopular First Dutch War* (1652-1654) on favorable terms, and he signed an uneasy alliance with France in 1655. He talked about a Protestant crusade and aided persecuted Protestants on the Continent. He was lured into what he thought would be a cheap war with Spain in 1655. Cadiz was blockaded, the plate fleet intercepted, and Dunkirk captured. His real aim, however, was to gain a foothold in the Spanish-dominated West Indies. He sent an expedition to capture Santo Domingo, but it was mismanaged and an embarrassing failure. His generals captured Jamaica on the rebound. The Spanish War of 1655-1659* was expensive and unpopular. But Cromwell's policy marks the beginning of systematic attempts by England to build an overseas empire.

Cromwell died on 3 September 1658, and the Protectorate crumbled within seven months. It had been held together for five years by respect for Cromwell and his strength of character. Political consensus had been impossible, and the unconstitutionality of the Protectorate could be resolved only by the Restoration*. Only two concrete Protectorate reforms were adopted after the Restoration; the abolition of dueling and, most important, the outlawing of feudal tenure.

Since the time of Gilbert Burnet*, the earl of Clarendon (Edward Hyde*), and Laurence Echard, all historians contemporary to the Protectorate, much has been written about the period. More has been written about Cromwell, including much nonsense, than about the Protectorate. Cromwell has been viewed as the prototype of the modern dictator and as the precursor of the Victorian liberal. C. H. Firth's *Oliver Cromwell* (1900, 1953) is still useful. The best modern efforts to understand Cromwell are R. S. Paul's *The Lord Protector* (1953) and Lady Antonia Fraser's *Cromwell* (1973). Christopher Hill's *God's Englishman* (1970) is as revealing about the author's interpretation of the period as about Cromwell. More recent additions to the literature include John Morrill, ed., *Oliver Cromwell and the English Revolution* (1990) and Barry Coward, *Oliver Cromwell* (1991).

The best detailed political narratives of the Protectorate are the old Whig interpretations of S. R. Gardiner, *The History of the Commonwealth and Protectorate* (4 vols., 1903), and C. H. Firth's follow-up, *The Last Years of the Protectorate* (2 vols., 1913). Godfrey Davies, *The Restoration* (1955), is the best detailed history of the 1658-60 period. The best succinct modern analysis of the Protectorate is by Ivan Roots, *Commonwealth and Protectorate* (1966). Christopher Hill's numerous works, though controversial because of his Marxist approach, have broadened our understanding of the era and opened new vistas for research. Research into local history begun by E. M. Everitt in the 1960s marks a significant departure in the historical approach to the period. A few detailed local studies, such as David Underdown's *Somerset* (1973), have followed, but much remains to be done in local history. The seventeenth century has undergone fundamental revision, but the

Protectorate has been overshadowed by research in the Civil War era. Much research remains to be done on the 1650s.

Bibliography: Antonia Fraser, *Cromwell, Our Chief of Men*, 1973; Ivan Roots, *Commonwealth and Protectorate*, 1966.

Wilson J. Hoffman

Protectorate Parliaments (1654-1655, 1656-1658, 1659). Three parliaments met during the Protectorate* of the Cromwells. Between 1653 and 1657 parliaments existed by authority of the Instrument of Government* and differed from their predecessors in that they consisted only of the House of Commons, had to meet five months every three years, and had representatives from Ireland* and Scotland*. Members had to be of known integrity, fearing God, and of good conversation. Catholics* and anyone who had warred against parliament* since 1641 were ineligible to sit. Representation was redistributed in favor of counties with the franchise based on property. The house was subordinate to the lord protector and the council of state*.

The Instrument required the first parliament to meet in September 1654. Elections occurred in the summer and were heated but were not influenced by the government, many of whose opponents were elected. The house immediately resolved to debate the Instrument and especially whether government should be by one person and parliament. After five days Oliver Cromwell* addressed the house and informed it that the issue was not debatable. When members returned to their chamber, they found the doors guarded by soldiers who refused to admit anyone without a signed pledge not to alter the government as settled in one person and parliament. All but three members complied. The only constructive work of this parliament was to recognize the protector and parliament as supreme legislative authorities. Members debated the Instrument clause by clause, and some of the most heated debates in parliamentary history occurred. Cromwell lost patience and dissolved the house in January 1655. No legislation was passed.

Two events forced the government to issue writs of election for a new parliament in July 1656: the storm created by Cromwell's resort to military rule in 1655 and mounting debts due to the Spanish War of 1655-1659*. Elections were held in August 1656, which the government tried to influence in hopes of having a more amenable parliament. John Thurloe* worked with the major generals* to prevent the election of opponents, and he used legal technicalities to keep key republicans from being elected. His success was limited. After the opening ceremonies in September, members again found their chamber doors guarded by soldiers who refused admission to anyone who did not have a ticket of approval from the council of state. About 100 members were excluded, and forty-one additional members left in protest. The first session of this parliament was moderately productive.

Two events raised basic constitutional issues that determined the nature of debates in 1657. The case of James Nayler, a Quaker* who at Bristol had parodied Christ's entry into Jerusalem, was brought before parliament. Though the house had no judicial authority, it tried and punished Nayler. The house in effect impugned the validity of the Instrument. The attempt of Miles Sindercome to burn Whitehall in January 1657 raised the question of Cromwell's successor, about which the Instrument was unsatisfactory. In response to these and other problems, Sir Christopher Packe in February introduced a remonstrance urging, among other things, that the Crown be offered to Cromwell, that he be empowered to name his successor, and that parliament be bicameral. Packe's proposals ultimately resulted in a new constitution, the Humble Petition and Advice*, which was adopted in May 1657.

The second session of the parliament of 1656 met in January 1658. According to the Petition, parliament now had two houses, the House of Commons and "the Other House." Little is known about debates in the Other House. In the Commons, however, republicans resumed their seats and steered debate again to the nature of government. Debate on matters of national importance was stymied. Cromwell dissolved his last parliament on 4 February 1658 in anger.

Richard Cromwell* met his only parliament in January 1659. Thurloe failed to keep the opposition from being elected, and Richard's call for reconciliation was to no avail. He was no more able to control parliament than his father was. In 1659 parliament was divided, not only by the usual factions (Independents*, republicans, Anabaptists, and royalists*) but also by conflict between army and civilian members. The civilians refused to vote arrears to the army* and were determined to get control of it. In frustration Richard dissolved parliament on 22 April 1659. The dissolution effectively ended his Protectorate and began a year of anarchy.

The Protectorate Parliaments were barren. In part the Cromwells were in an impossible situation, for their parliaments reflected the deep political division of the country. The army's power was unacceptable to most people, and the fact that its political wishes could not be ignored was divisive and ultimately fatal. The Cromwells were also to blame for difficulties, for they were inept parliamentarians who made little effort to manage parliament. Ironically, Oliver, an admirer of Elizabeth I, did not emulate her methods of parliamentary management. It is also ironic that the only sovereign to serve in the house was its most incompetent manager.

Bibliography: Ivan Roots, *Commonwealth and Protectorate*, 1966; H. R. Trevor-Roper, "Oliver Cromwell and His Parliaments," in H. R. Trevor-Roper, *The Crisis of the Seventeenth Century*, 1956.

                                                                        Wilson J. Hoffman

Prynne, William (1600-1669). Lawyer and Puritan* controversialist, he was an irrepressible critic of Charles I's* royal court* and the religious policies of Archbishop William Laud* during the 1630s. He became a national hero in 1637, when he was tried for seditious libel, imprisoned, and suffered having his ears clipped.

Born during 1600 in Somerset, William Prynne graduated from Oriel College, Oxford, in 1621 and from there went on to study law at Lincoln's Inn. While in London* he developed into a strict Puritan, an adherent of Presbyterianism*, and an opponent of the growing power of Arminianism* within the Church of England (see Anglicanism*). The year 1627 marked the beginning of Prynne's controversial pamphleteering, which brought him popularity among the Calvinists* and hatred from the Arminian bishops. He published *Historio-Mastix*, an attack on the theater, in 1632. The government considered it to be a criticism of Queen Henrietta Maria's* participation in court masques, as well as a criticism of magistrates who allowed theaters to remain open. After imprisoning Prynne in the Tower of London, the court of Star Chamber (see Prerogative Courts*) tried and sentenced him to life imprisonment and to the first clipping of his ears in 1634.

While in prison Prynne continued to write pamphlets attacking the bishops and promoting Sabbatarianism*. This activity once more brought him before the Star Chamber in 1637, where he was convicted along with his fellow Puritan controversialists Henry Burton and John Bastwick of the crime of seditious libel. They were sentenced to large fines, the loss of the rest of their ears, and branding. Unfortunately for Charles I, the public pillorying and ear clipping of Prynne, Burton, and Bastwick resulted in popular demonstrations in their favor and a general discrediting of the government and the bishops. Afterwards, the three men were returned to prison, where they remained until the Long Parliament* released them in 1640.

Prynne supported the parliamentarian* cause in the First Civil War*. Although a religious Presbyterian*, he supported the Erastian position granting the state control over the church. He was an opponent of the army* and the Political Independents*, which resulted in his being barred from the parliament* and imprisoned during Pride's Purge* in 1648. Later he denounced Charles I's trial*, and starting in 1650 the government of the Commonwealth* imprisoned him for three years. Undeterred by such adversities, the uncompromising Prynne criticized first the Protectorate* and then the Restoration* monarchy of Charles II* until his death on 24 October 1669. Although his efforts were largely ineffectual after 1640, Prynne's earlier writings and criticisms helped to weaken the authority of Charles I and Archbishop Laud.

Bibliography: William Lamont, *Marginal Prynne, 1600-1669*, 1963.

Ronald H. Fritze

Puritanism. Over the years many historians have attempted to define the nature and composition of this ubiquitous and amorphous religious movement within English Protestantism. It is generally agreed that Puritans placed great emphasis on Bible* reading and living an activist Christian life. The problem is that many non-Puritans also shared those same emphases. Still, historians such as Christopher Hill and Lawrence Stone have tended to base their historical interpretations on that broad and loose definition. Others, like Michael Finlayson, have found such a descriptive definition to be so broad as to be meaningless because it places too many diverse people into the category of Puritans.

Other historians have added to the basic descriptive definition the requirement that Puritans sought a further reformation of religion. Thus Puritans were the people who felt that the Church of England (see Anglicanism*) had retained too many inappropriate and even dangerous remnants of the popish church of Rome (see Catholics*). Within this aspect of the definition of Puritanism, some historians insist that only those who worked to reform the Church of England from within should be called Puritans. As a result the various Separatist* groups are excluded from consideration as Puritans. Most historians, however, consider any definition of Puritanism that excludes Separatists to be too narrow. Still, some historians have tended to equate Puritanism with resurgent Presbyterianism* within the Church of England. The problem with that approach is that modern research has discovered that most Jacobean and Caroline Protestants were content with the episcopal structure of the Church of England. In effect they were episcopalian Puritans. It took the excesses of the Arminian* bishops and the turmoil of the Civil War* to reactivate the support for Presbyterianism that had been effectively suppressed by Archbishop John Whitgift during the latter half of Elizabeth's reign. Meanwhile Puritans obviously continued to exist in Jacobean and Caroline England, even while Presbyterianism was dormant. That makes Puritanism broader than merely Presbyterianism.

Many historians have pointed out that the name *Puritan* originated as an insult. That is generally how people living in the late sixteenth through the seventeenth centuries tended to use the word. For people of that era, a Puritan or "Precisian" was a sanctimonious hypocrite, a religious subversive, or both. On the other hand, the people whom historians tend to identify as Puritans referred to themselves as the Godly or Godly People or as professors of true religion. For Patrick Collinson, perhaps the leading authority on Elizabethan and Jacobean Protestantism, Puritans were a hotter or more enthusiastic sort of Calvinistic* Protestant in matters of social morals, church policies, and anti-Catholicism. The activities of Puritans that sought the uplifting of morality, promoted the further reformation of the church, and combated actual or imagined popery in English society constituted Puritanism. While some people find this definition to be overly loose, it has the virtue of being reasonably consistent with what is known about "Puritans" and "Puritanism" during the late sixteenth and the first half of the seventeenth centuries.

Collinson's conception of Puritanism has been bolstered by the research of Peter Lake and R. T. Kendall on the division within English Calvinists between credal and experimental (or experiential) Calvinism. Adherents of credal Calvinism accepted all aspects of Calvinistic doctrine, including predestination, as an intellectual system, but they also placed particular emphasis on the Calvinistic belief that it was impossible to determine those who were elected to salvation and those who were among the reprobate. As a result, credal Calvinists did not believe that the doctrine of predestination had or should have much impact on the policies of the church or the life of the individual Christian. They discouraged speculation and preaching about predestination because it would create an unanswerable and unnecessary anxiety about salvation among ordinary Christians. Instead credal Calvinists emphasized the role of the church in encouraging a proper obedience to authority among the laity.

Experimental Calvinists differed radically from credal Calvinists because they contended that predestination should have a large impact on the life of individual Christians. This contention stemmed from their belief that individual Christians could discover whether they were among the elect, although only God knew with certainty who was saved. If Christians determined that they were among the elect, they had a duty to attempt the transformation of the world into a godly society. This task meant they were engaged in an apocalyptic struggle with both the morally corrupt among their fellow Protestants and the anti-Christian machinations of the papacy and its English minions. Puritans adhered to experimental Calvinism, which was the source of their religious activism. That is not to say that all experimental Calvinists and the adherents of anti-papal opinions were Puritans. Many were not. The existence of experimental Calvinism, however, provides a convincing explanation for the activism and attitudes of English Puritans.

Connecting Puritanism to experimental Calvinism and the sternest aspects of predestinarian theology also helps to explain its rapid decline after the Restoration*. Richard Greaves has shown that significant religious radicalism survived the Restoration and the period of repression that followed (see Baptists*; Dissenters*; Quakers*). Still, the ultimate defeat of republicanism and Puritanism proved profoundly discouraging to the Godly People of English society. Popular support for extreme predestinarian ideas also suffered a decline after 1660, and the classic form of Puritanism faded, even though people like Richard Baxter* fought hard to preserve it.

Bibliography: Patrick Collinson, *English Puritanism*, 1983; Patrick Collinson, *The Religion of Protestants: The Church in English Society, 1559-1625*, 1982; Michael G. Finlayson, *Historians, Puritanism, and the English Revolution: The Religious Factor in English Politics before and after the Interregnum*, 1983; R. T. Kendall, *Calvin and English Calvinism to 1649*, 1979; Peter Lake, "Calvinism and the English Church, 1570-1635," *Past and Present* 114 (1987): 32-76.

                                                                                   Ronald H. Fritze

Putney Debates (1647). The debates in the general council of the army* (and its committees) held in late October and early November 1647, which began in the church at Putney (in Surrey), were primarily about the proposals for settlement that the army should put to the king. A detailed and accurate record of the first three days of debate (28-29 October and 1 November) was kept by William Clarke, secretary to the army council. These sessions of the general council were initiated in order to discuss the radical proposals put forward by a small group of army agents stirred up by the Leveller* leader John Lilburne* and others. The proposals were contained in *The Case of the Armie Truly Stated* and in the first Agreement of the People* and went much beyond those contained in the army's own Heads of the Proposals* of July-August 1647. It was the Agreement, read to the council on 28 October, that formed the basis of the recorded debates. Most prominent in defending its proposals were Colonel Thomas Rainsborough and two civilian Levellers invited to the meeting, John Wildman and Maximilian Petty; the burden of presenting the contrary case was taken up chiefly by Oliver Cromwell* and, above all, Henry Ireton*.

On the first day (28 October), following the reading of the Agreement, discussion focused on the question of whether the army was bound by its previous engagements and declarations to principles incompatible with those in the new radical proposals. Cromwell and Ireton argued that the army had already bound itself to preserving and defending king, Lords, and Commons; their opponents tried to argue that it was impossible to be bound morally, even by one's own engagements, to defend something that was inherently unjust.

The second day of debate (29 October) was not a formal session of the general council of the army and may have been a meeting of a committee, set up during the debates on the previous day, to consider the Levellers' proposals in the light of the army's previous engagements. It met at the quarters of the quartermaster-general. The meeting began with much expression of uncertainty about its purpose and agenda, but eventually the Agreement of the People was read, and debate focused on its first article. That article appears to have been concerned with the need to establish electorates of roughly equal population, but Ireton took it as implying a demand for universal manhood suffrage. He argued that such a demand was contrary to the ancient constitution, upon which all "civil right" depended and which rightly decided that political power should be in the hands of those with "a permanent fixed interest" (property) in the nation. Government existed to protect that property, and giving a voice to the propertyless would endanger this protection. Rainsborough at least was prepared to defend what Ireton excoriated, asserting that "every man that is under a government ought first by his own consent to put himself under that government." Others were more guarded, and Petty wished to enfranchise only those "that have not lost their birthright." The qualification was ambiguous; it may have covered no more than royalists* but could possibly have excluded apprentices, servants, beggars, and wage earners as well. These latter groups Petty was to specify as possible exclusions later in the day, following a compromise suggestion made by Captain Edmund Rolfe. Though the day's proceedings descended into acrimony and Clarke's record of them breaks off abruptly, it is possible that the committee did reach a decision to extend the franchise to all save beggars and servants, which is broadly what Rolfe proposed.

Clarke's record of a third day of debate is again of a session of the general council of the army, though ad hoc committee meetings occurred on the preceding days. The debates on 1 November did not initially consider, as seems to have been intended, the conclusions reached in committee over the previous days but instead became a discussion of the king's legislative veto. Eventually the committee proposals were given a reading. The meeting adjourned without much agreement being achieved. At this point Clarke's record ends, though both the general council and its committee continued to meet over the following days. While concentration on the franchise question can distort the historical significance of the Putney Debates, it is undeniable that the discussion of manhood suffrage on 29 October gave the debates an assured place in the history of democratic thought.

Bibliography: A. S. P. Woodhouse, ed., *Puritanism and Liberty: Being the Army Debates (1647-9) from the Clarke Manuscripts*, 1951; Austin Woolrych, *Soldiers and Statesmen: The General Council of the Army and its Debates, 1647-1648*, 1987.

Glenn Burgess

Pym, John (1584-1643). The man whose leadership of the opponents of Charles I's* policies in the Long Parliament* earned him the derogatory sobriquet "King Pym" was born 20 May 1584 in Somerset. His father died when he was four. He grew up among the thoroughly Puritan* kindred of his stepfather, Sir Anthony Rous of Halton St. Dominic in Cornwall. Pym's stepbrother Sir Francis Rous, a vigorous Puritan and anti-Arminian, remained close to him throughout his political career. Pym studied at Broadgates Hall, Oxford, and the Middle Temple, London*, and in 1607 he was appointed receiver of Crown lands* for Wiltshire, Hampshire, and Gloucestershire. After the death of his wife, Anne Hooke of Bramshott in Hampshire, he did not remarry. Until the beginning of his parliamentary career in 1621, little is known about him. In the parliament of 1621*, his first speech demanded the punishment of a fellow member who had denounced a bill for being "Puritan." Throughout his career Pym was deeply opposed to Roman Catholicism* and thus concerned to promote unity among Protestants as a means of maintaining a common front against the Catholics.

In the parliament of 1624*, Pym initiated the attack on the alleged theological Arminianism* of a cleric, Richard Montagu (appointed bishop of Chichester by Charles I in 1628). Thinking he could count on the Calvinist* orthodoxy of James I*, Pym believed he was sounding an alarm that the king would heed. In the parliament of 1625*, Pym held a seat that was in the gift of Francis Russell (earl of Bedford from 1627). Pym continued his drive to impeach "Arminian" clergy (for him tantamount to Roman Catholics) in 1625 and thereafter. By 1626 he had concluded that the Arminian cause was being advanced by Charles I and his favorite, the 1st duke of Buckingham (George Villiers*). In the parliaments of 1626* and 1628*, Pym was selected to present the Commons's case against Montagu to the House of Lords, but the sessions ended before he could do so. In 1628 Pym joined in the struggle for the Petition of Right* for atypical reasons. Lacking a county power base of his own, Pym was unlike many members whose main concerns were to preserve local autonomy against central encroachment and to oppose royal taxation* because their constituents disliked it. He supported efforts to vote the king additional moneys because he knew that otherwise the English parliament* might disappear, as had representative assemblies elsewhere in Europe. His goal was an English Crown powerful enough to defend the doctrines he considered "Protestant" against the forces of the Counter-Reformation.

During Charles I's Personal Rule*, Pym worked closely with groups of peers and gentlemen, many of them Puritan, in the Saybrooke (Connecticut), Providence Island, and Massachusetts Bay companies. They sought to establish colonies in America where Puritan worship could occur free of the ceremonialism favored by Archbishop William Laud* and the king (see Colonization*). Pym and his colleagues gained the forum they needed when Charles I's failure to suppress the prayer book rebellion in Scotland forced him to call the Short Parliament* in 1640. Four days after the session began, Pym and Rous made powerful speeches stating the subjects' grievances on religious and constitutional grounds. In the Long Parliament*, Pym's great political skills were employed at every decisive moment. He was intimately involved in negotiations with the king for a settlement that would have brought him and his friends into the privy council* early in 1641. He managed the campaign to bring down Charles's hated adviser, Thomas Wentworth*, earl of Strafford, and to get the king to sign a bill prohibiting the dissolution of the parliament without its consent. Like many other members of the Long Parliament, Pym was shocked and frightened by indications that Catholic plotters were influencing royal decisions (e.g., the Army Plots*), and he used these fears to advance his agenda among members of parliament and the citizenry of London. News of the Irish Rebellion* greatly stimulated fears of "popery" and assisted Pym's drive toward passage of the Grand Remonstrance* by the House of Commons in November 1641. The king's failed bid to arrest the Five Members*, one of whom was Pym, was an outrageous breach of parliamentary privilege that had the effect of stiffening the resolve of his opponents and making a negotiated escape from the drift toward Civil War* more unlikely than ever.

It had never been Pym's goal to make parliament sovereign and Charles I a puppet, but when the First Civil War* began in the summer of 1642, he could preserve what had been gained only by working to enable the parliamentarians* to resist the king militarily. In the time that remained before his death on 8 December 1643, Pym continued to walk a fine line between extremist positions, either one of which would have doomed his cause politically. He blocked both those who would have given up what had been won for peace and those who wanted total victory over royalism*. Ironically some of the means to this end (e.g., the passage of ordinances establishing the excise tax and the weekly assessment) came to be no less hated than the fiscal feudalism of Charles I in the 1630s.

Besides the fiscal structure Pym created, the most important component of his strategy was the Scottish alliance, which was consummated in September 1643. It may be doubted that he would have approved of Charles I's trial and execution* or of the growth of sectarianism that occurred as the decade wore on. But the parliamentarians would almost certainly have lost the Civil War without the groundwork that Pym laid.

Bibliography: J. H. Hexter, *The Reign of King Pym,* 1941; Conrad Russell, "The Parliamentary Career of John Pym, 1621-29," in Peter Clark, A. G. R. Smith, Nicholas Tyacke, eds., *The English Commonwealth,* 1979; Conrad Russell, *The Fall of the British Monarchies, 1637-42,* 1991.

J. Sears McGee

Q

Quakers. The Religious Society of Friends, commonly known as the Quakers, was founded by George Fox* (1624-1691) during the chaos of seventeenth-century England as a protest against the formalism and uniformity of the state religion. Known originally as Children of the Light, Publishers of Truth, Friends of Truth, and eventually as the Religious Society of Friends, they received their popular name, Quakers, from a magistrate who used the term in 1650 in response to Fox's statement in court, "to tremble at the word of the Lord." Originally a term of derision, it also applied to people who shook or quaked during religious experiences.

The doctrine of the inner light, the voice of God that spoke to each human, became the core of Quaker thought. It was a seed of divinity within each soul, and thus one could have an immediate experience of the divine. By following the light, the disciple came to know right from wrong. Consequently one arrived at the knowledge of God without the aid of externals or intermediaries. At worship the Quakers sat in silence and waited for the word of God to speak. Reacting against "steeple houses" and a "hireling ministry," Quakers disavowed sacraments, ceremonies, and an organized ministry. The inner light created a priesthood of all believers and a spiritual equality, though "elders" supervised worship and "overseers" took care of pastoral concerns of the group.

Consequently the Quakers developed practices that challenged contemporary social and ecclesiastical conventions. They did not pay tithes or take oaths, rejected conscription and compulsory church attendance, and refused to use titles or to doff their hats to a superior. In speech they used the terms *thee* and *thou* instead of the formal *you*. Quakers avoided the fine arts, sports, and dancing and dressed plainly. They denounced formal creeds and externals of religion, and they shared the anti-papal bias of the age. Departing from traditional Christian customs, they practiced a spiritual baptism and communion. In the spirit of equality, the Quakers also preached the equality of women*, abhorred slavery, advocated educational and prison reforms, and supported numerous social programs.

On account of these principles, Quakers suffered some persecution during the first half of the seventeenth century at the hands of the Puritans*, but because of the limited religious toleration associated with the Commonwealth*, their membership increased. The Restoration* of Charles II* in 1660 and the Clarendon Code* ended toleration for non-Anglicans. In 1664 and 1670, for example, two Conventicle Acts (16 Car. 11, c. 4; 22 Car. 11, c. 1) accounted for persecutions and numerous mass arrests of the Quakers. The 1664 act prohibited meetings for worship in homes by more than five people (in addition to members of the family) who did not worship according to the Book of Common Prayer. Records estimate that approximately 13,562 were imprisoned, over 500 died in gaol, and 198 were transported. In 1666, Fox believed that 1,000 of his disciples were in prison.

Their courage won them many converts, such as the theologian Robert Barclay (1648-1690), William Penn (1644-1718), and Isaac Penington (1616-1679). In 1681, after obtaining a grant from Charles II, Penn founded Pennsylvania, the "Holy Experiment" based on Quaker principles, especially freedom of religion. This colony soon became a refuge for Quakers fleeing the persecutions in England. The Quakers experienced a taste of religious freedom in 1687 and 1688 when James II* (1685-1688) issued two Declarations of Indulgence* giving liberty of conscience to his subjects. After the Glorious Revolution* of 1688, penalties against Quakers and other Nonconformists were removed by the 1689 Toleration Act (I Gul. & Mar., c. 18). Quakers were allowed to make an affirmation rather than take an oath. Nonconformists were eventually admitted to civil office in 1828.

Fox had no plans to establish another religious sect. He believed each person should rely on the inner light for inspiration and action, but Fox soon came to realize that some organization was necessary for worship and business. The basic unit of Quaker organization was the meeting. Monthly meetings dealt with the business of a town or small area. Representing a larger area such as a county, monthly meetings came together for fellowship, worship, and business in the quarter meeting. The yearly meeting legislated for the entire body. These meetings registered births, marriages, and deaths, and made provisions for the poor. After the Restoration, Fox required a separate woman's monthly meeting for business. Established in 1675, the meeting for suffering, which met monthly in London*, addressed concerns growing out of their persecution.

Quakers believed that divine guidance would direct the deliberations of these gatherings, and thus they would sit in silence and allow inspiration to work in a manner similar to worship. They did not debate or vote on matters discussed, but instead waited for a consensus, recorded by a clerk, to emerge from the meeting.

The main beliefs of the Quakers are contained in Barclay's *Theologiae Verae Christianae Apologia* (1676), which emphasized how the Quakers differed from other Christians, and Penn's *Primitive Christianity* (1696), which stressed the similarities between the Quakers and the early Christian church. Numerous tracts by Fox, pamphlets by Penington, and communications from the yearly meetings also contain the main beliefs of the Quakers. With the death of their founders and the arrival of religious toleration, the Quakers lost some of their original zeal and fervor and lapsed into quietism.

Bibliography: Hugh Barbour, *The Quakers in Puritan England*, 1964; W. C. Braithwaite, *The Beginnings of Quakerism*, 1955.

René Kollar

R

Raleigh, Sir Walter (c.1552-1618). A controversial figure during both Elizabeth and James I's* reigns, Raleigh personified Renaissance versatility; he was a poet, historian, courtier, explorer, and colonist.

Born in Devon, Raleigh briefly attended Oxford, then fought in France on the Huguenot side for several years. When Raleigh returned to London*, he quickly became a favorite of Queen Elizabeth, who showered him with gifts of land and lucrative government appointments. Although the anecdote told by Thomas Fuller about Raleigh's throwing his cloak over a puddle for the queen to walk over may be apocryphal, he was nonetheless her dear "Water" until his clandestine marriage in 1592 to Elizabeth Throckmorton, one of the queen's ladies-in-waiting, led to his disgrace and brief imprisonment.

Raleigh was always engaged in several projects. He was a tireless advocate of colonization* and trade*, and between 1584 and 1589 he sent three expeditions to found a colony on Roanoke Island near North Carolina, which Raleigh named Virginia in honor of his ruler, the Virgin Queen. Unfortunately these settlements were unsuccessful, and when Raleigh's marriage led to a falling out with the queen, he was unable to send subsequent expeditions. The information gathered from these trips, however, was invaluable to future explorers.

Raleigh's next project, conceived in part to regain the queen's favor, was a trip to the Orinoco River in 1595 to discover gold in the region of El Dorado. Although Raleigh did not find the legendary city, he returned with some gold and wrote an account of his trip, *The Discovery of the Large, Rich, and Beautiful Empire of Guiana* (1596).

When James succeeded to the throne in 1603, he had already formed an ill opinion of Raleigh, thanks to Raleigh's enemies at the royal court*. Raleigh was notoriously anti-Spanish, whereas James was anxious to keep peace with Spain. Furthermore, James disliked Raleigh's alleged atheism, as well as his promotion of tobacco, a drug James considered repellent.

Right after James's accession, Raleigh was arrested on trumped-up charges of conspiracy with Spain to place Arabella Stuart* on the throne. During his trial, led by Sir Edward Coke*, Raleigh conducted himself so well that popular opinion grew sympathetic and saw Raleigh as the victim of a setup. He was nonetheless condemned to death, though James commuted his sentence to imprisonment in the Tower of London, where Raleigh stayed for almost thirteen years with his family.

In 1616 Raleigh was released to lead another expedition to Guiana in search of gold, on the condition that he would not fight with the Spanish settlers; unfortunately, there was a battle with the Spanish in which Raleigh's son Walter was killed. When Raleigh returned to England, James had him beheaded.

In his lifetime, few of Raleigh's poems were printed, and the publishing history of his verse has been plagued with questions of dates and authorship. Among the more famous poems are his cynical reply to Christopher Marlowe's "The Passionate Shepherd" and a long tribute to Elizabeth, "The Ocean to Cynthia," which is now lost, although a 520-line fragment in Raleigh's own handwriting is still extant. Raleigh wrote many of his prose works during his imprisonment, including numerous political treatises, a guidebook of parental advice, and, most important, the beginning of his ambitious *History of the World*. Many of Raleigh's writings were dedicated to his friend Prince Henry* of Wales, who unlike his father appreciated Raleigh's many talents (see Historical Thought*; Literature*; Political Thought*).

Bibliography: Stephen Greenblatt, *Sir Walter Raleigh*, 1973; E. A. Strathman, *Raleigh: A Study in Elizabethan Skepticism*, 1951.

Jo Eldridge Carney

Ranters. Pejorative term given to a supposed radical Protestant sect, largely comprised of urban poor, with significant representation in the army*, first identified after the death of Charles I*. The movement, if it could be called such, was active throughout the 1650s and had neither a recognized leader nor organization. Its members championed pantheism, mysticism, a pronounced rejection of social and contemporary religious convention, and militant skepticism.

Radical millenarian* hopes of a society ready to usher in King Jesus faded after the dissolution of the monarchy, with the consolidation of power by moderate and conservative Puritan* elements. Radical anger and frustration grew, along with a conviction that the Reformation was left incomplete, if not deliberately betrayed. These sentiments found expression in beliefs and behavior reprehensible to the Puritan leadership, Anglicans*, and Catholics*.

Puritan animosity rose from this Ranter denial of Interregnum* society and religion. Pantheism directly contradicted prevailing religious standards and social institutions. Ranters stripped the Bible* of a literal resurrection, a physical heaven and hell, Trinitarianism, and the promotion of society based on Judeo-Christian standards of behavior.

Ranters repudiated Puritan moralism with drunkenness or tobacco use (which reputedly enhanced spiritual awareness), swearing in the place of preaching, blasphemously parodying Puritan worship, and ignoring contemporary standards of sexual conduct. Individual Ranters condemned monogamous families, rejected the practice of church marriage, and advocated wife swapping.

Ranters also raised societal animosity because of their refusal to recognize the prevailing English social structure. Their profound disrespect of the established clergy, suspicion that social institutions simply served to buoy class dominance, and conviction that any form of authority represented the exploitation of the poor set them at odds with an England that had rejected the Ranters' radical vision in 1649. Antisocial manifestations therefore naturally rose from radical feelings of disenfranchisement, isolation, and betrayal.

The Ranter phenomenon faded during the 1650s, finally perishing after the Restoration* of the monarchy, much of it subsumed within an increasingly quietist Quakerism*, as George Fox* wrested control from James Nayler. It also faded with the same lack of structure that made it so difficult to identify and categorize in the first place.

Significant historiographic controversy surrounds both the Ranter and related Seeker* movements. Opinions range from those advocating the existence of a definable, organized Ranter structure, to others who simply see the Ranters as a projection of conventional sixteenth-century society's fears. The ambiguity largely results from the fact that the Ranters were first identified and named, if not invented, by others. No self-confessing Ranter church existed. There is little, if any, evidence that indicates that Ranters had any awareness of themselves as a group. Ranters had no official membership, property, or confessional statements. They were primarily defined by detractors such as John Bunyan* or Richard Baxter*, interested in defending conventional Puritanism and Protestant Separatism* from what they considered radical extremists. Some recent scholarship also takes exception to the identification of Ranters as a distinct sect by disagreeing with the characteristics that Ranters held in common. Thus it is asserted that it is impossible to develop a list of identifying characteristics held in common by people historically considered to have been Ranters. It is, however, certain that Interregnum Puritanism and Restoration Anglicanism did experience significant radical opposition.

Bibliography: J. C. Davis, *Fear, Myth and History*, 1986; Jerome Friedman, *Blasphemy, Immorality and Anarchy: The Ranters and the English Revolution*, 1987; Christopher Hill, *The World Turned Upside Down: Radical Ideas During the English Revolution*, 1972; A. L. Morton, *The World of the Ranters: Religious Radicalism in the English Revolution*, 1970.

William Nikides

Recusancy. Recusancy, from the Latin word *recusare* (to refuse), was the name given to the refusal to acknowledge the 1559 Act of Uniformity (1 Eliz. I, c. 2) and the resistance to attending Anglican* church services. The term came to indicate Roman Catholics* who would not accept the state religion. Plots against the queen, threats of rebellion or invasion, and distrust of Catholicism forced the government to act. During the reign of Elizabeth (1558-1603), several statutes excluded recusants from public office, professional life, and the universities* and made priests liable to the penalties of treason, but the state did not enforce these laws with uniformity. Because of these penal laws, recusants remained a small minority of the population*, and some left the country and settled on the Continent.

The Catholics experienced some leniency under the first two Stuarts, and under James I* there was some relaxation in the enforcement of these laws. Catholic involvement in the Bye Plot* (1603) and the Gunpowder Plot* (1605) produced additional penalties against recusants. In 1606, a statute (3 Jac. I, c. 4) imposed a sacramental test for public office, required a new oath of allegiance*, which denied the temporal power of the pope and his power to depose, and placed additional restrictions on the movements of Catholics within the realm. It also confirmed existing laws against Jesuits and seminary priests and declared that property might be seized to meet the £20 fine for absence from Anglican services. In spite of parliamentary protests, Catholics experienced some toleration during James's last years. They openly practiced their rites, and eighty were justices of the peace (see Local Government*). Nonetheless, during his reign twenty-six Catholics were executed.

Early in the reign of Charles I*, parliament* again wanted to apply the full force of the recusancy laws, but he continued his father's policy of tolerance. The king's marriage to Henrietta Maria*, displays of Catholicism in public and at the royal court*, and renewed contact with the pope alienated many and increased the fears of Roman Catholicism. However, Charles did issue proclamations ordering priests to leave England, and he asked parents to recall their children from foreign schools. Two Catholics were executed during his reign, but after 1629 the prosecution of recusancy laws fell into abeyance.

During the Civil War*, Catholics supported the king against parliament, a body from which they could expect no justice or religious liberty. To help finance their cause, however, both sides extracted fines from recusants throughout the war and sometimes confiscated their estates. The king's opponents identified Catholicism with the royalist* cause, and the Long Parliament* of 1640 applied stringent laws against the Catholics. Eleven priests were executed between 1641 and 1642, and in 1643 parliament introduced an oath of allegiance required of all recusants. After 1646 the laws were applied with less severity. The Rump Parliament* in 1650 repealed compulsory attendance at Anglican services. Between the Long Parliament and the death of Oliver Cromwell* in 1658, approximately twenty-six recusants were executed.

Roman Catholics welcomed the Restoration* in 1660 and expected favorable treatment from Charles II*. His promise in the secret Treaty of Dover* (1670) to become a Roman Catholic, which he did on his deathbed, his marriage to the Catholic Catherine of Braganza*, and his attempts to modify anti-Catholic legislation seemed to justify this expectation. His Declaration of Indulgence of 1662 sought to restore rights to non-Anglicans, but it failed to pass the House of Commons. In an attempt to strengthen Anglicanism, parliament passed a series of laws known as the Clarendon Code*. Although it was directed specifically against Nonconformists, Catholics also suffered. In 1672 Charles issued a second Declaration of Indulgence*, which suspended laws against non-Anglicans, but he withdrew it in the face of parliamentary opposition. Parliament responded in 1673 with a Test Act* (25 Car. II, c. 2), which required reception of the Anglican sacrament and a declaration against transubstantiation from officeholders. In 1678 a second Test Act (30 Car. II, c. l) excluded Catholics from the House of Lords. The Popish Plot* (1678) claimed the lives of many Catholics, including St. Oliver Plunket (1681), the last person executed for his religion in England.

The Catholicism and policies of James II* aroused suspicion, and many feared a restoration of Catholicism. In 1687 he issued a Declaration of Indulgence*, which repealed the laws against Catholics and Nonconformists and allowed freedom of public worship. A second declaration the following year and his attempt to force it on the nation contributed to the Glorious Revolution* of 1688. Additional laws discriminated against Catholics and excluded them from the throne. During the eighteenth century, religious toleration began. The Catholic Relief Act of 1791 (18 Geo. III, c. 60) repealed many of the recusancy laws, and in 1829 the Catholic Emancipation Act (10 Geo. IV, c. 7) permitted Catholics to sit in parliament.

Bibliography: J. C. H. Aveling, *The Handle and the Axe*, 1976; John Bossy, *The English Catholic Community, 1570-1850*, 1976.

René Kollar

Regicides. When negotiations between the Long Parliament* and Charles I* collapsed in November 1648, extreme members of the army* led by Colonel Thomas Pride purged the House of Commons of members who favored further negotiation. Within days of Pride's Purge*, the remaining Rump Parliament* passed an act establishing a high court of justice to try the monarch (see Charles I, Trial, Execution, and Cult of*).

There were 135 men named to serve on the court. Few had been asked, and only about half actually sat as judges. Those who became regicides were at court on the day the king was sentenced to death or signed the warrant for his execution. As might be expected, most came from the army and the Rump. Several of Oliver Cromwell's* loyal colonels were named to the court, and fourteen signed the king's death warrant. About three-quarters of those named on the commission were members of the Rump, and forty-three actually agreed that the king should die.

Although several men with legal training were named to try the king, very few were actually lawyers. Of those who sat during the trial, none had any distinction. Only John Bradshaw, the president of the court, was a practicing judge, and like the lawyers he was not a particularly brilliant star in the legal firmament. Three other judges were named in the commission, but they refused to sit and left London*. No peers participated, the House of Lords having unanimously rejected the Commons's plan to try the king. The closest to nobility who joined in condemning the monarch were Lord Grey of Groby and Thomas Lisle, sons of English peers. Landed and commercial interests had heavy representation, which belies the common claim that the court was composed of the dregs of the people. Several, such as Edmund Ludlow, belonged to families with deep roots in the landed interests of England.

After the trial and execution, Cromwell could not keep this group united behind him. At the end of the Commonwealth* period, several strong republicans, such as Thomas Scott, refused to have anything to do with the Protectorate*. Others, like Thomas Harrison and John Jones, assumed responsible positions in the Commonwealth and made an easy transition to the Protectorate.

With the Restoration* in 1660, the Convention Parliament*—following Charles II's* long declared wishes—passed an Act of Indemnity and Oblivion* (12 Car. II, c. 11), which forgave all but a small list of the king's opponents. The notable exception was the regicides, who were denied royal pardon and made subject to either execution or life in prison. By this time eighteen of these men—including Cromwell, Henry Ireton*, and Bradshaw—had died. In a fit of petty revenge, the Convention ordered their bodies exhumed, their heads cut off, and the remains thrown into a common burial pit. Several regicides, feeling the change in political winds, fled the country. Many, like Ludlow, went to Switzerland, where they formed a colony of radical discontents. Others settled in Germany. Edward Whalley, John Dixwell, and William Goffe traveled to the American colonies. Although most were warmly received, they lived in fear of the new English regime. John Lisle was murdered in Germany and three others—John Okey, Thomas Barkstead, and Miles Corbet—were kidnapped in 1662 and returned to England, where they were summarily executed. All who fled died abroad, although Ludlow made a brief return to England after the Glorious Revolution*. He quickly left when a warrant for his arrest was issued.

A large group of regicides turned themselves in, relying on a proclamation from the king offering some mercy. They were not executed but were convicted of treason and jailed for life. Of the sixty-seven men who had agreed to the king's sentence of death, only six were tried for their lives. Also tried as regicides were John Cook, the king's prosecutor; Daniel Axtell and Francis Hacker, guards at the trial; and Hugh Peter, an obnoxious antimonarchical preacher. Twelve others pled guilty and were sentenced to life in prison. Thomas Harrison and John Crew, millenarians* and Fifth Monarchy Men*, went to their deaths unrepentant. Others who had agreed to the king's death, especially those not executed, were not so faithful to their cause, pleading ignorance, lack of malice, or youth.

Several of the king's judges escaped punishment altogether. Most notable was Richard Ingoldsby, who frustrated an army attempt to overthrow the government immediately before the Restoration, for which he was knighted. No other regicide was as fortunate, and those who avoided execution or prison did so through the pleas of families and friends to the House of Commons when it drafted the Act of Indemnity and Oblivion.

The king's opposition went underground after the Restoration, made martyrs of the executed regicides, and spread copies of their dying speeches. Thomas Venner, inspired in part by these words, led an abortive rebellion against Charles II's new government in 1661. It failed, as did all of the other uprisings and plots against the monarchy. Nevertheless, the spirit of the regicides lived on, maintaining in part the "Good Old Cause"*.

Bibliography: William L. Sachse, "England's 'Black Tribunal': An Analysis of the Regicide Court," *The Journal of British Studies* 12 (May 1973), pp. 69-85; C. V. Wedgwood, *A Coffin for King Charles: The Trial and Execution of Charles I*, 1964.

David A. Davis

Remonstrance of the Army (1648). By 21 September 1648, Lord Thomas Fairfax*, commanding the Long Parliament's* New Model Army*, had withdrawn his force to St. Albans. With the end of the Second Civil War*, radical elements in the army* demanded a cessation of the Treaty of Newport* negotiations with Charles I*. Among the rank and file, the serious arrears in pay turned troops against parliament's* efforts to reach a settlement and contributed to the charged atmosphere. Fairfax resisted Henry Ireton's* advice that the army should occupy London* and purge the House of Commons. Ireton, as leader of the army radicals and frustrated by Fairfax's inaction, drew up the document called the Remonstrance of the Army in November 1648.

Fairfax, forced to address Ireton's Remonstrance, convened a council of officers at St. Albans from 7 to 11 November. The document chronicled the misconduct of Charles, laying blame on the king for the outbreak of the Second Civil War* and calling for the abolition of the monarchy and swift justice for Charles. Fairfax and a majority of the officers objected to the radical tone of the document, which further drove Ireton toward an antimonarchical position. A conference of Levellers* and Ireton's followers, held on 15 November at the Nag's Head Inn in London, resulted in additional demands: the requirement for parliament to dissolve itself and for successor bodies to be elected by a revised electoral system, either annually or biennially. Parliament would be the supreme governing body, but a king, if elected only to serve as head of state, would have no veto power. The meeting did not discuss either the status of the House of Lords or a religious settlement.

Fairfax and his supporters attempted private negotiations with Charles based on the continuance of the Lords, control of the armed forces by a council of state*, and a reformed electoral system returning a biennial parliament. Charles rejected these terms on 18 November, forcing Fairfax to assent to Ireton's Remonstrance. On 20 November 1648 the council of officers adopted and sent to the Commons the Remonstrance, along with a demand for army pay. The document had now grown to over 25,000 words and presented the Commons with the problem of digesting its contents. Debate on the Remonstrance was postponed first to 27 November, then to 1 December. For the Long Parliament, the delay proved decisive. Fairfax, goaded by Ireton and the Levellers, occupied London on 2 December and demanded £40,000 from the city for army arrears. The army moved the king from the Isle of Wight to Hurst Castle, Hampshire, an action parliament declared illegal.

Once again Fairfax refused to dissolve parliament, which prompted Ireton to act. An army committee of action formed to "put a stop to such proceedings." On 6 December Colonel Thomas Pride purged parliament by arresting forty-one and excluding 140 members of parliament from Westminster Hall. Pride's Purge* resulted in the more radical 154-member Rump Parliament*, which then resolved to deal with the king. The Long Parliament's failure to address the Remonstrance of the Army expeditiously set in motion events which culminated in Charles I's trial, conviction, and execution* in January 1649.

Bibliography: John Kenyon, *The Civil Wars of England*, 1988.

Stanley D. M. Carpenter

Restoration. The term *Restoration* is applied to both Charles II's* return to England after the Interregnum* and the period following that return. Charles's contribution to his return was limited. The Republic was brought down not by royalist* insurrection but by its own internal divisions. By late 1659 the army* was politically isolated, with few civilian supporters. Seeking a parliament* that could provide a civilian front for military rule and vote taxation* to pay the soldiers, its leaders recalled the Rump Parliament* but soon expelled it again. By so doing, they split the army. General George Monck*, commander of the forces in Scotland*, demanded the reinstatement of the Rump as the legitimate parliament.

As Monck led his forces into England on 1 January 1660, the army leaders faced mounting civilian resistance and a threatened tax strike. In desperation they again recalled the Rump. Confident that Monck would obey its commands, the Rump ordered him to march into the City of London* and crush popular opposition there. Monck demanded instead that it readmit those members of parliament (MPs) excluded from the Long Parliament* in Pride's Purge*. He thus reestablished the Commons as they had been in 1648, when a majority had favored negotiations with Charles I*. He also ordered parliament to dissolve itself and hold fresh elections.

Before it broke up, the old parliament tried to ensure that the elections would produce a body similar to itself. Former royalists were debarred from voting, but the electors had other ideas. The Convention Parliament*, which met in April, was fairly evenly divided between members of royalist and parliamentarian* backgrounds. Within days it invited the king to return.

The sudden collapse of the military regime has been explained in various ways. Some blame a panic response to the threat of disorder. Others blame the regime's lack of support, compounded by the split in the army and the abandonment of Oliver Cromwell's* policy of "healing and settling." The soldiers' demoralization in the winter of 1659-1660 in the face of civilian hostility suggests that the latter interpretation is the more convincing.

Charles II returned to England without preconditions. His position was defined after his return by two bodies: the Convention, which sat from April to December 1660, and the Cavalier Parliament*, which was elected early in 1661 and remained in being until 1679. The Convention liquidated some of the major problems left by the Interregnum. The Act of Indemnity and Oblivion* of 1660 (12 Car. II, c. 11) removed the danger that former parliamentarians could be punished by the new regime. The New Model Army* was paid off, and the soldiers dispersed quietly into civilian life. Other issues, such as the church, the militia, the extent of the royal prerogative*, were left open and were decided by the Cavalier Parliament.

The Cavalier Parliament's first act declared that all legislation which had not received the royal assent was null and void. Constitutionally, therefore, England returned to the position after the reforming legislation of 1641. By this the king had lost the prerogative courts* and the power to raise money without the consent of parliament, but he retained overall control of the government and in particular continued to choose his own ministers and to direct the armed forces. The Cavalier Parliament said nothing on the former point, thus tacitly allowing Charles II a free choice of advisers; on the latter, the Militia Act of 1661 (13 Car. II, c. 6) stated that the king had full and sole control of the armed forces. Parliament also strengthened the new king's powers. The Corporation Act of 1661 (13 Car. II, st. 2, c. 1) enabled him to appoint commissioners to remove "disaffected" members of town corporations (see Clarendon Code*; Local Government, Towns*). An Act against Tumultuous Petitioning in 1661 forbade mass lobbies of parliament. The Licensing Act* of 1662 (14 Car. II, c. 33) gave Charles statutory power to censor the press (see Printing*).

This rebuilding of the king's power was quite deliberate. Scared by twenty years of social, political, and religious upheaval, the Cavalier House of Commons wanted a strong king (and a strong church) to hold down the disaffected elements in society. Their world must not be turned upside down again. In addition, by handing back executive responsibility to the king, the Commons freed themselves of a burden that they had taken on only to conduct the war effort against Charles I* and that most MPs found excessive.

In reestablishing the powers of the Crown, the Cavalier Parliament sought to return to the situation that should have existed before the Civil War*. They were not, however, prepared to trust the new king too far. The power to purge corporations and censor the press was only temporary. The Commons voted that the king should control the armed forces but ignored his requests for a larger army; while the main military force was the militia, officered by country gentlemen like themselves, they need not fear military rule. But the balance parliament sought to strike was most apparent in the case of taxation and revenue*.

Charles II returned with no revenues of his own. Since 1641 the Crown had depended for money on what parliament would grant. Charles was in no position to demand an independent revenue. Nevertheless the Convention assessed the annual cost of the government in peacetime and voted, in principle, to provide him with the necessary revenue for life. Some of the calculations proved overly optimistic, but the principle behind the vote was clear: the king ought to enjoy a measure of financial independence; he should not have to keep begging the Commons for money.

Yet just as the Commons were careful not to extend the king's powers too far, so they were careful not to give him too much money. They wished him to call parliament regularly, and his main reason for doing so would be to ask for additional grants. Moreover, if he needed money he would be more inclined to remedy grievances and heed the Commons's advice as "the price of money." While willing to vote him additional temporary grants, therefore, the Commons refused to add significantly to his permanent revenue, which remained for much of the reign insufficient to support his government.

The Restoration settlement, then, can be seen as an attempt to reestablish the balance between the powers of the king, who directed government, and of parliament, who financed that government and advised on how it should be carried on. How effectively he governed would depend on his ability to work with parliament. There was thus a certain ambiguity in the settlement, which has led historians to interpret it in different ways. The formal powers of the king were restored virtually intact, but he could no longer raise revenue except in ways approved by parliament. Some scholars therefore stress the institutional strengths of the monarchy. Others remark that Charles II found it hard to exploit those strengths in practice because of his deteriorating relationship with parliament. Others again argue that whatever its institutional strengths, the monarchy had lost much of its moral authority because of Charles I's defeat and execution*. There are no definitive answers to these questions, not least because of the ambivalent legacy of the recent past. The upheavals of the 1640s and 1650s may for some have discredited monarchy; for others they showed the need to restore an effective monarch as the linchpin of the restored old regime. It was also difficult to forget Charles I's misgovernment, so while they wanted the king to rule effectively, they were careful not to give him too much power. This placed the onus on Charles II to work with parliament in order to make the most of his opportunities, and this he failed to do.

Bibliography: Ronald Hutton, *The Restoration: A Political and Religious History of England and Wales, 1658-67*, 1985; John Miller, *Restoration England: The Reign of Charles II*, 1985.

John Miller

Root and Branch Bill and Petition (1641). Due to financial constraints, Charles I* summoned the Long Parliament* in 1640. The parliament was predominately Puritan* in spirit, even though its leaders were Anglicans*. Ecclesiastical change dominated the early concerns of the body as petitions poured in upon it. One of those was the Root and Branch Petition, which carried with it 15,000 signatures and advocated the abandonment of the episcopacy.

The bill, when finally proposed to parliament*, took its name from the earlier petition that advocated the elimination of the episcopacy with all its "roots and branches." Sir Edward Dering presented the bill to parliament, but he denied authorship and claimed he received the document from Sir Arthur Haselrig. Apparently Haselrig obtained it from Oliver Cromwell* and Sir Henry Vane the younger. The authorship was likely a joint effort of Haselrig, Vane, and Cromwell.

Parliament abandoned the bill, but the House of Commons did pass several Puritan measures, which show the bill's influence. For example, forbidding sports on the Lord's Day, eliminating corporal bowing at the name of Jesus, taking down communion rails, and removing pictures considered scandalous (like the Virgin Mary's) all indicate that while the bill did not pass, the debate over it led to a certain Puritan direction in subsequent legislation.

Led by Cromwell, debates over the Book of Common Prayer and sermons occupied the Puritan agenda for the rest of the session. Sermons, it was decided, should be presented in the afternoons in all parishes. On 20 October, at the beginning of parliament's next session, Cromwell backed a bill to remove bishops from the House of Lords. Of course, the house rejected this measure, but Cromwell continued to rail against the bishops' right to vote there.

By 1641 the Commons ordered images, altars, crucifixes, and relics of idolatry removed from the churches. At the invitation of London* ministers, a delegation from the Scotch Assembly, led by Alexander Henderson, visited London to set up a presbytery. In 1642 parliament abolished episcopacy and the liturgy. By this time the royalist* and parliamentarian* armies were in the field.

The Root and Branch Bill and Petition can be viewed as an early political step for advancing the Puritan cause within parliament. Although it officially was not adopted by that body, it did wield considerable influence on later measures that passed the assembly. Its strident message of abolishing the episcopacy set the tone for the Puritans to pressure parliament toward an ecclesiastical Calvinism*.

Bibliography: Antonia Fraser, *Cromwell the Lord Protector*, 1973; J. P. Kenyon, *Stuart England*, 1978.

John S. Erwin

Roundheads. During the English Civil Wars* *Roundhead* was the epithet applied by the royalist* propagandists to the parliamentary party and its adherents. It seems to have come into use slightly before the rejoinder *Cavalier** was first applied by the parliamentary propagandists to their royalist opponents.

The origins of the term presumably came from the observation that parliamentary officers of strong religious views tended to wear their hair close-cropped, showing the shape of their heads—though the practice was by no means universal among them—in contrast to the fashion among royalist courtiers of wearing their hair long. In fact, many, if not most, parliamentary officers, Oliver Cromwell* among them, seem to have worn their hair to shoulder length, as long as Charles I* wore his. Mrs. Hutchinson reported that when the war began, parliamentary soldiers—presumably enlisted men rather than their officers—wore their hair short, the style favored by London* apprentices at the time, but that by the war's end they did not. As a term of abuse *roundhead* was effective, for contemporary evidence suggests that it rankled and was resented by parliamentarians*.

The *Oxford English Dictionary*, relying on the earl of Clarendon (Edward Hyde*), notes that the use of the term appears to have begun in late 1641, before the outbreak of the Civil War. In his *Historical Collections*, John Rushworth attributed its first specific use in this sense to an officer named David Hide, who applied it to the anti-Episcopalian party in December 1641.

Bibliography: *Oxford English Dictionary*.

S. J. Stearns

Royal College of Physicians. Henry VIII chartered the Royal College of Physicians (RCP) in 1518 as the licensing body and regulatory board for the profession. No doctor could practice medicine* within seven miles of London* unless he were a fellow or licentiate. In 1522 the college's jurisdiction was extended to all of England, but lack of enforcement procedures made this moot. During Tudor times the RCP's monopoly went unchallenged, and the fellows avoided professional disputes through compromise.

The college was challenged in the seventeenth century on two fronts. Most fellows, especially those with Oxford or Cambridge medical degrees (see Universities*), still followed Galenic medicine and humoral theory, while continentally trained doctors adopted Paracelsus's empiricism. By mid-century disputes about diagnostic approaches threatened the harmony and elite status of the RCP. It also faced encroachment by medical personnel not university trained as physicians. In 1618, when it issued a pharmacopoeia including traditional and iatrochemical recipes, the RCP had only thirty-eight members, and by 1663 just two more, too few for London's burgeoning population*. Discrete functions for surgeons and apothecaries had existed since the Middle Ages, but spurred by debates over tradition and authority in English politics, they and other "irregular" practitioners contended for patients' fees. By 1650 the ratio of surgeons to physicians was five to one, by 1700 ten to one. Monitored by the Barber-Surgeons Company since 1540, surgeons had gained great expertise during wartime. The RCP spent an increasing amount of time policing the activities of surgeons, apothecaries, and even midwives.

The RCP and the early Stuarts were mutually supportive, but politics required a shift after 1642 toward parliamentary forces in London. Association with the Cromwellian party, however, did little to halt the college's decline; the Commonwealth's* questioning of traditional monarchical government undermined it. The Restoration* witnessed further diminution of the RCP, whose fellows believed they could demonstrate an awareness of public charges of elitism simply by keeping the college minutes in the vernacular rather than Latin. But no new charter conferring privileges was forthcoming from parliament*, in part due to lobbying by surgeons and apothecaries. During the plague of London* in 1665, few RCP physicians remained in the city, further weakening that group's claim to primacy (see also Epidemics and Plague*). A rival Society of Chemical Physicians further threatened the RCP's exclusivity. Worse, Charles II* enthusiastically supported empiricism, for example, in the Royal Society*, which eclipsed the RCP in scientific importance in the 1670s. Charles showed such preference for new methods that he forced the RCP to issue licenses to virtual charlatans and foreign mountebanks. The traditionally trained fellows were reluctant to experiment with or approve new drugs from the Western Hemisphere like cinchona or ipecac; medical irregulars were less inhibited.

The RCP fought back. Claiming to act in patients' best interests, in 1695 it established a dispensary, maintaining sufficient stock to treat impoverished patients at cost, in hopes that this would compare favorably to overmedicating, overpriced apothecaries. But some fellows refused to support this, their names were published, and the RCP was lampooned in the press. In 1702 apothecaries were given the right to supply medicines to the army* and navy* without RCP approval. In 1704 the college pressed suit against William Rose, an apothecary "practicing physick." Though King's Bench upheld the college's right to determine who could practice in London, the judgment was reversed in the House of Lords. Reflecting Whig* sentiment for demystifying the profession and the popular notion that the RCP had failed to protect medical consumers, the verdict overturned a century of pro-RCP precedent, virtually eliminated the RCP monopoly over medicine, and awarded to apothecaries the right to recommend as well as dispense medicines.

Bibliography: George N. Clark, *History of the Royal College of Physicians of London*, 3 vols., 1964-72; Harold J. Cook, *The Decline of the Old Medical Regime in Stuart London*, 1986; William Munk, *Roll of the Royal College of Physicians*, 3 vols., 1861.

Elizabeth Lane Furdell

Royal Society. Britain's first formal public organization devoted to the advancement of science*, organized in 1660 and chartered in 1662. The Royal Society sprang from the intellectual soil of the 1640s. To millenarian* Protestants like Samuel Hartlib, John Pell, and John Dury, the Civil Wars* heralded the reorganization of society and a blossoming of knowledge. They took hope from utopian visions like Francis Bacon's* *New Atlantis* and J. V. Andreae's *Christianopolis* and *Modell of a Christian Society*. Real-world intellectual organizations included the Académie Française (founded 1635) and Mersenne's circle of correspondents (1635-1648), which included Hartlib and future fellows Theodore Haak, Seth Ward, Kenelm Digby, and William Petty.

After Charles I's* defeat at the Battle of Naseby* in 1645, many intellectuals settled in London*. John Wallis recounts weekly meetings at physician Dr. Jonathan Goddard's lodgings or at mathematician Samuel Foster's lecture and lodgings at Gresham College. Attendees included Haak, John Wilkins, and eminent physicians, disciples of William Harvey. After the Second Civil War* (1648) Wallis, Goddard, and Wilkins moved to Oxford. Physical scientists continued meeting at Gresham College, while physiologists and anatomists centered their activities on the Royal College of Physicians*. Robert Boyle and friends met informally at the London residence of his sister, Lady Ranelagh.

Throughout the period, Hartlib maintained a voluminous correspondence with intellectuals of all sorts and promoted Comenian proposals for reformed grammar schools and new libraries. In this same vein Petty, and later John Evelyn* and Abraham Cowley, proposed new colleges (see Universities*). All this activity expressed a faith that science could be advanced through institutions.

At Oxford, Wallis and his friends joined a thriving scientific community. In 1649 they organized formally, meeting in Petty's lodgings. From 1651 they held regular meetings, mostly at Wilkins' lodgings at Wadham College. Membership rolls were kept; members included the astronomer Ward, physician Thomas Wilkins, Christopher Wren, and later Boyle. Admission was by majority vote, and as in London subscriptions paid for experimental demonstrations in chemistry, microscopy, and other subjects. The Oxford Experimental Philosophy Club continued until 1690 or so.

The Restoration* brought the opportunity to establish a national institution for promoting scientific development. Boyle, Ward, Sir Robert Moray, and Lord Brouncker led the effort, and on 28 November 1660 the Royal Society held its inaugural meeting, organizing along the lines of the Oxford group. Its public philosophy, projected in Boyle's essays, Robert Hooke's *Micrographia* (1665), and Thomas Sprat's *History of the Royal Society* (1667), was Baconian experimentalism and induction. However, the actual diversity of interests reflected the ferment of the previous decade, experimentation coexisting with occult philosophy as possible foundations for "real" science.

The membership, effectively limited to well-to-do male Londoners, was otherwise heterogeneous. Eager to recruit the most accomplished practitioners in a variety of fields, the fellows proposed friends and relatives for membership, electing poets, scholars, and churchmen as well as scientists. The election of Charles II, the duke of York (see James II*), and Prince Rupert gave the Royal Society and the new science establishment credentials and international prestige. Some nonscientists, including Samuel Pepys*, were among the most active fellows. Society was an attractive feature of membership. Meetings, comprising twenty to as many as sixty fellows, were often associated with dinner parties or coffee-house* discussions, and in the 1660s lecture-going was something of a courtly fashion.

The Royal Society met at Gresham College until the Great Fire of London* in 1666, when it moved to Arundel House, returning in 1673. Experimental demonstrations often took center stage at meetings. Hooke, the first curator of experiments, and his successors prepared exhibitions of barometrics, falling bodies and specific gravity, microscopy, magnetism, and anatomy, including transfusions, injections, and the famous air pump experiments on respiration. Nonetheless, over the first two decades, public experiment declined in favor of lectures, reports of research, discussion, and debate.

Early on, the Royal Society's supporters sought endowment as a national research institution and hoped to build and endow a college. These efforts failed, but the society did develop a museum, a collection of scientific instruments, and a library based on that collected by Thomas Howard, earl of Arundel. It also made some grants for special projects, such as Nehemiah Grew's work on plant anatomy (1672).

The early society's greatest scientific contribution was made in the person of Henry Oldenburg, its first secretary. Oldenburg maintained an international scientific correspondence, forging connections with Huygens (optics), Leeuwenhoek (microscopy), Hevelius (astronomy), Leibnitz (mathematics), and the Bolognese empiricists. From 1665 he published *Philosophical Transactions,* the first science periodical. Immensely popular at home and abroad, it ceased publication at his death in 1677. Replaced between 1679 and 1682 by Hooke's *Philosophical Collections*, it was revived in 1683, edited by Robert Plot.

Bibliography: R. G. Frank, *Harvey and the Oxford Physiologists*, 1980; M. B. Hall, *Promoting Experimental Learning: Experiment and the Royal Society, 1660-1727*, 1991; Michael Hunter, *The Royal Society and Its Fellows, 1660-1700*, 1982.

Mark Heumann

Royalism. *Royalist* was the label given to an adherent of the king's cause in the Civil War*, and thus *royalism* has served historians as a name for that cause itself. Other than loyalty to the king, there were few defining principles to royalism. It certainly should not be confused with the idea of absolutism*. Some royalists were absolutists, but many others were not. The term must be seen primarily as a political rather than a theoretical one. Royalists were supporters of the king and his policies, not believers in a single set of political theories.

Although the word *royalist* is recorded in the *Oxford English Dictionary* as being first used in 1643 by William Prynne* (*royalism* is not recorded until its use by Edmund Burke in 1793), it seems that the word in fact originated in the 1620s. Isolated occurrences of *royalist* can be found as early as 1624, and in 1627 Robert Sibthorpe used it to refer to those who rejected the view that subjects had a right to resist their king. Sir Robert Filmer's reference to "the new coined distinction of subjects into royalists and patriots" may refer to the 1620s, though this is not certain.

Nevertheless, the word did not come into common usage until the 1640s, and it is on this usage that historians have built their term *royalism*. A royalist grouping is generally seen to have emerged in the Long Parliament* over the years 1641-1642, as many who had supported the attack on the financial and constitutional abuses of Charles I's* Personal Rule* (1629-1640) began to believe that the majority in the Commons were themselves threatening to undermine the ancient constitution. These men came to see the preservation of the traditional powers of the king as essential to the preservation of England's traditional mode of government. Eventually they were to fight for the king in the Civil War.

For most, the heart of this royalism was not the adoption of a simple monarchical loyalism but a willingness to defend the common law* and the ancient constitution. Monarchy itself was defended on the grounds that it was a customary component of England's legal and constitutional system. Most royalists remained firmly attached to the principle of legal and limited government (a position sometimes labeled "constitutional royalism"). From *His Majesties Answer to the xix Propositions* (1642), written by Viscount Falkland and Sir John Culpepper, to the writings of Judge David Jenkins in the middle and late 1640s, royalist propaganda stressed the themes of moderation, conservatism, and legality. For some of them, loyalty to the king seemed to be a simple consequence of loyalty to the law.

Not all royalists accepted this moderate position. A few of them, including Filmer and Thomas Hobbes*, were prepared to invest something close to arbitrary authority in rulers. These thinkers showed much less concern for legality, since they tended to see all laws as derived from the king's will anyway. This absolutist position does not appear to have been typical of royalism in the 1640s. There was indeed almost no theoretical unity to royalism. Some accepted patriarchal theory (Filmer), others did not; many were theorists of divine right monarchy*, some were not (Hobbes); some believed that monarchy originated in the consent of the people (Hobbes and Dudley Digges), many believed that monarchical authority came immediately from God. Not all royalists were even agreed on the principle of nonresistance*. It was perhaps closer to a defining principle than anything else, but some (including Henry Ferne and, more surprisingly, Hobbes) were willing to concede to individuals a natural right to defend themselves. About all that royalists had in common was the belief that in England in the 1640s, one king, Charles I, should be supported against his enemies.

    Royalism has been much less used by historians of the later Stuart period. Nevertheless, the writings of many royalists of the 1640s were republished over the period 1660-1689, and many of the ideas expressed in defense of Charles I in the 1640s were found in later Tory* thinking. Filmer's writings in particular were central to the polemical interchange of the 1680s. But the continuity between the 1640s and later periods was possibly clearest in the area of ecclesiology. Just as royalists in the 1640s had been on the whole defenders of the Church of England by law established (as well as defenders of king and common law), so the chief use of their ideas in the Restoration* period was by "Anglican* royalists," defenders of the integrity of the established church against demands for the toleration of nonconformity. These people, in the crucial years 1688-1689, tended to call themselves members of the church party and are called by historians Tories rather than royalists. They may have been more responsive than their predecessors of the 1640s to absolutist varieties of royalism, but neither this nor their different name should obscure the continuities between the royalism of the 1640s and later Tory thinking. (See Political Thought*.)

Bibliography: James Daly, "The Origins and Shaping of English Royalist Thought," *Canadian Historical Association: Historical Papers* (1974): 15-35; Mark Goldie, "John Locke and Anglican Royalism," *Political Studies* 31 (1983): 61-85; J. P. Sommerville, "Absolutism and Royalism," in J. H. Burns and Mark Goldie, eds., *The Cambridge History of Political Thought, 1450-1700*, 1991.

                                                                            Glenn Burgess

Rump Parliament. At the end of the Civil War* the Long Parliament* split into moderate and extremist wings. The moderate Presbyterians* tried to halt the revolution in midcourse by an abortive compromise with Charles I*, incurring the wrath of Independents* determined to destroy the monarchy and backed by the army*. On 6 December 1648 Colonel Thomas Pride, commanding a strong force and aided by Lord Grey of Groby and Edmund Ludlow, stood outside the House of Commons and arrested or turned away the majority of members (Presbyterians). (See Pride's Purge*.)

    The purged parliament* or "Rump" excluded about three-fifths of the members then eligible to sit. Initially it consisted of fewer than sixty members of parliament, but later some were readmitted and new ones elected. Although as many as 200 may have sat at one time or another after December 1648, average attendance was well under 100. Numerous constituencies had only one sitting representative; many had none.

The Rump ended negotiations with the king, a prelude to Charles's trial and execution* on 30 January 1649. Administratively it abolished the House of Lords and the monarchy, established the council of state*, and declared England a Commonwealth*. It faced up to threats from Ireland*, Scotland*, and the Dutch but failed to cooperate with the army or achieve internal reconstruction. It was able to collect substantial revenue through the monthly assessment, the customs revenue, and the excise tax (see Taxation and Revenue*), yet members accepted bribes and practiced nepotism.

The Rump was less successful in four areas of policy where change was expected: religion, law, social reform, and parliamentary reform. Religious chaos continued after the abolition of episcopacy and the failure of the Presbyterian system to win general acceptance.   Some opposed any form of established church.   Oliver Cromwell* was against reviving religious persecution, disestablishing the church, and abolishing titles without first making financial provision for ministers. The Rump's inability to achieve any clear-cut religious settlement was largely the result of internal division between Presbyterians and Independents, but most Rumpers put enforcement of a Puritan* code of morality ahead of religious liberty. Several repressive acts were passed in 1650, including a strict sabbath observance law (see Sabbatarianism*), a measure imposing the death penalty for adultery, and acts against blasphemy and unlawful swearing.

Legal reform, opposed by the lawyers, was urgently needed to change what Cromwell called "wicked and abominable laws," but the Rump did little to remedy abuses. At least two committees proposed reforms, but the Commons undercut them with constant debate. Much reform was held up or rejected by disagreements between radicals and reform-minded lawyers, such as a bill to establish courts for probate, marriage, and divorce cases. Still the Rump achieved some positive legal reforms. Between 1649 and 1650 acts were passed for the relief of prisoners' debts and for the redress of delays to litigants in the appeals procedure.

Social reform produced little. There was a measure to pay schoolmasters out of sequestered tithes, and the Rump was anxious to control the ideological content of the curriculum. Committees were formed but nothing else done regarding other matters, including the building of a northern university (see Universities*) and the relieving of poverty (see Poor Laws and Poverty*), an activity which was unprecedented in 1649 since the country had still not recovered from the war.

Parliamentary reform was crucial to the Rump's survival; its failure in this area caused its destruction. The army continued to demand its dissolution and new elections under a reformed franchise and a redistribution of constituencies. Civilian Rumpers clung stubbornly to power, proposing that their own seats should be guaranteed in the next parliament and that elections be held only in constituencies that were vacant because of Pride's Purge. This conflict continued throughout the Commonwealth. It was intense during the dispute over the dissolution of the Long Parliament, though after some persuasion the army decided not to turn the Rump out in 1648. It still continued to seek its dissolution, and in 1651 the members set the date of 3 November 1654 to end the session; but as their incapacity to effect reform grew, Cromwell and others tried to advance the date of a general election.

The Rump prepared a "bill for a new representative" in February 1653 but made no move to disband. The bill, which would have allowed members to keep their seats without having to be reelected, was too much for Cromwell, who summoned a conference with the parliamentary leaders and urged them to suspend the bill on 19 April. The next morning the bill was hurriedly rushed through parliament. Cromwell heard about it, hastened to the house with his musketeers, and listened briefly to the debate until the speaker put the question that the bill be passed. Suddenly he rose, praised the good work parliament had done formerly, upbraided members individually for corruption and evil living, and summoned his soldiers. He then dissolved the Rump and the council of state on 20 April 1653.

Thus the army rid itself of the "transparent veil of constitutionalism." However, the populace applauded this ejection of the highly unpopular Rump. Still the "interruption," as the expulsion was called, divided civilian and military supporters of the republic and wrecked successive Cromwellian parliaments. Army leaders replaced the Rump with Barebone's Parliament* of 140 "divers persons fearing God, and of approved fidelity and honesty" (129 from England, five from Scotland, six from Ireland). It elected a new council of state, or rather added a civilian majority; appointed committees; drafted bills; voted taxes to carry on the war at sea but not to maintain the army at home; and chose a date (the symbolic 3 November 1654) for its end. On 12 December 1653 the majority of members resigned, while the minority were expelled. The army then installed Cromwell as lord protector. Protectorate Parliaments*, all of short duration, followed in 1654-1655, 1656, and—under Richard Cromwell*—1659.

In April 1659 the army overthrew the Protectorate* because of its moderation and on 6-7 May recalled the Rump. A few old Commonwealthmen*, including hardened republicans like Thomas Scot and Arthur Haselrige and religious zealots like Henry Vane and Richard Salwey, came back with enthusiasm, but others were more reluctant. The army petitioned parliament on 12 May for a commonwealth without a single person at its head, an act of oblivion for all public acts committed since April 1653, free expression of faith for all Christians excepting popery or prelacy, removal of all royalists* and Levellers* from offices of trust, speedy election of members of parliament, and administration by a council of state. These demands met with mixed results from the Rump. The army was angered by the appointment of commissioners to nominate officers, which gave the Rump complete control over the armed forces since the navy* was treated the same way. The Rump quickly alienated all sections of the army.

The Rump ceased sitting on 13 October, then reassembled on 26 December. George Monck*, preliminary to the Restoration*, secured the readmittance of members expelled in 1648. They resumed sitting with a new council of state on 21 February 1660, the restored Long Parliament dissolved itself on 16 March, and Charles II* issued his Declaration of Breda* on 4 April.

If the Rump achieved so little, it was not from lack of talent. Many of its members would have been an asset to any government (e.g., the younger Henry Vane, Thomas

Scott, Oliver St. John, Richard Salwey, Henry Nevile, Algernon Sidney, George Thomson, and Arthur Hesilrige, the only survivor of the Five Members*). Whatever their religious background, many were practical men but found routine, daily administration too complex to leave much time for long-range planning. Their first priority was defense against internal and external enemies, which meant dealing with Ireland, Scotland, France, the militia, the navy, and foreign policy, and winning the First Dutch War* (1652-1654). With inefficient parliamentary management and an ineffective council of state unskilled in handling routine house business, reform was a secondary concern. This caused interminable argument and delay, stonewalling in committees, and months of unnecessary debate. Finally the Rump's original members were, like Cromwell, architects of the revolution and dedicated Puritans but also country gentlemen unwilling to change the social order. Disturbed by party disharmony, worried by their isolation, and surrounded by Levellers and royalists, they embraced the conformists, who were even less interested in change. Ultimately the Rump destroyed itself.

Bibliography: David Underdown, *Pride's Purge*, 1971; Blair Worden, *The Rump Parliament, 1648-1653*, 1974.

Martin J. Manning

Rye House Plot (1683). Because of the dominating influence of Whig* historiography, the Rye House Plot has often been discounted as a fiction propagated by Charles II's* government to destroy the Whigs*. This interpretation has been reinforced by extraordinarily difficult evidentiary problems, caused in large part by confessions that intersperse fiction with fact. However, most Stuart specialists, having reexamined the evidence, are now agreed that the plotting was real. The so-called Rye House Plot involved a series of intertwined conspiracies, one of which entailed an insurrection intended to compel Charles to exclude the duke of York (see James II*) from the line of succession and the other an attempt to assassinate the royal brothers.

The idea of a general insurrection was initially broached by Anthony Ashley Cooper*, earl of Shaftesbury, shortly after the House of Lords rejected the Exclusion Bill in November 1680 (see Exclusion Crisis*). The duke of Monmouth, William Lord Howard, and Sir Thomas Armstrong discouraged him at that time, but the idea was revived when the king became ill in May 1682; after Charles recovered, planning ceased. The following summer, Archibald Campbell*, 9th earl of Argyll, sought unsuccessfully to obtain £30,000 from Shaftesbury and his supporters to mount a rebellion in Scotland. Argyll subsequently fled to the Netherlands, from whence he continued to plot with English and Scottish militants until his ill-fated expedition in 1685. Shaftesbury, who distrusted Argyll, began thinking anew of an insurrection after the Tory* victory in the 1682 London* shrieval election. The discussions, which involved Monmouth, Russell, Ford Lord Grey, and probably Armstrong, set the stage for Monmouth's tumultuous progress through Cheshire in September. So enthusiastic was the duke's reception that he was prepared to rebel, but Russell demurred, primarily because preparations for a simultaneous uprising in the southwest were not complete.

An increasingly distrustful Shaftesbury went into hiding shortly thereafter, though plotting continued. Shaftesbury now considered the possibility of assassinating Charles and James, a proposal apparently first suggested by John Wildman. Plans were made for a party of assassins led by Richard Rumbold to strike as Charles and James passed the Rye House in Hertfordshire on their return from Newmarket. From Robert Ferguson, one of Monmouth's agents, the duke learned of this scheme and prevailed with Shaftesbury to call it off and cooperate instead on plans for a general rebellion. After the uprising, scheduled for 2 November, was postponed until 19 November and then delayed again, Shaftesbury, fearing imminent arrest, fled to the Netherlands.

The Monmouth cabal did not meet again until after Shaftesbury's death in January 1683, but another group of conspirators, the key members of which were Colonel John Rumsey and the attorneys Robert West and Richard Goodenough, continued to plot in London. As Monmouth's agent, Ferguson had worked with this group before he accompanied Shaftesbury to the Netherlands. West and his cohorts discussed both insurrection and assassination, but nothing had come of their talks by the time Ferguson returned to London at their behest in February 1683. By this point the so-called council of six (Monmouth, Russell, the earl of Essex, William Lord Howard of Escrick, Algernon Sidney, and John Hampden) was pondering a general uprising in connection with dissident Scots led by such men as Lord Melville, Sir John Cochrane, and Sir Hugh Campbell of Cessnock. The Scots in fact sent representatives to London but not until April and May 1683, ostensibly to discuss settlements in Carolina.

Well before the arrival of the Scots, the West cabal had revived the scheme to assassinate Charles and James as they returned from Newmarket. Monmouth monitored their planning, primarily through Ferguson. Although recruiting for the party of assassins had already begun, the conspirators were not ready to act when a fire forced the royal party to leave Newmarket earlier than planned. Undeterred by this failure, both cabals continued to scheme, Monmouth's for a major insurrection coordinated with the Scots (including Argyll's people, who sought at least £10,000), West's for an uprising centered in London. Recruiting for the latter was in progress when one of the conspirators, Josiah Keeling, lost his nerve and confessed on 12 June. Sweeping arrests followed; authorities seized both incriminating documents and weapons, though not as many of the latter as had been anticipated. For their role in the various conspiracies, Russell, Sidney, Hampden, Rumbold, and others were executed. Monmouth, Howard, Grey, West, Rumsey, and Keeling saved themselves by confessing, and Ferguson and Goodenough (both of whom would later acknowledge their involvement) escaped to the Netherlands. Essex died in the Tower, having ostensibly committed suicide, though he was probably murdered, in part to increase the likelihood of Russell's conviction. The Monmouth and Argyll rebellions in 1685 were in part the outgrowth of the failed plans for uprisings in 1682-1683 (see Monmouth Rebellion*).

Bibliography: R. L. Greaves, *Secrets of the Kingdom: British Radicals from the Popish Plot to the Revolution of 1688-89*, 1992; Richard Ashcraft, *Revolutionary Politics & Locke's Two Treatises of Government*, 1986.

Richard L. Greaves

S

Sabbatarianism. Attitudes to Sabbath observance polarized by the 1630s, contributing to the tension that led to the Civil War*. Points of disagreement included whether Christians were bound to observe Sunday rather than Saturday, whether observance was instituted by divine or human law, which nonreligious activities were allowable on the Sabbath, and who exercised jurisdiction over them. Deeper controversies were reflected in these issues as well: the relative merits of Scripture versus church tradition, competing secular and ecclesiastical authority, and questions of public order and morality.

By 1603 there was considerable agreement among the governing class that there should be neither work, travel, nor trade on Sunday. Some recreations after divine service were generally acceptable, but blood sports, dancing, excessive drinking, and plays were often criticized. Elizabethan parliaments* and church records reveal anxiety over jurisdiction but considerable cooperation between ecclesiastical and lay officials, the latter increasingly preoccupied with the disorderly potential of communal recreations.

In 1603 enthusiastic Puritans* presented their new king with the Millenary Petition*. One demand was better Sabbath observance. James I*, perhaps wary of disorderly crowds or keen to pacify the petitioners, issued a proclamation against blood sports, plays, and "other like disorders" on Sundays. He instructed justices of the peace to stop Sundays being "prophaned" by "bear baiting, piping, dancing, bowling." At the Hampton Court Conference* in 1604, all present supported better Sabbath observance. Jacobean canons* and visitation articles suggest episcopal consensus on the undesirability of attending alehouses and considerable disapproval of games, dancing, and blood sports on Sundays. Influential lay support for this Sabbatarianism was demonstrated in the 1606 bill passed by the Commons (see Parliament of 1604-1610*). It provided for the punishment of abuses, including bear and bull baiting, plays, church ales, and dancing. It was delayed in the Lords, perhaps at James's instigation, but reintroduced in the parliament of 1614* and strongly supported in both houses. Football was added to the undesirable activities. In the Lords, the future Laudian Richard Neile supported the bill. Bishop James

Montague objected, favoring moderate recreation and punishment in ecclesiastical courts* alone. Montague was editing James's *Basilikon Doron*, wherein moderate recreation was supported. This perhaps explains Montague's lonely stand on the bill, which died with parliament's* dissolution.

In 1617, fresh from clashes with Scottish Presbyterians*, James visited Lancashire. Local magistrates, harsher than their bishop, had recently forbidden even piping and dancing at any time on Sundays. Resentful laymen petitioned James, who criticized the magistrates. Within days, piping and dancing occurred outside a Lancashire church during services. James turned the offenders over to Bishop Morton. Morton drafted the Book of Sports*, prohibiting blood sports, plays, and bowling. Recusants* could do sports only after attending church. James's preface rebuked Lancashire's "Puritans and precise people". Such attacks on "lawful recreations" could increase drunkenness and recusancy, leaving men unfit for war. James now saw no harm in piping, dancing, archery, and vaulting, and he associated strict Sabbatarianism with Puritans, lumping them with "Judaizing Sabbatarians," who would not even prepare food on Sundays.

In 1618 James made the Book of Sports a national declaration. The Lancashire episode perhaps suggested that secular authorities exceeded their authority in religious matters, threatening James's royal supremacy. Coupled with the trial of the Saturday Sabbath advocate John Traske, it indicated a need for moderation and clarification. However, the result in some localities was disorder outside churches or clashes between justices of the peace over enforcement. The subject was becoming increasingly controversial. A Sabbatarian bill sailed through the parliaments of 1621*, 1624*, and 1625*. Prince Charles (see Charles I*), perhaps courting popularity, supported the bill and as king assented to it in 1626, making Sunday blood sports, plays, church ales, and dancing illegal.

The controversy was revived and aggravated by Charles I's primate. Although London's* lay and ecclesiastical officials traditionally cooperated over Sabbath enforcement, Archbishop William Laud* resented mayoral involvement in 1629 and 1633. West country judges had long issued orders against church ales and punished offenders. Laud resented such orders being read in Somerset pulpits in 1633; the judges were invading episcopal jurisdiction and prohibiting traditional church festivals. He persuaded Charles to reissue the Book of Sports with an amendment protecting church ales in 1633. Laud no doubt liked James's preface, which ordered bishops to handle "Puritans and precisians" firmly. The book was to be published in all churches. Laud made obedience therein a test of clerical conformity. Many ministers, not just "Puritans," were distressed. Some were suspended.

Opinion was dangerously polarizing. Anti-Sabbatarians like Peter Heylyn depicted opposition to Sunday recreation as new and extremist. Enthusiastic Sabbatarians like the popular London rector Henry Burton blamed Laud for the reissuing and other "popish" innovations. Burton was deprived and his ears cut off in the pillory at Westminster.

Sabbatarianism had become a symbol of anti-Laudianism. Laud's downfall ensured a backlash. In 1643 the Long Parliament* ordered all copies of the Book of Sports burned. A 1644 act prohibited all Sunday recreations, although more detailed acts of 1650 and 1657 suggest enforcement difficulties.

Thus Sabbath recreations became another bone of contention between the early Stuart monarchy and some influential county gentry and clergy. In the tense 1630s extremism flourished on both sides. The calmer atmosphere of the Restoration* effectively reverted to pre-Book of Sports positions on recreations, wherein lack of clarification facilitated workable compromises at the local government* level.

Bibliography: Kenneth L. Parker, *The English Sabbath*, 1988, and reviews of it by Anthony Milton, *Journal of Ecclesiastical History* 41 (1990): 491-495 and Nicholas Tyacke, *English Historical Review* 106 (1991): 1002-1003.

                                                                     Vivienne C. Sanders

Salisbury, Earl of. See Cecil, Robert.

Sancroft, William (1617-1693). Archbishop of Canterbury who, through his leadership of the Seven Bishops* and the non-jurors, attempted to protect the Church of England's (see Anglicanism*) independence and moral integrity during the crises of James II's* tyranny and the Glorious Revolution*.

Sancroft was born into a yeoman family of Suffolk on 30 January 1617 and received his education at Emmanuel College, Cambridge, where he became a fellow in 1642. Ejected from his fellowship in 1651 for refusing to swear an oath of loyalty to the Commonwealth*, from 1657 to 1660 he went into self-imposed exile on the Continent. Upon his return, his friend John Cosin, the bishop of Durham, made Sancroft his chaplain. Further advancement rapidly followed, and in 1662 he was elected master of Emmanuel College and served as dean of St. Paul's Cathedral from 1664 to 1677. He succeeded Gilbert Sheldon* as archbishop of Canterbury in 1678 and devoted much attention to fruitless efforts to reconvert James II to Anglicanism.

Sancroft believed strongly in the subject's duty to give obedience to legitimate monarchs. Initially he agreed to serve on James II's ecclesiastical commission but quickly resigned when he discovered that the layman Judge George Jeffreys was to be its head (see Bloody Assizes*). In 1688 he opposed James II's order for Anglican clergy to read the Declaration of Indulgence* of 1687 during services in their churches. Along with six other bishops, he petitioned the king to withdraw his order and for his efforts was imprisoned in the Tower of London on the charge of seditious libel. Massive public support for the Seven Bishops helped to secure them a not guilty verdict. But in spite of his problems with James II, Sancroft loyally continued to advise the king to moderate his policies and refused to participate in any of the opposition activities that brought about the Glorious Revolution. After parliament* declared William* and Mary* to be the king and queen of England, Sancroft along with eight other bishops and 400 other ministers, who became known as the non-jurors, declined to take the required oaths of allegiance and supremacy. They argued that they were barred from taking the new oaths because of the earlier oaths of allegiance and supremacy they had sworn to James II. No arguments or threats could change their minds. As a result of his recalcitrance, parliament suspended Sancroft from the office of archbishop in 1689 and forced him out of Lambeth Palace in 1691. He died on 24 November 1693 during his forced retirement in the country, having established a reputation for unyielding integrity.

Bibliography: Norman Sykes, *From Sheldon to Secker*, 1959.

Ronald H. Fritze

Savoy Conference (1661). This conference between twelve Puritan* divines and twelve bishops, with nine assistants attending on each side, was held at the Savoy Palace, London*, from 15 April through 25 July 1661. These religious leaders met to discuss the revision of the Book of Common Prayer. As events leading up to the Restoration* had unfolded, Puritans had become more and more dissatisfied with the worship service. After the Restoration, English sentiment was strongly royalist*, and the bishops successfully resisted the attempts by the Puritans to revise sections of the worship service. Many of the observances and parts of the service appeared to the Puritans to reflect Roman Catholicism*. Puritan leaders' intransigence blinded them to the shifting of lay support toward Roman Catholicism and caused them to become disillusioned with the proceedings of the conference. This fact, coupled with the January uprising in London of the Fifth Monarchy Men*, undermined the prospects of the Savoy Conference called by Charles II*. The purpose of the meeting, to find a basis of accommodation between the Presbyterians* and the Anglicans* by revising the prayer book, was drastically reduced by the recent Fifth Monarchy revolt. The result of the conference was simply the continued use of the unrevised prayer book, a subtle but important loss for the Puritans in their attempt to retain a modicum of control over ecclesiastical concerns.

Bibliography: J. H. Blunt, *Annotated Book of Common Prayer*, 1908; J. P. Kenyon, *Stuart England*, 1978.

John S. Erwin

Saye and Sele, Lord. See Fiennes, William.

Science and the Scientific Revolution. During the seventeenth century, men and women interested in investigating the natural world developed new theories and discoveries, a new methodology, and a new structure for scientific practice. The combination of these elements created what has become known as the Scientific Revolution. The Scientific Revolution was a European rather than simply an English phenomenon, but English participation was extremely important and in some cases crucial. This was the century in which the English scientific community developed and took its place at the forefront of European scientific investigation. Indeed the English scientific community supplied a number of crucial elements that would unite to create modern science: a significant number of innovative and insightful thinkers, a national stake in a new methodology that stressed cooperative experiment and objectivity, and a gentlemanly coterie of scientists who applied their social standards of behavior to the ideology of modern science.

The Scientific Revolution is most clearly identified with the development of a heliocentric model of the universe. This began with Nicholas Copernicus (1473-1543), who claimed that the earth revolved around the sun and developed a mathematical model to explain the movement of the planets. The first true Copernican was Johannes Kepler (1571-1630), who showed that the planets moved around the sun in elliptical, rather than circular, orbits. Galileo Galilei's (1564-1642) telescopic observations of the craters on the moon and sunspots, repeated by the Englishman Thomas Harriot (1560-1621) in 1609, proved that the part of the universe above the moon was not perfect, as Aristotle had claimed, but was similar to the earthly sphere. This finding encouraged the great English astronomer and mathematician, Sir Isaac Newton (1642-1727), to devise a mathematical model of motion that would explain heavenly and earthly movement in a single system based on his concept of universal gravitation.

Newton was the most famous scientist of his generation. He received many important marks of honor indicative of his high status, including positions as Lucasian Professor of Mathematics at Cambridge, master of the mint, and president of the Royal Society*. Even Newton's opulent state funeral in 1727 demonstrated his exalted position, made plain to French contemporaries by Voltaire's eye-witness accounts. Yet it would be a mistake to equate Stuart science only with Isaac Newton. By the 1660s a lively community of scientific scholars had grown up, focused both at the universities* and increasingly in London*. Gresham College, established in London in 1598 by Sir Thomas Gresham's bequest, provided a focus for many enthusiastic natural philosophers and scientists, acting as an adjunct to the scientific training and programs at Oxford and Cambridge. The cooperation, rather than competition, of Gresham and the universities can be seen by the career of Sir Henry Briggs (1561-1630). Briggs was educated at Cambridge, then moved to London to become Gresham Professor of Geometry (1598-1620), finally returning to Oxford to become the first Savilian Professor of Astronomy in 1620. Thus Oxford and Cambridge provided a venue for scientific investigation, as well as the status of university appointments and a network of likeminded individuals. Still, London was proving to be an increasingly important locale for scientific discussion, due in the early part of the century to the presence of the royal courts* (especially those of James I* and of Henry*, prince of Wales), the Inns of Court, and Gresham, and encouraged still further after 1663 by the presence of the Royal Society.

Many men studied the natural world in the Stuart period and made important contributions to the larger revolution taking place. In mathematics, John Napier (1550-1617) and Briggs developed logarithms. An interest in simplifying calculations also led Edmund Gunter (Gresham Professor of Astronomy, 1619-1626) to develop a series of calculating instruments, including a slide rule. Many mathematicians, such as Briggs, John Pell (1611-1685), John Wilkins (1614-1672), Sir Isaac Barrow (1630-1677), and James Gregory (1638-1675), labored to find answers to algebraic problems such as squaring the circle. The work of these men, especially of Barrow, directly influenced Newton in his development of the calculus (or fluxions as he called it) in the 1660s. This development led to a priority dispute, since Gottfried von Leibniz claimed that he had invented the calculus several years earlier. A pamphlet war ensued between Leibniz and Samuel Clarke (1675-1729), Newton's champion, which produced much vitriol and little resolution. Today the credit for the invention of the calculus is generally awarded to both men.

In astronomy, the work of continental astronomers dominated the field in the first half of the century. The early work of Thomas Harriot established English astronomy, but he did not publish, so his work was little known beyond his immediate circle. Gunter, Thomas Lydiat (1572-1646), John Bainbridge (1582-1643), Henry Gellibrand (Gresham Professor of Astronomy, 1627-1636), and William Oughtred (1575-1660), all avowed Copernicans, studied the paths of the planets and the positions of the stars. Their work in the period before and during the Interregnum* was extended in the years after the Restoration* by Newton and Edmund Halley (1656-1742). Newton's great opus, *The Mathematical Principles of Natural Philosophy* (1687), laid out his theory of universal gravitation and established a mathematical and mechanical model for the motion of the whole universe. Halley's investigation of comets resulted in the demonstration that comets, like planets, orbited the sun. The Great Comet of 1682, which Halley identified from historical accounts and whose return in 1754 he predicted, now bears his name.

Closely akin to the study of astronomy was the field of cosmology and magnetic research. England had established its preeminence in this discipline with the earlier work of William Gilbert, whose *De Magnete* (1600) had introduced the theory that the earth was a large magnet. In the early years of the seventeenth century, English magnetic philosophers maintained Gilbert's picture of the earth as a static lodestone, arguing against French magnetic philosophers who claimed that the interior of the earth was movable. Gilbert's views won the day, an outcome that tells us a great deal about the growing English claim to intellectual hegemony. Gilbert's work was followed by Gunter and Gellibrand, who studied secular variation (the changing nature of the variation of compass needles from true north) and demonstrated that the magnetic variation of the earth varied over time. This was a disturbing finding, since it seemed to cast much magnetic information in doubt and was only partially counteracted by Halley's isogonic map in 1701, which connected all areas of similar magnetic variation on the globe.

English natural philosophers also investigated the behavior of light and vision. Newton took a lead in this area, developing a theory of light based on a series of simple and elegant experiments, published in *Opticks* (1704). By passing a beam of sunlight through a series of prisms, Newton demonstrated that white light was not pure light, as had been previously supposed, but rather was a composite of many colors of light (the spectrum). Newton believed that light was composed of particles and that their differing speeds resulted in a differing angle of refraction when passed through a prism. This theory was hotly debated, the French preferring a wave theory of light, but Newton's *Opticks* provided a foundation for a new English school of optical research throughout the eighteenth century. English natural philosophers and instrument makers also used prisms and lenses to create telescopes and microscopes.

Newton developed the first reflecting telescope, while Robert Hooke (1635-1703), curator of experiments of the Royal Society, examined the subvisual world through the newly developed microscopes. His book *Micrographia* (1665) reported the shape of things too small to be seen by the naked eye.

Equally important were investigations of the chemical makeup of the world. Robert Boyle (1627-1691) and Newton were involved in alchemical investigations, looking both for the philosopher's stone and the basic substance of matter. This was a respectable study in seventeenth-century natural philosophy, and both men's investigations were the result of a belief in God's ordering of the universe. Boyle later denounced old-fashioned alchemical investigations and in *The Skeptical Chymist* (1661) laid a foundation for the new study of chemistry. As well, Boyle and Hooke began to investigate the air, using a newly devised air pump. They demonstrated that air had weight, that a vacuum could exist, and that part of the air was necessary for respiration and combustion. Thomas Hobbes*, a natural philosopher as well as moralist, strongly criticized the work of Boyle and Hooke. Hobbes claimed that the air pump did not work (probably accurate) and that it in no way represented a vacuum, as they had claimed. Although Hobbes had many sound arguments, Boyle's rising status, both socially and scientifically, ensured that his was the winning side of this disagreement.

English natural philosophers also made important contributions in the field of biology and medicine*. Several herbals and bestiaries were written during the seventeenth century, and botany was taught at the medical faculties of the two universities. During the Interregnum, anatomical demonstrations were performed, especially at Oxford, although most anatomy followed the work of Italian physicians. William Harvey (1578-1657), who had received his medical training at Padua, returned to London in 1602, worked as Charles I's* royal physician, and conducted a series of experiments on blood in animals. This resulted in the publication of *On the Movement of the Heart and Blood in Animals* (1628), in which Harvey demonstrated that the blood in animals and in human beings circulated through the entire body, returning to the heart. In his preface Harvey drew the political parallel between this circulation and the movement of citizens around their king.

All of these men and their investigation show the liveliness of the scientific community in seventeenth-century England. Equally important, however, was the development of a new method of scientific inquiry, a new "scientific method." In England, this methodology sprang from the writing of Sir Francis Bacon*.

Bacon, although not himself a natural philosopher, proposed a reform of natural philosophy in the *Novum Organum* (1620) and *The New Atlantis* (1627). This program of reform was part of a grander scheme to reform all knowledge, especially legal knowledge and moral philosophy. Bacon believed that all human knowledge was flawed because of the idols that all men carried with them. These were the prejudices and preconceived ideas through which human beings observed the world. Bacon felt that the only way for natural philosophers to disabuse themselves of these idols was to look at small, discrete bits of nature, isolated from their environs. Using this assumption Bacon introduced what has come to be called the inductive method. He suggested that increments of information could be gathered by armies of investigators, put together in tabular form, and explained by an elite cadre of interpreters. Thus Bacon's methodology, although it appeared more democratic than earlier scholastic methods, was actually a means to control truth and knowledge by a small elite group who determined what could be studied and what answers were acceptable.

This methodology was challenged on the continent by René Descartes and his followers, who preferred a deductive style based on skepticism. In England, however, Baconianism reigned supreme, at least rhetorically. When the Royal Society was founded, it adopted Baconianism as its methodology, partly as a way of distancing itself from what it saw as "godless" Cartesianism and partly as a call to national superiority. This allegiance to Baconianism was more rhetorical than real but demonstrates a growing belief in the superiority of English science.

The development of an English methodology was extremely important, for both the maturity of English science and the development of the larger Scientific Revolution. Of even greater significance in the creation of modern science was the new locale of scientific discussion and the new ideology and code of conduct established in seventeenth-century London. Science had previously been the property of clerics and academics. The upheaval of the Interregnum and Restoration created an opportunity for a new group of practitioners, gentlemen in London, to develop a new standard for scientific conduct and a new place to practice science.

Robert Boyle was particularly instrumental in this transformation. He set up his pneumatic laboratory in his sister's house on Pall Mall in London, and people interested in natural philosophy gathered to witness his experiments. Since he was a gentleman and since the codes of conduct concerning the new experimental science had not yet been established, Boyle and his gentleman colleagues took over the codes of ethics from their social position. A scientist's word became his bond, scientists collectively determined who could achieve the status of a scientist, and the polite discourse of the town club became the accepted mode for scientific conversation. More than any scientific discovery, this development of rhetoric and behavior helped create the science we recognize today.

One of the most enduring historiographic controversies concerning science in this period is the question of the relationship between science and religion. From Robert Merton's *Science, Technology and Society in Seventeenth-Century England* (1938) came the contention that Protestantism, and especially Puritanism*, helped create the Scientific Revolution, which led Christopher Hill and others to claim that the Puritan universities of the Interregnum provided the first real impetus for English science. In recent years, historians have denied a relationship between strongly held Puritan beliefs and scientific investigation, claiming instead that natural philosophers pursued science as a way of avoiding the religious controversies of the day. Founders of the Royal Society wanted to avoid the taint of either atheism or "enthusiasm." Early supporters of the Royal Society, such as Thomas Sprat (1635-1713) and Joseph Glanvill (1636-1680), claimed that natural philosophy allowed a worship of God and His works that would not interfere with church politics.

Most of this discussion of seventeenth-century science has focused on the contributions of men of science; however, this was a period when women* were attempting to make their mark on the study of the natural world. Both Anne Finch, viscountess of Conway (1631-1679), and Margaret Cavendish, duchess of Newcastle (1617-1673), were interested in breaking into this previously clerical and male preserve. The same social and intellectual upheaval that made science a gentlemanly pursuit gave women a brief window of opportunity to become involved in natural philosophy. Anne Conway corresponded with Leibniz and developed a theory of "monads" that became the basis of his particulate philosophy of the universe. Margaret Newcastle wrote many books of natural philosophy and attended a meeting of the Royal Society. Both women, however, were exceptions rather than the beginning of a trend. The eighteenth century saw a restriction in women's sphere in science as in much else.

During the seventeenth century, English natural philosophers arrived as players in the larger continental Scientific Revolution. Where the sixteenth century had been a period of scientific apprenticeship, in the seventeenth century Englishmen took their place at the forefront of scientific discovery and change. They supplied new ideas, theories, and experimental discoveries, a new methodology of science, and a new ethical ideology. These ingredients led to the development of a new scientific culture that would rapidly assume a recognizably modern face and would affect all aspects of English life.

Bibliography: Michael Hunter, *Science and Society in Restoration England*, 1981; Charles Webster, *The Great Instauration: Science, Medicine and Reform, 1626-1660*, 1975; R. S. Westfall, *Never at Rest: A Biography of Isaac Newton*, 1980.

Lesley Cormack

Scotland (1603-1688). Absentee monarchy, religious strife, and the rise of parliamentary government complicated seventeenth-century Scottish politics. Until 1641 the kings ruled Scotland through the privy council, with the Scottish estates playing a subordinate role. The rise and triumph of the Covenanters* witnessed the creation of a parliamentary state. The English conquerors utilized both military and conciliar government. The Restoration* revived royal control through the privy council but also added the post of royal secretary to advise the king on Scottish affairs. Finally, James VII (and II*)—as heir, then king—restored rigid royal supervision.

Having achieved political dominance during his personal rule, James VI (and I*) had the advantages of intimate knowledge of the means of government and of the men who formed the political nation. The king's boast, "I write and it is done, and by a clerk of the council I govern Scotland now, which others could not do by the sword," was not wide of the mark. With the ennobling of holders of church lands (mainly royal civil servants) in 1606, James solidified the commitment of nobles to Crown as opposed to Presbyterian* policies. The mutual trust between these men (exemplified by the earls of Dunbar, Dunfermline, and Melrose/Haddington) and the king ensured the implementation of royal policies in the council and estates. By setting the venue and date of meetings of the Church of Scotland's (see Kirk*) general assemblies and by wielding the financial carrot and stick over the clergy, the king also controlled religious affairs. From a distance James managed the reestablishment of episcopacy, pacification of the Borders and Highlands, and the establishment of justices of the peace. Parliament, whose business was set by the committee of articles (a body where bishops, in their capacity as royal servants, selected the noble members), was of importance only for setting taxation* and approving royal policies. Furthermore, the king kept the nobles and Presbyterian ministers, lairds, and burgesses divided to prevent any threat to royal power.

Declining mental faculties, the rise of nobles unknown to the king, royal arrogance, and a belief that the Scots Calvinists* would agree with their king that Anglican* practices were more reverent inspired James during his visit in 1617 to propose five articles. These innovations in religion were a religious calendar, kneeling while receiving communion, confirmation, and private baptism and communion. A general assembly rejected them in November. In a packed clerical assembly at Perth in January 1618, one-third voted against the king. As the Presbyterians rallied to oppose the Five Articles of Perth*, James believed withdrawal would weaken the Crown. Consequently the articles were pushed through a managed parliament in 1621, but two-fifths of the estates voted against them. James canceled his plans to align the Scottish Kirk more closely with the English church, in order to preserve a firm control of Scottish politics.

Charles I*, of Scottish birth and English breeding, proved a disaster. His arrogance, aloofness, and ignorance contrasted sharply with his father's skill. Charles made a string of missteps, which eroded the loyalty of the nobles and antagonized much of the country. His sweeping Acts of Revocation (challenging royal land grants back to 1542) terrorized all landholders, their provisions for freeing lairds from the feudal power of the aristocracy infuriated the latter, and the aim of bettering episcopal finances angered Presbyterians. That Charles intended his Scots government to fulfill his orders, not to advise him, was equally worrisome. To obtain an amenable council, the king packed it with bishops to whom he assigned important political duties. Royal declarations of war against France (an important trading partner) and Spain (possessor of numerous privateers) struck the thriving Scottish economy (see French War of 1627-1629* and Spanish War of 1625-1630*). The king's reliance on the despised Robert Maxwell, earl of Nithsdale, reinforced the political nation's fear of their monarch.

The royal visit in 1633 convinced a party of nobles that desperate measures were essential to preserve their class's role in governing Scotland. The Scots viewed Charles's worshipping with the full panoply of High Anglicanism insulting at best and smacking of popery. The king also disappointed those hoping for peerages or further advancement. Furthermore, he treated the nobles with coolness and contempt. The nadir of the visit was the Balmerino affair, in which the heir of one of James's trusted servants was charged, tried, and condemned to death for preparing to present a petition of grievances to Charles. The visit demonstrated to the Scots that their absentee English monarch intended to impose alien policies by absolutist* means upon them.

After his tour, Charles intended to draw Scotland into alignment with England in religious practices. To solidify royal power in the council, he made Archbishop John

Spottiswoode of St. Andrews chancellor in 1635. Nobles of all religious stripes were outraged by the first elevation of a churchman to the country's preeminent political office since the Reformation. The council's leading noble, Lord Treasurer John Stewart, earl of Traquair, had talent only for elevating himself, not in building a royal faction. In 1636 the imposition of a Book of Canons on the Kirk without the approval of even a managed general assembly hardened Presbyterian opposition to the king. Already the nobles, led by the earl of Rothes and Lord Loudoun, and the Presbyterian-inclined clergy had begun to prepare for overt opposition to royal policies.

The rotten edifice of Caroline royal government collapsed during the prayer book controversy in face of national fury. The prayer book, introduced in July 1637, attempted to bring Scottish worship practice closer to that of Laudian England (see William Laud*). The landholders, leagued with the Presbyterians, mounted a sustained campaign of civil disobedience and limited violence. The privy council, assailed by the protesters to the book, became a mere formality in national politics by late 1637. That November the supplicants (Covenanters after February 1638) formed a national committee called the Tables, which became Scotland's de facto government. After the two Bishops' Wars* (1639-1640), the king visited Scotland and acceded to all of the Covenanters' demands.

For a decade (1638-1648) the Covenanters ran a well-organized parliamentary system that withstood internal and foreign enemies. The Covenanters produced a two-tier government with the privy council (1641-1643), the estates, or the committee of estates (1643-1648) setting national policy and the civil presbyteries/committees of war (or of the shire) implementing it in the localities. The 8th earl (later 1st marquis) of Argyll (Archibald Campbell*) was the leading politician of the Covenanters, but many other nobles and lairds assisted him until the movement split over the Engagement* in spring 1648. Roman Catholics* and militant royalists* (such as the marquis of Montrose) were excluded from the noble-led government. While lairds acted with political initiative on occasion, the burgesses followed on the heels of men like Argyll or his rivals the duke of Hamilton and the earl of Lanark. In British politics the Covenanters played an active part, allying with the English to intervene in Ireland* and England.

The Covenanters split in 1648 over the grounds for a treaty with Charles. With national unity lost when the Kirk party* rejected the Engagement, the chances for survival of an independent Scotland diminished. While the governmental system created by the Covenanters persisted, internal rebellions and hostility from the English parliamentarians* weakened its prestige. The Covenanters accepted Charles II* as their king in 1649, but only in spring 1650 did he accept their assistance. The royalist stance of the Kirk party precipitated war with the English Commonwealth* that summer.

After the English conquest in September 1651, the Scots lost any significant political role. From 1651 to 1655 an English military governor (John Lilburne* or George Monck*) ruled the country. The union of parliaments in 1652 provided Scotland with members of parliament at Westminster, but their selection depended upon the approval of the English army*. In 1655 a council of state under Robert

Boyle, Lord Broghill, began governing Scotland from Edinburgh. Glencairn's Rising (1653-1655), the most serious attempt by the Scots to restore Charles II and regain independence, failed. In 1660, when Monck marched south to intervene in English politics, he left a supine country in which the natives lacked a real political voice.

The Restoration of Charles II as king of Scots in 1660 brought changes to Scottish politics. The king repudiated the union* of parliaments and restored Scotland's status as an independent kingdom. He followed James VI in assigning the daily government of Scotland to the privy council and by restoring episcopal church government. Royal commissioners—the earls of Middleton and Lauderdale (John Maitland*)—managed the meetings of the estates, which repealed all Covenanter legislation in 1661. The king's secretary in London* (Lauderdale, 1660-1681) initiated many of the royal policies for Scotland.

Initially repression of all Presbyterians and the suppression of opponents to royal policy were the hallmarks of the new regime. Middleton's control of the council (1661-1663) witnessed the removal of one-third of the clergy for adhering to Presbyterianism, the execution of the marquis of Argyll, the passage of high customs and excise duties, and the growth of rampant corruption in government. In a political coup Lauderdale expelled Middleton from power in 1663, replacing him with the debauched earl of Rothes. Repression (in line with Edward Hyde*, earl of Clarendon's policy in England) continued to drive government policy until the Pentland Rising* in 1666.

Lauderdale's ascent to near total control of Scottish affairs in 1667 initially brought a change in policy. With the earls of Tweeddale and Kincardine as allies, Lauderdale granted toleration to the less extremist Presbyterians (indulgences of 1669 and 1672). Opposition remained checked, despite the increasingly obvious corruption of Lauderdale's government. From 1673 he governed Scotland with the assistance of cronies. Repression of all opponents, Presbyterian or political, became the new keynote of the regime. The quartering of the "Highland Host" (anti-Presbyterian militia) in the southwest Lowlands capped the regime's willingness to crush religious nonconformity. The southwestern Presbyterians (also known as Covenanters for their stubborn adherence to the Covenants) rebelled in 1679, only to be crushed by James, duke of Monmouth. As a result of the Covenanter Rebellion*, Lauderdale lost his political influence.

From 1679 until Charles's death in 1685, two royal dukes controlled Scottish affairs. Monmouth pursued a policy of toleration for the Presbyterians. His replacement as vice-regent, the Roman Catholic James, duke of York and Albany (heir to the throne), restored anti-Presbyterian policies. York served as vice-regent in 1679 and 1680-1682, but from his arrival until his flight from England in 1688, his views dominated Scottish politics. Passage of a Test Act in 1681 obliged any Scotsman who wished to maintain secure title to his lands or hopes of political office to accept total royal supremacy in religion and civil affairs. Some of those dissatisfied with government policies fled to the Netherlands. With the exception of the fanatical Presbyterians (Cameronians), who were fighting a guerrilla war against the Crown, the rest of Scotland became as muzzled as it had been under the English.

The accession to the throne of York as James VII in 1685 emphasized the demoralized condition of Scots. The rising of the 9th earl of Argyll (Archibald Campbell*), in conjunction with Monmouth's Rebellion* in England, was easily crushed by overwhelming forces. Parliament voted the king the excise for life and addressed the most extravagant claims of loyalty to him. The legislature also passed more ferocious acts against Presbyterians of all stripes. An attempt to bribe the estates into granting Roman Catholics toleration in exchange for free trade with England failed in 1686. From that point James encouraged conversion to Catholicism and advanced his co-religionists into important posts. In declarations issued by the council in 1687, the king extended religious toleration to all. The Presbyterian clergy used the new situation to establish a church parallel to the national episcopal one, hardly the king's intention. Opposition to pro-Roman Catholic policies extended from Protestants on the council throughout society. Still there was no Scottish element in the Glorious Revolution* of 1688 until James fled England. Then popular discontent against Episcopalian clergy and Roman Catholics erupted. The stage was set for further constitutional and religious upheavals in Scotland, which exceeded those in England in the character of the changes they wrought. As James VI had so wisely warned, only the division of the nobility and the Presbyterians could ensure royal control of Scotland.

Bibliography: Gordon Donaldson, *Scotland: James V to James VII*, 1971; Rosalind Mitchison, *Lordship to Patronage: Scotland, 1603-1745*, 1983.

Edward M. Furgol

Seekers. Term describing supposed radical millenarian* group born during the reigns of James I* and Charles I*. Seekers were most visible during the revolutionary period and comprised a portion of the radical wing of English religion throughout the Interregnum*. Seekers sought to rediscover the religious purity of the apostolic age and to prepare the saints for the triumphant return of Christ; they harshly criticized established religion in the sixteenth century. Their lack of an identifiable organization and their extreme individualism render Seekers difficult to define or categorize precisely, though some evidence may point to the sporadic existence of informal groups of Seekers.

Seekers, like other radical sects, reflected a loss of confidence in the established church. Radicals interpreted victory in the Civil War* as a sign trumpeting the arrival of a new apostolic age. The failure to carry through radical religious and social changes drove Seekers away from both the Church of England (see Anglicanism*) and Presbyterians*, toward a Separatist* position.

They also promoted Martin Luther's priesthood of believers as the justification for social equality. Any social status would be based on spiritual experience rather than birth. Seekers such as William Erbery sought an equalization of the classes through increased poor relief (see Poor Laws and Poverty*) and higher taxation* for the wealthy. They discounted the power and authority of the established church in favor of an extreme individualism. Their focus on inward faith and experience made an outward, visible church no longer necessary.

The millennial hope that Christ would build a new church under a new apostolic dispensation contributed to the Seekers' rejection of contemporary ecclesiastical authority. They acquired the title "Seeker" because they were waiting for someone with the requisite apostolic ordination to usher in this new dispensation and endue them with power. Seekers therefore represented the yearnings of radical millenarians looking forward to the replacement of the corrupt visible church by a purified institution led by new apostolic authority and marked by emphasis on inner light rather than outward conformity to religious dogma. This inner light was manifested through a belief in miracles and the charismatic gifts. Seekers, along with Ranters*, faded during the Interregnum and disappeared after the Restoration*. Both lacked the organization necessary for surviving against powerful opposition. Both were also largely assimilated by other groups such as the Quakers*, who retained a strong emphasis on the inner light but had a far stronger and more resilient organization.

Both Ranters and Seekers are historiographically difficult topics of study. Seekers and Ranters both were identified and labeled by their detractors. Since they never identified themselves as formal groups, there is considerable doubt as to whether either existed as such. "Ranter" and "Seeker" may simply be terms given to individuals who shared a common deviation from Protestant or Catholic* norms.

Bibliography: Christopher Hill, *The World Turned Upside Down: Radical Ideas During the English Revolution*, 1972; R. M. Jones, *Mysticism and Democracy in the English Commonwealth*, 1965; J. F. McGregor and Barry Reay, *Radical Religion in the English Revolution*, 1984.

William Nikides

Selden, John (1584-1654). Lawyer, scholar, textual editor, historian, and not least of all vocal parliamentarian*, Selden made important contributions in each of these spheres in the course of his long life. He was born in West Tarring, Sussex, in December 1584; his mother was a gentleman's daughter and his father a local minstrel of some means. Selden's intellectual gifts were evident early on. From early training at Chichester Free School to his undergraduate years at Hart Hall Oxford, Selden proceeded, as did most other young men with legal ambitions, first to Clifford's Inn in London* in 1602 and then to the Inner Temple in 1604. He would remain associated with the Temple for the rest of his days and lived there through much of the early part of his adult life.

Selden soon acquired renown as a legal adviser and was employed in that capacity by several noble families, in particular by Henry Grey, 7th earl of Kent (d. 1639), and subsequently by his widow, Elizabeth (d.1651). But Selden never practiced law as a full-time occupation, so devoted was he to scholarship. Fluent in Latin, Greek, and Old English, and able to read Hebrew and some Arabic as well, he was among the most skillful linguists of his time, and he turned this immense erudition, enhanced by familiarity with the most up-to-date French and Dutch philological treatises, to the study of the past. His earliest works, such as *Jani Anglorum Facies Altera* (1610), dealt with the history of English law from remote antiquity to the Norman Conquest. In *Titles of Honor* (1614; second, expanded edition 1631) he investigated the origins and history of various English and continental titles of nobility and gentility, by way of comparing the political and hierarchical structures of different societies, past and present. He also displayed in *De Dis Syris* (1617) the familiarity with Oriental languages and scholarship that would establish him as a polymath of European (as opposed to merely English) reputation and would figure more prominently in many of his later works.

Selden remains most famous for two works. The first, written when he was still in his thirties, was the *History of Tithes* (1618), a marvelous example of philological scholarship and the early achievements of seventeeth-century historical thought*. An immensely learned work, it demonstrated from scrupulously careful comparison of texts and attention to manuscript sources that the English clergy's claim to tithes was in fact historically based and of relatively recent, thirteenth-century origins. This sparked, unusually for the early seventeenth century, a major historical controversy between Selden and the clergy, in which Selden's superior sense of historical development and his ability to muster sources have left him in modern eyes as the clear winner. The second work, difficult to date because it was published only in 1689 by his secretary Richard Milward (1609-1680), was the *Table-Talk*, a record of Selden's thoughts and sayings on a variety of subjects, including religion and politics, in the last two decades of his life. This book contains the clearest expression of some of Selden's views, free of the convoluted prose that obfuscates many of his major Latin and English works.

Beginning in the later 1620s, Selden largely abandoned the study of English history and began to pursue the study of comparative jurisprudence and especially natural law while also beginning to edit several texts that he would publish over the next quarter century, such as the eleventh-century chronicler Eadmer and the Arabic patriarch Eutychius; in the 1640s he would write an important commentary on the medieval legal treatise known as *Fleta*. Selden also engaged in the study of the law of the sea as it related to the concept of property, a central issue in seventeenth-century political thought. His *Mare Clausum* was composed under James I* in response to a treatise by the Dutch scholar and philosopher Hugo Grotius. It was first published in 1635 to assert the Stuart claim to sovereignty over the near seas, and it remains an interesting document in the history of international jurisprudence. Selden's works were collected and reprinted in 1726 by David Wilkins.

Like his older contemporary, the antiquary Sir Robert Cotton* (1571-1631), Selden was also an important political figure. He was imprisoned briefly for his part in preparing the Commons Protestation of 1621*. He first served as a member in the parliament of 1624*, being returned again to the parliaments of 1626* and 1628-1629*, when he was active as a client of William Seymour, earl of Hertford (1588-1660), and the Seymour interest. Selden's antiquarian skills proved indispensable to parliamentarians, and he was often placed on committees charged with searching the Tower of London records for precedents to justify parliamentary privileges or to disprove the historical arguments being adduced by officers of the Crown on behalf of unpopular practices such as billeting, forced loans*, and arbitrary imprisonment. He was prominent in the debate arising from the Five Knights Case* of 1627 and would participate in the framing of the Petition of Right* in 1628. Once again imprisoned, together with Sir John Eliot* and seven other members for his part in the stormy parliamentary session of 1629, Selden was released two years later at the intervention of Arundel. He spent the next decade immersed once more in scholarship and was sometimes connected with the Tew circle of intellectuals and philosophers associated with Lucius Cary, viscount Falkland (1610-1643) and Edward Hyde*, later earl of Clarendon, a group that also included Selden's friend, the philosopher Thomas Hobbes*. In the election to the Long Parliament*, he was returned for Oxford University. In addition to serving on several important committees, he was appointed clerk and keeper of the Tower records from 1643 and one of twelve commissioners of the Admiralty in the following year. Of moderate opinions in religion, he also sat for a time in the Westminster Assembly of Divines*, where he became an outspoken opponent of the Presbyterian* clergy. Selden's devotion to the rule of law, so pronounced in the 1620s, caused him to waver from the parliamentary cause in the 1640s as various unprecedented and unconstitutional measures were enacted before and during the Civil War*. He gradually withdrew from public affairs, and although he kept silence during Charles I's trial and execution*, he almost certainly disapproved of it. Occasionally consulted by the Commonwealth* and Cromwellian regimes (see Oliver Cromwell*; Richard Cromwell*, Protectorate*), Selden spent his last few years principally engaged in Hebraic and Arabic scholarship, while serving as the friend and legal adviser (and husband, as some contemporary opinion had it) of Elizabeth, dowager countess of Kent, until her death in 1651. He died on 30 November 1654, still living in her London residence, Carmelite House, and was buried in the Inner Temple. Most of his books, several thousand volumes in manuscript and print (including copious correspondence that remains largely unedited even today), ended up in the Bodleian Library, Oxford. Clarendon, though somewhat critical of his friend's prose style, praised Selden nonetheless as having "the best faculty in making hard things easy and present to the understanding of any man that hath ever been known."

Bibliography: David S. Berkowitz, *John Selden's Formative Years,* 1988; P. Christianson, "Young John Selden and the Ancient Constitution," *Proceedings of the American Philosophical Society* 128 (1984): 271-315.

Daniel R. Woolf

Self-Denying Ordinance (1644). The parliamentary armies' indifferent record since the summer of 1644, combined with their officers' repeated tendency to fracture along political and religious lines, provided compelling reasons for establishing a new military dispensation at the end of that year. Accordingly, on 9 December, the House of Commons adopted the following motion by Zouch Tate, chairman of the committee for the army*, seconded by Sir Henry Vane, Jr., "that during the time of this war, no member of either house shall have or execute any office or command, military or civil, granted or conferred by both or either of the houses of parliament or any authority derived from both or either of the houses, and that an ordinance be brought in accordingly."

The ordinance was widely perceived as a radical maneuver, since far more Peace Party than War Party commanders stood to lose their posts. To the radicals' surprise, the ordinance passed, over the bitter opposition of supporters of Robert Devereux*, earl of Essex in the Commons. But in spite of unremitting pressure exerted by the Commons on the upper house, Essex—who commanded a majority in the Lords—was able to block the measure. Not until four months later, when the New Model Army* had already been created in accordance with the principles of self-denial, did the Lords finally recognize the fait accompli. Having resigned their military commissions at the end of March 1645, the earls of Essex, Manchester, and Denbigh also lifted their veto of the Self-Denying Ordinance, which duly became law on 3 April.

In its final form the ordinance differed significantly from the resolution adopted by the Commons in December. Instead of rendering parliamentarians* incapable of executing any office or command for the duration of the war, it now simply dismissed them with forty days' notice. Furthermore, lords lieutenant*, deputy lieutenants, keepers of the rolls, justices of the peace (see Local Government*), and commissioners of oyer and terminer and gaol delivery (see Common Law and Courts*) were all exempted from the ordinance's provisions. Also protected were those who had enjoyed royal office before 1640 but were displaced by the king and later restored to their offices by parliamentary authority. Ironically the Lords retrieved their civilian appointments, whereas what had offended them most about the ordinance was that the nobility was robbed of its historic military function in the state.

Even more ironic, the amended ordinance paved the way for Oliver Cromwell's* appointment as lieutenant general of the New Model cavalry. At the beginning of May the Commons extended Cromwell's existing command by another forty days, since he was still fighting the royalists* and mobilizing fresh troops. The Lords grudgingly concurred. Early in June Sir Thomas Fairfax* wrote to both houses of parliament, requesting Cromwell's appointment to the New Model. The Commons granted Fairfax's request, but the Lords refused it. Cromwell defiantly took command at Naseby* and, by dint of his dazzling performance on the battlefield, compelled the Lords' acquiescence in his appointment. But they approved it only for a three-month period, which they later extended several times. It should be noted that Cromwell was not the only member of parliament to be exempted from the terms of the Self-Denying Ordinance. Major General Richard Browne's command was extended, while the earl of Warwick was later appointed admiral of the parliamentary navy*. Thus the Self-Denying Ordinance turned into a supple instrument whose main function was to exclude from the parliamentary war effort men whose service had been half-hearted or incompetent.

Bibliography: J. S. A. Adamson, "The Baronial Context of the English Civil War," *Transactions of the Royal Historical Society*, 5th series, 40 (1990): 93-120; A. N. B. Cotton, "Cromwell and the Self-Denying Ordinance," *History* 62 (1977): 211-231.

Ian Gentles

Separatism. The name *Separatist* was given to those English Protestants who rejected the Church of England (see Anglicanism*) as unreformable and separated themselves from it during the late sixteenth and early seventeenth centuries into "gathered" congregations, voluntary associations of like-minded believers living under a Christian covenant. Separatists believed that they were restoring the pristine purity of the church of the New Testament and used the Bible* as their sole guide for determining what constituted a true church.

Separatism had its origin during the reigns of the Tudor queens, Mary and Elizabeth, with its outstanding leaders being Robert Browne (c.1550-1633) and Henry Barrowe (c.1550-1593). Roman Catholics* naturally found the Separatists to be heretics, but even the Protestant Elizabethan Church of England found their schismatic teachings to be totally unacceptable and subjected them to vigorous persecution in the 1580s and 1590s. Barrowe and several other Separatist leaders suffered death for their beliefs in 1593. At that point many of the London* Separatists moved to Amsterdam, where they formed a congregation with Francis Johnson (1562-1618) serving as their pastor and Henry Ainsworth (1571-1622) acting as their teacher. Separatists who remained in England went into a period of quiescence.

Separatism revived in the reign of James I*, but it also experienced schisms that led to the end of the Elizabethan style of Separatism and the appearance of various competing groups who became the progenitors of some of the Civil War* sects and of the post-Restoration* Dissenters*. One of these revivers was John Smyth (c.1554-1612), who received his education at Christ's College, Cambridge, where he later became a fellow. Although definitely a Puritan* in his religious sympathies, he was not at first a Separatist and instead took great pains to stress his adherence to the Church of England. His initial problems with ecclesiastical authorities stemmed from his proclivity to engage in unauthorized preaching. When he first assumed the pastorate of Gainsborough parish in early 1606, he had not yet converted to Separatism. Then sometime in late 1606 or early 1607, his study of the teachings of Francis Johnson persuaded him to become a Separatist. That action led Smyth and some of his congregation in 1608 to join the Separatist community in Amsterdam.

Unfortunately for Johnson and his flock, John Smyth and his followers proved to be a highly divisive addition to their church. Smyth's religious beliefs continued to evolve, and in 1609 he concluded that the Church of England's baptism was invalid and so rebaptized himself. He also began promoting the practice of believer baptism and defended his ideas in *The Character of the Beast* (1609). Such ideas were highly controversial and caused a rift among the exiled Separatists. Meanwhile Smyth also adopted the theological ideas of Jacob Arminius (1560-1609) concerning Christ's having died for all people and humans possessing the free will to do good and achieve salvation (see Arminianism*). In taking up these positions Smyth rejected the

Calvinism* that dominated English Protestantism and Puritanism. Smyth's interlude as a traditional Separatist was brief. His theology continued to evolve, and in 1610 he even asked to join the fellowship of neighboring Dutch Mennonites. They had not yet decided on his admission when he died in 1612, although they finally did accept some of his followers in 1615. Thanks to these new theological positions and his close associations with Thomas Helwys (c.1550-c.1616), Smyth is considered a founder of the denomination of the General Baptists*.

A different Separatist church appeared at Scrooby in Nottinghamshire under the leadership of John Robinson (c.1575-1625). Faced by persecution, Robinson and his followers fled to Amsterdam in 1608 but found the dissensions among the English Separatists there over the controversial teachings of Smyth and Ainsworth to be most uncongenial, so they moved to Leyden in 1609. As time passed, these English Separatists increasingly came to fear that their theology was being corrupted by the proximity of Dutch Arminians and Mennonites. In 1617 Robinson and others began to plan to transplant their community into the emptiness of North America. That plan led to the famous voyage of the *Mayflower* in 1620 and the establishment of the Plymouth Colony by the Pilgrim fathers. Robinson was unable to accompany the original party and died in 1625 before he was able to travel to America. His followers there helped to shape the unique character of New England Puritanism and its theocracy.

Henry Jacob (1563-1624) represented yet another branch of early Stuart Separatism. Although an active opponent of Francis Johnson and his strict Separatism, Jacob came to believe that the established Church of England was not a true church. He took the Separatist position that only a gathered church constituted a true church. Unlike the Elizabethan Separatists, Jacob did not renounce all contact with the Church of England. Otherwise his doctrinal positions were true to the traditional Calvinism of most Separatists. Scholars have dubbed Jacob's theological position as semi-Separatism or moderate Separatism. In 1616 he founded a church at Southwark, considered to be the first religious Independent* or Congregational* church in England. Jacob's congregation later would also serve as the seedbed for the first Particular Baptists.

Separatism revived in Jacobean England, but the fluidity of its leaders' theological positions and their contentiousness caused the movement to fissure. General Baptists, Particular Baptists, and Independents were all directly born out of Separatism, while other Civil War sects and denominations of Dissenters owed Separatism credit for substantial indirect inspiration.

Bibliography: Stephen Foster, *The Long Argument: English Puritanism and the Shaping of New England Culture, 1570-1700*, 1991; Michael R. Watts, *The Dissenters: From the Reformation to the French Revolution*, 1978; and B. R. White, *The English Separatist Tradition: From the Marian Martyrs to the Pilgrim Fathers*, 1971.

Ronald H. Fritze

Settlement, Act of (Ireland, 1652). The Irish Act of Settlement was passed through the Rump Parliament* on 12 August 1652. It was designed for the "total reducement and settlement" of Ireland* following the end of the Irish Rebellion* of 1641-1652.

Though there was still guerrilla activity going on at this time, it was assumed that the Cromwellian conquest had resulted in the equivalent of unconditional surrender by the rebels. Under no obligation to protect either the lives or property of Irish Catholics*, the parliamentary authors considered any concession to them generous. The prime concern of the act was to establish the culpability of the entire Irish nation in the rebellion and the alleged massacre of Protestants in 1641 in order to justify the dispossession of Irish landowners. Since large expanses of Irish land had been promised to adventurers* who financed the conquest and soldiers who carried it out, this was absolutely essential for parliament*.

The act divided all Irish Catholics into four categories, each assigned a level of penalty. All those who owned goods less than £10 in value were issued a broad pardon on submission to English authorities. Among those of greater wealth, all who could not prove continuous loyalty were liable to forfeit up to one-third of their property. Anyone who had held a command in the forces opposing the parliamentary army* were liable to the forfeiture of two-thirds of their family estates and personal banishment. Both of these landed categories were to surrender their properties and receive the equivalent values of land in whatever area the parliament might designate.

The final category of Irish were those who were liable for both estate and life. This status included 105 specifically named prominent rebels, all those in rebellion before 10 November 1642, all those who committed "murder" during the rebellion, and all Jesuits or priests involved with the rebellion. It has been estimated that over 80,000 people were liable for the death penalty under these criteria, and it was probably so widely declared to add legal force to the confiscation measures. Courts convened to try rebels of this status actually executed fewer than 1,000 people. Nevertheless, the act laid the legal foundation for the widespread transplantation of Irish Catholic landowners to a "reservation" in Connaught carried out in the following years.

Bibliography: T. C. Barnard, *Cromwellian Ireland*, 1975.

John Nolan

Settlement Acts (England, 1662, 1685, 1692, 1697). In 1662 Parliament passed "An Act for the Better Relief of the Poor of this Kingdom" (13 & 14 Car. II, c. 12). This statute, often described as the Law of Settlement and Removal, specified that persons moving to a new parish could be removed within forty days by order of a justice of the peace (see Local Government*) if they occupied property worth less than £10 a year. Later acts of 1685 and 1692 tightened these restrictions—the first by ordering that the forty days should be counted from the time an immigrant gave notice in writing to the parish, the second by specifying that the clock began running only after publication of a notice in the parish church (1 Jac. II, c. 17; 3 Gul. & Mar., c. 11). The regulations were relaxed, however, in a statute of 1697, which stated that persons holding certificates from their former parishes could not be removed until they became charges in new parishes.

Few other pieces of Stuart legislation created more litigation than the settlement laws. To this day, despite the ravages of time, parish chests and county archives overflow with settlement examinations, certificates, and removal orders. Few other Stuart statutes, moreover, created as much controversy. For two centuries after 1662, reformers attacked the laws as time-consuming, costly, and unjust. One critic claimed that by the 1730s fully half of quarter sessions cases involved settlement disputes. Another reformer stated in 1832 that since the Glorious Revolution*, settlement litigation had cost the country £10 million. Proponents of free trade thought residence restrictions constituted a new feudalism. To deny someone the right of settlement, Adam Smith observed, was a denial of natural rights and liberties. From a different perspective, in their history of the early poor laws*, Beatrice and Sidney Webb concluded that the legislation sought to immobilize ninety percent of the population. The ultimate absurdity of residence regulations was shown in a case in 1815 at Clerkwell sessions, where two parishes fought over how much of a pauper's body belonged to each parish because his house lay on the boundaries of them both.

The critics of the Old Poor Law were correct in thinking that settlement litigation was expensive, wasteful, and cruel, but they tended to ignore the fact that the stakes were extremely high, reflecting the great costs of statutory poor relief. The act of 1662 did not alter the right to relief in one's native parish or last place of residence, which dated back to the Elizabethan poor laws. In reality, the statute tended to cause relief provision to increase. The mid-seventeenth century saw rising poor rates because of increased hardship, and they continued to rise after the Restoration*. To support a pauper was a very costly business, because in practice parishes gave assistance almost from the cradle to the grave, including weekly doles, housing, fuel, medical care, burial expenses, and even apprenticeships and education. Of course, not all parishes were generous, and many reluctantly obeyed the orders of justices to fulfill their legal obligations. But that authorities were increasingly meeting those obligations explains why they were prepared to fight lengthy cases involving immigrants who might become needy.

The settlement laws also tended to ensure that assistance was provided. Denied settlement in one parish, poor immigrants were returned to previous places of abode, which were obliged by law to take them and, if necessary, to assist them. In fact, the obstacles to immigration probably came down in many places with the requirement of forty days' residence in the act of 1662. Prior to that legislation, 365 days was the rule to qualify for settlement under the vagrancy clauses of the poor laws. In addition, up to 1662 a host of local regulations hindered free movement, including town bylaws and manorial customs, which required newcomers to provide sureties and to pay poor rates before they were accepted. So before 1662 there was a good chance that the migrant who became indigent would be treated as a vagrant. This situation began to change from the 1620s as justices increasingly ordered parishes to treat people as immigrants rather than vagabonds. Under the later Stuarts, vagrancy charges were mainly directed against the thoroughly uprooted: itinerant traders, Scots and Irish, gypsies, and military personnel.

The history of the Stuart settlement legislation suggests that the criticisms of later poor law reformers tell only part of the story. The act of 1662 and its successors had benefits as well as costs.

Bibliography: P. Styles, "The Evolution of the Law of Settlement," reprinted in his *Studies in Seventeenth-Century West Midlands History*, 1978; J. S. Taylor, "The Impact of Pauper Settlement, 1691-1834," *Past and Present* 73 (1976): 42-74.

A. L. Beier

Seven Bishops, Trial of the (1688). An incident in the reign of James II* that centered on Archbishop William Sancroft* and six other bishops' refusal to read publicly James's Declaration of Indulgence* of April 1688. The king had the Seven Bishops imprisoned and tried for seditious libel; the jury's finding of not guilty encouraged the burgeoning resistance to James's authority.

When James II issued his Declaration of Indulgence on 4 April 1687, the Anglican* clergy were not directly threatened by its attempts to impose religious toleration for Roman Catholics* and Dissenters*, and their misgivings were muted. The same reaction greeted the king's reissuing of the declaration one year later on 27 April 1688. This time, however, he followed it up by ordering on 4 May that the clergy of the Church of England read his Declaration from the pulpit. The clergy of London* were to read the order on 20 and 27 May, and the rest of the English clergy were to follow on 3 and 10 June. The *London Gazette* was not able to publish the king's order until 7 May, which did not allow much time for discussion.

Although there was some initial uncertainty about how to respond among the clergy, those in London resolved to disobey. One important meeting took place at Lambeth Palace on 12 May, when Archbishop Sancroft and several other bishops and prominent clergy decided to summon some of the other bishops to London for a show of solidarity against the king's order. On 18 May Sancroft and six bishops: William Lloyd of St. Asaph, Francis Turner of Ely, John Lake of Chichester, Thomas Ken of Bath and Wells, Thomas White of Peterborough, and Jonathan Trelawney of Bristol, drew up a petition explaining that their refusal to read the Declaration of Indulgence was based on it being an illegal use of the dispensing power* of the royal prerogative*. That same night they presented their petition to James II, who indignantly accused them of fomenting treason. In response, the bishops strenuously professed their loyalty but did not withdraw the petition. Meanwhile, someone conveyed a garbled version of the petition to a printer so that printed copies were spread throughout London in a matter of hours. James II blamed the Seven Bishops for the disclosure, but it seems more likely that someone in the palace released the flawed version of the original document.

When 20 May arrived, only a handful of the clergy read the declaration, and their congregations refused to listen. The same thing occurred on the following Sunday. Some of James II's advisers counseled moderation, but the harsh Judge George Jeffreys (see Bloody Assizes*) advocated prosecuting the recalcitrant bishops. Jeffreys's opinion prevailed, and on 27 May the privy council* summoned the Seven

Bishops to appear on 8 June. On that day the bishops refused to say anything that might incriminate them, so the government decided to charge them with seditious libel and demanded recognizances. When the Seven Bishops refused, based on the privileges associated with their high office, the king had them committed to the Tower of London. It was a foolish act, as the people of London came out en masse to support the bishops in their time of trouble. A week later on 15 June the court of King's Bench (see Common Law and Courts*) bailed the bishops on their own recognizances and scheduled them for trial on 29 June.

The trial of the Seven Bishops attracted great attention. The courtroom was packed with spectators, including much of the peerage, and sympathetic crowds thronged the streets outside. The four judges had previously proved themselves to be the willing tools of any royal policy, and one was even a known Catholic. Great attention had been taken to ensure the selection of an impartial jury, and some of the greatest lawyers in England represented the Seven Bishops.

Initially the Seven Bishops were almost acquitted on a technicality over the need to prove that they had published their allegedly libelous petition in Middlesex. Once that issue was decided, the point of contention became whether the Seven Bishops' petition was either libelous or seditious. After the opposing lawyers delivered their arguments, Lord Chief Justice Robert Wright instructed the jury to find them guilty. The Catholic Judge Richard Allibone concurred, but the other two judges dissented. Sir Richard Holloway denied that the petition was a libel, while Sir John Powell took a bolder course, declaring that the royal dispensing power was illegal. It has been suggested that Holloway and Powell may have acted so courageously more out of the greater fear of later being impeached by an angry parliament* than out of any principled defense of the law and the English constitution. With that instruction the jury withdrew and deliberated all night, finally emerging the next morning, 30 June, to declare the Seven Bishops not guilty.

The joy of the English people over the decision was universal, as Anglicans and Dissenters all considered the Seven Bishops to be national heroes and defenders of Protestantism. Such unity boded ill for the defeated and humiliated James II and helped to make the Glorious Revolution* possible. Meanwhile the Seven Bishops continued to act as always, with great dignity and circumspection. They even loyally advised the king to stop promoting illegal and dangerous policies, but by then it was too late for James II to save his tottering monarchy.

Bibliography: G. V. Bennett, "The Seven Bishops: A Reconsideration," in Derek Baker, ed., *Religious Motivation: Biographical and Sociological Problems for the Church Historian*, 1978; J. R. Jones, *Country and Court: England, 1658-1714*, 1979; Thomas Babington Macauley, *The History of England from the Accession of James II*, 6 vols., 1914; Roger Thomas, "The Seven Bishops and Their Petition, 18 May 1688," *Journal of Ecclesiastical History* 12 (1961): 56-70.

Ronald H. Fritze

Shaftesbury, Earl of. See Cooper, Anthony Ashley.

Shakespeare, William (1564-1616). In his prefatory poem to Shakespeare's first folio of 1623 (the first collected edition of the plays), Ben Jonson* said the playwright was "not of an age, but for all time." The fame of William Shakespeare, a son of the middle class like Geoffrey Chaucer, has proved the truth of Jonson's comment. He is the greatest playwright in the English language, able to convey the spirit of his own era as well as the enduring variety of human nature. He was baptized in Stratford-on-Avon on 26 April 1564, son of Mary Arden and John Shakespeare, a glove-maker and dealer in grain and timber, who rose to be high bailiff of the town but later fell into debt. Shakespeare attended the free grammar school in Stratford. He married Anne Hathaway when he was eighteen and she probably about twenty-six and likely pregnant. In 1583, a daughter Susanna was born, followed by twins, Hamnet and Judith, in 1585.

Between their births and his first activity in London* around 1592, little is known of him; suggestions as to his activities are conjecture. Evidence of his early impact on the London stage appears in Robert Greene's *Groats-worth of Wit* (1592), which parodies a line from *Henry VI*, part 3. Greene chides "an upstart Crowe, beautified with our feathers, that with his *Tygers heart wrapt in a Players hide* . . . is in his owne conceit the onely Shake-scene in a countrie." After the reopening of the theaters in 1594 following a two-year hiatus due to plague (see Epidemics and Plague*), Shakespeare established a firm link with the Lord Chamberlain's acting company, later known as the King's Men when its patronage changed. When Richard Burbage built the Globe Theater in 1599, Shakespeare became a principal playwright and shareholder and acted a bit in minor roles such as the ghost of Hamlet's father. By this time he apparently was able to assist his debt-ridden father and in 1597 had bought a comfortable home, New Place, in Stratford. While residing in London he retained his link to Stratford, inheriting his parents' holdings and purchasing land and rental property. He moved from London to Stratford around 1610, two years after his father's death, and probably completed some plays there. Hamnet died in 1596, and his two daughters married, but three grandsons never married and one granddaughter died childless; he thus left no direct descendants. He died on 23 April 1616, his will of 25 March bearing one of only six known genuine signatures by him.

Unlike the controversial Christopher Marlowe or the cantankerous Jonson, Shakespeare's life was free of outward disturbance, and his last years especially were those of a comfortable gentleman. Attempts to derive biographical background from the plays are foiled by his consummate skills at "losing" himself in the infinite variety of his characters. The relative scarcity of biographical facts and his lack of any post-grammar school education has made the question of authorship a perennial topic for non-scholars, yet the extant evidence and the irrefutable reputation he gained in his own day make other claimants for authorship—such as Marlowe, Sir Francis Bacon*, the earl of Oxford—finally unconvincing.

Shakespeare gained his earliest reputation as a poet as well as a dramatist. When Francis Meres praised him in *Palladis Tamia* (1598), he listed twelve plays plus two amatory poems: *Venus and Adonis* (1593) and *The Rape of Lucrece* (1594). Shakespeare also had begun his sequence of sonnets by 1599; the entire group of 154 (the final two are spurious) was published in 1609. The degree to which these poems depict biographical events is debatable. The identities of "Mr. W. H." (to whom they are dedicated) and the "dark lady" of the poems, for example, have not conclusively been resolved. This sequence represents the highest example of the English sonnet form. In 1601 his elegy *The Phoenix and the Turtle* appeared.

The dates of final completion for the thirty-seven plays are not precise; no manuscripts exist and dating must be based on internal and external evidence such as style, publication dates, the Stationer's register, or contemporary notices. Harbage offers the following chronology: *The Comedy of Errors* (1590); the three parts of *Henry VI* (1590-1592); *Richard III* (1593); *The Taming of the Shrew* (1593); *Titus Andronicus* (1594); *Two Gentlemen of Verona* (1594); *King John* (1594); *A Midsummer Night's Dream* (1595); *Richard II* (1595); *Love's Labour's Lost* (1596); *Romeo and Juliet* (1596); *The Merchant of Venice* (1597); *1 Henry IV* (1597); *2 Henry IV* (1598); *As You Like It* (1598); *Henry V* (1599); *Julius Caesar* (1599); *Much Ado About Nothing* (1599); *Twelfth Night* (1600); *Merry Wives of Windsor* (1600); *Hamlet* (1601); *Troilus and Cressida* (1602); *All's Well That Ends Well* (1603); *Measure for Measure* (1604); *Othello* (1604); *King Lear* (1605); *Macbeth* (1605); *Timon of Athens* (1606); *Pericles* (1607); *Antony and Cleopatra* (1607); *Coriolanus* (1608); *Cymbeline* (1609); *The Winter's Tale* (1610); *The Tempest* (1611); *Henry VIII* (1613).

Four broad stages appear in the growth of Shakespeare's plays. Those written before 1595 demonstrate a fairly obvious reliance on sources, especially Roman comedy, relatively narrow character development, and a beginner's concern for the development of a poetically dramatic language. *The Comedy of Errors* and *Two Gentlemen of Verona* display the confused-identity plot common to the comedies of Plautus and Terence, while *Love's Labour's Lost* and *The Taming of the Shrew* employ extensive rhyming, puns, and self-conscious word play. *Richard III*'s character is rather one-dimensional, a stage villain in historical dress.

The Merchant of Venice signals a greater pathos and sense of character in Shylock, and comedies in the second phase display a sharper realism in figures such as Rosalind in *As You Like It*, the tone at times even darkly sinister in "problem comedies" such as *Measure for Measure* or *Troilus and Cressida*. The histories of this phase, though like all his other history plays not always factually precise, depict more rounded personalities confronting complex situations, as in *Henry IV*.

The dark comedies and *Hamlet* reflect the introspective and morally confused world common to Jacobean tragedy and usher in the third period of the great tragedies. Figures such as Lear, Othello, Macbeth, and Hamlet are poignant and evocative explorations of the individual confronting conflict on personal, social, and spiritual levels; to many these are the greatest dramatic works ever composed. Their language is often colloquial, not artificially poetic, yet Shakespeare's insights are conveyed in masterfully symbolic terms.

The final period of the romances or tragicomedies *Pericles, Cymbeline, The Winter's Tale,* and *The Tempest* offer themes of reconciliation rather than conflict and are usually read as the poet's artistic farewell to his craft. In *The Tempest*, Prospero, the wise father and magician, is able to transform the crude, destructive forces on his island (probably modeled on the newly discovered Bermuda) to educate those around him in self-knowledge and to relinquish willingly his magical power and accept his life's end. Shakespeare's work thus ends on a note of fulfillment and acceptance.

Bibliography: Alfred Harbage, *William Shakespeare, a Reader's Guide*, 1963; Kenneth Muir and Samuel Schoenbaum, *A New Companion to Shakespeare Studies*, 1971; Schoenbaum, *William Shakespeare, A Documentary Life*, 1975.

Christopher Baker

Sheldon, Gilbert (1598-1677). Archbishop of Canterbury, he was the prime architect of the reestablishment of the Church of England (see Anglicanism*) after the Restoration* of Charles II* in 1660.

Gilbert Sheldon was born on 19 July 1598, the son of Roger Sheldon, a servant of the 7th earl of Shrewsbury. He joined Trinity College, Oxford, and after graduating won a fellowship at All Souls, where he became warden in 1626. Although he supported the basic Laudian (see William Laud*) concept of a strong, disciplined, national church, he was not a zealous Arminian*. During the Civil Wars* he was a staunch royalist* and a close adviser of Charles I* from 1646 until Charles's execution*. Sheldon encouraged the king not to compromise on religious matters with the parliamentarians*. Imprisoned briefly in 1648, he lived in retirement during the 1650s. Soon after the Restoration, he became bishop of London and, upon the death of William Juxon* in 1663, succeeded to the archbishopric of Canterbury. Due to Juxon's age and ill health, Sheldon had been functioning as a de facto archbishop for some time.

Sheldon, in partial alliance with Edward Hyde*, the earl of Clarendon, was largely responsible for the form and nature adopted by the post-Restoration Church of England, which in most essentials has continued into the twentieth century. One of his objectives was to create a high-quality body of clergy that was loyal to the episcopal form of government and the Thirty-nine Articles. Using great care, he was able to achieve that goal in spite of the large loss of clergy due to the purges of Presbyterians* and other Nonconformists. He also formed an alliance between the Church of England and the gentry, which quickly transformed them into firm supporters of the clergy. Bishops and parish clergy were encouraged to cultivate the neighboring gentry as Sheldon did with his frequent wining and dining of members of parliament* at Lambeth Palace. Much effort also went into recovering property lost by the church during the Interregnum* and refurbishing dilapidated buildings. Sheldon was planning a massive renovation of St. Paul's Cathedral even before the Great Fire of London* destroyed the medieval structure. One of his unfortunate legacies was his support for the Act of Uniformity of 1662 (14 Car. II, c. 4) with its rigid insistence on complete conformity (see Clarendon Code*), which institutionalized the divide between the Church of England and Protestant Dissenters* that persisted well into the nineteenth century.

Sheldon was a sincere defender of the Church of England as he envisioned it. He did not hesitate to criticize the moral irregularities of Charles II or to oppose the king's attempts to provide toleration for Dissenters* and Roman Catholics*. He successfully blocked Charles II's Declaration of Indulgence in 1662 and vociferously opposed the Declaration of Indulgence* of 1672. After his friend the earl of Clarendon fell from power in 1667, Sheldon found himself out of favor with the king and largely remained in political isolation until his death on 9 November 1677.

Bibliography: R. A. Beddard, "Sheldon and Anglican Recovery," *Historical Journal* 19 (1976): 1005-1017; V. D. Sutch, *Gilbert Sheldon*, 1973.

Ronald H. Fritze

Sheriffs. The sheriff of an English county was a local official responsible to the Crown for the performance of certain traditional administrative duties. Unlike civic sheriffs, who were usually merchants chosen by the constituents of an urban oligarchy, sheriffs of counties were selected annually by the king from a bill of nominees prepared in the Exchequer*. During the early part of the century, most sheriffs were, in keeping with contemporary aspirations, greater gentry, but after the Civil War* it was not uncommon for a lesser gentleman to hold a shrievalty. After being sworn and obtaining his patent of office, the sheriff selected those who attended to the routine duties of his office, including an undersheriff, who was often a lawyer, and several bailiffs and stewards of courts, who were likely to be of yeoman status. The chief tasks of the sheriff's office were the collection of royal revenues (see Taxation and Revenue*), the execution of process from the law courts at Westminster (see Common Law and Courts*), and the impanelment of juries for assizes, quarter sessions, and various commissions and inquests. The shrievalty also summoned the *posse comitatus* in an emergency, disseminated royal proclamations, and entertained the judges at the assizes. The sheriff's courts, the tourn and county court, dispensed plebeian justice, the latter becoming the center of local attention when it chose knights of the shire for parliament*.

Despite the sheriff's involvement in most local administrative activities, historians have traditionally portrayed his office as being in decline during the seventeenth century. This interpretation is based on the undeniable reality that Stuart gentry often sought to avoid the costs and burdens associated with the shrievalty. In fact the administrative character of the shrievalty depended primarily on the social status of sheriffs, which in turn depended partly on the fiscal constraints the Exchequer applied to the office. Until the reign of Charles I*, a sheriff was not expected to function as a quasi-bureaucrat, but as the guarantor of his county's order and fiscal integrity. During the Personal Rule* (1629-1640), when it was charged with the collection of ship money*, the shrievalty became a focal point of Charles I's efforts to transform local administration in order to rule without a parliament. Despite the stresses occasioned by that experiment, the shrievalty remained an integral local institution until the Civil War, when land sales required a change in the sheriff's accounting procedures at the Exchequer, the eventual upshot of which was to open the office to those who were socially marginal and politically malleable.

The shrievalty embodied the principle that local government* should be shared between Crown and county and that the gentlemen who coordinated that relationship ought to be drawn rotationally from among the gentry community. The experience of sheriffs during the seventeenth century transformed that tradition. Henceforth the ideal of a shrievalty capable of integrating the concerns of local and central government would yield to the reality of a division between local and central authority and the concurrent relegation of the sheriff's office to an essentially vestigial status. Acceptance of that arrangement by gentry was an enduring legacy of the English Revolution of the 1640s.

Bibliography: T. G. Barnes, *Somerset, 1625-1640: A County's Government During the Personal Rule*, 1961; M. C. Noonkester, "Charles I and Shrieval Selection, 1625-6," *Historical Research* 64 (1991): 305-311.

Myron C. Noonkester

Ship Money. In 1634 Charles I* issued writs for the collection of ship money from coastal areas. Ship money had its basis in the traditional obligation of port towns to provide ships for the navy*. In 1628 Charles had considered but then abandoned the idea of levying ship money upon the entire kingdom, not just upon the port towns. By actually doing this in 1635 and again in every year thereafter through 1640, he raised considerable sums of money. Even in 1638-1639, when the amount of ship money to be levied was reduced from the intended £200,000 to £70,000 because of plague and poverty (see Epidemics and Plague*; Poor Laws and Poverty*), the potential revenue compared favorably to the £55,000 raised by one parliamentary subsidy in 1628. Ship money, however, also stirred up a storm of protest.

The protests against ship money did not focus on its purpose of improving the navy. Memories of the Spanish Armada and support for the Protestant cause in Germany gave naval defense legitimacy, and Elizabethan precedents reinforced the medieval ones for the collection of ship money. Evidence in the State Papers, Domestic and in the records of the privy council* suggests that disputes focused on administration of the levy, but examination of personal letters and papers shows that people also had doubts about ship money's legality. The king's repeated imposition of ship money on the entire kingdom instead of summoning a parliament* and requesting subsidies aroused suspicions that he was seeking to avoid demands for redress of his subjects' grievances that would arise in parliament.

The legal questions about ship money were publicly debated in the Exchequer* in 1638 in the trial of John Hampden* for refusing to pay. Crowds packed the court to hear the attorneys for Hampden and the Crown argue the case and then to hear the judges deliver their opinions. Correspondents quickly informed friends and relatives in the country about what had happened and how each judge had ruled. Although people knew that the decision against Hampden had not been unanimous, most recognized that the ruling meant that further legal challenges at that time would be futile.

Disputes about rating of ship money were far more numerous. People protested against the fact that instead of relying on the commissioners who made the assessments for the parliamentary subsidies, the council had directed the sheriffs* to rate their counties for the amount of ship money due therefrom. Individuals claimed that they had been unfairly rated; so did towns. Some complained that the sheriff had been malicious; others argued about what proportions were supposed to be used in distributing local levies. In some instances counties themselves protested that they had been overcharged.

While attempting to deal with a flood of complaints, the privy council enforced ship money by threatening and cajoling the sheriffs, who were held personally accountable until they had paid the amount due from their counties for their year of office. The council also put pressure on the constables who did much of the actual work of collection on the local level. The council's efforts had considerable success. Ultimately only a very small percentage of the money assessed remained outstanding, and ship money made a significant contribution to royal revenue.

Expedience discouraged prolonged resistance either from sheriffs and constables who found their responsibilities distasteful or from citizens. While complaints could make a point, the consequences of continued resistance could mean the loss of property or place. Most people who initially refused to pay ultimately submitted, even though they may have subsequently joined in the petitions against ship money that went to parliament in 1640. Proceedings in parliament when it met after the end of the period of Personal Rule* (1629-1640) show that the political cost of ship money was high (see Short Parliament*; Long Parliament*). In return for his profits from ship money, Charles I lost goodwill. (See also Local Government*.)

Bibliography: Kenneth Fincham, "The Judges' Decision on Ship Money in February 1637: The Reaction in Kent," *Bulletin of the Institute of Historical Research* 57 (1984): 230-37; Peter Lake, "The Collection of Ship Money in Cheshire During the Sixteen-Thirties," *Northern History* 17 (1981): 44-71.

Esther S. Cope

Short Parliament (1640). The Short Parliament of 17 April to 5 May 1640, so called for its brief duration, marked the transition from the ideal of cooperative government to a more combative and factional system of politics. Parliament* and Crown could pursue conflicting agendas to the detriment of the realm. The policies of the Crown could be opposed for the good of the nation. The Short Parliament also ended the Personal Rule* (1629-1640) of Charles I* and played a key role in the breakdown of his regime on the eve of the Civil War*. Having mobilized for the First Bishops' War* in 1639 without benefit of parliamentary subsidies, the king and privy council* decided that a subsequent war must have income from parliamentary assessments, even if they were not as substantial as subsidies once were due to inflation and undervaluation (see Taxation and Revenue*). During the session, a minority alienated by Charles's government strove to sabotage any accommodation with the Crown, therefore denying the king the means to conquer Presbyterian* Scotland*. Many of these men—notably John Pym*, Lord Saye and Sele (William Fiennes*), Lord Brooke, Oliver St. John, Nathaniel Fiennes, Sir Walter Earle, John Hampden*, and Francis Rous—probably consulted with rebel Scots and in effect aided them. The saboteurs engaged in this flirtation with treason because they mistrusted the man Charles Stuart and his absolutist* polices for church and state. The king, too, sabotaged the parliament, though inadvertently. Neither the Lords nor Commons was managed effectively, largely because Charles I misgauged sentiments in parliament and the local constituencies. The king had summoned the members to vote a quick infusion of cash so that he could get on with mobilization, the rendezvous of forces being scheduled less than two-and-a-half months away, on 1 June 1640. Many members, however, were determined to discuss grievances as well as grant supply. Those grievances were framed by Pym in a tripartite configuration, held together by the themes of liberty and property, which in themselves were related. Privilege of parliament was arguably the most pressing grievance, given that the previous session in 1629 (see Parliament of 1628-1629*) had been abruptly dissolved and no subsequent parliament called for eleven years. The most pervasive grievance and the cause of the Scottish War was Arminianism*, which Pym and others saw as part of a conspiracy to bring Britain back to Roman Catholic* practice. Finally there were numerous royal fiscal devices employed without parliamentary (and, some thought, legal) sanction, such as ship money*, coat-and-conduct money, monopolies*, impositions*, fines for violating the forest laws*, and others.

The king demanded immediate supply in an amount that most members of parliament, regardless of their religious or political viewpoint, found staggering. The cost of the Scottish war was estimated at £1 million, and the Crown needed about fourteen, perhaps as many as eighteen, parliamentary subsidies. The Crown asked for twelve and showed some willingness to abandon ship money. However, even twelve was an extraordinarily heavy assessment, considering that few Englishmen expressed enthusiasm for the war and that the nation was in a recessionary economy. At this juncture, around 4 May, the "saboteurs," through Pym, raised the issue of the Bishops' Wars themselves, effectively fragmenting opinion so that no bargain was struck that day. With no money in the offing and the Commons poised to discuss the justification of the Scottish war, Charles swiftly dissolved the houses the following morning, 5 May 1640.

The Short Parliament made explicit and national the grievances that had troubled many in the localities during the 1630s. It also demonstrated the inability of the anti-Arminians and the king to come to any compromise agreement. Its precipitous dissolution meant that the next parliament would deal with the king in a more tenacious and belligerent fashion, thus moving England a little further on the road to Civil War.

Bibliography: Mark Charles Fissel, "Scottish War and English Money: The Short Parliament of 1640," in Fissel, ed., *War and Government in Britain, 1598-1650*, 1991: 193-223; Conrad Russell, *The Fall of the British Monarchies, 1637-1642*, 1992.

Mark Charles Fissel

Social Structure and Ranks. One of the great historiographical debates about Stuart England concerns the question of whether the revolutions of the seventeenth century were political, religious, social, economic, or some combination thereof. Thus, the study of social history has been central to scholarly inquiry about the period and often highly contentious. The question of whether the gentry in this period were rising—with an attendant crisis of the aristocracy—or falling is dealt with elsewhere in this volume (see Gentry Controversy*). That there was an inflation of honors*, an increase in peerages and knighthoods, is unquestionable, though whether this was detrimental is also a matter of debate. Arguments about the existence of class conflict, a fundamental division between court and country (see Court versus Country*), or identifiable county communities are not finally settled here, nor is the question about whether conflict or consensus was the normal state of affairs in Stuart England. These issues are likely to remain controversial. The family in the early modern era has been much studied, but there is not complete uniformity of opinion about it. Women* have received too little attention from historians (and too much from literary critics) for many concrete conclusions to be reached, though much work now is being done.

A number of factors exerted influence on the social structure of Stuart England. Population* grew rapidly in the early modern period, almost doubling between 1540 and 1640 and continuing to increase thereafter. Changes in agriculture*, notably enclosure and fen drainage*, led to considerable dislocation, an increase in internal migration, a growing agricultural proletariat, a rising number of landless paupers, and a higher potential for social disorders like the Midland Rising of 1607*. Coupled with the commercial revolution and the gradual introduction of new industrial techniques, this led to increased urbanization, particularly in London*, which by 1640 had a population of over 400,000, ten times that of 1500. Elsewhere it proceeded more slowly; only Norwich exceeded 20,000 inhabitants, while Bristol, Newcastle, and York each had over 10,000. The agricultural sector, hampered by the "little ice age" of 1550-1700 and by a great deal of bad weather, was unable to keep pace with this growth. Inflation was pervasive, but the rise in the price of food far surpassed any other product. At the same time real wages dropped precipitately, so that there was a decline in the standard of living. Medicine* lagged behind in the scientific revolution (see Science and Scientific Revolution*), hygiene was horrendous, epidemics and plague* remained common, and the average life expectancy at birth was somewhere in the mid-thirties.

English society remained distinctly hierarchical, although there was a fair amount of mobility up and down the social ladder. At the apex of society, except during the Interregnum* (1649-1660), stood the monarch. Just below came the five ranks of titled nobility (in descending order): duke, marquis, earl, viscount, and baron. These peers owed their prestige to tradition, their right to sit in the House of Lords, and ownership of enormous landed estates; the feudal role the nobility had once exercised had largely ceased to exist. During the early Stuart period the number of peers grew spectacularly; whereas there were only fifty-five at the end of Elizabeth's reign in 1603, there were 126 by 1628, and Charles I* created more near the end of his Personal Rule* (1629-1640). Though the aristocracy may have been in crisis in the late Elizabethan period as the result of inflationary pressure on income from lands normally granted to tenants for lives, by 1641 they were better off than at the beginning of Elizabeth's reign, thanks to raising rents and entry fines. Of course during the Civil War* and Interregnum, their fortunes suffered a sharp but temporary decline.

Next in status after the nobility came the gentry, who dominated local government in the counties and formed the bulk of the membership of the House of Commons. This group showed enormous variety, their ownership of land and "gentle" status (they did not work the land themselves) being the primary common denominators. In wealth some equaled members of the peerage, while others were no better off than the mere yeomen beneath them in the social hierarchy. As a group, their status improved in the seventeenth century. There were three ranks of gentry (in descending order): knight, esquire, and gentleman. Knighthood was an honor normally conferred by the Crown or its designate; however, James I* created a new category of hereditary knights known as baronets. The number of knights rose sharply as part of the inflation of honors. There were about 600 at Elizabeth's death; James created over 900 in his first four months in England. Knighthood could be a dubious honor, as the furor over distraint of knighthood* during the Personal Rule indicated. Honor aside, it may be more meaningful to subdivide the gentry into greater gentry (those with lands in several shires), county gentry, and parochial gentry, according to the amount of land they owned.

Among the nongentle members of society, the highest ranking in the countryside were the yeomen. Though this group is notoriously difficult to define with clarity, they may be described as free landowners who may have owned up to 100 acres, worked the land themselves or with a few servants, and were in general achieving a higher standard of living in the Stuart era. Next came the husbandmen, with holdings ranging from about twelve to fifty acres, often on the margin of survival. Below these were cottagers, with still less land, and the landless laborers, who found themselves in a subsistence crisis as the result of inflation. Those who lost their land or were unable to gain employment swelled the numbers of landless paupers, putting ever greater pressure on local government* officials charged with administering the poor laws*. The extent to which the term *peasant* can be used to describe any of the rural agrarian population is hotly debated, with Alan Macfarlane denying that there were any peasants in England at all. But the number of families living in peasant-like subsistence conditions declined over the course of the century.

The cities and towns were usually dominated by a handful of wealthy merchant oligarchs, though most merchants had far less wealth than these powerful few. Often merchant families intermarried with members of the gentry or even of the peerage who often had townhouses in London or other cities and were eager to exchange monetary wealth for social status. A significant and increasing number of urban dwellers belonged to one of the three professions: legal, medical, and ecclesiastical. In what might be loosely termed the lower middle class were various artisans and shopkeepers. Below these came wage laborers and an increasing number of paupers. Merchants and artisans still belonged to powerful guilds, and there were professional organizations as well, like the Royal College of Physicians*. Within the craft guilds, apprenticeship was still the normal route to advancement. Though fewer overall than the apprentices, an increasing number of young men now found advancement through education. The number of endowed grammar schools rose to around 700 by about 1650, with almost twice that many private schools. Enrollment at Oxford and Cambridge increased dramatically, as did the number of young men seeking legal education at one of the Inns of Court. The incidence of literacy was greater with social status and tended to be higher in towns. Women, generally barred from owning property, except by inheritance or marriage, were also much less likely to be educated, though many upper-class females were literate.

The family was an integral part of the social structure. Among the upper ranks of society, preservation of status and family wealth was generally a factor in selecting a spouse, but even lower down the social scale the choice of a marriage partner was in part determined by the ability to make a living. In seventeenth-century England, marriages came rather late. In the difficult conditions of the first half of the century, men married at average of between twenty-seven and twenty-nine years of age; at mid-century the age for women might be even higher. In part marriage was delayed until a couple could afford to support children, but even after marriage, English families managed to keep the birth rate fairly low and the size of families relatively small. Coupled with the rarity of the extended family in a single household—the nuclear family was the norm—this enabled English families to avoid poverty of the severity found on the Continent, and in the second half of the century, it combined with a gradually improving economy to produce a rise in living standards. As for inheritance, primogeniture was the general rule, but partible inheritance (e.g., gavelkind in Kent) was not unusual.

The Civil War and Interregnum, if they did not quite turn the world upside down, certainly threw the social structure out of kilter, with the regicide*, the abolition of the House of Lords and the episcopate, and the confiscation and sale of Crown, church, and royalist* lands. Groups wanting more radical change emerged, such as the quasi-democratic Levellers* and the communistic Diggers*, but failed to accomplish their goals. By the time of Charles II's return in 1660, many of the gentry who had opposed his father joined the nobility in welcoming him back.

With the Restoration* came a resumption of the *status quo ante bellum*. Lands, offices, and influence were returned to those accustomed to having them, though a certain unease persisted in those who had now experienced revolution. The Restoration era was marked, however, by a decline in the lesser gentry, burdened by increased poor rates and taxation* for England's foreign wars, continued low productivity in agriculture, low rents, and lack of capital to make the improvements that advances in science had made possible for wealthier landowners. One of the most important changes in the latter part of the century, though more evident after the Glorious Revolution*, was the rising importance of the moneyed interest, which assumed political influence on a par with or even surpassing that of many gentry and lower nobility. A related development was the ever-increasing role of London in the national political, economic, and cultural life of England.

Bibliography: Derek Hirst, *Authority and Conflict: England, 1603-1658*, 1986; J. R. Jones, *Country and Court: England, 1658-1714*, 1978.

William B. Robison

Solemn League and Covenant (1643). During the First Civil War*, the failure of the marquis of Hamilton's plan for establishing Henrietta Maria* as regent of Scotland* and the numerous military reverses experienced by the English parliamentarians* by mid-1643 created an opening for an alliance of the king's English enemies with the Covenanters*. Desperate for assistance against the three royalist* armies advancing on London*, John Pym* sent Sir Henry Vane the younger to Edinburgh as the parliamentarian ambassador. The Covenanters, anxious as always to secure the settlement of 1641 against royal machinations, prepared to meet Vane.

With the convention of estates (political nation) and the general assembly (ecclesiastical nation) both in session when Vane arrived on 7 August, the potential for a rapid Scottish response existed. Both bodies established committees to negotiate with Vane. The assembly convened under the chair of the Rev. Alexander Henderson (assembly moderator), Archibald Johnston of Wariston (its clerk), the Rev. Robert Baillie, and other ministers, along with members of the nobility. Wariston successfully persuaded the committee to abandon mediation in the English Civil War for intervention on parliament's* side.

The nature of the alliance known after the name of its treaty, the Solemn League and Covenant became more overtly religious in tone than the parliamentarians had planned. Wariston, worried about sects in England and later repudiation of the alliance (religious and security concerns as always influencing the Covenanters), argued for a "religious covenant" to be sworn by the Scots and English. The treaty went through two drafts, with the largest contention arising over the pattern of the British religious settlement. On 17 August the convention and assembly ratified the second version of the new Covenant. The document was then sent to England for parliament to debate. On 26 August the estates approved a treaty for sending a Scots army to England (to be paid by parliament) and against a separate peace. By mid-September parliament and the Westminster Assembly of Divines* amended the first clause of the Covenant, allowing the possibility of toleration for the Protestant sects. The relief of the royalist siege of Gloucester and the imminent end of the military season allowed parliament to take this liberty without hindrance from the Scots. Specifically, the call for church reform in England was to be "according to the word of God." They added Ireland* to the countries where the Covenant's religious settlement (first clause) would apply. They also changed the fifth clause from a specific adherence to the 1641 Treaty of London to a more general call for preservation of peace between the two kingdoms.

The Covenant consisted of six clauses. The first dealt with the religious settlement to be determined for Britain and Ireland. The second and fourth called for the suppression of Catholicism*, episcopacy, religious error, and royalists. Clause three promised preservation of the kingdoms' parliaments and liberties, as well as the maintenance of royal authority. The fifth muttered vague hopes for the continuance of peace between the kingdoms. Clause six exhorted signatories of the Covenant to mutual defense. The Covenant should be seen as another attempt to create a stable religious-political situation in the three kingdoms by Charles I's* opponents.

Following parliamentary ratification, the Covenant immediately was circulated for signatures. The covenanting Scots enthusiastically embraced it; the English parliamentarians split between those who hoped it would usher in a new age and those who merely sought preservation against royalists. In Ulster the Protestant settlers and the Scots army eagerly swore allegiance, while the colonels of British regiments allowed their men to do so in order to secure supplies and assistance from the Scots. The refusal of English Independents* (among the parliamentarians) to endorse the Westminster Assembly of Divines and the 1645 act of parliament establishing Presbyterianism* in England led the Scots to condemn them as covenant breakers. The religious (first) clause of the Solemn League and Covenant served as the inspiration for the Kirk* and Protester parties in Scotland (see Kirk Party*).

By 1660 the document lay forgotten under the horrors of English occupation, with its toleration and cultivation of Protestant sects. Only the radical Covenanters of the Restoration* era clung to the document as an expression of policy.

Bibliography: Walter Makey, *The Church of the Covenants, 1637-1651*, 1977; David Stevenson, *The Scottish Revolution, 1637-1644*, 1973.

                                                                        Edward M. Furgol

Somerset, Earl of. See Carr, Robert.

Spanish Match. The Spanish marriage negotiations constitute one of the best known and longest running events of James I's* reign. For all their ultimate futility and comic opera qualities, they grew logically out of the personalities and the imperatives of the early seventeenth century.

Following the Treaty of London* (1604), negotiations began that envisioned marrying Prince Henry* to the eldest Spanish princess, Donna Anna. Offers and counteroffers endured for twenty years, shifting upon Henry's death to the future Charles I* and upon Donna Anna's marriage to Louis XIII to her sister Donna Maria.

The pacifist James saw distinct advantages: furtherance of his plans to be the arbiter of European peace, dynastic enhancement, and protection through a match with the most powerful family in Europe. There were also potential trade* advantages: the English had long been dazzled by the allure of commerce with the Spanish empire. Given the king's nature, he was pursuing a rational policy. It is also a policy that explains a great deal about the ascendancy of the Spanish ambassador, Count de Gondomar, at the court of St. James from 1613 to 1622.

For the Spanish the advantages were more obvious. An English marriage meant an entrée to secure liberty of conscience for English Catholics*, extravagant freedoms for the Infanta in Britain, and a serious attempt to sway the Stuart dynasty to a Catholic future (the resulting children would be raised Catholic for the first twelve years of their life according to treaty terms enunciated just before the breakdown of negotiations). John Pym* the parliamentarian* may not have been too far wrong when he complained that to give the Catholics a legal foothold in England would ultimately lead to the downfall of the entire Protestant edifice. Indeed the influential but utterly myopic Gondomar encouraged such expectations in his Spanish superiors.

The plight of James's only daughter, Elizabeth*, and her husband, Frederick of the Palatinate of the Rhine, sometime king of Bohemia, sharpened for the English by the early 1620s the need for progress in the on-again, off-again bargaining (see Thirty Years War*). By 1623 this unlucky pair were in exile in Holland. In London* the Stuarts hoped unrealistically to rectify that situation by tying the Spanish match to a promise for Spanish Habsburg troops to drive imperial Habsburg troops from the Palatinate.

While the negotiations intensified in 1622 as the result of the earl of Bristol's embassy to Spain, there were no breakthroughs. At this point the unshakable pacifism of the king, the romanticism of princely youth, and the naiveté of the 1st duke of Buckingham (George Villiers*) produced Charles and Buckingham's notorious trip to Madrid to breach the impasse. It is uncertain who originated the idea, but the two secured James's reluctant sanction. Traveling incognito they would reveal themselves once in Spain, where love would triumph (Charles truly believed this) and Buckingham's self-acclaimed negotiating skills would prevail against an interminably refractory Spanish court.

It was a dangerous journey, especially for two essentially unaccompanied and identifiably well-born travelers. They left London on 17 February 1623. Fortune attended them, as did a certain amount of French solicitousness. Once they were in Spain by 7 March the tempo of negotiations did quicken. The Spanish were sure the prince would never have come without planning a conversion; Charles was equally sure that the Spanish would ensure the future of his sister and her husband. Given the highly unorthodox nature of the scheme, surprising progress was made. Buckingham, who while abroad secured his dukedom from an anxious James, displayed more ability than might have been expected. His failure to carry all, however, caused a debilitating rupture with the Spanish favorite, Olivares, in whose hands the twists and turns of the matter finally rested. Charles's actions were rather more impetuous (e.g., climbing a wall to be alone with his future bride) but floundered on stiff Spanish propriety and insistence on ceremony.

For a time the marriage seemed at hand, as the English made it clear that they would suspend the penal laws against Catholics (see Suspending Power*) and recommend to parliament three years hence their complete revocation. The Spanish pledged the troth of the Infanta, but insisted on keeping her in Spain, much to Charles's annoyance, until the articles of the marriage treaty were effected in England. They also began at papal behest to demand complete liberty of conscience for English Catholics. However, neither side was willing to make the final concessions that it would have taken to effect the marriage: Frederick's restoration to the Palatinate through Spanish intervention and a complete reversal of religious policy toward Catholics in England. Although Buckingham and Charles left Madrid on 28 August with promises of an imminent marital treaty, the further they withdrew, the more disillusioned they became.

Their reception in London confirmed that the domestic political winds did not support their previous course. The English were exultant at the safe return of the unwed prince and what this connoted for the future of Protestantism. Buckingham was sufficiently piqued that his strong pro-Spanish policies shifted to embrace the French instead. After a formidable number of diplomatic missions and a romantic gamble on what personal diplomacy could accomplish, the long-standing marriage negotiations floundered in the huge gulf that separated Catholic and dynastically sensitive Spain from a Protestant and relatively impotent England.

Bibliography: Charles Carlton, *Charles I, The Personal Monarch*, 1983; Roger Lockyer, *Buckingham*, 1981.

Gary M. Bell

Spanish War of 1625-1630. In seeking to marry his son and heir, the future Charles I*, to a Spanish Infanta, James I* hoped to secure Spanish involvement in mediating peace for the Palatinate of the Rhine in the Thirty Years War* (see also Elizabeth, Electress of the Palatinate*). The breakdown of the marriage negotiations in 1623 ruined his hopes, leaving Charles and the royal favorite, the 1st duke of Buckingham (George Villiers*), scouting ways to intervene in the Palatinate while thirsting for revenge on Spain. Parliament*, which had opposed the Spanish match*, sought a self-financing war against Spain, a revival of Elizabethan glories. James began raising a mercenary army for the Palatinate, negotiated for a French marriage for his son, and concluded a treaty with the Dutch. Armed with the power of the purse, the parliament of 1624* voted less money than James required and demanded that he break off relations with Spain. The Palatinate army starved in the Netherlands, the French ignored the Palatinate and demanded English ships to besiege the Huguenots in La Rochelle, and James died in March 1625 with his realm in a state of undeclared war with Spain.

Before his death, a fleet had been forming for a Spanish venture, since the Dutch treaty required that an English fleet blockade the Spanish coast. Comprising navy* ships as well as merchantmen and colliers, this fleet was manned by about 5,000 seamen and carried about 10,000 soldiers. Charles I came to the throne committed to a sea war against Spain. In June he sought funding for the fleet from his first parliament (of 1625*), which, hoping that the venture could be pursued by privateers and unable to wring from him a clear statement as to the aims of his policy or to the amount required, voted him a sum that was obviously insufficient. Emboldened by Buckingham, who was unwilling to surrender such an opportunity for military glory and personal gain, Charles dissolved parliament and gambled that the fleet would be able to capture the annual Spanish bullion fleet from Mexico, enrich the Crown, subsidize the Palatinate army, and overawe future parliaments.

The Cadiz expedition* sailed on 8 October, ninety Dutch and English ships under Sir Edward Cecil's command, and was a fiasco from the outset. The men pressed for it were untrained and unfit. The merchant captains wasted the opportunity to surprise a Spanish fleet at Cadiz, while the colliers made a botch of bombarding Fort Puntales. After a landing party captured the fort, the army's advance on the city bogged down when the men became hopelessly drunk. Cecil put to sea on 4 November to intercept the treasure fleet but deployed too far to seaward and missed the galleons, which slipped up the coast from Africa and into Cadiz harbor two days after the English left. Unaware that he had been thwarted, Cecil maintained station until 16 November, giving up the effort then because of unseaworthy ships, rotten food, and the spread of disease. Thirty of the ships never made it home.

Though the war lasted for four more years, there were no other campaigns of this magnitude. Furious at Buckingham's arrogance and dissembling when asking for funds for the Spanish expedition, parliament blamed him for its failure and refused to provide more funds for war against Spain while he exercised power. Privateering by the earl of Warwick and Sir Kenelm Digby achieved little against the Spanish, while raiders from Dunkirk harried English trade. Charles in any case was preoccupied after spring 1626 with hostilities against France (see French War of 1627-1629*) and interested in diplomatic efforts to separate France and Spain. Successful diplomacy by Peter Paul Rubens on Spain's behalf led to the ending of the war on 5 November 1630 by the Treaty of Madrid, which largely reproduced the terms of the Treaty of London* of 1604.

Bibliography: Charles Dalton, *Life and Times of Sir Edward Cecil, Viscount Wimbledon*, 1885; S. R. Gardiner, *History of England from the Accession of James I to the Outbreak of the Civil War, 1603-1642*, vols. 5-7, 1883-1884; John Glanville, *The Voyage to Cadiz in 1625*, 1883.

                                                        Joseph M. McCarthy

Spanish War of 1655-1659. Though hostilities began with the departure of the English fleet for raids on Spanish colonies on 20 December 1654, officially England did not declare war until 26 October 1655. Effectively, hostilities between England and Spain ceased when the English ally France signed the Treaty of the Pyrenees with Spain in November 1659.

In July 1654 Lord Protector Oliver Cromwell* announced his intention of a crusade against the Antichrist in the form of a war on Spain. Cromwell believed that a campaign in the West Indies, striking at Spanish bullion convoys and colonies, would weaken this great Catholic* power. He saw this Western Design as the first stage of a millenarian* conflict leading to the fall of Rome itself. His enthusiasm was encouraged by a nostalgic view of the Elizabethan maritime campaigns. Like many other leading Puritan* opponents of Charles I* before the Civil War*, he had resented the government's inaction when Spain destroyed the English Caribbean colonies at Tortuga in 1634 and Providence Island in 1640. The grand and ambiguous nature of the Western Design confounded its planning from the very beginning. Under the influence of a former Dominican who had lived in the West Indies, Thomas Gage, Cromwell gravely underestimated the difficulty of such a campaign. And though it was apparent that Cromwell had colonial ambitions, exactly where was never determined (see Colonization*).

Command of the first West Indies expedition was divided awkwardly between Admiral William Penn and General Robert Venables, who proved to be entirely incompatible. The fleet, carrying 2,500 troops of uneven quality, arrived on 29 January 1655 at Barbados. By recruiting among the West Indies English colonists, the force was increased to 9,000. Supplies, weapons, and food were short, and by no means were the recruits properly equipped or necessarily reliable troops.

On 13 April, after a long-suffering and disease-ridden stay on the Barbados, the fleet arrived off Spanish Santo Domingo. Though they landed without opposition, on 25 April, the English were routed at San Geronimo by a numerically inferior Spanish force. On 4 May the expedition abandoned Santo Domingo and embarked for Jamaica. There the fleet anchored on 11 May and easily occupied the Spanish settlement at Santiago de la Vega. Venables and Penn entered prolonged negotiations with the Spanish, only to discover that it was a ruse. However, Jamaica was captured and successfully annexed. But the conduct of the campaign so appalled Cromwell that when the commanders returned to England in September, both were imprisoned in the Tower.

The war with Spain ran concurrently with a lukewarm war with France, which ended in October 1655 with an Anglo-French treaty. During that previous summer, an English fleet under Admiral Robert Blake had cruised the Mediterranean to harass French shipping, block the duke de Guise's invasion of Naples, and force treaties on the North African ports. In June Blake turned from these duties to an attempt to seize the Spanish bullion fleet. He cruised off the coast of Portugal and Spain until August, then abandoned the enterprise.

The alliance with France was principally commercial, but its clauses included the expulsion of Charles II* from France. In April 1656 Charles made a treaty with Spain and adopted the Spanish Netherlands as his base. In April-May 1656 Blake and Edward Montague blockaded Cadiz. But the first important naval success for Britain was on 20 April 1657, when Blake destroyed a bullion fleet out of Santa Cruz.

Cardinal Mazarin of France promised Cromwell the port city of Dunkirk in exchange for English troops in a campaign against the Spanish Netherlands. Cromwell sent 6,000 men as part of the Anglo-French army under Turrenne. On 4 June 1658 the Anglo-French army met the Spanish-royalist* regiments at the Battle of Dunes and soundly defeated the Spanish and Charles II's regiments. Dunkirk became an English beachhead for Cromwell's planned crusade. There was never much enthusiasm for the war among England's merchants, and the support for an anti-Catholic crusade was sporadic. The death of Cromwell in October 1658 and the subsequent political instability reduced interest in the war, which effectively ended with the Restoration* of Charles II, who was on amiable terms with Spain. Of this war there is no comprehensive history. (See also Army*; Navy*.)

Bibliography: S. R. Gardiner, *History of the Commonwealth and Protectorate*, vol. 3, 1901; Christopher Hill, *God's Englishman*, 1970.

John H. F. Hughes

Star Chamber, Court of. See Prerogative Courts.

Stop of the Exchequer (1672). The Stop of the Exchequer was a fiscal expedient adopted in January 1672 by which Charles II*, probably acting at the behest of Lord Thomas Clifford*, issued letters patent formally suspending payments on certain loans in the Exchequer*. Although Charles had suggested that the stop would last only ten months, it was renewed one year later, and in 1674 its duration became indefinite. Such extreme action seemed necessary in response to the increasingly serious cash flow problems, bordering on bankruptcy, suffered by the Crown. By stopping payment on some of its obligations, the government revised the terms of a scheme inaugurated earlier by Sir George Downing, which had provided that ordinary subjects would advance money to the Crown in anticipation of the collection of a particular body of revenue such as a parliamentary grant. Subjects who participated would receive from the Treasury Lords signed, chronologically numbered orders, which would authorize repayment in strict sequence in an "unalterable course" of half-yearly installments at six percent interest. The orders, which matured during the time it took to collect the revenue, could be endorsed over to others, thereby becoming on occasion a form of paper money. The purpose of this credit scheme, which imitated Dutch practice, was to draw on the resources of small investors in order to finance government borrowing, thereby lessening dependence on city bankers and providing cheap, dependable credit for the government and a reliable savings vehicle for the public. By halting payments on such orders, the stop violated the premise that holders of orders would be repaid according to a prearranged schedule.

Many members of the privy council* opposed the stop, but their resistance was ineffective because there was no ready alternative to meet the costs of current operations, much less war with the Dutch (see Third Dutch War*, 1672-1674). Despite large grants in parliament* since 1669, by 1672 the government owed debts exceeding £2 million, part in existing debt, part in anticipation of a year's revenue. By stopping payments at the Exchequer of a portion of its debt, the Crown obtained a respite from its cash crisis and could thereby devote incoming revenue to wartime expenditure. Another advantage of this approach was that it potentially lessened any requests for supply that might have to be made to parliament, which would likely have demanded political concessions in exchange for new revenue.

The stop revealed that Downing's ambition of a government capable of borrowing directly from the public had not yet been realized, since it turned out that bankers had acquired most of the repayment orders. The bankers were eventually compensated but only after they had suffered a loss estimated at £1 million. In 1674 they received two years' interest on their capital, and in the later 1670s an annuities scheme further eased their burden. The order system continued, however, ultimately linking the fiscal reforms of 1667-1672 with those undertaken by the post-1688 regime.

Historians once characterized the Stop of the Exchequer as a symbol of the moral and fiscal bankruptcy of later Stuart England, but in fact it represented one of a series of hesitant steps toward a funded national debt (see Taxation and Revenue*).

Bibliography: A. Browning, "The Stop of the Exchequer," *History* 14 (1930): 333-337; C. D. Chandaman, *The English Public Revenue, 1660-1688,* 1975.

Myron C. Noonkester

Strafford, Earl of. See Wentworth, Thomas.

Stuart, Arabella (1575-1615). Arabella (or Arbella) Stuart was the only child of Charles Stuart, earl of Lennox, the younger brother of Henry Stuart, Lord Darnley, and Elizabeth Cavendish, the daughter of Bess of Hardwick. Born in England in 1575 and a cousin of James VI* of Scotland*, Arabella was perceived as an alternate potential claimant to the English throne after Elizabeth I.

Orphaned as a child, Arabella was under the control of her maternal grandmother, the countess of Shrewsbury, and at times lived in the same household as Mary Stuart, who was under the guard of the earl of Shrewsbury. Plans for Arabella's marriage were met with suspicion by Elizabeth I, who insisted that Arabella be kept closely guarded. Robert Dudley, earl of Leicester, considered a marriage between Arabella and his infant son, but the boy died at the age of four in 1584. In 1587 and 1591 Elizabeth had Arabella brought to the royal court* to show her off when there was discussion of her marriage with Rainutio, son of the duke of Parma, but these negotiations came to nothing, and in 1592 Elizabeth sent Arabella back to her grandmother; she did not return to court for the rest of Elizabeth's reign. In the summer of 1602 Arabella felt desperate. She was unmarried and had little prospect of a marriage being arranged for her. She wrote to the earl of Hertford suggesting she marry his grandson, Edward Seymour. Hertford informed Robert Cecil*, and Elizabeth and her grandmother were both furious with her initiative.

When James ascended the English throne in March 1603, he invited Arabella to court. James refused to believe that Arabella was linked with the treasonable plots of Sir Walter Raleigh* and Lord Cobham, and Cecil cleared her name at their trial. James did not treat Arabella with much generosity; he was parsimonious with her and also did not arrange a marriage for her. Though they were warned against it, Arabella secretly married William Seymour, the younger grandson of the earl of Hertford, on 22 June 1610. By 8 July the marriage was known to the court; William was summoned by the privy council* and sent to the Tower of London. Arabella was placed under the care of Sir Thomas Perry. Queen Anne (of Denmark*), Prince Henry*, and Cecil all counseled forgiveness, and most at court believed James would be merciful; instead he was adamant. Arabella and William planned an escape; William got to Holland, but Arabella was captured and then lodged in the Tower, as was her aunt Mary Talbot for aiding her escape. Though rumors spread that while in the Tower Arabella suffered insanity, this is unlikely to have been true as there is no suggestion of it in the official records. Arabella finally refused all sustenance and died on 25 September 1615. After her death James allowed William to return to England. His second wife was a daughter of the earl of Essex. They named one of their daughters for Arabella.

Bibliography: E. T. Bradley, *Life of the Lady Arabella Stuart*, 1889; David Durant, *Arabella Stuart: A Rival to the Queen*, 1978; Sara Jayne Steen, "Fashioning an Acceptable Self: Arabella Stuart," in Kirby Farrell, Elizabeth H. Hageman, and Arthur F. Kinney, eds., *Women in the Renaissance*, 1988.

Carole Levin

Suspending Power. A royal prerogative* through which the monarch could suspend a statute. Many regarded this as an unconstitutional encroachment on the authority of parliament*. Following the Restoration*, Charles II* and James II* attempted to use this power to suspend legislation directed against Catholics* and Dissenters*, thereby straining the relationship between monarch and parliament.

Prior to the Restoration, in his Declaration of Breda* of 1660, Charles II promised liberty of conscience to his subjects regarding religion. However, between 1661 and 1665 the Cavalier Parliament* (1661-1679), strongly Anglican* in sentiment, passed a series of acts to enforce religious conformity known as the Clarendon Code*, which included the Act of Uniformity of 1662 (14 Car. II, c. 4). Parliament refused the king's request to add provisions to the act that would have allowed him to dispense from the act Catholics who were not clergymen and to dispense loyal ministers from wearing the surplice or making the sign of the cross during baptism. Therefore, in May 1662 Charles attempted to suspend the act for three months, but he was thwarted by the opposition of the judges and bishops. In December he proposed his first Declaration of Indulgence and attempted to secure passage of an act that would have broadened the dispensing power* (technically to benefit Dissenters), but parliament rejected it in 1663. In keeping with the secret pro-Catholic provisions of the Treaty of Dover* (1670), Charles attempted to suspend the entire act with his Declaration of Indulgence of 1672*, but the judges opposed him, and in February 1673 the Commons passed a resolution asserting that the penal laws regarding religion could not be suspended except by act of parliament. In March Charles withdrew the declaration, and parliament subsequently passed the first Test Act* (25 Car. II, c. 2), which restricted both Catholics and Dissenters.

The accession of the Catholic James II in 1685 led to renewed conflict. Unable to persuade the parliament of 1685* to repeal the Test Act (supplemented in 1678 by 30 Car. II, st. 2, c. 1, in response to the Popish Plot*), James used the dispensing power to admit Catholics to the army*, privy council*, commissions of the peace (see Local Government*), and the universities*. This was upheld by King's Bench (see Common Law and Courts*) in the case of *Godden v. Hales* (1686), but the judges remained suspicious of the suspending power. Therefore, when James issued his first Declaration of Indulgence* in April 1687, he suspended the penal laws against Catholics and Dissenters, but did not attempt to overturn the Test Act entirely; rather, he merely suspended the requirements that officeholders take the oaths of allegiance and supremacy and declare that they had received the Anglican sacrament (he also offered them individual dispensations).

James provoked a new crisis when he issued his second Declaration of Indulgence in April 1688. Its provisions employing the suspending power were essentially the same, but in May James ordered that it be read from the nation's pulpits, which would have required the tacit approval of the clergy. When Archbishop William Sancroft* and six of his episcopal colleagues refused, arguing that parliament had declared the suspending power illegal, they were charged with seditious libel, but were acquitted in the famous trial of the Seven Bishops* in June. This brought jubilation from Anglicans and Dissenters, embarrassed the king, and helped bring about the Glorious Revolution*.

The Convention Parliament of 1689* called for the abolition of the suspending power and limits on the dispensing power in its Declaration of Rights*, and these provisions were later enacted as part of the Bill of Rights* (1 Gul. III & Mar., sess. 2, c. 2)

Bibliography: John Bossy, *The English Catholic Community, 1570-1850*, 1976; J. P. Kenyon, ed., *The Stuart Constitution: Documents and Commentary*, 1966; J. R. Tanner, *English Constitutional Conflicts of the Seventeenth Century, 1603-1689*, 1928; E. N. Williams, ed., *The Eighteenth Century Constitution: Documents and Commentary*, 1960.

William T. Walker

T

Taxation and Revenue (1603-1689). When James I* became king, the royal treasury was in desperate need of funds. The Tudors had made and spent vast amounts of money, and James inherited a massive debt and an empty treasury. James accepted the queen's debts, and when he ended the war with Spain in 1604 (see London, Treaty of*) parliament* became reluctant to vote financial aid for the Crown. Combined with these problems was the fact that parliament would use money as leverage against James and the other Stuarts in order to gain power for themselves.

James's revenue came from the income of Crown lands* and from taxes that parliament voted on a temporary and inconsistent basis. Out of these revenues the king had to pay all the expenses of his government. Parliament expected the monarch to live "of his own" (revenue from Crown lands and other personal sources) except in time of emergency (usually war), when it would levy taxes to pay the extraordinary expenses. But Crown land revenues had been inadequate for centuries to pay for the expenses of the government, so the king continually asked for taxes to supplement his income and meet his expenses of government.

Common taxes used in 1603 were subsidies, and fifteenths and tenths. A subsidy was a tax of 4 shillings on land and 2s. on goods; it amounted to £70,000. In addition, a £20,000 subsidy was levied on the clergy. One or more subsidies at a time might be granted by parliament. In the seventeenth century a fifteenths and tenths tax amounted to £29,000. Originally it was a tax of one fifteenth or one tenth on movables, but a valuation was taken in the fourteenth century, and the tax was thereafter based on the valuation. Counties paid the fifteenth, and towns paid the tenth.

Parliament became increasingly reluctant to continue these taxes for James. In 1601 parliament voted Elizabeth four subsidies and eight fifteenths and tenths. In 1606 it gave James three subsidies and six fifteenths and tenths, and in 1610 only one subsidy and one fifteenths and tenths were levied (see parliament of 1604-1610*). No taxes of this type were again given until 1621.

In 1610 James's lord treasurer, Robert Cecil*, attempted to negotiate the Great Contract* with the House of Commons. The Crown would give up its rights of purveyance and wardship and some other medieval sources of income in exchange for a parliamentary grant of £200,000 per annum. Because of other problems between the Crown and the Commons, the Great Contract was never concluded. James imposed medieval prerogative taxes and feudal dues on the country between 1610 and 1620 in order to finance his government (see royal prerogative*). Crown lands revenue increased during most of James's reign, and he sold land for £654,952 to provide additional income.

Customs duties were "farmed" between 1605 and 1671. Financiers would bid for the privilege of collecting the duties, agreeing to pay the Crown a specific sum. Duties on imports and exports were increased, and in 1604 a new book of rates was published with the higher duties.

During the 1620s direct taxes were resumed to pay for the wars of the period (see French War of 1627-1629*; Spanish War of 1625-1630*; Thirty Years War*). Two subsidies were granted in the parliament of 1621*, three subsidies and three fifteenths and tenths were levied in the parliament of 1624*, two subsidies were given in the parliament of 1625*, and five more were appropriated in the parliament of 1628*. The rate of return from these taxes continually decreased.

In the early part of Charles I's* reign, the government generally abandoned direct taxes (subsidies and fifteenths and tenths). Commons also decided to vote tonnage and poundage (a customs duty of five percent) for only one year. Income from the Crown estates continued to increase, and Charles continued to sell Crown lands, raising a total of £642,000 by this method during his reign.

Lack of money led Charles to pressure Englishmen for loans in 1627, totaling an amount that was to equal five subsidies (£300,000). Many resisted the pressure, and some gentry were imprisoned for resisting the forced loans*, but in that year £243,750 pounds was collected from the loans. In 1628 parliament forbade any gift, loan, or tax without its consent, severely limiting the king's arbitrary power in finance. Parliament granted five subsidies to the king in return for his signature on the Petition of Right*.

Between 1629 and 1640 the king operated the government and collected revenue without calling parliament (see Personal Rule*). He collected several archaic taxes: fines for distraint of knighthood*, forest fines (see Forest Laws*), ship money*, wardships, and enforcement of statutes against enclosures (see Agriculture*). He also granted monopolies*, which had been made illegal in 1624. By these measures and customs collections and by ignoring the Crown debt of about £1 million, Charles was able to keep his government solvent during this decade. His income in 1641 has been estimated at £862,000. The Long Parliament*, however, eliminated many of these sources in 1641.

After 1650 the expenses of the English government increased dramatically. In 1651 they amounted to £2,750,000. During the Interregnum* period (1649-1660) customs brought more than £300,000 into the Exchequer* annually, and much money was brought in by fines of royalists* and sale of Crown lands. Nevertheless, increased expenditures required more revenue, and the government created new taxes to fill the gap. Monthly assessments were laid on the counties, and the assessment was to be collected as an income tax. This tax later became merely a land tax, which became an important part of the tax structure throughout the eighteenth century. The excise tax was another important addition to the revenue. A tax on consumer goods, this levy was first put on some alcoholic beverages in 1643, and it was quickly extended to other goods. Opposition and riots greeted this new tax, but it became a permanent part of the tax structure.

By 1660 and the Restoration* of Charles II*, government revenue sources were greatly changed and modernized. The feudal taxes that James I and Charles I utilized had been eliminated, and the fifteenths and tenths had been superseded by customs, excise, and land taxes. A hearth tax of two shillings per hearth per annum was levied in 1662, but it was abolished in 1689. The farming of customs ended in 1671, and collection was controlled by commissioners.

The Commons established its right of initiating all money bills, and it began the practice of appropriation of supply. Each item of expenditure was funded by a specific tax, and if that tax did not produce its expected revenue, then that item of expenditure was short of money. This unhappy result was most often the case. Parliament did assume responsibility for the expenses of the army* and navy* during Charles II's reign, but the revenue often fell short.

An important new income for the Crown was an automatic grant of £1.2 million per year from parliament. This sum was an estimate of government expenses in the 1630s, with eight percent added for inflation. Originally suggested in the Great Contract of 1610, this grant was an admission by parliament that government expenses were the responsibility of the nation as well as the king. The estimate was too low for actual government needs in the 1660s, and the amount was never actually raised during any year. In order to supplement his income, Charles secretly accepted subsidies from Louis XIV of France (see Dover, Treaty of*). He also sold Crown lands that brought in hundreds of thousands of pounds.

In the 1680s, after the end of his wars (see Second and Third Dutch Wars*, 1665-1667, 1672-1674), the financial condition of Charles and the English government improved substantially. Total annual income reached £1,370,000, and annual expenditures declined to £1,175,000, allowing a reduction of £500,000 in the king's debt.

Parliament granted James II* an annual income of £2 million, but he still resorted to illegal and arbitrary taxation and accepted money from France. The revolutionary settlement of 1689 finally destroyed any financial independence of the Crown (see Glorious Revolution*). The Bill of Rights* made the levying of any money without consent of parliament illegal, and the Appropriations Act limited the life of a money bill to one year.

Important financial developments during the reigns of William III* and Queen Anne* included creation of the Bank of England in 1694 as a lending agency to the government, creation of a national debt (as opposed to a royal debt) in 1693, and the creation of exchequer bills as currency (paper money).

Bibliography: Stephen Dowell, *A History of Taxation and Taxes in England*, 4 vols., 1888, rprt. 1965.

                                                                                        W. Calvin Dickinson

Test Acts (1673, 1678). Two laws whose primary purpose was to bar Roman Catholics* from holding government offices or sitting in parliament*. The political pressures engendered by the Third Dutch War* (1672-1674) and the Popish Plot* (1678) forced Charles II* to accept them.

The first Test Act of 1673 (25 Car. II, c. 2) had its origin in the anti-Catholic agitation associated with the beginning of the Third Dutch War and the Declaration of Indulgence* in 1672. England's alliance with France had aroused fears of a conspiracy to reestablish Catholicism and arbitrary rule in England. Those fears received additional reinforcement when Charles II issued the Declaration of Indulgence, which granted religious toleration to both Dissenters* and Roman Catholics. Charles II claimed the power to suspend the penal statutes concerning religion as part of his royal prerogative*. Parliament, however, rejected the king's claim to possess the suspending power* and warned that such a power posed the threat of arbitrary rule.

To counter the Declaration of Indulgence, parliament passed the Test Act, specifically directed against Catholics. It barred anyone from holding civil or military office who had not performed a number of tests. These tests consisted of taking the oaths of supremacy and allegiance, communing in the Church of England (see Anglicanism*), and subscribing to a declaration that transubstantiation did not occur during the Lord's Supper. Although Charles II did not agree with the Test Act, he needed to cooperate with parliament or it would not vote the taxes (see Taxation and Revenue*) he needed to support the Third Dutch War. Dissenting Protestants could fulfill the requirements of the Test Act by occasional conformity (i.e., taking communion in the Church of England), while Catholics could not because of the declaration regarding transubstantiation. By accepting the Test Act, Charles II greatly restricted his ability to appoint his own officials and distribute patronage. It also forced his brother and heir, the duke of York (see James II*), to resign his office as lord admiral, which fueled speculation about how many other Catholics there still were in high places.

Parliament passed the second Test Act of 1678 (30 Car. II, st. 2, c. 1) in the midst of the turmoil of the Popish Plot. It required that anyone sitting in parliament, either the Lords or the Commons, take the oaths of supremacy and allegiance and make a declaration rejecting transubstantiation and other forms of Roman Catholic doctrine. Its provisions also applied to the Scottish and Irish parliaments (see Ireland*; Scotland*), although James was exempted from its provisions. Political pressures again forced Charles II to acquiesce to the legislation even though he personally found it objectionable. His brother and heir would later try to overturn the law when he became king. However, the Glorious Revolution* prevented James II from achieving his goal, and the Test Acts remained in force until 1829.

Bibliography: J. R. Jones, *Country and Court: England, 1658-1715,* 1979; J. P. Kenyon, *The Stuart Constitution,* 2d ed., 1986.

Ronald H. Fritze

Thirty Years War (1618-1648). There were three important ways in which the Thirty Years War had an impact on the English Civil War*. All have been acknowledged, but none has been accorded sufficient influence. First, England was a participant in the early stages of the Thirty Years War, and that participation, which was both expensive and militarily disastrous, did much to poison relations between Crown and parliament* throughout the 1620s. Charles I* was obliged to summon parliament because he needed funds to support his war policy on the Continent, and the ensuing struggle about war strategy, funding the war, and the legality of the king's extraparliamentary expedients to carry it on led to a serious constitutional uproar. Had there been no foreign war, there would have been no Petition of Right* and all that went with it. Arguably, the troubles that led to the Civil War began with the parliamentary crisis that the foreign wars created. Looking back from the 1640s, Edward Hyde* (later earl of Clarendon) suggested as much. Charles I's Personal Rule* (1629-1640) was possible only because the king had abandoned his participation in the continental wars, leaving him free to find—still with extraparliamentary expedients—the more modest sums required for a normal peacetime administration.

Second, once the Civil War had broken out, the fact that the major European states were heavily engaged in their own struggle on the continent meant that the contending parties in Britain were left to fight out their conflict without interference or much outside assistance. This worked heavily in the favor of the parliamentary side. Charles I might have been expected to raise some substantial assistance from France, which was not forthcoming largely because of the continental war. The first two years of the Civil War were essentially a stalemate militarily, broken only by the re-entry of the Scots, which tipped the balance against the king and created the momentum that proved fatal to his cause.

Third, not only was the king prevented by the Thirty Years War from appealing to monarchical solidarity abroad for help, but that war exacerbated religious hostility, which hardened political feelings in Britain as well. Charles's dynastic connection to Catholic France through his wife, Henrietta Maria*, had been a political liability from the beginning of his reign, and the cost of that association was even higher in the inflamed conditions created by the religious war on the Continent. While this brought the king devoted support from his Catholic subjects, that very fact alienated many more, who had long feared that the European-wide war was a terrible test both at home and abroad upon which the existence of the Protestant faith depended, and who assumed that upon that faith depended the survival of the traditional liberties of Englishmen. The European war reinforced the tendency to see the war at home in transcendent terms and thus to make any negotiated settlement with a king, perceived as a crypto-Catholic, more difficult.

The recent historiography of the origins of the Civil War has provided both support for these views and ammunition for denying them much significance. Conrad

Russell's work in studying the details of parliamentary politics has represented a determined assault on the Whiggish view of the Civil War as a conscious struggle about the constitution, in defense of civil and religious liberty. In so doing he has shown how important to the political crisis were the contingent effects of the military misadventures against France and Spain in the 1620s (see French War of 1627-1629*, Spanish War of 1625-1630*). However, another line of revisionist argument, best represented by Anthony Fletcher's *The Outbreak of the English Civil War*, has gone even further and argued in effect that no real connection at all can be established between the parliamentary troubles of the 1620s and the outbreak of the Civil War. The earlier issues, which had left the king isolated and without support, had been settled, and thus the Civil War can only be accounted for as the consequence of the overbearing parliamentary radicalism in late 1641 or as some kind of large accident, the product perhaps of misunderstanding or lack of communication. This debate remains unsettled. For the role played by the general hostility to Catholicism*, which did much damage to the king's cause, Michael Finlayson's *Historians, Puritanism, and the English Revolution*, among others, is helpful. On the direct impact of the later years of the fighting in the Thirty Years War on British affairs and political thought, less is available. Ian Roy has drawn attention to the way in which the brutality of the campaigns in central Europe, which was amply reported in Britain, led to great fear that continental methods would be employed in the Civil War, to the kingdom's utter ruin.

Bibliography: "England Turned Germany," *Transactions of the Royal Historical Society*, 5th Series, Vol. 28: 127-144.

                                                                                    S. J. Stearns

Thorough. First conceived by Archbishop William Laud* and Thomas Wentworth* (later earl of Strafford) in the early 1630s, "thorough" meant to govern absolutely, efficiently, in the interest of the Crown alone. This meant not only exploiting all royal offices to their fullest potential but also limiting the profits from patronage positions that flowed into private hands rather than the royal treasury. As such, it was the theoretical backbone of Charles I's* attempt at Personal Rule* between 1629 and 1640.

Thorough was first employed by Wentworth as lord president of the Council of the North from 1629 to 1632. It was mainly an improved method of collecting taxes by eliminating profiteering tax farmers (see Taxation and Revenue*), though it also entailed an attack on the independence of the northern lords. Charles's need for revenue during the period of personal rule led to its application in other branches of government. It almost always engendered resistance, for it deprived court favorites of personal income. Thorough particularly angered the queen's partisans, and Charles often undercut the policy to meet their demands. Nevertheless, during the mid-1630s it was put into action in the Anglican* church by Laud, who tried to make the church a source of financial and political support for the king. It was believed that "thorough" implementation of theological conformity was the first step in asserting the king's absolute authority. The most prominent application of thorough, however, was in Ireland*.

Wentworth, lord deputy of Ireland from 1632 until 1641, established a system often compared to such continental practitioners of absolutism* as Cardinal Richelieu in France and Count Olivares in Spain. He intended to make Ireland a source of new revenue for Charles rather than a drain on the royal treasury. In action, this meant focusing on increasing revenue in Ireland, reforming its army, and controlling its justice system. Appointed in 1632, Wentworth by 1634 had established dominance over the Irish parliament by playing off the factions of "Old" and "New" English. He obtained funds to revitalize the Irish army and authority to reform the Calvinistic* Irish church along Anglican lines. Henceforth, he exercised a relatively free hand in implementing thorough.

Wentworth encouraged fledgling industries, increasing the prosperity of Ireland. The flax industry, the iron industry, and the export of tallow were all promoted with some success. Royal revenue increased dramatically in the late 1630s with the direct collection of Irish customs duties. Wentworth also hoped to Anglicize the island and plotted a plantation* in Connaught. He also looked into the earlier plantations, taking care that the conditions of plantation had been observed. His investigations led to the dispossession of Derry from the City of London*, which had failed to settle enough Englishmen. In keeping with the spirit of thorough, Derry was returned to Crown management.

The greatest problems encountered in thorough administration of Ireland arose from the attempt to Anglicize the Irish church. The Puritan* "New English" and the Presbyterian* Scots in Ulster objected strenuously. The powerful earl of Cork, Richard Boyle, became an implacable opponent over the administration of church lands. Wentworth's policy of polarizing the various Irish factions in the interests of the Crown eventually earned him the scorn of all. Further, his policy of government without concern toward private interests did not extend to his own affairs, making his growing fortune the object of resentment in Ireland and England alike. Nevertheless, Charles I was pleased with Wentworth's progress, in 1640 elevating him to earl of Strafford and extending his powers. His failed attempt to use these broad powers to generate Irish support for Charles I against the Scots led to Wentworth's downfall, and his Irish adversaries eagerly used his attainder trial to discredit thorough. The policy, along with the other elements of Charles I's attempt at Personal Rule, ended with the coming of Civil War* in 1642.

Bibliography: H. F. Kearney, *Strafford in Ireland, 1633-1641: A Study in Absolutism*, 1989.

John Nolan

Thurloe, John (1616-1688). Historians have ignored Thurloe until recently. He was, however, well known at home and abroad during the Cromwellian Protectorate* of the 1650s.

Thurloe was not an army* man. Through the patronage of Oliver St. John, he served as clerk and secretary to various government committees and missions from 1645. Because of his efficiency and loyalty, he attracted the attention of the council of state* and Oliver Cromwell*. In 1653 he became sole manager of foreign intelligence, member of the council of state, and secretary of state. As secretary he was one of the most influential men in England. In 1655 he became postmaster general and was given authority to censor the printing* of public news.

As secretary of state, Thurloe was active in all aspects of government, both domestic and foreign, though he did not determine policy. He was a member of Cromwell's parliaments (see Protectorate Parliaments*) and manipulated the elections of 1656 to exclude as many of Cromwell's opponents as possible. He acted as Cromwell's spokesperson in parliament*, administered the details of foreign affairs efficiently, and was the most knowledgeable person in government about European affairs. He admired Cromwell and was loyal and incorruptible.

Thurloe's chief contribution to Cromwell was in his role as master spy. Because of extensive plotting to assassinate Cromwell and overthrow the Protectorate, an efficient intelligence system was essential. Thurloe used his position as postmaster general to intercept letters, employed local postmasters as spies, worked closely with the major generals* to gather information, and had agents at Charles II's* court in exile and at every other major court in Europe. One spy at Charles's court was exposed and summarily shot. Because of his extensive spy network, Thurloe foiled every plot against Cromwell. As a spy, he was legendary, and it was said that because of him, Cromwell carried the secrets of Europe in his girdle.

Thurloe was the mainstay of Richard Cromwell's* brief Protectorate. It was on Thurloe's word that Richard had been named by his father as his successor that the younger Cromwell became lord protector. Thurloe was Richard's backbone and acted as his spokesperson in the parliament of 1659. Upon its recall by General George Monck* in 1660, the Long Parliament* renamed Thurloe as secretary of state since he was the only knowledgeable person for the post.

At the Restoration* Thurloe was charged with high treason and committed to the Tower of London. He was soon released and lived until his death in Great Milton or in his chambers at Lincoln's Inn. It was rumored that he was treated gently because he had a black book that would reveal the disloyalty of many royalists*. The book has never been found, but he had the knowledge to be a threat. Charles's officials often consulted him about foreign affairs. He died suddenly in 1688 and is buried beneath the chapel at Lincoln's Inn. His papers were subsequently found in a false ceiling in his chambers.

Bibliography: Philip Aubrey, *Mr. Secretary Thurloe: Cromwell's Secretary of State*, 1990; D. L. Hobman, *Cromwell's Master Spy*, 1961.

Wilson J. Hoffman

Tories. One of the two political parties that came into existence during the Exclusion Crisis* (1678-1681), the Tories opposed the Whig* attempt to exclude the duke of

York, the future James II*, from the succession. Tories defended James's right to succeed to the throne because to deny his right would amount to an attack on the property rights of all citizens. *Tory*, a term of abuse, originally referred to one of the dispossessed Irish who became bandits. Supporters of the duke of York were first labeled Yorkists and later abhorrers* because they produced abhorring petitions to counter Whig petitions. Finally the term *Tory* was used because the duke had supported the Irish and was Catholic*, as the majority of Irish were.

Like the Whigs, the core of Tories developed during the latter stages (1674-1678) of the Cavalier Parliament*, where they were supporters of Thomas Osborne*, earl of Danby. Former royalists* from the Civil War* period, staunch Anglicans*, and some members of the royal court* assisted Charles II* in defending James's rights during the Exclusion Crisis. Like the Whigs, the Tories did not view themselves as a party, but claimed to represent the best and most sound segment of English society, the landed interest. Because of electoral defeats in 1679, Tories copied Whig methods and produced abhorrences to counter Whig petitions (see Petitioners*) and also later produced instructions for members of parliament*, which called for opposition to exclusion and enforcement of penal laws against Dissenters* to protect the Church of England. They feared that the earl of Shaftesbury (Anthony Ashley Cooper*) and the Whigs were pushing the country toward civil war by insisting on exclusion. While the Whigs maintained control in the House of Commons throughout the Exclusion Crisis, the Tories were strong in the House of Lords and defeated exclusion bills passed by the House of Commons.

In the Tory reaction (1681-1685) after the dissolution of the Oxford Parliament* (1681), Charles II worked with the Tories to break the power of the Whigs. Tories cooperated in the *quo warranto* proceedings against municipal charters, using that as an opportunity to get rid of local Whig rivals when the new charters were reissued. A bitter political struggle in London* during the autumn of 1682 resulted in the selection of two Tories as sheriffs*, which enabled Charles II and the Tories to break Whig control of London's political machinery and led to the eventual surrender of London's charter. Tories developed the doctrines of passive obedience, nonresistance*, and indefeasible hereditary succession, defending these ideas with examples from the Bible*, history (see Historical Thought*), and nature. The Anglican church and the Crown were the two institutions that received unqualified support during Charles II's reign; however, during the reign of James II, when the Tories were forced to choose between support of monarch or church, most of them chose the church.

The election of 1685 after James II's accession produced a very strong Tory majority in the House of Commons, which James relied on for support. Tories reacted against James II's expansion of the army* and inclusion of Catholic officers, use of suspending* and dispensing* powers, issuance of Declarations of Indulgence*, and the trial of the Seven Bishops*. Such actions, which were designed to procure toleration for Catholics, led the Tories to believe that the Anglican church was under attack, and they rallied to its defense. James II abandoned his attempt to rely on the Tories and turned to Whigs and Dissenters for support. He managed to alienate them too, and Whigs and Tories deserted James II during the Glorious Revolution* (1688-

1689) as prominent Tories and Whigs were signatories of the famous invitation to William of Orange*.

During the Convention Parliament* (1689), the Tories in general urged delay and caution in reaching a settlement; in contrast the Whigs sought a speedier resolution of the constitutional issues. The famous resolution of the House of Commons that James II had "subverted" the constitution by breaking the "original contract" between the people and king and had "abdicated the government," leaving the throne "vacant," was a combination of Whig and Tory arguments, and the resolution passed because of Whig and moderate Tory support. Other Tories had promoted the concept of a regency or upheld the proposition that the Crown had devolved upon Mary* alone and also disagreed with the Whig notion of an "original contract."

In the House of Lords, the Tories had greater strength; led by Daniel Finch, earl of Nottingham, Henry Hyde, 2d earl of Clarendon, and Lawrence Hyde, earl of Rochester, they unsuccessfully attempted to change the wording of the House of Commons's resolution from "abdicated" to "deserted" and delete the phrase that the throne was "vacant." Whig and Tory support was necessary for the offer of the Crown to both William and Mary, and both parties had agreed to bar a Catholic king from the throne of England.

William distributed offices to both Whigs and Tories, although some Tories were discontented in being overlooked. Controversy over the form of the oath of allegiance to be sworn to William and Mary caused a split within the Tories. The oath that recognized the de facto rather than de jure nature of William and Mary's rule was still unacceptable to a number of Tories, who refused to swear it. Some Tories maintained that the Convention was not legal because writs had not been issued by a legal king. Tories lost this fight; a bill was passed legalizing the Convention as a parliament, which enabled it to enforce the oath.

Concern for protecting the church led Tories to oppose vehemently a proposal from William that parliament repeal the Test Act*, and they successfully worked to amend the coronation oath, inserting the words "as by law established," which bound William to protect the Church of England. In April 1689 a large group of Tories met at the Devil Tavern in London to urge William to protect the church, demonstrating that they were concerned about the religious settlement. In August 1689 when the clergy had to take the oaths of allegiance, over 400 led by William Sancroft*, archbishop of Canterbury, refused, indicating that many of the Tory clergy were concerned about the political settlement. Some Tories had difficulty in accepting the religious and political settlement reached during the Glorious Revolution, while the Whigs had adhered to it. This set the stage for political squabbles in the post-1689 period between Tories and Whigs.

Bibliography: Keith Feiling, *A History of the Tory Party, 1640-1714*, 1924; J. R. Jones, "Parties and Parliament," in Jones, ed., *The Restored Monarchy, 1660-1688*, 48-70, 1979; W. A. Speck, *Reluctant Revolutionaries*, 1989.

Mark C. Herman

Trade, Foreign. In the years leading up to the seventeenth century, England and Europe in general experienced dramatic changes in the way foreign trade was conducted, the products involved, and the geographic areas of focus. The great age of exploration and discovery brought on prospects of new markets, new trade items, and a reorientation of international trade from the Mediterranean to the Atlantic, a situation that placed England in a propitious position to develop overseas trade. Moreover, the tremendous growth of European overseas trading activity had a substantial impact on England in expanding its markets, supplying raw materials, encouraging domestic consumer demands for a greater variety of goods, and fostering a growing reexport trade.

Accompanying these changes in foreign trade was the elimination of foreign monopolies (particularly those of the Venetians and the Hanseatic League) in England itself during the late Tudor period and the collapse of the Antwerp market, England's most important source of overseas trade. In general, however, the chief characteristic of English foreign trade in the overall economy of Europe at the beginning of the Stuart period was as a source of raw materials rather than a supplier of finished goods (as was later the case by the end of the Stuart period). Certainly one of the reasons for this rather undeveloped facet of the English economy was the fact that in spite of some substantial inroads made in international trade by the great trading companies* of the late Tudor period (the Muscovy, Levant, Barbary, Guinea, and Eastland companies and the Merchant Adventurers), foreign competition for both old and new markets was particularly keen, as well as dangerous. While the perils of dealing with the Barbary pirates were legend long before the accession of James I*, as late as 1609 there were estimated to be over a thousand pirates roving the Irish and English coasts. Even in 1603 Sir Walter Raleigh* (in his "Observations Concerning the Trade and Commerce of England with the Dutch and Foreign Nations") decried that the Dutch were cutting deeply into the English trade by the "roominess of their shipping, holding much merchandise, though sailing with fewer hands" in ships "each as large as two of ours."

Nonetheless, early foreign trade helped to develop economic growth in England by bringing in raw materials that cut the overall costs of manufactures and led to greater production and marketing of goods. Business skills developed in foreign trade were used for domestic industry, and the profits from foreign trade encouraged the middle class both to invest in overseas trade and to support those parts of the domestic economy that fostered the growth of foreign trade. As trade increased and profits grew, foreign commodities became cheaper and created a greater market for foreign goods as well as English goods overseas. As a result of this increased activity, English exports witnessed about a seventy-five percent increase between 1600 and 1640. While the Civil War* caused some problems in trade because of internal disruption and the negative European reaction to the execution of Charles I*, by the 1650s the reexport trade began to flourish, although hampered somewhat by the First Dutch War* (1652-1654). From the Civil War through the Restoration*, the overall foreign trade of England grew between a third and two-thirds primarily as a result of the new reexport trade (with the latter growing about ninefold during the same period). By the end of the 1660s reexports accounted for about a third of England's total export trade.

As for the specifics of the export-import trade itself, while increases in the metal trade were substantial by mid-century, the woolen trade continued to be the dominant export product of England throughout the century, with the export trade creating employment in support industries. During the Stuart period, foreign trade increased by about 500 percent; the labor employed in that trade increased considerably more because the volume and distances involved in the new trade were so much greater. Even the financing of overseas trade underwent substantial change to accommodate the longer time needed to see a turnaround from initial investment to eventual return. Although the volume of overseas trade increased substantially, the individual commodity value of goods did not. Also, the value of trade grew much more rapidly than national income, with the capital and labor requirements needed to accommodate that increase rising even faster.

The opening of the southern European trade was stimulated by the high cost of textiles in Spain and Italy, the decline in population in both areas, and the development of the lightweight woolens (the "new drapery") in England, a development prompted by the immigration of highly skilled Low Country textile craftsmen to the already developing worsted-producing areas of southeastern England. To this was added the lucrative broadcloth trade to central Europe up to mid-century, when that market declined but was picked up by the Turkish and Indian trades. Nonetheless, the overall decline of heavy woolens in favor of lightweight worsteds, serges, bays, and camlets and other lightweight cloths like cotton and linen characterized the great export and reexport trade of England during the Stuart period, a change that was stimulated by a shift to lightweight fashions by Europeans (see Cloth Trade*).

As for imports, grains and ship stores were supplied mostly from the Scandinavian and Baltic trade, which trebled during the Stuart period. Fruit, wines, oil, and wood were secured from Iberia, while the Italians provided silk and Middle Eastern products. The Levantine trade itself provided spices, textiles (raw silk and cotton), and dried fruits. Up to mid-century most English foreign trade was still focused on Europe and the Mediterranean areas. After the Civil War, however, the appeal of tobacco, sugar, indigo, calicoes, and other exotic goods prompted an increased shift to America, Africa, and the Far East. Indeed, the Asian-American trade, almost non-existent at the outset of the Stuart period, constituted over a third of the total overseas trade by 1688, with London* and Bristol handling most of that trade (Bristol increasing its total volume by 1,300 percent during the century, while London handled between two-thirds and three-quarters of the total trade of the nation).

To accommodate this vast increase in foreign trade, service industries to international commerce, such as the shipping industry, saw equally impressive development. Shipping tonnage alone doubled between the reign of James I and the Restoration. Legislative support of the growing reexport trade in the form of the Navigation Acts* of 1651 and 1660 (the latter 12 Car. II, c. 18) not only cut into the dominant Dutch carrying trade but furthered the development of English manufactures and the overall emulation of the mercantilist* policies developed in France by Colbert.

The proliferation of the enumerated commodities acts both stimulated English manufactures and reduced competition from the Europeans and American colonial manufacturing and shipping. The Spanish War of 1655-1659* and the subsequent improvement of relations with the Portuguese added the Portuguese colonial trade of Brazil, Africa, and Asia to English markets, as well as Jamaica and its rich sugar crop to the English empire. At the same time, competition from Irish agricultural products (mainly livestock, cloth, and dairy products) was reduced considerably by legislation in 1667 and 1681.

From the Restoration to the Glorious Revolution*, then, England experienced a commercial boom. In part this was due to the new mercantilist legislation and the growth of the American trade, but also to the expansion of the empire and further opening of the Eastern trade (particularly in North Africa, India, and China). While some of this new trade activity can be attributed to the growth of a few of the trading companies (especially the East India*, Royal African, and Hudson's Bay companies), it was the actual decline or destruction of the monopolies* of these trading companies and the opening up of trade with northern Europe and the Middle East to an increasing number of independent merchants that produced such dramatic economic results. While the growth of trade in the third quarter of the seventeenth century was never smooth because of the Second and Third Dutch Wars* (1665-1667 and 1672-1674, respectively), the Great Fire of London*, and numerous other disruptions, the overall foreign trade in exports increased by about half during the reign of Charles II* (to about £6.5 million per annum), while the accompanying merchant shipping tonnage nearly doubled to 400,000 tons. Indeed, Stuart foreign trade reached its zenith by the time of the Glorious Revolution and thereafter declined due to an influx of Eastern fine cloth in Europe and the subsequent reduction in the European demand for English cloth. Scottish dominance in the tobacco trade and the French incursion into the sugar trade also took its toll on the English export market in Europe, as did the protectionist policies adopted by many European countries at the turn of the century.

In spite of these later developments, however, the overall view of foreign trade during the Stuart period must be as one of increased expansion in most areas brought on by a change in governmental policy toward legislatively backed mercantilist policies; reorientation of market goods (the "new drapery," sugar, and oriental products); the focus on new markets in Asia, Africa, and the West; the refortification of the traditional European market by product adjustment and geographic refocusing to the Mediterranean; the opening up of business opportunities from the large, restrictive trade monopolies of the trading companies to smaller, private investors; and market adaptation to the more profitable carrying and reexport trade. The cumulative effect of these changes was that while England underwent the violent throes of political and constitutional discord (the Civil War, Interregnum*, and Glorious Revolution), the country remained economically prosperous at a time when most of the rest of Europe saw the collapse of their economies due to war, famine, and the collapse of the great banking houses. In part because of this failure and the trade vacuum it created (especially in Spain and Italy), Europe still remained the prime source of most English exports and imports. More important, the English, along with the Dutch, adapted readily to market conditions and as a result developed diversified economies that ensured domestic prosperity through the exploitation of external as opposed to limited internal sources of wealth.

Because of its very nature, foreign trade was extremely visible to the average Englishman and therefore drew a great deal of attention and commentary from contemporary observers. In turn, it is easy to overstate the importance of foreign trade in the overall economy of England especially since as late as the end of the Stuart period nearly two-thirds of the English population* was still engaged in agriculture*, while another sizable portion of the population was employed in domestic service. Still, at the same time a quarter of all English manufactures and half of all woolen products were exported, while almost a quarter of consumed household manufactures were imported. A more realistic interpretation of the role of foreign trade (measuring probably no more than ten to twelve percent of the gross national product) in the Stuart period, then, is that it not only had a substantial impact on the daily lives of most Englishmen, but as a facet of the overall economy of England it was growing at a much faster rate than any other segment of the economy.

Bibliography: Ralph Davis, *English Overseas Trade, 1500-1700,* 1973; W. E. Minchinton, ed., *The Growth of English Overseas Trade in the Seventeenth and Eighteenth Centuries*, 1969; G. D. Ramsey, *English Overseas Trade During the Centuries of Emergence*, 1957.

James I. Miklovich

Trading Companies. One of the more interesting phenomena of the early modern period in England, indeed all of Europe, was the proliferation of overseas trading companies. While certainly not indigenous to the Stuart period, the rise of trading companies in England as a means to conduct foreign trade* (as well as to carry out foreign policy and imperial defense) reached its peak during the seventeenth century.

In general the origins of English trading companies are tied inexorably to the origins of the corporate concept, in which merchants sought to extend the idea of guild control to overseas trade. Seeking to regulate employment, the volume and quality of goods, pricing, and self-governance without confronting the law on matters of unlawful organization and operation, groups of merchants attempted to secure written royal approval (in the form of grants and charters) to conduct their activities. Hence the earliest formation of trading companies came as "regulated" companies—those that allowed every member to trade on his own but within the stated regulation of the company. The regulated companies also took on the medieval form of trade guilds in that each member purchased a license to carry on trade within the company's sphere of influence, but at his own—rather than the company's—risk. His liability extended to his personal, as well as commercial, possessions, and no outsider was allowed to trade in the licensed domain of the company unless the necessary membership fees were paid.

Joint-stock companies, a later form of trading company, carried on the principles of regulated companies and provided some distinct features. Like regulated companies, joint-stock companies received exclusivity and protection of privilege by

Crown charter; its members traded independently but with corporate protection and backing; and upon withdrawal no member could make claims to any portion of the company's common shares. Unlike regulated companies, however, the focus was on the good of the company as a whole rather than on the individual (the assumption that since liability of the individual was limited only to the amount he had invested in the company's stock, his fortunes were to be tied to the company's survival and prosperity). Moreover, whereas regulated company membership took on an apprenticeship aspect to it, with no transfer of membership from one individual to another without company approval, joint-stock membership allowed for such a provision. Also unlike regulated membership, joint-stock members could withdraw from the association at any time without due notice, and joint-stock membership could include all forms of investors, not just traders. Because of these liberties, joint-stock companies became increasingly more popular by the seventeenth century although only three—the East India*, Hudson's Bay, and Royal African companies—were present by 1688. Nonetheless, the combined resources of these three eclipsed all other trading companies put together.

In terms of actual development, the earliest notable English trading companies were the Merchants of the Staple in the thirteenth century and the Merchant Adventurers in the fourteenth century, with only the latter surviving into the Stuart period. The real beginnings of trading company development, however, came in the late Tudor period and were designed to expand England's trade to certain geographic regions, conduct exploration and settlement (see Colonization*; Plantations*), and establish diplomatic relations with the foreign potentates they contacted in trying to establish trade. Hence the first of these great companies, the Muscovy or Russia Company (1555), was charged with discovering and securing a northeast passage to China as well as establish trade with Russia. Similarly, the Eastland Company (1579) was created to carry on the Baltic trade; the Barbary or Morocco Company (1585), the North African trade; the Guinea Company (1588), the West African trade; the Levant or Turkey Company (1581), the Levant and Persian trade; and the East India Company (1599), the East African, Indian, and East Asian trade.

Certainly an interesting feature of the development of these early companies is that many investors in one company often became financial backers or "adventurers" in other companies or trading schemes. Hence, many backers of the early Barbary trade were involved in both the Guinea and Baltic trade (e.g., of the thirty-four merchants interested in the 1558 Guinea expedition, twenty-two are found in the 1555 Muscovy Company charter), and although fierce rivals in the later Stuart period, a number of the early Levant Company merchants were responsible for the funding of the East India Company. Though competition between companies was often keen, sometimes a company provided assistance to a potential rival (as in the case of the East India Company's loaning of money to the Muscovy Company during James I's* reign) or a company was forced to buy out the charters of rivals (as in the case of the duplistic charters issued by James I and Charles I* to both Scottish and English companies trading in the Far East and Greenland).

In spite of the growing wave of protest against privilege and monopoly* at the accession of James I and throughout much of the early Stuart period, the number of trading companies grew dramatically: the London (1606), Virginia (1606), Plymouth (1620), and Massachusetts Bay companies (1628) in America; the Greenland adventurers (1620) and the Hudson's Bay companies (1670) in Canada and Greenland; the Somers (Bermudas) Islands (1615) and Canary Islands companies (1665) in the mid-Atlantic; the Amazon (1620), Guiana (1627), and Providence companies (1630) in Latin America; and the London Adventurers (1618) and Royal African companies (1672) in Africa.

The reasons for this proliferation of companies in spite of public and parliamentary protest are quite simple. Aside from the foreign policy and diplomatic reasons outlined above, Stuart monarchs saw trading companies as a mechanism by which they could both apply pressure on the trades at home and oversee English subjects abroad. Moreover, they also saw these corporate entities' goals and objectives as easy to read and, in terms of performance, equally easy to assess. Trading companies were ready sources of Crown revenue and could be easily intimidated by threats of charter revocation (as in the case of the powerful Merchant Adventurers, who lost their privileges from 1621 to 1634). Finally, the Crown saw the trading companies (as stated in the Eastland Company's charter) as a means to accomplish "the resistance of exactions and the suppression of unskillful and disorderly trade."

Ironically, it is for many of these reasons—as well as company rivalry, challenges from individual English and foreign traders, and the contemporary view that monopolies hindered England's commercial potential—that the trading companies declined by the end of the Stuart period. The fact that they were often economic and political tools of the Crown at a time when the Crown's bid to assert its royal prerogative* came under increasing resistance meant that trading company power was inevitably to come under the same constraints as the Crown's. Indeed, while it might be argued that recent studies have suggested that the great companies never really hindered the expansion of overseas trade, they also did little to affect its growth since the majority of the seventeenth-century trade was controlled by individual traders and small partnerships rather than the trading companies. There is also further evidence that the companies themselves felt that after the Civil War*, and certainly by the Glorious Revolution*, privilege guarantees by royal charter were far less reliable than those promulgated by statute. Therefore, the companies often offered little resistance to relinquishing their trade privileges when parliamentary statute so dictated (e.g., the opening of the Eastland Company's Baltic trade by the statute of 1672 and the Muscovy Company's trade by similar means in 1698). Finally, it must be noted that one of the major shifts in the focus of English overseas trade in the Stuart period, the new southern European markets, did not find the trading company as an appropriate vehicle by which to exploit that trade.

At the beginning of the seventeenth century, then, trading companies were a viable means to secure overseas trade, to protect it, and serve as a conduit to promote England's interests overseas; by the end of the century they were considered bulwarks against English trade expansion and tools of a quasi-absolute monarchy. Therefore, the attacks on the companies and their monopolistic privileges by parliament* and independent merchants were as much an attempt to weaken the economic and political power of the Crown as they were an attempt to destroy the exclusivity of trading rights maintained by trading companies. Yet in a Darwinian sense of adaptation and survival of the fittest, trading companies that did survive (particularly the Hudson's Bay and East India companies) found their greatest development in the late eighteenth and early nineteenth centuries. Later attempts like the South Sea Company brought both personal ruin and national embarrassment. While others certainly survived, they never achieved the levels of prominence that the early companies had gained, and the monopolistic trading company concept died hard in the wake of the free trade movement. Still, the great trading companies of the Tudor and Stuart period paved the way for Britain's economic dominance of foreign trade in the early modern and modern periods, as well as providing a mechanism by which the British empire was both expanded and, to a large degree, governed. The great trading fleets, the employment of colonials in company military, and the constant confrontation with foreign powers as a routine exercise in survival provided a blueprint for later British imperial management and provided service to the realm in securing foreign intelligence and safeguarding national interests overseas.

Bibliography: C. T. Carr. ed., *Select Charters of Trading Companies A.D. 1530-1707*, 1970; George Cawston and A. H. Keane, *The Early Chartered Companies (A.D. 1296-1858)*, 1968; W. R. Scott, *The Constitution and Finance of English, Scottish and Irish Joint-Stock Companies to 1720*, 3 vols., 1910-1912.

James I. Miklovich

Triennial Act (1641, 16 Car. I c.1). In 1641 William Strode introduced a bill into the House of Commons entitled, An Act for the Preventing of Inconveniences Happening by the Long Intermission of Parliaments. More commonly known as the Triennial Act, this statute attempted to prevent the return of Charles I's* Personal Rule* (1629-1640) by establishing procedures that would ensure that parliament* met regularly.

The Triennial Act proposed a complex mechanism. It required the king to issue a writ announcing the forthcoming parliament by 10 September of the third year after the last meeting of parliament. Should the king fail to do so, a series of procedures would be implemented. First, by 16 September the lord keeper of the great seal and the commissioners had to circulate writs to the lords commanding them to attend parliament. Various local officials, including sheriffs*, the constable of the castle of Dover, the lord warden of the Cinque Ports, and the mayor and bailiffs of Berwick upon Tweed would also receive writs advising them to hold elections for the forthcoming parliament. A solemn oath bound the lord keeper and the commissioners to enforce the act. Should they fail to do so, they would be deemed incapable of holding office, and an alternative electoral process would be implemented. Specifically the statute authorized a dozen or more peers to issue writs in the name of the king to direct the sheriffs to hold elections the following January. If the peers were negligent, the Triennial Act authorized sheriffs to hold elections. Finally, should the sheriffs refuse to issue the necessary warrants and supervise the elections, the act permitted freeholders to do so. The statute assessed fines of £1,000 for negligent sheriffs and constables. The Triennial Act guaranteed that parliaments and their members who were assembled under this act would have the same rights and privileges as if they had been summoned under the traditional great seal of England. Furthermore, members of parliament were no longer required to take the oaths of supremacy or allegiance.

In addition to guaranteeing that parliament would be held at least every three years, the Triennial Act ensured that its meetings would be more than perfunctory. The statute stipulated that parliament could not be dissolved or prorogued within fifty days of its meeting without the consent of the king and both houses of parliament. Furthermore, the act gave each house the right to approve its own speaker. In order to ensure that the English people were aware of the provisions of the statute, judges were to read the act at every general session and every assize court once a year.

Commons passed the bill on 30 January 1641 and the Lords on 5 February. Succumbing to public pressure, Charles approved the statute on 16 February. Ironically the Triennial Act never went into effect. The act itself provided that it would not go into effect with the current parliament, and thus it was not effective until the Restoration*, when the Cavalier Parliament* significantly changed it with the Triennial Act of 1664* (16 Car. II, c. 1).

Bibliography: J. P. Kenyon, *Stuart Constitution, 1603-1688*, rev. ed., 1986.

David B. Mock

Triennial Act (1664, 16 Car. II, c. 1). Earlier questions concerning the procedure for summoning parliament* and the duration of a particular parliament before the holding of a new election arose again following the Restoration*. As early as May 1661 a bill was introduced in the House of Lords to repeal the Triennial Act of 1641 (16 Car. I, c. 1). In January 1662 the Lords voted to repeal the act, and the House of Commons ordered that a bill be prepared in April 1662 and again in March 1663.

However, it was not until Charles II* directly raised the issue on 21 March 1664 that the Cavalier Parliament* acted decisively. The timing of the king's request was apparently deliberate, waiting for parliament to resolve more pressing needs. In his speech, Charles contended that after the most recent prorogation of parliament, plotters against him had been using computations of time under the 1641 act to raise doubt among his subjects about whether he planned to call parliament again. He also complained that others used the formulas in that act to contend that the sitting parliament had lapsed and that they planned to assemble themselves and choose a new parliament.

Parliament acted promptly in response on the king's speech. It took only slightly more than two weeks from the date of Charles II's request for it to pass the bill. The proponents of the repeal argued that the 1641 act should be treated as void because Charles I* had agreed to its passage under pressure of the London* mob. Furthermore, they asserted that the act's procedure for calling a parliament when the king failed to do so took away the royal prerogative*. They noted that the king's coronation oath required him to observe the law and that nothing further was necessary.

The 1641 act's defenders countered that the act should not be attacked because it was passed in "bad times" and that the act protected both the king and parliament from evil ministers. They argued that the repeal would mean that parliaments would not be regularly called. Others lamented that the repeal of the act would result in the loss of their liberties under Magna Carta.

With the passage of the new act, the king made a short speech stating that the 1641 act had discredited parliament and that no one would doubt again that England was a monarchy. The act repealed the 1641 act because it was in derogation of the king's "just rights" and his inherent prerogative in the "Imperial Crown." In its place, the new act required the sitting and holding of parliaments at least every three years. Although the act was adopted quickly, there were accounts of riots and a general uneasiness with the lack of certainty that parliament would regularly meet. The new act failed to establish any procedure for enforcement and ultimately was not effective. Indeed the failure to include a mechanism for parliament to be called allowed Charles II after the dissolution of the Oxford Parliament* in March 1681 to rule without a parliament until his death in February 1685. If there had been a procedure for calling a new parliament without the king's consent, then the radical Whig* design in part to force the calling of a parliament might not have been necessary. Instead the Whigs continued to scheme, which resulted in the prosecutions and executions after the "discovery" of the Rye House Plot* (1683).

It was not until after the Glorious Revolution* of 1688 that the problem of the calling and duration of parliament was adequately addressed. The political reality of William III's* wars, with the resulting need for money and the Mutiny Act of 1689 (1 Gul. & Mar., c. 5) (and those thereafter), which required the yearly authorization of the army*, forced the king to call parliament frequently. Nonetheless the Bill of Rights* observed only weakly that "parliaments ought to be held frequently." The Triennial Act of 1694 (6 & 7 Gul. & Mar., c. 2), however, required a meeting of parliament every three years and stipulated that no parliament could legally continue for over three years (later changed to seven years). The Act for the Continued Sitting of Parliament of 1696 (7 & 8 Gul. III, c. 15) provided that on the death of the king the existing parliament, or if there was no parliament, then the prior parliament would continue to function for a period of six months.

Bibliography: C. Robbins, "The Repeal of the Triennial Act in 1664," *Huntington Library Quarterly* 12 (1949): 121-140; Paul Seaward, *The Cavalier Parliament and the Reconstruction of the Old Regime, 1661-67,* 1989.

John Harrison Rains III

Triers and Ejectors. The triers were created by ordinance on 20 March 1654 and the ejectors by ordinance on 28 August 1654. The two ordinances (of six religious ordinances during the Protectorate*) formed the cornerstone of Oliver Cromwell* and Richard Cromwell's* church, along with the religious provisions of the Instrument of

Government* (1653) and the Humble Petition and Advice* (1657). Parliamentary ejectors had existed in the 1640s, but the Protectorate triers and ejectors were based on John Owen's* proposals of 1651. Separate ordinances created triers in Ireland* (1652) and Scotland* (1654).

The triers were a commission of thirty-eight laymen and ministers who met in Whitehall to approve the appointment of all ministers living in England and Wales*. Candidates in remote areas were examined by local ministers, who recommended to the commission. The power of the triers was retroactive to 1 April 1653. Ministers—including Independents*, Presbyterians*, and Baptists*—dominated the commission. Three commissioners, one of whom had to be a minister, certified that candidates were persons of godliness and integrity, of good conversation, and fit to preach the gospel. The purpose of the examination was to ensure quality and to prevent unqualified persons, especially layman, from preaching. The right of patrons to present candidates was untouched, and there was no mention of forms of worship, liturgy, ordination, or sacraments.

The triers reflect Cromwell's policy of religious toleration and his vision of an English church as a multitude of congregations practicing religion in diversity. Comprehension, according to the Instrument of Government, did not extend to popery or prelacy, and the Humble Petition and Advice further limited toleration by requiring ministers to believe in the Holy Trinity and the Bible* as the revealed Word of God. Within these limits, however, the triers were liberal and accepted ministers from various sects, non-Laudian (see William Laud*) Anglicans*, and many previously ejected clergymen. Richard Baxter*, no friend of Cromwell, praised the triers for saving congregations from ignorant, ungodly, and drunken ministers.

The ejectors were organized into county commissions, consisting of fifteen to thirty laymen (mostly gentry) and eight to ten divines, appointed by the government. They had the power to eject—when sitting with five approved ministers—preachers and schoolmasters who lived scandalously, held blasphemous ideas (defined by the Blasphemy Act of 1650) or atheistic or popish opinions, persisted in using the Book of Common Prayer (replaced by the *Directory* in 1644), declared publicly their disaffection from the government, or did not perform the duties of their office. The commissioners could give one-fifth of a successor's income to support the family of an ejected minister.

The ejectors were not generally active before 1655. In that year the major generals* were instructed to check on the effectiveness of the ejectors in their districts, and many of them reported that there had been no activity or that not enough commissioners had been appointed to achieve a quorum. The generals recommended acceptable names to Whitehall, and the local commissions were quickly filled. Ejections occurred but apparently not in large numbers during the Protectorate. Some seventy percent of the parishes were untouched by the ejectors.

The work of the ejectors has not been adequately studied and is controversial among modern scholars. Historians agree that about one-third (approximately 3,000) of the ministers were ousted between 1640 and 1660. Most activity, however, seems to have been by the parliamentary ejectors of the 1640s and directed against Laudian prelates. Because of the broad and ill-defined charges to the ejectors, some incumbents were abused; others refused to be ejected peacefully. Some ministers approved by the commission had trouble securing the church and parsonage from an incumbent. A preacher in Gloucestershire ousted an incumbent himself, only to be stoned in the pulpit by the congregation and sued after Cromwell's death to prevent his collecting tithes.

The triers and ejectors remained in power until the Restoration*, when over 100 Independent ministers were ejected from their livings. They accomplished Cromwell's policy of establishing a broad, comprehensive Christian Protestant church maintained by the state. This was the first time in England that the state established an ecclesiastical system in which more than one form of churchmanship was possible. Cromwell believed that his experiment was successful and that religion flourished as never before. His religious settlement is perhaps his most appealing and successful achievement.

Bibliography: Claire Cross, "The Church in England, 1646-1660," in G. E. Aylmer, ed., *The Interregnum: The Quest for Settlement*, 1972; Barry Coward, *The Stuart Age*, 1980.

Wilson J. Hoffman

Triple Alliance (1668). Originated in the Netherlands, whose maritime supremacy England failed to overcome in the Second Dutch War* (1665-1667). Dutch military weakness on land previously had not mattered because of the 1662 Franco-Dutch alliance. But Louis XIV claimed the neighboring Spanish Netherlands by "devolution" through his wife, Marie Theresa, Philip IV of Spain's oldest daughter, and in May 1667 invaded and soon overran them, forcing Johan De Witt, architect of Dutch policy, to abandon the French alliance and look to England.

Since the peace of the Pyrenees (1659), Spain had ceased to be a serious threat to other European powers, whose fear now focused on France. However, it was after the Second Dutch War, which ended with the humiliating Treaty of Breda, that England's reversal of national attitude began. Seeking Dutch friendship, the earl of Arlington (Henry Bennet*) requested William Temple, the English ambassador, to invite the Netherlands to join in forcing Louis to make peace with Spain.

De Witt was receptive, though from the beginning it was an uneasy relationship, less important to Charles II than "revenge on Holland." Charles hoped the alliance would help with domestic problems, including a bankrupt treasury and an anti-French and anti-Catholic House of Commons. The alliance sounded Protestant and might elicit more money from parliament* (see Taxation and Revenue*); it also prevented the Netherlands from joining with France against England.

In January 1668 English and Dutch representatives agreed in a treaty for the pacification of France and Spain to defend each other and to persuade France to make peace with Spain if the latter yielded its possessions in the Low Countries and consented to the cessation of hostilities there. For its part, France would return other territory taken from Spain; if not, England and the Netherlands would join Spain against France.

The Temple-De Witt agreement is usually called the Triple Alliance; Sweden was the third ally. This was a temporary departure from normal Swedish policy since it had no concern in the disputes of France and Spain. Sweden's rivalry with Denmark interested the Dutch, who wanted an ally to support their Baltic commercial interests. Now Sweden was weak, and its recent affairs in the Baltic had estranged it from France, which had not supported a Swedish candidate for the Polish throne and had acted in other matters against Sweden. Finally, Count Dohna, the Swedish representative at The Hague, was a relation of the House of Orange. Soon, however, Sweden returned to its accustomed position; England was to do the same.

The Triple Alliance was first signed at The Hague on 13 January 1668 and completed on 15 April, when England and the Netherlands negotiated a promise for Spain to pay Sweden a subsidy of 480,000 crowns. For the rest of 1668 the English experienced difficulties with their new allies. Competition with the Dutch for tropical markets continued; negotiations to ameliorate this foundered when rival trading companies* refused to make concessions. The two countries also disagreed over evacuation of English settlers from Surinam, and Spain refused to pay the agreed price for Swedish inclusion in the alliance. However, the English government worked to bolster the alliance, expressing a readiness to admit other Protestant states and proposing that England and the Netherlands pay Sweden part of the money owed by Spain. Meanwhile, France made peace, first between Spain and Portugal (February 1668), then with Spain (April 1668) in the Treaty of Aix-la-Chapelle, by which France returned the Franche-Comté to Spain but kept her conquests in Flanders.

Although long regarded as a diplomatic master-stroke in the chain of events preceding the Third Dutch War* (1672-1674), the alliance was never effective in restraining France, though its purpose so thoroughly reflected national aspirations that for many years it was regarded as the standard of what English foreign policy should be. However, it was undone by Charles II, whose strong feelings for France ran counter to English sentiment, a situation made worse because a French alliance abroad was associated with a pro-Catholic* policy at home. Indeed Charles may have considered it a step toward a French alliance, a move that would force Louis XIV to detach England from the Netherlands. In August 1668 Louis sent Charles de Croissy to London* to break the alliance and conclude another with England, which he did with the 1670 Treaty of Dover*.

Bibliography: *English Historical Documents, 1660-1714*, 1953; K. H. D. Haley, *An English Diplomat in the Low Countries*, 1986.

Martin J. Manning

U

Union (of England and Scotland). The Tudors, monarchs of Ireland* after 1540, occupied two thrones. But in 1603 the accession in England of James VI of Scotland* (as James I*) created a more complex "multiple kingdom," where the interaction of two contiguous nations—each with long-differing political, social, and economic traditions—worked intermittently, but recurrently, for a century as a mutually destabilizing force. From the start the "Union of Crowns" of 1603 begged questions about what had in fact been united, how, and with what effects. The failure of the first negotiated union in 1604-1607 did much to introduce ideological division and mutual distrust into English politics. Thereafter James I and Charles I* promoted union by ensuring Scots were represented (indeed over-represented) at the royal court*—for now the only "transnational" institution—and by bringing Scotland (especially its Presbyterian Kirk*) more closely in line with England. The first caused strains in England, and when Charles I pressed the latter too far, it led to the Bishops' Wars*, the collapse of Charles's government in both kingdoms, and then during 1640-1644 to attempts by his English and Scottish opponents to strengthen their common political cause in formal union, bringing the English church in line with the Scottish. That in turn helped create divisions in England, first between parliamentarians* and royalists*, then among the parliamentarians—between Presbyterians* and Independents*. The victory of the latter (and the New Model Army*) and Oliver Cromwell's* conquest in 1651 of Scotland closed off the Presbyterian option in England but hardly solved the underlying problem. The Restoration* simply shelved it. In 1667-1670 further union negotiations failed. Only after yet another failure (in 1702) did a parliamentary union succeed, on the eve of the Stuart demise, in 1706-1707, and even then the two realms' legal systems and churches remained (and remain) distinct.

James I's aim in 1603 was parliamentary recognition of the union established by his accession as a springboard for further changes. First, in 1604, would come a name change (from England and Scotland to Britain), while each parliament* would nominate commissioners to frame legislation on trade*, hostile laws, and, most important, mutual naturalization. This would pave the way to eventual "perfect union" of laws, institutions, parliaments, and churches. But despite James's staking the entire royal prestige on the scheme in 1604 and 1607, the English House of Commons rejected it, for reasons both practical and principled. Against James's view of a union established by the prerogative of his succession, the Commons claimed that the accession of a private man who also happened to be king of Scots had no practical consequences for England, appealing to the judges against the name change (who in ruling against it agreed it would abrogate all existing laws) and setting up the 1604 commission as a body to negotiate with a foreign country for their "common weale." In their view the English polity was rooted in the public sovereignty of king-in-parliament; to admit James's claims would be to deny the supremacy of statute, recognize a superior British authority in the royal prerogative*, and thereby reduce the English (and Scottish) parliaments to mere provincial estates. James's response to English resistance fueled these suspicions; he insisted his accession had concrete consequences for union and asserted them by prerogative. With the name change rejected, in October 1604 he assumed by proclamation the style "King of Great Britain" for use in all but formal legal documents. The proclamation also published an opinion he had obtained from the judges that Scots born since 1603 (the *post-nati*) were already automatically naturalized in England. When in 1607 the Commons refused to recognize this in legislation, James's ministers brought a test case—Calvin's Case* (1608)—which established the principle in law. Lord Chancellor Ellesmere's judgment, published by royal authority, denounced the Commons's distinction between the powers of private king and public kingdom as potentially treasonable and cited the 1604 proclamation as having some force as a legal precedent. Since the parliamentary scheme was dropped in 1607, naturalization and the invention of the Union Jack was where union formally rested. But by 1610 the questions raised by union—in combination with James's lavish patronage to his Scots bedchamber, his support for his prerogative courts*, the extension of prerogative impositions* on trade in 1608, and the collation and publication of the proclamations—had created widespread distrust of the king's regard for the English common law* and of his use of his prerogatives. This distrust wrecked the parliament of 1610* and the Addled Parliament of 1614 (where the legal case against union was redeployed against impositions) and, since it was never resolved, remained part of Charles I's English inheritance in 1625.

Charles I also inherited his father's Scottish policy, a thirty-year campaign to impose bishops and a royal supremacy on the Scots Presbyterian Kirk. James's greatest progress came after his English overdraft gave him decisive leverage in managing Scottish parliaments and general assemblies. But in 1634-1637 Charles I's completion of the Kirk's Anglicization, with an essentially English prayer book and canons*, was imposed without consultation, solely by prerogative. The massive opposition this aroused in Scotland found an answering response in England, and in 1639-1641 Charles faced a precariously united Anglo-Scottish opposition that put forward a mechanism for consultation between Scots and English parliaments. This opposition had substantial negative grounds for unity in constitutional grievances against the prerogative (as exercised in both church and secular affairs) and in using allegations of a "Popish Plot"* around Charles as a basis for popular appeal in both realms. But in 1640-1641 positive Scots demands for a settlement of both kingdoms, by presbyterianizing the Church of England (see Anglicanism*) to match the Kirk, split the Long Parliament* (and were a key factor in giving Charles I enough support to fight the Civil War*). For now the English parliament sidelined the divisive question. Only when parliament appeared to be losing the war in 1643 did it re-emerge, as the Scots dictated terms for their alliance involving the imposition of the Solemn League and Covenant* and a Presbyterian church in England. In January 1644 the alliance was embodied in a Committee of Both Kingdoms*. But it was largely powerless, and the growing power of Independency and the New Model Army in 1645-1646 shifted the balance, as Scots military aid was no longer seen as decisive. By mid-1647 Scots hopes for a secure union were pinned on the Presbyterians in England and on negotiations with Charles I, while the army's* Heads of Proposals* ignored the Scots and the Covenant. The divide was worked out in Charles's Engagement* with the Scots of December 1647, the Second Civil War* of 1648 (where the royalist threat was embodied almost wholly in a Scots army), and the political purges in both Edinburgh and London* that followed the New Model's victory. But though Pride's Purge* effectively neutralized the Presbyterians in England, Scotland remained unstable. There was no basis for a federal union of the English Republic with the Scots, who at once proclaimed Charles II* the covenanted king of all three realms, on condition he impose Presbyterian uniformity on Britain. Cromwell's preemptive conquest of first Ireland and then in 1650-1651 of Scotland ruled that out, securing Independent toleration in England and imposing on Scotland between 1651 and 1660 "an alien, oppressive police state, detested by all but a tiny minority of republicans and sectarians" (Brown). This incorporating "Imperial" union was reflected in notional Scottish representation in Barebone's* and Protectorate* parliaments, but in fact those who filled the thirty Scots seats in 1654, 1656, and 1659 were either army nominees or Englishmen.

The Restoration broke this union and returned the relationship to its prewar limbo as a union of crowns. By 1662 bishops had been restored in the Scots Kirk, but the suppleness of the chief operator in Scots politics henceforth (until 1680)—the earl of Lauderdale (John Maitland*), Scottish secretary and gentleman of the bedchamber—ensured this was not divisive. In 1667 an initiative came from Scotland for a union scheme related to trade questions. It ran into the sand due to English lack of interest but was then turned into a scheme for political union—of parliaments, but not of the law or the church—by Charles II and Lauderdale. Part of the aim of the 1669 scheme seems to have been to increase royal influence in a British House of Commons with a reliable phalanx of Scots votes. Despite Scottish suspicions Lauderdale could probably have delivered agreement north of the border. But again English indifference was decisive, and the scheme was dropped. It did form a basis, however, for the later union plans of 1702 and 1706-1707. The success of the latter was due largely to an urgent new English interest in changing the status quo after the Act of Settlement of 1701 (12 & 13 Gul. III, c. 2), for since Scotland rejected the Hanoverian succession, a real prospect opened up of further, and more acute, long-term instability.

Bibliography: K. M. Brown, *Kingdom or Province? Scotland and the Regal Union, 1603-1715*, 1992; Bruce Galloway, *The Union of England and Scotland, 1603-1608*, 1986; Brian Levack, *The Formation of the British State: England, Scotland, and the Union, 1603-1707*, 1987; Conrad Russell, *The Causes of the English Civil War*, 1991.

Neil Cuddy

Universities. At the beginning of the seventeenth century, London*—with Gresham College (1595), the Inns of Court, and the Inns of Chancery—had joined Oxford and Cambridge as "the third university." Inevitably the increasingly parlous politics of the time began to affect these institutions. Responding to growing criticism of their educational effectiveness, the universities accelerated this process by abandoning the political aloofness of the Elizabethan age and demanding representation in parliament*, the better to defend themselves. This representation, granted in 1604, failed of its purpose. One of the university representatives in parliament, Francis Bacon*, became at James I's* behest the most trenchant critic of the Cambridge curriculum's drift toward professional studies and of the faculty's sterile religious bickering.

At the same time the Stuart regime was encouraged to draw the universities further into the political arena by systematic appointment of Arminians*, especially at Oxford. The bitterly fought election that brought William Laud*, bishop of London and the king's chief minister, to the chancellorship in 1630, three years before he was raised to the archbishopric of Canterbury, capped this process. Chancellor until his execution in 1645, though he had ceased to exercise the function after 1641, he reformed student behavior, revived the college system, censored heterodox preaching, replaced university officials with men he considered politically and religiously reliable, and procured more than 1,300 manuscripts for the Bodleian Library. He also obtained a charter for the Oxford University Press, an early consequence of which was the flood of books and pamphlets supporting the royalist* cause in the Civil War* (see Printing and Book Trade*). His greatest legacy was the Laudian Code, a set of procedural rules accepted by the convocation in 1636 as the fundamental laws by which the university was to be governed (and which were in force until midway through the nineteenth century).

In the early years of the century, Oxford and Cambridge were at a population peak. Cambridge was slightly larger, with 3,000 students to Oxford's 2,900, and between 1625 and 1630 it graduated more students than in any other five-year period until this century. The coming of the Civil War eroded the population of both masters and students. Oxford was occupied by parliamentary forces from August to October of 1642 and for the ensuing four years was royalist headquarters, doubling as a depot for arms, food, and other military supplies. Lectures and disputations ceased, and graduations dropped from 200 bachelors in 1642 to thirty in 1645, and from 112 masters in 1642 to twenty in 1645. At Cambridge the university supported the king, while the townspeople were loyal to parliament. The parliamentarians* seized the university in 1642 and lodged 200 prisoners of war there. The earl of Manchester was sent by parliament to reform the university, a process that resulted in the dismissal of about 200 fellows and most heads of colleges, as well as a good deal of vandalizing of art works.

After parliament's victory, visitors were sent to reform Oxford in 1647, expelling about 350 of its fellows and nominating "godly" persons to succeed them. Barebone's Parliament* discussed in 1653 the abolition of the universities (Durham was initially founded at this time as an alternative), but despite parliamentary attacks on the universities, their endowments, curriculum, and scholarship, they survived with some diminution in the quality of dons. More lip-service to Puritanism* and a slight shift of the student population to persons of middle-class background marked the general extent of the accommodation of the universities to the Commonwealth*, even after Oliver Cromwell* took the chancellorship of Oxford.

Upon the Restoration* in 1660, a further reform brought back many who had been purged, so that royalism* and Anglicanism* held sway even more firmly than before the Civil War. The 1662 Act of Uniformity (14 Car. II, c. 4) drove Nonconformists from the universities and left them much less representative of the population* as a whole. Royal favor was expressed not only in royal appointments but in Charles II's* convening of parliament at Oxford in 1681 (see Oxford Parliament*) and his numerous visits to Cambridge (coincident with his attendance at Newmarket races). His successor, James II*, provoked opposition by interfering with the universities in pursuit of his Catholic* agenda, most notably by replacing Protestant fellows with Catholics and by ordering the fellows of Magdalen College to elect the bishop of Oxford as their new president. The coming of the Calvinist* William III* finally brought to the universities a political and religious equilibrium in which they were able to settle into more than a century of egregious mediocrity.

At the Inns of Court and of Chancery, the seventeenth century was an era of decline. Learning from textbooks replaced the older method of learning from lectures and disputations (moots), and by the end of the Civil War the old method of instruction had so far broken down that lectures were formally abandoned in 1677.

Despite the downturn in endowments in the middle of the century, the physical growth of the universities in the Stuart era was continuous and remarkable. Cambridge added the Second and Third Courts of St. John's, the Great Court, Nevile's Court, Peterhouse Chapel, and the Fellow's Building at Christ's College, capping the century with Christopher Wren's Pembroke Chapel, Emmanuel Chapel, and the library at Nevile's Court. Gothic in inspiration early in the century, university architecture tended more toward a mix of the classical and baroque by the century's end (see Art*). Oxford saw the founding of Wadham and Pembroke colleges, the addition of the Botanical Garden, the rebuilding of Oriel and University colleges, and Laud's project of finishing St. John's. The most remarkable development of all was the work of Thomas Bodley, former fellow of Merton College and Elizabethan ambassador, who devoted fifteen years of his life to buying books, recruiting benefactors, and rebuilding and extending Duke Humphrey's Library to produce the magnificent Bodleian Library. The agreement of the stationer's office to provide copies of all books registered with it ensured the continuous expansion of the library's collection.

Despite the dislocations of the century and an inevitable preoccupation with sectarian controversy, there were some noteworthy developments in the intellectual life of the universities during the Stuart era. The early part of the century saw a revival of scholastic philosophy and theology, a conservative reaction to Ramist logic and Calvinist theology. The Jesuit Counter-Reformation thinkers Carlo Borromeo and Francisco Suárez were much studied along with Aristotle, and both monographs and textbooks were written in the scholastic mode. By midcentury the Cambridge Platonists provided an alternative. A group of thinkers of Puritan background led by Benjamin Whichcote, they recoiled from Calvinism and Anglicanism alike, arguing for a tolerant, rational, and moral Christianity not hemmed in by ritual and dogma. By mid-century Oxford was the scientific center of the nation, but the removal of the Baconians in the Restoration* led to the founding of the Royal Society* (already emerging in the "Invisible Society" founded at Oxford in 1645) and its role as a powerful alternative to university-based research. Isaac Newton's ascension to the Lucasian Chair of Mathematics in 1669 began the transformation of mathematical knowledge and laid the foundation for Cambridge's later strength in mathematics and science*.

During the seventeenth century the colleges became immensely powerful and consequential entities, supporting themselves by rentals and leases of their properties, endowments, and undergraduate fees. Teaching was the province of the colleges, and university professorships declined in importance. The role of the university was to matriculate, examine, and discipline students. Its governing board was composed of the heads of the various colleges, whose importance made for hotly contested elections marred by outside interference. The student population was quite stratified, with wealthy gentlemen-pensioners and fellow commoners wearing distinctive garb, occupying luxurious quarters, and sending out for meals or messing together, while scholarship boys subsisted more modestly and some, servitors or sizars, waited on table or performed other menial tasks to cover their tuition. Whatever their state, the undergraduates were ruled by their dons, who oversaw not only their intellectual progress but also their moral development, their conduct, and even their finances.

Bibliography: V. H. H. Green, *A History of Oxford University,* 1974; John Prest, *The Illustrated History of Oxford University,* 1993; John Twigg, *The University of Cambridge and the English Revolution,* 1990.

Joseph M. McCarthy

V

Villiers, George, 1st Duke of Buckingham (1592-1628). A powerful court favorite during the reigns of James I* and Charles I*, Villiers was introduced to James in 1614 by George Abbott*, archbishop of Canterbury. The long-time royal favorite, Robert Carr*, was falling out of favor with the king, and Villiers was advanced to replace him. James was immediately captivated by the handsome, athletic Villiers and generously endowed him with titles and honors.

Villiers's rise was rapid. In 1615 he became a gentleman of the bedchamber; in 1616 he became master of the horse, knight of the garter, and a viscount; in 1617 he was given an earldom; and in 1618 he became marquis of Buckingham. At the age of twenty-six, Buckingham had become the most influential person in James's life, and from 1618 until his death ten years later, he dominated the royal court*. In contrast to Carr, Buckingham possessed some intelligence and political skill in addition to his physical charms. James came to depend completely on Buckingham to fulfill his complex emotional needs.

In 1620 Buckingham married Lady Catherine Manners, rich heiress of the earl of Rutland. Buckingham became extremely wealthy, amassing honors, estates, and bribes. Urged by his scheming mother, he used his power to place his relatives and friends in lucrative positions and marriages. His network of patronage and monopolies* exacerbated popular disillusionment over the corruption of James's court.

James's third parliament (of 1621*) was particularly significant for its criticism of both the domestic and foreign policies of Buckingham's regime. Parliament* attacked the abuses of Buckingham's monopoly* system, and numerous officials—including Lord Chancellor Francis Bacon*—were impeached (see Impeachment*); Buckingham sacrificed them to save himself. Parliament also criticized current foreign policy. Under the influence of the count of Gondomar, the shrewd ambassador from Spain, James and Buckingham adopted a pro-Spanish stance and advocated marriage between Prince Charles (see Charles I*) and the Infanta. Parliament opposed a Spanish match* and criticized Buckingham's involvement in foreign affairs, which so infuriated James that he dissolved parliament.

In 1623 Buckingham and Charles went to Madrid to negotiate a marriage settlement. While they were there, James created his favorite 1st duke of Buckingham. Their Spanish mission, however, was unsuccessful; angry and humiliated, they returned home resolved to promote war against Spain. James's fourth Parliament (of 1624*), fearful of a pro-Catholic alliance, applauded Buckingham's reversal of policy. Finance minister Lionel Cranfield*, trying to stabilize the treasury, opposed war, so Buckingham had him impeached. James, usually peace-loving, was persuaded to approve war preparations; by this time he was growing senile, and Buckingham and Charles ruled his kingdom.

James's death in 1625 did not diminish Buckingham's power; he had overcome Charles's earlier jealousy of him and forged a strong friendship with the heir to the throne. Cooperative relations between the Crown and parliament did not last, however. It became increasingly obvious that there were insufficient funds for military operations, but Buckingham was nonetheless determined to fight Spain (see Spanish War of 1625-1630*).

In March, England's attack on the Spanish Netherlands failed miserably; most of the troops died aboard ship amid appalling conditions, without even meeting the enemy. To make matters worse, Buckingham began controversial negotiations with France that eventually led to another war. Attempting to create an alliance with France against Spain, Buckingham had arranged marriage between Charles and Louis XIII's sister, Henrietta Maria*, but Buckingham had to promise leniency for the English Catholics*. This angered the Commons, which became even more furious when Buckingham sent English ships to suppress a Huguenot rebellion at La Rochelle.

Charles's first parliament (of 1625*) criticized Buckingham's pro-French policy and his military incompetence and refused to approve monies necessary for war. Charles, defending his favorite, angrily dissolved parliament. Buckingham then sent out the Cadiz expedition*, which was also a disaster, due to poor preparation and ill management.

Buckingham's campaign against Spain was an utter failure; his treaty with France fared no better. As negotiations broke down, Buckingham reversed his policy, reinstated Catholic penalties, and decided to aid the Huguenots against the French.

Charles's second parliament (of 1626*), led by Sir John Eliot*, demanded Buckingham's impeachment. Charles came to Buckingham's rescue and again dissolved parliament. Buckingham forged ahead, and the war with France began in 1627 (see French War of 1627-1629*). Buckingham himself led an expedition to the Ile de Rhe to relieve the Huguenots, but ill-prepared troops and inadequate planning led to another failure.

Charles's third parliament (of 1628*) again demanded Buckingham's dismissal, and Charles again prorogued it. Buckingham, ever persistent, went to Portsmouth to prepare a third expedition against France. However, John Felton, one of the many soldiers there angry with Buckingham's leadership, stabbed him to death on 23 August 1628.

When Buckingham died, he was certainly the most hated man in England; London* crowds rejoiced at his murder. His great wealth and power aroused envy, and his rule contributed to much of the strain between the king and parliament that led to the Civil War*, though he was only one of many causes.

Bibliography: Roger Lockyer, *Buckingham*, 1981.

Jo Eldridge Carney

Villiers, George, 2d Duke of Buckingham (1628-1687). Born 30 January 1628, the eldest surviving son of George Villiers*, 1st duke of Buckingham, and Katherine Manners. After Buckingham's assassination in August 1628, Charles I* adopted George and his brother, Francis (whose mother had become Catholic*). The young duke was educated at Cambridge.

In the Civil War* the boys fought with Prince Rupert in 1643. After the Long Parliament* sequestered Buckingham's lands, they went abroad with the earl of Northumberland. Buckingham returned in 1647, and parliament* restored his lands, but he joined the royalists* in the Second Civil War* in 1648, was declared a traitor, and fled to Holland (Francis died in battle). His twenty-first birthday was the day of Charles I's execution*.

Charles II* named Buckingham to the Order of the Garter in 1649 and the privy council* in 1650. He was with Charles in Scotland in 1650-1651, during the Third Civil War*, commanding his "Eastern Association." Escaping to Holland, he tried in 1652 to contact Oliver Cromwell*, met the Leveller* John Lilburne*, and outraged Henrietta Maria* by attempting to marry her daughter, Mary, the widowed princess of Orange. In 1654 he was estranged from Charles, in 1655 he traveled secretly to England, and in 1656 he attempted a reconciliation, foiled by Edward Hyde*, later earl of Clarendon. Back in England in 1657, he married Lord Thomas Fairfax's* daughter Mary on 15 September. Cromwell tried to arrest him in October but relented in 1658. He was arrested, however, in August and put in the Tower until February 1659.

At the Restoration* Buckingham regained favor, becoming a gentleman of the bedchamber and lord lieutenant of the West Riding of Yorkshire in 1661 and a privy councilor in 1662. At sea during the Second Dutch War* (1665-1667), he was briefly in the Tower for fighting the marquis of Dorchester in 1666 and was arrested for treasonous acts in 1667 and sent there again. Released in September, he helped engineer the fall of Clarendon.

The Cabal*, which headed the government from 1667 to 1673, was not united. Buckingham and the earl of Arlington (Henry Bennet*), its most powerful members, were enemies. Buckingham managed parliament poorly, obtaining only £300,000 in supply in 1668 and nothing in 1669 (see Taxation and Revenue*). Seeking allies among the opposition and Dissenters*, he proposed religious toleration bills in 1668 but was defeated by Archbishop Gilbert Sheldon*. In a duel he fatally wounded the earl of Shrewsbury, whose wife was his mistress; he intrigued against Queen Catherine*, the duke of York (see James II*), and the duke of Ormonde (James Butler*); and feuded in 1669 with William Coventry, who challenged him to a duel and whom Charles fired.

The king excluded Buckingham, Anthony Ashley Cooper* (later earl of Shaftesbury), and the earl of Lauderdale (John Maitland*) from negotiations for the secret Treaty of Dover* in 1670 and concocted a bogus treaty to divert them. Buckingham, who received a pension from Louis XIV, claimed to be France's best friend, hoping to command an army against the Dutch, obtain French support for becoming chief minister in England, and promote English trade*. But he failed to win a command in the Third Dutch War* (1672-1674). Meanwhile, lampooned by John Dryden*, he retaliated in verse and with the drama, *Rehearsal*, first performed in 1671.

In 1673 Buckingham learned of the secret treaty and threatened to impeach Arlington (see Impeachment*), but Charles intervened. Soon he was supplanted by Thomas Osborne*, later earl of Danby. In 1674 parliament attacked him over the French alliance and accused him of popery. He twice appeared in Commons, an unprecedented action for a ministerial peer, but failed in efforts to blame Arlington for the Triple Alliance*, to court the opposition by trumpeting his work with Shaftesbury, or otherwise win favor. Instead he antagonized the king, and the Commons voted to remove him from office.

In 1675 Buckingham spoke against a nonresistance* oath and introduced a failed bill to protect Dissenters. He and Shaftesbury attempted to claim in 1677 that parliament was dissolved as the result of a fifteen-month prorogation, incurring the wrath of the Lords, who put both in the Tower. Out in July, he recovered some influence, obstructed supply in 1678 and 1679, noisily damned the Popish Plot* (1678), was accused (along with Shaftesbury) of being involved in the bogus Meal Tub Plot* in 1679, and supported the Whigs* in elections, though he was absent from the vote to exclude York from the throne in 1680 (see Exclusion Crisis*). Upon James II's accession, he published a pamphlet calling for religious toleration, but in 1686 he retired from public life and died bankrupt on 16 April 1687.

Bibliography: Hester W. Chapman, *Great Villiers*, 1949; J. R. Jones, *Country and Court, England, 1658-1714*, 1978.

                                                                    William B. Robison

Vote of No Addresses (1648). The end of the First Civil War* ushered in a constitutional crisis characterized by personal negotiations with Charles I* for a political settlement with the Long Parliament* and for the security of the kingdom. The king's flight on 11 November 1647 from Hampton Court to Carisbrooke Castle on the Isle of Wight caused the parliamentary representatives, Oliver Cromwell* and Henry Ireton*, to cease negotiations.

Faced with the growing possibility of an alliance between the king and the Scottish Covenanters*, the House of Lords initiated a conference with the Commons on 26 November to prepare the Four Bills, which were designed to protect the security of the kingdom and parliament* and to serve as a basis for settlement. By a vote of 115 to 106, the Commons agreed to the bills on 11 December 1647, with the nay votes coming largely from radicals who opposed further negotiations and Presbyterians* who disagreed with the harsh terms. The nonnegotiable provisions required Charles to grant parliament control over all armed forces for twenty years; relinquish the right to veto bills dealing with the armed forces; annul all oaths, declarations, and proclamations against parliament and its supporters; revoke all sentences and forfeitures against parliament; void all peerages created since May 1642, with no new peerages to be created without parliamentary consent; and allow the sitting parliament to determine the date of its own adjournment. Attached to the fourth bill came negotiable provisions provided that the king accept the four bills *in toto*. These included the abolition of episcopacy and the proscription of the Book of Common Prayer and the sale of religious offices.

On 24 December a joint delegation presented Charles with the bills and requested a reply within four days. But on 26 December Charles and the Scottish lords of the commission signed the Engagement*, calling for Charles to go to London* to sign a personal treaty with parliament and for the disbanding of all armies; otherwise, the Scottish army would invade England. With this Charles abrogated all hopes of a negotiated settlement. On 28 December he rejected the bills and attempted to flee to the Continent, but ill winds aborted the escape.

By New Year's Day 1648, the general council of the army* assured parliament that the army stood firmly in its camp. Encouraged, parliament debated the king's reply on 3 January. Cromwell urged that no new negotiations be opened with Charles, and the Commons passed the Vote of No Addresses 141 to 91, which also declared further talks without parliament's permission to be treason. The general council publicly declared its support on 8 January, which induced a hitherto reluctant Lords to convene a committee on 13 January and approve the Vote of No Addresses on 17 January. Its preamble states that the Four Bills pertained only to the kingdom's security and safety and that Charles acted unreasonably in rejecting them. In light of the king's "absolute negative," parliament obliged itself "speedily to settle the present government."

Following Cromwell and John Lambert's defeat of the Scots at Preston in August 1648, parliament repealed the Vote of No Addresses on 24 August. The need for a political and religious settlement, shown by the extent of royalist* support during the Second Civil War*, brought renewed negotiations, resulting in the proposed Treaty of Newport*. It had become clear that no settlement imposed by parliament without the king's consent would be acceptable for the security and safety of the kingdom.

Bibliography: Austin Woolrych, *Soldiers and Statesman: The General Council of the Army and Its Debates, 1647-48*, 1987.

Stanley D. M. Carpenter

W

Wales. It is difficult to discern a coherent theme to the history of Wales in the seventeenth century, still less one that is distinct from that of its overawing eastern neighbor. The legislation of the 1530s that had formalized the relationship between them was merely one important step along the path by which Wales lost its distinctive, independent status and was united with and firmly under England. The Welsh, of course, had their own language and culture, history, and traditions, but by the seventeenth century they had long lost their political and administrative independence. In almost all the key political and religious developments of the century—most of them centered on Whitehall and Westminster—there were few uniquely Welsh experiences and reactions. Instead, events in Wales generally mirrored those in England as a whole or in English regions which, like Wales, were physically distant from the political and economic leadership of London* and the southeast.

It is, moreover, often misleading to talk of a single Wales in this period. Socially Wales was deeply divided between the gentry elite—powerful, rich and getting richer, generally English speaking, and increasingly Anglicized in outlook and activities—and the common people, the rural masses who made up most of the 300,000 to 400,000 souls who lived in Stuart Wales—many of them trapped in poverty, generally Welsh speaking, and inward looking. Geography also divided Wales physically, socially, and economically, for life in the eastern marches, the Vale of Glamorgan, the lowlands in the far southwest, and along the western and northern coastal strips was very different from that in the moors, uplands, and mountains that covered most of Wales. Even the language of the masses was no longer a completely unifying force, for by this time spoken Welsh took different forms in the north and the south. No Welsh town served in theory or in practice as a national capital, and few could lay claim to being regional centers. Instead most Welsh men and women looked across the border to the towns of Chester, Shrewsbury, and Bristol, which served as trading centers and more for the people of north, middle, and south Wales respectively.

The opening decades of the seventeenth century were probably the most harmonious of the whole century. Wales had been bled white to pay for Elizabeth I's European wars. In contrast, James I's* policy of avoiding war—so greatly reducing royal demands for men, money, and material—proved popular in England and Wales alike. The years 1603-1620 saw not only generally good harvests, leading to lower food prices and rising standards of living, but also few major political controversies to inflame or divide the Welsh. The potential for religious unrest was enormous; the Protestant Reformation had come late to Wales, and, as well as significant Roman Catholic* minorities, especially in the northeast and southeast, much of the rural population* had been only recently and shallowly won over to the new faith and probably retained some affection for the more ceremonial Catholic church of their parents or grandparents. The size and relative poverty of the four Welsh bishoprics and of many Welsh parishes hindered the work of full conversion and of the ministry in general. However, James's policy of allowing a broad range of Protestants, high and low, to worship within the Church of England (see Anglicanism*), which encompassed Wales, and of usually permitting discrete Roman Catholics to follow their faith unmolested, maintained religious peace within Wales.

The years 1620-1640 saw this peace collapse. Repeated harvest failures produced poverty, distress, and starvation. The heavy financial demands imposed first to pay for the French War of 1627-1629* and the Spanish War of 1625-1630*, and then to support Charles I's* Personal Rule* in the 1630s strained the limited resources of Wales, exacerbating distress and dissent. Some Welshmen went further and criticized these exactions, particularly the repeated collection of ship money* in the 1630s, on political grounds, as unjust non-parliamentary taxation* tending towards royal tyranny. At the same time the king's implementation of Arminianism* upset the fragile religious peace in Wales. During the 1630s three of the Welsh bishoprics were in the hands of bishops who fully supported and implemented Arminian reforms. To many in Wales with lingering affection for the old religious ways and customs and little love for the increasingly austere Church of England, these reforms may have been welcome. But to others they smacked of anti-Protestantism and an attempt to re-impose hated Roman Catholicism by stealth. It was the 1630s, with the work of a handful of fiercely anti-Arminian preachers, that saw the birth of the radical, nonconforming Protestantism that became a feature of Wales.

Thus as the crisis with Scotland* in the late 1630s' turned to political crisis in England and to full-scale Civil War* from 1642, there was good reason to have expected many in Wales to support the Long Parliament*. But in reality almost all of Wales came out for the king at the outbreak of war and remained overwhelmingly loyal to him until conquered by parliament* in 1645-1646. Throughout the war Wales was one of the royalist* heartlands, supplying men, materials, and money to support the royalist war effort. Welsh royalism might be explained by the political and religious conservatism of the rural masses or by the weakness of the more radical, urban-based "middle class" within Wales, though such sweeping generalizations are dangerous and open to criticism. More plausibly, the allegiance of Wales may have been decided by the Welsh gentry, the intermarrying elite who ran Stuart Wales. The gentry had done very well out of royal government in the century or so before the Civil War, gaining property from the Crown at the dissolution of the monasteries and power, status, and money by holding office under the Crown. A natural conservatism, traditional allegiance to the Crown, self-interest, and fear of the social, political, and religious changes that parliamentary rule might produce motivated the Welsh gentry to carry Wales into the royalist camp.

Most of Wales escaped large-scale bloodshed. Welsh men and money were siphoned off to support the war effort elsewhere, but there was surprisingly little fighting on Welsh soil. There were occasional parliamentary raids across the border and a more permanent penetration up the Severn Valley in the latter half of 1644. But before 1645 the only prolonged fighting occurred in the far southwest, the one corner of Wales that had declared for parliament in 1642. Royalist and parliamentary troops crossed and recrossed Pembrokeshire in repeated waves, the royalists never quite able to flush their opponents out, the parliamentarians* unable to sweep beyond the county and undermine royalism in the heart of Wales. Not until autumn 1645, with the king clearly defeated and a spent force in England and with Welsh enthusiasm for the royalist cause tempered by physical and financial exhaustion, did the parliamentarians make real headway. Quickly and with little open resistance in the field, the Welsh accepted the inevitable and made their peace with parliament. Only a few castles or walled towns stood out—Raglan in the southeast; Aberystwyth in the west; Denbigh, Conwy, Harlech, and others in the north—to be starved or bombarded into submission during 1646-1647.

Renewed resistance in the south and northwest in 1648, led by a mixture of old royalists and embittered former parliamentarians, was effectively crushed. Thereafter peace and something approaching normality returned to Wales. Many prominent royalist gentry were fined and found themselves out of office until 1660, though few families were completely ruined, and most survived to come into their own again at the Restoration*. Local administration during the 1650s rested in the main with lesser gentry—men who had been neutral, inactive, or tactful and low-key royalists during the Civil War—though they had to share power with a few outsiders, including garrison commanders and other military figures from obscure backgrounds who had risen rapidly in parliament's service during the 1640s. Some traditional forms of local government*, particularly the work of justices of the peace and quarter sessions, quickly returned. Other functions, particularly local defense and the collection of the regular and heavy taxes imposed during the 1650s (see Taxation and Revenue*), were exercised by specialist committees which included members drawn from beyond the ranks of the traditional local gentry.

Post-Civil War developments in religion ran much deeper. Parliament regarded Wales, like several English regions far from London, as dark corners of the land, where popery, paganism, ignorance, and profanity allegedly flourished and godly reformation needed a boost. The Civil War had seen the collapse of the old Church of England and with it the removal of the bishops. At the parish level well over 300 Welsh clergy were ejected in 1645-1660 for their overt royalism, political and religious views, pluralism and nonresidence, or lax morals (see Triers and Ejectors*). It was hard to find suitable replacements for these often poor, Welsh-speaking parishes, but committees set up by parliament did succeed in filling some of the vacancies with approved, godly ministers. Others were appointed as itinerant preachers, roaming the Welsh counties. The most intense period of activity was 1650-1653, when—under the Act for the Better Propagation and Preaching of the Gospel in Wales—special commissioners (many of them non-Welsh) organized the work of ejection and appointment. But religious change went deeper still, for with the collapse of the established church and censorship and with de facto religious toleration in operation, large numbers of Protestant sects sprang up, most notably Congregationalists*, Baptists*, and Quakers*. Again this was by no means a uniquely Welsh experience.

In England and Wales alike, religion proved the greatest source of tension and division in the post-Restoration period. Purely political divisions were few and fleeting in 1660-1689, and Wales settled down under the rule of Charles II* and the now almost totally Anglicized Welsh gentry. The Church of England was restored in 1660 and with it the four Welsh bishoprics, presiding over a poor but hard-working church within Wales. However, the reimposition of narrow, intolerant conformity caused at least 130 ministers to leave their livings in Wales in or before 1662 and led to a quarter of a century of persecution. Congregationalists, Presbyterians*, and Baptists went underground; the Quakers, more open, bore the brunt of persecution down to the 1680s, when many Welsh Quakers gave up the struggle and emigrated to the more tolerant shores of New England. Welsh Roman Catholics were also persecuted, at least four of them losing their lives in the wake of the Popish Plot* (1678), sacrificed on the altar of bitter Welsh anti-Catholicism. In 1688 many in Wales gave moral if not active support to the Glorious Revolution* and welcomed the replacement of Catholic James II* with solidly Protestant William* and Mary*, though the mood of Tory* Anglicans quickly changed in Wales, as in England. Protestant dissent (see Dissenters*) emerged from a generation of physical and psychological pressure to enter the promised land created by the Toleration Act (1 Gul. & Mar., c. 18). From modest beginnings, nonconformity was to change the face of Wales in the eighteenth and nineteenth centuries.

Bibliography: Peter Gaunt, *A Nation Under Siege, The Civil War in Wales, 1642-48*, 1991; G. H. Jenkins, *The Foundations of Modern Wales, 1642-1780*, 1988; G. Williams, *Recovery, Reorientation and Reformation, Wales, c.1415-1642*, 1987.

Peter Gaunt

Wentworth, Thomas, Earl of Strafford (1593-1641). The case of Thomas Wentworth, earl of Strafford, dominated the early months of what was to become known as the Long Parliament*. Accused of treason by the House of Commons in November 1640, Strafford was tried in the spring of 1641 and executed by virtue of an act of attainder on 11 May of that year. At the time of his impeachment*, Strafford, who had attained his earldom in January 1640, was among Charles I's* closest advisors. Rather than focusing on one allegedly traitorous act, the articles the Commons brought against Strafford included a grabbag of charges. Particularly prominent were his conduct as lord deputy of Ireland* from 1632 to 1640 and his role in urging the king to summon and then to dissolve the Short Parliament* of the spring of 1640. Strafford denied that the charges against him were treason. He was after all serving, not resisting, the Crown. Worried that his defense would be successful, the Commons switched to proceedings by a bill of attainder. The House of Lords passed the bill in the wake of the Army Plot*, and Charles, whom Strafford had written to free his conscience, gave his consent. Strafford's execution followed immediately.

The eldest son of a family of Yorkshire gentry, Thomas Wentworth went to university* (St. John's, Cambridge) and to the Inns of Court (the Inner Temple). Through ability and ambition he gained power and fame. He also made enemies. His rivalry with Sir John Savile, another Yorkshire gentleman, extended from local politics to parliament*, where Wentworth first sat in 1614 (see Addled Parliament*). Having participated actively in the parliaments of 1621* and 1624*, he attracted attention in the parliament of 1625* by his attempts to respond to a challenge to his election and later, after that dispute had been resolved, by verbally confronting the king's favorite, the 1st duke of Buckingham (George Villiers*). Charles consequently made Wentworth sheriff* of Yorkshire to prevent him from sitting in the parliament of 1626*.

Wentworth's parliamentary career reached its climax in 1628 when he, who had been among those imprisoned for refusing the forced loan*, was among the Commons's leaders. Especially vocal in attacking the billeting of troops, he wanted rights protected but in return was willing to grant the king subsidies (see Taxation and Revenue*).

The ability and leadership that Wentworth had demonstrated in parliament brought him to the king's attention and led to the offer of a peerage and royal appointments that represented the goals of ambitious men of his era. After the parliament of 1628* adjourned, Charles made him Baron Wentworth and appointed him lord president of the council of the north. As the king's chief representative first in northern England and subsequently in Ireland, Wentworth stirred controversy with his fiery temper and his efforts to consolidate royal authority and increase royal revenue. In correspondence with his friend Archbishop William Laud*, he shared his hopes and fears about the future for both Ireland and England. With King Charles, his relationship was more formal. Only after Strafford's death did Charles realize how much he owed this loyal servant. (See Thorough*.)

Bibliography: Hugh F. Kearney, *Strafford in Ireland, 1633-41*, 1960; William Knowler, ed., *The Earl of Strafford's Letters and Despatches*, 2 vols., 1739.

Esther S. Cope

Westminster Assembly of Divines and Westminster Confession (1643-1652). This synod was the culminating act in the struggle between the Anglican* and Puritan* factions in England during the Civil War* and Interregnum*. Because of the distinction of the men who attended it, the quality of the documents it sent forth, and the magnitude of the group that accepted these precepts, it occupies first place among the synods of the Reformed church. The membership was fixed by the Long Parliament* at 151, with 121 clergy and thirty laymen, twenty of whom were chosen from the House of Commons and ten from the House of Lords. The clergymen were taken two from each county; two each from Cambridge, the Channel Islands, and Oxford; one each from the counties of Wales*; and four from London*. A delegation was sent from the Scots assembly, and three delegates were invited from New England.

All members were Calvinist* in doctrine, though differences existed on the subject of church government. The assembly met every weekday except Saturday and generally convened from nine in the morning until one or two in the afternoon. There was freedom of debate, and speakers spoke as long as they thought necessary. The assembly is best known for its revision of the Thirty-nine Articles to bring them into Calvinist form and the preparation of a Confession of Faith, Catechisms, and the Book of Discipline.

The Confession took over two years to complete, while the Catechisms and Book of Discipline were completed simultaneously. The Confession, in its completed form, extends to thirty-three chapters, each containing a small group of propositions. The chapters address Scripture, the Trinity, God's decree, Creation, Providence, the Fall, sin and its punishment, God's covenant with man, Christ the mediator, free will, effectual calling, justification, adoption, sanctification, saving faith, repentance unto life, good works, the perseverance of saints, assurance of grace and salvation, the law, Christian liberty and liberty of conscience, worship and the Sabbath, lawful oaths and vows, the civil magistrate, marriage and divorce, the church, the communion of the saints, the sacraments, baptism, the Lord's Supper, church censures, synods and councils, the state after death and the Resurrection, and the Last Judgment. In its comprehensiveness, the Westminster Confession marked the most complete formulation of biblical revelation as it appeared to the most learned Puritan divines. It was the last creed of Calvinism and represented the harvest of years of theological debate.

Four principles emphasized by the assembly are the authority of the Scriptures, which began the Confession, the sovereignty of God, the rights of conscience, and the sole jurisdiction of the church within its own domain. Each of these remain to this day an essential part of English-speaking Presbyterian* churches throughout the world with only slight modifications.

Simultaneous to the drafting of the Confession, the Larger Catechism was eventually approved in 1648, but its 196 questions made it too elaborate to be popular. Historically it has served as a commentary on the Confession and as the foundation for the popular Shorter Catechism. The Shorter Catechism followed in formation the Larger Catechism and was also approved in 1648. The Shorter Catechism contained 107 questions and began and ended with the same questions as its longer predecessor. It lent itself better to memory and hence was more useful to the catechumen and teacher alike.

Antiepiscopal in church government and Calvinistic in doctrine, the Westminster documents are the compact historical expression of the Puritan impulse in Great Britain.

Bibliography: F. L. Cross, *The Oxford Dictionary of the Christian Church*, 1957; A. F. Mitchell and B. Struthers, eds., *Minutes of the Sessions of the Westminster Assembly of Divines*, 1874.

John S. Erwin

Whigs. One of two political parties that came into existence during the Exclusion Crisis* (1678-1681), the Whigs pushed for the exclusion of the duke of York, the future James II*, from the English succession. They viewed his Catholic religion as a threat to Protestantism and English liberties because they connected Catholicism* with arbitrary and absolute government. The term *Whig*, originally one of vilification, derived from *Whiggamore*, which had been applied to extreme Scottish Covenanters* or Presbyterians*, who had rebelled against royal authority in Scotland*. Hence the Whigs were regarded by their opponents, the Tories*, as being nothing more than extremists and rebels whose policies, like those of opponents of Charles I* in 1641 and 1642, would lead to civil war. Other terms of abuse used before the term *Whig* gained widespread currency were *Presbyterian, petitioners**, and *men of '41*.

Neither the Whigs nor the Tories regarded themselves as a party, and there was not a two-party system in existence. They functioned as parties only intermittently during election campaigns and sessions of parliament*. Both Whigs and Tories viewed "party" in a negative way; "party" represented a small, narrow interest. Whigs and Tories claimed that they represented the best interests of the nation and that their opponents were the ones representative of a narrow, corrupt faction.

Different geographic and social sections were evident within the Whigs, although they were to gain a firm grip on London* during the Exclusion Crisis. The core of those regarded as the first Whigs developed as opposition to Thomas Osborne*, earl of Danby, in the latter stages (1674-1679) of the Cavalier Parliament*. The struggle for exclusion imposed a degree of organization and discipline and provided a rallying point for several different groups: the "Old Presbyterians" opposed to the Clarendon Code*; the country opposition of prominent gentry critical of the royal court*; men who attacked government ministers hoping to attain office themselves; those who gathered around James Scott, duke of Monmouth, and promoted his interests; and republicans and former Levellers* from the Civil War* period. All of these different groups were united in the policy of exclusion by the leadership of Anthony Ashley Cooper*, earl of Shaftesbury.

The Whigs won the elections of 1679 and 1681 and mobilized mass support by making exclusion a national issue. Through the use of petitions, pamphlets geared toward different educational levels, songs, bonfires, and pope burning processions on the anniversaries of the Gunpowder Plot* and the accession of Elizabeth I, the Whigs raised the level of political awareness in London and throughout the country and heaped abuse on the Tories. Whigs organized the Green Ribbon Club to promote these undertakings and also developed instructions for members of parliament (MPs), which took the form of addresses from constituents insisting that parliament vote no money for Charles II* until certain conditions were met: that Protestantism was protected from popery, English liberties were secured, and abhorrers* were punished.

The purpose of the instructions was to encourage MPs to remain firm in insistence on exclusion; these instructions did bring the Whigs closer to constituents.

Skillful use of royal prerogatives* by Charles II defeated the Whig attempt at exclusion. Use of prorogation and dissolutions removed parliament as a national forum. After dissolution of the Oxford Parliament* in 1681, Charles II dismissed Whigs from the militia, commissions of peace, and the judiciary, had Shaftesbury indicted for treason, procured election of Tory sheriffs* in London, and introduced *quo warranto* proceedings against municipal charters, while working in conjunction with the Tories (see Local Government*). After Shaftesbury's flight into exile and death abroad and the executions of other Whig leaders as a result of the Rye House Plot* (1683), the first Whig party was reduced in strength to a group of London Whigs of lower social origin and some noble supporters of the duke of Monmouth.

The election of 1685, after the accession of James II, revealed the Whigs to be in a very weak position with only fifty or so MPs out of 513 in the House of Commons, a position much weaker than that of the Tories during the Exclusion Crisis. After Monmouth's Rebellion* (1685), James used Tories to uphold his policies of attempting to procure wider toleration for Catholics. Whig strength was so weak that they were unable to provide the basis for any unified opposition. Tory refusal to go along with James's policies led the king to seek support from Whigs by late 1687. By 1688 James II had alienated both Whigs and Tories, causing them to desert James and support William of Orange*.

In the Convention Parliament* (1689) moderate Whigs were in the majority in the House of Commons, and a Whig was selected as speaker. The struggle over the constitutional settlement during the Glorious Revolution* (1688-1689) brought about some divisions between Whigs and Tories. In general the Whigs pushed for a quicker settlement of the issues involved and promoted the view of John Locke* that James II had broken the "original contract" between the ruler and the people and had "abdicated the government," leaving the throne "vacant." Whigs in the House of Lords defended this view, contained in the House of Commons's resolution, against attempts by Tory leaders to change the word *abdicated* to *deserted* and against the attempts of some Tories to declare a regency. During the debates concerning the constitutional settlement, Whigs expressed greater concern for wider religious toleration that would encompass Protestants. After accepting the Crown, William III awarded offices to both Whigs and Tories because he was beholden to them both, but he never came to be dependent upon one to the exclusion of the other.

Bibliography: J. R. Jones, *The First Whigs,* 1961; J. R. Jones, "Parties and Parliament," in Jones, ed., *The Restored Monarchy, 1660-1688*, 1979: 48-70; W. A. Speck, *Reluctant Revolutionaries*, 1989.

                                                                Mark C. Herman

William III (1650-1702). Born at The Hague, William Henry was the son of Mary, eldest daughter of Charles I* of England, which put him in line for the throne. His father was William II, prince of Orange and stadholder of the United Provinces, who died of smallpox eight days before William III was born. William III was put in his mother's custody and educated by Dr. Cornelis Trigland, who instructed him in the Calvinist* principles of the Dutch Reformed faith. Later his household was established in Leyden, and Dr. Henry Bornius of the university directed his studies. English was his native language, but he could speak Dutch, French, German, Latin, and Spanish. In 1660 his mother died. She attempted to leave his care to Charles II*, but the Dutch intervened, and Johan de Witt, leader of the States General of Holland, took control of his education. De Witt tried to remove all English influence on William, including sending all his English servants home.

In 1668 William began to take control of his life and play a more active part in affairs of state. He proved very popular with the army and the people. In November 1670 he visited England for the first time, to try to collect a debt from Charles II. William was cordially greeted and entertained by his uncle and received some satisfaction regarding the debt. More important, he achieved instant popularity with the English.

In February 1672 William received the military title of captain general and in July was made stadholder. This put William in position to lead the Dutch army against the French threat. The de Witt brothers were murdered by an angry mob in August, and the prince of Orange now assumed leadership of the Dutch provinces. Although a capable soldier and a natural leader, William had few victories against the overwhelming French armies in the next four years. Nevertheless, France's allies, including England, withdrew from the conflict one at a time, and in 1678 William concluded the Treaty of Nijmegen with France.

In 1677 William married Mary*, oldest daughter of the duke of York (see James II*), still a girl of fifteen. William was in line for the English throne, and the marriage consolidated the two strongest claims to the throne. William hoped to gain some control of England's foreign policy through the marriage. Mary was so unhappy that she wept for a day and a half. William knew the match would be unpopular in his country, so he attempted to keep his plans secret. They were married on 4 November in Mary's bedroom, with neither the queen nor the duchess of York attending.

In the Exclusion Crisis* (1678-1681), William initially remained neutral. He would take no action prejudicial to either Charles or James. He respected them and had actually courted James when seeking Mary's hand. But he told a French agent that if parliament* summoned him to the throne, he would respond positively. At this point, however, there was very little support for William among English party leaders. By 1680, however, he reversed himself and was a proponent of James's exclusion. After this Charles and James were hostile toward him, and William maintained contact with Whig* party leaders. In 1683 William opposed the marriage of James's daughter, Anne*, to Prince George of Denmark, which had been proposed by the French. William and Anne were never on cordial terms after this time, and William, as king, treated Anne shabbily.

When James became king in 1685, William determined to improve relations with him because his wife was next in line for the throne. He sent an ambassador to make his submission to the new king, who accepted him with some conditions. By 1687, however, relations between James and his government were so hostile that William was repeatedly requested to intervene, and the relationship between William and James soured.

Once James's son was born in 1688, a revolution was going to take place with or without William. He intervened to prevent another republic in England, which would be detrimental to Dutch interests, and because he needed English military might against France, which James would not provide.

Contrary to the wishes of his English cohorts, William invaded England with a large army in case James's army* was willing to fight. On 5 November William's army landed at Torbay. James's army was at Salisbury, and when he arrived to take command, he was too nervous to assume leadership. Instead of engaging William he retreated toward London*. These weak decisions proved to be his defeat. His officers and his army began to desert. On 17 November the remainder of the royal army marched out of London on William's orders. On the next day, James left London, and in the afternoon William entered the city.

Mary had supported the revolution, much to her father's surprise. She was a fervent Protestant and did not want a continuation of Catholic* monarchy. She accepted the convenient story that James Edward was an impostor. Some Englishmen, led by the earl of Danby (Thomas Osborne*), wanted to make Mary queen, others wanted a regency for James, and a few wanted to restore James with conditions. William would accept none of this. He would remain in England only as king. The final compromise was that William and Mary became joint monarchs, a unique situation in English history. In practice William was the ruler, and Mary was not even accorded some of the ceremonial symbols of ruler. Mary died of smallpox in 1694, and William never remarried; there were no children. The Declaration of Rights* (and subsequently the Bill of Rights*) settled the Crown on Mary's issue, then on Anne and her issue, then on William's issue.

All his life William was cursed by ill health. He had a humpback and chronic asthma. A naturally poor appetite weakened his body further. In character William was shy and retiring. He had a temper, which he expressed by kicking his valets. William paid little attention to women*, although he did engage in at least one extramarital affair. He showed enthusiasm only for government business, warfare, and hunting.

Bibliography: Stephen B. Baxter, *William III*, 1966.

W. Calvin Dickinson

Witchcraft. Witch hysteria in Stuart England cannot be understood without a knowledge of the general European origins of the witch craze that gripped Europe for over two centuries. Sixteenth- and seventeenth-century society saw witchcraft as a dangerous and potent blend of sorcery and heresy. Sorcery itself is a cultural universal that links European witchcraft with similar phenomena in primitive societies. What made the European witch craze unique was the fusion of sorcery with heresy to create a double crime, a *crimen exceptum*. According to contemporaries, the witch's act of making an explicit pact with Satan to obtain her magical powers threatened to undermine and subvert all of Christian society.

While both sorcery and heresy had existed throughout the medieval period, Pope Innocent VIII issued a papal bull in December 1484 advertising that this new compound crime was of sufficient magnitude for the Roman church to take action to eradicate its threat to Christianity. In 1486 two Dominican inquisitors, Heinrich Kramer and Jacob Sprenger, created the *Malleus Maleficarum*, the first encyclopedia of witchcraft and demonology. An extremely mysogynistic work, the *Malleus* elaborated the supposed conspiracy of Satan to destroy mankind, articulated the reasons why women* were the chosen agents of the Devil for this purpose, and set out procedures for conducting a witch trial.

Witch hysteria came to England over seventy-five years later, not beginning in earnest until the reign of Elizabeth I. While the first English witchcraft law was passed under Henry VIII in 1542, it has been assumed by scholars that it was not widely enforced. A parliamentary statute of 1563 (5 Eliz. I, c. 16) set the legal standard for the subsequent persecution of witches in England. Some historians have attributed the arrival of continental witch fears in England to the return of the Marian exiles from Calvin's Geneva and other "witch-infested" parts of Europe upon Elizabeth's accession to the throne.

Whatever the reasons for the escalation of legal prosecution of witches after 1563, few historians of English witchcraft have disputed that many, maybe even a majority, of English witches were executed in the Elizabethan era. This fact stands despite the fact that under the Elizabethan statute a crime committed by means of witchcraft had to be proved at law. That is, evidence had to be supplied that the alleged witch had murdered, caused damage to crops or cattle, or committed other *maleficia* by means of witchcraft.

By contrast the subsequent statute of 1604 (I James I, c. 12), which the parliament (of 1604-1610*) passed to pander to James I's* expertise on witchcraft, made prosecution for this crime much simpler. The Jacobean statute made even the act of consulting with, covenanting with, or entertaining evil spirits punishable by death. Moreover, this act, which was not repealed until 1736 (9 George II, c. 5), influenced legal handbooks in North America, spreading the witch hysteria across the Atlantic. In the colonies, individuals convicted of witchcraft were hanged just as they were in England; on the Continent and in Scotland*, officials administered the traditional penalty for heresy: burning at the stake.

The widespread publication of the *Daemonologie*, James I's book on witchcraft practices, which he authored in 1597 while already king of Scotland, aided the more facile legal process in England. James's interest in witchcraft dated from an alleged attempt on his own life by the North Berwick witches in 1591. *Daemonologie* later served as a kind of handbook for the justices of the peace, magistrates, and assize court judges in England in much the same way the *Malleus* had functioned on the Continent (see Common Law and Courts*; Local Government*).

With the legal, theological, and intellectual premises for witchcraft more accessible, the Stuart period produced many additional witch trials. The English Civil War* was the most fertile period for hunting witches. Professional witch finders like Matthew

Hopkins and John Stearne located many witches in East Anglia. Nineteen women, the largest number of witches known to be executed at one time in England, were hanged at Chelmsford in Essex in 1645. In contrast with the 1640s, magistrates, justices of the peace, and assize judges of the Cromwellian era were somewhat less enthusiastic about hunting witches. Many women who were accused of witchcraft in this period were acquitted, and others who were convicted were later pardoned.

While the Restoration* period was also a time of great interest in witchcraft, scholars and theologians were more intensely debating the reality of witchcraft. Joseph Glanvill, a fellow of the Royal Society*, reaffirmed the popular belief in the reality of witches in his widely published *Sadducismus Triumphatus* (1666), while John Webster, a Nonconformist minister and later a physician, championed skepticism in his *The Displaying of Supposed Witchcraft* (1677).

The Restoration period, despite debate, produced additional witch trials and allusions in the records to large witch panics in various parts of England. In 1682 three women from Bideford in north Devon were executed in a notorious case, but most trials in this period—as earlier—involved a sole female singled out by her neighbors for this charge. Alice Molland, the last woman known to have been executed for witchcraft in England, died in Exeter in 1685. The last recorded witch trial in England occurred in 1717 at Leicester, when the alleged witch was acquitted. Although parliament* finally repealed the Jacobean witchcraft statute in 1736, unofficial and illegal abuse of women accused of witchcraft in English villages persisted into the twentieth century.

Since witchcraft became a topic for serious study by scholars in the nineteenth century, there have been two main approaches to the study of witchcraft. The first treatment of witchcraft, the rationalist approach, deals with this episode in European society as intellectual history. Early representatives of the rationalist approach to English witchcraft were Wallace Notestein (*A History of Witchcraft in England, 1558-1715*, 1911) and C. L. Estrange Ewen (*Witch Hunting and Witch Trials*, 1929, and *Witchcraft and Demonianism*, 1933). Notestein delineated the general course of the witch hysteria in England, while Ewen was responsible for cataloging many additional witch trials in the home counties and elsewhere in England. The second witchcraft school explains the witch craze as social interaction. More recently, during the last two decades, the social school of witchcraft interpretation has dominated English witchcraft scholarship. The year 1970 saw the publication of Alan Macfarlane's *Witchcraft in Tudor and Stuart England* and in the following year Keith Thomas's *Religion and the Decline of Magic* revolutionized witchcraft studies.

Trained as both historian and anthropologist, Macfarlane confined his study of witchcraft accusations and prosecutions to the county of Essex. He amassed considerable data on the personality, sex, age, and marital status of the accused witches, their accusers, and the witnesses. He examined kinship networks for possible motivations toward witchcraft accusations, as well as other common factors such as illness and religion. Deemphasizing the intellectual and elitist fears of Satanic conspiracies, Macfarlane viewed the supposed fear of witches' *maleficia* as disguised guilt. He explained the rise of witch beliefs in connection with population* growth and changes in land ownership between 1560 and 1650. He also saw a conflict between the medieval Catholic* communal ideal of neighborliness, still held by Protestant Christianity in spite of its individualistic spirit, and the necessities of economic and social change. Labeling one's neighbor a witch served to end one's own guilt at refusing him or her charity. According to Macfarlane, witch prosecution declined after 1650 when workhouses were established and it was considered a Christian's duty to abstain from indiscriminate charity (see Poor Law and Poverty*).

While subscribing to the same socioeconomic causation for witch trials in England, Thomas's book was vaster in scope and far more ambitious. Trying to relate these beliefs to the religious ideas of the period, he dealt at great length with numerous occult subjects. Thomas demonstrated that occult arts, including witchcraft, were sometimes parasitic upon Christian teaching, while at other times they were in sharp competition with both the medieval Catholic church and its Protestant rivals. Thomas pointed out that there was always much legitimate magic in the special state and function of the priesthood in Roman Catholicism, particularly in sacraments such as the Eucharist, wherein the priest's words facilitate the act of transubstantiation. The Reformation doctrines of Martin Luther, John Calvin, and others tended to undermine the magical basis for religion and thus robbed the priesthood of its monopoly on legitimate magic. Witchcraft and sorcery, by contrast, always involved illegitimate magic in the eyes of church authorities of whichever persuasion.

Since neither Macfarlane nor Thomas provided much explanation in their theories as to why the witch was usually female, several scholars began to address this subject as one of the central issues of the witch craze. In Europe at large, the percentage of accused witches who were female averaged above seventy-five percent, reaching a high of ninety-five percent in certain areas. Even in Macfarlane's Essex the percentage of women accused as witches was extremely high, at ninety-two percent. Feminist historians began to view the witch hysteria as cultural misogyny which has been part of Western civilization since the classical period. Christina Larner's book *Enemies of God* (1981) broke new ground for English and Scottish witchcraft in articulating questions about this issue.

Several other historians have dealt with the gender factor in parts of the Continent and in North America; their work has been instrumental in focusing more attention in English witchcraft studies toward this end. One of the first scholars to explain the preponderance of women with respect to the mechanisms of witch trials was Erik Midelfort (*Witch-Hunting in Southwestern Germany, 1562-1684*, 1972), who discussed the stereotype of the witch as a woman and demonstrated that it broke down during the larger witch panics. In large panics, almost anyone male or female, young or old might be accused of witchcraft. Others, including Lyle Koehler (*A Search for Power: The "Weaker Sex" in Seventeenth-Century New England*, 1980) and Carol F. Kraals (*The Devil in the Shape of a Woman*, 1987), have analyzed the social factors in New England that caused women to be the principal victims of this crime.

Because witchcraft has always been a multifaceted, interdisciplinary topic, there has been a plethora of writing on this subject in other disciplines. Recently sociologist Marianne Hester (*Lewd Women and Wicked Witches*, 1992) reviewed the Essex material on witchcraft as part of a larger project to link various kinds of societal violence against women. Hester sees rape as the modern-day equivalent to a witchcraft accusation as a means of socially controlling female behavior.

Beyond the gender issue, the trend in English witchcraft studies is toward specialized regional studies of witchcraft in parts of England hitherto neglected, with the emphasis on East Anglia that Macfarlane began. Brian P. Levack's *The Witch-Hunt in Early Modern Europe* (1987) has provided an excellent synthesis of witchcraft studies in England and Europe.

Bibliography: E. William Monter, *European Witchcraft*, 1969, and "The Historiography of European Witchcraft," *Journal of Interdisciplinary History* 2 (1972): 435-451.

Janet A. Thompson

Women. The history of women in the Stuart period (as in most other periods of history) is still at an early stage of development historiographically. The serious historical study of the agency of women was provoked by the feminist movements of the 1960s, and much work on women still displays the signs of its birth. Many historians of women believe that their history should trace the changes in the structures of patriarchal domination of the institutions of government, economy, and society. To counteract the perceived male bias of previous generations of historians, efforts have been made to retrieve the writings of seventeenth-century women. Women's history of the early modern period has also tended strongly toward social, and in particular family, history. Because so little has yet been done and so much more remains to be done, it would be rash to offer firm conclusions on the place of women in Stuart Britain, but it is possible to sketch out the main fields of research.

The debate on the social and economic forces acting upon women in the early modern period has taken as its starting point Alice Clark's *Working Life of Women in the Seventeenth Century*. Clark argued that during the late sixteenth and early seventeenth centuries, the forces of nascent capitalism destroyed the household's role as the primary unit of economic production and consumption. In the medieval period, women had been in a position of rough and ready equality with men because their contribution to the household economy was, and was perceived to be, of equal value. In Clark's view capitalism afforded to males the positions of wage laborers, bourgeois middlemen, and capitalists but created no female role except the decorative and parasitical one of the modern housewife. Women's status fell accordingly.

Clark's thesis has been attacked from many quarters. Medievalists (such as Judith Bennett) have denied the accuracy of Clark's characterization of women's place before capitalism and maintained instead that women had always worked in the least prestigious and rewarding sectors of the economy. With the waning of Marxist historiography, the belief that English society changed essentially in the early-modern period has been questioned. Alan Macfarlane has argued that there was a fundamental continuity in English social and economic relations from the fourteenth to the nineteenth centuries; throughout this period women played a key part in a stable society. By accumulating dowries in domestic service, marrying late, and then restricting their fertility, women contributed to the steady accumulation of wealth that produced the agricultural and industrial revolutions. For Macfarlane, far from being drudges valued only for their childbearing services, Stuart Englishwomen and their progenitors and posterity had unusually high legal and social status compared with women outside northwest Europe. The position of women also lies at the heart of Lawrence Stone's *The Family, Sex and Marriage*. Stone has utterly rejected Macfarlane's "changeless family," instead viewing the Stuart period as a key transitional stage between the "open lineage" family of the fifteenth and sixteenth centuries and the modern "closed domesticated nuclear" family. The strongly patriarchal elements of the Stuart family did place restrictions on women's freedom, but counteracting this was the growth of affective relationships between parents and children and of companionate marriages, and these led eventually to a decrease in male authoritarianism. The growth of the nuclear family based on sentiment was a precondition for an improvement in women's status after the mid-seventeenth century, when the strains of religious, social, and political divisions decreased.

The paucity of evidence for the roles of women in the Stuart economy, both because of limitations in the sources themselves and the previous neglect of the female dimension by historians, makes it very difficult to judge the truth or falsity of the rival theses. In sharp contrast, seventeenth-century views of women and their role are amply evidenced in literary, religious, and legal publications and in private letters and memoirs. This massive quarry of evidence has as yet been little mined. Scholars of English literature, such as Juliet Dusinberre and Linda Woodbridge, have begun the formidable task of analyzing attitudes to women in Renaissance drama and prose. Many are following in their footsteps, often under the influence of post-structuralist and new historicist theories, which sometimes render their conclusions less than immediately comprehensible to the average student of Stuart history. Hardly surprising, Stuart literature was no more univocal on women than on any other topic. Dramatic portraits of strong-minded, independent heroines vie with didactic exhortations on the need for submission in wives and daughters; both were elements in the Stuart portrayal of woman and her proper role. The relative importance of these dissonant elements and the tensions between them provide the focus for the best studies of women in Stuart literature.

Historians' assessment of the position of women in the English legal system suffered at first from an excessive concentration on the common law* and in particular on its doctrine that every wife was a *feme couvert*. Common law was based on the legal fiction that husband and wife became one person at marriage and that only the husband could represent this "person" in actions at law; the wife's legal position, termed *coverture*, significantly restricted her independence. Early studies tended to neglect the importance of equity and ecclesiastical law in mitigating the consequences of this fiction. A more balanced history of Stuart women's legal position is now being developed on the basis of studies of the operation of equity (for example, by Maria Cioni and Amy Louise Erickson). Similarly, the investigation of the ecclesiastical court records (for example, by G. R. Quaife and Martin Ingram) offers new insights into the actual effect of law on some of the most important areas of women's lives. All these studies indicate how misleading it is to characterize women as no more than the passive victims of a hostile legal system. Women constituted a significant proportion of plaintiffs and defendants in Chancery and the ecclesiastical courts*; widows were the key group in the administration of wills.

Church history is also benefiting from the study of women's place in religion. An understandable, but unfortunate, tendency to read only readily available Puritan* popular sermons had initially led to an exaggeration of the contrasts between woman's relative position in Catholicism* and Protestantism. However, works such as Margo Todd's allow a more sophisticated assessment of the impact of the Reformation on women. Wealthy women's significance as patronesses of the clergy, Catholic women's role in the survival of recusancy*, the female place in Puritan piety, and women's importance in the Separatist* sects (many of whose congregations consisted of more women than men) are all being considered anew. Two historians whose works exemplify what can be learned from adding the feminine dimension to religious thought are Christina Larner, who has shown the importance of gender in early modern witch hunts (see Witchcraft*), and Phyllis Mack, in her sensitive analysis of Quaker* women's preaching.

As yet Stuart political and constitutional history does not show the impact of women's history very clearly, yet even in this area, study of what women were doing while their husbands, fathers, and sons maneuvered in parliament* and on the battlefield has added a new dimension to our appreciation of the nature of Stuart society. How differently would gentlemen have conducted central political affairs had not their wives been competently running their estates?

Women's history in the Stuart period is still young, but it already poses important questions in its own right. How were women affected by and how did they affect the major religious, social, and political changes of the period? Did women's status change significantly, or was the seventeenth century merely one phase in a seamless continuity of female experience? Did these years witness the consolidation or the subversion of patriarchy? At present there are more questions than answers, but questions so interesting that they will not easily be laid aside. The research needed suggests that women's history, like a woman's work, will never be done.

Bibliography: Judith M. Bennett, "Women's History: A Study in Continuity and Change," *Women's History Review* 2 (1993): 173-184; Maria L. Cioni, *Women and Law in Elizabethan England*, 1985; Alice Clark, *Working Life of Women in the Seventeenth Century*, 1919; Juliet Dusinberre, *Shakespeare and the Nature of Women*, 1975; Amy Louise Erickson, "Common Law versus Common Practice: The Use of Marriage Settlements in Early Modern England," *Economic History Review*, 2d series, 42, no. 1 (1990): 21-39; Martin Ingram, *Church Courts, Sex and Marriage in England, 1570-1640*, 1987; Christina Larner, *Enemies of God: The Witch-Hunt in Scotland*, 1981; Alan Macfarlane, *Marriage and Love in England: Modes of Reproduction, 1300-1840*, 1986; Phyllis Mack, *Visionary Women: Ecstatic Prophecy in Seventeenth-Century England*, 1992; G. R. Quaife, *Wanton Wenches and Wayward Wives*, 1979; Lawrence Stone, *The Family, Sex and Marriage in England, 1500-1800*, 1977; Margo Todd, *Christian Humanism and the Puritan Social Order*, 1987; Linda

Woodbridge, *Women and the English Renaissance: Literature and the Nature of Womankind, 1540-1620*, 1984.

Margaret R. Sommerville

Chronology

1603	24 March	Death of Elizabeth I and accession of James VI of Scotland
	10 April	James VI proclaimed James I, king of England, Scotland, France, and Ireland
	23 June	Proclamation of James I ending war with Spain
		Millenary Petition
		Bye and Main Plots
1604-1610		Parliament of 1604-1610
1604	14-18 January	Hampton Court Conference
	19 March	First parliament of James I convened
	June	Apology of the Commons
	19 August	Treaty of London ends war with Spain
	September	Canons of 1604 announced to Church of England
		Goodwin v. Fortescue
1605	5 November	Gunpowder Plot discovered

1606		Penal laws and oath of allegiance directed against disloyal Roman Catholics
		Bate's Case
1607		Jamestown settlement established in colony of Virginia
		Suppression of John Cowell's legal dictionary, *The Interpretor*
1608	26 June	Treaty with the Netherlands
		Book of Rates
1609	9 April	Beginning of Twelve Years' Truce between Spain and the Netherlands
	17 June	Alliance with the Netherlands and France to guarantee Twelve Years' Truce
1610	9 June	Arabella Stuart imprisoned for marrying William Seymour
		Great Contract of Robert Cecil debated by parliament
1611	9 February	First parliament of James I dissolved
		Creation of the rank of baronet
		Publication of the Authorized Version of the Bible
1612	24 May	Death of Robert Cecil
	5 November	Death of Henry, prince of Wales
		Establishment of first General Baptist congregation in England by Thomas Helwys
1613-1617		Cockayne Project

1613	14 February	Wedding of Elizabeth, daughter of James I, to Frederick V, elector of the Palatinate of the Rhine
1614	5 April-7 June	Addled Parliament (the second parliament of James I)
1615	27 September	Death of Arabella Stuart
1617	7 March	Appointment of Sir Francis Bacon as lord keeper
		Publication of the Book of Sports
1618-1648		Thirty Years War
1618-1619		Synod of Dort
1618	7 June	Appointment of Sir Francis Bacon as lord chancellor
		Spanish match first proposed
	August	Five Articles of Perth
	29 October	Execution of Sir Walter Raleigh
1620	12 November	*Mayflower* lands on North America
1621	30 January	Third parliament of James I convened
		Forced dismissal of Bacon by parliament
	18 December	Protestation of the Commons
1622	6 January	Third parliament of James I dissolved
		English forces assist in capture of Hormuz from Portuguese
1623	7 March-30 August	Charles, prince of Wales, and the duke of Buckingham travel to Spain but fail to secure the Spanish match
		Amboina Massacre

1624	19 February- 24 March	Fourth Parliament of James I
		Monopolies Act
		Ernst of Mansfeld's failed expedition to recover the Palatinate
	20 July	Marriage treaty between England and France for marriage of Charles, prince of Wales, and Henrietta Maria
		Publication of Richard Montague's *A New Gag for an Old Goose*, which asserted a non-Calvinist vision of English Protestantism
1625-1630		Spanish War
1625	27 March	Death of James VI and I
	18 June- 12 August	First Parliament of Charles I
	October	Cadiz expedition
		Publication of Richard Montague's *Appello Caesarum*, which strongly asserted Arminian doctrines
1626-1633		Feoffees for Impropriations
1626	6 February- 15 June	Second Parliament of Charles I
	16 June	Declaration against controversy
		Levying of a forced loan
1627-1629		French War
1627		Levying of a forced loan
	November	Five Knights' Case

		Duke of Buckingham leads unsuccessful expedition to the Isle of Rhé to relieve besieged city of La Rochelle
		First colonization of Bermuda
1628-1629		Parliament of 1628-1629
1628		Further unsuccessful attempts to relieve La Rochelle
	17 March	Third parliament of Charles I convened
	June	Petition of Right
	11 June	Commons's Remonstrance for enforcement of Penal Laws
	23 August	Assassination of duke of Buckingham
1629	2 March	Three resolutions passed by Commons
	10 March	Third parliament of Charles I dissolved
	24 April	Treaty of Susa ends war with France
		Massachusetts Bay Colony founded
1629-1640		Personal Rule of Charles I
1630	January	Beginning of collection of fines for distraint of knighthood
	15 November	Treaty of Madrid ends war with Spain
		Providence Island Company founded
1631		Book of Orders
1633		Reissuing of Book of Sports
1634		Beginning of levying of ship money
1635		Collection of ship money extended to inland counties

1636-1642		First Popish Plot
1636		Code of Canons in Scotland
1637		Hampden's Case
		Punishment of Prynne, Burton, and Bastwick
		Charles I orders Scots to adopt Book of Common Prayer
	23 July	Riot at St. Giles against prayer book
1638	28 February-1 March	Signing of Scottish National Covenant
	November	Meeting of General Assembly of Scots Kirk at Glasgow
1639		First Bishops' War
	18 June	Pacification of Berwick
1640	13 April-5 May	Short Parliament
	June	Canons of 1640 published
	August-November	Second Bishops' War
	28 August	Battle of Newburn
	26 October	Completion of Treaty of Ripon
	3 November	Beginning of Long Parliament
	11 December	Root and Branch Petition
	16 December	Parliament declares canons of 1640 illegal
	18 December	Impeachment and imprisonment of Archbishop Laud
1640-1648		Long Parliament

1641-1653		Irish Rebellion
1641	16 February	First Triennial Act
	23 March	Beginning of trial of earl of Strafford
	3 May	Revelation of First Army Plot
	10 May	Act of Attainder for earl of Strafford and Act against Dissolution
	12 May	Execution of earl of Strafford
	24 June	Ten Propositions
	5 July	Parliament abolishes Star Chamber and High Commission
	13 August	Charles I travels to Scotland
	23 October	Beginning of Irish Rebellion
	30 October	Revelation of Second Army Plot
	1 November	News of Irish Rebellion arrives in London
	25 November	Charles I returns to London
	1 December	Grand Remonstrance
1642-1646		First Civil War
1642	4 January	Attempted arrest of Five Members
	13 February	Clerical Disabilities Act
	4 March	Militia Ordinance
	23 April	Charles I denied entry into Hull
	1 June	Nineteen Propositions of parliament delivered to Charles I
	11 June	Charles I issues Commission of Array to raise troops

	12 June	Parliament establishes Westminster Assembly of Divines
	4 July	Committee of Safety appointed
	22 August	Charles I raises his standard at Nottingham
	2 September	Parliament orders closing of all theaters
	22 September	Suspension of episcopacy
	23 October	Battle of Edgehill
	13 November	Battle of Turnham Green
1643-1652		Westminster Assembly of Divines
1643	1 February-14 April	Oxford Negotiations
	March	Sequestration Ordinance
	24 June	Death of John Hampden
	1 July	Beginning of Westminster Assembly of Divines
	13 July	Battle of Roundway Down
	22 July	First Excise ordinance
	26 July	Fall of Bristol to royal forces
	3 August	Peace resolutions by House of Lords
	7 August	House of Commons rejects peace resolutions
	20 September	First Battle of Newbury
	25 September	Solemn League and Covenant and alliance with Scots
	5 December	Death of John Pym
1644-1648		Committee of Both Kingdoms

1644	19 January	Scottish army invades England
	16 February	Establishment of Committee of Both Kingdoms
	2 July	Battle of Marston Moor
	14 July	Henrietta Maria leaves England
	16 July	Surrender of York to Parliamentary forces
	21 August	Battle of Lostwithiel
	27 October	Second Battle of Newbury
1645	4 January	Abolition of Book of Common Prayer
	10 January	Execution of Archbishop Laud
	29 January-22 February	Uxbridge Negotiations
	15 February	Establishment of New Model Army
	3 April	Self-Denying Ordinance
	14 June	Battle of Naseby
	10 July	Battle of Langport
	23 July	Battle of Bridgwater
1646	24 February	Abolition of Court of Wards and Liveries
	5 May	Charles I surrenders to Scots army
	14 July	Propositions of Newcastle
	9 October	Abolition of episcopacy
1647-1648		Second Civil War

1647	30 January	Scots hand Charles I over to parliament
	16 May	Declaration of the Army
	May-June	First and Second Indemnity Ordinances
	4 June	Coronet Joyce moves king to Newmarket
	15 June	Declaration of the Army
	1 August	Heads of the Proposals
	6-7 August	Army enters London
	28 October	First Agreement of the People
	28 October–8 November	Putney Debates
	11 November	Charles I flees to Isle of Wight
	26 December	Engagement between Charles I and the Scots
1648	3 January	Establishment of Derby House Committee
	17 January	Vote of No Addresses
	23 March	Revolt in Pembrokeshire begins Second Civil War
	21-26 May	Royalist rising in Kent
	8 July	Scottish army invades England
	17-19 August	Battle of Preston
	27 August	Surrender of Colchester
	11 September	Humble Petition presented to Parliament
	18 September	Treaty of Newport
	4 October	Cromwell enters Edinburgh
	7 October	Cromwell leaves Scotland

	20 November	Remonstrance of the Army
	30 November	Declaration of the Army
	2 December	Army reenters London
	6 December	Pride's Purge and creation of Rump Parliament
1648-1653		Rump Parliament
1649-1660		Interregnum
1649-1651		Third Civil War
1649-1653		Commonwealth
1649-1654		Engagement Controversy
1649-1660		Various Councils of State form part of government
1649	20-27 January	Trial of Charles I
	30 January	Execution of Charles I
	5 February	Charles II proclaimed king in Scotland
	17 March	Abolition of monarchy by Rump Parliament
	19 March	Abolition of House of Lords by Rump Parliament
	14-15 May	Army mutineers defeated at Burford
	19 May	Rump Parliament declares England a Commonwealth
	15 August	Cromwell lands at Dublin
	12 September	Cromwell captures Drogheda
	16 October	Cromwell captures Wexford

1650	2 January	Engagement Act
	10 May	Adultery Act
	26 May	Cromwell leaves Ireland
	23 June	Charles II takes the Covenant
	9 August	Blasphemy Act
	3 September	Battle of Dunbar
1651	1 January	Coronation of Charles II in Scotland
	3 September	Battle of Worcester
	9 October	Navigation Act
	16 October	Charles II escapes to France
	7 November	Death of Henry Ireton
1652-1654		First Dutch War
1652	24 February	Act for Pardon and Oblivion
	19 May	Beginning of First Dutch War
	28 September	Battle of Kentish Knock
1653-1659		Protectorate
1653	18-20 February	Three Days Battle of Portland
	20 April	Cromwell dismisses Rump Parliament
	6 July- 12 December	Barebone's Parliament
	31 July	Battle of Texel
	16 December	Beginning of Protectorate and publication of Instrument of Government

1654	19 January	Repeal of Engagement
	20 March	Ordinance for Triers
	5 April	Treaty of Westminster ends First Dutch War
	12 April	Ordinance for Union between England and Scotland
	18 August	Planning for Western Design against Spanish West Indies
	28 August	Ordinance for Ejectors
	3 September	First Protectorate Parliament convened
1655-1659		Spanish War
1655	22 January	First Protectorate Parliament dissolved
	12-16 March	Penruddock's Rising
	14 April-4 May	Naval operations against Santo Domingo fail
	12 May	Parliamentary forces land on Jamaica
	9 August	Naming of first ten major generals
	22 August	First instructions to major generals
	21 September	Commission to major generals for supervision of counties
	11 October	Revision of commission to major generals
	24 October	Treaty between France and England
	26 October	Formal beginning of war between England and Spain
	2 November	Major generals begin their work of local government
	4-18 December	Readmission of the Jews into England

1656	February	Spain formally declares war on England
	29 July	Imprisonment of Henry Vane
	17 September	Second Protectorate Parliament convened
	22 September	Exclusion of opposition members from parliament
	6-16 December	Debate over blasphemy case of James Nayler
1657	13 March	England allies with France
	31 March	Humble Petition and Advice presented to Cromwell
	3 April	Cromwell first refuses crown
	9 April	Fifth Monarchist uprising by Thomas Venner
	25 May	Humble Petition and Advice accepted without provisions for kingship
1658	20 January	New session of Second Protectorate Parliament begins
	4 February	Second Protectorate Parliament dissolved
	14 June	Battle of the Dunes
	3 September	Death of Oliver Cromwell and proclamation of Richard Cromwell as lord protector
1659	27 January-23 April	Richard Cromwell's parliament
	6-7 May	Rump Parliament reassembled
	25 May	Abdication of Richard Cromwell
	12 July	Act of Pardon and Indemnity
	31 July-16 August	Booth's Rising

	13 October	Rump Parliament disbanded again
	15 October	Establishment of Committee of Ten
	26 December	Rump Parliament reassembled again
1660	1 January	Monck enters England with army
	3 February	Monck and army enter London
	18 February	Act for a new parliament passed
	21 February	Long Parliament reassembled as secluded members allowed to join the Rump Parliament
	15 March	Act for new parliamentary elections
	16 March	Long Parliament dissolved
	15 April-25 July	Savoy Conference
	24 April	Declaration of Breda
	25 April-9 December	Convention Parliament
	25 May	Charles II lands in Kent
	29 May	Charles II enters London
	October	Trial of regicides
1661-1679		Cavalier Parliament
1661-1665		Enactment of Clarendon Code
1661	6 January	Fifth Monarchist Uprising in London
	8 May	Cavalier Parliament convened
		Corporation Act
1662	May	Act of Uniformity

	21 May	Charles II marries Catherine of Braganza
		Declaration of Indulgence
		Licensing Act
		Royal Society of London founded
1664		Conventicle Act
		Second Triennial Act
1665-1667		Second Dutch War
1665	4 March	Charles II declares war on Dutch
		Five Mile Act
	3 June	Battle of Lowestoft
	June-September	Plague of London
1666	1-4 June	Four Days Battle
	25 July	Battle of North Foreland
	2-6 September	Great Fire of London
1667-1673		Cabal Ministry
1667	June	Dutch attack English fleet in the Medway
	21 July	Treaty of Breda ends Second Dutch War
1670	22 May	Treaty of Dover
1672-1674		Third Dutch War
1672	17 March	England declares war on Dutch
	March	Declaration of Indulgence
	28 May	Battle of Solebay

		Stop of the Exchequer
1673		First Test Act
	28 May	Battle of Schoonveldt Channel
	11 August	Battle of Texel
	30 September	James (II), duke of York, marries Mary of Modena
1674	19 February	Treaty of Westminster ends Third Dutch War
1678-1681		Exclusion Crisis
1678	September	Supposed revelation of Popish Plot
		Second Test Act
1679	24 January	Cavalier Parliament dissolved
	6 March-12 July	Habeas Corpus Parliament
	1-22 June	Covenanter Rebellion
	July	First Exclusion Bill
	October	Meal Tub Plot
	7 October	Exclusion Bill Parliament convened but repeatedly prorogued without meeting until 21 October 1680
	October	Exclusion Bill Parliament prorogued
1680	21 October	Exclusion Bill Parliament reconvened
	October	Second Exclusion Bill
1681	18 January	Exclusion Bill Parliament dissolved
	21-28 March	Oxford Parliament

	April	Third Exclusion Bill
1683	April	Rye House Plot
1685	6 February	Death of Charles II and accession of James II
	19 May	James II's parliament convened
	11 June-7 July	Monmouth's Rebellion
	5-6 July	Battle of Sedgemoor
	September	Bloody Assizes
		Revival of the Licensing Act
	2 November	James II's parliament prorogued (never met again)
1686		*Godden v. Hales*
1687	4 April	Declaration of Indulgence
	2 July	James II's parliament dissolved
1688	25 April	Declaration of Indulgence
	10 June	Birth of James Edward (the Old Pretender)
	29-30 June	Seven Bishops Case ends in acquittal
	30 June	Invitation to William of Orange to assume English Crown
	5 November	William of Orange lands at Torbay
	23 December	James II flees England for France
1689	22 January-6 February	Convention Parliament

1689   23 February   Declaration of Rights formally accepted by
                        William and Mary, who are formally
                        proclaimed king and queen

                        Bill of Rights

Bibliography

This bibliography is intended simply to provide a list of important and recent books dealing with topics of general interest to beginning students of the years 1603-1689. Most of these books will contain footnotes and bibliographies that will guide the reader to other more specialized books and articles.

BIBLIOGRAPHIES AND OTHER REFERENCE WORKS.

Aylmer, G. E., and J. S. Morrill. *The Civil War and Interregnum: Sources for Local Historians*. London: Bedford Square Press, 1979.

Cook, Chris, and John Wroughton. *English Historical Facts 1603-1688*. Totowa, N. J.: Rowman and Littlefield, 1980.

"Great Britain, Commonwealth, Ireland, and Canada." In *Recently Published Articles*. Washington, D. C.: American Historical Association, 1976-1990.

Greaves, Richard L., and Robert Zaller. *Biographical Dictionary of British Radicals in the Seventeenth Century*. 3 vols. Brighton: Harvester, 1982-1984.

Keeler, Mary Frear, ed. *Bibliography of British History: Stuart Period, 1603-1714*. 2d ed. Oxford: Oxford University Press, 1970.

Laurence Urdang Associates, comp. *Lives of the Stuart Age, 1603-1714*. New York: Barnes & Noble, 1976.

Morrill, John S. *Seventeenth Century Britain*. Folkestone: Archon Books, 1980.

Newman, Peter R. *Companion to the English Civil Wars*. New York: Facts on File, 1990.

Royal Historical Society Annual Bibliography of British and Irish History. Brighton: Harvester Press, 1976-.

Sachse, William L. *Bibliographic Handbooks: Restoration England, 1660-1689*. Cambridge: Cambridge University Press, 1976.

Writings on British History. London: Institute of Historical Research, 1937-.

COLLECTIONS OF PRIMARY SOURCES

Abbott, W. C., ed. *Writings and Speeches of Oliver Cromwell*. 4 vols. Cambridge, Mass.: Harvard University Press, 1937-1947.

Clarendon, Edward Hyde, 1st Earl of. *History of the Rebellion*. 6 vols. Edited by W. D. Macray. Oxford: Oxford University Press, 1888.

Firth, C. H., and R. S. Rait, eds. *Acts and Ordinances of the Interregnum*. 3 vols. London: Her Majesty's Stationery Office, 1911.

Gardiner, S. R., ed. *The Constitutional Documents of the Puritan Revolution, 1625-1660*. Oxford: Oxford University Press, 1906.

Haller, William, ed. *Tracts on Liberty in the Puritan Revolution*. 3 vols. New York: Columbia University Press, 1934.

Keeler, J. F., and P. L. Hughes, eds. *Stuart Royal Proclamations of James I*. Oxford: Oxford University Press, 1973.

Kenyon, J. P., ed. *The Stuart Constitution 1603-1688*. 2d ed. Cambridge: Cambridge University Press, 1986.

Larkin, James L., ed. *Stuart Royal Proclamations: II. Royal Proclamations of King Charles 1625-46*. Oxford: Oxford University Press, 1982.

Prothero, G. W., ed. *Select Statutes and Other Constitutional Documents Illustrative of the Reigns of Elizabeth and James I*. Oxford: Oxford University Press, 1913.

Tanner, J. R., ed. *Constitutional Documents of the Reign of James I*. Cambridge: Cambridge University Press, 1930.

Winstanley, Gerard. *The Law of Freedom and Other Writings*. Edited by Christopher Hill. Harmondsworth: Penguin Books, 1973.

Wolfe, D. M., ed. *Leveller Manifestoes of the Puritan Revolution*. New York: Nelson, 1944.

Woodhouse, A. S. P., ed. *Puritanism and Liberty*. London: Dent, 1938.

Wooton, David, ed. *Divine Right and Democracy: An Anthology of Political Writings in Stuart England*. Harmondsworth: Penguin Books, 1986.

GENERAL SURVEYS AND MULTIPERIOD WORKS

Ashton, Robert. *Reformation and Revolution, 1558-1660*. London: Granada, 1984.

Clark, J. C. D. *Revolution and Rebellion: State and Society in England in the Seventeenth and Eighteenth Centuries*. Cambridge: Cambridge University Press, 1986.

Coward, Barry. *The Stuart Age*, 2d ed. London: Longman, 1993.

Gardiner, S. R. *History of England from the Accession of James I to the Outbreak of the Civil War 1603-1642*. 10 vols. London, 1884

Hill, Christopher. *The Century of Revolution, 1603-1714*. London: Thomas Nelson, 1961.

Hirst, Derek. *Authority and Conflict: England, 1603-1658*. London: Edward Arnold, 1986.

Jones, J. R. *Country and Court: England, 1658-1714*. London: Edward Arnold, 1978.

Lockyer, Roger. *The Early Stuarts: A Political History of England 1603-1642*. London: Longman, 1989.

Miller, John. *Bourbon and Stuart: Kings and Kingship in France and England in the Seventeenth Century*. New York: Franklin Watts, 1987.

Russell, Conrad. *The Crisis of Parliaments*. Oxford: Oxford University Press, 1971.

Smith, A. G. R. *The Emergence of a Nation State: The Commonwealth of England, 1529-1660*. London: Longman, 1984.

Solt, Leo. *Church and State in Early Modern England, 1509-1640*. Oxford: Oxford University Press, 1990.

REIGNS OF JAMES VI AND I AND CHARLES I

Akrigg, G. P. V. *Jacobean Pageant or the Court of King James I*. Cambridge: Harvard University Press, 1962.

Aylmer, G. E. *The King's Servants: The Civil Service of Charles I, 1625-42*. New York: Columbia University Press, 1961.

Carlton, Charles. *Charles I: The Personal Monarch*. London: Routledge and Kegan Paul, 1983.

Cogswell, Thomas. *The Blessed Revolution: English Politics and the Coming of War, 1621-1624*. Cambridge: Cambridge University Press, 1989.

Cust, Richard. *The Forced Loan and English Politics, 1626-1628*. Oxford: Oxford University Press, 1987.

Cust, Richard, and Ann Hughes, eds. *Conflict in Early Stuart England: Studies in Religion and Politics, 1603-1642*. London: Longman, 1989.

Gregg, Pauline. *King Charles I*. London: J. M. Dent, 1981.

Lee, Jr., Maurice. *Great Britain's Solomon: James VI and I in His Three Kingdoms*. Urbana: University of Illinois, 1990.

Lockyer, Roger. *Buckingham: The Life and Political Career of George Villiers, First Duke of Buckingham, 1592-1628*. London: Longman, 1981.

Nicholls, Mark. *Investigating the Gunpowder Plot*. Manchester: Manchester University Press, 1991.

Parry, Graham. *The Golden Age Restor'd: The Culture of the Stuart Court, 1603-42*. Manchester: University of Manchester Press, 1981.

Peck, Linda Levy, ed. *The Mental World of the Jacobean Court*. Cambridge: Cambridge University Press, 1991.

Reeve, L. J. *Charles I and the Road to Personal Rule*. Cambridge: Cambridge University Press, 1989.

Russell, Conrad. *Parliaments and English Politics, 1621-1629*. Oxford: Oxford University Press, 1979.

Sharpe, Kevin. *Criticism and Compliment: The Politics of Literature in the England of Charles I*. Cambridge: Cambridge University Press, 1987.

—— and Peter Lake, eds. *Culture and Politics in Early Stuart England*. Stanford, CA: Stanford University Press, 1993.

——, ed. *Faction and Parliament: Essays on Early Stuart History*. Oxford: Oxford University Press, 1978.

——. *The Personal Rule of Charles I*. New Haven: Yale University Press, 1992.

——. *Sir Robert Cotton, 1586-1631: History and Politics in Early Modern England*. Oxford: Oxford University Press, 1979.

Smith, A. G. R., ed. *The Reign of James VI and I*. London: Macmillan, 1973.

Tomlinson, Howard, ed. *Before the English Civil War: Essays on Early Stuart Politics and Government*. London: Macmillan, 1983.

Wedgwood, C. V. *The King's Peace, 1637-1641*. London: Collins, 1955.

——. *Thomas Wentworth, First Earl of Strafford, 1593-1641*. New York: Macmillan, 1962.

White, Stephen D. *Sir Edward Coke and "The Grievances of the Commonwealth," 1621-1628*. Chapel Hill: University of North Carolina Press, 1979.

Willson, David Harris. *King James VI and I*. London: Cape, 1956.

——. *The Privy Councillors in the House of Commons: 1604-1629*. Minneapolis: University of Minnesota Press, 1940.

CAUSES OF THE CIVIL WAR

Finlayson, Michael G. *Historians, Puritanism, and the English Revolution*. Toronto: University of Toronto Press, 1985.

Fletcher, Anthony. *The Outbreak of the English Civil War*. New York: New York University Press, 1981.

Hill, Christopher. *The Intellectual Origins of the English Revolution*. Oxford: Oxford University Press, 1980.

Hughes, Ann. *The Causes of the English Civil War*. London: Macmillan, 1991.

Richardson, R. C. *The Debate on the English Revolution Revisited*. 2d ed. London: Routledge, 1988.

Russell, Conrad. *The Causes of the English Civil War*. Oxford: Oxford University Press, 1990.

——, ed. *The Origins of the English Civil War*. London: Macmillan, 1973.

————. *The Fall of the British Monarchies, 1637-1642.* Oxford: Oxford University Press, 1991.

Stone, Lawrence. *The Causes of the English Revolution.* New York: Harper & Row, 1972.

Zagorin, Perez. *The Court and the Country: The Beginning of the English Revolution.* London: Routledge & Kegan Paul, 1969.

THE CIVIL WAR AND INTERREGNUM

Ashton, Robert. *The English Civil War: Conservatism and Revolution, 1603-1649.* London: Weidenfeld and Nicolson, 1978.

————. *Counter-Revolution: The Second Civil War and Its Origins, 1646-1648.* New Haven, CT: Yale University Press, 1995.

Aylmer, G. E. *The Interregnum: The Quest for Settlement.* London: Macmillan, 1972.

————. *The Levellers in the English Revolution.* Ithaca, N.Y.: Cornell University Press, 1975.

————. *Rebellion or Revolution? England from Civil War to Restoration.* Oxford: Oxford University Press, 1986.

————. *The State's Servants: The Civil Service of the English Republic, 1649-1660.* London: Routledge and Kegan Paul, 1973.

Barnard, Toby. *The English Republic, 1649-1660.* London: Longman, 1982.

Brailsford, H. N. *The Levellers and the English Revolution.* London: Cresset Press, 1961.

Brunton, D., and D. H. Pennington. *The Members of the Long Parliament.* London: George Allen and Unwin, 1954.

Coward, Barry. *Oliver Cromwell.* London: Longman, 1991.

Davis, J. C. *Fear, Myth and History: The Ranters and Historians.* Cambridge: Cambridge University Press, 1986.

Firth, Charles H. *Oliver Cromwell and the Rule of the Puritans in England.* New York: G. P. Putnam, 1900.

Haller, William. *Liberty and Reformation in the Puritan Revolution.* New York: Columbia University Press, 1955.

Hexter, J. H. *The Reign of King Pym.* Cambridge, Mass.: Harvard University Press, 1941.

Hibbard, Caroline. *Charles I and the Popish Plot. Chapel Hill: University of North Carolina Press, 1983.*

Hill, Christopher. *God's Englishman: Oliver Cromwell and the English Revolution.* New York: Dial Press, 1970.

Holmes, Clive. *The Eastern Association in the English Civil War.* Cambridge: Cambridge University Press, 1974.

Hutton, Ronald. *The British Republic, 1649-1660.* London: Macmillan, 1990.

Keeler, Mary F. *The Long Parliament*. Philadelphia: American Philosophical Society, 1954.

Kishlansky, Mark A. *The Rise of the New Model Army*. Cambridge: Cambridge University Press, 1979.

Manning, Brian S. *The English People and the English Revolution*. London: Heinemann, 1976.

Morrill, John, ed. *Oliver Cromwell and the English Revolution*. London: Longman, 1990.

————, ed. *Reactions to the English Civil War, 1642-1649*. London: Macmillan, 1982.

————. *The Revolt of the Provinces: Conservatives and Radicals in the English Civil War, 1630-1660*. London: George Allen and Unwin, 1976.

Richardson, R. C., ed. *Images of Oliver Cromwell: Essays for and by Roger Howell, Jr.* Manchester: Manchester University Press, 1993.

Roots, Ivan. *The Great Rebellion*. London: Batsford, 1966.

Snow, Vernon F. *Essex the Rebel: The Life of Robert Devereux, the Third Earl of Essex, 1591-1646*. Lincoln: University of Nebraska Press, 1970.

Underdown, David. *Pride's Purge: Politics in the Puritan Revolution*. Oxford: Oxford University Press, 1971.

————. *Revel, Riot and Rebellion: Popular Politics and Culture in England, 1603-1660*. Oxford: Oxford University Press, 1985.

————. *Royalist Conspiracy in England, 1649-1660*. New Haven: Yale University Press, 1960.

Walzer, Michael. *The Revolution of the Saints*. New York: Atheneum, 1968.

Wedgwood, C. V. *The King's War, 1641-1647*. London: Collins, 1958.

Woolrych, Austin. *Commonwealth to Protectorate*. Oxford: Oxford University Press, 1982.

————. *Soldiers and Statesmen: The General Council of the Army and Its Debates*. Oxford: Oxford University Press, 1987.

Worden, A. B. *The Rump Parliament*. Cambridge: Cambridge University Press, 1974.

RESTORATION AND REIGNS OF CHARLES II AND JAMES II

Earle, Peter. *Monmouth's Rebels: The Road to Sedgmoor, 1685*. London: Weidenfeld and Nicolson, 1977.

Fraser, Antonia. *Royal Charles: Charles II and the Restoration*. New York: Alfred Knopf, 1979.

Greaves, Richard L. *Deliver Us From Evil: The Radical Underground in Britain, 1660-1663*. Oxford: Oxford University Press, 1986.

————. *Enemies Under His Feet: Radicals and Nonconformists in Britain, 1664-1677*. Stanford: Stanford University Press, 1990.

Haley, K. H. D. *The First Earl of Shaftesbury.* Oxford: Oxford University Press, 1968.

Harris, Tim. *Politics Under the Later Stuarts: Party Conflict in a Divided Society 1660-1715.* London: Longman, 1993.

Holmes, Geoffrey. *The Making of a Great Power: Late Stuart and early Georgian Britain, 1660-1722.* London: Longman, 1993.

Hutton, Ronald. *Charles II: King of England, Scotland, and Ireland.* Oxford: Oxford University Press, 1989.

——. *The Restoration: A Political and Religious History of England and Wales, 1658-1667.* Oxford: Oxford University Press, 1987.

Jones, J. R. *Country and Court: England, 1658-1714.* London: Edward Arnold, 1979.

——, ed. *The Restored Monarchy.* London: Macmillan, 1979.

Kenyon, J. P. *The Popish Plot.* London: Heinemann, 1972.

Knights, Mark. *Politics and Opinion in Crisis, 1678-1681.* Cambridge: Cambridge University Press, 1995.

Miller, John. *James II: A Study in Kingship.* Hove: Wayland, 1978.

——. *Popery and Politics in England, 1660-1688.* Cambridge: Cambridge University Press, 1973.

——. *Restoration England: The Reign of Charles II.* London: Longman, 1985.

Ogg, David. *England in the Reign of Charles II.* 2d ed. Oxford: Oxford University Press, 1956.

——. *England in the Reigns of James II and William III.* Oxford: Oxford University Press, 1955.

Seaward, Paul. *The Cavalier Parliament and the Reconstruction of the Old Regime, 1661-1667.* Cambridge: Cambridge University Press, 1989.

——. *The Restoration.* London: Macmillan, 1991.

THE GLORIOUS REVOLUTION

Kenyon, J. P. *Revolution Principles: The Politics of Party, 1689-1720.* Cambridge: Cambridge University Press, 1977.

Schwoerer, Lois G., ed. *The Revolution of 1688-89.* Cambridge: Cambridge University Press, 1992.

Speck, W. A. *Reluctant Revolutionaries: Englishmen and the Revolution of 1688.* Oxford: Oxford University Press, 1988.

CONSTITUTIONAL HISTORY

Ashcraft, Richard. *Revolutionary Politics and John Locke's Two Treatises of Government.* Princeton: Princeton University Press, 1986.

Hirst, Derek. *Representative of the People? Voters and Voting in England Under the Early Stuarts*. Cambridge: Cambridge University Press, 1975.

Judson, M. A. *The Crisis of the Constitution: An Essay in Constitutional and Political Thought, 1603-1645*. New Brunswick: Rutgers University Press, 1949.

Kishlansky, Mark A. *Parliamentary Selection: Social and Political Choice in Early Modern England*. Cambridge: Cambridge University Press, 1986.

Little, David. *Religion, Order and Law: A Study of Pre-Revolutionary England*. New York: Harper and Row, 1969.

MacPherson, C. B. *The Political Theory of Possessive Individualism: Hobbes to Locke*. Oxford: Oxford University Press, 1962.

Martinich, A. P. *The Two Gods of Leviathan: Thomas Hobbes on Religion and Politics*. Cambridge: Cambridge University Press, 1992.

Phillipson, Nicholas, and Quentin Skinner, eds. *Political Discourse in Early Modern Britain*. Cambridge: Cambridge University Press, 1993.

Pocock, J. G. A. *The Ancient Constitution and Feudal Law*. Cambridge: Cambridge University Press, 1957.

Sommerville, J. P. *Politics and Ideology in England, 1603-1640*. London: Longman, 1986.

LEGAL HISTORY

Brooks, C. W. *Pettyfoggers and Vipers of the Commonwealth: The "Lower Branch" of the Legal Profession in Early Modern England*. Cambridge: Cambridge University Press, 1986.

Cockburn, J. S. *A History of English Assizes, 1558-1714*. Cambridge: Cambridge University Press, 1972.

Herrup, Cynthia B. *The Common Peace: Participation and the Criminal Law in Seventeenth-Century England*. Cambridge: Cambridge University Press, 1987.

Levack, Brian P. *The Civil Lawyers in England, 1603-1641: A Political Study*. Oxford: Oxford University Press, 1973.

Prall, S. E. *The Agitation for Law Reform during the Puritan Revolution*. The Hague: Martinus Nijhoff, 1966.

Prest, Wilfred R. *The Rise of the Barristers: A Social History of the English Bar, 1590-1640*. Oxford: Oxford University Press, 1986.

Sharpe, J. A. *Crime in Early Modern England, 1550-1750*. London: Longman, 1984.

Veall, Donald. *The Popular Movement for Law Reform, 1640-1660*. Oxford: Oxford University Press, 1970.

LOCAL, REGIONAL, AND URBAN STUDIES

Barnes, Thomas G. *Somerset, 1625-1640: A County's Government During the "Personal Rule."* Cambridge, Mass.: Harvard University Press, 1961.

Blackwood, B. G. *The Lancashire Gentry and the Great Rebellion.* Manchester: Chetham Society, 1978.

Clark, Peter, and P. Slack, eds. *Crisis and Order in English Towns.* London: Routledge, 1972.

Coate, Mary. *Cornwall in the Great Civil War and Interregnum.* Oxford: Oxford University Press, 1933.

Coleby, Andrew M. *Central Government and the Localities: Hampshire, 1649-1689.* Cambridge: Cambridge University Press, 1987.

Everitt, Alan. *The Community of Kent and the Great Rebellion, 1640-1660.* Leicester: Leicester University Press, 1966.

Fletcher, Anthony. *A County Community in Peace and War: Sussex, 1600-1660.* London: Longman, 1975.

———. *Reform in the Provinces: The Government of Stuart England.* New Haven: Yale University Press, 1986.

Howell, Roger. *Newcastle-upon-Tyne and the Puritan Revolution.* Oxford: Oxford University Press, 1967.

Hughes, Ann. *Politics, Society and Civil War in Warwickshire, 1620-1660.* Cambridge: Cambridge University Press, 1987.

Hunt, William. *The Puritan Moment: The Coming of Revolution to an English County.* Cambridge, Mass.: Harvard University Press, 1983.

Morrill, John. *Cheshire, 1630-1660: County Government and Society during the "English Revolution."* Oxford: Oxford University Press, 1974.

Pearl, Valerie. *London and the Outbreak of the Puritan Revolution.* Oxford: Oxford University Press, 1960.

Underdown, David. *Somerset in the Civil War and Interregnum.* Newton Abbot: David and Charles, 1973.

RELIGIOUS HISTORY

Capp, B. S. *The Fifth Monarchy Men A Study in Seventeenth Century Millenarianism.* London: Faber, 1976.

Carlton, Charles. *Archbishop William Laud.* London: Routledge, 1987.

Champion, J. A. I. *The Pillars of Priestcraft Shaken: The Church of England and Its Enemies, 1660-1730.* Cambridge: Cambridge University Press, 1992.

Collinson, Patrick. *The Religion of Protestants: The Church in English Society, 1559-1626.* Oxford: Oxford University Press, 1982.

Cragg, G. R. *Puritanism in the Age of the Great Persecution.* Cambridge: Cambridge University Press, 1957.

Cross, Claire. *Church and People, 1450-1660*. Fontana, 1976.

Davies, Julian. *The Caroline Captivity of the Church: Charles I and the Remoulding of Anglicanism*. Oxford: Oxford University Press, 1992.

Doran, Susan, and Christopher Durston. *Princes, Pastors, and People: The Church and Religion in England, 1529-1689*. London: Routledge, 1991.

Fincham, Kenneth. *Prelate as Pastor: The Episcopate of James I*. Oxford: Oxford University Press, 1990.

Firth, Katherine R. *The Apocalyptic Tradition in Reformation Britain, 1530-1645*. Oxford: Oxford University Press, 1979.

Green, I. M. *The Reestablishment of the Church of England, 1660-1663*. Oxford: Oxford University Press, 1978.

Haller, William. *The Rise of Puritanism or, The Way to New Jerusalem as Set Forth in Pulpit and Press from Thomas Cartwright to John Lilburne and John Milton, 1570-1643*. New York: Columbia University Press, 1938.

Hill, Christopher. *A Turbulent Seditious and Factious People: John Bunyan and His Church*. Oxford: Oxford University Press, 1988.

———. *The World Turned Upside Down*. New York: Viking, 1972.

Ingle, H. Larry. *First Among Friends: George Fox and the Creation of Quakerism*. Oxford: Oxford University Press, 1994.

Jordan, W. K. *The Development of Religious Toleration in England*. 4 vols. Cambridge, Mass.: Harvard University Press, 1932-1940.

Katz, David S. *Philo-Semitism and the Readmission of the Jews to England, 1603-1655*. Oxford: Oxford University Press, 1982.

Kendall, R. T. *Calvin and British Calvinism to 1649*. Oxford: Oxford University Press, 1979.

Lamont, William M. *Godly Rule: Politics and Religion, 1603-60*. London: Macmillan, 1969.

———. *Richard Baxter and the Millennium*. London: Rowman and Littlefield, 1979.

McGregor, J. F., and Barry Reay, eds. *Radical Religion in the English Revolution*. Oxford: Oxford University Press, 1984.

Reay, Barry. *The Quakers and the English Revolution*. London: Temple Smith, 1985.

Seaver, Paul. *The Puritan Lectureships: The Politics of Religious Dissent, 1560-1662*. Stanford: Stanford University Press, 1970.

Sommerville, C. John. *The Secularization of Early Modern England: From Religious Culture to Religious Faith*. New York: Oxford University Press, 1992.

Spurr, John. *The Restoration Church of England, 1646-1689*. New Haven: Yale University Press, 1991.

Tolmie, Murray. *The Triumph of the Saints*. Cambridge: Cambridge University Press, 1977.

Trevor-Roper, H. R. *Archbishop Laud, 1573-1645*. 2d ed. London: Macmillan, 1962.

Tyacke, Nicholas. *Anti-Calvinists: The Rise of English Arminianism, c.1590-1640*. Oxford: Oxford University Press, 1987.

Vann, Richard. *The Social Development of English Quakerism*. Cambridge, Mass.: Harvard University Press, 1969.

Wallace, Dewey. *Puritans and Predestination: Grace in English Protestant Theology, 1528-1695*. Chapel Hill: University of North Carolina Press, 1982.

Watts, M. R. *The Dissenters from the Reformation to the French Revolution*. Oxford: Oxford University Press, 1978.

White, B. R. *The English Baptists of the Seventeenth Century*. London: Baptist Historical Society, 1983.

————. *The English Separatist Tradition*. Oxford: Oxford University Press, 1971.

White, Peter O. G. *Predestination, Policy and Polemic: Conflict and Consensus in the English Church from the Reformation to the Civil War*. New York: Cambridge University Press, 1992.

SOCIAL AND ECONOMIC HISTORY

Appleby, Andrew. *Famine in Tudor and Stuart England*. Stanford: Stanford University Press, 1978.

Appleby, Joyce O. *Economic Thought and Ideology in Seventeenth Century England*. Princeton: Princeton University Press, 1978.

Brenner, Robert. *Merchants and Revolution: Commercial Change, Political Conflict, and London's Overseas Traders, 1550-1653*. Princeton: Princeton University Press, 1993.

Capp, B. S. *Astrology and the Popular Press: English Almanacs, 1500-1800*. London: Faber, 1979.

Clay, C. G. A. *Economic Expansion and Social Change: England, 1500-1700*. 2 vols. Cambridge: Cambridge University Press, 1984.

Cliffe, J. T. *The Puritan Gentry: The Great Puritan Families of Early Stuart England*. London: Routledge and Kegan Paul, 1984.

Coleman, D. C. *The Economy of England, 1450-1700*. Oxford: Oxford University Press, 1977.

Cressy, David. *Literacy and the Social Order: Reading and Writing in Tudor and Stuart England*. Cambridge: Cambridge University Press, 1980.

Friedman, Jerome. *The Battle of the Frogs and Fairford's Flies: Miracles and the Pulp Press during the English Revolution*. New York: St. Martin's, 1993.

Heal, Felicity, and Clives Holmes. *The Gentry in England and Wales, 1500-1700*. Palo Alto, CA: Stanford University Press, 1995.

Hill, Christopher. *Reformation to Industrial Revolution, 1530-1780*. London: Weidenfeld and Nicolson, 1967.

Houlbrooke, Ralph. *The English Family, 1450-1700*. London: Longman, 1984.

Hoyle, R. W., ed. *The Estates of the English Crown, 1558-1640*. Cambridge: Cambridge University Press, 1992.

Hutton, Ronald. *The Rise and Fall of Merry England: The English Ritual Year 1400-1700*. Oxford: Oxford University Press, 1994.

Ingram, Martin. *Church Courts, Sex and Marriage in England, 1570-1640*. Cambridge: Cambridge University Press, 1990.

Laslett, Peter. *The World We Have Lost: England Before the Industrial Age*. 3d ed. London: Scribners, 1983.

Macfarlane, Alan. *The Family Life of Ralph Josselin: A Seventeenth Century Clergyman*. Cambridge: Cambridge University Press, 1970.

———. *The Justice and the Mare's Ale: Law and Disorder in Seventeenth-Century England*. Cambridge: Cambridge University Press, 1981.

Manning, Roger B. *Hunters and Poachers: A Cultural and Social History of Unlawful Hunting in England, 1485-1640*. Oxford: Oxford University Press, 1993.

O'Day, Rosemary. *Education and Society in Tudor and Stuart England, 1500-1800: The Social Foundations of Education in Early Modern Britain*. London: Longman, 1982.

Reay, Barry, ed. *Popular Culture in Seventeenth-Century England*. London: Crome Helm, 1985.

Seaver, Paul S. *Wallington's World: A Puritan Artisan in Seventeenth-Century London*. Stanford: Stanford University Press, 1985.

Slack, Paul. *The Impact Plague in Tudor and Stuart England*. London: Routledge, 1985.

———. *Poverty and Policy in Tudor and Stuart England*. London: Longman, 1988.

Spufford, Margaret. *Contrasting Communities: English Villagers in the Sixteenth and Seventeenth Centuries*. Cambridge: Cambridge University Press, 1974.

———. *Small Books and Pleasant Histories: Popular Fiction and Its Readership in Seventeenth-Century England*. Cambridge: Cambridge University Press, 1981.

Stone, Lawrence. *The Crisis of the Aristocracy, 1558-1641*. Oxford: Oxford University Press, 1965.

———. *Family, Sex and Marriage in England, 1500-1800*. New York: Harper and Row, 1977.

Thirsk, Joan, ed. *The Agrarian History of England and Wales. Vol. 4: 1500-1640*. Cambridge: Cambridge University Press, 1967.

Thomas, Keith. *Man and the Natural World: A History of Modern Sensibility*. New York: Pantheon, 1983.

———. *Religion and the Decline of Magic*. New York: Scribners, 1971.

Watt, Tessa. *Cheap Print and Popular Piety, 1550-1640*. Cambridge: Cambridge University Press, 1991.

Wilson, Charles. *England's Apprenticeship, 1603-1763*. New York: St. Martin's Press, 1965.

Wrightson, Keith. *English Society, 1580-1680*. London: Hutchinson, 1982.

Wrigley, E. A., and R. S. Schofield. *The Population History of England, 1541-1871*. London: Edward Arnold, 1981.

MILITARY AND NAVAL HISTORY

Adair, John. *Roundhead General: A Military Biography of Sir William Waller*. London: Macdonald, 1969.

Andrews, Kenneth R. *Ships, Money and Politics: Seafaring and Naval Enterprise in the Reign of Charles I*. New York: Cambridge University Press, 1991.

Carlton, Charles. *Going to the Wars: The Experiences of the British Civil Wars, 1638-1651*. London: Routledge, 1992.

Firth, C. H. *Cromwell's Army*. London: Methuen, 1902.

———, and G. Davies. *The Regimental History of Cromwell's Army*. 2 vols. Oxford: Oxford University Press, 1940.

Gentles, Ian. *The New Model Army in England, Ireland, and Scotland, 1648-1653*. Cambridge, Mass.: Blackwell, 1992.

INTELLECTUAL HISTORY AND HISTORY OF SCIENCE

Greengrass, Mark, ed. *Samuel Hartlib and Universal Reformation: Studies in Intellectual Communication*. Cambridge: Cambridge University Press, 1995.

Jacob, Margaret C. *The Cultural Meaning of the Scientific Revolution*. New York: A. A. Knopf, 1988.

———. *The Newtonians and the English Revolution, 1689-1720*. Hassocks: Harvester Press, 1976.

Kroll, Richard; Ashcraft, Richard; and Zagorin, Perez, eds. *Philosophy, Science and Religion in England, 1640-1700*. Cambridge: Cambridge University Press, 1992.

Martin, Julian. *Francis Bacon, the State and the Reform of Natural Philosophy*. Cambridge: Cambridge University Press, 1992.

Morgan, John. *Godly Learning: Puritan Attitudes Toward Reason, Learning and Education, 1560-1640*. Cambridge: Cambridge University Press, 1986.

Webster, Charles. *The Great Instauration: Science, Medicine and Reform, 1626-1660*. London: Duckworth, 1975.

Westfall, Richard S. *Never at Rest: A Biography of Isaac Newton*. Cambridge: Cambridge University Press, 1980.

———. *Science and Religion in Seventeenth-Century England*. New Haven: Yale University Press, 1958.

Wormald, B. H. G. *Francis Bacon: History, Politics and Science, 1561-1626.* Cambridge: Cambridge University Press, 1993.

IRELAND

Barnard, T. C. *Cromwellian Ireland.* Oxford: Oxford University Press, 1975.
Bottigheimer, K. S. *English Money and Irish Land.* Oxford: Oxford University Press, 1970.
Moody, T. W.; Martin, F. X.; and Byrne, F. J., eds. *A New History of Ireland.* Vol. 3: *Early Modern Ireland, 1534-1691.* Oxford: Oxford University Press, 1976.

SCOTLAND

Donald, P. H. *An Uncounselled King: Charles I and the Scottish Troubles.* Cambridge: Cambridge University Press, 1990.
Donaldson, Gordon. *Scotland: James V to James VII.* Edinburgh: Oliver and Boyd, 1965.
Dow, Frances. *Cromwellian Scotland.* Edinburgh: John Donald, 1979.
Stevenson, David. *The Scottish Revolution, 1637-45.* Newton Abbott: David and Charles, 1973.
———. *Revolution and Counter-Revolution in Scotland.* London: Royal Historical Society, 1975.

WALES

Dodd, A. H. *Studies in Stuart Wales.* Cardiff: University of Wales Press, 1952.
Jones, J. Gwynfor. *Early Modern Wales, c.1525-1640.* London: The Macmillan Press Ltd., 1994.
Williams, Glanmor. *Recovery, Reorientation and Reformation: Wales, c. 1415-1642.* Oxford: Oxford University Press, 1987.

Index

ISBN 0-313-28391-5

90000>

EAN

9 780313 283918

HARDCOVER BAR CODE